Brill's Encyclopedia of Hinduism

HANDBOOK OF ORIENTAL STUDIES
HANDBUCH DER ORIENTALISTIK

SECTION TWO
INDIA

edited by

J. Bronkhorst
A. Malinar

VOLUME 22/6

Brill's Encyclopedia of Hinduism

Volume VI:
Index

Edited by
Knut A. Jacobsen
(*Editor-in-Chief*)

Associate Editors
Helene Basu
Angelika Malinar
Vasudha Narayanan

TUTA SUB AEGIDE PALLAS · 1683 ·

BRILL

LEIDEN • BOSTON
2015

Library of Congress Cataloging-in-Publication Data

Brill's encyclopedia of Hinduism / edited by Knut A. Jacobsen (editor-in-chief); associate editors, Helene Basu, Angelika Malinar, Vasudha Narayanan.
p. cm. — (Handbook of oriental studies. Section three, India, ISSN 0169-9377; v. 22/6)
ISBN 978-90-04-26555-4 (hardback : alk. paper)
1. Hinduism—Encyclopedias. I. Jacobsen, Knut A., 1956- II. Basu, Helene. III. Malinar, Angelika. IV. Narayanan, Vasudha.
BL1105.B75 2009
294.503—dc22

2009023320

ISSN 0169-9377
ISBN 978 90 04 26555 4

Table of Contents, Volume VI

Table of Contents, Volumes I–VI

Religious Specialists

Religious Traditions

Philosophy

Some Modern Religious Groups and Teachers

Preface

This is the sixth and final volume of *Brill's Encyclopedia of Hinduism*. The goal of the *Encyclopedia* is to present the latest scholarship on all aspects of the Hindu religious traditions. The *Encyclopedia* makes available in-depth critical scholarship, and the depth and breadth of information provided in this work are unmatched by any reference work on Hinduism. I hope it will appeal to a wide range of readers. At the foundation of the *Encyclopedia* is a fascination with a phenomenon that we as humans share, and in the examination of this phenomenon, the emphasis is on critical knowledge. Hinduism as a religious tradition functions on a number of different levels, from the most complex architecture, philosophy, and linguistic activity to the performance of short ritual acts: a woman connecting for a brief moment to a statue of the god Gaṇeśa in a wayside shrine on her way to work, a Hindu holy man performing his morning rituals in the Himalaya, a young boy learning to recite Sanskrit ritual texts at a school for priest education in South India, a dance performance in a temple, an astrologer giving advice to a client, the tying of a short thread to a tree by a pilgrim at a Hindu sacred place, a meeting of the organizational committee of a Hindu temple anywhere in the world, a philosophical discussion at an assembly of learned persons in Benares, artisans making stone sculptures for temples, Vedic sacred formulas and texts recited daily, and manuscripts of Hinduism being preserved in facilities and libraries worldwide. In these and many other ways, the Hindu traditions are performed by hundreds of millions of people every day. The goal of the *Encyclopedia* is to present the Hindu traditions as they take place on all these levels. Hinduism, it is often observed, has no common church and no common creed, and it is not based on a holy book or a single founder. That may be so, but Hinduism has many organizations, many creeds, many sacred texts, and founders of a number of organizations and knowledge traditions. The vision of this work is to approach the mosaic and network of Hindu traditions in all their multiplicity, and as both historical and contemporary institutions from different angles and in a variety of contexts, and to document a number of connections and networks.

For many scholars whose work is dedicated to understanding the history, structure, and pluralism of Hindu traditions, Hinduism is definitely the world's most exciting religion. This enthusiasm for the subject is displayed in the articles of the *Encyclopedia*. The articles are clear, comprehensive, interesting and exciting, and they do justice to the Hindu traditions both in the context of ancient civilizations and as global living traditions.

I am thankful to the many authors who shared their great knowledge of the Hindu traditions and contributed the articles to volume VI of the *Encyclopedia*. They represent the best of scholarship on Hinduism in Indology, religious studies, history, anthropology, sociology, art history, and other academic disciplines.

Knut A. Jacobsen

List of Editors and Contributors

Editor in chief

Jacobsen, Knut A., is professor in the history of religions at the University of Bergen and author and editor of many books and numerous articles in journals and edited volumes on various aspects on religions in South Asia and in the South Asian diasporas. He is the author of *Prakṛti in Sāṃkhya-Yoga: Material Principle: Religious Experience, Ethical Implications* (1999; Indian edition 2002), *Kapila: Founder of Sāṃkhya and Avatāra of Viṣṇu* (2008), and *Pilgrimage in the Hindu Tradition: Salvific Space* (2013). Other recent publications include the edited volumes *South Asians in the Diaspora: Histories and Religious Traditions* (2004), *Theory and Practice of Yoga: Essays in Honour of Gerald James Larson* (2005), *South Asian Religions on Display: Religious Processions in South Asia and in the Diaspora* (2008), *South Asian Christian Diaspora: Invisible Diaspora in Europe and North America* (2008), *Modern Indian Culture and Society* (2009), *Sikhs in Europe: Migration, Identities and Representations* (2011), *Sikhs across Borders: Transnational Practices among European Sikhs* (2012), and *Yoga Powers: Extraordinary Capacities Attained through Meditation and Concentration* (2012).

Associate Editors

Basu, Helene, is professor of anthropology at Westfaelische Wilhelms-Universitaet, Münster. Her main areas of research are contemporary Indian religions (Hinduism, Islam), Indian Ocean studies, African migrations to India, Indian migrations to Africa, and cultural psychiatry. She has conducted several fieldwork projects in western India and East Africa. She is author of *Habshi-Sklaven, Sidi-Fakire. Muslimische Heiligenverehrung im westlichen Indien* (1994) and *Von Barden und Königen.Ethnologische Studien zur Göttin und zum Gedächtnis in Kacchch* (2004). Her publications include numerous articles as well as coedited and edited collections such as *Embodying Charisma: Modernity, Locality and the Performance of Emotion at Sufi Shrines* (1998, with P. Werbner) and *Journeys and Dwellings: Western India and the Indian Ocean* (2007).

Malinar, Angelika, is professor of Indology at the University of Zürich, Switzerland. Her main areas of research are the history of Hinduism, Sanskrit epics and Purāṇas, Indian philosophy and aesthetics, and contemporary South Asian religions and Hindi literature. She has conducted several research projects, most recently on Hindu monasticism in Orissa, and is author of *Rājavidyā. Das königliche Wissen um Herrschaft und Verzicht. Studien zur Bhagavadgītā* (1996), *The Bhagavadgītā: Doctrines and Contexts* (2007; paperback ed. 2009), and *Der Hinduismus* (2 vols., 2009) and coauthor of *Studien zum Nārāyaṇīya/Studies in the Nārāyaṇīya* (1997). Her publications include numerous articles as well as edited and coedited volumes, such as *Charisma and Canon: Essays on the Religious History of the Indian Subcontinent* (2001), *Text and Context in the History, Literature and Religion of Orissa* (2004), *Time in India: Concepts and Practices* (2007), and *Un/Reinheit. Konzepte und Erfahrungsmodi im Kulturvergleich* (2009).

Narayanan, Vasudha, is distinguished professor in the Department of Religion at the University of Florida and a past president of the American Academy of Religion. She was educated at the Universities of Madras and Bombay and at Harvard University. She is the author or editor of seven books and over a hundred articles, chapters in books, and encyclopedia entries. Her books include *The Life of Hinduism* (2007, with J. Stratton Hawley), *Hinduism* (2004, 2009), *The Vernacular Veda: Revelation, Recitation,* *and Ritual* (1994), *The Way and the Goal: Expressions of Devotion in the Early Śrīvaiṣṇava Tradition* (1987), and *The Tamil Veda: Piḷḷan's Interpretation of the Tiruvāymoḻi.* Her research has been supported by several organizations, including the Centre for Khmer Studies, the American Council of Learned Societies, National Endowment for the Humanities (1987, 1989–1990, and 1998–1999), the John Simon Guggenheim Foundation, the American Institute of Indian Studies/Smithsonian, and the Social Science Research Council. She is currently working on research into Hindu traditions in Cambodia.

Contributors

Acevedo, Deepa Das, received her PhD in anthropology from the University of Chicago in 2013 and is currently a JD student at the University of Chicago Law School. Her dissertation examined the executive and judicial regulation of public Hindu temples in Kerala, India, with a focus on the prominent Ayyappan temple at Sabarimala. Separately, she has also written on the treasures unearthed in 2011 at the Padmanabhaswamy temple in Trivandrum, Kerala (*Modern Asian Studies*, forthcoming) as well as on secular governance in India (*Law & Social Inquiry*, 2013) and the development of "Hindu law" (*Religion Compass*, 2013). Her work uses social science methodologies to explore legal practices and institutions.

Arweck, Elisabeth, is a Senior Research Fellow in the Warwick Religions and Education Unit (WRERU) in the Centre for Educational Studies at the University of Warwick, UK. She completed her PhD at King's College London in 1999 on the subject of New Religious Movements. Since joining WRERU, she has worked on a number of research projects focusing on young people and religious socialization, (religious) education, and religion and spirituality. Recent research has been concerned with young people growing up in mixed-faith families and young people's attitudes to religious diversity. Publications include articles in peer review journals, book chapters, edited volumes, and single authored volumes. Dr Arweck is a member of a range of national and international associations, both for the sociology of religion and religious education, and she is the editor of the *Journal of Contemporary Religion.*

Bhargava, Rajeev, is professor and former director of Centre for the Study of Developing Societies, Delhi (2007-2014). He was professor at Jawaharlal Nehru University, New Delhi (1980-2005), and head of the Department of Political Science, University of Delhi (2001–2005). He is Honorary Fellow of Balliol College, Oxford, and Professorial Fellow of Australian Catholic University, Sydney. He has been a Fellow at Harvard University, University of Bristol, Institute of Advanced Studies, Jerusalem, Institute for Advanced Study, Berlin, and the Institute for Human Sciences, Vienna. He has also been Distinguished Resident Scholar, Institute for Religion, Culture and Public Life, Columbia University, and Asia Chair at Sciences Po, Paris. R. Bhargava's publications include *Individualism in Social Science* (1992), *What Is Political Theory and Why Do We Need It?* (2010), and *The Promise of India's Secular Democracy* (2010). His edited works are *Secularism and Its Critics* (1998) and *Politics and Ethics of the Indian Constitution* (2008). His work on secularism and methodological individualism is internationally acclaimed.

Cozad, Laurie Ann, received a master s degree from the School of Foreign Service at Georgetown University and a master s degree and PhD from the University of Chicago Divinity School in the history of religions. She has written several articles on religion and politics and published the book *Sacred Snakes: Orthodox Images of Indian Snake Worship.* She is presently working on a book for Lexington Press, *God on High: Religion, Cannabis, and the Quest for Legitimacy* as well as an article entitled Disaster and Divinity: Hurricane Katrina 10 Years After. Dr Cozad served as an associate professor at the University of Mississippi in a joint appointment in the Croft Center for International Studies and the Department of Philosophy and Religion. She is currently an associate professor at Lesley University's Graduate School for Arts and Social Sciences in the Division of Interdisciplinary Inquiry where she specializes in mindfulness studies, religious studies methodology, indigenous religions, and religion, politics and public policy.

Greenberg, Yudit Kornberg, is the George D. and Harriet W. Cornell Endowed Chair of Religion and Founding Director of the Jewish Studies Program at Rollins College in Winter Park, Florida. Her fields of teaching and research include modern and contemporary Jewish thought, comparative religion, women and religion, and cross-cultural views of love and the body. Dr. Greenberg is the author of *Better than Wine: Love, Poetry and Prayer in the Thought of Franz Rosenzweig*, the two-volume *Encyclopedia of Love in World Religions*, nominated for the American Academy of Religion Book award for 2009, and is editor of *From Spinoza to Levinas: Hermeneutical, Ethical, and Political Issues in Modern and Contemporary Jewish Philosophy*. She has written numerous articles and essays in modern and contemporary Jewish thought, is presently completing her book *Reading Love and Eros in Jewish Thought*, and recently began writing a textbook titled *Body in Religion: Cross-cultural Perspectives* due for publication by Bloomsbury Publishers in 2016.

Hutter, Manfred, is professor in the history of religions at the University of Bonn, Germany, authoring or editing 20 books and numerous articles in journals and edited volumes on various aspects of religions in the ancient Near East and Iran as well as on religions in Southeast Asia. His books include *Das ewige Rad* (2001), *Die Weltreligionen* (32008), and *Handbuch Bahāʾī. Geschichte, Theologie, Gesellschaftsbezug* (2009). Among his edited volumes are *Religionsgeschichte Syriens* (with P.W. Haider and S. Kreuzer [1996]), *Lexicon der christlichen Antike* (with J.B. Bauer [1999]), *Religionsinterne Kritik und religiöser Pluralismus im gegenwärtigen Südostasien* (2008), and recently *Between Mumbai and Manila: Judaism in Asia since the Founding of the State of Israel* (2013).

Neuß, Jürgen, has had his education at the former Institute for Indian Philology and Art History of the Free University Berlin, the South Asia Institute of the Humboldt-University Berlin and the University of Allahabad (India). His special interest lies in the change of Indian society, specifically the conflicts between tradition and modernization. Neuß earned his PhD in 2008 at the Free University in Berlin, with his dissertation *Narmadāpradakṣiṇā. Circumambulation of the Narmadā River*, recently published by Brill as *Narmadāparikramā: Circumambulation of the Narmadā River: On the Tradition of a Unique Hindu Pilgrimage* (2012). Other recent publications include *Chili, Chai, Chapati. Geschichten aus Indien* (2011) and *Untersuchungen zur Textgeschichte der Yamasmṛti* (2011).

Rigopoulos, Antonio, earned his PhD at the University of California-Santa Barbara and is associate professor of Sanskrit and religions and philosophies of India at the Ca' Foscari University of Venice, Italy. His main field of research concerns the ascetical and devotional traditions of medieval and modern Maharashtra. Among his publications are *The Life and Teachings of Sai Baba of Shirdi* (1993), *Dattātreya: The Immortal Guru, Yogin, and Avatāra: A Study of the Transformative and Inclusive Character of a Multi-faceted Hindu Deity* (1998), *Hinduismo* (2005), *The Mahānubhāvs* (2005), and *Guru: Il fondamento della civiltà dell'India* (2009). He has edited the volume *Guru: The Spiritual Master in Eastern and Western Traditions: Authority and Charisma* (2004).

Sanderson, Alexis, after taking an undergraduate degree first in classics (1969) and then in Sanskrit (1971) at Balliol College, Oxford, spent six years in Kashmir studying with a scholar and traditional *guru* of Śaivism. He was Associate Professor in Sanskrit at the University of Oxford and a Fellow of Wolfson College from 1977 to 1992. From 1992 to the present, he has been the Spalding Professor of Eastern Religions and Ethics at the same university and a Fellow of All Souls College. His field is early medieval religion in India and Southeast Asia, focusing on the history of Śaivism, its relations with the state and Brahmanism, and its impact on the development of Vaiṣṇavism, Buddhism, and Jainism.

Notes for Users

Organization. The *Encyclopedia of Hinduism* contains in-depth, critical research articles that are thematically organized, rather than short, alphabetically organized dictionary entries containing only information that would be easily retrieved from the internet. The organization of articles within each theme is alphabetical. Many local gods and goddesses, festivals, castes, sacred places, saints, organizations, and so on are not given separate entries, but information about them is nevertheless found in a number of articles. The index, to be included in volume VI, will be comprehensive for all volumes and will serve as the alphabetical tool of the *Encyclopedia*.

Common terms and concepts. Some terms – such as those for certain bodies of Hindu sacred texts such as Śruti ("Revealed Texts"), Smṛti ("Texts Committed to Memory": texts based on revelation but composed by humans), Āgama ("Scripture": texts considered revelation by certain Hindu traditions), and those for the three major divisions of the Hindu traditions, Vaiṣṇava (traditions related to the worship of the god Viṣṇu and his embodiments), Śaiva (traditions related to the worship of the god Śiva and his entourage), and Śākta (traditions related to the worship of the Goddess, Śakti, and goddesses identified with her) – are used and referred to in a number of articles and are explained and treated in articles (for Śruti and Smṛti, see articles in section *Sacred Texts and Languages* [vol. II]; for Vaiṣṇava, Śaiva, and Śākta, articles in section *Religious Traditions* [vol. III]), in addition to being index words and searchable through the index.

Hinduism includes many gods and goddesses, but many Hindus and many Hindu textual traditions also insist that behind the multiplicity of gods there is in reality only one God, or that all the goddesses similarly are manifestations of one and the same great Goddess. To cope with this plurality of conceptions of the divine, the generic term God is used when speaking of the one God of whom it is believed that all distinct gods or goddesses are but forms, and the term Goddess is used when speaking of the one Goddess, of whom all distinct goddesses are believed to be manifestations. The Devī refers to the Goddess, while *devī* refers to one of the many goddesses, *devīs*.

Bodies of literatures (Vedas, Purāṇas, etc.) are printed in roman, but separate publications are italicized.

References. Cross-references (symbol: →) to other articles indicate that the subject is dealt with there or that supplementary information is available in those articles. Sometimes the article to which reference is made is shortened (e.g. → *tīrtha* instead of → *tīrtha* and *tīrthayātrā*).

Transliteration. *Brill's Encyclopedia of Hinduism* recognizes the diversity and plurality of Hinduism and the terminology that can be applied to it, but for the purposes of the publication, we have for the most part used one spelling style for each term, while avoiding unnecessary Sanskritization and allowing for some local spellings. We have tried to keep diacritics to a minimum: if diacritics were applied to all words derived from Indian languages, then even the word Hindu would be spelled Hindū; adhering to such a strict linguistic practice would serve little purpose. Diacritics are used for a number of terms and concepts from Sanskrit and other Indian languages, for gods, goddesses, texts, schools, and for personal names, but not for most persons and organizations from 19th and 20th centuries who have become part of English-language discourse (e.g. Mahatma Gandhi and not Mahātmā Gāndhī, Jawaharlal Nehru and not Javāharlāl Nehrū, Vivekananda and not Vivekānanda, Bhaktivedanta and not Bhaktivedānta, Ramnamis and not Rāmnāmīs). We do not use diacritics on many Anglicized words derived from Sanskrit or other Indian languages such as brahmanic(al), upanisadic(al), puranic(al), agamic(al) and shastric(al). To emphasize the *Encyclopedia*'s contemporary character, we do not use diacritics on place names, states, regions, languages, scripts, eras, periods, dynasties, kingdoms, and empires (e.g. Maharashtra and not Mahārāṣṭra, Varanasi and not Vārāṇasī, Allahabad and not

Allāhābād, Kushanas and not Kuṣāṇas), except mythical and literary place names. We have used diacritics for rivers such as Gaṅgā and Yamunā to emphasize their feminine gender. Literary periods have diacritics (e.g. Caṅkam period). For transliteration from Sanskrit, we have used the scheme issued by the Transliteration Committee of the Geneva Oriental Congress (September 1894), which is the standard for academic works (now called International Alphabet of Sanskrit Transliteration [IAST]). For Chinese transliteration, the Pinyin transliteration system is used. We have allowed for some traditional spellings such as Sri Chand instead of Sri Cand, which would be unrecognizable to the Sikhs. For caste names and months, we have allowed for different local spellings. A member of the caste (*varṇa/jāti*) spelled in Sanskrit Brāhmaṇa is spelled here Brahman for the sake of full-text search, the collective body of texts is spelled Brāhmaṇas, the god is Brahmā, while the transcendent absolute is spelled *brahman* (lowercase and italics). The four *varṇa*s are capitalized, not italicized (e.g. Kṣatriya); *jāti*s (castes) are capitalized and not italicized and have mostly been printed without the required diacritics. Brāhmaṇa is sometimes used for the Brahman caste when the *caturvarṇa* (four class) system is referred to. Months have been written in many languages and in many ways (e.g. Kartik, Karttik, Kārttik, Kārttika [Oct–Nov]) but are accompanied by the Gregorian-calendar equivalents in brackets. For Tamil transliteration, one of the common schemes is used, in which the palatal s is usually rendered as c, and the alveolars as *ṉ, ṟ, ḻ*.

Pronunciation. Hindu religious traditions, textual as well as oral, are followed, observed, and performed in a number of different languages, mostly South Asian, and even Sanskrit words are pronounced differently in the different regions of India. Nevertheless, some readers might find the following guide for pronunciation of Sanskrit words useful: vowels are pronounced as they are written and pronounced in Latin, Italian, and German. A line above a vowel means length. Consonants correspond, with a few exceptions, to English consonants. Aspirate consonants should be pronounced with an aspiration immediately followed (examples: gh pronounced as in doghouse, th as in hothouse), while unaspirated stops should be pronounced without any aspiration; the dentals (ṭ, ṭh, ḍ, ḍh, and ṇ) should be pronounced with the tip of the tongue touching the teeth, and c and ch are pronounced tsj; ṅ is pronounced like ng in singer, and ñ is pronounced nj; ś is pronounced with the tongue in the same position as in ya; and ṣ is like English sh. Tamil is economical in its use of consonants, and unlike in Sanskrit the same letter may be pronounced in several ways. The letter transliterated as k, for instance, may be pronounced as k, g, or h, depending on the position of the letter and also the geographic origin of the speaker.

Sources. Primary sources are listed in the prelims section of each volume, secondary sources at the end of each article. The * denotes a manuscript. The (*) means that besides print edition(s) also manuscript(s) were consulted.

Authorship. The articles are signed with the name of the author. The author's academic affiliation and additional biographical information are given in the List of Contributors.

Online. The contents of volumes I through V of *Brill's Encyclopedia of Hinduism* are made available online, in full, at http://referenceworks.brillonline.com/browse/brill-s-encyclopedia-of-hinduism. Volume VI will appear on the Web site in 2015; the index included therein will be fully hyperlinked online, allowing users to click directly to the place in an article where an index term occurs. Articles in print and online are the same, but cross-references are hyperlinked and occasional typos and mistakes may have been corrected in the latter. New articles will be continuously added to the online edition of the encyclopedia as part of planned regular updates. Once enough new material has been brought together, the publication of supplementary print volume will be considered.

KNUT A. JACOBSEN

Primary Sources

Abhidānacintāmaṇi	*Hemacandra's Abhidānacintāmaṇi: Ein systematisch angeordnetes sysnonymisches Lexikon*, trans. O. Böthlingk & C. Rieu, St. Petersburg, 1847.
Abhidharmakośa	*L'Abhidharmakośa de Vasubandhu: Traduction et annotations*, trans. L. de la Vallée Poussin, Brussels, 1923–1931, repr. 1971.
	Abhidharmakośa of Vasubandhu, Chapter I: Dhātunirdeśa, ed. Y. Ejima, Tokyo, 1989.
Abhidharmakośa(bhāṣya)	*Abhidharmakośa(bhāṣya) of Vasubandhu*, ed. P. Pradhan, Patna, ^{2}1975.
Abhidharmakośavyākhyā	*Abhidharmakośavyākhyā of Yaśomitra*, vol. I, ed. D. Shastri, Varanasi, ^{2}1981.
Abhijñānaśākuntala	*Abhijñānaśākuntala by Kālidāsa with Vaikhānasaśrīnivāsācārya [= Tirumalācārya Śrīnivāsācārya]'s Vyākhyā and Rāghavabhaṭṭa's Dyotanikā*, 1954.
Abhinayadarpana	*Nandikeṣvara's Abhinayadarpanam: A Manual of Gesture and Posture Used in Hindu Dance and Drama: English Translation, Notes and the Text Critically Edited with Illustrations*, ed. and trans. M. Ghosh, Calcutta, 1957.
Ādeśapadavyākhyā	**Ādeśapadavyākhyā*, ms. 1285(B) at the Maharaja Mansingh Pustak Prakash, Jodhpur, n.d.
Advaitasiddhi	*Advaitasiddhi of Madhusudana Sarasvati*, ed. K. Bhattacharya, Delhi, 1992.
Āgamaḍambara	*Much Ado about Religion by Bhaṭṭa Jayanta*, ed. C. Deszö, New York, 2005.
Āgamaprāmāṇya	*Āgamaprāmāṇya of Yāmunācārya*, ed. M. Narasimhachary, Baroda, 1976.
	Yāmuna's Āgamaprāmāṇyam or Treatise on the Validity of Pāñcarātra: Sanskrit Text and English Translation, J.A.B. van Buitenen, Madras, 1971.
Agastimata	"Agastimata," in: L. Finot, ed., *Les Lapidaires Indiens*, Paris, 1896, 77–139.
Agnipurāṇa	*Agnipurāṇa of Maharṣi Vedavyāsa*, ed. U. Baladeva Upādhyāya, Vārāṇasi, 1966.
	The Agni Purana, N. Gangadharan, Delhi, 1985.
Ahirbudhnyasaṃhitā	*Ahirbudhnya-Saṃhitā of the Pāñcarātrāgama*, 2 vols., ed. by M.D. Ramanujacharya under the Supervision of F. Otto Schrader, rev. by V. Krishnamacharya, ALS 4, Madras, 1916, ^{2}1986 (first repr.).
	Pāñcarātra Saṃhitās and Early Vaiṣṇava Theology with a Translation and Critical Notes from Chapters on Theology in the Ahirbudhnya Saṃhitā, M. Matsubara, Delhi, 1994.
Aikkiyaviyal	*Śrīmaṟaiñāṉacampantanāyaṉar aruḷicceyta caivac ciṟu nūlkaḷ (mutaṟpakuti)*, ed. T.C. Mīṉāṭcicuntaram Piḷḷai, Thiruvavaduthurai, 1954.
Āʾīn-i Akbarī	*ʿAllāmī, Abūʾl-Fażl: The Āʾīn-i-Akbar*, trans. and ed. H. Blochmann & S.L. Goomer, Delhi, 1871, 1965.
	Āʾīn-i Akbarī, Abū al-Fażl, 3 vols., trans. H. Blochmann, D.C. Phillott, H.S. Jarrett & J. Sarkar, Calcutta, 1929–1948.
Aitareyabrāhmaṇa	*Aitareya Brāhmaṇa*, ed. T. Aufrecht, Bonn, 1897.

	The Aitareya and Kauṣītaki Brāhmaṇas of the Rigveda, trans. A.B. Keith, HOS 25, Delhi, 1971.
	Aitareyabrāhmaṇa with the Commentary of Bhaṭṭa Bhāskara Miśra, ed. A.M. Sastri & L. Srinivasacharya, Delhi, repr. 1985.
Aitareyāraṇyaka	*Aitareyāraṇyaka*, ed. A.B. Keith, Delhi, repr. 1995.
Ajitāgama	*Ajitāgama*, 3 vols., ed. N.R. Bhatt, PIFI 24, Pondicherry, crit. ed. 1964, 1967, 1991.
Alakhbānī	*Alakhbānī or Rushdnāmā of Shaikh Abd-ul-Quddus Gangohi*, ed. S.A.A. Rizvi & S. Zaidi, Aligarh, 1971.
Al-Qawl al-jamīl	*Al-Qawl al-jamīl*, Šāh Walī Allāh, Delhi, n.d.
Amanaskayoga	"Amanaskayoga," ed. J. Birch, BA thesis, University of Sydney, 2006.
	Amanaskayoga, ed. R.L. Shrivastav, Gorakhpur, 1980.
Amarakośa	*Amarakośa with Unpublished South Indian Commentaries*, crit. ed. A.A. Ramnathan, Adyar, 1971.
Amaraughaprabodha	"Amaraughaprabodha," ed. K. Mallik, in: *idem*, *The Siddha Siddhānta Paddhati and Other Works of Nāth Yogis*, Poona, 1954.
Amaraughaśāsana	*Amaraughaśāsana of Gorakṣanātha*, ed. P. Mukund Rām Śāstrī, KSTS 20, Srinagar, 1918.
Amṛtānubhava	*Amṛtānubhava*, B.P. Bahirat, Bombay, 1963.
	Amrutanubhav (= *The Nectar of Divine Experience*), Madhava, Pune, 1981.
	Jñāndev's Anubhavamrut: The Immortal Experience of Being, D. Chitre, New Delhi, 1996.
Amṛtasiddhi	**Amṛtasiddhi*, mss. 1242 and 1243 at the Maharaja Mansingh Pustak Prakash, Jodhpur, n.d.
Aṅguttaranikāya	*Aṅguttaranikāya*, ed. R. Morris & E. Hardy, London, 1888–1900.
Anteṣṭividhi	"The Anteṣṭividhi: A Manual on the Last Rite of the Lakulīśa Pāśupatas," D. Acharya, *JA* 298/1, 2010, 129–152.
Anurāg Sāgar	*The Ocean of Love: The Anurag Sagar of Kabir*, ed. and trans. A. Singh Ji, New Hampshire, 1982.
Aparokṣānubhūti	*Aparokṣānubhūti or Self-realization or Rājayoga of Śaṅkarācārya*, ed. and trans. J.L. Gupta "Chaitanya", Delhi, 2004 (Hind., Eng.)
	Rāja-Yoga: Being a Translation of the Vākyasudha or Dṛgdṛśyaviveka of Bhāratitīrtha [Part I] and the Aparokṣānubhūti of Śrī Śankarāchārya [Part II]: With Introduction and Notes, trans. M.N. Dvivedi, Ahmedabad, 1890.
Āpastambadharmasūtra	*Dharmasūtras: The Law Codes of Āpastamba, Gautama, Baudhāyana and Vasiṣṭha*, trans. P. Olivelle, Dehli, 1999.
Āpastambaśrautasūtra	*The Śrauta Sūtra of Āpastamba*, 3 vols., ed. R. Garbe, Calcutta, 1882–1902, repr. Delhi, 1990.
	Das Śrautasūtra des Āpastamba, trans. W. Caland, Göttingen, 1921.
	Āpastamba-Śrauta-Sūtra, ed. G.U. Thite, Delhi 2004.
Āṟāyirappaṭi	*Bhagavad Viṣayam*, 10 vols., ed. S. Kirusnasvami Ayyankar, Madras, 1924–1930.
Arthaśāstra	*The Kauṭilīya Arthaśāstra*, 3 vols., ed. and trans. R.P. Kangle, R.P., Bombay, [2]1969.
Āryabhaṭīya	*Āryabhaṭīya of Āryabhaṭa: Critically Edited With Introduction, English Translation, Notes, Comments, and Indexes*, ed. K.S. Shukla, New Delhi, 1976.
	The Āryabhaṭīya of Āryabhaṭa: An Ancient Indian Work on Mathematics and Astronomy, W.G. Clark, Chicago, 1930.

Āryāsaptaśatī
Āryāsaptaśatī: With the Commentary of Ananta by Govardhana, ed. Pandit Durgaprasad, Kasinath Pandurang Parab & Vasudev Laxman Sastri Pansikar, Delhi, 1988.
Āryāsaptaśatī o Gauḍavaṅga: Sanskrit Text with Bengali Translation and Commentary, ed. and trans. Śrī Jāhnavī Kumār Chakrabarty, Calcutta, 1972.

Aṣṭādaśabhedanirṇaya
Aṣṭādaśabhedanirṇaya: Explication des dix-huit différences (entre les deux branches de l'École de Rāmānuja) de Śrī Vātsya Raṅganātha. Édition critique, Traduction et Notes, S. Siauve, Pondicherry, 1978.

Aṣṭādhyāyī
Aṣṭādhyāyī: Pâṇini's Grammatik. Herausgegeben, übersetzt, erläutert und mit verschiedenen Indices versehen von Otto Böhtlingk, Delhi, 1998.
Kātyāyana's First Vārttika on Pāṇini's Aṣṭādhyāyī, Mahābhāṣya of Patañjali, ed. F. Kielhorn, vol. 1/2, Pune, ^{3}1962.

Atharvapariśiṣṭa
"The Pāśupata Observance (*Atharvapariśiṣṭa* 40)," P. Bisschop, & A. Griffiths, *IIJ* 46/4, 2003, 315–348.

Atharvaveda
Atharvaveda, ed. V. Bandhu, Hoshiarpur, 1960–1964.

Atharvavedasaṃhitā
Atharvaveda Saṃhitā, trans. W.D. Whitney, 2 vols., Cambridge MA, 1905; ed. R. Roth & W.D. Whitney, 2 vols., Berlin, 1924.
Atharvaveda-Saṃhitā, W.D. Whitney, Delhi, 1996.
Atharva-Veda Saṃhitā: Text with English Translation, Śloka Index and Names of Ṛṣis and Devatās. W.D. Whitney, 2 vols., Delhi, 1987.

Ātmabodha
Self-Knowledge (Atmabodha), trans. Swami Nikhilananda, New York, 1946.

Avadhūtagītā
Avadhūtagītā, ed. P. Thomi, RTÜ 4, Wichtrach, 1996.

Bālakṛṣṇanāṭakamu
Bālakṛṣṇanāṭakamu by T. Veṅgamāmba, ed. K.J. Krishnamurti, Tirupati, 2007.

Basavapurāṇa
Basavapurāṇa [*of Bhimakavi*], ed. R.C. Hiremath, Dharwar, 1971. (Kan.)
Basava Purāṇamu [*of Pālkurike Sōmanātha*], Madras, 1966. (Tel.)
"The Basava-Purāṇa of the Lingaits," trans. G. Würth, *JBombayBRAS* 8/24, 1865, 65–97.

Baudhāyanadharmasūtra
Dharmasūtras: The Law Codes of Āpastamba, Gautama, Baudhāyana and Vasiṣṭha, trans. P. Olivelle, Dehli, 1999.
The Baudhayana-Dharmasutra, ed. with Govinda's *Vivaraṇa* commentary by Umesa Chandra Pandeya, KSS 104, Varanasi, 1972.

Baudhāyanagṛhyasūtra
Baudhāyana Gṛhya Sūtra, Shama Sastri, New Delhi, 1982.

Baudhāyanaśrautasūtra
The Baudhāyana Śrauta Sūtra, 3 vols., ed. by W. Caland, Calcutta, 1982.
The Baudhāyana Śrautasūtra, crit. ed. and trans. C.G. Kashikar, New Delhi, 2003.

Bhagavadgītā
Bhagavad Gītā with Eleven Commentaries, ed. S.G.S. Sadhale, Delhi, 2000.
Bhagavadgītā, trans. B. Miller, New York, 1986.
Bhagavadgītā with Śaṅkara's Bhāṣya, ed. N. Vilinatha, Madras, 1971.
Die Bhagavadgītā, trans. R. Garbe, Leipzig, 1905.
The Kashmir Recension of the Bhagavadgītā, ed. F.O. Schrader, Stuttgart, 1930.
The Bhagavadgītā, with the Sanatsujatīya and the Anugītā, ed. and trans. K.T. Telang, Oxford, 1882.
Śrīmad Bhagavadgītā-rahasya or Karma-Yoga-Śāstra: Including an External Examination of the Gītā, the Original Sanskrit Stanzas, Their English Translation, Commentaries on the Stanzas, and a Comparison of Eastern and Western Doctrines etc., 2 vols., trans. B.S. Sukthankar, ed. B.G. Tilak, Poona, 1935.

	The Bhagavad-Gītā with a Commentary Based on the Original Sources, ed. and trans. R. Zaehner, Oxford, 1969.
	Śrīmadbhagavadgītā (with Rāmānuja's Commentary), ed. V.G. Apte, ĀSS 92, 1923.
	Bhagavadgītā, trans. S. Radhakrishnan, London, 1971.
Bhagavaī	*Viyāhapannatti (Bhagavaī): The Fifth Anga of the Jaina Canon*, J. Deleu, LSJRS 10, Delhi, 1970, repr. 1996.
	Bhagavaī Viāhapaṇṇattī, ed. Muni Nathamal, Anga Suttāni 2, Ladnun, V.S. 2031.
	Viyāhapaṇṇattisuttaṁ, ed. Bechardas J. Doshi & Amritlal Mohanlal Bhojak, 3 vols., Jaina-Āgama-Series 4, Bombay, 1974–1982.
Bhāgavatapurāṇa	*Śrīmadbhāgavata Śrīdharī Ṭīkā*, Varanasi, 1962.
	Bhāgavata Purāṇa of Kṛṣṇa Dvaipāyana Vyāsa with Sanskrit Commentary Bhāvārthabodhinī of Śrīdharasvāmin, ed. J.L. Shastri, Delhi, 1983.
	Srimad-Bhāgavatam with Notes from a Dozen Commentaries, trans. N. Raghunathan, 2 vols., Madras, 1976.
	Srimad Bhagavata: The Holy Book of God, trans. S. Tapasyananda, 4 vols., Madras, 1980–1992.
	Srimad-Bhāgavata-Mahāpurāṇa with Sanskrit Text and English Translation, trans. C.L. Goswami, 2 Vols, Gorakhpur, 1971, [2]1982.
	The Bhāgavata-Purāṇa, 4 vols., trans. and annotated by G.V. Tagare, Delhi, 1992.
	Śrīmadbhāgavata: dvādaśa skandha sampūrṇa, Śaṅkaradeva, Dibrugarh, 1989.
	Śrīmad Bhāgavata Mahāpurāṇam, with the Sanskrit commentaries of Śrīdhara Svāmin's Bhāvārthadīpikā, Śrī Vaṃśīdhara's Bhāvārthadīpikāprakāśa, Śrī Rādhāramaṇadāsa Gosāmin's Dīpinī, Śrīmad Vīrarāghava's Bhāgavatacandrikā, Śrīmad Vijayadhvajatīrtha's Padaratnāvalī, Śrīmad Jīva Gosvāmin's Kramasaṃdarbha, Śrīmad Viśvanātha Cakravartin's Sārārthadarśinī, Śrīmad Śukadeva's Siddhāntapradīpa, Śrīmad Vallabhācarya's Subodhinī, Śrī Puruṣottamacaraṇa Gosvāmin's Subodhinīprakāśaḥ, Śrī Giridharalāla's Bālaprabodhinī, ed. Kṛṣṇaśaṅkara Śāstrī, Ahmedabad, 1965.
Bhāgavatasandarbha	*Bhāgavatasandarbha (with the Gopālatoṣaṇī Commentary of Śyāmdās)*, 6 vols., Jīva Gosvāmī, Hindi trans., Śyāmdās, Vrindavan, 1984–1999.
Bhaktalīlāmṛt	"Bhaktalīlāmṛt [of Bhīmasvāmī Śirgāvkar]," in: *Rāmdās āṇi Rāmdāsī: Bhāg Dusrā*, Dhule, 1906, 1–170.
Bhaktalīlāmṛta	*Life of Eknath: Śrī Eknath charitra, Translated from the Bhaktalīlāmṛta*, ed. J.E. Abbott *et al.*, Poona 1928, 1981.
	Life of Tukaram: Translation from Mahipati's Bhaktalilamrita Chapters 25 to 40, ed. J.E. Abbott *et al.*, Poona, 1930, 1980.
	Nectar from Indian Saints, ed. J.E. Abbott *et al.*, Poona, 1935.
Bhaktamāla	*Bhakta-māla, Gosvāmī Śrī Nābhājī kṛta Śrī-bhakta-māla, Śrī Priyādāsajī praṇīta ṭīkā-kavitta*, ed. S.B. Rupakala, Lucknow, 1977.
	Bhaktamāl, Priyādāsjī praṇit ṭīkā-kavitta, Sītārāmśaraṇ Bhagavānprasād Rūpkalā viracit Bhaktisudhāsvad tilak sahit, Nābhādās, Lucknow, 1903, 1914, [6]1977.
	Rāghavdās kṛt bhaktmāl, ed. A. Nāhṭā, Jodhpur, 1965 (Hind.).
	Nābhādās: Śrī Bhaktamāl, ed. Rupkala (Rūpkalā = S. Bhagavānprasād), Lucknow, 1961.
Bhaktavijaya	*Stories of Indian Saints: A Translation of Mahipati's Marathi Bhaktavijaya*, ed. J.E. Abbott *et al.*, Poona 1933, 1982.

Bhaktirasāmṛtasindhu — *The Bhaktirasāmṛtasindhu of Rūpa Gosvāmin*, ed. and trans. D.L. Haberman, Delhi, 2003.
Bhaktirasāmṛtasindhu by Rūpa Gosvāmī, ed. Haridāsa Dāsa, Navadvipa, 1961.

Bhaktiratnākara — *Bhaktiratnākāra of Narahari Cakravartī [Ghanaśyāma Dāsa]*, ed. by Rāmanārāyaṇa Vidyāratna, Murshidabad, 3rd ed. Bengali San 1332 (= 1926).
Bhaktiratnākara of Narahari Cakravartī Ṭhākura, Kolkata, 1987.
Bhaktiratnākara, Śaṅkaradeva, Patiala, 1982.
Narahari Cakravartī, Bhaktiratnākara, ed. Nandalāl Vidyāsāgara, Calcutta, 1960.

Bhaktiratnāvalī — *Bhakti Ratnāvalī*, Mādhavadeva, New Delhi, 2009.

Bhārgavatantra — *Bhargava Tantram (A Pancaratragama Text)*, ed. by Raghava Prasad Chaudhary, KSV 8, Allahabad, 1981.

Bhāṣāpariccheda — *Bhāṣāpariccheda with Siddhānta-muktavālī by Viśvanātha-nyāya-pañcānana*, trans. by Swami Madhvananda, Kolkata, 2004.
Bhāṣāpariccheda of Viśvanātha Nyāyapañcānana Bhaṭṭācārya, ed. E. Roer, BI 8, Osnabrück, 1980.

Bhāṣāvaṃśāvalī — *Bhāṣāvaṃśāvalī*, ed. N. Pauḍela & D. Laṃsāla, 2 vols., Vikram 2020, 2033.

Bhaviṣyapurāṇa — *Bhaviṣyamahāpurāṇa*, ed. K. Śrīkṛṣṇadāsa, Bombay, 1910.

Bhāvopahārastotra — *The Bhāvopahārastotra of Cakrapāṇi Nātha with the commentary (-vivaraṇa) of Ramya Deva Bhatta*, ed. Mukundarāmaśāstrī, Bombay, 1918.

Bījagaṇita — "Bījagaṇita of Bhāskara," ed. T. Hayashi, *SCIAMVS* 10, 2009, 3–302.

Bījak — *Kabīr bījak*, ed. S. Singh, Allahabad, 1972 (Hind.).
The Bijak of Kabir, trans. L. Hess & S. Singh, Delhi, 1983, 2001.

Brahmāṇḍapurāṇa — *Brahmāṇḍapurāṇa*, trans. G.V. Tagare, Delhi, 1983.
The Brahmāṇḍa-Mahāpurāṇam, ed. K.V. Sarma, Varanasi, 1983.
Brahmāṇḍa Purāṇa, ed. J.L. Shastri, Delhi, 1973.

Brahmapurāṇa — *Sanskrit Text and Indices of the Brahmapurāṇa*, ed. P. Schreiner & R. Söhnen, Wiesbaden, 1986.

Brahmasaṃhitā — *Brahma-Samhitā with Commentary by Shri Shrila Jeeva Goswāmi* by Jīva Gosvāmī; ET: *Bhakti Siddhānta Saraswati*, ed. Bhakti Vilās Tirtha, Madras, 1973.

Brahmasiddhi — *Brahmasiddhi of Maṇḍana Miśra*, ed. S.K. Sastri, Madras, 1937.

Brāhmasphuṭasiddhānta — *Brāhmasphuṭasiddhānta*, ed. S. Dvivedī, Benares, 1901–1902.

Brahmasūtra — *Le Vedanta: Etude sur les Brahma-sutra et leurs cinq commentaires*, V.S. Ghate, Paris, 1918; ET: *The Vedānta: A Study of the Brahma-sūtras with the Bhāṣyas of Śaṃkara, Rāmānuja, Nimbārka, Madhva, and Vallabha*, Poona, 1981.
The Brahmasutrabhashya of Srikanthacharya with the commentary Sivarkamanidipika by Appayadikshita edited with Sutrarthacandrika, 2 vols., ed. R. Halasyanatha Sastri, New Delhi, 1986.

Brahmasūtrabhāṣya — *Brahma Sutra Bhashya*, ed. Panchamukhi, Delhi, 1994.
Brahmasūtraśāṃkarabhāṣyam, ed. J.L. Shastri, Delhi, 1980.
Brahmasūtraśāṅkarabhāṣya, ed. with three subcommentaries by Pt. A. Shastri & V.L. Shastri Pansikar, Varanasi, 2000.
Śrīmad-dvaipāyana-praṇīta-brahmasūtrāṇi. Ānandagiri-kṛta-ṭīkā-saṃvalita-śāṃkara-bhāṣya-sametāni, ed. Nārāyaṇa Śāstrī Ekasaṃbekare, ĀSS 21/1–2, 1890–1891.

The Sacred Books of the East, vols. XXXIV, XXXVIII: The Vedānta Sūtras of Bādarāyaṇa: With the Commentary by Śaṅkara, trans. G. Thibaut, Oxford, 1890, 1896.

Brahmasūtragovindabhāṣya — *Brahma-sūtra-govinda-bhāṣyam of Baladeva Vidyābhūṣaṇa*, ed. with Hindi trans. by Rāsavihāri Dāsa and Narasiṃha Dāsa, Mathura, Vikram 2011 (= 1955).

Brahmasūtranimbārkabhāṣya — *Brahmasūtra-Nimbārkabhāṣyaṃ Vedāntakaustubha-Vedāntakaustubhaprabhā-Bhāvadīpikā-Vyākhyātrayopetam: With an Exhaustive Introduction, Contents, Notes, and Thirteen Appendices*, ed. M.M. Agrawal, 4 vols., Delhi, 2000.

Brahmayāmala — **Brahmayāmala*, ms. 3–370 at the National Archives Kathmandu (= unpublished transcription and partial edition by S. Hatley & C. Kiss based on manuscript 3–370 [palm-leaf] of the National Archives, Kathmandu [Nepal-German Manuscript Preservation Project, reel n. A 42–46]), Kathmandu, dated 1052 CE.

Bṛhadāraṇyakopaniṣadbhāṣya — *Śhrimat Sureswaráchárya-viracitaṃ Bṛihadáraṇyakopanishadbháshyavártikam with its Commentary by Śrímat Ánandajnyána*, ed. Pandit Kasínátha Śasrtrí Ágáśe, ĀSS 16/1–3, Puṇyākhyapattana (= Pune), 1892–1894.

Bṛhadbhāgavatāmṛta — *Śrī Bṛhad Bhāgavatāmṛta of Śrīla Sanātana Gosvāmī*, G. Dasa (Dāsa), vol. I, Los Angeles, 2002.

Bṛhajjātaka — *The Bṛihajjâtakam of Varâha Mihira*, trans. S. Vijnanananda, New Delhi, [1]1912, 1979.

Bṛhaspatismṛti — *Bṛhaspatismṛti (Reconstructed)*, ed. K.V. Rangaswami Aiyangar, GaOS 85, Baroda, 1941.

Bṛhatkhecarīprakāśa — **Bṛhatkhecarīprakāśa*, ms. 14575 at the Scindia Oriental Research Institute Library, Ujjain, n.d.

Bṛhatsaṃhitā — *Bṛhatsaṃhitā*, vols. I–II, ed. with the commentary of Bhaṭṭotpala by A.V. Tripāṭhī, SBG 97, Varanasi, 1968.

Varāhamihira's Bṛhat Saṃhitā [then follows] Bṛhatsaṃhitā [in Nāgarī] With English Translation, Exhaustive Notes and Literary Comments, 2 parts, by Prof. M. Ramakrishna Bhat, Delhi, 1981–1982.

Bṛhatstotraratnākara — *Bṛhat-stotra-ratnākaraḥ I and II*, ed. R.N. Ācārya, Varanasi, 1983.

Caitanyabhāgavata — *Caitanyabhāgavata* of Vṛndāvana Dasa, Mayapur, 1997.

Caitanyacandrāmṛta — *Caitanya Candrāmṛtam* of Prabodhānanda, trans. Sarvabhāvana Dāsādhikarī, Vrindavan, 2004.

Caitanyacaritāmṛta — *The Caitanya Caritāmṛta of Kṛṣṇdāsa Kavirāja: A Translation and Commentary*, trans. E.C. Dimock Jr., ed. T.K. Stewart, Cambridge MA, HOS 56, 2000.

Murāri Gupta, Kṛṣnacaitanyacaritāmṛta, ed. Swami B.V. Bhāgavata, Vrindavan, 2006.

Śrī Caitanya-Caritāmṛta of Kṛṣṇadāsa Kavirāja Gosvāmī with Original Bengali Text, ed. and trans. Kṛṣṇadāsa Kavirāja & A.C. Bhaktivedanta Swami Prabhupāda, Los Angeles, 1975, [2]1996, 2002.

Caitanyacaritāmṛta by Kṛṣṇadāsa Kavirāja, ed. Bhakti Kevala Auḍulomi, Calcutta, 1957.

Cāṇakyarājanīti — *Cāṇakya-Rāja-Nīti*, trans. L. Sternbach, Madras, 1963.

Candraśekhar — *Candraśekhar kāhinī bā candranāth māhātmya*, Caṭṭagrām, n.d.

Candrāvalokana — **Candrāvalokana*, ms. D 4345 at the Government Oriental Manuscripts Library, Chennai, n.d.

Caṅkaṟpanirākaraṇam — *Meykaṇṭacāttiraṅkal*, publ. Department of Saivasiddhanta, University of Mandras, Chennai, 1988.

	Śrīmaṟaināṉacampantanāyaṉar aruḷicceyta caivac ciṟu nūlkaḷ (mutaṟpakuti), ed. T.C. Mīṉāṭcicuntaram Piḷḷai, Thiruvavaduthurai, 1954.
Carakasaṃhitā	*Carakasaṃhitā of Agniveśa, with the Āyurveda-Dīpikā Commentary of Cakrapāṇidatta*, ed. J. Trikamji, New Delhi, [5]1992.
	The Caraka Saṃhitā, 6 vols., Translations in Hindi, Gujarati and English by the Shree Gulabkunverba Ayurvedic Society, Jamnagar, 1949.
Caryāgītikoṣa	*Caryāgītikoṣa: With a Modern Bengali Translation and Facsimile of the Manuscript*, ed. Nilaratan Sen, Calcutta, 2001.
Catuḥślokibhāṣya	*Catuḥślokibhāṣyam, Stotraratnabhāṣyam, Gadhyatrayabhāṣyañca*, ed. C.V. Śrīvatsāṅkācāryar, Madras, 1968.
Caturvargacintāmaṇi	*Caturvargacintāmaṇi of Śrī Hemādri*, ed. Bharatacandraśiromaṇi, Varanasi, 1985.
Caurāsī Baiṭhak Caritra	*Chaurasi Baithak: Eightyfour Seats of Shri Vallabhacharya*, Shyam Das, Baroda, 1985.
Caurāsīpad	*The Caurāsī Pad of Śrī Hit Harivaṃś*, C.S.J. White, Honolulu, 1977; repr. "'The Love of Rādhā': A Translation of the Caurāsī Pad of Śrī Hit Harivaṃś with Commentary," *JVS* 7/1, 1998, 101–180.
	The Eighty-four Hymns of Hita Harivaṃśa: An Edition of the Caurāsī Pada, R. Snell, Delhi, 1991.
Cencunāṭakamu	*Cencunāṭakamu*, ed. K.J. Krishnamurti, Tirupati, 2007.
Chāndogyopaniṣad	*The Early Upaniṣads: Annotated Text and Translation*, ed. P. Olivelle, New York, 1998.
Chāndogyopaniṣadbhāṣya	*The Chha'ndogya Upanishad with the Commentary of Sankara A'cha'rya and the Gloss of A'nanda Giri*, ed. E. Röer, Calcutta, 1850.
Cintyāgama	**Cintyāgama*, paper transcript (T.13) at the French Institute of Pondicherry, n.d.
Civanāṉacittiyār	*Civanāṉacittiyār cupakkam civākkirayōkikaḷ uraiyuṭaṉ* (with Śivāgrayogī's commentary), publ. Thiruvavaduthurai Adheenam, Thiruvavaduthurai, 1965.
	Aruṇanti Civācāriyar Civañānacittiyār, J.M. Nallaswamy Pillai, Madras, 1913.
Civanāṉapōtam	*Civanāṉaptamum vārttikameṉṉum poḻippuraiyum civanāṉacuvāmika ceyta tirāviṭamāpāṭiyam eṉṉum Civanāṉapōtamāpāṭiyamum*, ed. Swaminathapanditar, 1906.
	Meykaṇṭacāttiraṅkal, publ. Department of Saivasiddhanta, University of Mandras, Chennai, 1988.
Civañānapōṭam	*Meykaṇṭatēvar Civañānapōṭam: Translated with Notes and Introduction*, J.M. Nallaswamy Pillai, Madras, 1895.
Civappirakācam	*Civappirakācam by Umāpati with the Commentary by Maturaiccivappirakācar*, ed. P. Ramanatha Pillai, Tirunelveli, 1975.
	Meykaṇṭacāttiraṅkal, publ. Department of Saivasiddhanta, University of Mandras, Chennai, 1988.
Dabistān-i maḏāhib	*The Dabistan or School of Manners*, D. Shea & A. Troyer, New York, [1]1843, 1901.
	Dabistān-i maḏāhib, Mīr Ḏu'l-Fiqār Ardistānī Mawbadšāh; ET: D. Shea & A. Troyer, *Hinduism during the Mughal India of the 17th Century*, Patna, 1998.
Dādūjanmalīlā	*The Hindī Biography of Dādū Dayāl (Janmalīlā)*, ed. and trans. W.M. Callewaert, Delhi, 1988.
Dādūvāṇī	*Śrī Dādūdayāljī kī vāṇī: With Hindi Translation and Commentary*, ed. Svāmī Nārāyaṇdās, Jaipur, n.d. (c. 1969) (Hind.).

	Śrī Dādūdayāljī kī vāṇī saṭīk, ed. Maṅgaldās Svāmī, Jaipur, n.d. (c. 1951) (Hind.).
Dānakelikaumudī	*Dānakelikaumudī* by Rūpa Gosvāmī, ed. Purīdāsa Mahāśaya, Vrindavan, 1947.
Dānasāgara	*Ballālasena, Dānasāgara*, ed. B. Bhattacharya, Calcutta, 1956.
Dasam Granth	*Sri Dasam Granth Sahib Text and Translation*, ed. J. Singh & D. Singh, 1999.
Daśaprakaraṇāni	*Daśaprakaraṇāni*, 4 vols., ed. P.P Lakṣmīnārāyaṇopādhyāya, Bangalore, 1971.
Daśavidhahetunirūpaṇa	[*Vaikhānasasmārtasūtra*]= *Vaikhānasagṛhyasūtra* [*with Vaikhānasadharmasūtra and -pravarasūtra*], with Śrīnivāsa-makhin [=-Dīkṣita]'s *Tātparyacintāmaṇi* commentary and his *Daśavidhahetunirūpaṇa*, and extracts from Nṛsiṃhāgnicit Vājapeyin [= Nṛsiṃha Vājapeyin]'s commentary, ed. R. Pārthasārathi Bhaṭṭācārya, Śaka 1889 (= 1967 CE).
Dattātreyayogaśāstra	*Dattātreyayogaśāstra*, ed. B. Avasthi, Delhi, 1982.
	**Dattātreyayogaśāstra*, mss. 1936 and 1937 at the Maharaja Mansingh Pustak Prakash, Jodhpur, n.d.
	**Dattātreyayogaśāstra*, ms. 4107 at the Oriental Institute Baroda, Vadodara, n.d.
	**Dattātreyayogaśāstra*, ms. 6/4–399 at the Prajna Pathashala Mandal, Mumbai, n.d.
	**Dattātreyayogaśāstra*, mss. 4369, R5579, and 5585 at the Government Oriental Manuscripts Library, Chennai, n.d.
Devībhāgavatapurāṇa	Devībhāgavatapurāṇa Vijnanananda, Swami, trans. Sri Mad Devī Bhāgavata Purāṇa, n.d.
Devīdvyardhaśatikā	*Devīdvyardhaśatikā*, ms. 1-242, NGMPP A161.12 (paper; Newari script), at the National Archives Kathmandu, Kathmandu, n.d., on: www.muktabodha.org (accessed August 2013).
Devīgītā	*The Devī Gītā, The Song of the Goddess: A Translation, Annotation, and Commentary*, trans. C.M. Brown, Albany, 1998.
	The Song of the Goddess, the Devi Gita: Spiritual Counsel of the Great Goddess, trans. C.M. Brown, Albany, 2002.
Devīkalottarāgama	**Devīkalottarāgama*, paper transcript (T.89) at the French Institute of Pondicherry, n.d.
Devīmāhātmya	*Devi-Mahatmya: The Glorification of the Great Goddess*, trans. V.S. Agrawala, Varanasi, 1963.
	Devī Māhātmyam, trans. S. Jagadiswarananda, Madras, 1953.
Devīnāmavilāsa	*The Devīnāmavilāsa of Sāhib Kaul*, ed. M. Kaul, Delhi, 1942, 1989.
Dhammasaṅgaṇi	*Dhammasaṅgaṇi*, ed. E. Müller, London, 1885.
Dharmottarapradīpa	*Dharmottarapradīpa*, ed. D. Malvania, TSWS 2, Patna, ²1971.
Dhūrtākhyāna	*Haribhadra: Ballade des coquins*, ed. J.-P. Osier & N. Balbir, Paris, 2004.
Dhvanyāloka	*The Dhvanyāloka of Ānandavardhana with the Locana of Abhinavagupta*, ed. with introduction by D.H.H. Ingalls, trans. by D.H.H. Ingalls *et al.*, Cambridge MA, 1990.
	Dhvanyāloka of Ānandavardhana with the Locana of Abhinavagupta, 3 vols., ed. R. Tripāṭhi, Delhi, 1975–1981.
Dhvanyālokalocana	*The Dhvanyāloka of Ānandavardhana with the Locana of Abhinavagupta*, ed. with introduction by D.H.H. Ingalls, trans. by D.H.H. Ingalls *et al.*, Cambridge MA, 1990.
Dīghanikāya	*Dīghanikāya*, ed. T.W. Rhys Davids & J.E. Carpenter, London, 1890–1911.

Digvijaya	*Sankara -Dig-Vijaya: The Traditional Life of Sri Sankaracharya, by Madhava-Vidyaranya*, trans. T. Swami, Madras, n.d.
Dīkṣātattvaprakāśa	*Dīkṣātattvaprakāśa, Paṇḍita Śrī Dulāreprasāda Śāstriṇā saṃgṛhītaḥ*, Calcutta, 1924, ^{2}1966.
Divyasūricarita	*The Divya Suri Caritam by Garudavahana Pandita*, Bombay, 1798.
Dvādaśastotra	*Dvādaśastotra of Śrī Madhvācārya*, Madras, 1975.
Dvipadabhāgavatamu	*Dvipadabhāgavatamu* by T. Veṅgamāmba, books 1 & 2, ed. Gopikrishna, Hyderabad, 2009.
Epigraphia Indica	*Epigraphia Indica*, 42 vols., Delhi, 1892–1978.
Etymologisches Wörterbuch des Altindoarischen	*Etymologisches Wörterbuch des Altindoarischen*, 3 vols., M. Mayrhofer, Heidelberg, 1992–2001.
Gadhyatrayabhāṣya	*Catuḥślokibhāṣyam, Stotraratnabhāṣyam, Gadhyatrayabhāṣyañca*, ed. C.V. Śrīvatsāṅkācāryar, Madras, 1968.
Gadyarāja	*Gadyarāja: A Fourteenth Century Marathi Version of the Kṛṣṇa Legend*, trans. I.M.P. Raeside, Bombay, 1989.
Gadyatraya	*Rāmānujagranthamālā*, ed. P.B. Annangaracariar, Kanci, 1974.
Gaṇakārikā	*Gaṇakārikā, with the Ratnaṭīkā of Bhāsarvajña*, ed., C.D. Dalal, GaOS 15, Baroda, 1920, repr. 1966.
Gaṇeśagītā	*Gaṇeśagītā: A Study, Translation with Notes and a Condensed Rendering of the Commentary of Nīlakaṇṭha*, ed. and trans. K. Yoroi, The Hague, 1968.
Gaṇeśapurāṇa	*The Gaṇeśa Purāṇa*, trans. G. Bailey, vols. I–II, Wiesbaden, 1995, 2008.
Gaṇeśatāpanīyopaniṣad	"Die Gaṇeśatāpanīya-Upaniṣad, Teil 1: Text und Übersetzung, Teil 2: Anmerkungen," (unpubl.) diss., Marburg University, 1965.
Gārgīyajyotiṣa	*The Yuga Purāṇa: Critically Edited, With an English Translation and a Detailed Introduction*, ed. and trans. J.E. Mitchener, Calcutta, 1986.
Garuḍapurāṇa	*The Garuḍapurāṇa (Sāroddhāra)*, trans. E. Wood & S.V. Subrahmanyam, Allahabad, 1911. *Garuḍapurāṇam*, ed. R. Bhattacarya, Varanasi, 1964.
Gāthā (Eknāth)	*Śrīeknāthmahārāj Yāñcyā Abhaṅgācī Gāthā*, ed. T.H. Āvaṭe, Poona, 1908. *Eknāthsvāmīkṛt Abhaṅgācī Gāthā*, publ. Induprakāś, Mumbai, 1906. *Śrīeknāth Mahārājāñcyā Abhaṅgāñcī Gāthā*, ed. T. Tātyā, Mumbai, 1903. *Eknāthī Gāthā*, ed. R.Ś. Gondhaḷekar, Poona, 1893.
Gautamadharmasūtra	*Dharmasūtras: The Law Codes of Āpastamba, Gautama, Baudhāyana and Vasiṣṭha*, trans. P. Olivelle, Dehli, 2.
Gheraṇḍasaṃhitā	*Das Indische Yoga-Lehrbuch Gheraṇḍa-Saṃhitā. Aus dem Sanskrit Übersetzt, Kommentiert und mit Abbildungen Herausgegeben*, ed. and trans. P. Thomi, Wichtrach, ^{2}2006. *Gheraṇḍasaṃhitā*, ed. J. Mallinson, New York, 2004.
Gītābhāṣya	*Rāmānuja on the Bhagavadgītā: A Condensed Rendering of His Gītābhāṣya with Copious Notes and Introduction*, ed. and trans. J.A.B. van Buitenen, The Hague, 1951. *Rāmānujagranthamālā*, ed. P.B. Annangaracariar, Kanci, 1974.
Gītagovinda	*Jayadeva's Gitagovinda: Love Song of the Dark Lord*, B. Stoler-Miller, Delhi, 1984. *Gītagovindakāvyam: With Kāntamiśra's Padabhāvārthacandrikā*, ed. Candraśekhara Hota, Allahabad, 1997. *Le Gītagovinda de Jayadeva: Texte, Concordance, et Index*, H. Quellet, Hildesheim, 1978. *Gītagovindakāvyam: With the Sañjivanī of Vanamālibhaṭṭa, Padadyotanikā of Nārāyaṇa Paṇḍita, and Jayantī of Kṛṣṇa*, Jayadeva, Hyderabad, 1969.

	Gītagovinda: With King Mānāṅka's Commentary, ed. V.M. Kulkarni, Ahmedabad, 1965.
	Gītagovinda, ed. Harekṛṣṇa Mukhopadhyāya, Calcutta, 1957.
	Gītagovindakāvyam: With the Raskapriyā of Kumbhakarṇa and the Rasamañjarī of Śaṅkaramiśra, ed. Mangesh Ramkrishna Telang & Vasudev Laxman Panshikar, Bombay, 1899.
Gītārthasaṃgraha	*Gītārthasaṅgraha of Abhinavagupta: Translation with an Introductory Study*, ed. and trans. A. Sharma, Leiden, 1983.
	Abhinavagupta's Commentary on the Bhagavad Gītā: Gītārtha Saṃgraha, trans. B. Marjanovic, Varanasi, 2002.
	Śrīmad Bhagavad Gītā With Commentary by Mahāmāheshvara Rājānaka Abhinava Gupta, ed. L.R. Brahamachārī, Srinagar, 1933.
Gobhilagṛhyasūtra	*Gobhilagṛhyasūtra*, ed. F. Knauer, Dorpat, 1884.
Gopālacampū	*Gopālacampū*, Jīva Gosvāmī, ed. Purīdās, Dhaka, 1947.
Gopālarājavaṃśāvalī	*Gopālarājavaṃśāvalī*, ed. and trans. D. Vajrācārya & Kamal P. Malla, Wiesbaden, 1985.
Gorakhbāṇī	*Gorakhbāṇī*, ed. P.D. Badathval, Allahabad, 1960.
Gorakṣasaṃhitā	*Gorakṣasaṃhitā*, ed. J.S. Pandeya, SBG 111, Varanasi, 1976.
Gorakṣaśataka	**Gorakṣaśataka*, ms. R 7874 at the Government Oriental Manuscripts Library, Chennai, n.d..
Gorakṣasiddhāntasaṃgraha	*Gorakṣasiddhāntasaṃgraha*, ed. J.S. Pandeya, SBG 110, Varanasi, 1973.
Gorakṣavijaya	*Gorakṣavijaya of Vidyāpati*, ed. H. Mishra, Patna, 1984.
Gosāīṃ Carit	*Gosāīṃ-carit*, K. Gupta, 1964.
Govindalīlāmṛta	*Govindalīlāmṛta* by Kṛṣṇadāsa Kavirajā, ed. Haridāsa Śāstrī, Vrindavan, 1981.
Guṇamālā	*Guṇamālā*, Śaṅkaradeva, Jorhat, 1975.
Gurū Granth Sāhib	(*Śrī*) *Gurū Granth Sāhib with Complete Index*, 2 parts, W.M. Callewaert, Delhi, 1996.
Haribhaktivilāsa	*Gopālabhaṭṭa Gosvāmī: Śrī Śrī Haribhaktivilāsaḥ*, Dacca, 1946.
	Haribhaktivilāsa of Gopāla Bhaṭṭa, ed. by Haridāsa Śāstri, Vrindavan, 1986.
Haripaṭh	*L'Invocation: Le Haripath de Dnyandev*, C. Vaudeville, Paris, 1969.
Harivaṃśa	*The Harivaṃśa: Being the Khila or Supplement to the Mahābhārata, for the First Time Critically Edited*, ed. P.L. Vaidya, 2 vols., Poona, 1969–1971.
Haṭha(yoga)pradīpikā	*Haṭhapradīpikā of Svātmārāma (10 chapters): With Yogaprakāśikā Commentary by Bālakṛṣṇa*, ed. M.L. Gharote & P. Devnath, Lonavla, 2001.
	Haṭhapradīpikā of Svātmārāma, ed. S. Digambarji & P. Jhā, Lonavla, 1970.
Haṭhapradīpikā Siddhāntamuktāvalī	**Haṭhapradīpikā Siddhāntamuktāvalī*, ms. 6756 at Maharaja Mansingh Pustak Prakash, Jodhpur, n.d.
Haṭhapradīpikājyotsnā	*Haṭhapradīpikājyotsnā of Brahmānanda*, ed. S. Maheśānand, B. Śarmā, J. Sahāy & R. Bodhe, Lonavla, 2002.
Haṭharatnāvalī	*Haṭharatnāvalī*, ed. M.L. Gharote, P. Devnath & V.K. Jha, Lonavla, 2002.
Hīr Vāris Śāh	*The Adventures of Hir and Ranjha*, Waris Shah, London, 1973.
Hitacaritra	*Hita-Caritra* by Uttamdās, Nagari Pracarini Sabha, Mayasankar Yajnik collection, MS 4822, 1760.
Īśānaśivagurudevapaddhati	*Īśānaśivagurudevapraṇītā*, ed. T. Ganapati Sastri, 4 vols., New Delhi, 1990.
Iṣṭasiddhi	*Iṣṭasiddhi of Vimuktātman*, ed. M. Hiriyanna, Baroda, 1933.

Īśvarapratyabhijñākārikā	*The Īśvarapratyabhijñākārikā of Utpaladeva with the Author's Vṛtti*, ed. F. Torella, Delhi, 2002.
Īśvarapratyabhijñākārikāvṛtti	*The Īśvarapratyabhijñākārikā of Utpaladeva with the Author's Vṛtti*, ed. F. Torella, Delhi, 2002.
	The Siddhitrayī and the Īśvarapratyabhijākārikāvṛtti, ed. M.K. Shastri, Srinagar, 1921.
Īśvarapratyabhijñāvimarśinī	*Bhāskarī: A Commentary on the Īśvarapratyabhijñāvimarśinī of Ācārya Abhinavagupta* (Abhinavagupta's text with Bhāskarī commentary), 3 vols., ed. and trans. K.A. Subramania Iyer and K.C. Pandey, Delhi, 1986.
Īśvarapratyabhijñāvivṛtivimarśinī	*The Īśvarapratyabhijñāvivṛtivimarśinī by Abhinavagupta*, 3 vols., ed. by M.K. Shastri, Delhi, 1987.
Īśvarasaṃhitā	*Īśvarasaṃhitā Anantācāryais saṃśodhitā*, Śāstramuktāvaḷī 45, Kanchipuram, 1923.
Jaiminīyabrāhmaṇa	*Jaiminīya Brāhmaṇa of the Sāmaveda Critically Edited*, ed. R. Vira & L. Chandra, Delhi, 1954.
Jātaka	*The Jātaka or Stories of the Buddha's Former Births*, vol. III, ed. E.B. Cowell, trans. H.T. Francis & R.A. Neil, London, 1957.
	The Jātaka Together with its Commentary Being Tales of the Anterior Birhts of Gotama Buddha, ed. V. Fausbøll, London, 1877–1897.
Jayadrathayāmala	*Jayadrathayāmala tantra*: *Ṣaṭka* 1, ms. 5/4650, NGMPP B122/7 [paper; Devanāgarī script]; Ṣaṭka 2, ms. 5/4650, NGMPP A153/2 [paper; Devanāgarī script]; Ṣaṭka 3, ms. 5/1975, NGMPP A152/9 [paper; Newari script]; Ṣaṭka 4, ms. 1/1468, NGMPP B122/4, [paper; Newari script], all at National Archives Kathmandu (= unpublished transcription by O. Serbaeva Saraogi, 2007–2009), Kathmandu, n.d., on: www.muktabodha.org (accessed August 2013).
Jayākhyasaṃhitā	*Jayākhyasaṃhitā of Pāñcarātra Āgama, Critically Edited with Introduction in Sanskrit, Indices, etc.*, ed. Embar Krishnamacharya, GaOS 54, Baroda, 1967.
Jīvābhigama	*Jīvājīvābhigamasūtra: mūlapāṭha, prastāvanā, artha, vivecana, tathā pariśiṣṭa, ādi yukta*, Byāvara, 2002.
Jñānāmṛtasārasaṃhitā	*The Nárada Pancha Rátra in the Original Sanscrit*, ed. by K.M. Banerjea, BI.NS. 17, 25, 34, 75, Calcutta, 1865.
Jnānāvaraṇabhāṣya	*Śivajnānabodha with with the Commentary Called Jnānāvaraṇabhāṣya by Veḷḷiyampalavāṇamuṉivar*, ed. T. Ganesan, forthcoming.
Jñāneśvarī	(*Śrī*)-*Jñāneśvarī of Jñānadeva*, ed. G.S. Naṇadīkar, 5 vols., Mumbai, 2001.
	The Jñāneśvarī, trans. R.S. Lokapur, Belgaum, 1995.
	Jnaneshwar's Gita: A Rendering of the Jnaneshwari, trans. S. Kripananda, Albany, 1989.
	Sri Jnanadeva's Bhāvārtha Dīpikā: Otherwise Known as Jnāneshwari, R.K. Bhagwat, Madras, 1979.
	Śrījñāneśvarī, V.K. Rajwade, Mumbai, 1977.
	Jnāneshvari (*Bhāvārthadipikā*), V.G. Pradhan & H.M. Lambert, London, 1967.
Kabīr Granthāvalī	*Kabīr Granthāvalī*, Pārasanātha Tivārī, Ilāhābād, 1989; Prayāga, 1961.
	Kabīr Granthāvali by Śyāmasundaradāsa, Prayāga, 1928; Kāśī, 1951.
Kabīr Vāṇī	*Kabīr Vāṇī*, Charlotte Vaudeville, Institut français d'Indologie, Pondichéry, 1982.
Kadaḷiya karpura	*Kadaḷiya karpura*, H. T[h]ipperudra Swamy, Mysore, [7]1986; ET: *Soul unto the Sublime*, Hubli, 1982.

Kalātattvakośa	*Kalātattvakośa*, vol. V: *Form/Shape (ākāra/ākṛti)*, ed. R.C. Sharma, New Delhi, 2002.
Kālikāpurāṇa	*Kālikāpurāṇa*, trans. B. Shastri, Delhi, 1991.
Kalyāṇ Tīrthāṅk	*Kalyāṇ Tīrthāṅk*, Gorakhpur, 1957 (Hind.).
Kāmasūtra	*The Kama sutra of Vatsyayana*, trans. R. Burton, New York, 1964.
	The Complete Kāma Sutra, trans. A. Danielou, Rochester, 1994.
Kāmikāgama	*Kāmikāgama*, vol. I: *Pūrvabhāga*, vol. II: *Uttarabhāga*, publ. South Indian Archakar Association, Chennai, 1975, 1988.
Kaṇādasūtravivṛti	*Vaiśeṣikadarśanam*, ed. N. Shiromani, Calcutta, 1886.
Kanhāvat	*Kanhāvat of Malik Muhammad Jāyasī*, ed. P.L. Gupta, Varanasi, 1981.
Kāśyapasaṃhitā	*Kāśyapasaṃhitā of Vṛddhajīvaka*, ed. J. Trikamji & S. Sharma, NSS 1, Kathmandu, (microfiche) 1938.
	Kāṭhaka. Die Saṃhitā der Kaṭha-Śākhā, ed. L. von Schroeder, 3 vols., Leipzig, 1900–1910, repr. ed. K.L. Janert, Wiesbaden, 1970.
Kathāsaritsāgara	*The Ocean of Stories* being C.H. Tawneys translation of Somadeva's *Kathā Sarit Sāgara*, ed. N.M. Penzer, 10 vols., Boston, 1924ff.
Kāṭhakasaṃhitā	*Kāṭhaka: Die Saṃhitā der Kaṭha-Śākhā*, 3 vols., ed. L. von Schröder, Leizig, 1900–1910, repr. 1979.
Kaṭhopaniṣad	*Kaṭhopaniṣad No. 3 in Daśopanishads, with the Commentary of Sri Upanishad-Brahma-Yogin*, ed. C. Kunhan Raja, vol. I, Madras, 1935.
Kātyāyanaśrautasūtra	*Kātyāyana-Śrautasūtra: Text with English Translation and Notes*, ed. G.U. Thite, Delhi, 2006.
	Kātyāyana Śrauta Sūtra, ed. and trans. H.G. Ranade, Poona, 1978.
Kaulajñānanirṇaya	"Kaulajñānanirṇaya," ed. P.C. Bagchi, in: *idem, Kaulajñānanirṇaya and Some Minor Texts of the School of Matsyendranātha*, CSS 3, Calcutta, 1934.
Kauśikasūtra	*Altindisches Zauberritual: Probe einer Uebersetzung der wichtigsten Theile des Kauśika Sūtra*, W. Caland, Amsterdam, 1900.
	Kauśika Sūtra, ed., Bloomfield, Delhi, 1972.
Kauṣītakibrāhmaṇa	*Kauṣītaki Brāhmaṇa: Text*, ed. S. Sarma, VOHD suppl. 9/1, Wiesbaden, 1968.
	The Aitareya and Kauṣītaki Brāhmaṇas of the Rigveda, trans. A.B. Keith, HOS 25, Delhi, 1971.
Kauṣītakyupaniṣad	"Kauṣītaki Upaniṣad," ed. A. Frenz, *IIJ* 11, 1968–1969, 79–129.
Kavitāvalī	*Tulsī Dās: Kavitāvalī*, F.R. Allchin, 1964.
Kāvyanirṇaya	*Bhikhārīdās: Kāvyanirṇaya*, ed. Ved Prakash (Ved Prakāś), Delhi, 2006.
	Bhikhārīdās: Kāvyanirṇaya, ed. J. Caturvedi (Caturvedī), Mathura, 1959.
Khaḍgamālāstotra	*Śrīvidyā Khaḍgamālā*, ed. S.S. Shastri, Madras, 1954.
Khecarīvidyā	*The Khecarīvidyā of Ādinātha: A Critical Edition and Annotated Translation of an Early Text of Haṭhayoga*, ed. J. Mallinson, London, 2007.
Kiraṇāgama	*Bhatta Ramakantha's Commentary on the Kiranatantra, vol. I, chs. 1–6*, ed. D. Goodall, crit. ed., PIFI 86/1, Pondicherry, 1998.
	Kiraṇāgama, ed. T.R. Panchapagesa Sivacharya & K.M. Subrahmanya Sastri, Devakottai, 1932.
Kiraṇatantra	*Bhaṭṭa Rāmakaṇṭha's Commentary on the Kiraṇatantra*, vol. I: *chapters 1–6*, ed. D. Goodall, Pondicherry, 1998.
Kiraṇāvalī	*Kiraṇāvalī*, ed. J.S. Jetly, GaOS 154, Baroda, 1971.
Kiraṇāvalīprakāśa	*Kiraṇāvālī*, appendix (617–706), ed. N.C. Vedantatirtha, BI 200/4, Calcutta, 1956.
Kiraṇāvalīṭīkā	*Kiraṇāvālī*, appendix (617–706), ed. N.C. Vedantatirtha, BI 200/4, Calcutta, 1956.

Kīrtanaghoṣa — *Kīrttana-ghoṣa āru Nāma-ghoṣa*, Śaṅkaradeva, Guwahati, 1962.

Kīrtanalu — *The Complete Kritis of Sri Thyagaraja: Compiled by Maddali Venkata Subbayya, Telugu Script with English Transliteration and Translation*, M.V. Subbayya, Hyderabad, 2008.
Tyagaraja Keertanalu, K.V. Shastri, 1975.

Kitāb taḥqīq mā li'l-Hind — *Kitāb taḥqīq mā li'l-Hind*, A.R. al-Bīrūnī; ET: E.C. Sachau, *Alberūnī's India*, London, 1910.

Kramasadbhāvatantra — *Kramasadbhāvatantra*, ms. 1–76 Śaivatantra 144, NGMPP A209/23 [material?], at the National Archives Kathmandu, Kathmandu, n.d., on: www.muktabodha.org (accessed August 2013).

Kriyādhikāra — *Kriyādhikāra*, ed. by R.B. Pārthasārathi Bhaṭṭācārya, Tirupati, 1953.

Kriyāsaṃgrahapañjikā — *Kuladatta's Kriyāsaṃgrahapañjikā*, ed. T. Tanemura, Groningen, 2004.

Kṛtyakalpataru — *Kṛtyakalpataru by Bhaṭṭa Lakṣmīdhara*, ed. K.V.R. Aiyyangar, 11 vols., GaOS 92, 98, 100–102, 106, 110–112, 119, 123, Baroda, 1941–1953.

Kṛṣṇasandarbha — *Kṛṣṇasandarbha and Its Critical Study* by Jīva Gosvāmī, ed., Chinmayi Chatterjee, Calcutta, 1986.

Kubjikāmatatantra — *The Kubjikāmatatantra. Kulālikāmnāya Version: Critical Edition*, eds. T. Goudriaan & A. Schoterman, Leiden, 1988.

Kumārasaṃbhava — *Kālidāsa's Kumārasaṃbhava*, trans. M.R. Kale, cantos I–VIII, 1981, repr. 1986.

Kūrmapurāṇa — *The Kūrma Purāṇa with English Translation*, trans. A. Bhattacharya, S. Mukherji, V.K. Varma & G.S. Rai, ed. A.S. Gupta, Varanasi, 1972.
Kūrmapurāṇa, ed. A.S. Gupta, Varanasi, 1972.
The Kūrma Purāṇa: A System of Hindu Mythology and Tradition, ed. N. Mukhopadhyaya, Calcutta, 1890.

Laghubhāgavatāmṛta — *Laghubhāgavatāmṛta* by Rūpa Gosvāmī, ed. Bhakti Prajnan Yati, Mayapura, 1995.

Lakṣmītantra — *Lakṣmī Tantra: A Pāñcarātra Text*, trans. S. Gupta, 1972, repr. 2003, 2007.

Lakṣmīviśiṣṭādvaitabhāṣya — *Lakṣmīviśiṣṭādvaitabhāṣya by Śrīnivāsa Dīkṣita, with Sundararāja's Nigamacūḍādarpaṇa commentary*, ed. Addaṅkitirumalai Śrīnivāsatātācārya, 1896.

Lalitāsahasranāma — *Lalitāsahasranāma (Taken from Brahmāṇḍapurāṇa), Containing "Saubhagyabhāskara" Sanskrit Commentary of Bhāskararāya, with Hindi Commentary by Shri Bharat Bhushan*, Vrajajivan Prachyabharati Granthamala 43, Delhi, 2009.

Lallā-Vākyāni — *Mystical Verses of Lallā*, J. Kak, Delhi, 2007. *Lallā-Vākyāni: Or The Wise Sayings of Lal Ded*, ed. and trans. G. Grierson & L.D. Barnett, London, 1920.

Laṅkāvatārasūtra — *Laṅkāvatārasūtra*, ed. P.L. Vaidya, BST 3, Darbhanga, 1963.

Lexikon der indogermanischen Verben — *Lexikon der indogermanischen Verben. Die Wurzeln und ihre Primärstammbildungen*, ed. H. Rix, Wiesbaden, 2001.

Līlāvatī — *Līlāvatī*, 2 vols., ed. V.G. Āpaṭe, Pune, 1937.

Liṅgadhāraṇacandrikā — *Lingadhāranachandrikā of Nandikeshwara*, ed. and trans. M.R. Sakhara, Belgaum, n.d. (c. 1942).
Liṅgadhāraṇacandrikā [of Nandikeśvara], Kāśī, 1905. (Skt.)

Liṅgapurāṇa — *Liṅgapurāṇa of Sage Kṛṣṇa Dvaipāyana Vyāsa, with Sanskrit commentary Śivatoṣiṇī of Gaṇeśa Nātu*, ed. J.L. Shastri, 1985.

Mādhavamahotsava — *Mādhavamahotsava* by Jīva Gosvāmī, Bengali trans. Haridās Dās, Nabadwip, 1942.

Mādhuryakadambinī — *Mādhurya-kadambinī of Viśvanātha Cakravartī*, version 3 (based on three editions), on: www.granthamandira.com (accessed January, 2011).

Mahābhāgavatapurāṇa — *Mahābhāgavatapurāṇa: An Ancient Treatise on Śakti Cult*, ed. P. Kumar, Delhi, 1983.

Mahābhārata — *The Mahābhārata for the First Time Critically Edited*, ed. V.S. Sukthankar, S.K. Belvalkar, F.D. Edgerton *et al.*, 19 vols., Poona, 1927–1966.
Mahabharata of Krishna-Dwaipayana Vyasa, trans. and ed. K.M. Ganguli, 4 vols., 1883–1896, repr. 2004.
The Mahābhārata: Book 11. The Book of the Women; Book 12. The Book of Peace. Part One, trans. J. Fitzgerald, Chicago, 2004.
The Mahābhārata, trans. K.M. Ganguli, New Delhi, 2004.
The Mahābhārata, vol. II/2: *The Book of the Assembly Hall*; vol. III: *The Book of the Forest*, trans. J.A.B. van Buitenen, Chicago, 1975.
Das Mahābhārata und seine Theile, 4 vols., ed. A. Holtzmann, Kiel, 1892–1895.
The Mahabharata of Krishna-Dwaipayana Vyasa, trans. P.C. Roy, 12 vols., Calcutta, 1952–1962.

Mahābhāṣya — *Kātyāyana's First Vārttika on Pāṇini's Aṣṭādhyāyī, Mahābhāṣya of Patañjali*, ed. F. Kielhorn, vol. I/2, Pune, [3]1962.
The Vyâkaranamahâbhâshya of Patanjali, ed. F. Kielhorn, 3 vols., Bombay, 1880–1885.

Mahādēviyakkanapurāṇa — *Cannabasavāṅkana Mahādēviyakkana purāṇa*, ed. B.N. Chandraiah, Mysore, 1968.

Mahānayakprakāśa — *Mahānayakprakāśa*, Arṇasiṃha Kulācārya, in Kālikākulapañcaśataka, ms. 5–358, NGMPP B30/26, ff. 103v1–130r5 [palm-leaf; Newari script] at the National Archives Kathmandu, Kathmandu, n.d., on: www.muktabodha.org (accessed August 2013).

Mahānayaprakāśa — *Mahānayaprakāśa*, ed. K. Sāmbaśiva Śāstrī, TSS 130/Citrodayamañjarī 19, Trivandrum, 1937.

Mahānuśāsana — *Mathamnay Setu or Mahanushasanam*, P. Mishra, Dwarka, 2001.

Mahārthmañjarī — *Mahārthmañjarī of Maheśvarānanda with the Autocommentary Parimala*, ed. V. Dvivedi, Varanasi, 1972.

Mahāvaṃśa — *Mahāvamsa: The Great Chronicle of Ceylon*, trans. W. Geiger, London, 1912.

Mahotsavavidhi — *A Priests' Guide for the Great Festival: Aghorashiva's Mahotsavavidhi*, R. Davis, Oxford, 2010.

Maḫzan al-ʿulūm — *Maḫzan al-ʿulūm*, Vraja Mohana, n.l., 1867.

Maitrāyaṇisaṃhitā — *Maitrāyaṇisaṃhitā: Die Saṃhitā der Maitrāyaṇīya-Śākhā*, ed. L. von Schroeder, 4 vols., Wiesbaden, 1970, 1881–1886.

Maitrāyaṇīyopaniṣad — *The Maitrāyaṇīya Upaniṣad: A Critical Essay, with Text, Translation and Commentary*, ed. and trans. J.A.B. van Buitenen, The Hague, 1962.
Maitrāyaṇyupaniṣad, in: V.P. Limaye and R.D. Vadekar, eds., *Eighteen Principal Upaniṣads*, vol. I, Poona, 1958, 325–357.

Majjhimanikāya — *Majjhimanikāya*, ed. V. Trenckner & R. Chalmers, London, 1888–1899.

Majmaʿ al-baḥrayn — *Majmaʿ al-baḥrayn*, M. Dārā Šikōh; ET: ed. M. al-Ḥaqq, *Majmaʿ-ul-Baḥrain or the Mingling of the Two Oceans*, Calcutta, 1998.

Mālinīślokavārttika — *Abhinavagupta's Philosophy of Revelation: Mālinīślokavārttika 1, 1–399*, J. Hanneder, Groningen, 1998.

Mālinīvijayavārttika — *Śrī Mālinīvijaya Vārttikam*, ed. M.K., Srinagar, 1921.

Mālinīvijayottaratantra — *The Yoga of the Mālinīvijayottaratantra: Chapters 1–4, 7, 11–17*, S. Vasudeva, Pondicherry, 2004.
Śrī Mālinīvijayottara Tantram, ed. M.K. Shastri, Delhi, 1984.

Manthānabhairavatantra — *Manthānabhairavatantram Kumārikākhaṇḍaḥ: The Section Concerning the Virgin Goddess of the Tantra of the Churning Bhairava*, 14 vols., ed. and trans. M. Dyczkowski, 2009.

Mantramahodadhi	*Mantramahodadhiḥsaṭīkaḥ*, Bombay, 1910, rev. ed. 1962, repr. 1983.
Manuśāstravivaraṇa	*Bhāruci's Commentary on the Manusmṛti* (*The Manu-Śāstra-Vivaraṇa, Books 6–12*), 2 vols., ed. J.D.M. Derrett, Wiesbaden, 1975.
Manusmṛti	*Manu's Code of Law: A Critical Edition and Translation of the Mānava-Dharmaśāstra*, ed. and trans. P. Olivelle, New York, 2005.
	Manusmṛti with the Sanskrit Commentary Manvarthamuktāvalī of Kullūka Bhaṭṭa, ed. J.L. Shastri, Delhi, 1983.
	Manu-Smṛti with the Manubhāṣya of Medhātithi, 2 vols., ed. and trans. G. Jha, 2 vols., Calcutta, 1932–1939.
	Manusmṛti: The Laws of Manu, transl. by W. Doniger with B.K. Smith, New Delhi, 1991.
	Manusmṛti, vols. I–VI, ed. with the commentaries of Medhātithi, Sarvajñanārāyaṇa, Kullūka, Rāghavānanda, Nandana, Rāmacandra, Maṇirāma, Govindarāja, & Bhāruci by J.H. Dave, Bombay, 1972–1984.
	The Laws of Manu, trans. G. Bühler, *Sacred Books of the East*, vol. XXV, Oxford, 1886.
	Manava-Dharma-Sastra or the Institutes of Manu, ed. G.C. Haughton, London, 1825.
Manvarthamuktāvalī	*Manusmṛti with the Sanskrit Commentary Manvarthamuktāvalī of Kullūka Bhaṭṭa*, ed. J.L. Shastri, Delhi, 1983.
Māpāṭiyam	*Civanāṉaptamum vārttikameṉṉum poḻippuraiyum civanāṉacuvāmika ceyta tirāviṭamāpāṭiyam eṉṉum Civanāṉapōtamāpāṭiyamum*, ed. Swaminathapanditar, 1906.
Mārkaṇḍeyapurāṇa	*The Márcaṇḍeya Puráṇa*, ed. K.M. Banerjea, Calcutta, 1862, repr. 1980.
	Mārkaṇḍeya Purāṇa, transl. F.E. Pargiter, Calcutta, 1904.
	Mārkaṇḍeya Purāṇa, Delhi, 1983.
	Mārkaṇḍeyapurāṇa, ed. K.M. Banerjea, Calcutta, 1862.
Mārkaṇḍeyasaṃhitā	*Mārkaṇḍeya Saṃhitā*, Tirupati, 1984.
Mataṅgapārameśvaratantra	*Mataṅgapārameśvaratantra: Kriyāpāda, Caryāpāda and Yogapāda, with the Commentary of Bhaṭṭa Rāmakaṇṭha up to Kriyāpāda 11:12b.*, ed. N.R. Bhatt, PIFI 65, Pondicherry, 1982.
Matsyapurāṇa	*Matsyapurāṇa*, ĀSS 54, Poona, 1907.
	Śrīmadvaipāyanamunipraṇītaṃ Matsyapurāṇam, ed. H.N. Apte, Pune, 1907.
Mayamata	*Mayamatam: Treatise of Housing, Architecture and Iconography*, ed. B. Dagens, 2 vols., New Delhi, 1994.
	Traité sanskrit d'architecture, vol. I: *Première Partie: Ch. I à XXV, Edition Critique, Traduction et Notes*, vol. II : *Deuxième Partie: Ch. XXVI–XXXVI et Index-glossaire général, Edition Critique, Traduction et Notes*, by Bruno Dagens, PIFI 40/1–2, Pondichéry, 1970–1976.
Meymmoḻiccaritai	*Iḷaṅkārikkuṭi meymoḻittēvar aruḷiya Meymmoḻiccaritai*, ed. M. Caṇmukam Piḷḷai, Chennai, 1977.
Mīmāṃsābhāṣya	*Śrīmajjaiminipräṇīte Mīmāṃsādarśane Ādita Ārabhya Dvitīyādhyāyaprathamapādāntaḥ* [...] *Śrīkumārilabhaṭṭviracitatantravārtikāsahitaśābarabhāṣyasametaś ca*, ed. Subbā Śāstrin & Vināyaka Gaṇeśa Āpaṭe [= Āpṭe], ĀSS 97, Pune, 1929.
Mīmāṃsāślokavārttika	*The Mimāṃsāślokavārtika with the Commentary Kāśikā of Sucaritamiśra*, ed. K. Sāmbaśiva Śāstrī, TSS 90, 99, 150, Trivandrum, 1926, 1929, 1943.
	(*Mīmāṃsā*)*ślokavārttika*, trans. G. Jha, Calcutta, 1907.
	A Hindu Critique of Buddhist Epistemology: Kumārila on Perception: The "Determination of Perception" Chapter of Kumārilabhaṭṭa's Ślokavārttika, Translation and Commentary, trans. J. Taber, London, 2005.

Mīmāṃsāsūtrabhāṣyanibandhana *Der Organizsmus des urheberlosen Veda. Ein Studie der Niyoga-Lehre Prabhākaras mit ausgewählten übersetzungen der Bṛhatī*, K. Yoshimizu, Vienna, 1997.

Miragāvatī "Miragāvatī of Kutubana: Avadhī Text with Critical Notes," ed. D.F. Plukker, diss., Universiteit van Amsterdam, 1981.

Mṛgendrāgama *Śrīmṛgendram kāmikopāgamam vidyāyogapādadvayamilitam śrībhaṭṭanārāyaṇakaṇṭh aviracitayā vṛttyā tadvyākhyayāghoraśivācāryaviracaitayā dīpikayā cālaṃkṛtam* (with the commentary *Vṛtti* by Nārāyaṇakaṇṭha and subcommentary *Dīpikā* by Aghoraśivācārya).

Mṛgendrāgamavṛtti *Śrīmṛgendram kāmikopāgamam vidyāyogapādadvayamilitam śrībhaṭṭanārāyaṇakaṇṭh aviracitayā vṛttyā tadvyākhyayāghoraśivācāryaviracaita yā dīpikayā cālaṃkṛtam* (with the commentary *Vṛtti* by Nārāyaṇakaṇṭha and subcommentary *Dīpikā* by Aghoraśivācārya).

Muhūrtadīpika *Vidyāmādhavīyam*, vol. I, ed. with Viṣṇu's *Muhūrtadīpika* commentary by R.S. Sastry, Mysore, 1998.

Mūlamadhyamakakārikā *Mūlamadhyamakakārikās (Mādhyamikasūtras) de Nagarjuna avec la Prasannapadā de Candrakīrti*, ed. L. de la Vallée Poussin, St. Petersburg, 1903.

Muttiniccayam *Muttiniccayam (Muttiniccayamūlamum veḷḷiyampalavāṇamuṉi variyaṟṟiyaruḷiya ciṟṟuraiyum. nāṉa campanta tēcikacuvāmika)*, publ. Progressive Accukkūṭam, Chennai, 1934.

Nācciyār Tirumoḻi *The Secret Garland: Antal's Tiruppavai and Nacciyar Tirumoli*, trans. A. Venkatesan, New York, 2010.

Naiṣadhacarita *Naiṣadhacarita of Śrīharṣa*, K.K. Handiqui, Poona, 1956.

Naiṣadhīyacarita *Naiṣadhīyacarita: With the Commentary of Nārāyaṇa* by Śrīharṣa, ed. Śivadattaśarmā, Lucknow, 1988.

Nāmaghoṣa *Nāma Ghoṣa*, Mādhavadeva, Jorhat, 1975.

Nālāyira Divya Prabandham *Nālāyirattivviyappirapantam*, ed. K.V. Rettiyar, Madras, 1981.
Sri Tivyappirapantam, 4 vols., Madras, 1956.
Nalayira Divya Prabandham, http://www.ramanuja.org/sv/prabandham/index.html.

Nāṉāmirtam *Vākīcamuṉivar aruḷicceyta nāṉāmirtam mūlamum paḻaiya uraiyum* (= *Nāṉāmirtam*), ed. Turaicāmi Piḷḷai, Chidambaram, 1987.

Nāradasmṛti *The Nāradasmṛti*, 2 vols., ed. and trans. R.W. Lariviere, Philadelphia, 1989.

Nareśvaraparīkṣā *Nareśvaraparīkṣā with the Commentary Prakāśa by Rāmakaṇṭha*, ed. M.K. Shastri, KSTS 45, Srinagar, 1926.

Narmadā kī kahānī *Narmadā kī kahānī*, D. Prasad (Prasād), Indore, 1990, ²2000, ³2008 (Hind.).

Narmadāmāhātmya *Śrīnarmadāmāhātmya*, S.B.N.G. Bule (Buḷe), Dadar, n.d.

Nārmadāpurāṇa *Atha bṛhat śrīnārmadāpurāṇam revākhaṇḍam*, Omkaranand Giri (Oṃkārānand Giri), Hoshangabad, 1965, ²1969, ³1994.

Nāṭyaśāstra *Nāṭyaśāstra of Bharatamuni with the Commentary Abhinavabharati*, GaOS 36, Baroda, ²1956.
Nāṭyaśāstra ascribed to Bharata-Muni (A Treatise on Ancient Indian Dramaturgy and Histrionics), 2 vols., trans. M. Ghosh, CSS 118, Varanasi, 1967, repr. 2007.
The Nāṭyaśāstra, trans. M. Ghosh, Calcutta, 1961.
The Nāṭyaśāstra: English Translation with Critical Notes, trans. A. Rangacharya, New Delhi, 1996.
Nāṭyaśāstra of Bharatamuni with the Commentary Abhinavabhāratī by Abhinavaguptāchārya, 4 vols., ed. Dr. R.S. Nagar and K.L. Joshi. Delhi, 1981–1984.

	Natyasastra of Bharatamuni, trans. Dr. N.P. Unni, Delhi, 1998.
	Nāṭyaśāstra: Text with Introduction, English Translation and Indices in Four Volumes, ed. N.P. Unni, Delhi, 2003.
Navanādhacharitra	*Navanādhacharitra of Gauraṇa*, ed. K. Ramakrishnaiya, MUTS 7, Madras, 1937.
Navyanyāyabhāṣāpradīpa	*Navyanyāya-bhāṣāpradīpaḥ*, ed. M. Nyayaratna, Calcutta, 1973.
Nemināthapurāṇa	*The Epic of Nemi (Neminātha-purāṇa) of Karṇapārya*, S. Anacker, Shravanabelagola, 2002.
Netratantra	*Netratantram (Mṛtyuñjaya Bhattārakaḥ) with the Commentary Udyota of Kṣemarājācārya*, ed. V. Dvivedi, Delhi, 1985.
	Netratantra with Commentary (Uddyota) by Kṣemarāja, ed. M.K. Shastri, KSTS 46, Srinagar, 1926.
Netratantroddyota	*Netratantra with Commentary (Uddyota) by Kṣemarāja*, ed. M.K. Shastri, KSTS 46, Srinagar, 1926.
Nigamacūḍādarpaṇa	*Lakṣmīviśiṣṭādvaitabhāṣya by Śrīnivāsa Dīkṣita, with Sundararāja's Nigamacūḍādarpaṇa commentary*, ed. Addaṅkitirumalai Śrīnivāsatātācārya, 1896.
Niśvāsatattvasaṃhitā	**Niśvāsatattvasaṃhitā*, ms. 1-227 at the National Archives Kathmandu, Kathmandu, n.d.
Nītisāra	*The Nītisāra by Kāmandaki*, ed. and trans. R. Mitra, Calcutta, 1861.
Nityāṣoḍaśikārṇava	*(Vāmakeśvaratantrāntargataḥ) nityāṣoḍaśikārṇavaḥ. Śrībhāskararāyonnītasetubandhākhyavyākhyāsahitaḥ*, ed. K.V. Abhyaṃkar, Pune, 1973.
Nityotsava	*Nityotsava of Umānandanātha (Supplement to Paraśurāma-kalpasūtra)*, ed. A. Mahadeva Sastri, rev. and enlarged by Trivikrama Tirtha, Baroda, 1977.
Nṛsimhaśatakamu	*Nṛsimhaśatakamu* by T. Veṅgamāmba, ed. K.J. Krishnamurti, Tirupati, 2007.
Nyāyakandalī	*Padārthadharmasaṅgraha*, ed. V.S. Dvivedin, VZS 4, Varanasi, 1895.
Nyāyakandalīpañjikā	*Nyāyakandalīpañjikā*, ed. J.S. Jetly & V.G. Parikh, GaOS 174, Baroda, 1991.
Nyāyakumudacandra	*Nyāyakumudacandra of Śrimat Prabhācandrācārya*, ed. M. Jain, Bombay, 1938.
Nyāyakusumāñjali	*Nyāyakusumāñjali: Edited with Hindi Translation*, D. Jha, Varanasi, 1973.
Nyāyalīlāvatī	*Nyāyalīlāvatī*, ed. H. Shastri & D. Shastri, CSS 64, Varanasi, 1927–1934.
Nyāyamañjarī	*Nyāyamañjarī of Jayantabhaṭṭa*, ed. K.S. Varadacharya, 2 vols., Mysore, 1969, 1983.
	Nyāyamañjarī, ed. Pt. Surya Narayan Shukla, Banaras, 1936.
Nyāyamañjarīgranthibhaṅga	*Nyāyamañjarīgranthibhaṅga of Cakradhara*, ed. N.J. Shah, Ahme-dabad, 1972.
Nyāyasāra	*Nyāyasāra*, ed. V.S. Abhyankar, Pune, 1922.
Nyayasūtra	*Nyayasūtras: Nyāyadarśana: Text with Vātsyāyana's Bhāṣya*, ed. by A. Thakur, Darbhanga, 1967.
	Gautama's Nyāyasūtras (with Vātsyāyana-Bhāṣya) Translated into English, trans. G. Jha, Poona, 1939.
	Nyāyadarśanam, ed. by Tarkatirthas, 1936–1944.
	Die Nyāyasūtra's, ed. W. Ruben, Leipzig, 1928.
Nyāyavārttika	*Nyāyavārttika*, ed. A. Thakur, NCG 2, New Delhi, 1997.
Nyāyavārttikatātparyaṭīkā	*Nyāyavārttikatātparyaṭīkā*, ed. A. Thakur, NCG 3, New Delhi, 1996.
Padārthadharmasaṃgraha	*Praśastapādabhāṣya (Padārthadharmasaṅgraha) with Commentary Nyāyakandalī of Śrīdharabhaṭṭa*, ed. D.J. Sharman, Varanasi, 1963.
	Padārthadharmasaṅgraha, ed. V.S. Dvivedin, VZS 4, Varanasi, 1895.

Padārthasaṃgrahaṭīkā — *Padārthasaṅgrahaṭīkā*, ed. G. Kaviraj & D. Shastri, CSS 61, Varanasi, 1930.

Padāvalī — *The Hindi Padāvalī of Nāmdev*, ed. W.M. Callewaert & M. Lath, Delhi, 1989.

Padmapurāṇa — *Padma Purāṇa*, ĀSS 131, Poona, 1893.
Padmamahāpurāṇa, Delhi, 1895, repr. 1984.

Pādmasaṃhitā — *Padma Samhita*, crit. ed. by Seetha Padmanabhan and R.N. Sampath (part 1), Seetha Padmanabhan and V. Varadachari (part 2), PPPS 3, 4, Madras, 1974, 1982.

Padmāvatī — *The Padumāwati of Malik Muḥammad Jaisi*, ed. G.A.Grierson & S. Dvivedi, Calcutta, 1911.

Paitāmahasiddhānta — "The Paitāmahasiddhānta of the Viṣṇudharmottarapurāṇa," ed. D. Pingree, *Brahmavidyā* 31/32, 1967/1968, 472–510.

Pampāmāhātmya — "Pampāmāhātmya," in: V. Filliozat, *Kālāmukha and Pāśupata Temples in Dharwar*, app. 2, 4, Chennai, 2000.

Pañcapādikā — *Pañcapādikā of Śri Padmapādācārya and Pañcapādikāvivaraṇa of Śrī Prakāśātman*, ed. S. Shastri, S., & S.R.K. Shastri, Madras, 1958.

Pañcapādikāvivaraṇa — *Pañcapādikā of Śri Padmapādācārya and Pañcapādikāvivaraṇa of Śrī Prakāśātman*, ed. S. Shastri, S., & S.R.K. Shastri, Madras, 1958.

Pañcaprakriyā — *Pañcaprakriyā of Sarvajñātman*, ed. T.R. Chintamani, Madras, 1946.

Pāñcarātrarakṣā — *Śrī Pāñcarātra Rakṣā of Śrī Vedānta Deśika*, crit. ed. with Notes and Variant Readings by M. Duraiswami Aiyangar and T. Venugopalacharya with an Introduction in English by G. Srinivasa Murti, ALS 36, Madras, 1942.

Pañcārthabhāṣya — "Pañcārthabhāṣya on Pāśupatasūtra 1.37–39: Recovered from a Newly Identified Manuscript," P. Bisschop, *JIPh* 33/5–6, 2005, 529–551.
Pāśupatasūtra with Kauṇḍinya's Pañcārthabhāṣya, ed. A. Sastri, TSS 143, Trivandrum, 1940.

Pañcasiddhāntikā — *The Pañcasiddhāntikā of Varāhamihira*, part 1–2, ed. and trans. D. Pingree; comm. O. Neugebauer & D. Pingree, HFS 6/1, Copenhagen, 1970.

Pañcāvaraṇastava — *The Pañcāvaraṇastava of Aghoraśivācārya: A Twelfth-Century South Indian Prescription for the Visualisation of Sadāśiva and His Retinue*, ed. D. Goodall *et al.*, Pondicherry, 2005.

Pannirunāmam — *Pannirunāmam*, by Vedānta Deśika, on: www.ibiblio.org/sripedia/ebooks/vdesikan/pannirunamam (accessed August, 2013).

Parabrahmotthāpanasthala — "Jain Arguments against Vedānta Monistic Theism: A Translation of the *Parabrahmotthāpanasthala* of Bhuvanasundarasūri," F. van den Bossche, *JIPh* 25/4, 1997, 337–374.

Parākhyatantra — *The Parākhyatantra: A Scripture of the Śaiva Siddhānta*, ed. D. Goodall, Pondicherry, 2004.

Paramārthasāra — *Introduction to Tantric Philosophy: The Paramārthasāra of Abhinavagupta with the Commentary of Yogarāja*, ed. L. Bansat-Boudon & K. Tripathi, London, 2010.
Paramārthasāra of Abhinavagupta with the Commentary of Yogaraja, publ. Kashmir Research Department, KSTS 7, Srinagar, 1916.

Paramasaṃhitā — *Paramasaṃhitā [of the Pāñcharātra]*, ed. and trans. into English with an introduction by S. Krishnaswami Aiyangar, GaOS 86, Baroda, 1940.

Pārameśvarasaṃhitā — *Pārameśvarasaṃhitā Govindācāryaiḥ saṃskṛtā, anekavidhādarśādibhiḥ saṃyojitā ca*, Srirangam, 1953.

Paramōpatecam — *Śrīmaṟaiṉāṉacampantanāyaṉar aruḷicceyta caivac ciṟu nūlkaḷ* (*mutaṟpakuti*), ed. T.C. Mīṉāṭcicuntaram Piḷḷai, Thiruvavaduthurai, 1954.

Parātriṃśikātattvavivaraṇa — *Il commento di Abhinavagupta alla Parātriṃśikā (Parātriṃśikātattvavivaraṇam): Traduzione e testo by Abhinavagupta*, ed. R. Gnoli, Rome, 1985.

Parātriṃśikāvivaraṇa — *Parātriṃśikāvivaraṇa: The Secret of Tantric Mysticism*, trans. J. Singh, Delhi, 1988.

Parātriśikālaghuvṛtti — *Parātriśikālaghuvṛtti and Parātriśikāvivṛtti*, ed. by J. Zadoo Shastri, Srinagar, 1947.

Parātrīśikāvivaraṇa — *A Trident of Wisdom: Translation of Parātrīśikā-Vivaraṇa*, trans. J. Singh, Albany, 1989.

Paripāṭal — *Paripāṭal*, ed. and Fr. transl. by F. Gros, 1968.

Pāśupatasūtra — *Pāśupatasūtra with Kauṇḍinya's Pañcārthabhāṣya*, ed. A. Sastri, TSS 143, Trivandrum, 1940.
"The Sūtrapāṭha of the Pāśupatasūtra," P. Bisschop, *IIJ* 49/1–2, 2006, 1–21.

Paticupācappaṉuvah — *Śrīmaṟaiṉāṉacampantaṉāyaṉar aruḷicceyta caivac ciṟu nūlkaḷ (mutaṟpakuti)*, ed. T.C. Mīṉāṭcicuntaram Piḷḷai, Thiruvavaduthurai, 1954.

Pātravidhi — "The Pātravidhi: A Lakulīśa Pāśupata Manual on Purification and Use of the Initiate's Pot," D. Acharya, in: C. Watanabe, M. Desmarais & Y. Honda, eds., *Saṃskṛtasādhutā: Studies in honour of Professor Ashok Aklujkar*, New Delhi, 2011, 1–28.

Pauṣkarāgama — *Pauṣkarasaṃhitā (jñānapādaḥ) śrīmadumāpatiśivācāryaviracitabhāṣyopetā*, ed. P. Ramasastri, Chidambaram, 1925.

Pauṣkarasaṃhitā — *Śrīpāñcarātrāgame Ratnatrayāntargatā Śrīpauṣkarasaṃhitā/Sree Poushkara Samhita, One of the Three Gems in Pancharatra*, ed. His Holiness Sree Yatiraja Sampathkumara Ramanuja Muni of Melkote, Bangalore, 1934.

Pavanadūta — *Pavanadūtam* by Dhoyī (Dhoyika), ed. Chintaharan Chakravarti, Calcutta, 1926. "Pavanadūtam: With an Appendix on the Sena Kings," in: Monmohan Chakravarti, ed., *Journal and Proceedings of the Asiatic Society of Bengal, New Series* 1, 1905, 41–71.

Picumata — see *Brahmayāmala*

Prabhuliṅgalīle — Basawanal, S.S., ed., *Cāmarasa kṛta Prabhuliṅgalīle*, Dharwar, 1971.

Prahlāda Bhakti Vijayam — *Tyāgarāja's Prahlāda Bhakti Vijayam*, P. Sambamoorthy, 1965.

Pramāṇavārttikabhāṣya — *Pramāṇavārttikabhāṣyam or Vārtikālaṅkāraḥ of Prajñākaragupta*, ed. R. Sāṅkṛtyāyana, Patna, 1953.

Pramāṇavārttikavṛttiṭīkā — *Pramāṇavārttikavṛttiṭīkā of KarṇakagominI*, ed. R. Sāṅkṛtyāyana, Allahabad, 1944.

Pramāṇaviniścaya — *Dharmakīrti's Pramāṇaviniścaya: Chapters 1 and 2*, ed. E. Steinkellner, Vienna, 2007.

Praśnatantra — *Tājikanīlakaṇṭhī* (including *Praśnatantra*), ed. with Viśvanātha's commentary, Hind. trans. and commentary by Kedāradatta Jośī, Delhi, 2008.

Pratimānāṭaka — *Pratimānāṭaka of Bhāsa: Edited with Introd., Translation, Critical and Explanatory Notes and Appendices*,by Shivaram Mahadeo Paranjape, Poona, 1927.

Pratiṣṭhālakṣaṇasārasamuccaya — *The Hindu Pantheon in Nepalese Line Drawings: Two Manuscripts of the Pratiṣṭhālakṣaṇasārasamucchaya*, G. Bühnemann, Varanasi, 2004.

Pratyabhijñāhṛdaya — *Pratyabhijñāhṛdayam: The Secret of Self-Recognition*, ed. J. Singh, Delhi, 1980.

Prāyaścittavidhi — "The Prāyaścittavidhi: A Manual on Atonement of the Lakulīśa Pāśupatas," D. Acharya, *JIS*, forthcoming.

Rādhākṛṣṇagaṇoddeśadīpikā	*Rādhākṛṣṇagaṇoddeśadīpikā* by Rūpa Gosvāmī, ed. Medinīndralāla Mitra, Calcutta, n.d.
Ragales	*Mahākavi Hampeya Hariharadevakṛta Nūtana Purātanara Ragalegalu*, ed. M.S. Sunkapura, Dharwar, 1976.
Raghuvaṃśa	*Raghuvaṃśa of Kālidāsa: with the Commentary Sañjīvanī of Mallinātha, Cantos I–V*, ed. and trans. M.R. Kale, Delhi, 1997.
	The Raghuvaṃśa of Kālidāsa, with the Commentary of Mallinātha, ed. G.R. Nandargikar, Delhi, ^{4}1971.
Rahasyatrayasāra	*Srimad Rahasyatrayasiira of Srf Vedantadesika*, trans. M.R. Rajagopala Ayyangar, Kumbakonam, 1956.
Rājamārtaṇḍa	*Yogasūtras of Patañjali with Bhojavṛtti called Rājamārtaṇḍa (in English Translation)*, J.R. Ballantyne & G.S. Deva, ed. with introduction by A.C. Sastri, Delhi, 1990.
Rājataraṅgiṇī	*Rājataraṅgiṇī of Jonarāja* by Jonaraja, trans. J.C. Dutt, Delhi, 1986.
Rājayogāmṛtasāramu	*Rājayogāmṛtasāramu*, ed. K.J. Krishnamurti, Tirupati, 2007.
Rāmabhadradīkṣita	*The Patañjali-charita*, KM 51, Bombay, 1985.
Rāmānandajanmotsava	*Rāmānandajanmotsava, Paṇḍit-Rāmnārāyaṇadāsajī kṛta bhāṣāṭīkayā'-laṅkṛtā*, Raṇahar Pustakālaya, Dakor, 1906.
Rāmavijaya	*Rāmavijaya: śabārtha ślokārtha o baragīta sahita*, Śaṅkaradeva, Darbhanga, 1989.
Rāmāyaṇa	*The Vālmīki Rāmāyaṇa: Critical Edition*, ed. G.H. Bhatt & U.P. Shah, 7 vols., Baroda, 1960–1975.
	The Ramayana of Valmeelti in the original Sungscrit with a Prose Translation and Explanatory Notes, 5 vols., ed. W. Carey & J. Marshman, Serampore, 1806–1810, repr. 1823.
	The Rāmāyaṇa of Vālmīki: An Epic of Ancient India, vol. I: *Bālakāṇḍa*, ed. R.P. Goldman, annotation by R.P. Goldman & S.J. Sutherland, Princeton, 1984.
	The Rāmāyaṇa of Vālmīki: An Epic of Ancient India, vol. II: *Ayodhyākāṇḍa*, trans. S.I. Pollock, ed. R.P. Goldman, Princeton, 1986.
	The Rāmāyaṇa of Vālmīki: An Epic of Ancient India, vol. III: *Araṇyakāṇḍa*, trans. S.I. Pollock, ed. R.P. Goldman, Princeton, 1991.
	The Rāmāyaṇa of Vālmīki: An Epic of Ancient India, vol. IV: *Kiṣkindhākāṇḍa*, trans. R. Lefeber, ed. R.P. Goldman, Princeton, 1994.
	The Rāmāyaṇa of Vālmīki: An Epic of Ancient India, vol. V: *Sundarakāṇḍa*, ed. R.P. Goldman & S.J. Sutherland, Princeton, 1996.
	The Rāmāyaṇa of Vālmīki: An Epic of Ancient India, vol. VI: *Yuddhakāṇḍa*, ed. R.P. Goldman & S.J. Sutherland, Princeton, 2009.
	The Rāmāyaṇa of Vālmīki, trans. H.P. Shastri, 3 vols., London, 1952–1959, rev. ed. 1962.
	Ramayana id es carmen epicum de Ramae rebus gestis poetae antiquissimi Valmicis opus. 3 vols., ed. and trans. A.W. von Schlegel, Bonn, 1829–1838.
	The Yuddhakāṇḍa: The Sixth Book of the Vālmīki-Rāmāyaṇa: The National Epic of India, ed. P.L. Vaidya, Baroda, 1971.
Rāmcaritamānas	*Tulsīdās, Rāmcaritamānas*, ed. S.N. Chaube, Kashi, 1947.
	The Rāmāyaṇa of Tulsi Dās, trans. F.S. Growse, Cawnpore, 1891, rev. ed. Delhi, 1978.
	Tulsi Ramayan in English Verse, S.D. Gupta, New Delhi, 2010.
	Tulasidasa's Shriramacharitamanasa, R.C. Prasad, 1988.
	The Gospel of Love: An English Rendering of Tulasi's Shri Rama Charita Manasa, C.L. Dhody, 1987.

	The Ramayana of Tulsidas, A.G. Atkins, 2 vols., 1966.
	The Holy Lake of the Acts of Rāma, W.D.P. Hill, London, 1952.
	Śrī Rāmacharitamānasa: Or the Mānasa Lake Brimming over with Exploits of Śrī Rāma, C. Goswami, 1949.
Rasagaṅgādhara	*The Rasagaṅgādhara: With the Commentary of Nāgeśa Bhaṭṭa by Jagannātha*, ed. Paṇḍit Durgāprasād & Kāśināth Parab, Bombay, 1888.
Rasasāra	*Rasasāra*, ed. G. Jha & G. Kaviraj, PWSBTS 5, Varanasi, 1922.
Rashasyatrayasāram	*Śrīmadrashasyatrayasāram: With the Commentary Sāravistaram of Abhinava Tēcika Vīrarākavācāryiar*, Veṅkaṭanātha (Vedāntadeśika), 2 vols., Madras, 1980.
Ratnaparīkṣā	"Ratnaparīkṣā of Buddhabhaṭṭa," in: *L. Finot, ed., Les Lapidaires Indiens*, Paris, 1896, 1–58.
Ratnaṭīkā	*Gaṇakārikā, with the Ratnaṭīkā of Bhāsarvajña*, ed., C.D. Dalal, GaOS 15, Baroda, 1920, repr. 1966.
Ratnatraya	*Aṣṭaprakaraṇam tattvaprakāśatattvasaṅgrahatattvatrayanirṇayaratnatrayabhogakārikānādakārikāmokṣakārikāparamokṣanirāsakārikākhyasiddhāntaśaivīyāṣṭagranthānām saṭī kānām samāhāraḥ*, ed. V. Dviveda, Varanasi, 1988.
Ratnāvalī	*Ratnāvalī of Harṣa*, ed. and trans. M.R. Kale, Delhi, 2002.
Rauravāgama	*Rauravāgama*, 3 vols., ed. N.R. Bhatt, PIFI 18, Pondicherry, crit. ed. 1961, 1985 (repr. 1972), 1988.
Record of Buddhistic Kingdoms	*A Record of Buddhistic Kingdoms Being an Account by the Chinese Monk Fa-Hein of Travels in India and Ceylon (AD 399–414) in Search of the Buddhist Books of Discipline*, trans. J. Legge, [1]1986, 1991.
Ṛgveda	*Ṛgveda-Saṁhitā: The Sacred Hymns of the Brāhmans Together with the Commentary of Sāyanāchārya*, ed. F.M. Müller, vols. 1–5, Varanasi, [1]1890.
	Der Rig-Veda, aus dem Sanskrit ins Deutsche, trans. K.F. Geldner, 3 vols., Cambridge MA, 1951.
	Rig Veda: A Metrically Restored Text With an Introduction and Notes, ed. B.A. van Nooten & G.B. Holland, HOS 50, Cambridge MA, 1994.
	Ṛg Veda, trans. W. Doniger, New York, 1981.
	Die Hymnen des Ṛigveda, T. Aufrecht, 2 vols., Bonn, 1887.
	Ṛg Veda, With the Commentary of Sāyana, eds., N.S. Sontakke, & C.G. Kashikar, Poona, 1933–1951.
Śābdabodhamīmāṃsā	*Śābdabodhamīmāṃsā: An Inquiry into Indian Theories of Verbal Cognition*, ed. N.S.R. Tatacharya, New Delhi, 2005–2008.
Sabhālakṣaṇa Mattu Prasaṅga Pīṭhike	*Yakṣagāna Sabhālakṣaṇa Mattu Prasaṅga Pīṭhike (Vaṃśāvaḷi Sahitavāgi)*, Udupi, 1967.
Ṣaḍdarśanasamuccaya	*Ṣaḍdarśanasamuccaya of Haribhadra*, ed. L. Suali, Calcutta, 1905; ET in: D. Chattopadhyaya & M.K. Gangopadhyaya, *Cārvāka/Lokāyata: An Anthology of Source Materials and Some Recent Studies*, Delhi, 1990, 257–297.
	Ṣaḍdarśanasamuccaya (of Rājaśekhara), ed. Haragovindadas & Becardas, ŚYJG 17, Varanasi, [2]1913.
Ṣaddarśanasamuccaya Laghuvṛtti	*Tarkarahasyadīpikā*, Appendix I, ed. M. Jain, JMGSG 36, New Delhi, [2]1981.
Sādhanadīpikā	*Sādhanadīpikā* by Rādhākṛṣṇa Gosvāmī, ed. Haridāsa Śāstrī, Vrindavan, n.d.
Saduktikarṇāmṛta	*Saduktikarṇāmṛta* by Śrīdharadāsa, ed. Sureś Chandra Banerji, Calcutta, 1965.

Śaivāgamādimāhātmyasaṃgraha	*Śaivāgamādimāhātmyasaṃgraha of Jnānaprakāśa*, ed. T. Ganesan, forthcoming.
Śāktānandataraṅgiṇī	*Brahmanandagiri's Sakatanandtarangini: Text with Hindi Translation*, ed. R.K. Rai, Varanasi, 1993.
Śāktopaniṣads	*The Śākta Upaniṣads*, tarns. A.G. Krishna Warrier, Madras, 1967.
Samāj Śṛṅkhalā	*Samāj-Śriṅkhalā*, ed. Govinda Saran Sastri, Vrindaban, 1988 (Hind.).
Sāmavidhānabrāhmaṇa	*Sāmavidhāna Brāhmaṇa*, Tirupati, 1964.
Saṃbandhavārtika	*The Saṃbandha-Vārtika of Sureśvarācārya*, ed. and trans. T.M.P. Mahadevan, Madras, 1972.
Sāṃkhyakārikā	"Sāṃkhyakārikā: Sanskrit and English," in: G.J. Larson, *Classical Sāṃkhya: An Interpretation of Its History and Meaning*, Delhi, 1979, 235–277.
	The Sāṅkhyakārikā of Īśvara Kṛṣṇa, trans. S.S.S. Sastri, Madras, repr. 1973.
	"Sāṃkhyakārikā," in: R.C. Pandeya, ed., *Yuktidīpikā: An Ancient Commentary on the Sāṃkhya-Kārikā of Īśvarakṛṣṇa*, Delhi, 1967, app. 1.
Sāṃkhyasāra	*Sāṃkhyasāra: Text and Translation with Notes by Dr. Shiv Kumar*, ed. and trans. S. Kumar, Delhi, 1988.
Sāṃkhyasūtra	*The Sāṃkhya Aphorisms of Kapila*, trans. and ed. I. . Ballantyne, Delhi, repr. 1984.
Saṃyuttanikāya	*Saṃyuttanikāya*, ed. L. Feer, 1884–1898.
Saṃkṣepaśārīraka	*Saṃkṣepaśārīrakam*, ed. H.N. Apte, Poona, 1918.
Saṃskāravidhi	"The Saṃskāravidhi: A Manual on the Transformatory Rite of the Lakulīśa-Pāśupatas," D. Acharya, in: D. Goodall & A. Padoux, eds., *Tantric Studies in Memory of Hélène Brunner*, CI 106, Pondicherry, 2007.
Śaṅkaradevamādhavadevar	*Śaṅkaradeva-Mādhavadevar Jīvana-caritra*, D. Ṭhākura, Tezpur, 1900.
Śaṅkaravijaya	*Śaṅkaravijaya*, ed. J. Tarkapaṉchánana, Calcutta, 1868.
Sant Guṇ Sāgar	*Śrī sant guṇ sāgar, by Mādhavdās, ed. and comm.*, ed. S. Śāstrī, Bhairana, VS 2056 (= 1999–2000) (Hind.).
Santavijaya	*Rāmdās: Translation of Mahipatī's Santavijaya*, J.E. Abbott, Poona, 1932.
	Mahārāṣṭrakavisantamālā, n. 8, Rāmdās, Mahipatīkṛta Santavijāyance, n.d.; ET: *The Poet-Saints of Mahārāshtra, No. 8, Rāmdās, Translation of Mahipatī's Santavijaya*, J.E. Abbott, 1932.
Saptapdārthī	*Saptapdārthī: Edited with Introduction, Translation, and Notes*, D. Gurumurti, Madras, 1943.
Saptatiratnamālikā	"Saptatiratnamālikā," in: *Guruparamparā Prabhāvam of Śrī Brahmatantrasvatantra Swāmi*, S. Aṇṇaṉ, Śrī Prativādi Bhayaṅkara, Madras, 1968, 53–67.
Śāradātilaka	*Śāradātilakam of Śrī Lakśmaṇadeśikendra [sic] with Padārthādarśa Commentary by Śrīmad Rāghava Bhaṭṭa*, ed. M. Jha Bakshi. Varanasi, [3]1986.
Śārṅgadharapaddhati	*Śārṅgadharapaddhati*, ed. P. Peterson, Bombay, 1888.
Sarvadarśanasaṃgraha	*Sarvadarśanasaṃgraha of Mādhavācārya: Sanskrit Text, English Translation, Notes and Appendix*, transl. by E.B. Cowell & A.E. Gough, ed. by K.L. Joshi, Delhi, 1986.
	Sarvadarśanasaṃgraha of Sāyaṇa-Mādhava: Edited with an Original Commentary in Sanskrit, ed. V.S. Abhyankar, Poona, 1924, [2]1978.
Sarvajnanottarāgama	**Sarvajnanottarāgama*, paper transcript (T.334) at the French Institute of Pondicherry, n.d.
Sarvamūlagrantha	*Sarvamūlagranthāḥ*, ed. Prabhanjanacharya, Bangalore, 1999.
	Sarvamūlagranthāḥ, ed. B. Govindācārya, 5 vols. Bangalore, 1969–1974.

Sarvāṅgī	*The Sarvāṅgī of Gopāldās*, ed. W.M. Callewaert, Delhi, 1993.
Sarvānukramaṇī	*Kātyāyana's Sarvānukramaṇī of the Rigveda, with Extracts from Shadgurusishya's Commentary Entitled Vedārthadīpikā*, ed. A.A. Macdonell, Oxford, 1886.
Sarvasamvādinī	*Sarvasamvādinī with Commentary Cūrṇikā by Jīva Gosvāmī* by Jīva Gosvāmī, ed. Purīdās, Vrindavan, 1953.
Śatakatrayādisubhāṣitasaṃgraha	*Śatakatrayādi-subhāṣitasaṃgraha: The Epigrams Attributed to Bhartṛhari*, ed. D.D. Kosambi, Bombay, 1948.
Śatapathabrāhmaṇa	*The Çatapatha Brāhmaṇa in the Mādhyandina-Çākhā with Extracts from the Commentaries of Sāyaṇa, Harisvāmin and Dvivedaganga*, ed. A. Weber, CSS 96, Varanasi, 1855, repr. 1964.
	Śatapathabrāhmaṇa, ed. C. Shastri, P. Shastri & R. Dikshita, Varanasi, [3]1998.
	Śatapatha Brāhmaṇa: Śrīmadvājasaneyimādhyandinaśatapathabrāhmaṇam (with Sāyaṇa's Commentary and the Commentary by Śrī Hari Svāmī), ed. by "Several Learned Persons," n.d.
	Śatapathabrahmaṇa, trans. by J. Eggeling, Part 1–4, Motilal Banarasidass, Delhi, 1963.
Śataratnasaṃgraha	*Śataratnasaṃgrahaḥ saṭīkaḥ umāpatiśivācāryasaṃgṛhītaḥ pancānana śāstrisampāditaḥ* (= *Śataratnasaṃgraha*), ed. P. Sastri, Calcutta, 1944.
Ṣaṭsāhasrasaṃhitā	*The Ṣaṭsāhasrasaṃhitā Chapters 1–5*, ed. and trans. J.A. Schoterman, Leiden, 1982.
Ṣaṭsthalasiddhānta	*Sri Siddalingeshwara Shatsthala Siddanta*, G.S. Bale, Edison, 1997.
Sāttvatasaṃhitā	*The Sāttvata Saṃhitā with Comment[a]ry by Alaśiṅga Bhaṭṭa*, Foreword by Dr. Gaurinath Shastri, ed. Vajra Vallabha Dwivedi, LRTP 6, Varanasi, 1982.
Śaunakīyācaturādhyāyikā	*Śaunakīyā Caturādhyāyikā: A Prātiśākhya of the Śaunakīya Atharvaveda*, ed. M.M. Deshpande, Cambridge UK, 1997.
Saundaryalaharī	*Saundarya-Laharī of Śrī Śaṃkarācārya: With Commentaries Saubhāgyavardhanī of Kaivalyāśrama, Lakṣmīdharā of Lakṣmīdharācārya, Aruṇāmodinī of Kāmeśvarasūrin, English Translation and Notes*, by R. Anantakṛṣṇa Śāstrī and K.R. Gāru, Prayogas illustrated with Yantras, Madras, 1957.
	Saundarya-Lahari of Sri Samkara-Bhagavatpada, ed. S. Sastri & S. Ayengar, Madras, 1937.
	Saundaryalaharī of Śaṅkarācārya with the Lakṣmīdhara Commentary, ed. S. Malaviya, Vrajajivan Prachyabharati Granthamala 101, Delhi, 2009.
	Saundarya-Laharī of Sri Sankaracārya, Tapasyananda, Chennai, 1987.
	The Saundaryalahari: Or Flood of Beauty Traditionally Ascribed to Śaṅkarācārya, ed. and trans. W.N. Brown, HOS 43, Cambridge, 1958.
Sekaśubhodaya	*Sekaśubhodaya of Halayudha Miśra*, ed. S. Sen, BIS, 286, Calcutta, 1963.
Siddhāntaleśasaṃgraha	*Appayya Dīkṣita: Siddhāntaleśasaṃgraha*, ed. and trans. S.S. Suryanarayana Shastri, Madras, 1937.
Siddhāntamuktavālī	*Bhāṣāpariccheda with Siddhānta-muktavālī by Viśvanātha-nyāyapañcānana*, trans. by Swami Madhvananda, Kolkata, 2004.
Siddhāntapaṭal	*Siddhānta Paṭal* by Rāmānanda, Śrī Durgā Pustak Bhaṇḍār, Allahabad, n.d.
Siddhāntasārāvali	*Siddhāntasārāvali of Trilocanaśiva* (with the commentary of Anantaśambhu), publ. in: *BGOMLM* 17–20, Chennai.
Siddhasiddhāntapaddhati	*Siddhasiddhāntapaddhati of Gorakṣanātha*, ed. M.L. Gharote & G.K. Pai, Lonavla, 2005.

Siddhasiddhāntasaṃgraha	*Siddhasiddhāntasaṃgraha*, ed. G.N. Kaviraja, PWSBT13, Benares City, 1925.
Siddhitrayī	*The Siddhitrayī and the Īśvarapratyabhijākārikāvṛtti*, ed. M.K. Shastri, Srinagar, 1921.
Siddhitrayī	*Sri Yamunacharya's Siddhi Trayi*, ed. R. Ramanujachari & K. Srinivasacharya, Madras, 1972.
Śivadṛṣṭi	*The Śivadṛṣṭi of Śrīsomānandanātha with the Vṛtti by Utpaladeva*, ed. M.K. Shastri, Pune, 1934.
Śivajnānabodha	*Śivajnānabodha with with the Commentary Called Jnānāvaraṇabhāṣya by Veḷḷiyampalavāṇamuṉivar*, ed. T. Ganesan, forthcoming.
	Śivajnānabodhaḥ: Śivajnānabodha with the Laghuṭīkā of Śivāgrayogī, ed. T. Ganesan, Chennai, crit. ed. 2003.
	Śivajnānabodhavṛttiḥ jnānaprakāśāyāryeṇa viracitā, ed. Muttukkumaracuvami, Jaffna, Kali year 5029.
	Śivajnānabodha with the commentary called Vṛtti by Sadāśivaśivācārya, publ. in: *BGOMLM* 16/1, Chennai, 1963.
	Śivajnānabodhaḥ śrīmacchivāgrabhāṣyopetaḥ, ed. D. Tampiran & K. Sastri, Kumbakonam, n.d.
Śivajnānabodhavṛtti	*Śivajnānabodhavṛttiḥ jnānaprakāśāyāryeṇa viracitā*, ed. Muttukkumaracuvami, Jaffna, Kali year 5029.
	Śivajnānabodha with the commentary called Vṛtti by Sadāśivaśivācārya, publ. in: *BGOMLM* 16/1, Chennai, 1963.
Śivajnānabodhopanyāsa	*Śivajnānabodhopanyāsaḥ: A Commentary on the Śivajnānabodha by Nigamajnānadeśika*, ed. T. Ganesan, New Delhi, crit. ed. 2009.
Śivamahimnastava	*Śivamahimnastava of Puṣpadanta*, ed. Narayanapatisarma, Varanasi, ^{2}1983.
Śivapurāṇa	*Śivamahāpurāṇam*, parts I and II, ed. K. Kṛṣṇadāsa & K. Puṣpendra, 1986.
	The Śivamahāpurāṇam, vol. I, Delhi, 1986.
	Śiva-Purāṇa, parts I–IV, 1969–1970, repr. 1982–1987.
Śivasaṃhitā	*Śivasaṃhitā*, ed. J. Mallinson, New York, 2007.
Śivasūtra	*Gli aforismi di Śiva, con il Commento di Kṣemarāja (Śivasūtravimarśinī)*, ed. and trans. R. Torella, Milan, 2013.
	The Aphorisms of Śiva: The Śiva Sūtra with Bhāskara's Commentary, the Vārttika, trans. M.S.G. Dyczkowski, Albany, 1992.
	Śivasūtras: The Yoga of Supreme Identity; Text of the Sūtras and the Commentary Vimarśinī of Kṣemarāja, ed. and trans. J. Singh, Delhi, 1979.
Śivasūtravārttika	*The Aphorisms of Śiva: The Śiva Sūtra with Bhāskara's Commentary, the Vārttika*, trans. M.S.G. Dyczkowski, Albany, 1992.
Śivasūtravimarśinī	*Śivasūtras: The Yoga of Supreme Identity; Text of the Sūtras and the Commentary Vimarśinī of Kṣemarāja*, ed. and trans. J. Singh, Delhi, 1979.
	Śivasūtra-vimarśiṇī of Kṣemarāja, ed. J.C. Chatterji, Srinagar, 1911.
Skandapurāṇa	*The Skandamahāpurāṇa*, ed. K. Śrīkṛṣṇadāsa, Delhi, 1867, repr. 1986.
	Skandamahāpurāṇam, ed. K. Kṣemarāja & N. Siṃha, 1986–1987.
	The Skandapurāṇa, Volume 1, Adhyāyas 1–25: Critically Edited with Prolegomena and English Synopsis, ed. R. Adriaensen, H.T. Bakker & H. Isaacson, Groningen, 1998.
	The Skanda-Purāṇa: Part XIV, trans., G.V. Tagare, Delhi, 1999.
	Studies in the Skandapurāṇa, vol. III: *Harānandalaharī: Volume in Honour of Professor Minoru Hara on his Seventieth Birthday*, ed. R. Tsuchida & A. Wezler, Reinbek, 2000.

Ṣoḍaśagrantha	*The Grace of Lord Krishna: The Sixteen Verse-Treatises (Ṣoḍaśagranthāḥ) of Vallabhacharya*, trans. J.D. Redington, Delhi, 2000.
Somaśambhupaddhati	*Somaśambhupaddhati*, 4 vols., ed. and trans. H. Brunner-Lachaux, Pondicherry, 1963–1998.
Spandakārikā	*The Stanzas of Vibration: The Spandakārikā with Four Commentaries*, M.S.G. Dyczkowski, Albany, 1992.
	Spanda-Kārikās: The Divine Creative Pulsation (With Kṣemarāja's Nirṇaya), ed. J. Singh, Delhi, 1980.
Śrāmaṇyaphalasūtra	*Das Śrāmaṇyaphala-Sūtra. Synoptische Übersetzung und Glossar der chinesischen Fassungen verglichen mit dem Sanskrit und Pāli*, K. Meisig, FBI 19, Wiesbaden, 1987.
Śrautakośa	*Śrautakośa (Encyclopaedia of Vedic Sacrificial Ritual Comprising the Two Complementary Sections, Namely the Sanskrit Section and the English Section)*, ed. R.N. Dandekar & C.K. Kashikar, Poona, 1958–1994.
Śrī Bayālīs Līlā	*Śrī Bayālīs-Līlā by Śrī Hita Dhruvadās Jī Maharāj*, ed. L. Goswami, Vrindaban, Vikram 2028 (= 1962).
Śrībhāṣya	*Śrī Bhāṣya of Rāmānujācārya*, ed. V.S. Abhyankar, Bombay, 1914.
	The Vedānta-Sūtras with the Commentary of Rāmānuja, trans. G. Thibaut, Oxford, 1904.
	Rāmānujagranthamālā, ed. P.B. Annangaracariar, Kanci, 1974.
Śrīkaṇṭhabhāṣya	The *Brahmasutrabhashya of Srikanthacharya with the commentary Sivarkamanidipika by Appayadikshita edited with Sutrarthacandrika*, 2 vols., ed. R. Halasyanatha Sastri, New Delhi, 1986.
Śrīkārabhāṣya	*Śrīkāra Bhāṣya*, 2 vols., ed. C. Hayavadana Rao, Bangalore, 1936. (Skt.)
	Śrīkara Bhāṣyaṃ [of Śrīpati Paṇḍita], Mysore, 1954. (Skt.)
Śrīkhaṇḍyākhyān	*Śrīsant Eknāth Mahārāj yāñce Ovibaddha Caritra (of Keśavsvāmī)*, ed. P.E. Pānse, Nagpur, 1980.
	"Eknāth-caritra [of Keśavsvāmī]," in: *Śrīeknāth Mahārājāñcyā Abhaṅgāñcī Gāthā*, ed. T. Tātyā, Mumbai, 1903, 1–124.
Śrīkṛṣṇakīrttana	*Śrīkṛṣṇakīrttana* by Baḍu Caṇḍīdāsa, ed. Basanta Rañjan Rāy Bidbadballabh, Kolkata, 1974.
	Śrīkṛṣṇakīrttana: With a Modern Bengali Translation and Facsimile of the Manuscript Śrīkṛṣṇakīrttan by Baḍu Caṇḍīdāsa, ed. Nilaratan Sen, 2 vols., Kolkata, 1974.
Śrīmadbhagavadarcāprakaraṇa	*Śrīmadbhagavadarcāprakaraṇa by Nṛsiṃha Vājapeyayājin [=Vājapeyin]*, ed. D. Raṃgācārya, 1936.
Śrīmukundamālā	*Śrīmukundamāla* [sic], ed. K.R. Pisharoti, Annamalainagar, 1933.
Śrīpraśnasaṃhitā	*Śrīpraśna Samhitā* [*sic*], ed. S. Padmanabhan with the Foreword of Dr. V. Raghavan, KSV 12, Tirupati, 1969.
Śrīrādhārasasudhānidhi	*Śrī Rādhā Rasa Sudhā-Nidhi of Śrī Hita Harivaṃś*, ed. S.K.S. Ali, Vrindaban, 1977.
Śrīrādhārasasudhānidhistotra	*Śrī Rādhā-Sudhā-Nidhi-Stotram*, ed. L. Goswami, Bombay, 1991.
	Śrī Rādhā-Sudhā-Nidhi of Śrī Hit Harivaṃś, ed. S.K.S. Ali, Vrindavan, 1977.
Śrīsūkta	*Śri Sūktam*, B.B. Konnur, Bombay, 1993.
Śrītēcikastōtramālā	*Śrītēcikastōtramālā* by Veṅkaṭanātha (Vedāntadeśika), ed. Śrī Rāmatēcikācāryar Svāmi, Madras, 1982.
Śrīvacanabhūṣaṇa(m)	*Śrīvacanabhūṣaṇa of Pillai Lokācārya: Edition with English Translation*, R. Lester, Madras, 1979.
	Srimatvaravaramunintrakrantamalai, ed. P.B. Annangaracariya, Kanci, 1966.

Śrīvallabhadigvijaya	*Śrīvallabhadigvijayam or Śrīyadunāthadigvijaya*, Yadunātha, Baroda, 1985.
Stotraratnabhāṣya	*Catuḥślokibhāṣyam, Stotraratnabhāṣyam, Gadhyatrayabhāṣyañca*, ed. C.V. Śrīvatsāṅkācāryar, Madras, 1968.
Stotrasamuccaya	*Stotrasamuccaya: A Collection of Rare and Unpublished Stotras [I]*, ed. K.P. Aithal, ALS 99, Madras, 1969.
Subhāṣitatriśatī	*Subhāṣitatriśatī*, ed. D.D. Kosambi, Bombay, 1957.
Subhāṣitratnakoṣa	*Subhāṣitratnakoṣa* by Vidyākara, ed. D.D. Kosambi & V.V. Gokhale, Cambridge MA, 1957.
Sumadhvavijaya	*Sumadhvavijayaḥ*, ed. B. Prabhanjanacharya, Bangalore, 1989, [2]1996. *Nārāyaṇa Paṇḍitācārya's Sumadhva Vijaya*, D.R.V. Rau, Visakhapatnam, 1982.
Sundarabāhustava	*Stotramālā*, ed. P.B. Annangaracariyar, Kanci, 1974, 15–42.
Śūnyasaṃpādane	*Śūnyasampādane*, 5 vols., ed. S.C. Nandimath, L.M.A. Menezes, R.C. Hiremath & M.S.Sunkapur, Dharwar, 1965–1972 (Kan.). *Śūnyasaṃpādane [of Gūḷūra Siddhavīraṇāryaru]*, Bijapur, 1930. (Kan.)
Sūrsāgar	*Sampūrṇ Sūrsāgar (Śrīkṛṣṇa Līlātmak)* by Sūrdās, ed. K.L. Gupta, 5 vols., Allahabad, 2005. *Sūrsāgar* by Sūrdās, ed. M. Gupta, Agra, 1979. *Sūrsāgar* by Sūrdās, ed. Jagannāthdās "Ratnākar" *et al.*, 2 vols., Varanasi, 1972, 1976.
Sūryasiddhānta	"Translation of the Sūrya-Siddhānta, a Textbook of Hindu Astronomy, with Notes and an Appendix," ed. E. Burgess, JAOS 6, 1858–1860, 141–498.
Suśrutasaṃhitā	*Suśrutasaṃhitā of Suśruta, with the Nibandhasaṅgraha Commentary of Śrī Ḍalhaṇāchārya and the Nyāyacandrikā Pañjikā of Gayadāsāchārya on Nidānasthāna*, ed. J. Trikamji & N. Ram, JaiAS 34. Varanasi, [7]2002. *Suśruta Saṃhitā: Text with English Translation, a Full and Comprehensive Introduction, Additional Text, Different Readings, Notes, Comparative Views, Index, Glossary and Plates*, ed. L. Dwivedi, 3 vols., Varanasi, 1998.
Sūyagaḍa	*Studien zum Sūyagaḍa. Die Jainas und die anderen Weltanschauungen vor der Zeitenwende*, W.B. Bollée, SSIUH 24, Wiesbaden, 1977.
Svacchandatantra	"The Svacchandatantram: History and Structure of a Śaiva Scripture," 2 vols., W.J. Arraj, diss., University of Chicago, 1988. *The Svacchanda Tantra with Commentary "Udyota" by Kṣemarājācārya*, ed. V. Dvivedi, Delhi, 1985. *Svacchandatantra with the Commentary of Kṣemarāja*, ed. M.K. Shastrī, KSTS 31, 38, 44, 48, 51, 53, 56, Bombay, 1921–1935. *Svacchandatantra*, ed. P. Madhusūdanakaulaśāstrī, Bombay, 1921–1935.
Svāyambhuvasūtrasaṃgraha	*Svāyambhuvasūtrasaṃgrahaḥ vidyāpādaḥ sadyojyotiṣkṛtaṭīkāsahitaḥ* (The Tantra of Svayambhū with the Commentary of Sadyojyoti), ed. and trans. P.-S. Filliozat, New Delhi, 1994.
Śvetāśvataropaniṣad	"Die Śvetāśvataropaniṣad: Einleitung – Edition und Übersetzung von Adhyāya I," ed. T. Oberlies, *WZKS* 39, 1995, 61–102.
Syādvādaratnākara	*Syādvādaratnākara of Vādidevasūri*, ed. L. Motilāla, Pune, 1926–1927.
Taḏkira-yi ġawṯiyya	*Taḏkira-yi ġawṯiyya*, Gul Hasan Qalandar Qadiri, Delhi, 1918.
Taittirīyabrāhmaṇa	*The Taittirīya Brāhmaṇa of the Black Yajur Veda, with the Commentary of Sāyaṇācārya*, ed. R. Mitra, vol. III, Calcutta, 1870.

	The Taittirīya Brāhmaṇa with the Commentary of Bhaṭṭa Bhāskara Miśra, ed. A.M. Sastri, A. Mahadeva, R. Shama Sastry & L. Srinivasacharya, Delhi, 1911–1921, repr. 1985.
	Taittirīya-Brāhmaṇa, ed. P. Kumar, vols. I–III, Delhi, 1998.
	Taittirīya-Brāhmaṇa: Searchable Non-accented Transliterated Text, ed. S. Sarma, Chennai, 2005, http://www.sanskritweb.net/yajurveda/tb-find.pdf.
	Taittirīyabrāhmaṇam. E. Mahādevaśāstriṇāsampāditā, Delhi, repr. 1985.
	The Taittirīyabrāhmaṇa of the Black Yajur Veda, ed. R. Mitra, Osnabrück, 1855.
Taittirīyasaṃhitā	*Taittirīyasaṃhitā*, ed. A. Weber, 2 vols., IS 11–13, Leipzig, 1871–1872, repr. 1973.
	Taittirīya-Saṃhitā, vol. I/2, ed. N.S. Sonatakke & T.N. Dharmadhikari, Poona, 1972.
	The Veda of the Black Yajus School Entitled Taittiriya Sanhita: Translated from the Original Sanskrit Prose and Verse by Arthur Berriedale Keith, HOS 18, Delhi, repr. n.d.
Taittirīyopaniṣad	*Taittirīyopaniṣad*, trans. by Swāmī Śarvānanda, Mylapore, 1965.
	Taittirīyopaniṣad with Śaṃkarabhāṣyam, ed. V.S. Islampurkar, Poona, 1929.
Taittirīyopaniṣadbhāṣya	*Taittirīyopaniṣad with Śaṃkarabhāṣyam*, ed. V.S. Islampurkar, Poona, 1929.
Tājikabhūṣaṇa	*Tājikabhūṣaṇa*, ed. with Hindi trans. by Sītārāma Śāstrī, Mumbai, 2008.
Tājikanīlakaṇṭhī	*Tājikanīlakaṇṭhī* (including *Praśnatantra*), ed. with Viśvanātha's commentary, Hind. trans. and commentary by Kedāradatta Jośī, Delhi, 2008.
Tantrāloka	*La lumiere sur le Tantras: Chapitres 1 a 5 du Tantrāloka*, ed. and trans. L. Silburn & A. Padoux, Paris, 1998.
	The Tantrāloka of Abhinavagupta with the Commentary of Jayaratha, 8 vols., ed. and trans. M.K. Shastri, Delhi, 1987.
	The Tantrāloka of Abhinava Gupta with Commentary by Rājānaka Jayaratha, ed. M.K. Shastri, 12 vols., Allahabad, 1918–1938.
Tantrālokaviveka	*The Tantrāloka of Abhinavagupta with the Commentary of Jayaratha*, 8 vols., ed. and trans. M.K. Shastri, Delhi, 1987.
Tantrasadbhāvatantra	*Tantrasadbhāvatantra*, (transcription by M. Dyczkowski), on: www.muktabodha.org (accessed August, 2013).
Tantrasāra	*The Tantrasāra of Abhinavagupta*, ed. by M.R. Shastri, Delhi, repr. 1982.
Tantravārttika	*Śrīmajjaiminiprāṇīte Mīmāṃsādarśane Ādita Ārabhya Dvitīyādhyāyaprathamapādāntaḥ* [...] *Śrīkumārilabhaṭṭviracitatantravārtikāsahitaśābara-bhāṣyasametaś ca*, ed. Subbā Śāstrin & Vināyaka Gaṇeśa Āpaṭe [= Āpṭe], ĀSS 97, Pune, 1929.
	Kumārila Bhaṭṭa's Tantravārttika (*A Commentary on Śabara's Bhāṣya on the Pūrvamīmāṃṣā Sūtras of Jaimini*), trans. G. Jha, 2 vols., Delhi, 1998.
Tāntrikābhidhānakośa	*Tāntrikābhidhānakośa: A Dictionary of Technical Terms from Hindu Tantric Literature*, (vol. I & II: ed. H. Brunner, G. Oberhammer & A. Padoux) vol. III: ed. D. Goodall, M. Rastelli, Vienna, forthcoming.
Tarkabhāṣā	*The Tarkabhāṣā of Keśavamiśra: Edited with an Introduction, Translation into English and Notes* (*Explanatory and Critical*), ed. A.B. Gajendragadkar & R.D. Karmarkar, Pune, 1991.
Tarkarahasyadīpikā	*Tarkarahasyadīpikā*, ed. M. Jain, JMGSG 36, New Delhi, ^{2}1981.

Tarkasaṃgraha	*Tarkasaṅgraha with Dīpikā*, ed. and trans. Y.S. Athalye, BSS 55, Pune, 1974.
Tātparyacintāmaṇi	[*Vaikhānasasmārtasūtra*]= *Vaikhānasagṛhyasūtra* [*with Vaikhānasadharmasūtra and -pravarasūtra*], with Śrīnivāsa-makhin [=-Dīkṣita]'s *Tātparyacintāmaṇi* commentary and his *Daśavidhahetunirūpaṇa*, and extracts from Nṛsiṃhāgnicit Vājapeyin [= Nṛsiṃha Vājapeyin]'s commentary, ed. R. Pārthasārathi Bhaṭṭācārya, Śaka 1889 (= 1967 CE).
Tattuvaviḷakkam	*Tattuvaviḷakkam of Campantacaranalayacuvamikal* (title page missing; to be found at the French Institute of Pondicherry).
Tattvabindu	*Tattvabindu by Vācaspatimiśra with Tattvavibhāvanā by Ṛṣiputra Parameśvara*, ed. V. Rāmaswami Sastri, Madras, 1936.
Tattvacintāmaṇi	*Pūrṇānanda's Śrītattvacintāmaṇi: Critically Edited from Original Manuscripts (Chapters I–XVIII) with an original commentary by Bhuvanmohan Sankhyatirtha and (Chapters XIX–XXVI) with Notes*, ed. C. Bhattacharya, Introduction by P. Bagchi, Delhi, repr. 1994.
	Tattvacintāmaṇi, ed. N.S. Ramanuja Tatacharya, Tirupati, 1972–1999.
Tattvakaumudī	*Tattvakaumudī: Vācaspati Miśra's Commentary on the Sāṃkhya-Kārikās*, trans. G. Jha, Poona, 1965.
Tattvapradīpikā	*Tattvapradīpikā*, ed. Yogindrananda, Benares, 1974.
Tattvaprakāśa	*Aṣṭaprakaraṇam tattvaprakāśatattvasaṅgrahatattvatrayanirṇayaratnatrayabhogakārikānādakārikāmokṣakārikāparamokṣanirāsakārikākhyasiddhānta śaivīyāṣṭagranthānām saṭī kānām samāhāraḥ*, ed. V. Dviveda, Varanasi, 1988.
Tattvaprakāśavṛtti	*Aṣṭaprakaraṇam tattvaprakāśatattvasaṅgrahatattvatrayanirṇayaratnatrayabhogakārikānādakārikāmokṣakārikāparamokṣanirāsakārikākhyasiddhānta śaivīyāṣṭagranthānām saṭī kānām samāhāraḥ*, ed. V. Dviveda, Varanasi, 1988.
Tattvasamāsasūtra	*Tattvasamāsasūtra with the Commentary of Bhāvāganeśa*, ed. R.S. Bhattacharya, Banaras, n.d.
Tattvasaṃgraha	*Tattvasaṅgraha of Śāntarakṣita with the Commentary of Kamalaśīla*, ed. E. Krishnamacharya, Baroda, 1926.
Tattvasandarbha	*Tattvasandarbha* by Jīva Gosvāmī; ET: *Gopiparāṇadhana Dāsa*, Los Angeles, forthcoming.
Tattvavaiśāradī	*The Yoga-System of Patañjali Or the Ancient Hindu Doctrine of Concentration of Mind Embracing The Mnemonic Rules Called Yoga-Sūtras of Patañjali and The Comment, called Yoga-bhāṣya, attributed to Veda-Vyāsa and the Explanation, called Tattva-Vaiśāradī, of Vāchaspati-Miśra translated form the original Sanskrit by James Haughten Woods, 1914*, Delhi, 1988.
Tattvavibhāvanā	*Tattvabindu by Vācaspatimiśra with Tattvavibhāvanā by Ṛṣiputra Parameśvara*, ed. V. Rāmaswami Sastri, Madras, 1936.
Tattvavinirṇaya	*Srimad-Viṣṇu-Tattva-Vinirṇaya of Śrī Madhvācārya*, S.S. Raghavachar, Mangalore, 1959.
Tattvopaplavasiṃha	*Jayarāśi Bhaṭṭa's Tattvopaplavasiṃha (An Introduction, Sanskrit Text, English Translation and Notes)*, E.A. Solomon, Delhi, 2010.
Tēvāram	*Tēvāram*, 2 vols., ed. T.V. Gopal Iyer, PIFI 68/1–2, Pondichery, crit. ed. 1984, 1985.
Ṭhāṇāṅgasutta/ Sthānāṅgasūtra	*Śrī-Sthānāṅgasūtram: Ghāsīlālajī-mahārāja-viracitayā sudhākhyayā vyākhyayā samalaṇkṛtaṃ Hindī-Gurjara-bhāṣā-›nuvāda-sahitam*, 2 vols., Rajkot, 1964–1966.
Theragāthā	*The Elders' Verses I: Theragāthā*, trans. K.R. Norman, London, 1969.

	The Thera- and Therī-gāthā: Stanzas Ascribed to the Elders of the Buddhist Order of Recluses, ed. H. Oldenberg & R. Pischel, London, 1966.
Tīrthacintāmaṇi	*Tīrthacintāmaṇi of Vācaspati Miśra*, ed. K. Smritirtīrtha, BI 195, Calcutta, 1912.
Tīrthakamalākara	*Tīrthakamalākara, i.e. Laghutristhalīsetu, by Kamalākara Bhaṭṭa*, Benares, 1953.
Tīrthenduśekhara	*Tīrthenduśekhara by Nāgeśabhaṭṭa*, ed. S.N. Sukla, PWSBTS 66, Benares, 1936.
Tirukkuṟaḷ	*Tirukkuṟaḷ*, W.H. Drew, J. Lazarus & F.W. Ellis, New Delhi, 1886, repr. 1989.
	The "Sacred Kurraḷ" of Tiruvaḷḷuva-Nāyanār, G.U. Pope, London, 1886.
Tiruneṟiviḷakkam	*Tiruneṟiviḷakkam*, publ. in: *Cittāntam*, malar 32, itaḻ 10, n.d.
Tiruppāvai	*Āṇṭāḷ: Antalarulicceyta Tiruppāvai*, Madras, 1976.
	The Poems of Āṇṭāḷ: Tiruppāvai and Nācchiyar Tirumoḻi, trans. P.S. Sunderam, Bombay, 1987.
	Consider our Vow: An English Translation of Tiruppāvai and Tiruvempāvai, trans. N. Cutler, Madurai, 1979.
	The Secret Garland: Antal›s Tiruppavai and Nacciyar Tirumoli, trans. A. Venkatesan, New York, 2010.
Tiruvāymoḻi	*Poems of Āṇṭāḷ: Tiruppāvai and Nācchiyar Tirumoḻi*, trans. P.S. Sunderam, Bombay, 1987.
	Tiruvāymoḻi, 10 vols., ed. P.B. Annangaraciyar, Kanci, 1949–1963.
	Tiruvāymoḻi English Glossary, 2 vols., Satyamurti Ayyangar, Bombay, 1981.
Tiruvempāvai	*Consider our Vow: An English Translation of Tiruppāvai and Tiruvempāvai*, trans. N. Cutler, Madurai, 1979.
Tristhalīsetu	*Tristhalīsetu by Nārāyaṇa Bhaṭṭa*, ed. G.Ś. Gokhale, ĀSS, Poone, 1915.
Tristhalīsetusārasaṃgraha	*Tristhalīsetusārasaṃgraha by Bhaṭṭoj Dikṣita*, ed. S.N. Sukla, PWSSTS 65, Benares, 1936.
Uḍutaḍiya Akkamahādēviya ragaḷe	*Hariharana Uḍutaḍiya Akkamahādēviya ragaḷe*, ed. T.S. Shama Rao, Mysore, ²2011.
Uṇmaiviḷakkkam	*Uṇmaiviḷakkkam*, publ. The Department of Saivasiddhanta, University of Madras, Chennai, 1988.
Upadeśasāhasrī	*Upadeśasāhasrī: A Thousand Teachings*, trans. S. Jagananda, Madras, 1941, ⁵1973.
	A Thousand Teachings: The Upadeśasāhasrī of Śaṅkara, ed. S. Mayeda, Albany, 1992.
Uttamabrahmavidyāsāra	*Uttamabrahmavidyāsāra*, ed. U.C. Śrīnivāsa Bhaṭṭācārya, B. Vīrarāghavācārya & U. Vēṃkaṭanarasiṃhācārya, 1921.
Uttarajjhayaṇa/ Uttarādhyayana	*Uttarajjhayaṇāṇī*, Calcutta, 1967.
Vacanas (Akkamahādēvi)	*Mahādēviyakkagaḷa Vacanagaḷu*, Dharwar, 1973. (Kan.)
	Vacanas of Akkamahādēvi [*Mahādēviyakka*], trans. A. Menezes & S.M. Angadi, Dharwar, 1973.
	Songs for Śiva: Vacanas of Akka Mahadevi, V. Chaitanya, Walnut Creek, 2005.
	Akkana vacanagaḷu, ed. S. Basavaraju, Mysore, ³1977.
	At the Lord's Feet: An English Translation of Selected Vachanas of Akka Mahadevi (A Woman Saint of Karnataka) and Some Mahādēviyakkana vacanagaḷu, ed. R.C. Hiremath, Dharwad, ²1973.
Vacanas (Allama Prabhu)	*Allama Prabhudēvara Vacanagaḷu*, Dharwar, 1976. (Kan.).
Vacanas (Basava)	*Basavaṇṇavara Vacanagaḷu*, ed. R.C. Hiremath, Dharwar, 1968. (Kan.)

Vachanas of Basavaṇṇa, ed. H. Deveerappa, trans. L.M.A. Menezes & S.M. Angadi, Sirigere, 1967.

Vādaratnāvalī — *The Jewel-Necklace of Argument: Vādaratnāvalī of Viṣṇudāsācārya*, trans. E. Gerow, New Haven, 1990.

Vaikhānasagṛhyasūtra — [*Vaikhānasasmārtasūtra*]= *Vaikhānasagṛhyasūtra* [*with Vaikhānasadharmasūtra and -pravarasūtra*], with Śrīnivāsa-makhin [=-Dīkṣita]'s *Tātparyacintāmaṇi* commentary and his *Daśavidhahetunirūpaṇa*, and extracts from Nṛsiṃhāgnicit Vājapeyin [= Nṛsiṃha Vājapeyin]'s commentary, ed. R. Pārthasārathi Bhaṭṭācārya, Śaka 1889 (= 1967 CE).

Vaikhānasasmārtasūtra — *Vaikhānasasmārtasūtram*, ed. W. Caland, Calcutta, 1927; trans. W. Caland, Calcutta, 1929.

Vaikhānasaśrautasūtra — *Vaikhānasaśrautasūtra*, ed. W. Caland, 1941.

Vaiśeṣikasūtra — *The Vaiśeṣika Sûtras of Kaṇâda With the Commentary of Śaṅkara Miśra and Extracts From the Gloss of Jayanârâyaṇa*, trans. N. Sinha, Allahabad, 1911.

Vaiśeṣikasūtras, trans. N. Sinha, New York, 1974.

Vaiśeṣikasūtra of Kaṇāda with the Commentary of Candrānanda, ed. Jambuvijayaji, GaOS 136, Baroda, 1961.

Vaiśeṣikasūtravārttika — *Vaiśeṣikasūtravārttika/Kaṇādasūtravārttika* called *Tarkasāgara* ("*Kaṇādasūtranibandha*"), ed. A. Thakur, MKG 21, Darbhanga, 1985.

Vaiśeṣikasūtravṛtti — *Vaiśeṣikasūtra of Kaṇāda with the Commentary of Candrānanda*, ed. Jambuvijayaji, GaOS 136, Baroda, 1961.

Vaiśeṣikasūtravyākhyā — *Vaiśeṣikasūtravyākhyā*, ed. A. Thakur, MGP 1, Darbhanga, 1957.

Vaiśeṣikasūtropaskāra — *Vaiśeṣikasūtropaskāra*, ed. N. Mishra, KSS 195, Varanasi, [2]1969.

Vaiṣṇavamatābjabhāskara — *Śrīvaiṣṇavamatābjabhāskara, Svāmī Rāmeśvarānandācārya praṇita Prabhā-kiraṇa sahitaḥ*, Rāmānandācarya, Porbandar, 1980.

Vājasaneyimādhyandinaśuklayajurvedasaṃhitā — *Vājasaneyi-Mādhyandina-Śukla-Yajurveda-Saṃhitā, with the Mantra-Bhāṣya of Uvaṭa, the Vedadīpa-Bhāṣya of Mahīdhara, Appendices, an Alphabetical List of Mantras and a Short Introduction*, ed. P.J. Shastri, Delhi, 1971.

Vākyapadīya — *Bhartṛharis Vākyapadīya / die mūlakārikās nach den Handschriften hrsg. und mit einem pāda-Index versehen*, ed. W. Rau, AKM 42, 4, Wiesbaden, 1977.

Bhartṛharis Vākyapadīya II : Text der Palmblatt-Handschrift Trivandrum S.N. 532 (= A), ed. W. Rau, AGSK 7, Stuttgart, 1991.

Vākyasudha — *Rāja-Yoga: Being a Translation of the Vākyasudha or Dṛgdṛśyaviveka of Bhāratitīrtha [Part I] and the Aparokṣānubhūti of Śrī Śankarāchārya [Part II]: With Introduction and Notes*, trans. M.N. Dvivedi, Ahmedabad, 1890.

Vāmakeśvarīmata — *Nityāṣodaśikārṇavaḥ Śivānandakṛtarjuvimarśinī-vidyānandakṛtārtharatnāvalī-bhāskararāyakṛtasetubandhākhyaṭīkātrayasahita-bhāṣābhāṣyavibhūṣitaḥ*, ed. S.N. Khaṇḍelavāla, Caukhamba Surabharati Granthamala 509, Varanasi, 2011.

The Vāmakeśvarīmatam with the Commentary of Rājānaka Jayaratha, ed. M.K. Shastri, Kashmir Series of Texts and Studies 66, Srinagar, 1945.

Vāmanapurāṇa — *The Vāmanapurāṇa, with English Translation*, ed. A.S. Gupta, Varanasi, 1968.

Varadarājapañcāśat — *Varadarājapañcāśat: With Sanskrit Commentary by Karūr Śrīnivāsācārya*, P.-S. Filliozat, Bombay, 1990.

Varadarājastava — *Stotramālā*, ed. P.B. Annangaracariyar, Kanci, 1974, 15–42.

Vārāṅ Bhāī Gurdās — *Vārāṅ Bhāī Gurdās*, ed. J. Singh, Patiala, 1998.

Vārttika — *Kātyāyana's First Vārttika on Pāṇini's Aṣṭādhyāyī, Mahābhāṣya of Patañjali*, ed. F. Kielhorn, vol. 1/2, Pune, [3]1962.

Vāsishṭarāmāyaṇamu — *Vāsishṭarāmāyaṇamu* by T. Veṅgamāmba, ed. K.J. Krishnamurti, Tirupati, 2007.

Vasiṣṭhadharmasūtra — *Dharmasūtras: The Law Codes of Āpastamba, Gautama, Baudhāyana and Vasiṣṭha*, trans. P. Olivelle, Dehli, 1999.

Vāsiṣṭhamahārāmāyaṇatātparyaprakāśa — *The Yogavāsiṣṭha of Vālmīki: With the Commentary Vāsiṣṭhamahārāmāyaṇatātparya Prakāsha*, 2 vols., Delhi, repr. 1981.

Vasiṣṭhasaṃhitā — *Vasiṣṭhasaṃhitā (Yogakāṇḍa)*, ed. S. Maheshananda, B.R. Sharma, G.S. Sahay & R.K. Bodhe, Lonavla, rev. ed. 2005.

Vātsyāyanabhāṣya — *Gautama's Nyāyasūtras (with Vātsyāyana-Bhāṣya) Translated into English*, trans. G. Jha, Poona, 1939.
Nyayasūtras: Nyāyadarśana: Text with Vātsyāyana's Bhāṣya, ed. A. Thakur, Darbhanga, 1967.

Vātūlanāthasūtra — *Vātūlanāthasūtravṛtti of Anantaśakti: The Vātūlanātha-Sūtras with the Vritti of Anantaśaktipāda*, ed. and trans. P. Madhusūdanakaulaśāstrī, KSTS 39, Bombay, 1923.

Vāyupurāṇa — *Mahāmuniśrīmadvyāsapraṇītaṃ Vāyupurāṇam. etat pustakam ānandāśramasthapaṇḍitaiḥ sapāṭhāntaranirdeśaṃ saṃśodhitam. tac ca Hari Nārāyaṇa Āpaṭe ity anena (...) prakāśitam*, Poona, 1905.
Vāyupurāṇa, ed. K. Krishnadas, Bombay 1895, repr. 1983.
Śrīmad-Vāyu-Mahāpurāṇam Śrīmad-Vāyu-Mahāpurāṇam, Bombay, 1933.
The Vāyu Purāṇa, trans. G.V. Tagare, 2 vols., Delhi, 1987–1988.

Vedāntakaustubha — *Vedāntapārijātasaurabha of Nimbārka and Vedāntakaustubha of Śrīnivāsa (Commentaries on the Brahma-sūtras)*, vol. I–II., ed. R. Bose, Calcutta, 1940–1941.

Vedāntaparibhāṣa — *Dharmarājādhvārīndra: Vedāntaparibhāṣa*, ed. and trans. S.S. Suryanarayana Shastri, Madras, 1942.

Vedāntapārijātasaurabha — *Vedāntapārijātasaurabha of Nimbārka and Vedāntakaustubha of Śrīnivāsa (Commentaries on the Brahma-sūtras)*, vol. I–II., ed. R. Bose, Calcutta, 1940–1941.

Vedāntasāra — *Sadānandayogīndra: Vedāntasāraḥ with Rāmatīrtha's Vidvanmanorañjanī*, ed. Brahmacārī Medhācaitanya, Calcutta, 1993.

Vedāntasūtra — *The Vedāntasūtras with Commentary of Rāmānuja*, ed. and trans. G. Thibaut, SBE 48, Oxford, 1904.
The Vedānta Sūtras of Badarāyaṇa with the Commentary by Śaṅkarācārya, trans. G. Thibaut, Delhi, 1992.
Vedāntasūtras with the Commentary of Śrī Madhvācharya, trans. S.S. Rao, Tirupati, 1936.

Vedārthasaṃgraha — *Introduction to the Vedārthasaṃgraha of Sri Rāmānujacharya*, S.S. Raghavachar, Mangalore, 1973
Rāmānuja's Vedārthasaṃgraha, ed. J.A.B. van Buitenen, Poona, 1956.
Rāmānujagranthamālā, ed. P.B. Annangaracariar, Kanci, 1974.
Vedārthasaṃgraha of Śrī Rāmānujācārya, S.S. Raghavachar, Mysore, 1956.

Verba Indoarica — *Verba Indoarica: die primären und sekundären Wurzeln der Sanskrit-Sprache*, C.H. Werba, Wien, 1997.

Vīdēvdād — *Vīdēvdād 10–12: Critical Edition, Translation and Commentary of the Avestan and Pahlavi Texts*, M.Á. Andrés-Toledo, Salamanca, 2009.

Vidhavavivāha — *Vidhavavivāha*, Ishwar Chandra Vidyasagar, Calcutta, 1856; ET: trans. B. Hatcher, *Hindu Widow Marriage*, New York, 2011.

Vidyāmādhavīya — *Vidyāmādhavīyam*, vol. I, ed. with Viṣṇu's *Muhūrtadīpika* commentary by R.S. Sastry, Mysore, 1998.

Vijñānabhairava — *Vijñānabhairava or Divine Consciousness: A Treasury of 112 Types of Yoga*, ed. J. Singh, Delhi, 1979.

Vikramacarita — *Vikrama's Adventures or The Thirty-two Tales of the Throne: A Collection of Stories about King Vikrama, as Told by the Thirty-two-Statuettes That Supported His Throne*, trans. F. Edgerton, 2 vols., Cambridge MA, 1926, repr. Delhi, 1993. (= *Vikramacarita*)

Vimānārcanākalpa — *Vimānārcanākalpa*, ed. Raghunāthacakravārtin & S. Mādhavācārya, Madras, 1926.

Vimānavatthu-Aṭṭhakathā — *Paramattha Dīpanī, Part 4: Commentary on the Vimāna-Vatthu*, JPTS 18, ed. E. Hardy, London, 1901.

Vinayapatrikā — *Tulsī Dās: The Petition to Rām*, F.R. Allchin, 1966.

Vinayapiṭaka — *Vinaya-Piṭaka: The Book of Discipline*, vol. I: *Suttavibhaṅga*, trans. I.B. Horner, London, 1938.

Vīramitrodaya — *Vīramitrodaya of Mitra Miśra*, ed. P. Śarmā *et al.*, 21 vols., CSS 30, Benares, 1913–1936.

Vīramitrodaya: Paribhāṣā-Prakāśa, ed. Mitramiśra, Benares, 1896.

Virūpākṣapañcāśikā — "Virūpākṣapañcāśikā (With Vidyācakravartin's Vivṛti)," in: G. Kaviraj, ed., *Tantrasaṁgraha (Part 1)*, Varanasi, 1970, 1–22.

The Teachings of the Odd-Eyed One: A Study and Translation of the Virūpākṣapañcāśikā with the Commentary of Vidyācakravartin, D.P. Lawrence, Albany, 2008.

Viṣṇudharmasūtra — *Viṣṇudharmāḥ: Precepts for the Worship of Viṣṇu*, part 1: *Adhyāyas 1–43*, part 2: *Adhyāyas 44–81*, part 3: *Adhyāyas 82–105*, ed. R. Grünendahl, Wiesbaden, 1983.

Viṣṇudharmottarapurāṇa — *Viṣṇudharmottara-purāṇa: Third Kaṇḍa Critically Edited with Introduction, Notes, etc. (Vol. 1: Text, Critical Notes, etc.)*, by Priyabala Shah, GaOS 130, Baroda, 1958.

The Viṣṇudharmottarapurāṇam, Delhi, 1985.

Viṣṇupārijātamu — *Viṣṇupārijātamu* by T. Veṅgamāmba, ed. U. Lakshmikantamma, Hyderabad, 1965.

Viṣṇupurāṇa — *The Viṣṇumahāpurāṇam*, Delhi, 1910, repr. 1985.

Śrīviṣṇupurāṇa, trans. Ś. Gupta, Gorakhpur, 1990.

Viṣṇu Purāṇa with Śrīdharasvāmin's Commentary and Śrīkālipadatarkācārya's Gloss, SaS 1, Calcutta, 1965.

The Vishnu Purana, trans. H.H. Wilson, Calcutta, 1972.

Viṣṇupurāṇa: Including the Hindi Translation of Munilāl Gupta, Gorakhpur, 1933.

Viṣṇusahasranāma — *Sri Visnusahasranama*, trans. S. Sathyamurthi Ayyangar, Bangalore, 1996.

Sri Vishnu Sahasranama with the Bhashya of Sri Parasara Bhattar, ed. A.S. Raghavan, Madras, 1983.

Viṣṇusaṃhitā — *The Viṣṇu Saṃhitā*, ed. by M.M. Gaṇapati Sāstrī, With an Elaborate Introduction by N.P. Unni, TSS 85, Delhi, rev. ed. 1991.

Viṣṇusmṛti — *The Law Code of Viṣṇu: A Critical Edition and Annotated Translation of the Vaiṣṇava-Dharmaśāstra*, ed. and trans. P. Olivelle, HOS 73, Cambridge MA, 2009.

Viṣṇutattvavinirṇaya — *Śrīmad-Viṣṇu-Tattva-Vinirṇaya of Śrī Madhvācārya*, ed. S.S. Raghavachar, Mangalore, 1959.

Vivekacūḍamaṇi — *Vivekachudamani of Sri Sankaracharya*, Swami Madhvananda, Mayavati, [5]1952.

Vivekamārtaṇḍa — *Das Gorakṣaśataka* (= *Vivekamārtaṇḍa*), ed. F. Nowotny, Cologne, 1976.
**Vivekamārtaṇḍa of Gorakṣadeva*, ms. 4110 at the Oriental Institute Baroda, Vadodara, n.d.

Vyāsabhāṣya — *Yoga Philosophy of Patañjali Containing his Yoga Aphorisms with the Commentary of Vyāsa in the Original Sanskrit, and Annotations Thereon with Copious Hints on the Practice of Yoga by Swāmi Hariharānanda Āraṇya*, Calcutta, 1981.

Vyāsavāṇī — *Vyāsa-Vāṇī: Harirām Vyāsa*, ed. S.R. Goswami, Mathura, 1973.

Vyavahāramayūkha — *The Vyavahára Mayúkha, in Original, with an English Translation*, ed. and trans. V.N. Mandlik, Bombay, 1880.

Vyomavatī — see *Padārthasaṃgrahaṭīkā*

Yajñādhikāra — *Yajñādhikāra*, Eguvarpalayam, 1931.

Yajurvedasaṃhitā — *Yajurveda Saṃhitā: Sanskrit Text with English Translation*, trans. R.T.H. Griffith, Delhi, 1899, repr. 1997.

Yantracintāmaṇi — *Yantracintāmaṇiḥ of Dāmodara*, crit. ed. by H.-G. Türstig, Stuttgart 1988.

Yatidharmaprakāśa — *Vāsudevāśrama Yatidharmaprakāśa: A Treatise on World Renunciation*, vol. II, ed. P. Olivelle, Leiden, 1977.

Yatidharmasummucaya — *Rules and Regulations of Brahmanical Asceticism: Yatidharma-summucaya of Yādava Prakāśa*, ed. and trans. P. Olivelle, Albany, 1995.

Yavanajātaka — *The Yavanajātaka of Sphujidhvaja*, ed., trans., and comm. D. Pingree, Cambridge MA, 1978.
The Yavanajātaka of Sphujidhvaja, ed. with annotated ET by D. Pingree, Cambridge USA, 1978.

Yogabīja — *Yogabīja*, ed. R.L. Śrīvāstav, Gorakhpur, 1982.

Yogapradīpakā — *Jogpradīpakā of Jayatarāma*, ed. M.L. Gharote, Jodhpur, 1999.

Yogaprakāśikā — *Haṭhapradīpikā of Svātmārāma (10 chapters): With Yogaprakāśikā Commentary by Bālakṛṣṇa*, ed. M.L. Gharote & P. Devnath, Lonavla, 2002.

Yogasārasaṃgraha — *Yogasārasaṅgraha*, trans. G.N. Jha, ed. A. Kumar, Delhi, 1995.

Yogasūtra — *Yoga Philosophy of Patañjali Containing his Yoga Aphorisms with the Commentary of Vyāsa in the Original Sanskrit, and Annotations Thereon with Copious Hints on the Practice of Yoga by Swāmi Hariharānanda Āraṇya*, Calcutta, 1981.
The Yoga-Sūtras of Patañjali: Sanskrit Text and English Translation Together with an Introduction and an Appendix, and Notes on Each Sūtra Based upon Several Authentic Commentaries – All in English, trans. M.N. Dvivedi, Madras, 1890.
The Yoga Philosophy: Being the Text of Patanjali, with Bhoja Raja's Commentary, with their translations in English by Dr. Ballantyne and Govind Shastri Deva, an Introduction by Col. Olcott and an Appendix, T. Tatya, [2]1885.

Yogasūtravṛtti — *The Yoga Philosophy: Being the Text of Patanjali, with Bhoja Raja's Commentary, with their translations in English by Dr. Ballantyne and Govind Shastri Deva, an Introduction by Col. Olcott and an Appendix*, T. Tatya, [2]1885.

Yogavāsiṣṭha — *The Yoga-Vāsiṣṭha-Mahārāmāyaṇa of Vālmiki: Translated From the Original Sanskrit*, trans. V.-L. Mitra, 4 vols., Delhi, repr. 1978.
The Yogavāsiṣṭha of Vālmīki: With the Commentary Vāsiṣṭhamahārāmāyaṇatātparya Prakāsha, 2 vols., Delhi, repr. 1981.
Muntaḫab-i Jūg-bāsasht (Selections from the Yoga-vāsiṣṭha), ed. F. Mujtabā'ī, Tehran, 2006.

Yoginīhṛdaya — *Yoginīhṛdayam Amṛtānandayogikṛtadīpikayā Bhāṣānuvādena ca Sahitam*, ed. V. Dviveda, Delhi, 2011.
Le Coeur de la Yoginī: Yoginīhṛdaya avec le commentaire Dīpikā d'Amṛtānanda, A. Padoux, PICI 63, Paris, 1994.
Yoginīhṛdayam with Commentaries Dipikā of Amṛtānanda and Setubandha of Bhāskararāya, G. Kaviraja, Varanasi, 1979.

Yuktidīpikā — *Yuktidīpikā*, ed. A. Wezler & S. Motegi, ANIS 44, Stuttgart, 1998.
Yuktidīpikā, trans. S. Kumar & D.N. Bhargava, Delhi, 1990.

Primary Source Abbreviations

AbhiBhā.	*Abhinavabhārati*
AbhiD.	*Abhinayadarpaṇa*
AbhK.	*Abhidharmakośa*
AbhKBh.	*Abhidharmakośabhāṣya*
AbhKVyā.	*Abhidharmakośavyākhyā*
ĀdHṛ.	*Ādityahṛdaya*
ĀG.	*Ādigranth*
AgMa.	*Agastimata*
AgP.	*Agnipurāṇa*
AhirSa.	*Ahirbudhnyasaṃhitā*
AitĀ.	*Aitereyāraṇyaka*
AitBr.	*Aitareyabrāhmaṇa*
AjiĀg.	*Ajitāgama*
ĀK.	*Ānandakanda*
AK.	*Amarakośa*
AmBU.	*Amṛtabindopaniṣad*
AmPrab.	*Amaraughaprabodha*
AN.	*Aṅguttaranikāya*
AṇuBh.	*Aṇubhāṣya*
Anuvyā.	*Anuvyākhyāna*
ĀpDhS.	*Āpastambadharmasūtra*
ĀpGS.	*Āpastambagṛhyasūtra*
ĀpŚS.	*Āpastambaśrautasūtra*
ĀpSulS.	*Āpastambaśulbasūtra*
Āry.	*Āryabhaṭīya*
ArŚ.	*Arthaśāstra*
AṣṭA.	*Aṣṭādhyāyī*
AṟTiVa.	*Aṟputattiruvantāti*
AṣṭHṛSa.	*Aṣṭāṅgahṛdayasaṃhitā*
AṣṭSa.Sū.	*Aṣṭāṅgahṛdayasaṃhitā.Sūtrasthāna*
ĀśvGS.	*Āśvalāyanagṛhyasūtra*
ĀtBo.	*Ātmabodha*
AthŚiU.	*Atharvaśirāsupaniṣad*
ĀtTatVi.	*Ātmatattvaviveka*
AV.	*Atharvaveda*
AVP.	*Atharvaveda: Paippalāda recension*
AVŚ.	*Atharvaveda: Śaunakīya recension*
AvvKu.	*Avvaikkuṟaḷ*
ĀyDīp.	*Āyurvedadīpikā*
Balarām.	*Balarāmāyaṇa*
BĀU.	*Bṛhadāraṇyakopaniṣad*
BĀUBh.	*Bṛhadāraṇyakopaniṣadbhāṣya*
BauDhS.	*Baudhāyanadharmasūtra*
BauGS.	*Baudhāyanagṛhyasūtra*
BhāgP.	*Bhāgavatapurāṇa*
BhaMā.	*Bhajanamālā*

BhārT.	*Bhārgavatantra*
BhaVai.	*Bhagavaī*
BheSa.	*Bhelasaṃhitā*
BhG.	*Bhagavadgītā*
BhKal.	*Bhāmākalāpamu*
BhMā.	*Bhaktamāl*
BhPr.	*Bhāvaprakāśa*
BhRaĀk.	*Bhaktiratnākara*
BhRaAm.	*Bhaktirasāmṛtasindhu*
BhRaĀv.	*Bhaktiratnāvalī*
BHSD	*Buddhist Hybrid Sanskrit Grammar and Dictionary*
BhVa.	*Bhaktivardhinī*
BīG.	*Bījagaṇita*
BISM	*Bhārat Itihāsa Saṁśodhak Mandal*
BrāṇḍaP.	*Brahmāṇḍapurāṇa*
BṛBh.	*Bṛhadbhāṣya*
BṛDhP.	*Bṛhaddharmapurāṇa*
BṛhBhAm.	*Bṛhadbhāgavatāmṛta*
BṛhSa.	*Bṛhatsaṃhitā*
BrP.	*Brahmapurāṇa*
BrS.	*Brahmasūtra*
ḄṛSaṃU.	*Ḅṛhatsaṃnyāsopaniṣad*
BrSBh.	*Brahmasūtrabhāṣya*
BrSi.	*Brāhmasphuṭasiddhānta*
BṛSm.	*Bṛhaspatismṛti*
BṛŚṛPad.	*Bṛhatśṛṅgadharapaddhati*
BrY.	*Brahmayāmala*
BuCar.	*Buddhacarita*
CaiBh.	*Caitanyabhāgavata*
CaiC.	*Caitanyacaritāmṛta*
CaiCan.	*Caitanyacandrāmṛta*
CarSa.	*Carakasaṃhitā*
CarSa.Ci	*Carakasamhitā.Cikitsāsthāna*
CarSa.Ni.	*Carakasaṃhita.Nidanasthāna*
CarSa.Śā.	*Carakasaṃhitā.Śārirasthāna*
CarSa.Sū.	*Carakasaṃhita.Sūtrasthāna*
CarSa.Vi.	*Carakasaṃhitā.Vimānasthāna*
CaŚat.	*Caṇḍīśataka*
CatVC.	*Caturvargacintāmaṇi*
ChāU.	*Chāndogyopaniṣad*
ChāUBh.	*Chāndogyopaniṣadbhāṣya*
Cilapp.	*Cilappatikāram*
CiMā.	*Ciṟiyamātal*
CiÑāCi.	*Civañāṉacittiyār*
CiÑāPō.	*Civañāṉapōtam*
CiPira.	*Civappirakācam*
CNāṭ.	*Ceñcu Nāṭakamu*
CūS.	*Cūladukkhakkhandhasutta*
CuVa.	*Cullavagga*
DāJLī.	*Dādūjanmalīla*
Daś.	*Daśakumāracarita*
DaśŚl.	*Daśaślokī*

DaU.	*Dattātreyopaniṣad*
DāVā.	*Dādūvāṇī*
DYŚa.	*Dattātreyayogaśāstra*
DBhāgP.	*Devībhāgavatapurāṇa*
DePañc.	*Devanāyakapañcāśat*
DhPra.	*Dharmottarapradīpa*
DhS.	*Dhammasaṅgaṇi*
DhvaĀl.	*Dhvanyāloka*
DN.	*Dīghanikāya*
DM.	*Devīmāhātmya*
EI.	*Epigrahia Indica*
EWA.	*Etymologisches Wörterbuch des Altindoarischen*
GaṇK.	*Gaṇakārikā*
GaP.	*Garuḍapurāṇa*
GāT.	*Gāyatrītantra*
GauDhS.	*Gautamadharmasūtra*
GauDī.	*Gauragaṇoddeśadīpikā*
GītaGov.	*Gītagovinda*
GobhGS.	*Gobhilagṛhyasūtra*
GoŚat.	*Gorakṣaśataka*
GovLī.	*Govindalīlāmṛta*
GTātp.	*Gītātātparya*
HanBā.	*Hanumānbāhuk*
HarC.	*Harṣacarita*
HirGS.	*Hiraṇyakeśīgṛhyasūtra*
HRat.	*Haṭharatnāvalī*
HV.	*Harivaṃśa*
H(Y)P.	*Haṭhayogapradīpikā*
HYPṬ.	*Haṭhayogapradīpikāṭīkā*
ĪśPraK.	*Īśvarapratyabhijñākārikā*
ĪśPraKVṛ.	*Īśvarapratyabhijñākārikāvṛtti*
ĪśPraVim.	*Īśvarapratyabhijñāvimarśinī*
ĪśSa.	*Īśvarasaṃhitā*
ĪśŚai.	*Īśānaśaivagurudevapaddhati*
ĪśU.	*Īśopaniṣad*
Ja.	*Jātaka*
JaiBr.	*Jaiminīyabrāhmaṇa*
JaiUBr.	*Jaiminīyopaniṣadbrāhmaṇa*
JaySa.	*Jayākhyasaṃhitā*
Jīv.	*Jīvābhigama*
JñāSa.	*Jñānāmṛtasārasaṃhitā*
JY.	*Jayadrathayāmala*
JyoVe.Ṛg	*Jyotiṣavedāṅga.Ṛgveda recension*
KaĀv.	*Kavitāvalī*
KaG.	*Kabīr Granthāvalī*
KālŚat.	*Kālahastīśvara Śatakamu*
KāmĀg.	*Kāmikāgama*
KāmS.	*Kāmasūtra*
KaṇC.	*Kaṇṇinuṉ Ciṟuttampu*
KāP.	*Kālikāpurāṇa*
KaPa.	*Kabīr Parcāī*
KārĀg.	*Kāraṇāgama*

KarBh.	*Karṇabhāra*
KarSto.	*Karpūrādistotra*
Kāś.	*Kāśikāvṛtti*
KāśSa.In.	*Kāśyapasaṃhitā.Indriyasthāna*
KāśSa.Ka.	*Kāśyapasaṃhitā.Kalpasthāna*
KāṭhGS.	*Kāthakagṛhyasūtra*
KāṭhSa.	*Kāṭhakasaṃhitā*
KaṭhŚU.	*Kaṭhaśrutyupaniṣad*
KaṭhU.	*Kaṭhopaniṣad*
KaṭhUBh.	*Kaṭhopaniṣadbhāṣya*
KātŚS.	*Kātyāyanaśrautasūtra*
KauS.	*Kauśikasūtra*
KauṣBr.	*Kauṣītakibrāhmaṇa*
KauṣU.	*Kauṣītakopaniṣad*
KāvĀd.	*Kāvyādarśa*
KāvAl.	*Kāvyālaṃkāra*
KāVil.	*Kāmakalāvilāsa*
KāvMī.	*Kāvyamīmāṃsā*
KCaic	*Kṛṣṇacaitanyacaritāmṛta*
KīGh.	*Kīrtanaghoṣa*
KeU.	*Kenopaniṣad*
KhVid.	*Khecarīvidyā*
KirĀg.	*Kiraṇāgama*
KirĀv.	*Kiraṇāvalī*
KirĀvṬī.	*Kiraṇāvalīṭīkā*
KirT.	*Kiraṇatantra*
KoS	*Koshur Samachar*
KrDī.	*Kramadīpikā*
KSS.	*Kathāsaritsāgara*
KumSambh.	*Kumārasambhava*
KūP.	*Kūrmapurāṇa*
KuT.	*Kulārṇavatantra*
LakṣT.	*Lakṣmītantra*
LaS.	*Laṅkāvatārasūtra*
LBhAm.	*Laghubhāgavatāmṛta*
LDC.	*Liṅgadhāraṇacandrikā*
Līlāv.	*Līlāvatī*
LiP.	*Liṅgapurāṇa*
LIV	*Lexikon der indogermanischen Verben*
LS	*Lokmat Sahitya*
MaBh.	*Mahābhāṣya*
MaBh.P.	*Mahābhāṣya.Paspaśāhnika*
MaiSa.	*Maitrāyaṇīsaṃhitā*
MaitriU.	*Maitryupaniṣad*
MaiU.	*Maitrāyaṇīyopaniṣad*
MāKad.	*Mādhuryakadambinī*
MālA.	*Mālavikāgnimitra*
MaMa.	*Mayamata*
MaMañ.	*Mahārthamañjarī*
MaNāU.	*Mahānārayaṇopaniṣad*
MāṇḍU.	*Māṇḍukyopaniṣad*
ManuBh.	*Manubhāṣya*

MārP.	*Mārkaṇḍeyapurāṇa*
MārSa.	*Mārkaṇḍeyasaṃhitā*
MāŚlVā.	*Mālinīślokavārttika*
MaSm.	*Manusmṛti*
MaSta.	*Mahimnaḥstava*
MatĀg.	*Mataṅgapārameśvarāgama*
MatKāñ.	*Maturaikkāñci*
MatP.	*Matsyapurāṇa*
MatSa.	*Matsyendrasaṃhitā*
MaVā.	*Mahāvāṇī*
MāViT.	*Mālinīvijayottaratantra*
MāViVā.	*Mālinīvijayavārttika*
MBh.	*Mahābhārata*
MBhāgP.	*Mahābhāgavatapurāṇa*
MBhPa.	*Mahābhāratatātparyanirṇaya*
MCT.	*Mahācīnatantra*
Megh.	*Meghadhūta*
Mitā.	*Mitākṣarā*
MīmS.	*Mīmāṃsāsūtra*
MīmSBh.	*Mīmāṃsāstrabhāṣya*
MIS.	*Marāṭhyāñcyā Itihāsācīṃ Sādhaneṃ*
MkP.	*Mārkaṇḍeyapurāṇa*
MLaSto.	*Mahālakṣmīstotra*
MMU.	*Mantramahodadhi*
MN.	*Majjhimanikāya*
MoMud.	*Mohamudgara*
MNirT.	*Mahānirvāṇatantra*
MṛgĀg.	*Mṛgendrāgama*
MSBh.	*Mīmāṃsāsūtrabhāṣya*
MŚlVāKā.	*Mīmāṃsāślokavārttikakāśikā*
MtP.	*Matsyapurāṇa*
MuDī.	*Muhūrtadīpikā*
MuMā.	*Mukundamālā*
MuTiVa.	*Mutal Tiruvantāti*
MūTiVa.	*Mūṉṟam Tiruvantāti*
MuU.	*Muṇḍakopaniṣad*
MuUBh.	*Muṇḍakopaniṣadbhāṣya*
NācTiMo.	*Nācciyār Tirumoḻi*
NāGh.	*Nāmaghoṣa*
NāPariU.	*Nāradaparivrājakopaniṣad*
NarParī.	*Nareśvaraparīkṣā*
NarParīPr.	*Nareśvaraparīkṣāprakāśa*
NāSm.	*Nāradasmṛti*
NāTiVa	*Nāṉmukaṉ Tiruvantāti*
NāṭŚā.	*Nāṭyaśāstra*
NB	*Nav Bhārat*
NeT.	*Netratantra*
NiLak.	*Nirodhalakṣaṇa*
Nir.	*Nirukta* (of Yāska)
NīSā.	*Nītisāra*
NīŚat.	*Nītiśataka*
NiŚe.	*Nighaṇṭuśeṣa*

NiṣTSa.	*Niṣvāsatattvasaṃhitā*
NPP	*Nāgarī Pracāriṇī Patrikā*
NyāBh.	*Nyāyabhāṣya*
NyāK.	*Nyāyakandalī*
NyāKPañj.	*Nyāyakandalīpañjikā*
NyāMañ.	*Nyāyamañjarī*
NyāVā.	*Nyāyavārttika*
NyāS.	*Nyāyasūtra*
NyāSVār.	*Nyāyasūtravārttika*
NyāVārTṬī.	*Nyāyavārttikatātparyaṭīkā*
NyāSVṛ.	*Nyāyasūtravṛtti*
PaDhSaṅg.	*Padārthadharmasaṅgraha*
PādSa.	*Pādmasaṃhitā*
PañBh.	*Pañcārthabhāṣya*
PāñRa.	*Pāñcarātrarakṣā*
PañBr.	*Pāñcaviṃśabrāhmaṇa*
ParĀg.	*Parākhyāgama*
ParSa.	*Paramasaṃhitā*
PārSa.	*Pārameśvarasaṃhitā*
PāS.	*Pāśupatasūtra*
PaSaṅgṬī.	*Padārthasaṅgrahaṭīkā*
PaTr.	*Parātrīśikā*
PaTrV.	*Parātrīśikāvivaraṇa*
PauṣĀg.	*Pauṣkarāgama*
PauṣSa.	*Pauṣkarasaṃhitā*
PāVi.	*Pātravidhi*
PdP.	*Padmapurāṇa*
PdSa.	*Pādmasaṃhitā*
PED	*Pali-English Dictionary*
PerTiMo.	*Periyatirumoḻi*
PeTiMo.	*Perumāl Tirumoḻi*
PrCU.	*Prabodhacandrodaya*
PrMā.	*Praśnamārga*
PrT.	*Praśnatantra*
PrU.	*Praśnopaniṣad*
PST.	*Prapañcasāratantra*
PūPr.	*Pūjāprakāśa*
Puṟ.	*Puṟanāṉūṟu*
RaĀv.	*Ratnāvalī*
RabR.	*Rabīndra Racanāvalī*
RaGa.	*Rasagaṅgādhara*
RaghV.	*Raghuvaṃśa*
RaiVā.	*Raidāsvāṇī*
RājSā.	*Rājayoga Sāramu*
Rām.	*Rāmāyaṇa*
RaMañ.	*Rasamañjarī*
RāmPTU.	*Rāmapūrvatāpanīyopaniṣad*
RāmRSto.	*Rāmarakṣāstotra*
RāmRU.	*Rāmarahasyopaniṣad*
RāmUTU.	*Rāmottaratāpinyopaniṣad*
RaSā.	*Rasasāra*
RasAr.	*Rasārṇava*

RasCu.	*Rasendracūḍāmaṇi*
RasHṛT.	*Rasahṛdayatantra*
RasRaSam.	*Rasaratnasamuccaya*
RaṬī.	*Ratnaṭīkā*
RatPa.	*Ratnaparīkṣā*
RaTr.	*Ratnatraya*
RaĀv.	*Ratnāvalī*
RCM.	*Rāmcaritmānas*
RKhV.	*Revākhaṇḍa.Vāyupurāṇa*
RūSi.	*Rūpasiddhi*
ṚV.	*Ṛgveda*
RVKh.	*Ṛgvedakhila*
SadKar.	*Saduktikarṇāmṛta*
SaṃgBh.	*Saṃgrahabhāṣya*
SāṃK.	*Sāṃkhyakārikā*
SaṃNir.	*Saṃnyāsanirṇaya*
SāṃS.	*Sāṃkhyasūtra*
SāṃSā.	*Sāṃkhyasāra*
SaṃsVi.	*Saṃskāravidhi*
SāṃTKau.	*Sāṃkhyatattvakaumudī*
SaṅgRaĀk.	*Saṅgītaratnākara*
ŚāṅkhGS.	*Śāṅkhāyaṇagṛhyasūtra*
SāPā.	*Sāmantapāsādikā*
SāPañc.	*Sāmbapañcāśikā*
Sar.	*Saroddhāra*
SarĀg.	*Sarvajñānottarāgama*
SarMūGr.	*Sarvamūlagrantha*
SātSa.	*Sātvatasaṃhitā*
ŚatSaṃg.	*Śataratnasaṃgraha*
ŚatTr.	*Śatakatraya*
SauLa.	*Saundaryalaharī*
SauP.	*Saurapurāṇa*
ŚāV.	*Śāktavijñāna*
SāViBr.	*Sāmavidhānabrāhmaṇa*
ŚBr.	*Śatapathabrāhmaṇa*
ŚBrK.	*Śatapathabrāhmaṇa: Kāṇvīya recension*
ŚBrM.	*Śatapathabrāhmaṇa: Mādhyandina recension*
ṢDSam.	*Ṣaḍdarśanasamuccaya*
ṢDSam.LVṛ.	*Ṣaddarśanasamuccaya.Laghuvṛtti*
SidPad.	*Siddhasiddhāntapaddhati*
ŚiDṛ.	*Śivadṛṣṭi*
ŚiDṛVṛ.	*Śivadṛṣṭivṛtti*
SidTr.	*Siddhitrayī*
ŚiJñ.	*Śivajñānabodha*
ŚiJñUpany.	*Śivajñānabodhopanyāsa*
ŚiJñV.	*Śivajñānabodhavṛtti*
SiMĀv.	*Siddhāntamuktāvalī*
SiRa.	*Siddhāntarahasya*
ŚiS.	*Śivasūtra*
ŚiStoĀv.	*Śivastotrāvalī*
ŚiSV.	*Śivasūtravimarśinī*
SmSth.	*Smṛtisthaḷ*

SN.	*Saṃyuttanikāya*
SPā.	*Sūtrapāṭha*
SpK.	*Spandakārikā*
SpN.	*Spandanirṇaya*
ŚrīBh.	*Śrībhāṣya*
ŚrīGuR.	*Śrīguṇaratnakośa*
ŚrīKaBh.	*Śrīkaṇṭhabhāṣya*
ŚrīKīr.	*Śrīkṛṣṇakīrtana*
ŚrīPrSa.	*Śrīpraśnasaṃhitā*
ŚrīRā.	*Śrīrādhārasasudhānidhi*
ŚṛṅPr.	*Śṛṅgāraprakāśa*
ŚṛṅŚat.	*Śṛṅgāraśataka*
ŚruSūM.	*Śrutisūktimālā*
ŚSaṃp	*Śūnyasaṃpādane*
ŚSS.	*Śrī Sāī Saccarita*
StC.	*Stuticintāmaṇi*
ŚTT.	*Śāradātilakatantra*
SuMVij.	*Sumadhvavijaya*
SūŚat.	*Sūryaśataka*
SuśrSa.	*Suśrutasaṃhitā*
SuśrSa.Ci.	*Suśrutasaṃhitā. Cikitsāsthāna*
SuśrSa.Sū.	*Suśrutasaṃhitā. Sūtrasthāna*
SvaT.	*Svacchandatantra*
ŚvetU.	*Śvetāśvataropaniṣad*
TĀ.	*Tantrāloka*
TāBhū.	*Tājikabhūṣaṇa*
TaiBr.	*Taittirīyabrāhmaṇa*
TaiSa.	*Taittīriyasaṃhitā*
TaiU.	*Taittirīyopaniṣad*
TarRahDī.	*Tarkarahasyadīpikā*
TātDī.	*Tātparyadīpikā*
TatK.	*Tattvakaumudī*
TatPr.	*Tattvaprakāśa*
TatSaṃkh.	*Tattvasaṃkhyāna*
TatVai.	*Tattvavaiśāradī*
TatVi.	*Tattvaviveka*
TĀVi.	*Tantrālokaviveka*
Ṭhāṇ.	*Ṭhāṇāṅgasutta/Sthānāṅgasūtra*
TiCaVi.	*Tiruccantaviruttam*
TiMā.	*Tirumalāi*
TiMu.	*Tirumuṟai*
TiMuP.	*Tirumuṟaikaṇṭapurāṇam*
TiMuPa.	*Tirumurukāṟṟuppaṭai*
TiNeVi.	*Tiruneṟiviḷakkam*
TiVāy.	*Tiruvāymoḻi*
TiViP.	*Tiruviḷaiyāṭaṟpurāṇam*
TiVir.	*Tiruviruttam*
TNŚat.	*Tarigoṇḍa Nṛsimhaśatakamu*
TSā.	*Tantrasāra*
TSadT.	*Tantrasadbhāvatantra*
TVā.	*Tantravārttika*
Ullekh.	*Ullekhanī*

UpāKh.	*Upādhikhaṇḍana*
UpaSāh.	*Upadeśasāhasrī*
UttJh.	*Uttarajjhayaṇa/Uttarādhyayana*
VādŚS.	*Vādhulaśrautasūtra*
VāgAl.	*Vāgbhaṭālaṃkāra*
VaiDhS.	*Vaikhānasadharmasūtra*
VaiS.	*Vaiśeṣikasūtra*
VaiŚat.	*Vairāgyaśataka*
VaiSmS.	*Vaikhānasasmārtasūtra*
VaiSUp.	*Vaiśeṣikasūtropaskāra*
VaiSVṛ.	*Vaiśeṣikasūtravṛtti*
VājPrāt.	*Vājasaneyiprātiśākhya*
VājSa.	*Vājasaneyisaṃhitā*
VākPad.	*Vākyapadīya*
VāMa.	*Vāmakeśvarīmata*
VāmP.	*Vāmanapurāṇa*
VaP.	*Varāhapurāṇa*
VarPad.	*Varuṇapaddhati*
Värtt.	*Vārttikā*
VasDhS.	*Vasiṣṭhadharmasūtra*
VAT.	*Vidyārṇavatantra*
VedKau.	*Vedāntakaustubha*
VedPāSau.	*Vedāntapārijātasaurabha*
VedSaṃg.	*Vedārthasaṃgraha*
VIA.	*Verba Indoarica*
ViCū.	*Vivekacūḍāmaṇi*
ViDhP.	*Viṣṇudharmottarapurāṇa*
VijBhai.	*Vijñānabhairava*
ViM.	*Vivekamārtaṇḍa*
VinP.	*Vinayapiṭaka*
VinPa.	*Vinaypatrikā*
ViP.	*Viṣṇupurāṇa*
ViPā.	*Viṣṇu Pārijatamu*
ViPā.	*Villipāratam*
ViSa.	*Viṣṇusaṃhitā*
ViSah.	*Viṣṇusahasranāma*
ViSm.	*Viṣṇusmṛti*
ViTatVinir.	*Viṣṇutattva(vi)nirṇaya*
ViyPa.	*Viyāhapannatti*
VvA.	*Vimānavatthu-Aṭṭhakathā*
VyāBh.	*Vyāsabhāṣya*
YCu.	*Yakoppu Cuṇṇam*
YHṛ.	*Yoginīhṛdaya*
YugŚa.	*Yugalaśataka*
YS.	*Yogasūtra*
YSBhV.	*Yogasūtrabhāṣyavivaraṇa*
YukDī.	*Yuktidīpikā*

Journals and Series

AA	*Arts Asiatiques*
AAA	*Archives of Asian Art*
AAAG	*Annals of the Association of American Geographers*
AAAPSS	*Annals of the American Academy of Political and Social Science*
AAE	*Arabian Archaeology and Epigraphy*
AaM	*Anthropology and Medicine*
AARAS	American Academy of Religion Academy Series
AASF-B/H	Annales Academiae Scientiarum Fennicae B/Humaniora
ABORI	*Annals of the Bhandarkar Oriental Research Institute*
ABS	*American Behavioral Scientist*
AcA	*Acta Asiatica*
ACK	*Amar Chitra Katha*
AE	*American Ethnologist*
AÉPHÉ	*Annuaire de L'École Pratique des Hautes Études*
AER	*American Economic Review*
AES	*Archives Européennes de Sociologie*
AfA	*African Affairs*
AFS	*Asian Folklore Studies*
AGSK	Abhandlungen der Geistes- und Sozialwissenschaftlichen Klasse
AHES	*Archive for History of Exact Sciences*
AI	*Art International*
AI (BASI).NS	*Ancient India (Bulletin of the Archaeological Survey of India). New Series*
AIP	*Archiv für Indische Philosophie*
AIRS	*Anantacharya Indological Research Series*
AJP	*American Journal of Philology*
AJPS	Asian Journal of Political Science
AJS	*American Journal of Sociology*
AJSS	*Asian Journal of Social Science*
AKAWB	*Abhandlungen der Königlichen Akademie der Wissenschaften in Berlin*
AKM	Abhandlungen für die Kunde des Morgenlandes
AL	*Annali Lateranensi*
ALB	*Adyar Library Bulletin*
ALS	Adyar Library Series
AM	*Asian Music*
AM	Aryan Miscellany
AmAn	*American Anthropologist*
AmAn.NS.	*American Anthropologist.NS*
AMM	*American Mathematical Monthly*
AMTM	*Asian Medicine – Tradition and Modernity*
ANIS	Alt- und Neu-Indische Studien
AnM	*Anthropology and Medicine*
Ansoc	*Anneé sociologique*
Ansoc. NS	*Anneé sociologique. Nouveau Style*
AO	*Acta Orientalia*
AOR	*Annals of Oriental Research*
AOSS	American Oriental Society Series

AP	*Antiquorum Philosophia*
APa	*Ancient Pakistan*
APh	*Asian Philosophy*
APQ	*American Philosophical Quarterly*
AQ	*Anthropological Quarterly*
AR	*Asiatick Researches*
AR/BR	*Archiv für Religionswissenschaft/Beiträge zur Religionswissenschaft*
ARA	*Annual Review of Anthropology*
ARO	*Archiv Orientalni*
ArsO	*Ars Orientalis*
ARSR	*Australian Religion Studies Review*
ArtA	*Artibus Asiae*
AS	*American Scientist*
AS/ÉA	*Asiatische Studien/Études Asiatiques*
ASB	*Archives of Sexual Behavior*
AsE	*Asian Ethnology*
ASMS	Asiatic Society Monograph Series
ASoR	*American Sociological Review*
ASR	*Asian Studies Review*
ĀSS	Ānandāśrama Sanskrit Series
ASSR	*Archives de sciences sociales des religions*
ASt	*Asian Studies*
ASu	*Asian Survey*
AT	*Anthropology Today*
ATASN	*Aura: Tidskrift för akademiska studier av nyreligiositet*
ATJ	*Asian Theatre Journal*
ATR	*Annals of Tourism Research*
BAI	*Bulletin of the Asia Institute*
BASI	*Bulletin of the Anthropological Survey of India*
BDCRI	*Bulletin of the Deccan College Research Institute*
BDIMB	*Boletim Do Instituto Menezes Bragança*
BEFEO	*Bulletin de l'École Française d'Éxtrême Orient*
BÉHÉ.SPhH	*Bibliothèque de l›École des Hautes Études, Sciences Philologiques et Historiques*
BÉHÉ.Sr	*Bibliothèque de l'École des Hautes Études, Sciences religieuses*
BEI	*Bulletin d'Études Indiennes*
BEPB	*Bulletin des Études Portuaises et Bresiliennes*
BF	Baghdader Forschungen
BGOMLM	*Bulletin of the Government Oriental Manuscripts Library Madras*
BI	Bibliotheca Indica
BIL	Brill's Indological Library
BIS	*Berliner Indologische Studien*
BIS	Bibliotheca Indica Series
BJ	*Basava Journal*
BJP	*British Journal of Psychiatry*
BJRE	*British Journal of Religious Education*
BKGA	Beiträge zur Kultur und Geistesgeschichte Asiens
BKI	*Bijdragen tot de Taal-, Land- en Volkenkunde van Nederlandsch-Indië*
BKSSL	Beiträge zur Kenntnis südasiatischer Sprachen und Literaturen
BMJ	*British Medical Journal*
BollS	Bollingen Series
BOS	Bhandarkar Oriental Series
BOS.NS	Bonner Orientalistische Studien. Neue Serie

BPP	*Bengal Past and Present*
BPWM	*Bulletin of the Prince of Wales Museum*
BRSS	Berkeley Religious Studies Series
BSOAS	*Bulletin of the School of Oriental and African Studies*
BSOS	*Bulletin of Oriental Studies*
BSPS	Bombay Sanskrit and Prakrit Series
BSR	*Bulletin for the Study of Religion*
BSS	Bombay Sanskrit Series
BST	Buddhist Sanskrit Texts
BTF	*Bangalore Theological Forum*
BtG	*Back to Godhead*
BV	Bharatiya Vidya
BWHO	*Bulletin of the World Health Organization*
CA	*Cultural Anthropology*
CAJ	*Central Asiatic Journal*
CAS	*Contributions to Asian Studies*
CaSA	Cahiers de la Société Asiatique
CC	*Cultural Critique*
CCi	*Collectanea Cisterciensia*
CCM	*Christian College Magazine*
CCP	*Commonwealth and Comparative Politics*
CCu	*Cross Currents*
CD	*Current Dialogues*
CEQ	*CoEvolution Quarterly*
CERO.NI	Collectio Editionum Rariorum Orientalum. Noviter Impressarium
CES	Collection Emile Senart
CGIP	*Computer Graphics and Image Processing*
CI	Collection Indologie
CII	*Corpus Inscriptionum Iranicarum*
CII	*Corpus Inscriptiorum Indicanum*
CIS	*Contributions to Indian Sociology*
CIS.NS	*Contributions to Indian Sociology. New Series*
CK	*Common Knowledge*
CMAJ	*Canadian Medical Association Journal*
CMEW	*Comparative Medicine East and West*
CMP	*Culture, Medicine and Psychiatry*
CO	*Christian Orient*
CONJ	*Canadian Oncological Nursing Journal*
CP	*Comprehensive Psychiatry*
CPh	*Classical Philology*
CQ	*Caribbean Quarterly*
CR	*China Report*
CrAS	*Critical Asian Studies*
CrC	*Cross Currents*
CrIS	*Cracow Indological Studies*
CRPRP	*Community Religions Project Research Paper*
CS	*Caribbean Studies*
CSA	*Contemporary South Asia*
CSAS	Cambridge South Asian Studies
CSS	Chowkhamba Sanskrit Series
CSSA	Cambridge Studies in Social Anthropology
CSSAAME	*Comparative Studies of South Asia, Africa and the Middle East*

CSSH	*Comparative Studies in Society and History*
CuA	*Current Anthropology*
CuS	*Current Science*
DC	*Dance Chronicle*
DCMS	Deccan College Monograph Series
DEP	*Development Economics Papers*
DGR	Diederichs Gelbe Reihe
DJAAAS	*Daedalus: Journal of the American Academy of Arts and Sciences*
DNRL	De Nobili Research Library
DRdM	Die Religionen der Menschheit
DRJ	*Dance Research Journal*
DRT	Disputationes Rheno-Trajectinae
DS	*Deccan Studies*
DUMOPS	Duke University Monographs and Occasional Papers Series
EA	*Eastern Anthropologist*
EaA	*Education about Asia*
EBHR	*European Bulletin of Himalayan Research*
EcW	*Economic Weekly*
EDCC	*Economic Development and Cultural Change*
EE	*Environmental Ethics*
ÉFEO.ÉT	École française d'Extrême-Orient, Études thématiques
ÉFEO.M	École française d'Extrême-Orient, Monographies
EFEO.R	L'École Française d'Extrême-Orient: Réimpressions
EH	*Ethnohistory*
EI	*Epighraphia Indica*
EIP	*Encyclopedia of Indian Philosophies*
EJCN	*European Journal of Cardiovascular Nursing*
EJS	*European Journal of Sociology*
EJVS	*Electronic Journal of Vedic Studies*
EM	*Ethnomusicology*
EoI	*Encyclopedia of India*
EPW	*Economic and Political Weekly*
ERC	*Ethnic and Racial Studies*
ERE	*Encyclopaedia of Religion and Ethics*
ESR	*Ethnic Studies Report*
ÉVP	Études védiques et pāṇinéennes
EW	*East and West*
FBI	Freiburger Beiträge zur Indologie
FCS/SAS	Foreign and Comparative Studies/South Asian Series
FEQ	*The Far Eastern Quarterly*
FiR	*Fieldwork in Religion*
FiU	*Folklore in Use*
FJEM	*Finnish Journal of Ethnicity and Migration*
FSSACS	French Studies in South Asian Culture and Society
GaOS	Gaekwad Oriental Series
GG	Geschichte und Gesellschaft
GGA	*Göttingische Gelehrte Anzeigen*
GGI	Gods and Goddesses in India
GH	*Gender and History*
GIAPA	Grundriss der Indo-Arischen Philologie und Altertumskunde
GJJ	*Goethe-Jahrbuch Japan*
GJKSV	*Ganganatha Jha Kendriya Sanskrit Vidyapeetha*

GOS	Groningen Oriental Studies
GR	Geographica Religionum
GR	*Geographical Review*
GS	*Gender and Society*
GS	Glasenapp Stiftung
HA	*Historische Anthropologie*
HAn	*History and Anthropology*
HdO	Handbuch der Orientalistiek
HeR	*Hedgehog Review*
HFS	Historisk-filosofiske Skrifter
HIL	History of Indian Literature
HiR	*Historical Research*
HLDW	*Hindi: Language, Discourse, Writing*
HLJ	*Hastings Law Journal*
HM	*Hommes et migrations*
HOS	Harvard Oriental Series
HOS.OM	Harvard Oriental Series, Opera Minora
HP	*The Hindoo Patriot*
HR	*History of Religions*
HRQ	*Human Rights Quarterly*
HSPCIC	History of Science, Philosophy and Culture in Indian Civilization
HT	*Hinduism Today*
HTM	*Hinduism Today Magazine*
HTR	*Harvard Theological Review*
HWJ	*History Workshop Journal*
IA	*Indian Antiquary*
IAn	*Indian Anthropologist*
IAQR	*The Imperial and Asiatic Quarterly Review*
IAR	Indian Archaeology in Retrospect
IAs	*Internationales Asienforum*
IAVRIB	*International Association of the Vrindavan Research Institute Bulletin*
IB	*India and Beyond*
IBK/JIBS	*Indogaku Bukkyōgaku Kenkyū/ Journal of Indian and Buddhist Studies*
IC	*Indian Culture*
ICQ	*India International Quarterly*
IDE	*Il Diritto Ecclesiastico*
IEPh	*Internet Encyclopedia of Philosophy*
IESHR	*Indian Economic and Social History Review*
IHQ	*Indian Historical Quarterly*
IHR	*The Indian Historical Review*
II	*Interreligious Insight*
IICQ	*India International Centre Quarterly*
IIJ	*Indo-Iranian Journal*
IJAHD	*International Journal of Aging and Human Development*
IJAHS	*International Journal of African Historical Studies*
IJCP	*International Journal of Cultural Property*
IJGS	*Indian Journal of Gender Studies*
IJGT	*International Journal of Group Tensions*
IJHS	*International Journal of Hindu Studies*
IJHSc	*Indian Journal of History of Science*
IJHSp	*International Journal of the History of Sport*
IJLC	*International Journal of Law in Context*

IJP	*Indian Journal of Psychiatry*
IJPN	*International Journal of Palliative Nursing*
IJPS	*International Journal of Punjab Studies*
IJSP	*International Journal of Social Psychiatry*
IJTS	*International Journal of Tantric Studies*
IL	*Indian Linguistics*
ILS	*Illustrated London News*
ILWCH	*International Labor and Working-Class History*
IM	*Immigrants and Minorities*
IMR	*International Migration Review*
IMW	*Indonesia and the Malay World*
IOCPS	Institute of Oriental Culture Special Series
IPA	*Indian Philosophical Annual*
IPC	*Indian Philosophy and Culture*
IrA	*Iranica Antiqua*
IS	Indische Studien
IS	*Iranian Studies*
IsC	*Islamic Culture*
ISPP	*Indian Studies Past and Present*
IT	Indica et Tibetica
IT	*Indologica Taurinensia*
JA	*Journal Asiatique*
JAAR	*Journal of the American Academy of Religion*
JAAS	*Journal of Asian and African Studies*
JAC.E	Jahrbuch für Antike und Christentum. Ergänzungsband
JAF	*Journal of American Folklore*
JAH	*Journal of African History*
JaiAS	Jaikrishnadas Ayurveda Series
JAOS	*Journal of the American Oriental Society*
JAR	*Journal of Anthropological Research*
JAS	*Journal of Asian Studies*
JASB	*Journal of the Anthropological Society of Bombay*
JASNAS	*Journal of Alternative Spirituality and New Ages Studies*
JASo	*Journal of the Asiatic Society*
JAsSB	*Journal of the Asiatic Society of Bombay*
JAsSM	*Journal of the Asiatic Society of Mumbai*
JBombayBRAS	*Journal of the Bombay Branch of the Royal Asiatic Society*
JBORS	*Journal of the Bihar and Orissa Research Society*
JBV	*Journal of Beliefs and Values*
JCG	*Journal of Cultural Geography*
JCH	*Journal of Contemporary History*
JCMC	*Journal of Computer-Mediated Communication*
JCR	*Journal of Contemporary Religion*
JCS	*Journal of Church and State*
JDH	*Journal of Design History*
JDL	*Journal of the Department of Letters*
JDS	*Journal of Developing Societies*
JEAS	*Journal of the European Ayurvedic Society*
JEMS	*Journal of Ethnic and Migration Studies*
JES	*Journal of Ecumenical Studies*
JESHO	*Journal of the Economic and Social History of the Orient*
JFSR	*Journal of Feminist Studies in Religion*

JGJRI	*Journal of the Ganganath Jha Research Institute*
JGOS	*Journal of the German Orientalist Society*
JH	*Jewish History*
JHA	*Journal for the History of Astronomy*
JHaCS	*Journal of Halacha and Contemporary Society*
JHCS	*Journal of Hindu-Christian Studies*
JHI	*Journal of the History of Ideas*
JHP	*Journal of Humanistic Psychology*
JHS	*Journal of the History of Sexuality*
JHSoc	*Journal of Historical Sociology*
JHSt	*Journal of Hindu Studies*
JIABS	*Journal of the International Association of Buddhist Studies*
JIAS	*Journal of the Indian Anthropological Society*
JIBS	*Journal of Indian and Buddhist Studies*
JICPR	*Journal of the Indian Council for Philosophy Research*
JIESMS	Journal of Indo-European Studies Monograph Series
JIF	*Journal of Indian Folkloristics*
JIFMC	*Journal of the International Folk Music Council*
JIH	*Journal of Indian History*
JIJS	*Journal of Indo-Judaic Studies*
JIMS	*Journal of the Indian Musicological Society*
JIntH	*Journal of Interdisciplinary History*
JIPh	*Journal of Indian Philosophy*
JIS	*Journal of Indological Studies*
JISOA	*Journal of the Indian Society of Oriental Art*
JJ	*Jain Journal*
JKS	*Journal of Kerala Studies*
JKUH	*Journal of the Karnatak University: Humanities*
JLM	*Journal of Law and Medicine*
JLS	*Journal of Lesbian Studies*
JMadrasU	*Journal of Madras University*
JMAS	*Journal of Modern African Studies*
JMGSG	Jñānapīṭha Mūrtidevī Granthamālā Sanskrit Grantha
JMSUB	*Journal of the Maharaja Sayajirao University of Baroda*
JMU	*Journal of the Mysore University*
JNRC	*Journal of the Nepal Research Centre*
JOI	*Journal of the Oriental Institute*
JOR	*Journal of Oriental Research*
JP	*Journal of Pain*
JPC	*Journal of Pastoral Care*
JPH	*The Journal of Pacific History*
JPHS	*Journal of the Pakistan Historical Society*
JPS	*Journal of Punjab Studies*
JPTS	*Journal of the Pali Text Society*
JRA	*Journal of Religion in Africa*
JRAI	*Journal of the Royal Anthropological Institute*
JRAI.NS	*Journal of the Royal Anthropological Institute. New Series*
JRAS	*Journal of the Royal Asiatic Society*
JRASBeng	*Journal of the Royal Asiatic Society Bengal*
JRASGBI	*Journal of the Royal Asiatic Society of Great Britain and Ireland*
JRE	*Journal of Religion in Europe*
JRH	*Journal of Religious History*

JS	*Journal for Semitics*
JSAH	*Journal of the Society of Architectural Historians*
JSAI	*Jerusalem Studies in Arabic and Islam*
JSAL	*Journal of South Asian Literature*
JSAS	*Journal of Southeast Asian Studies*
JSAS	*Journal of South Asian Studies*
JSeAS	Journal of Southeast Asian Studies
JSL	*Journal of Symbolic Logic*
JSR	*Journal of Social Research*
JSR	*Journal of Social Research*
JSS	*Journal of Social Sciences*
JSSA	*Journal of Sociology and Social Anthropology*
JSSR	*Journal for the Scientific Study of Religion*
JTS	*Journal of Tamil Studies*
JUB	*Journal of the University of Bombay*
JUH	*Journal of Urban History*
JUP	*Journal of the University of Poona*
JUPHS	*Journal of the University of Poona Humanities Section*
JVieS	*Journal of Vietnamese Studies*
JVS	*Journal of Vaishnava Studies*
JWH	*Journal of World History*
KM	Kāvyamālā
KPAWPHKS	Königlich Preussischen Akademie der Wissenschschaften, Philologisch-historische Klasse, Sitzungsberichte
KS	*Kannada Studies*
KSAS	Key Studies in Asian Studies
KSEW	Kleine Schriften Ernst Windisch
KSHJ	Kleine Schriften Hermann Jacobi
KSHO	Kleine Schriften Hermann Oldenberg
KSMW	Kleine Schriften von Michael Witzel
KSPH	Kleine Schriften Paul Hacker
KSPT	Kleine Schriften Paul Thieme
KSS	Kashi Sanskrit Series
KSTS	Kashmir Series of Texts and Studies
KSV	Kendriya Sanskrit Vidyapeetha
KZ	*Zeitschrift für vergleichende Sprachforschung auf dem Gebiet der indogermanischen Sprachen, begründet von A. Kuhn*
LAHPOP	Linguistics, Archaeology and the Human Past: Occasional Paper
LCPh	*Les Cahiers de Philosophie*
LHR	*Law and History Review*
LNAI	Lecture Notes in Artificial Intelligence
LRTP	Library Rare Texts Publications
LSJRS	Lala Sundarlal Jain Research Series
LT	*Literature and Theology*
Man.NS	*Man. New Style*
MAQ	*Medical Anthropology Quarterly*
MARG	*Mitteilungen für Anthropologie und Religionsgeschichte*
MAS	*Modern Asian Studies*
MASI	Memoirs of the Archaeological Survey of India
MBJ	*Meher Baba Journal*
Mcb	*Mélanges chinois et bouddhiques*
MD	*Modern Drama*

MeA	Münchner ethnologische Abhandlungen
MedA	*Medical Anthropology*
MEZW	*Materialdienst der Evangelischen Zentralstelle für Weltanschauungsfragen*
MGP	Mithilāvidyāpīṭha Granthamālā Prācīnācāryagranthāvālī
MGSI	*Memoir of the Geological Society of India*
MHJ	*Medieval History Journal*
MHSI	Monumenta Historica Societatis Iesu
MIH	*Modern Intellectual History*
MiI	*Man in India*
MIO	*Methodological Innovations Online*
MIS	Mithila Institute Series
MJLS	*Madras Journal of Literature and Science*
MKAW.AL	Mededeelingen der Koninklijke Akademie van Wetenschappen, Afdeeling Letterkunde
MKG	Mahārājādhirāja Kāmeśvarasiṃha Granthamālā
ML	*Medical Law*
MQ	*Mystics Quarterly*
MR	Machikaneyama Ronso
MR	*Material Religion*
MRDTB	*Memoirs of the Research department of Toyo Bunko*
MSC	Manuscripts in the Schøyen Collection
MSFOu	Mémoires de la Société Finno-Ougrienne
MSLS	*Modern Sri Lanka Studies*
MSS	*Münchener Studien zur Sprachwissenschaft*
MTSR	*Method and Theory in the Study of Religion*
MUTS	Madras University Telegu Series
NAWG.PHK	*Nachrichten der Akademie der Wissenschaften in Göttingen. Philologish-historische Klasse*
NC	*The Nineteenth Century*
NCG	Nyāyacaturgranthikā
NCo	*New Community*
NCTRA	*Numazu College of Technology Research Annual*
NGJI	*National Geographical Journal of India*
NH	*Natural History*
NJSH	*Nidān: Journal for the Study of Hinduism*
NNGMCP	*Newsletter of the Nepalese German Manuscript Cataloguing Project*
NR	*Nova Religio*
NRT	*Nouvelle revue théologique*
NSS	Nepal Sanskrit Series
NZG	New Zealand Geographer
NZJAS	*New Zealand Journal of Asian Studies*
OA	*Oriental Art*
OA.NS	*Oriental Art.New Style*
ÖAWPHKD	Österreichische Akademie der Wissenschaften, Philosophisch-Historische Klasse, Denkschriften
ÖAWPHKS	Österreichische Akademie der Wissenschaften, Philosophisch-historische Klasse, Sitzungsberichte
ÖAWVKSKS	Österreichische Akademie der Wissenschaften, Veröffentlichungen der Kommission für Sprachen und Kulturen Südasiens
OHJRI	*Online – Heidelberg Journal of Religions on the Internet*
OLA	Orientalia Lovaniensia Analecta
OLP	*Orientalia Lovaniensia Periodica*

OP	Orientamenti Pedagogici
OR	*Orissa Review*
ORIS	*Oriental Research Institute Series*
OS	*Orientalia Suecana*
OTF.NS	Oriental Translation Fund, New Series
PAPS	*Proceedings of the American Philosophical Society*
PB	*Prabuddha Bharata*
PCR	*Perspectives in Clinical Research*
PDI	Publications du département d'Indologie
PDNRL	Publications of the De Nobili Research Library
PDR	*Population and Development Review*
PÉFEO	Publications de l'École française d'Extrême-Orient
PEW	*Philosophy East and West*
PG	Population Geography
PH	*Pakistan Horizon*
PICI	Publications de l'institut de civilisation indienne
PIEA	Philosophia Indica: Einsichten-Ansichten
PIFI	Publications de l'Institut Français d'Indologie
PiH	Perspectives in History
PO	*Poona Orientalist*
POS	Poona Oriental Series
PoS	*Postcolonial Studies*
PP	*Past and Present*
PPl	People and Place
PPPS	Pāñcarātra Parisodhanā Pariṣad Series
PR	*Paragrana*
PRe	*Performance Research*
PRPT	Purāṇa Research Publications Tübingen
PSc	Philosophy of Science
PSM	Poet-Saints of Maharashtra
PSPSH	Poznan Studies in the Philosophy of the Sciences and the Humanities
PSt	*Population Studies*
PTJSTCW	Postscripts: The Journal of Sacred Texts and Contemporary Worlds
PV	*Pacific Viewpoint*
PW	Pacific World
PWSBTS	Princess of Wales Saraswati Bhavana Texts and Studies
PWSBTS.RS	Princess of Wales Saraswati Bhavana Texts and Studies. Reprint Series
QDPE	Quaderni di diritto e politica ecclesiastica
QEHWPS	Queen Elizabeth House Working Paper Series
QJMS	*Quarterly Journal of the Mythic Society*
QJSA	*Quarterly Journal of Studies on Alcohol*
RAI.NS	*Royal Anthropological Institute. New Style*
RBN	*Religieuze Bewegingen in Nederland*
RC	*Religion Compass*
ResAA	*Res: Anthropology and Aesthetics*
RG	*Religion and Gender*
RGG	*Religion in Geschichte und Gegenwart*
RH	*Rays of the Harmonist*
RHR	*Revue de l'Histoire des Religions*
RL	*Roopa Lekha*
RO	Rocznik Orientalistyczny
RPP	*Religion Past and Present*

RRP	Religious Research Paper
RRR	*Review of Religious Research*
RS	Religionswissenschaftliche Studien
RSA	*Religions of South Asia*
RSO	*Rivista degli Studi Orientali*
RSR	*Religious Studies Review*
RSS	*Rivista di studi Sudasiatici*
RSSSR	*Research in the Social Scientific Study of Religion*
RST	*Religious Studies and Theology*
RTÜ	Reihe Texte und Übersetzungen
RU	*Religionen Unterwegs*
RUS	Rice University Studies
RWA	Reihe Wort und Antwort
SA	*South Asia*
SAA	*South Asian Archaeology*
SACS	*South Asian Cultural Studies*
SAD	*South Asian Diaspora*
SAR	*South Asia Research*
SARel	*South Asian Religions*
SarS	Sarasvatī Suṣamā
SAS	*South Asian Studies*
SaS	Sanātanaśāstram Series
SATR	Studies in Asian Thought and Religion
SB	*Sociological Bulletin*
SBE	Sacred Books of the East
SBG	Sarasvatī Bhavana Granthamālā
SC	*Social Compass*
SchAS	Schweizer Asiatische Studien
SCI	Studies of Classical India
SdR	Symbolik der Religionen
SES	*Senri Ethnological Studies*
SF	*Sikh Formations*
SFS	*Studies in Formative Spirituality*
SGDOS	Sri Garib Dass Oriental Series
SGKAS	Schriften zur Geschichte und Kultur des Alten Orients
SGM	*Scottish Geographical Magazine*
SHR	Studies in the History of Religions
SI	*Studia Indolognicze*
SIASMS	Scandinavian Institute of Asian Studies Monograph Series
SiH	*Studies in History*
SII	*Studien zur Indologie und Iranistik*
SII.M	Studien zur Indologie und Iranistik, Monographie
SiIS	Sikhism and Indian Society
SiP	*Siddha Path*
SiR/SR	*Studies in Religion/Science Religieuses*
SIS	*South Indian Studies*
SITES.NS	*SITES: A Journal of Social Anthropology and Cultural Studies, New Series*
SIUH	Studia Indologica Universitatis Halensis
SJLS	*Singapore Journal of Legal Studies*
SJoA	*Soutwestern Journal of Anthropology*
SJWCS	*Signs: Journal of Women in Culture and Society*

SN	*Sangeet Natak*
SNP	*Sri Narasimha Priya*
SO	ScriptOralia
SoAn	*Social Analysis*
SoAr	*Sovietskaya Arkheologiya*
SoC	*Senses of Cinema*
SocA	*Social Anthropology*
SocAn	*Sociological Analysis*
SoES	Social and Economic Studies
SoF	*Social Forces*
SOR	Serie Orientale Roma
SoR	*Sociology of Religion*
SoS	*Social Scientist*
SP	*Social Problems*
SP	Sanmati Publication
SPBMS	Studia Philologica Buddhica Monograph Series
SPHKKAW	*Sitzungsberichte der philosophisch-historischen Klasse der kaiserlichen Akademie der Wissenschaften*
SPP	Sino-Platonic Papers
SPP	*Sociologia Problemas e Práticas*
SR	*Social Research*
SRAA	*Silk Road Art and Archaeology*
SRP	*Sri Ranganatha Paduka*
SRV	*Sri Ramanuja Vani*
SS	*Social Scientist*
SSIUH	Schriftenreihe des Südasien-Instituts der Universität Heidelberg
SSM	*Social Science and Medicine*
SSPS	Sanskrit Sahitya Parishad Series
ST	*Social Text*
StA	*Studia Asiatica*
StII	*Studien zur Indologie und Iranistik*
StM	*Studia Missionalia*
StO	*Studia Orientalia*
StOR	Studies in Oriental Religions
StR/SR	*Studies in Religion/Sciences religieuses*
STT	*Stud Tribes Tribals*
SuA	*Suomen Antropologi*
SuS	Subaltern Studies
SWP	Sociology Working Paper
ŚYJG	Śrīyaśovijayajainagranthamālā
TA	*Tamilian Antiquary*
TAB	*The Art Bulletin*
TAPLA	*Transactions and Procdeeings of the American Philological Society*
TBM	*The Burlington Magazine*
TC	*Tamil Civilization*
TDR	*The Drama Review*
TG	*Tourism Geographies*
TH	Theosophical History
TKVNM	*Tijdschrift van de Koninklijke Vereniging voor Nederlandse Muziekgeschiedenis*
TMS	*The Midwest Sociologist*
TNA	*The Nation and Athenaeum*
TP	*Textual Practice*

TPa	*T'oung Pao*
TPS	*Transactions of the Philological Society*
TS	*Tantric Studies*
TSAM	*Traditional South Asian Medicine*
TSS	Trivandrum Sanskrit Series
TSSR	*Trends in Social Science Research*
TSWS	Tibetan Sanskrit Works Series
UCeylonR	*University of Ceylon Review*
ULR	*Utrecht Law Review*
VBA	*Visva-Bharati Annals*
VIJ	*Vishveshvaranand Indological Journal*
VKNAW.AL.NR	Verhandelingen der Koninklijke Nederlandse Akademie van Wetenschappen, Afdeling Letterkunde, Nieuwe Reeks
VR	*Visible Religion*
VS	*Victorian Studies*
VZS	Vizianagaram Sanskrit Series
WA	*World Archaeology*
WECR	*Worldviews: Environment, Culture, Religion*
WES	*World Ethno-national Studies*
WM	*Waste Management*
WSIQ	*Women's Studies International Quarterly*
WSTB	Wiener Studien zur Tibetologie und Buddhismuskunde
WZKM	*Wiener Zeitschrift für die Kunde des Morgenlandes*
WZKMUL	*Wissenschaftliche Zeitschrift der Karl-Marx-* Universität Leipzig
WZKSAIP	*Wiener Zeitschrift für die Kunde Südasiens und Archiv für Indische Philosophie*
YI	*Young India*
YJ	*Yoga Journal*
ZAA.S	Zeitschrift für Anglistik und Amerikanistik, Studies
ZDMG.S	*Zeitschrift der Deutschen Morgenländischen Gesellschaft. Supplementband*
ZE	*Zeitschrift für Ethnologie*
ZMR	*Zeitschrift für Missionswissenschaft und Religionswissenschaft*
ZR	*Zeitschrift für Religionswissenschaft*
ZRG	*Zeitschrift für Religions- und Geisteswissenschaft*
ZS	Zentralasiatische Studien
ZVR	*Zeitschrift für vergleichende Rechtswissenschaft*

General Abbreviations

app.	appendix
approx.	approximately
Arab.	Arabic
arch.	archeological
Ardh.	Ardhamagadhi
Ass.	Assamese
astr.	astronomical
Aves.	Avestan
Avest.	Avestan
b.	born
Bah.	Bahasa Indonesia
Bal.	Balinese
BCE	before the Common Era
Beng.	Bengali
bot.	botanical
Braj.	Brajbhasha
Burm.	Burmese
c.	circa
CE	Common Era
cent./cents.	century/centuries
ch./chs.	chapter/chapters
Chn.	Chinese
cit.	cited by
comm.	commentary
crit. ed.	critical edition
d.	died
dir.	director
diss.	dissertation
Drav.	Dravidian
ed./eds.	editor, edited by/editors
ET	English translation
et al.	and others
etym.	etymology
f./ff.	following page/following pages
fem.	feminine
fig.	figure
Fij.	Fijian
fl	*floruit*
Fr.	French
FS	*Festschrift*
Ger.	German
Germ.	Germanic
Grk.	Greek
Guj.	Gujarati
h.	here
Heb.	Hebrew

Hind.	Hindi
HSkt.	Hybrid Sanskrit
incl.	including
Intro.	Introductory section
Iran.	Iranian
Ital.	Italian
Jav.	Javanese
Jpn.	Japanese
Kan.	Kannara
Kash.	Kashmiri
km/km2	kilometer/kilometer squared
Kon.	Konkani
Lat.	Latin
lit.	literally
m	meter
Mah.Pr.	Maharashtri Prakrit
Mal.	Malayam
Mar.	Marathi
masc.	masculine
Mid. Jav.	Middle Javanese
ms./mss.	manuscript/manuscripts
myth.	mythological
n.d.	no date
Nep.	Nepali
New.	Newari
n.l.	no location
n/nn	note/notes
NGO	nongovernmental organization
no./nos.	number/numbers
nom.	nominative
Old Hind.	Old Hindi
Old Jav.	Old Javanese
Old Mar.	Old Marathi
Old Pers.	Old Persian
Ori.	Oriya
p./pp.	page/pages
Pahl.	Pahlavi
Pal.	Pali
Pers.	Persian
pl.	plate
pl.	plural
Port.	Portuguese
prod.	producer
Pt.	Paṇḍit
publ.	published by/publisher
Punj.	Punjabi
r.	reigned
Raj.	Rajasthani
recon.	reconstructed
repr.	reprint
rev. ed.	revised edition
Rs.	Rupee

Rus.	Russian
s.v.	*sub voce*
Sarn.	Sarnami
sing.	singular
Skt.	Sanskrit
śl.	*śloka*
Śmt.	Śrīmatī (Mrs.)
spec.	special
st.	stanza
Sum.	Sumerian
suppl.	supplement
Tam.	Tamil
Tel.	Telegu
Tha.	Thai
Tib.	Tibetan
Toch.	Tocharian
Tul.	Tulu
trans.	translator, translated by, translation
unpubl.	unpublished
Urd.	Urdu
v/vv.	verse/verses
Ved.	Vedic
Viet.	Vietnamese
vol./vols.	volume/volumes
WHO	World Health Organization

Appendix
Volume I

Gods, Goddesses, and Divine Powers

Narmadā

Appendix
Volume II

Sacred Texts and Languages

Śaiva Texts

Appendix
Volume IV

Relations to Other Religions and Traditions

Hinduism and Judaism

Hinduism and Contemporary Issues

Secularism and Religion-State Relations in Modern India

Secularism: A Search for Conceptual Spaces

Appendix
Volume V

Religious Symbols

Nāgas

Trimūrti

Hinduism and Migration: Contemporary Communities outside South Asia

Austria

Germany

Some Modern Religious Groups and Teachers

Brahma Kumaris and Dada Lekhraj

Narmadā

The Narmadā is the fifth-largest river of India with a total length of 1,312 km. Flowing from east to west, it originates in Amarkantak in the Maikal hills on the eastern border of present Madhya Pradesh and joins the Arabian Sea near Bharuch in Gujarat. For almost its entire length, the river and the valley adjoining its banks are enclosed by massive rock formations, the Vindhya range in the north and the Satpura in the south, forming a natural border between North India and the Deccan. The Narmadā Valley and the surrounding mountain ranges represent the western half of the great central Indian tribal belt, which extends eastward into Jharkhand, Orissa, and Chhattisgarh. Recent finds of remains of two different types of hominines trace human settlement in the central Narmadā Valley back to the Middle Pleistocene, about 200,000–250,000 years ago (Sankhyan *et al.*, 2012). The inaccessibility of the terrain and the resulting geographical isolation of the region have ensured the relative autonomy of a number of tribal peoples in various tracts of the Narmadā Valley and adjoining mountain ranges up to the advent of → British rule. Major tribal groups in the valley comprise the Gond and Baiga in the eastern part of the valley (from Amarkantak to Jabalpur), the Gond, Kol, and Korku in the central part (from Narsinghpur to Harda), and the Bhil in the western part (from Harda to the Gujarat border) with a particular stronghold in the districts of Jhabua and Barwani (see Srivastav & Caldirola, 2005). This ethnic background must be borne in mind as it is crucial for an assessment of the cultural history of the Narmadā Valley and, particularly, the significance of the river goddess Narmadā in Hinduism. The Narmadā River plays, if at all, an insignificant role in the religious beliefs and practices of the different tribal peoples of the Narmadā Valley as far as can be judged from what has been recorded by anthropologists of their exclusively oral traditions. Hence, available sources for the religious veneration of the Narmadā uniformly belong to the Hindu tradition.

A brief summary of references to the Narmadā in Sanskrit literature provides a chronological and geographical framework for the increasing cultural importance of the Narmadā and her adoption into the Hindu pantheon. At the same time, it conveys an idea of the process of proliferation of Hinduism in a large forested tribal terrain.

Probably the earliest references to the Narmadā in Sanskrit literature are found in the epics. The → *Rāmāyaṇa* locates it near the Vindhya and Ṛkṣavat mountains and describes the river and the surrounding terrain as inaccessible and infested with wild animals. The → *Mahābhārata* additionally associates the river with the Vaiḍūrya Mountain and enumerates a number of rivers south of the Narmadā. By the mid-1st century CE, the difficulties of navigation near the Narmadā estuary up to the ancient port town of Bhṛgukachcha (present-day Bharuch) were described in the *Periplus Maris Erythraei*. Barygaza, as the place is called in the *Periplus Maris Erythraei*, is

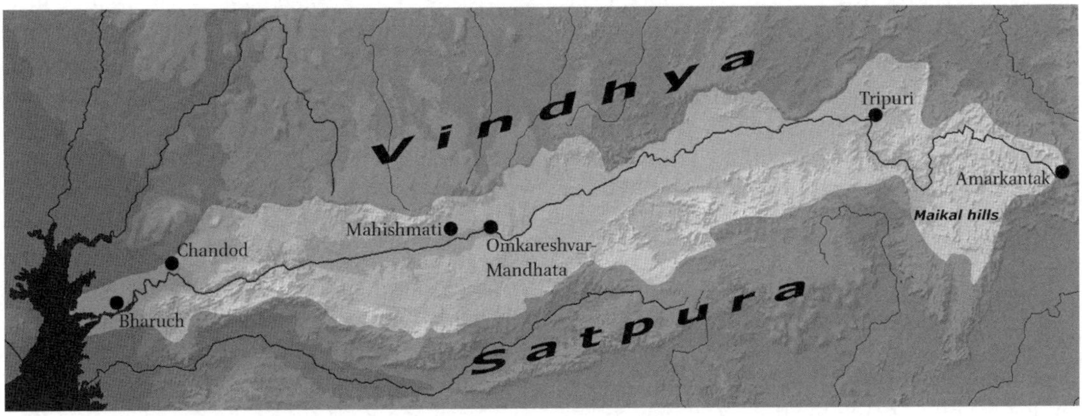

Map of the Narmadā Valley.

characterized as a bustling market town and an important center of commerce in western India by that time. The place also occurs in the *Mahābhārata* along with two other important centers, Māhiṣmatī (present-day Maheshwar) and Tripurī (present-day Tewar, near Jabalpur). While all three places have a long history going back to prehistoric times, they still figure as the most prominent places in the Narmadā Valley in the early historical period. However, as the scarcity of references in early Sanskrit works suggests, most parts of the Narmadā Valley seem to have been largely unknown and unexplored well into the second half of the 1st millennium CE.

This situation began to change considerably around the early 2nd millennium CE, when a Narmadā-specific corpus of Sanskrit literary works gradually began to evolve; in it, increasing numbers of → *tīrtha*s along the banks of the Narmadā are enumerated and eulogized. The earliest examples of such texts are short *Narmadāmāhātmya* sections incorporated into some of the → Purāṇas. Quotations of the relevant section of the *Matsyapurāṇa* found in Lakṣmīdhara Bhaṭṭa's *Kṛtyakalpataru*, which was composed in the second quarter of the 12th century CE at Varanasi, contain a eulogy of the Narmadā River. However, only a few *tīrtha*s are mentioned, most notably the Amarakaṇṭaka Mountain and several places located on it, and the Narmadodadhisaṅgama, that is, the Narmadā's confluence with the sea. These text passages seem to represent an original core, which, in the course of time, was gradually expanded in two different ways: firstly, by the inclusion of lists of an ever increasing number of *tīrtha*s along the riverbanks, as can be seen, for example, in the *Kūrmapurāṇa*, which mentions altogether 67 *tīrtha*s, of which 39 are treated in just a single stanza (*KūP*. 39–40; see Gupta, 1971, 519–531); secondly, Māhātmyas of individual *tīrtha*s were elaborated on by the inclusion of legends (*itihāsa*). Perhaps the most prominent example of this kind of expansion is found in the *Matsyapurāṇa*, with a version of the Tripurāntaka legend localized in the region around the ancient city of Tripurī and the Amarakaṇṭaka Mountain (*MatP*. 187.6–188.84; see Apte, 1907, 410–416). Eventually, however, the redaction of the *Narmadāmāhātmya* chapters in the Purāṇas was apparently given up in favor of the composition of an independent text, the *Revākhaṇḍa* (Revā is another popular name for the river), which has come down to us in two largely different versions (Omkaranand Giri, 1994), one containing 116 and the other one 232 *adhyāya*s (chapters). In contrast to manuscript evidence, which shows that at indeterminable points of time the shorter version was incorporated into the *Skandapurāṇa* and the longer one into the *Vāyupurāṇa*, the latter is found in almost all printed editions of the *Skandapurāṇa* and commonly regarded as one of its integral parts (*khaṇḍa*s). Both versions are genetically linked, as they share a common core of about 39 *adhyāya*s, which were apparently borrowed from the shorter version into the longer one (Neuß, 2012, 45–46). A first datable testimony to the existence of a *Revākhaṇḍa* is found in Ballālasena's *Dānasāgara*, composed in 1169/1170 CE in Bengal, where the text, however, is listed among works the author regarded unfit for reference (Bhattacharya, 1953, 7). About a century later, Hemādrī, who hailed from Devagiri (present-day Daulatabad, Maharashtra), cites in his *Caturvargacintāmaṇi* about 39 stanzas from a *Revākhaṇḍa* in almost the same sequence as they are found in the extant shorter version.

The historical essence of literary evidence (see Neuß, 2012, 19–53) may be summarized as follows. The earliest testimonies to a veneration of the Narmadā are closely connected with the Amarakaṇṭaka Mountain and were probably composed there, at the source of the river, but probably not before the 8th century CE. Additions to this original core originate in Gujarat, as almost all new *tīrtha*s mentioned in respective sections of the Purāṇas are situated here. In the 12th century, the *Revākhaṇḍa* appears in quotations as an originally independent text. While the *Narmadāmāhatmya* sections of the Purāṇas continue to be quoted even centuries later in works related to *tīrthayātrā* written north of the Narmadā, the *Revākhaṇḍa* is apparently held more authoritative in regions to the south of the river. While the bulk of material contained in the extant versions of the text is concerned with *tīrthayātrā*, other → *dharmaśāstra* topics are also dealt with but these show few particularities specifically related to either the river or the goddess Narmadā. The shorter and older version seems to have been compiled about the 11th century in the region around Tripurī, but the additions found in the longer version were certainly composed later in Gujarat, probably somewhere near the city of Chandod. As the *Revākhaṇḍa* strives to define the Narmadā Valley as a coherent religio-cultural landscape, it was probably intended to serve as an authoritative text regulating religious and social life in the Narmadā Valley.

The earliest dated testimony to the religious veneration of the Narmadā is found in an unpublished eulogy of the Narmadā contained in a rock inscription in the Amareśvara Temple at Omkareshwar-Mandhata, one of the main sacred centers in the Narmadā Valley. It is part of a larger record engraved in 1063 CE by a single scribe. Other portions of the inscription contain details of the Amareśvara Temple that clearly show that it was a → Pāśupata establishment at that time (Chakravarti, 1948).

The character and content of the literary sources as well as the legends woven around the goddess Narmadā suggest that the religious veneration of the river evolved in circles of wandering Śaiva ascetics. The most frequently quoted account of the "birth" of the Narmadā is found in the longer version of the *Revākhaṇḍa* in the course of a dialogue between the *ṛṣi* Mārkaṇḍeya and Yudhiṣṭhira, the eldest of the Pāṇḍava brothers:

> Formerly Śiva Śaṅkara of quiescent body performed extensive penance along with Umā for the sake of the welfare of all the worlds. The Lord of self-control, the immanent soul of all living beings, climbed the mountain Ṛkṣaśaila and performed a severe penance. He was invisible to all living beings. As that Lord was performing penance, perspiration issued forth from his body. The (drops of) sweat originating from Rudra flooded that mountain. The highly meritorious, excellent river was born of it. (*RKhV*. 4.13–17; trans. Tagare, 1999, 14–15)

After her birth, the Narmadā is said to have initially assumed the form of a woman in the *kṛtayuga* (see → cosmic cycles) and propitiated Rudra for ten thousand years in order to obtain a boon from him. The boon that she asks for provides a characterization of the goddess Narmadā's nature and summarizes the blessings that her devotees may expect from her:

> By your grace, O Lord of Devas, let me be imperishable at the advent of Pralaya when all mobile and immobile beings are destroyed. When the rivers, oceans and mountains have perished, O Lord of Devas, let me be holy and imperishable, with your favour. Devout persons who have taken a bath in me should be rid of all their sins, even if they have committed major and minor sins. O Śaṅkara, Jāhnavī destroys great sins in the northern region. I should become so in the southern region. Then only I shall be worshipped by the gods. Just as the celestial river coming down from Svarga became well-known on the earth as Gaṅgā, O Lord of Devas, so let me be the Dakṣiṇagaṅgā (Southern Gaṅgā). A man who devoutly takes his holy bath in me, O Maheśvara, should acquire that merit which is usually obtained by taking holy bath in all the Tīrthas of the earth. O Lord, may the sin of Brāhmaṇa-slaughter and others like that which have remained accumulated be destroyed by taking the holy plunge for the period of a month. My desire is that, due to the holy dip in me, O Śaṅkara, one shall get all those benefits that accrue from the study of all the Vedas and performance of all the Yajñas. From my water, O Śaṅkara, let there be that benefit which usually arises from all sorts of Dānas and fasts and the holy plunge in all the Tīrthas. Those who adore Maheśvara on my banks should repair unto your Loka, O Śiva. Let this happen, O Lord, O Maheśāna; O Lord of the world, this alone is the boon. I desire that you do stay always on my banks along with Umā and other deities. Let every living being that dies in my waters go to Amarāvatī, whether they have done excellent

Fig. 1: Narmadā statue, Narmadā temple, Amarkantak (photo by Jürgen Neuß).

Karmas or ignoble Karmas, whether they are mentally calm with full control over the sense-organs or not. O Lord of the chiefs of Devas, if you are pleased and if you consider it proper, let me be well-known in all the three worlds as the destroyer of great sins. (*RKhV.* 4.20–32; trans. Tagare, 1999, 15–16)

This passage suggests that the goddess Narmadā was modeled after the river goddess → Gaṅgā, whom she – according to the *Revākhaṇḍa*, however – excels in her purificatory abilities:

Narmadā is the most excellent one among all rivers. It is destructive of all sins. It shall redeem all living beings, both mobile and immobile… Gaṅgā is auspicious in Kanakhala; Sarasvatī in Kurukṣetra; but Narmadā is auspicious everywhere, whether it be a village or a forest. The water of Sarasvatī sanctifies one in three days; the water of Yamunā in seven days; the water of Gaṅgā sanctifies one immediately; but the water of Narmadā does so through the very sight. (*RKhV.* 21.3–6; trans. Tagare, 1999, 81)

According to a local legend chronicled in the *Central Provinces District Gazetteers*, the Gaṅgā herself must come every year to wash off the sins burdened on her by her devotees. She comes in the form of a coal-black cow, takes a dip in the Narmadā, and returns home white (see Russell, 1908, 251).

That the Gaṅgā goddess served as a model for the Narmadā goddess is further corroborated by the iconography of available pictorial representations. Like the Gaṅgā, she rides on a crocodile and is four armed, holding a lotus and a waterpot. The most striking difference is the presence of *ṛṣis* that are often depicted surrounding the goddess, as, for example, in what is perhaps the oldest-known stone sculpture of the Narmadā from Amarkantak (Banerji, 1931, plate LII a, now lost). The scarcity of stone images of the goddess Narmadā – only a few such sculptures are known – significantly points to the fact that her veneration has probably never been an independent rite. Indeed, there are very few temples in which the goddess is the central object of worship, most notably the Narmadā temple in Amarkantak. But even this is a twin temple, with two sanctums facing each other in a west-east axis. The western shrine houses an image of Narmadā made of black stone, the eastern one contains as its central deity a → *liṅga* called Amarakaṇṭakeśvara and a separate image of → Pārvatī carved from white marble.

Fig. 2: Narmadā temple complex, Amarkantak (photo by Jürgen Neuß).

Tradition has it that each and every stone in the river is a representation of → Śiva. The famous and much sought-after *bāṇaliṅgas*, egg-shaped stones of a particular variety of rock, are said to come from Dhavrikund, a deep pool in the Narmadā near Omkareshwar-Mandhata (now submerged), and sold in large numbers at several places in the valley. Apparently, Narmadā has always remained subordinate to Śiva, notwithstanding the fact that almost everywhere in the valley, people greet one another with "*narmade har*" – a pious reference to both, Narmadā and Hara (i.e. Śiva) – and that the Narmadā is the object of what is probably one of the most compelling pilgrimages in India.

The *narmadāparikramā* (circumambulation of the Narmadā), as the pilgrimage is called, requires the pilgrim to completely circumambulate the river, covering a distance of more than 2,600 km. It has to be undertaken in the most humble manner: the pilgrims should walk barefoot and keep only the most indispensable articles with them – ideally a set of clothes, a blanket, a waterpot, and a walking stick. The *parikramāvāsīs*, as these pilgrims are called, should beg for food and be content with whatever they are offered by the people living on the riverbanks. They may eat only what is cooked by themselves or their hosts. They must always walk with their right shoulder pointing to the Narmadā, the obligatory manner for any kind of circumambulation (*pradakṣiṇa*) in Hindu ritual, which must follow a clockwise course. Finally, they may never cross the Narmadā except at its confluence with the sea, where this is unavoidable. If they have crossed a tributary once, they may never turn back and cross it in the opposite direction. The pilgrimage should ideally be completed in three years, three months, and thirteen days, though walking is prohibited in the rainy season (*caturmāsya*), which the pilgrims should spend with a *guru* in an *āśram* or *maṭh*.

The earliest references to the performance of the *narmadāparikramā* are found in colonial reports of the late 19th century. *The Imperial Gazetteer of India* states the following:

> The most meritorious act that a pilgrim can perform, is to walk from the sea up to the source at Amarkantak, and then back along the opposite bank. This pilgrimage, called parikrám or pradakshana is chiefly undertaken by devotees from Gujarát and the Deccan, and takes from one year to two years in accomplishment. (Hunter, 1881, 58–59)

Two years later, M. Williams reports that

> a pilgrim starts from the source of the Narbadā, at Amara-kaṇṭaka – a peak of the Vindhya chain in Goṇḍwāna – and walks to the mouth, near Broach, and back. This takes nearly three years. (Williams, 1883, 348)

R.V. Russell notes, 25 years later, that

> [e]very year 300 or more pilgrims start to perform the *pradakshnā* of the Nerbudda, that is, to walk from its mouth at Broach to its source at Amarkantak on one side, and back on the other, a performance of the highest religious efficacy. (Russell, 1908, 251)

Evidently, the *narmadāparikramā* was already established by the late 19th century. Its origins and age, however, are hard to determine. According to tradition, the *narmadāparikramā* was first undertaken by the *ṛṣi* Mārkaṇḍeya, who is said to have performed the most extensive *parikramā* possible: he circumambulated the Narmadā including all her tributaries. However, there is no clear evidence to show that the pilgrimage was performed before the "dark period" in the Narmadā Valley, which ended after the third Anglo-Maratha war in 1818 (see → Maratha). This period of about half a century was marked by conquests of rivaling Maratha leaders (foremost among them the descendants of the Scindia and Holkar lineages), tribal insurgencies, the ravages of the Pindaris (bands of marauders usually attached to one of the Maratha chiefs), and retaliating military campaigns by the British. It is very likely that the practice of the *parikramā* terminated during these decades if it was at all performed before. Even though the *Revākhaṇḍa* contains numerous references to the circumambulation of individual *tīrthas* and is regarded to represent the basis for the *narmadāparikramā*, we find in it just a passing reference to the circumambulation of the river:

> There is no doubt about this that those who have reached Narmadā, those who circumambulate her, and those who drink her water are meritorious. (*RKhV*. 29.37; trans. Tagare, 1999, 120)

Also, in its description of the numerous *tīrthas* situated along the river, the *Revākhaṇḍa* does not follow a circumambulatory course but rather jumps from one bank to the other. Only the *Vasiṣṭhasaṃhitā*, a nonextant text with an undated Marathi rendering (Bule, n.d.), lists the *tīrthas* that it eulogizes separately for the north and south bank of the river. This may perhaps reflect the practice of the *parikramā* at some time prior to the 19th century, but the vagueness of these literary references leaves this question undecided. The revival (or, perhaps, initiation) of the *parikramā*, however, may possibly be credited to one Svami Kamal Bharati, who is said to have performed the *parikramā* thrice and founded an organization (*jamāt*) of *parikramāvāsī*s in Koksar near Hoshangabad around the mid-19th century (Neuß, 2012, 139–140; Prasad, 1990, 128–129).

The construction of a number of large dams during the last decades notwithstanding, the *narmadāparikramā* presently enjoys high popularity even though long stretches of the traditional pilgrimage path and a large number of temples and hermitages have been submerged in the reservoirs. Considerable numbers of pilgrims – *sādhus* and laypersons alike – embark on this spiritual journey every year. While many still follow the traditional mode and walk, others now use modern modes of transport. Such practices are increasingly promoted by the government of Madhya Pradesh, which recently announced its intention to build a road all around the river. Organized bus tours already conveniently carry pilgrims to the main holy spots on the river, but this practice misses out the ultimate goal of the *narmadāparikramā*. The experience of solitude, hardships, and austerities as well as the complete dependence on the grace of the goddess is regarded as the fundamental prerequisite for the spiritual success of the pilgrimage. Accordingly, the traditional way of hiking is still held in high esteem, although some rules have undergone considerable modifications. For example, many *parikramāvāsī*s now begin (and end) their pilgrimage at Omkareshwar-Mandhata with a visit to the famous Oṃkāreśvara Temple, which houses one of the twelve *jyotirliṅgas*. When the *parikramā* is begun in the older fashion at either the source or the estuary, this temple – which stands on an island in the Narmadā – cannot be visited at all, because the pilgrim is strictly forbidden to cross the river in any way.

More grave, however, are the changes caused by the reservoirs, which now compel the pilgrims to walk extensive stretches on busy roads and highways quite far away from the riverbanks, because no alternatives have yet been established for the submerged portions of the original pilgrimage path. The fact that this means a violation of fundamental rules of the *parikramā*, which bind the pilgrim to exclusively drink Narmadā water, to daily have *darśan* of the river, not to leave its banks for any mundane reason, and to visit and bathe at all the *tīrthas* mentioned in the ancient tradition, is, however, of no consequence. As is the fact that the dams have converted the once vividly rushing river into a series of stagnant lakes. In many conversations with *parikramāvāsī*s, *sādhus*, or laypersons in the valley, I have never experienced any considerable kind of change in the common religious perception of the Narmadā. It is venerated in the same way, held in the same esteem, and worshipped with the same fervor as before. While, given the sanctity of the river, one might have expected some kind of protest against the dams from orthodox Hindu circles, their critique of these projects was astonishingly marginal.

Strong resistance, however, was organized in the early 1980s among the tribal population, mainly in the submergence zone of the Sardar Sarovar Dam on the Madhya Pradesh-Gujarat border. The continuing struggle of their organization, the Narmada Bachao Andolan ("Save the Narmada Movement"), for the right to proper compensation and rehabilitation of these marginalized people, who were and continue to be forced to sacrifice their sheer humble existence for what in political parlance is termed the "greater common good," is well documented in numerous academic and non-academic publications as well as a couple of documentaries. It reveals a great deal about the inner structure of Indian society and its relation to the functioning of the Indian state. Tribal resistance against the dams is the latest example in a historical series of periodically recurring, (comparatively) peaceful, tribal rebellions against governmental policies and legislations that chronically disregarded tribal interests and rights.

Earlier-documented examples of tribal insurgencies in the Narmadā Valley periodically occurred in the Rajpipla-Barwani area – the very region where the Narmada Bachao Andolan has its stronghold – and was directed against colonial legislation concerning forest use, the ban on swidden cultivation, and land taxation, which ultimately deprived the tribals of their economic resource base and irrevocably ruined most of their distinct cultural identity (see Kela, 2012). These legislations were often justified by the claim that the tribal peoples, who were commonly perceived by the majority of colonial legislators as pitiable savages, had to be uplifted and integrated into mainstream society.

This claim, with all its underlying 19th-century racism and colonial arrogance, has been one of the main arguments of the proponents of the dams, who promised a bright future for those to be displaced, euphemistically termed the "project-affected people" (or just: PAP). Still, for many tribal communities, this promise remains nothing but an empty phrase. Their land, which was earlier of little economic interest, has been ultimately appropriated by the Indian state and lies submerged in reservoirs that now water the fields of those who can afford agricultural land, pump sets, and electricity. The Narmadā River, which once sprang from the body of Śiva, is now blocked by dams made of concrete, into which countless stones from the river – all representations of the Narmadā's mythical father – were crushed.

Bibliography

Apte (Āpṭe), H.N., *Śrīmadvaipāyanamunipraṇītaṃ Matsyapurāṇam*, Pune, 1907.

Banerji, R.D., *The Haihayas of Tripuri and Their Monuments*, Calcutta, 1931.

Bhattacharya, B., *Dānasāgara of Ballāla Sena*, Calcutta, 1953.

Bule (Buḷe), S.B.N.G., *Śrīnarmadāmāhātmya*, Dadar, n.d.

Chakravarti, N.P., "A Note on the Halayudha Stotra in the Amaresvara Temple," *EI*, vol. XXV, 1948, 183–185.

Gupta, A.S., *The Kūrma Purāṇa*, Varanasi, 1971.

Hunter, W.W., *The Imperial Gazetteer of India*, vol. VII: *Narf to Rangmagiri*, London, 1881.

Kela, S., *A Rogue and Peasant Slave: Adivasi Resistance, 1800–2000*, New Delhi, 2012.

Neuß, J., *Narmadāparikramā: Circumambulation of the Narmadā River*, Leiden, 2012.

Omkaranand Giri (Oṃkārānand Giri), *Atha bṛhat śrīnārmadāpurāṇam revākhaṇḍam*, Hoshangabad, 1965, 2 1969, 3 1994.

Prasad (Prasād), D., *Narmadā kī kahānī*, Indore, 1990, 2 2000, 3 2008 (Hind.).

Russell, R.V., ed., *Central Provinces District Gazetteers: Nimar District, Volume A, Descriptive*, Allahabad, 1908.

Sankhyan, A.R., L.M. Dewangan, S. Chakraborty, S. Kundu, S. Prabha, R. Chakravarty & G.L. Badam, "New Human Fossils and Associated Findings from the Central Narmada Valley, India," *CS* 103/12, 2012, 1461–1469.

Srivastav, L., & S. Caldirola, *The Tribes of Narmada Valley*, New Delhi, 2005.

Tagare, G.V., *The Skanda-Purāṇa: Part XIV*, Delhi, 1999.

Williams, M., *Religious Thought and Life in India: Part I, Vedism, Brāhmanism, and Hindūism*, London, 1883.

JÜRGEN NEUẞ

Śaiva Texts

Those engaged in the study of Śaivism have before them in manuscript collections in the Indian subcontinent and around the world a great abundance and variety of textual sources, providing a rich record of what Śaivas of various persuasions were instructed to do and think as adherents of their religion, beginning from the period between the Maurya and Gupta empires and then increasing to a flood from the 5th century CE onwards, when Śaivism emerges into view as the dominant faith of the Indian subcontinent and large parts of Southeast Asia. During the last four decades our knowledge of this literature and its connections with the related textual traditions of tantric Buddhism, Pāñcarātrika Vaiṣṇavism (→ Pāñcarātra), and the Jaina Mantraśāstra, has increased greatly through the study of the contents of these collections by a growing number of scholars. The progress of this research has been accelerated by two major undertakings. The first is the Nepal-German Manuscript Preservation Project (1970–2002) and its continuation, the Nepal-German Manuscript Cataloguing Project (2002–), which, as a result of an agreement between the Deutsche Forschungsgemeinschaft (German Research Council) and the Government of Nepal, has microfilmed and made readily accessible to scholars about 140,000 Nepalese and East Indian manuscripts preserved in the relative isolation and mild climate of the Kathmandu valley, dating in the case of Śaiva manuscripts from the 9th century onwards. The second is the collection amassed from the 1950s onwards by the Institut Français de Pondichéry (French Institute of Pondicherry) of 8600 predominantly Śaiva South Indian palm-leaf manuscripts and 1144 Devanagari paper transcripts, of which the latter, containing approximately two thousand texts, have in recent years been scanned and made available on the Internet, with images of the former to follow. There are many other important collections with substantial holdings of Śaiva manuscripts in India and in Europe. But the task of mapping the literature in those collections has been facilitated by the fact that these two major projects have enabled scholars to acquaint themselves with some rapidity with large quantities of previously unknown texts, or texts known only through citations, and so to identify and classify more readily than might otherwise have been feasible the riches preserved in these other libraries. The work is far from complete, but I offer here as one who has been engaged in this research throughout this period my present understanding of what the Śaiva literature preserved in these various collections contains. I shall be comprehensive, in the sense that I shall cover the literatures of all the major branches of the Śaiva tradition of which I am aware; but I cannot attempt to be exhaustive by mentioning every work that I have seen in all of these. For in the case of many of these branches, especially those that developed or continued to develop from the 12th century down to the recent past, it is feasible to mention in a survey of this compass only the major among the works that have reached us and, among minor and ancillary texts, such as anonymous ritual handbooks and devotional hymns, only some examples. For the same reason I have excluded from consideration surviving Śaiva textual materials that were produced outside the subcontinent, on the islands of Java and Bali, and also the numerous Indian and Southeast Asian belletristic works whose narratives are taken from Śaiva mythology. My primary aim is to provide scholars with a chronologically ordered map of the main divisions of the literature and their interlocking religious contexts as they appear to me at present, reporting the regions in which texts were composed where evidence is available.

Lay Śaivism

First there are texts followed by traditions of lay devotion to → Śiva. They include in the Śaiva perspective all instruction for the propitiation of the vedic deity Rudra found in the → Vedas and their ancillary corpora. But the principal sources in this domain are the texts of what may be called the Śivadharma corpus after the work that is probably the earliest and precedes the others in manuscripts that contain all or most of them. These are the *Śivadharma, Śivadharmottara, Śivadharmasaṃgraha, Umāmaheśvarasaṃvāda, Uttarottaramahāsaṃvāda, Śivopaniṣad, Vṛṣasārasaṃgraha, Dharmaputrikā*, and *Lalitavistara*. They advocate the veneration of Śiva and the dedication of a third of one's wealth to the support of his followers, the creation and maintenance of temples and other Śaiva institutions, and donations thereto, promising the devotee success and security in this life and, after death, the finite reward of ascension to the deity's paradise (Śivaloka, Rudraloka), followed, once the merit that earned that reward has been exhausted, by the most desirable of incarnations in the human world. They claim, moreover, that the rewards of adherence extend in various degrees to the devotee's patriline and dependents.

Also in this lay Śaiva domain are certain → Purāṇas, notably the *Skandapurāṇa, Vāyupurāṇa, Liṅgapurāṇa, Devīpurāṇa*, and *Śivapurāṇa*, and a great number of short compositions promoting Śaiva sacred sites (*śivakṣetra, śivāyatana*) that have been given the status of scripture by attribution to one of these, most commonly the *Skandapurāṇa*, often in large collections covering the sites of whole regions. Thus we have, for example, a *Himavatkhaṇḍa*, a *Revākhaṇḍa*, an *Avantikhaṇḍa*, a *Sahyādrikhaṇḍa*, a *Prabhāsakhaṇḍa*, a *Nāgarakhaṇḍa*, a *Kāśīkhaṇḍa*, and a *Pauṇḍrakhaṇḍa* assigned to the *Skandapurāṇa*. But perhaps even greater is the number of those that circulated locally and were never redacted into larger wholes, their claim to scriptural status being sustained by no more than an assertion in their colophons that they are parts of some Purāṇa. Examples are the *Nepālamāhātmya* attributed to a *Himavatkhaṇḍa* of the *Skandapurāṇa*, the *Pampāmāhātmya* attributed to a *Hemakūṭakhaṇḍa* of the same, the *Āmardakamāhātmya* attributed to a *Kāverīkhaṇḍa* of the *Padmapurāṇa*, and the *Ekaliṅgamāhātmya* attributed to the *Vāyupurāṇa*. In some cases the loci of attribution appear to have had no independent existence. Thus in → Kashmir it was conventional to attribute such compositions to the *Bhṛṅgīśasaṃhitā* or *Ādipurāṇa*, though no manuscripts of works bearing these names have come to light, let alone manuscripts of them containing these supposed parts.

Since this literature is composed for the laity, it is generally written in undemanding Sanskrit that could be expected to be readily understood by a larger public, but there is also much writing of this kind that recognizes the limitation in this regard of even this simple form of the learned lingua franca by adopting Tamil, Telugu, and other vernacular languages. As for the Śivadharma corpus, the same limitation prompts the *Śivadharmottara* to recommend that it be taught to its audiences in the languages of their regions. The text probably envisages its being chanted in Sanskrit with each verse or group of verses followed by an explanation in the vernacular. But it could also be taken as advocating the production of translations. One survives: the Tamil *Civatarumōttaram* authored by Vedajñāna I in the 16th century.

Initiatory Śaivism

Then there are the literatures of forms of Śaivism for initiates, which set themselves far above that for the laity by offering the individual alone the attainment of the non-finite goal of → liberation (*mokṣa*). This initiatory Śaivism comprises (1) the systems of the Atimārga, namely those of the Pāñcārthika → Pāśupatas (Atimārga I), the Lākulas, also known as Kālamukhas (Atimārga II), and the → Kāpālikas, also known as Mahāvratins or adherents of the Somasiddhānta (Atimārga III), which arose in that order, (2) those of the Mantramārga or "tantric Śaivism" that developed on the basis of the second and third, coexisted with all three, and promised not only liberation but also, for those initiates consecrated to office, the ability to accomplish supernatural effects (*siddhi*) such as the averting or counteracting of calamities (*śānti*) and the warding off or destruction of enemies (*abhicāra*), and (3) those of the predominantly Śākta Kulamārga, which offered the same goals as the Mantramārga, but propagated distinct "Kaula" methods that have more in common with the practices of Atimārga III than with those of the Mantramārga and indeed, I propose, developed directly from that source, preserving most of its distinctive features.

Chronology

The dating of these traditions cannot be determined with any precision from the available data; but we may say that the Atimārga came into existence probably no later than the 2nd century CE and reached its third stage not later than the 5th, the earliest dateable reference to the Kāpālikas of Atimārga III being found in Agastyasiṃha's 5th-century commentary on the Jaina *Dasaveyāliyasutta*, supposed earlier references being based on misconceptions concerning the date of the sources in question. The Mantramārga and Kulamārga emerged thereafter, the earliest text of the former, the *Niśvāsamūla*, assignable to the period 450–550 CE, presupposing Atimārga II, whose cosmic hierarchy it has inherited and extended.

Mantramargic learned exposition on the basis of an already constituted corpus of scriptural texts is in evidence not later than the 8th century and was at its height in both the Mantramārga and the Kulamārga from the 9th to the 12th. The earliest unambiguous dateable evidence of the Kulamārga is in the early 9th century, in the *Haravijaya* of the Kashmirian Ratnākara. There may be a reference to followers of the Kulamārga in the description of the temple of the goddess Vindhyavāsinī in the Prakrit Kāvya *Gauḍavaho* of Vākpatirāja, written in the first half of the 8th century; but this is not beyond doubt, the reference there to what may be "Kaula women," that is to say, to female initiates in the Kulamārga or to the wives of male initiates, being more probably to women of the Kol tribe that lived in the region in which that temple is located.

The literature of lay devotion began when the Atimārga was already established and continued to grow after the emergence of the Mantramārga. It might be assumed that it was produced by adherents of the initiatory traditions for the guidance of their uninitiated followers. However, while these texts show some awareness of the initiatory traditions, either of the Atimārga alone or of both that and the Mantramārga, and while the initiatory traditions promoted this literature as valid prescription for their lay followers, divergences in matters of doctrine argue against the assumption that they themselves produced it. It is rather the product of an old and widespread tradition that the initiatory systems acknowledged when they rose to prominence, just as they took over preexisting Śaiva temple cults.

The Atimārga

The corpus of texts known to us from the Atimārga is small. From the Pāñcārthika Pāśupatas (Atimārga I) we have their foundational text, the *Pañcārtha* or *Pāśupatasūtra*, probably much the earliest of our texts of initiatory Śaivism, perhaps of the 2nd century CE, containing practical religious instruction and the *mantra*s of this system, with the commentary (*Pañcārthabhāṣya*) of Kauṇḍinya. The latter, poorly transmited in three manuscripts of which only one is complete, was probably composed at some time between 400 and 550 CE. We also have five short verse texts. Of these the *Saṃskāravidhi*, the *Pātravidhi*, the *Prāyaścittavidhi*, and the *Anteṣṭividhi*, which have come down to us in a single manuscript, are devoted as their titles reveal to the procedure of the initiation ceremony, rules concerning the ascetic's begging bowl, penances, and the procedures for the disposal of the dead, principally burial. The fifth, the *Gaṇakārikā*, arranges the various key elements of the teaching pertaining to initiation and the stages of the post-initiatory discipline contained in the *Pañcārthabhāṣya* under nine sets (*gaṇa*s) of items, comprising eight pentads and one triad. This too, together with a commentary, the *Ratnaṭīkā*, has reached us through a single manuscript, which was preserved by good fortune in a bundle of Jaina texts in a Jaina library in Patan (Pāṭan).

I consider it probable that these five texts, like the *Pañcārtha*, were taught as revelation rather than as works of human scholarship. For the Sanskrit of the *Gaṇakārikā* and the four *vidhi* texts does not conform throughout to the norms expected of writing claimed by authors as their own. Rather its transgressions of the rules of the grammarians associate it with the register of Sanskrit seen in the surviving early Śaiva scriptures of the Mantramārga. In support of the position that the *Gaṇakārikā* was considered to be scripture rather than mere human exegesis we may also cite the fact that the author of the commentary on the text presents it as the answer given to a question of a disciple that begins with the words "Is it the case, O Bhagavat...?". For this is how Kauṇḍinya introduces the *Pañcārtha* in his *Pañcārthabhāṣya*, as the answer given by Śiva as the first teacher (named Lakulīśa in later sources) to a question by Kuśika, his first disciple, which begins with the words "O Bhagavat, is there or is there not a definitive removing of all these forms of suffering?". This strongly suggests that the author of the *Ratnaṭīkā* considered the propagation of the *Gaṇakārikā* to be on a par with that of the *Pañcārtha*. Furthermore, the *Prāyaścittavidhi* is said in its first colophon to have been "taught by the Venerable Gārgya". This attribution may be to the Gārgya who was the second of the four disciples of Lakulīśa held to have been the progenitors of the four Pāñcārthika lineages (*gotra*). This is consistent with a belief that the text is revelation, since a tradition seen in the earliest *Skandapurāṇa* holds that these four were created from the four faces of Śiva and instructed to take birth in the world for the salvation of Brahmans. It is further supported by the colophon's expression "taught by" (*-upadiṣṭa*) as opposed to "composed by" (*-viracita*) or the like.

Four other small Pāñcārthika works are contained in the bundle of Jaina manuscripts that contains the *Gaṇakārikā* and its commentary. The first comprises 21 verses on the universal ethical principles (*yamas*) of the Pāñcārthikas following the *Pañcārthabhāṣya*, and the second, in 13 verses, follows obeisance to the 28 incarnations of Rudra, from Śveta to Lakulīśa, with a prayer to the last that the author may master his doctrine. Both inform us that they are the work of an otherwise unknown ascetic called Viśuddhamuni. The third, in 26 *āryā* verses, summarizes, without indication of authorship, what Kauṇḍinya teaches in the *Pañcārthabhāṣya* on the nature of Śiva/Rudra as the cause (*kāraṇa*) of all things, the first of the five topics (*padārtha, artha*) that give the foundational text its name (*Pañcārtha*) and thereby its followers theirs (Pāñcārthika). This is only the first part of a work that summarized the teaching of the *Pañcārthabhāṣya* on all five topics, namely *kāraṇa* (cause), *kārya* (effect), *vidhi* (observance), *yoga* (union), and *duḥkhānta* (the end of suffering). The fourth is a hymn of seven verses in which Rudra is invoked under 21 names followed by instruction to the reader that the recitation of these names or even one of them at the end of his worship will lead him to Śiva when he dies and the information that this teaching was given by Rudra in the *Skandapurāṇa* at the request of Gaurī, followed by a verse of obeisance to the goddess as the *pañcārthavidyā* (gnosis of the *Pañcārtha*).

Apart from these sources we have in the Mantramārga's *Niśvāsamukha* a brief versified account of Atimārga I based on the instructional parts of the *Pañcārtha* with the addition of a rule that one should offer Śiva only flowers that have withered and fallen to the ground, and another in a puranic work from Karnataka, the *Pampāmāhātmya*, which incorporates a modified version of the eight verses of the *Gaṇakārikā* and elaborates the discipline following our known sources, but also provides revealing information not found in those, notably that when in the last stage of the Pāñcārthika's ascetic disciple he retires to die in a cremation ground, it is envisaged that he will do so by ending his life through → *yoga*, by extracting his soul from his body through → meditation, a practice only alluded to in the *Pañcārtha* and its commentary but much stressed in the Mantramārga, particularly in the *Mataṅgapārameśvara*, which in its prescriptions for ascetic initiates perpetuates the discipline of the Atimārga.

Pāñcārthika tradition is also reflected in a number of puranic works. These are of uncertain value as evidence of properly Pāñcārthika beliefs and practices, representing rather modifications through accommodation to Brahmanical orthopraxy. But the *Pampāmāhātmya* is exceptional in this regard, as is the earliest, and probably original *Skandapurāṇa*, a work whose first redaction, in North India, was probably produced within the period 550–650 CE, and which reaches us in manuscripts of which the earliest was penned in 810/811 CE. For this contains valuable traditions concerning the early history of this form of Śaivism, its lineages, and sacred sites.

As for the scriptures of Atimārga II, we have, apart from their titles, only a few verses quoted from one of them, the *Pañcārthapramāṇa*, in a mantramargic commentary. Knowledge of the textual prescriptions of this tradition can be gained at present only from the account of it given in the Mantramārga's *Niśvāsamukha* and from scattered remarks in other sources. We also have an account in the *Pampāmāhātmya*; but this, being secondary, is of uncertain reliability in the absence of more detailed primary sources.

The situation with the Kāpālika/Mahāvratin tradition of Atimārga III, also known as the Somasiddhānta, is much the same, though it is now clear that much of its practice was carried forward into the more antinomian traditions of the Mantramārga and Kulamārga and that with it may have come textual material of which some, such as the *Yoginīsaṃcāra* incorporated in the *Jayadrathayāmala*, may have undergone little redactional modification. Here too we have a secondary source of uncertain value in the *Pampāmāhātmya*.

In the prescriptive evidence of the Atimārga the emphasis is on meditative absorption in the deity and countercultural asceticism (→ *tapas*), that is to say, on practices that draw their strength and appeal from their contravention of the norms of conduct imposed by the dominant, Brahmanical culture. Nonetheless this is transcendence from within. For initiation and thence the practice of the discipline are stated in our sources to be accessible only to Brahmans and only to those who have duly passed through the ceremony that qualifies a boy to begin the study of the Veda. This requirement excludes women, though we have epigraphic evidence in an inscription of 1208/1209 from Mount Abu that this exclusion was not always enforced.

The Mantramārga

In the texts of the Mantramārga access is extended to Śiva devotees in all the four caste-classes (*varṇa*), and also to women, though in the last case usually only as passive beneficiaries of initiation rather than as active initiates with access to office. By "passive beneficiary" I mean those who have received the form of initiation termed "without seed" (*nirbījā dīkṣā*), in which the destruction of the soul's bonds effected by the ritual is made to include that of the post-initiatory discipline (*samayapāśa*). Such persons are promised the benefit of initiation, namely liberation at death, but freed of the inconvenience of the ritual obligations that bind ordinary initiates. They are passive beneficiaries, then, in the sense that they do not have to do what ordinary initiates do. They are expected instead to maintain the duties they had as lay Śaivas before their initiation. Moreover, although meditation and asceticism are carried over into these texts it is the prescription of ritual that now dominates; and this comprises not only ritual worship as the regular duty of initiates but also, and more crucially, the ritual of initiation itself (*dīkṣā*), which, greatly elaborated, is promoted as the means by which Śiva himself chooses to destroy the bonds of souls ripe for liberation, acting through the person of his consecrated officiants (*ācārya*, → *guru*), who alone are empowered to perform the ritual. This shift justifies the giving of initiation to devotees such as women, and also to rulers, who by reason of their duties of governance are not able thereafter to take on any additional ritual commitments. Only for others was initiation promoted as both liberating and qualificatory. The substantial rewards bestowed on officiants for performing such initiations for kings was no doubt among the principal drivers of the growth and spread of the Mantramārga's institutions. In addition the literature sets out rituals for the installation (*pratiṣṭhā*) of → *liṅga*s, other substrates of worship, and the temples that enshrine them, and for the accomplishment of the supernatural effects mentioned above.

The Saiddhāntika Scriptures

The Mantramārga comprises two main divisions. The first of these came to call itself the Siddhānta ("The Definitive Doctrine"; see → Śaiva Siddhānta). Its texts dominate the prescription of the more visible domains of the Mantramārga, presenting its officiants as performing the consecration of *liṅga*s and temples where worship was to be performed for the collective benefit of all, holding office as the superintendents of the monasteries (*maṭha*) commonly attached to them, and taking the office of the king's preceptor (*rājaguru*), offering the monarch the benefit of Śaiva initiation and consecrating him in his office in a Śaiva variant of the Brahmanical ceremony of royal consecration (*rājyābhiṣeka*), thus promoting its officiants as vital to the welfare of the whole society.

Of its early scriptures those that survive completely or substantially are the *Niśvāsa* corpus (*Niśvāsamukha, Niśvāsamūla, Niśvāsanaya, Niśvāsottara, Niśvāsaguhya*, and *Niśvāsakārikā*, the last including the *Dīkṣottara*), various texts that are or claim to be redactions of the *Kālottara* (*Jñānapañcāśikā, Śatika, Sārdhaśatika, Dviśatika, Sārdhatriśatika, Saptaśatika, Trayodaśaśatika*, and *Bṛhatkālottara*), the *Sarvajñānottara*, the *Pārameśvara* (*Pauṣkarapārameśvara*), the *Svāyambhuvasūtrasaṃgraha*, the *Rauravasūtrasaṃgraha*, the *Mataṅgapārameśvara*, the *Kiraṇa*, the *Mṛgendra*, and the *Parākhya*. These scriptural sources are supplemented by two digests, the *Prāyaścittasamuccaya* of Hṛdayaśiva and the *Nityādisaṃgraha* of Takṣakavarta, which preserve for us passages of several scriptures of the Mantramārga that have not otherwise reached us, both Saiddhāntika and non-Saiddhāntika.

The Saiddhāntika Exegesis

We also have a body of learned exegesis on some of these works. On the doctrinal chapters of the *Svāyambhuvasūtrasaṃgraha* we have a running prose commentary, the *Svāyambhuvavṛtti*, by Sadyojyotis, also known as Kheṭabāla or Kheṭanandana, and on those of the *Rauravasūtrasaṃgraha* we have the following parts of a commentary (*Rauravavṛtti*) in verse by the same author, transmitted to us as independent treatises: the *Bhogakārikā*, the *Mokṣakārikā*, and the *Paramokṣanirāsakārikā*. We also have his *Tattvatrayanirṇaya* and *Tattvasaṃgraha*, in which he sets out Saiddhāntika ontology following, according to a later authority, the *Svāyambhuvasūtrasaṃgraha* and *Rauravasūtrasaṃgraha* respectively, and the *Nareśvaraparīkṣā*, a systematic philosophical treatise in which he formulates his understanding of the Siddhānta's doctrines of the soul and god without explicit dependence on any individual scripture. A near contemporary, Bṛhaspati, wrote a *Rauravavārttika*, a commentary in verse on the *Rauravasūtrasaṃgraha*, and the *Śivatanu*, a verse treatise of unknown scriptural affiliation. But of these two works we now have only citations in the works of others. We have no evidence of where either of these early commentators was active. As for their date, both lived before the 9th century, probably within the period 675–750 CE.

From the Kashmirian Bhaṭṭa Nārāyaṇakaṇṭha we have an exhaustive commentary on the *Mṛgendra*. We know that he also wrote a subcommentary (*-ṭippaṇaka*) on Sadyojyotis' *Svāyambhuvavṛtti* and a long commentary (*bṛhaṭṭīkā*) called the *Śarannisā* on the same author's *Tattvasaṃgraha*; but as yet no manuscript of either has been located.

From his son Bhaṭṭa Rāmakaṇṭha we have elaborate prose commentaries on the doctrinal chapters of the *Kiraṇa* and on the *Sārdhatriśatika* recension of the *Kālottara* and the *Mataṅgapārameśvara*, these covering the whole of those Tantras and therefore not only doctrine (*jñāna*) but also ritual (*kriyā*), meditation (*yoga*), and ascetic discipline (*caryā*). We also have his prose commentaries on four of the works of Sadyojyotis: the *Mokṣakārikā*, the *Paramokṣanirāsakārikā*, the *Tattvatrayanirṇaya*, and the *Nareśvaraparīkṣā*. The last of these, the *Nareśvaraparīkṣāprakāśa*, is a work of rigorous philosophical argument in which Rāmakaṇṭha attempts to establish Sadyojyotis' Siddhānta against the positions of the Buddhists and others. He also composed a commentary on the *Svāyambhuvasūtrasaṃgraha* (*Svāyambhuvoddyota*), but no manuscript of this has surfaced. These two Kashmirian authors, father and son, were active in Kashmir and neighbouring Darvabhisara (Dārvābhicāra) during the second half of the 10th century.

Two other Saiddhāntika treatises in verse have been transmitted from the period up to the 12th century: the *Ratnatrayaparīkṣā* of Śrīkaṇṭha and the *Tattvaprakāśa* of King Bhojadeva. Śrīkaṇṭha has been assumed to be a Kashmirian and to have been a predecessor in the teaching lineage that produced Bhaṭṭa Nārāyaṇakaṇṭha and Bhaṭṭa Rāmakaṇṭha. But there is no evidence that supports or refutes either claim. If the King Bhojadeva to whom the *Tattvaprakāsa* is attributed is, as seems probable, the Mahārājādhirāja Bhojadeva to whom an important Saiddhāntika Paddhati, the *Siddhāntasārapaddhati*, is attributed, then this work is a product of Malwa (Mālava) and of the first half of the 11th century.

From Aghoraśiva, a South Indian scholar active in Chidambaram around the mid-12th century, who perpetuated the exegetical tradition of Bhaṭṭa Nārāyaṇakaṇṭha and Bhaṭṭa Rāmakaṇṭha, we have the *Mṛgendravṛttidīpikā*, his subcommentary on Bhaṭṭa Nārāyaṇakaṇṭha's commentary on the *Mṛgendra*, commentaries on the *Dviśatika* recension of the *Kālottara*, the doctrinal chapters of the *Sarvajñānottara*, the *Bhogakārikā* and *Tattvatrayanirṇaya* of Sadyojyotis, the *Ratnatrayaparīkṣā* of Śrīkaṇṭha, the *Tattvaprakāśa* of Bhojadeva – this provides the only firm limit for the date of the last two works – and the *Nādakārikā* of Bhaṭṭa Rāmakaṇṭha, 25 verses extracted from the latter's commentary on 1.5ab of the *Sārdhatriśatika* recension of the *Kālottara*.

We also have in a single South Indian manuscript a commentary called *Bālabodhinī* on some chapters of the doctrinal section (*Jñānakāṇḍa*) of the *Kiraṇa* by an author who is identified in the colophon of the first chapter as Aghoraśiva, in those of the rest as Vyākhyānikācārya, and in the closing verses before the last as Siṃharāja, son of Kāmarūpeśa and pupil of Nīlakaṇṭha, the pupil of a pupil of a *guru* at Āmardakapura (i.e. Aundah [Auṃḍhā] in the Marathawada [Marāṭhavāḍā] region of Maharashtra). It is followed without any indication that a new work commences by a commentary on the *Kiraṇa*'s section on ritual (*Kriyākāṇḍa*) – only the first nine *paṭala*s (13–21) survive in our manuscript – which four of the chapter colophons call the *Cintāmaṇiṭīkā* and two attribute to Aghoraśiva. On stylistic grounds it is improbable that the two commentaries are by one individual with the common Saiddhāntika initiation name Aghoraśiva and very improbable that either author is the Aghoraśiva of Chidambaram whose works have been mentioned above.

We have another commentary on the *Kiraṇa* by a certain Tryambakaśambhu about whom the text contains no further information. It draws on Kṣemarāja's commentary on the *Svacchanda*, which places it after circa 1000 CE, and the *Vimalāvatī* of Vimalaśiva, which places it after 1101/1102.

We may wonder what proportion of the Saiddhāntika commentaries that once existed has reached us. That is impossible to determine for the earliest period, but we are able to know which scriptures could be studied with commentaries by South Indian Saiddhāntikas in the 12th century from a review of all the sources of knowledge of the Siddhānta available at that time given by Aghoraśiva's pupil Vaktraśambhu. Distinguishing between those scriptures that have received commentaries and those that have not, he gives a closed list of the first. They are the *Raurava(sūtrasaṃgraha)*, the *Svāyambhuva(sūtrasaṃgraha)*, the *Mṛgendra*, the *Kiraṇa*, the *Parākhya*, the *Mataṅga(pārameśvara)*, the *Sūkṣmasvāyambhuva*, the *Dviśatika*, *Sārdhatriśatika*, and *Catuḥśatika* (recensions of the *Kālottara*), the *Sarvajñānottara*, and the *Mohaśūrottara*. Of these we lack the commentaries on the *Parākhya, Sūkṣmasvāyambhuva, Catuḥśatika*, and *Mohaśūrottara*. In the case of the *Sūkṣmasvāyambhuva* and *Catuḥśatika* we lack manuscripts of the scriptures themselves. The *Mohaśūrottara* does survive and will be mentioned under another heading.

From early South Indian authors we also have an independent summary of the Saiddhāntika system in the *Siddhāntadīpikā*, composed in 1071/1072 by Rāmanātha, abbot of the eastern *maṭha* at Thiruvarur (Tiruvārūr); and in the *Siddhāntasamuccaya* and *Siddhāntarahasyasāra* of Trilocanaśiva we have a presentation of the ontology and soteriology of the Siddhānta built around a digest-like compendium of citations from the Saiddhāntika scriptures and the works of Sadyojyotis. The author, who is described in its colophonic verse as the abbot of a *maṭha* in Śvetāraṇya (i.e. Thiruvenkadu), may not be the Trilocana whose works will be mentioned below. But we can be confident that he is a relatively early author, since his work is closely allied with the other South Indian Saiddhāntika works of this period in the range of its scriptural sources and in its Kashmirian doctrinal stance. To these we may add two others works. The first is the *Śataratnasaṃgraha* of an Umāpatiśiva of Chidambaram. Though that is undoubtedly a later work than the *Siddhāntadīpikā* and *Siddhāntasamuccaya*, since the sources from which it has been compiled include two scriptures that are never mentioned by these or earlier exegetes and are not transmitted in manuscripts north of the Deccan, namely the *Devīkālottara* and the *Viśvasārottara*, it nonetheless adheres strictly, as the earlier treatises do, to the view of the Siddhānta espoused by Sadyojyotis, Bhaṭṭa Nārāyaṇakaṇṭha, Bhaṭṭa Rāmakaṇṭha, Aghoraśiva and others, as does its anonymous commentary (*Śataratnollekhanī, Śataratnollekha*). The second is the *Siddhāntaprakāśikā* of a certain Sarvātmaśambhu, since that too adheres to the basic dualistic and ritualistic tenets of the classical Siddhānta of the early commentators.

The later works of this exegetical literature, that is to say, all but the works of Sadyojyotis, add to our knowledge of the scriptural corpus, since they are rich in citations, drawing on more scriptural texts than have survived independently. However, their principal interest for the historian lies in the fact that they follow Sadyojyotis by adhering to a strictly ritualistic reading of the scriptures, holding that only the ritual of initiation, performed by a consecrated officiant, or rather by Śiva through such a person, can effect the liberation of the soul, this being accomplished subliminally at the time of initiation and becoming fully manifest only when the initiate is separated from his body through death. The sense of this doctrine in the broader context of the religion is that it constitutes a claim that the gift of liberation is entirely in the hands of the ritualists, extruding the gnostic and visionary tendencies that were present in the early Siddhānta and continued to flourish in the non-Saiddhāntika traditions of the Mantramārga as alternative routes to liberation, and challenging the claims of those traditions to be able to bring about liberation through ecstatic experience before death (→ *jīvanmukti*).

One may wonder with good reason at the large span of time, two hundred years at least, that separates Sadyojyotis' and Bṛhaspati's works from the rest of the Saiddhāntika exegetical literature that has reached us. The reason for this lacuna is not that no such literature was produced in the interim but rather that the Kashmirian exegesis of the 10th to 11th centuries was a dogmatic return to the strictly ritualistic soteriology of Sadyojyotis after a period during which alternative, more flexible readings of the scriptural corpus had been current. The success of this fundamentalist reformation appears to have ousted alternative readings to the extent that no manuscripts of the commentaries that taught them have come down to us. Indeed we would know nothing of these readings were it not that some non-Saiddhāntika authors have referred to them.

In addition to commentaries we have a good number of surviving Paddhatis ("Guides") produced by various Saiddhāntika pontiffs. These go beyond the somewhat discrepant and incomplete prescriptions of the scriptures to provide systematic and comprehensive accounts of the rituals, propagating a simpler and uniform system in the place of the diversity and complexity seen the scriptures by basing it on the Mantra system and deity set of one of these, the *Kālottara* in its *Dviśatika* or *Sārdhatriśatika* recension, and supplementing their parsimonious prescriptions – as their titles declare, the first contains only 200 verses and the second only 350 – by drawing on other scriptural sources. Notable among these Paddhatis are the *Nityakriyānusaṃdhāna* and *Naimittikakriyānusaṃdhāna* of the Paddhati of Brahmaśambhu (*Brahmaśambhupaddhati*), the latter completed in 937/938 CE, the *Siddhāntasārapaddhati* of Mahārājādhirāja Bhojadeva, composed in Malwa at an unrecorded date during the first half of the 11th century, the *Kriyākāṇḍakramāvalī* of Somaśambhu, abbot of the major Saiddhāntika monastery at Golagī (i.e. Gurgi) in the kingdom of the Kalacuris of Tripurī (i.e. Tewar), composed in 1048/1049, the *Naṭarājapaddhati* of Rāmanātha of the "Southern Golagī Monastery" founded at Thiruvarur, some 1,500 km to the South, by Brahmaśiva, an east Indian (*gauḍadeśīya*) missionary from the original foundation, composed in 1057/1058, the *Kriyāsaṃgrahapaddhati* of Vāladhārin, composed before 1090, the date of its only manuscript known to me, the *Vimalāvatī* of Vimalaśiva, *rājaguru* of the ruler of Magadha and resident in Banaras, composed in 1101/1102, the *Kriyākramadyotikā* of Aghoraśiva of Chidambaram, composed in 1157/1158, the undated *Jñānaratnāvalī* of his contemporary Jñānaśiva, originally from Chidambaram but living in Banaras when he wrote this work, the *Siddhāntasārāvalī* of the South Indian Trilocanaśiva, a disciple of both Aghoraśiva and Jñānaśiva, the undated and incompletely transmitted *Tattvaratnāvalī* of Vimalācārya, also called Paramaśrotriya Sadāśiva, whose only know manuscript, written in the Pala script, is probably of the 12th century, the *Siddhāntaśekhara* of Viśvanātha, who was active in Banaras in or close to the first half of the 13th century, and the *Siddhāntasāra* of the Keralan Īśānaśiva (the *Īśānaśivagurudevapaddhati*) of uncertain date. Based on the *Mṛgendra* rather than the *Kālottara* we have the *Mṛgendrapaddhati* of the Aghoraśiva who wrote the *Kriyākramadyotikā* in 1157/1158. We also have the brief *Varuṇapaddhati* of Varuṇaśiva, which summarizes the topics of *dīkṣā* and *pratiṣṭhā* in about two hundred verses without going into the details of procedure. Its date cannot be determined at present beyond noting that it echoes the *Kriyākāṇḍakramāvalī* of 1048/1049 and is attested by no dateable author before Vedajñāna II of Chidambaram, the 16th-century author of a commentary on the text. This same Vedajñāna composed two digest-like Paddhatis of his own: the *Ātmārthapūjāpaddhati* and the *Dīkṣādarśa*, both of which have reached us intact. Also from the 16th century we have the Paddhati *Śivārcanacandrikā* of Appayya Dīkṣita, written under the patronage of Cinna Bomma Reddi, the ruler of Vellore.

We have commentaries on five of these Paddhatis. On the *Mṛgendrapaddhati* we have that of the author's pupil Vaktraśambhu. On the *Kriyākāṇḍakramāvalī* of Somaśambhu we have that of Trilocanaśiva, the 12th-century author of the *Siddhāntasārāvalī*. He tells us in that commentary that he also commented on the Paddhati of Brahmaśambhu; but no manuscript of this work has reached us. It is probable that this Trilocanaśiva is identical with the author of that name who wrote the *Prāyaścittasamuccaya*, a Saiddhāntika compendium on penances. On the *Siddhāntasārāvalī* we have a commentary by one Anantaśambhu, concerning whose date I can say only that he postdates Viśvanātha, since he quotes him. On the *Kriyākramadyotikā* of Aghoraśiva we have a commentary by Nirmalamaṇi, another late South Indian author, possibly of the 16th or 17th century but certainly later than Viśvanātha, since he too quotes the *Siddhāntaśekhara*, and another by Kacchapeśvaraśiva of Kāñcī (Kanchipuram), of whose date I can cite no evidence other than that he, like Nirmalamaṇi, quotes Viśvanātha. On the *Varuṇapaddhati* of Varuṇaśiva we have in addition to the commentary of Vedajñāna II already mentioned another by a Bhaṭṭa Śivottama, for whose date we have no evidence other than the fact that his commentary is mentioned by Vedajñāna as his guide.

We also have compendia that prescribe the penances to be undertaken for intentional or accidental infringements of the rules binding initiates, and the rules governing the states of impurity occasioned by a death, the correct timing of the various rituals, notably the *Prāyaścittasamuccaya* of Hṛdayaśiva, the *Prāyaścittasamuccaya* of Trilocanaśiva, the *Āśaucacandrikā* of Uttuṅgaśiva, and the *Āśaucadīpikā* and *Śaivakālaviveka* of Vedajñāna II; and we have treatises that give us systematic analyses of questions concerning the ritual rights and obligations of the various social groups among the Śaivas, such as the *Antyeṣṭiprakaraṇa* on the various types of Śaiva cremation ritual and the periods of impurity that ensue, the *Varṇāśramacandrikā*, which gathers and analyses evidence from Śaiva scriptural sources and Paddhatis bearing on the application of the Brahmanical caste-classes and disciplines within Saiddhāntika practice and in particular on the qualification of Śūdras (Vēḷāḷas) to receive Śaiva initiation and consecration to office, and the *Śaivasaṃnyāsapaddhati* of Śivāgrayogīndra Jñānaśivācārya, which establishes the related qualification of Śaiva Vēḷāḷas to enter the discipline of the renouncer.

The Siddhānta's Pratiṣṭhātantras and Pratiṣṭhāpāddhatis

In addition to the general scriptural works of the Siddhānta we have a number of specialized scriptures called Pratiṣṭhātantras that treat only the rituals of installation (*pratiṣṭhā*) and such ancillary subjects as iconography, iconometry, and the plans of various types of temple, royal palaces, monasteries, and new settlements, from royal centers to villages. Of scriptures of this kind we have the *Devyāmata*, the *Mohaśūrottara*, the *Piṅgalāmata*, and the *Mayasaṃgraha*. The first three have reached us in their entirety, while for the *Mayasaṃgraha* we have at present only a single incomplete witness. We also have the *Bhāvacūḍāmaṇi*, a commentary, fortunately complete, written on the whole of that work by the Kashmirian Vidyākaṇṭha, a pupil of the Bhaṭṭa Rāmakaṇṭha who has given us commentaries on the *Kālottara, Mataṅgapārameśvara*, and *Kiraṇa*. Commentaries also existed on the *Piṅgalāmata* and the *Mohaśūrottara* by Bhaṭṭa Nārāyaṇakaṇṭha of Kashmir (or his son Bhaṭṭa Rāmakaṇṭha) and Aghoraśiva of Chidambaram respectively, but neither of these, it seems, has reached us.

Here too we find a number of Paddhatis, works whose purpose, like that of those that pertain to the whole range of Saiddhāntika rituals, was to provide fuller, more systematic coverage of the rituals, in this case those of installation alone, and of all that pertains to them. Notable in this category are the *Pratiṣṭhāsārapaddhati* composed in Banaras by a pupil of a Kumāraśiva who was a contemporary of Mūlarāja I, founder of the Caulukya dynasty of Gujarat, who ruled from 941 to 997/998 CE, the *Lakṣaṇasaṃgraha* of the east Indian Vairocana, probably of the same century, the *Śaivāgamanibandhana* of Murāribhaṭṭa, probably a Keralan, and the *Prayogamañjarī* of the Keralan Ravi, written no later than the 15th century.

Saiddhāntika Liturgical Hymnography

Within the corpus of surviving Saiddhāntika Śaiva sources we have also a small body of hymns (*stava, stuti,* → *stotra*) composed for recitation in the course of worship. The earliest will be the *Vyomavyāpistava* if the Rāmakaṇṭha to whom it is attributed by its 16th-century commentator Vedajñāna II is the Kashmirian Saiddhāntika Bhaṭṭa Rāmakaṇṭha. Of certain attribution are the *Pañcāvaraṇastotra* of Aghoraśiva and the *Śivapūjāstava* of his contemporary Jñānaśiva. Closely related is the *Dhyānaratnāvalī* of their pupil Trilocanaśiva, which consists of verses to be recited for the visualization of all the deities of the Saiddhāntika pantheon in the order in which they are worshipped.

The Scriptures of the Non-Saiddhāntika Mantramārga

The Siddhānta is strictly Śaiva, in the sense that the regular rites prescribed by its scriptures are focused on Śiva alone (in his mild five-faced and ten-armed Sadāśiva form), worshipped without his consort. The rest of the Mantramārga, which, as we shall see, has been variously classified by the Śaivas, comprises texts that teach cults with a Śākta-Śaiva orientation, whose deities are generally more ferocious in character and who for the most part differ from the Siddhānta's lacto-vegetarian Sadāśiva by requiring offerings such as meat and alcoholic liquor. They are principally the following:

1. the four goddesses Jayā, Vijayā, Ajitā (also called Jayantī), and Aparājitā (with their brother Tumburu);
2. Svacchandabhairava and his consort (Aghoreśvarī, Bhairavī);
3. Kapālīśabhairava and his consort Aghorī (Caṇḍā Kāpālinī);
4. the triad of the goddesses Parā, Parāparā, and Aparā, with or without their Bhairava consorts; and
5. Kālasaṃkarṣaṇī (Kālī) and her many variants.

In the texts of all but the first of these cults we find to a greater or lesser extent elements of the cremation ground practices found in Atimārga II and III, practices lacking in the Saiddhāntika scriptures with the exception of the very early *Niśvāsa* corpus, in which the polarization of the Saiddhāntika and non-Saiddhāntika traditions seems not yet to have emerged.

With these non-Saiddhāntika works Śaiva accounts of the scriptural literature also group texts known as the Gāruḍatantras and Bhūtatantras concerned with therapeutic and exorcistic procedures, which invoke such wrathful Rudra forms as Nīlakaṇṭha, Khaḍgarāvaṇa, Lohaka, Krodheśvara, Devatrāsa, Aghora, and Jvareśvara.

In addition to texts of these traditions we have the *Netra* (also called *Amṛteśavidhāna* and *Mṛtyujit*), which teaches the cult of Amṛteśvarabhairava and Amṛtalakṣmī. This text, which does not appear in any early account of the Śaiva canon and was produced in Kashmir between circa 700 and 850 CE, probably after 800, overrides the distinctions between the various branches of the Mantramārga listed here and that between the Mantramārga and the Kulamārga by propagating a form of worship for use by royal officiants that can be inflected as required to take on the character of any of these divisions and indeed of others outside Śaivism.

The texts of the non-Saiddhāntika traditions for the most part do not enter the territory of worship performed in temples for the public good, their cults being mostly conceived as courses of propitiatory worship to be undertaken by individuals in the private domain for the benefit of none but themselves or designated beneficiaries. Moreover, although the scriptures of the Siddhānta taught rituals for the accomplishment of supernatural effects, it was the non-Saiddhāntika scriptures that provided the most elaborate accounts of such rituals; and the ferocious character of many of their deities no doubt rendered them particularly appealing to royal and other clients eager to invest in supernatural assistance against enemies and calamities. As a result we may say that in the Mantramārga's engagement with society rather than in the domain of personal religion the Siddhānta came to operate principally in the fields of regular piety, state legitimation, and social stability, aspiring to subsume and preserve the Brahmanical socio-religious order and therefore tending to free itself of the countercultural elements of its atimargic antecedents, while the non-Saiddhāntika Śākta-Śaiva systems, which maintained and developed those elements, came to the fore in the domain of rituals commissioned to avert danger in response to particular events or as regular, institutionalized programmes of state protection.

This duality of function is not readily observed by reading the insiders' texts, since these belong to one or other of the divisions and all claim to be offering the same goals. But it can be detected not only in the greater emphasis on rituals for supernatural effects in the non-Saiddhāntika corpus but also, for example, in the ruling of the Saiddhāntika *Mṛgendra* that a person may inflect his worship to accomplish supernatural effects by propitiating Śiva in one or other of the secondary aspects of Sadāśiva considered to be the sources of the non-Saiddhāntika traditions, in the Saiddhāntika *Kālottara*'s brief account of how one may use the Saiddhāntika Mantra of the *Kālottara* system in non-Saiddhāntika Sādhanas to attain supernatural effects by propitiating either Bhairava and the Mothers (*mātṛkā*) or Tumburu and the Four Sisters (*bhāgini*), that is to say, the deities of the Dakṣiṇa or Vāma streams respectively, and in a passage in the anonymous commentary on the Saiddhāntika *Śataratnasaṃgraha* which distinguishes between the Siddhānta and the other four streams by saying that the first bestows liberation and the others the counteracting of poisons (by means of the Gāruḍatantras), the exorcising of dangerous spirits (by means of the Bhūtatantras), the subjecting of others to one's will (by means of the Vāmatantras), and the destruction of enemies (by means of the Dakṣiṇatantras, also called Bhairavatantras).

This same duality can be detected in the *Uttarārdha* of the Śaiva *Liṅgapurāṇa*. For that text in spite of its claim to be a Purāṇa covers Saiddhāntika worship as the norm and adds Bhairava-centered and Śākta rituals specifically for the destruction of the king's enemies and the promoting of his victory in battle. Other examples of the role of the non-Saiddhāntika traditions in this domain are the cult of Bhadrakālī for the king's success in war seen in the *Āṅgirasakalpa* corpus of the Paippalādins of Orissa, the South Indian Mātṛtantra tradition, and the cult of Tumburu and his Sisters established for state protection in Cambodia early 9th century. We may compare in this regard the commissioning by kings in the Brahmanical domain both of status-enhancing Śrauta ceremonies and of atharvavedic rituals performed by specialists in the office of the royal chaplain for the warding off of dangers of all kinds from the royal household and the kingdom.

Nonetheless, however great the divergence between the Saiddhāntika and non-Saiddhāntika cults of the Mantramārga in terms of their primary function or emphasis, they are essentially variants of a single ritual system.

Classifications of the Mantramārga's Scriptures

Five Streams (*srotas*)

Of the classifications of the Mantramārga's scriptures found in works within it the earliest and most comprehensive divides it into five streams of revelation held to have come forth from the mouths of the five faces of Sadāśiva: the scriptures of the Siddhānta, divided artificially into two subcanons (the 10 Śivabhedas and the 18 Rudrabhedas) from the upper and upward-gazing Īśāna face – this then is a Saiddhāntika classification – and those of the non-Saiddhāntika systems from the four faces below, which look towards the cardinal directions: the Vāmatantras, teaching the cult of the four Sisters and their brother Tumburu from the north/left-facing mild Vāmadeva face, the Dakṣiṇatantras, teaching cults of Bhairavas and goddesses from the south/right-facing ferocious Aghora face, the Gāruḍatantras from the front/east-facing Tatpuruṣa face, and the Bhūtatantras from the rear/west-facing face of Sadyojāta. We find this classificatory schema in the *Śrīkaṇṭhī-Srotobheda* with long lists of the texts and subtexts in each category, in a shorter passage prefixed to a manuscript of the *Jñānapañcāśikā*, also seen in Vairocana's *Lakṣaṇasaṃgraha*, giving only the primary texts in each division, in the *Mṛgendra*, mentioning only one text as an example of each stream, and in a number of other Saiddhāntika sources, both scriptural and exegetical, that merely mention the classification and emphasise the superiority of the Siddhānta that it articulates.

The Three Streams: Siddhānta, Vāma, Dakṣiṇa

In the non-Saiddhāntika scripture *Picumata*, also called *Brahmayāmala*, we encounter a modification of this classification evidently designed to express the view that the non-Saiddhāntika traditions are superior to the Saiddhāntika and to push the Gāruḍatantras and Bhūtatantras to the margin. It divides the Śaiva scriptures into three principal streams, central (*madhyama*), left (*vāma*) and right (*dakṣiṇa*), as emanations of three corresponding powers of the deity, termed Madhyamā, Vāmā, and Dakṣiṇā, in ascending order, assigning the Siddhāntatantras to the first, the Vāmatantras to the second, and the Dakṣiṇatantras, among which it counts itself, to the third. Ascent through this hierarchy is compared to the process of preparing rice. The system of the Śivabhedas and Rudrabhedas, that it to say, the Siddhānta, is likened to the removing of the husks (*tuṣa*) from the grains, that of the Vāmatantras to the cleaning of the grains by the removing of the bran (*kambūka*), and that of the Dakṣiṇatantras to the cooking of the pure white grains that remain. The Gāruḍatantras and Bhūtatantras, together with a number of other tantric systems, including the Vaiṣṇava → Pañcarātra, are assigned to what it calls the lower stream (*adhaḥsrotas*).

Siddhāntatantras and Bhairavatantras

Later classifications, of which there are two, submerge the Vāma within the Dakṣiṇa and reflect, I propose, a time when the former had become marginal, overtaken and engulfed by the forms of Śākta-Śaiva observance found in the Dakṣiṇatantras that carried forward the tradition of Atimārga III. Both classifications, like that of the *Picumata*, leave the Bhūtatantras and Gāruḍatantras out of their account, no doubt for the same reason. The first presents the canon in terms of a simple dichotomy between Saiddhāntika and non-Saiddhāntika Tantras, the former comprising ten Śivatantras, 18 Rudratantras, and satellites of these, and the latter listed with evident artificiality as the 64 Bhairavatantras, divided into eight ogdoads. Vāmatantras are found among the 64 listed in this classification, but the great majority are, or appear to be, works of Dakṣina character.

Mantrapīṭha and Vidyāpīṭha

The second classification, while recognizing this basic dichotomy, subdivides the non-Saiddhāntika category into Bhairava-centered and Goddess-centered texts in works that belong to the latter subcategory. It articulates, then, a Śākta perspective on the canon. It divides the non-Saiddhāntika scriptures, excluding the Bhūtatantras and Gāruḍatantras, into two collections termed Pīṭhas: the Mantrapīṭha for the Bhairava-centered tradition and the Vidyāpīṭha for the Goddess-centered. Texts assigned to the Vidyāpīṭha generally refer to themselves in their colophons as belonging to the Vidyāpīṭha within the Bhairava stream (*bhairavasrotas*), the latter term evidently denoting the whole non-Saiddhāntika corpus other than the Gāruḍatantras and Bhūtatantras.

The Mantrapīṭha is dominated by the *Svacchanda*, also known as the *Lalitasvacchanda*, the Tantra of the cult of Svacchandabhairava and his consort Aghoreśvarī. This work is the preeminent text of this category in the scriptural accounts. It also the only one that has come down to us in its entirety. The only other works of this category that have reached us through citation or the incorporation of passages in compendia are its satellites: the *Aghoreśvarīsvacchanda*, the *Dvādaśasāhasra/Mantrapīṭhasvacchanda*, and the *Rasasvacchanda*.

The importance of the *Svacchanda* is evident (1) from the fact that it has come down us in manuscripts in widely separated parts of the subcontinent, namely the Kathmandu Valley, Kashmir, and Tamil Nadu, (2) from the survival of various Paddhatis for worship and initiation based on it in the Kathmandu Valley, and, above all, in Kashmir, where it became, with the *Netra*, the principal basis of the rituals of the region's Śaivas down to recent times, and (3) from the the fact that it is the unacknowledged source of much of the wording and content of the prescription of the ritual of Saiddhāntika initiation set out by Bhojadeva in his influential *Siddhāntasārapaddhati*, stripped, of course, of all non-Saiddhāntika *mantras* and deities, these being replaced by those of the Saiddhāntika *Kālottara*.

The Vidyāpīṭha is divided into three subcollections in the only known account of it, which is contained in the first *ṣaṭka* of the *Jayadrathayāmala*: the Vāmatantras, Yāmalatantras, and Śaktitantras. The first of these comprises, according to that source, three lead texts: the *Nayottara*, the *Mahāraudra*, and the *Mahāsaṃmohana*. The *Picumata* also recognizes three Tantras in this category: the *Saṃmoha*, the *Nayottara*, and the *Śaukra*. The Cambodian Sdok Kak Thom inscription of 1052 names four Vāma scriptures: the *Śiraścheda*, the *Vināśikha* (*sic* for *Vīṇāśikha*), the *Saṃmoha*, and the *Nayottara*, and implies by referring to them as the four mouths of the four-faced deity Tumburu that they were understood to constitute a complete canon, at least of the tradition's core texts.

Of these texts we now have only the *Vīṇāśikha*, which reaches us in an undated palm-leaf manuscript in a proto-Bengali hand of the 12th or 13th century. Since the *Vīṇāśikha* refers to the *Saṃmohana/Mahāsaṃmohana*, *Nayottara*, and *Śiraścheda* as its antecedents, we learn that it is the most recent of the four texts and that its absence from the Vāma canons of the *Jayadrathayāmala* and *Picumata* may be because it was not in existence when their accounts of the Śaiva revealed literature were drawn up.

We may safely assume that *Saṃmoha*, *Saṃmohana*, and *Mahāsaṃmohana* are variant titles of one and the same work. As for the *Śiraścheda*, the *Jayadrathayāmala* claims this as another name for itself. So might not this, or rather its first *ṣaṭka*, which is the original text to which the three subsequent *ṣaṭka*s were added, be the Vāmatantra referred to by the Sdok Kak Thom inscription and the *Vīṇāśikha*? The first *ṣaṭka* does refer to itself as a Vāma text. But this claim is hardly supported by its contents. For though there are some Vāma elements in the first *ṣaṭka* they are incidental and subordinated within a Dakṣiṇa framework. At best we can accept the *ṣaṭka*'s own characterization of itself in its listing of the Vidyāpīṭha's lead texts as a Vāma-Dakṣiṇa hybrid. Moreover, that same account speaks of the original *Śiraścheda* revelation's having split into two transmissions of which the available work represents only one. This may well have been intended to account for the existence of another, purely Vāma *Śiraścheda*, now lost.

We have, then, only one of the core scriptures of the Vāma canon. In addition we have testimony of a lost work whose title may tentatively be reconstructed as *Devītantrasadbhāva* in the form of a two-folio fragment of a birchbark manuscript, possibly from as early as the mid-6th century, containing a précis of this text, to be discussed under the heading of Vāma exegesis, and also an incomplete 11th-century Nepalese manuscript of the *Siddhayantrārṇava* (The Ocean of Empowered *Yantras*), which attributes itself to the *Umātilaka* of the *Saṃmohana* cycle.

The other two text groups in the Vidyāpīṭha are the Yāmalatantras and Śaktitantras. The lead texts of the first are said by the *Jayadrathayāmala* to be five: *Rudrayāmala, Brahmayāmala, Viṣṇuyāmala, Skandayāmala*, and *Umāyāmala*. The treatment of these in the *Jayadrathayāmala* makes it clear that the *Brahmayāmala* was the preeminent work of this class; and indeed it is this alone that has reached us intact, as a work of about 12,000 verses variously entitled *Brahmayāmala*, *Picumata*, and *Ucchuṣma*, surviving in a well-preserved Nepalese palm-leaf manuscript dated in 1052. We also have three of its satellite texts: the *Mahābhairavamaṅgalā*, the *Piṅgalāmata*, and the *Matasāra*, which teaches a cult of the same pantheon as the *Picumata* but with additions that are its signature.

The *Brahmayāmala* is strongly Kāpālika in character, carrying forward into the Mantramārga the antinomian and sanguinary culture of Atimārga III; and the relative antiquity of this current of mantramargic Śaivism is evident in many details of its doctrines and prescriptions. As to how old it is, the earliest verifiable citations of the work are found in the *Tantrāloka* of → Abhinavagupta, who was active in Kashmir around the late 10th and early 11th centuries CE; but it is mentioned indirectly, together with the *Viṣṇuyāmala* and *Rudrayāmala* in the hymn *Bhairavīvardhamānaka* that survives in a codex of 819 CE, and the earliest and probably original *Skandapurāṇa* of the 6th or early 7th century lists seven Mātṛtantras with *-yāmala* titles, beginning with the *Brahmayāmala*, all but two of which are named in accounts of the Yāmalatantras seen in our mantramargic sources.

Connected with this early *Brahmayāmala* are two texts under this title surviving in South India. These claim to be part of the *Brahmayāmala* and indeed are derived from it to the extent that they share its core pantheon and an number of other formal features; but they differ from it radically in that they prescribe a regular cult of Cāmuṇḍā/Bhadrakālī and the seven Mothers to be conducted before fixed idols in temples by non-Brahman priests of the Pāraśava caste for the protection of the state and its subjects and the enhancement of royal power. The antiquity of this South Indian variant of what was originally a purely private form of worship undertaken by individual initiates of any caste for their own benefit alone cannot be determined from the surviving manuscripts, but the textual prescriptions of the cult are closely reflected in two Tamil inscriptions that set out the provisions for the funding of the temple of the goddess Kolārammā at Kolar (Kolār) in Nolambavadi (Noḷambavāḍi), detailing the yearly allowances for the staff, who include a teacher of grammar and Yāmala, the deities, and the various ceremonies. The first is dated in the second regnal year of Kō-Rājakesarivarma, alias Rājendracoladeva (Kulottuṅga I), that is to say, in 1071/1072. The second is undated but appears to be the continuation of the first, recording the same witnesses to its provisions.

The third subcollection, that of the Śaktitantras, is said by the *Jayadrathayāmala* to contain seven lead texts: the *Sarvavīrasamāyoga*, the *Siddhayogeśvarīmata*, the *Pañcāmṛta*, the *Viśvādya*, the *Yoginījālaśaṃvara*, the *Vidyābheda*, and the *Śiraccheda*. Of these, two have reached us: (1) the *Siddhayogeśvarīmata*, in what is evidently a much shorter redaction that that which is frequently quoted in the Kashmirian exegetical literature, and (2) the *Śiraccheda*, otherwise known as the *Jayadrathayāmala*, at this stage only the work that would later be the first of four *ṣaṭka*s passing under this title.

These two are at the base of the other two traditions that are well-represented in our surviving sources. The first, taught in the former, is the cult of the goddesses Parā, Parāparā, and Aparā. This gave rise to the *Mālinīvijayottara*, which became the base scripture of the Śākta system known as the Trika, and is part of a larger corpus of scriptures that also includes the *Tantrasadbhāva* and, known for the most part only through citations and other testimonia, the *Triśirobhairava*, the *Devyāyāmala*, the *Trikakularatnamālā*, the *Trikasadbhāva*, the *Trikasāra*, the *Yogasaṃcāra*, the *Bhairavakula*, and the *Vīrāvalī*. In addition we have chapters from three other texts of this tradition assigned in their colophons to (the cycle of) the *Siddhayogeśvarīmata* in Hṛdayaśiva's *Prāyaścittasamuccaya*: the *Bījabheda*, the *Bhairavodyāna*, and the *Trikasārottara*. We also have the *Parātriṃśikā/Parātrīśikā* or *Anuttaratriṃśikā*, a short work teaching an essentialized form of Trika worship that is directed to the goddess Parā alone, a system also known as the Anuttara or Parākrama.

Finally, we have the *Vijñānabhairava*. This scripture is concerned entirely with the outlining of a 112 meditation exercises, with one verse for each, these being referred to as *nistaraṅgopadeśa* (teachings concerning the Waveless). It does not engage with the specifics of tantric ritual in a manner that would enable us to conclude that it is a work of the Trika or some other ritual tradition. But its Trika background is apparent from verses in which this transcendence of ritual is formulated as the transcendence of the Trika's ritual. This is, in other words, a Trika work that advocates practices that are free of the specifics of its *mantra* deities.

The second surviving Śaktitantra tradition, taught in the *Jayadrathayāmala*, also called *Tantrarāja* and *Tantrarājabhaṭṭāraka*, is that of the cult of the goddess Kālasaṃkarṣaṇī or Kālī. This, in its expanded form created by the addition of three subsequent *ṣaṭka*s, probably in Kashmir, adds a vast array of texts that prescibe the procedure to be followed for the propitiation of variant forms of this goddess and introduces material closely related to the Kaula tradition of Kālī worship known as the Kālīkula, Krama, Mahānaya, Mahārtha, or Devīnaya, whose scriptural sources will be covered below under the literature of the Kulamārga.

As for the Gāruḍatantras and Bhūtatantras, pushed into the background by the non-Saiddhāntika classificatory systems, we have lists of titles both in the passage prefixed to a manuscript of the *Jñānapañcāśikā* and seen in Vairocana's *Lakṣaṇasaṃgraha* and, with lists of subtexts, in the *Śrīkaṇṭhī-Srotobheda*; but nearly all of this extensive canon seems not to have reached us, the only survivors being two texts in Nepalese palm-leaf manuscripts that claim to be parts of the *Trottala*, also known as the *Tottala*, *Trotula*, or *Totula*, a work that appears in the lists of the primary Gāruḍatantras and has been quoted by the Kashmirian scholar Kṣemarāja. These are the *Tvaritāmūlasūtra* and the *Tvaritājñānakalpa*. We also have the *Kriyākālaguṇottara*. This is not listed in the canonical accounts, but it contains material pertaining to both these streams, has been quoted by Kṣemarāja in his *Netroddyota*, and reaches us complete in a number of Nepalese manuscripts, the earliest penned in 1184/1185 for the preceptor of a feudatory ruler in the kingdom of Dhavalasrota in the west of Nepal. The assumption that its exorcistic sections draw on our lost Bhūtatantras is supported by the fact that it includes a *Khaḍgarāvaṇakalpa* and a *Caṇḍāsidhārakalpa*, sections devoted to the rites of the Rudras Khaḍgarāvaṇa and Caṇḍāsidhāra. For Tantras bearing the names of these *mantra* deities are found in the canonical lists. There is evidence of the same kind of its having drawn on the lost Gāruḍatantras. For it also contains a *Devatrāsakalpa* and there is a *Devatrāsatantra* among the listed scriptures of that class.

In addition we have in other Śaiva scriptural sources, particularly the *Jayadrathayāmala*, a quantity of Gāruḍa material, that is to say, prescriptions whose purpose is devenomation and the control of snakes, both actual snakes and the mythical → *nāga*s, and through the latter the control of rainfall, believed to lie in their power, and hence the protection of crops. The working of such material into the major Tantras may account at least in part for the atrophy of the original sources.

The Non-Saiddhāntika Mantramārga's Exegesis

The exegetical literature on the non-Saiddhāntika Tantras may be presented most aptly within the categories given by the *Jayadrathayāmala*, since it is this perception of the components of the Śaiva revelation that the authors of this literature adopted, that is to say, in terms of the dichotomy between the Bhairava-centered Mantrapīṭha and the Devī-centered Vidyāpīṭha, and within the latter between the Tantras of the Vāma stream, the Yāmalatantras, and the Śaktitantras, and within the last, between the Trika and the cult of Kālasaṃkarṣaṇī taught in the *Jayadrathayāmala* itself.

On the *Svacchanda*, the principal scripture of the Mantrapīṭha, we have an extensive and exhaustive commentary (*Svacchandoddyota*) composed by the Kashmirian Kṣemarāja (*fl.* c. 1000–1050). He refers to an earlier commentary on the text by Rājānaka Bhullaka, another Kashmirian, as his title Rājānaka reveals. No manuscript of his work has reached us. We have only its title – Kṣemarāja refers to it as *Bṛhaṭṭīkā* (Long Commentary) – and some of its interpretations, which Kṣemarāja cites to reject. We also have Kṣemarāja's commentary on the *Netra*, which though not explicitly claimed for the Mantrapīṭha – indeed this Tantra is mentioned to my knowledge in no early account of the Śaiva canon – may nonetheless be considered as an auxiliary text of that division.

We have in addition a substantial body of Kashmirian Paddhatis based on either or both of these two Tantras, though they also incorporate ancillary material from Saiddhāntika and Śākta sources. Notable among these are the *Śiṣyasaṃskārapaddhati* for the neophyte's initiation (*samayadīkṣā*), the *Kalādīkṣāpaddhati*, originally composed by the Kashmirian Guru Manodadatta/Manoda in 1335/1336 and subsequently expanded with the development of somewhat divergent versions down to at least the 17th century, for the full initiations (*nirvāṇadīkṣā* and *sādhakadīkṣā*) and consecrations to office (*ācāryābhiṣeka, sādhakābhiṣeka,* and Śaiva *rājyābhiṣeka*), the anonymous *Agnikāryapaddhati* in full and abbreviated versions for the fire sacrifice, the *Śivanirvāṇapaddhati* for cremation, usually anonymous but sometimes attributed to a *guru* called Manohara, and, commonly transmitted with the last, Paddhatis covering the various rituals that follow cremation, from the offerings of the first ten days to the annual *śrāddha*. Based on the *Netra* we have in the *Gurupustikā/Gurupustaka* of Rājānaka Śitikaṇṭha, a Kashmirian who was active circa 1375–1425, a comprehensive Paddhati, covering regular worship, penances, initiation, consecration of officiants, and installation. In the domain of the regular obligatory worship of initiates we have a Paddhati for the worship of Svacchandabhairava, and, representing a variant tradition, an anonymous Paddhati setting out Śaiva worship both regular (*nityapūjā*) and on special occasions (*naimittikapūjā*) such as the annual *śivarātri* festival, the first centered on Amṛteśabhairava (Netrabhaṭṭāraka) and the second on Sakalasvacchanda, his consort Aghoresvarī, and Niṣkalasvacchanda drawn from the *Svacchanda*, culminating in the worship of a new form not found there, namely Mahāsvacchandabhairava, which has its own, postclassical scripture, the *Vṛddhasvacchanda*, and which combines in one seven-faced and thirty-six-armed figure not only Svacchandabhairava but also the Nārasiṃha and Vārāha faces of the trademark Vaikuṇṭha icon of Kashmirian Pāñcarātrika Vaiṣṇavism, the face of the sun (Kulamārtaṇḍabhairava) representing the Saura tradition, and the face of Heruka embodying the Buddhism of the Yoginītantras, an innovation not found in any of the other Kashmirian Paddhatis mentioned here.

Nepal too has preserved *Svacchanda*-based Paddhatis for the worship of Svacchandabhairava, notably the *Svacchandadevārcanavidhi* and *Svacchandadevalakṣahomayāga*, and *Netra*-based Paddhatis for the worship of Amṛteśvarabhairava: the *Apratihatamahādīkṣāsuṭippaṇaka*, also called *Netroddyota*, of Viśveśvara, probably of the 12th century, and the *Amṛteśvarapūjana* composed by the Nepalese king Abhayamalla (r. 1216–1255). Other relevant manuscripts in this category are the *Amṛteśvarapūjāgnikāryavidhāna*, the *Amṛtasūryapūjāvidhi* with drawings of the deities, and the *Pūjākāṇḍa*, which contains an *Amṛtabhairavārcanavidhi* penned in 1277/1278, an *Amṛtīśabhairavabhaṭṭārakāhnikavidhi*, and an *Amṛtasūryārcanavidhi*.

Within the Vidyāpīṭha we have no exegetical material on the scriptures of its Vāma division other than the fragment already mentioned, the first two folios of a work that we may call **Devītantrasadbhāvasāra* – its title is not contained in the surviving portion – because it claims at its beginning to be a precis in the *āryā* meter of the key parts (*sāra*) of what it calls *devīnāṃ tantrasadbhāvam* ("the essence of the Tantras of the goddesses"). The latter appears to have been a scriptural work, since our fragment describes it as having been received from Śiva by a sage who is described as the adornment of the line of Atri and is therefore probably Durvāsas, the son of Atri, who is widely encountered in the role of the intermediary through whom Śiva's teachings have reached mankind. The identification of the text as a work in the Vāma tradition is secured by its subject matter, since that is the attaining of supernatural effects (*siddhi*) through the correct formation and modification of the *mantra*s of Tumburu, his four Sisters, and the secondary deities of that pantheon of worship. Though our text claims to be only a precis, and indeed preserves the form of its source to the extent that it begins after the opening verses in the manner of scripture as a dialogue in which Śiva teaches in response to the sage's enquiry, its declaration of intent in the opening verses and the choice of the *āryā* meter both suggest that this work wished to be seen as a product of human learning rather than as scripture. This work reaches us from a very early period in the development of the Mantramārga. For the two birchbark folios, which were preserved against all odds by inclusion in the famous mass of Buddhist manuscripts, mostly fragmentary, discovered in 1931 by shepherds in a ruined *stūpa* near Gilgit in the Gilgit-Baltistan territory of Pakistan, are written in an early variety of the Kashmirian script whose archaic features suggest that it may be as early as the mid-6th century CE. In that case it is older by three centuries than what are otherwise our oldest tantric Śaiva manuscripts, those that have survived from the 9th century in Nepal: *Niśvāsatattvasaṃhitā, Sarvajñānottara, Pārameśvara*, and *Mahābhairavamaṅgalā*.

Up to the 8th century at least this tradition enjoyed considerable popularity in the Indian subcontinent, and also in Southeast Asia, where it may have lingered for several centuries. We can infer this popularity from a wide range of evidence found in Buddhist, Jaina, and Brahmanical textual sources, and also, in the case of Southeast Asia, in inscriptions. However, evidence from the 10th century and after suggests that by then the Vāma system had faded from view. The surviving works of the Śaiva exegetes of this period make no references to its primary texts in their citation-rich works; and this silence is particularly striking in the case of the digests of Hṛdayaśiva and Rājānaka Takṣakavarta. The former's *Prāyaścittasamuccaya* draws extensively on the whole range of the non-Saiddhāntika Mantramārga, both Mantrapīṭha and Vidyāpīṭha, but includes no Vāma text. The same applies to Takṣakavarta's *Nityādisaṃgraha*, except that he has included a long passage from a *Vīṇāśikhottara*, which is a Vāma text if we may judge from its title alone, though it contains nothing that proves or indicates that affiliation. In his detailed presentation of scriptural sources bearing on the regular duties of initiates he illuminates only worship that follows the Siddhānta, the *Svacchanda*, or the *Netra*. Nor to my knowledge have any of the South Indian authors from the 11th century onwards cited Vāma scripture. The same absence is seen in the Saiddhāntika Paddhati *Vimalāvatī* of the east Indian Vimalaśiva (1101/1102), although he, like the Saiddhāntika Hṛdayaśiva, has cited numerous non-Saiddhāntika works of the Mantrapīṭha, the Vidyāpīṭha, and the Kulamārga.

The Yāmala division of the Vidyāpīṭha seems also to have fared poorly in the times of our exegetes, though not as poorly as the Vāmatantras. We have no commentary on the *Brahmayāmala*, and no report of one in our sources. But the text was still well known around the turn of the 1st and 2nd millennia, since it is cited quite frequently by Abhinavagupta. Moreover, its deities were sufficiently important in Kashmir to enter, albeit as a minor element, the region's *Svacchanda*-based Paddhatis. Its chief goddess Caṇḍā Kāpālinī is included among the recipents of oblations in the *Agnikāryapaddhati* and the *Śivarātripūjāpaddhati*; and she is worshipped with her four subordinates Raktā, Karālā, Caṇḍākṣī, and Mahocchuṣmā and their attendants (*dūtī*s) Karālī, Danturā, Bhīmavaktrā, and Mahābalā as the deities of the *śrāddha* lamp in the Kashmirian Śaivas' *śivadīpaśrāddha*.

The *Brahmayāmala* materials derived from this source whose context is the South Indian tradition of temple-based Yāmala worship have also reached us without a commentary. However, we do have the *Mātṛsadbhāva*, an explanatory work of professed human authorship that sets out to provide a summary account of the rituals of this tradition as found in various Yāmala texts, collating their teachings, which, we are told, are not complete in any one of these sources, to present a comprehensive, ordered account of the cult of the Mothers. When compared to the scriptural texts of this tradition the *Mātṛsadbhāva* differs primarily not only in its lucid and generally correct Sanskrit but also in its extensive expurgation of most of the strongly Kāpālika elements of this tradition while in spite of this recalling the tradition's roots in Atimārga III by, for example, describing the officiant as "one who has mastered the Somasiddhānta." The expurgation of counter-Brahmanical elements and the fact that it survives in Kerala and is cited in the Keralan tantric Paddhati literature inclines me to think that the work was produced in that region among the Nambūtiri Brahmans. As for its date, I can say at present only that it predates the 15th-century Keralan author Śaṅkaran Nambūtiri, since he refers to it as the principal authority for the Keralan tradition of the worship of the Mothers accompanying Cāmuṇḍā/Bhadrakālī as the slayer of the *daitya* Ruru, Rurujit. However, the text or one or more of the lost Yāmala texts on which it draws, has a wider geographical horizon. For it relates the myth of the conquest of the *daitya* enemies of the gods by Cāmuṇḍā/Karṇamoṭī and the other Mothers at Koṭivarṣa (Kotivarsha) in the far north of Bengal, that of the origin of its sacred Śūlakuṇḍa ("Pool of the Trident") and the drinking of its water, the granting of the boon to the *mātṛka*s as the reward for their victory that those who worship them with devotion will attain whatever *siddhi* they desire and salvation at death, and the presence there of Śiva together with the Mothers as the Bhairava Hetukeśvara. This material, probably in its original form, appears in the *Skandapurāṇa* of the 6th or early 7th century in its account of how Cāmuṇḍā/Bahumāṃsā and the other Mothers came to be worshipped with the rites of the Yāmalatantras. The memory of Koṭivarṣa as the source of the tradition is also embedded in the ritual system. For when the Śākta sacred sites are installed one by one in vases on the site of worship Koṭivarṣa is to be in the central vase surrounded in the directions by Prayāga (Prayag) and the rest.

In the manuscript in which I have accessed this text the *Mātṛsadbhāva* is followed by a *Balikalpa*, a prose Paddhati that sets out the procedure for the making of *bali* offerings in a temple of the goddess established following this tradition. There are certainly other Keralan materials of this kind awaiting recognition or close study, such as the *Rurujidvidhānapūjāpaddhati* governing the procedures for the cult of Cāmuṇḍā and the Mothers and the already published Paddhati of that cult that occupies *paṭala*s 7–9 of the *Śeṣasamuccaya* and its autocommentary composed by Śaṅkaran Nambūtiri in the 15th century.

As for exegesis in the Śaktitantra division of the Vidyapīṭha, we have an abundance in the case of the Trika, the system of worship represented by the *Siddhayogeśvarīmata* in the *Jayadrathayāmala*'s list of primary scriptures (*mūlasūtra*). We have no commentary on that work itself. But on the *Mālinīvijayottara*, which rightly places itself in the cycle of that text, we have in the *Tantrāloka, Mālinīślokavārttika*, and *Tantrasāra* of the Kashmirian Abhinavagupta, active circa 975–1025 CE, what is undoubtedly the most extensive, elaborate, intellectually sophisticated, and influential exegesis in the Śaiva literature. Though these works are formally exegesis of the *Mālinīvijayottara* alone they develop on that base a comprehensive Śākta Śaivism that subsumes within itself the entire Mantramārga, both Saiddhāntika and non-Saiddhāntika, and grounds this complex both in the Kulamārga, drawing strongly on the Kālī-focused form of that tradition known as the Krama, and in the doctrine of dynamic nondual consciousness expounded philosophically by Somānanda, Utpaladeva, and Abhinavagupta himself. We also have an elaborate commentary (*vivaraṇa*) by Abhinavagupta on the *Parātriṃśikā*, the scripture of the Trika subsystem known as the Parākrama or Anuttara. But that lies in the domain of the Kulamārga.

The Trika system expounded in the *Tantrāloka* had a great impact on Śākta-Śaiva theory in Kashmir and throughout the subcontinent in subsequent centuries, but it seems not to have put down deep roots in Kashmir as a system of ritual-based observance. Apart from the vast running commentary of Rājānaka Jayaratha on the whole of this text, written in Kashmir in the 13th century, we have no other Trika works from that region; and even this commentary suggests that its author was not an initiate in the Trika as a living system of rituals, his own ritual expertise being rather in the cult of the goddess Tripurasundarī, to which we shall return. The *Kalādīkṣāpaddhati* that guided Śaiva initiation in Kashmir until, in the first quarter of the 20th century, that ceremony ceased to be performed, recognizes that some initiands passing through its *Svacchanda*-based ceremonies retained a connection with the Trika, probably through family tradition, and so ordains that in their case the officiant should insert during the fire sacrifice some additional oblations for the Trika's principal *mantra* deities; but it is a striking fact that this is one of the very rare evidences of Trika ritual practice in Kashmir. Among the many Kashmirian manuscripts that have reached us I have encountered no Paddhati for the regular worship or initiation ceremonies of this tradition.

On the *Vijñānabhairava*, the Trika scripture concerned with meditation practices, there was a commentary by Abhinavagupta's pupil Kṣemarāja, of which only the commentary on the introductory 23 verses is known to have reached us. Śivopadhyāya, a Kashmirian author writing during the governorship of Sukhajīvana (1753–1762), tells us that he could find no manuscript that contained more and so composed a work in which he added to the surviving portion of Kṣemarāja's work his own commentary on the remaining verses (24–163). We have another commentary (*Vijñānakaumudī*), written on the whole work by the Kashmirian Bhaṭṭāraka Ānanda in 1672, during the time of Akbar.

As for exegesis on the *Jayadrathayāmala*, the other Śaktitantra that has reached us in manuscripts, its huge extent and encyclopaedic character may have discouraged any aspiration to write a running commentary on the whole. Nonetheless some exegesis on the teachings of this Tantra has reached us. We have the *Bhuvanamālinīkalpaviṣamapadavivṛti* of the Kashmirian Śrīvatsa, a commentary on the chapter of the fourth *ṣaṭka* that gives the text for the rites of Bhuvanamālinī, also known as Dīkṣādevī, which served among the

Śaiva officiants of Kashmir as a brief substitute for the elaborate form of *Svacchanda*-based initiation to be adopted in times of hardship or emergency. We also have Nepalese manuscripts of an anonymous *Jayadrathayāmalaprastāramantrasaṃgraha*. This work, probably Kashmirian, comments on and decodes the passages of the work that give the *mantra*s of its numerous deities in encrypted form, covering the whole text, though not exhaustively, and also provides line drawings of some of the encryption diagrams (known as *prastāra*) referred to in the text. The manuscripts that contain this useful manual preface it with the *Tantrarājatantrāvatārastotra*, a hymn to the tradition of this Tantra by one Viśvāvarta, whose name reveals him to have been a Kashmirian. This states the first *ṣaṭka*'s view of its position in the Śaiva canon and adores what it takes to be the principal Kālīs of the four *ṣaṭka*s: Kālasaṃkarṣaṇī in the first, Siddhalakṣmī in the second, the three goddesses, Trailokyaḍāmarā, Matacakreśvarī, and Ghoraghoratarā, in the third, and, in the fourth, Siddhayogeśvarī and the Krama's innermost pantheon of the 13 Kālīs. Finally, a section of Abhinavagupta's *Tantrāloka*, though it is a work of the Trika, is a Paddhati following the *Mādhavakula*, a Kaula text contained in the fourth *ṣaṭka*, though it is not beyond doubt that it was already part of the *Jayadrathayāmala* at that time.

That the text was influential in Kashmir can be seen in the fact that a number of the forms of Kālī the procedure for whose worship it teaches were taken into the *Svacchanda*-based *Agnikāryapaddhati* that guided until recent times the fire sacrifices performed in the major Śaiva ceremonies. In the section of that sacrifice in which goddesses are worshipped with oblations of clarified butter (*devīnām ājyahoma*) we find several of the *Jayadrathayāmala*'s deities, namely Bhuvanamālinī, Pāpāntakāriṇī, Vidyāvidyeśvarī, Vāgbhaveśvarī, Vāgīśī, Siddhalakṣmī, Mantramātṛkā, Mantraḍāmarikā, Saptakoṭīśvarī, Bhāgyādhirohiṇī and Nityākālī. The sections in the Paddhatis devoted to each of these goddesses use verse passages from the *Jayadrathayāmala*'s treatments of their worship as recitation texts for the goddesses' gratification (*tarpaṇaśloka*) when making the oblations to them into the fire, and give their *mantra*s, both the primary (*mūlamantra*) and the six ancillaries (*ṣaḍaṅgas*). We also have a Kashmirian *Jayadrathayāmala*-based Paddhati for the worship of Siddhalakṣmī (*Siddhalakṣmīpūjāpaddhati*) and a so-called *Pratyaṅgirāstotra*, which contains materials on the four *pratyaṅgirās* of the *Jayadrathayāmala*, namely Siddhalakṣmī, Mantramātṛkā, Mantraḍāmarikā, and Saptakoṭīśvarī, giving the *mantra*s, visualizations, and ritual procedure, drawing on this scripture but also going beyond it. Thus its text for the visualization (*dhyāna*) of Mantraḍāmarikā accords with the prescription of the *Mantraḍāmarikāpaṭala* of the third *ṣaṭka* but is an independent composition, and supplements that text by supplying the weapons in four of her sixteen hands, which are unspecified there. In the case of Saptakoṭīśvarī it supplies a visualization verse not found there. These materials exhibit accurate interpretation of the text of the *Jayadrathayāmala*, since while that gives the *mantra*s in encrypted form the Kashmirian Paddhatis report them as they are.

The cults of the *Jayadrathayāmala*'s goddesses were by no means restricted to Kashmir. A detailed view of the geographical range of this tradition, as of most tantric traditions, is not possible from the materials currently known; but we have abundant evidence of the importance of the cult of the goddess Siddhalakṣmī in the kingdoms of the Kathmandu Valley down to modern times, where she is generally referred to with a small inaccuracy as Siddhilakṣmī. She was adopted as a royal deity and her worship, in conjunction with that of Kubjikā, Guhyakālī, and Tripurasundarī, appears in the ritual manuals of the Newars as the constant frame in which other rituals are contained. Moroever, of these royal goddesses, Guhyakālī too is *Jayadrathayāmala*-based to the extent that the goddess and her cult, though not found in the *Jayadrathayāmala*, are very much in its spirit and draw heavily upon it.

As for post-scriptural literature in the traditions of the Gāruḍatantras and Bhūtatantras we have a rich tradition of learned exposition among the Nambūtiri Brahmans of Kerala in the Mantravāda section of, or rather added to, the *Siddhāntasāra* of the Keralan Īśānaśiva and in the *Tantrasārasaṃgraha* or *Nārāyaṇīya* (*nārāyaṇīyo mantravāda*) of Nārāyaṇa of Śivapura (Shivapura) with the commentary *Mantravimarśinī* of Vāsudeva, which owes its title according to its author to the fact that it is a summary (*sārasaṃgraha*) of the teachings of such Tantras as the *Śikhāyoga*, which is one of titles in the canonical lists of the Gāruḍatantras. We have also the *Saṃhitāsāra*, a work in fine Prakrit verse by Śaṅkuka, which, as its title and content declare, claims to have extracted the essentials from the Gāruḍa scriptures, with an anonymous Sanskrit commentary which almost certainly was written by a Kashmirian, probably in the 10th or 11th century, surviving in an undated but probably early 12th-century Nepalese manuscript. The *Yogaratnāvalī* of Śrīkaṇṭhaśambhu, perhaps a Keralan, does the same in Sanskrit for both the Gāruḍatantras and the Bhūtatantras in its first and second chapters respectively.

The Kulamārga

As for the Kulamārga, its texts share with those of the non-Saiddhāntika Mantramārga the counter-Brahmanical character of its offerings and observances. But it is more extreme in this regard and also departs markedly by following a distinct ritual system, which was inherited, I propose, with some modifications and additions, from the Kāpālika Atimārga III. It is found both in its own independent texts (the Kulaśāstras), such as the *Kulapañcāśikā*, the *Kulasāra*, the *Kulānanda*, the *Kaulajñānanirṇaya*, and the *Timirodghāṭana*, and within texts of Śākta orientation that are assigned to the Mantramārga such as the *Mālinīvijayottara* and the second, third, and fourth *ṣaṭka*s of the *Jayadrathayāmala*, so that in such traditions we are offered two distinct cults of their deities, one following the Mantramārga and the other, seen as more elevated, following the Kulamārga. In the latter, instead of the elaborate and time-consuming process of initiation through offerings into a consecrated fire (*hautrī dīkṣā*) seen throughout the Mantramārga, we see initiation through → possession (*āveśa*) by the goddess and the consumption of "impure" sacramental substances (*caruprāśana*, *vīrapāna*). We also find sexual intercourse with a consecrated consort (*dūtī*) as a central element of private worship, sanguinary sacrifices, and collective orgiastic rites celebrated by assemblies of initiates and women of low caste. The proposition that the essentials of this ritual system were carried forward from the Kāpālika tradition of the Somasiddhānta (Atimārga III) must be argued in detail elsewhere. Here I merely point out that the salient features of the latter show a marked similarity between the two traditions, setting them apart from the rest of Śaivism. These features are in brief:

1. erotic ritual with a female companion;
2. sanguinary practices for the propitiation of the fierce gods Mahābhairava/Bhairava and Cāmuṇḍā;
3. the notion that supernatural powers may be attained through the extraction by yogic means of the vital essences of living beings;
4. initiation through the consumption of consecrated liquor; and
5. the centrality of states of possession.

Here we may seem to be in the presence of a purely personal, largely secret, and mystical cult. But, as in the cults of the non-Saiddhāntika Mantramārga, the public value of this form of Śaivism for the protection of society and the state is also stressed.

The texts of the Kulamārga, also called the Kula teaching (Kulaśāsana, Kulāmnāya, and the like), or simply the Kula, were focused on the propitiation of the goddess Kuleśvarī with or without Bhairava (Kuleśvara) surrounded by the eight Mothers, and attended by Gaṇeśa and Vaṭuka, with ancillary worship of the four *yuganātha*s (the *siddha*s who propagated the tradition in the four ages) together with their consorts, ending with Macchanda and Koṅkaṇā in the present *kaliyuga*, and the six non-celibate *rājaputra*s who were the sons of this couple, together with their consorts; but in course of time this was variously inflected and modified in liturgical systems differentiated most obviously by the identity of the central deity. Thus in an early classification, seen in the *Ciñciṇīmata*, we are given accounts of four systems of Kaula teaching, called the Āmnāyas ("Traditions"), assigned to the four directions, east (Pūrvāmnāya), north (Uttarāmnāya), west (Paścimāmnāya), and south (Dakṣiṇāmnāya), each with a distinctive pantheon of worship.

Of these the Pūrvāmnāya as outlined in this text appears to be the uninflected, original form of the Kula; and it is closely related to that which was taught for the Trika by the *Mālinīvijayottara* (11.3–16), Abhinavagupta's *Tantrāloka* (29.18–55), and Jayaratha's commentary thereon. Indeed there is textual continuity between this part of the *Ciñciṇīmata* and the passages of the *Kulakrīḍāvatāra*, a text that has not otherwise survived to my knowledge, which Jayaratha quotes at length in his commentary on this section of the *Tantrāloka* to provide the scriptural authority that remains unstated in Abhinavagupta's presentation. The only significant difference is that the Trika has superimposed its own distinctive *mantra* deities on to the underlying model.

The Kashmirian Śākta Śaiva exegetes of the 9th to 11th centuries do not use this classification into Āmnāyas. But later Kashmirian sources do support the close connection between the Trika and the Pūrvāmnāya that I am proposing. The

Kalādīkṣāpaddhati tells us that at a certain point in the preparatory rituals offerings into fire should be made in the case of the Pūrvāmnāya, that is to say, in the case of adherents thereof, to the three Bhairavas (Bhairavasadbhāva, Ratiśekhara, and Navātman), three goddesses (Parā, Parāparā, and Aparā), and Mātṛsadbhāva. These, as the text of the Mantras that follows this statement shows, are the core *mantra* deities that define the Trika. Likewise in a fragmentary birchbark manuscript that contains parts of the text guiding the Kashmirian *śivarātri* worship as performed by Śaiva initiates we find the Trika's alphabet goddess Mālinī receiving offerings as the goddess of the Pūrvāmnāya after the recitation of a meditation verse that identifies her with the Trika's high goddess as embodied in the three goddesses enthroned on the lotuses on the tips of the trident at the center of the Trika's initiation → *maṇḍala* as the nondual ground of the agent, means, and object of cognition. Mālinī is also worshipped as the goddess of the Pūrvāmnāya in the Kashmirian Śaiva *gurus*' *Agnikāryapaddhati*, in the section on the fire offerings of clarified butter to the goddesses (*devinām ājyahoma*), with a meditation verse addressed to Parā, the Trika's highest goddess, as embodied in her seed syllable *sauḥ*.

The Trika produced several scriptures with a predominantly or exclusively Kaula orientation. Unfortunately these survive for the most part only in citations in the *Tantrāloka* and Jayaratha's commentary thereon. The principal among them are the *Triśirobhairava*, the *Trikakularatnamālā*, the *Yogasaṃcāra*, the *Trikasāra*, the *Bhairavakula*, and the *Vīrāvalīkula*. The citations do not reveal much about the character of these texts on the level of the specifics of ritual; but we can at least see that the *Vīrāvalīkula* was considered to pertain to a higher form of Kaula practice in which external elaborations were rejected in favor of inner experience. Thus in initiation the *Vīrāvalī* advocated in place of the outer Kula's method of possession (*āveśa*), in which there occurs a paralysis (*stobha*) of the initiand's physical agency as his body and consciousness are taken over by the goddess, a higher method of spontaneous fusion of the initiator's and initiand's consciousness (*sāmarasya*). This evidence of distinction between different levels of practice within the Trika is confirmed by a passage in the *Siddhakhaṇḍa* of the Paścimāmnāya-Kaula *Manthānabhairava*. For that teaches a ladder of higher and higher means of liberation in which the Bhairavatantras are followed in ascending order by the methods of the *Mālinīvijayottara*, the *Bhairavakula*, and the *Vīrāvalī*, with the last transcended in turn by the Krama, and that by the form of Kaula practice espoused by the *Manthānabhairava* itself.

The Paścimāmnāya, with which the *Ciñciṇīmata* aligns itself, is that of the cult of the goddess Kubjikā and her consort Navātman, a system whose scriptural corpus comprises principally the *Kubjikāmata*, *Laghvikāmnāya*, and *Ṣaṭsāhasrakulālikāmnāya*, but also such works as the *Śrīmatottara/Gorakṣasaṃhitā*, *Kularatnoddyota*, and *Manthānabhairava*. The last contains several remarks that reveal its provenance to be the Deccan plateau, more specifically Deśa (Desh), the central subregion of the modern state of Maharashtra. It tells us that it is in the Deccan (*dakṣiṇāpatha*) that the initiatory tradition (*ājñā*) of the Kubjikā cult is maintained; that it is "here in Deśa" that *siddhi* can be achieved; that those in the Konkan, the coastal region of Maharashtra, Goa, and Karnataka, should travel up to the Deccan plateau to obtain the scriptures, since without them this tradition will bear no fruit; and that the *Khañjinīmata* of 24,000 verses, which was brought back to earth from the subterranean paradise at the beginning of the current *kaliyuga*, is (already) well known in the Deccan in the form of the *Kulālikāmata*, its redaction in 3,500 verses. That redaction is surely the *Kubjikāmata* in the principal of its three redactions. That and that alone is of this length; and it is referred to in its colophons with the synonym *Kulālikāmnāya*. That the *Manthānabhairava* was composed in the Deccan is confirmed by its practice of compounding the names of goddesses with -avvā. This is surely a reflex of the vernacular usage in this region, where goddess names of this kind are commonplace, *avvā* ("mother") being used in Kannara as a feminine title of respect and affection. This feature is also found in the *Kubjikāmata*. It is probable, then, that it too is a product of the Deccan, and therefore that the whole tradition emerged and developed in that region. This should be taken to include the Konkan. For the claim of the *Siddhakhaṇḍa* that those in the Konkan should go to Desh for this Tantra admits that teaching is found in the Konkan too, claiming only that the best tradition is to be found inland. Moreover, the *Ṣaṭsāhasrasaṃhitā* begins with the information that it was at Candrapurī/Candrapura in the Konkan, probably the ancient port town of Goa now called Chandor, that Śrīnātha first propagated this teaching at the beginning of the current *kaliyuga*.

This evidence establishes, moreover, that the Trika (Pūrvāmnāya) was present in the Deccan, and that it was so before the literature of the Paścimāmnāya was redacted. For the *Kubjikāmata* drew extensively on the Trika's scriptures, embedding the cult of its deities in a modified Trika substrate. Nor is there good reason, in spite of the later prominence of the Trika in Kashmir, to suppose that it must have travelled from Kashmir to the Deccan before it exerted this influence. There is no need, then, to seek a connection with Kashmir to explain the fact that the Jaina Somadevasūri has referred to the Trika in his *Yaśastilaka*, completed in 959 CE at Gaṅgādhārā (Gangadhara), near Vemulawada in the Karimnagar district of Andhra Pradesh.

The *Ciñciṇīmata*'s account of the Uttarāmnāya shows this to be the system for the worship of the goddess Kālī (Kālasaṃkarṣaṇī) known variously as the Krama, Mahānaya, Mahārtha, Devīnaya, or Kālīkula that we find in a number of liturgical variants in parts of the *Jayadrathayāmala*'s later *ṣaṭka*s, the *Kālikākulapañcaśataka*, the *Devīdvyardhaśatikā*, the *Kālīkulakramasadbhāva*, the *Yonigahvara*, and, known only through their utilization in the Paddhati *Kālīkulakramārcana* of Vimalaprabodha, the *guru* of King Arimalla of Nepal (r. 1200–1216), the *Pañcacāmaraśekhara, Dvīpamata, Dvīpottara, Śaktikaulika, Kaulakamala, Kharapuccha, and Mahārthakramabheda.*

The *Kālikākulapañcaśataka* and *Kālīkulakramasadbhāva* identify Uḍḍiyāna, that is to say, the Swat Valley, in the far northwest of the subcontinent, as the place of their revelation. But there are several pieces of evidence that encourage us to suspect that this is myth rather than fact. In Vimalaprabodha's account in the *Kālīkulakramārcana* of the Krama ritual in which male and female adepts are worshipped collectively with offerings of food and drink (*cakrakrīḍā*) he gives a secret jargon (*samayachommaka*) that should be used by the sponsor with all the invited participants to refer to the five phases of the Krama, from emission (*sṛṣṭi*) to radiance (*bhāsā*). The expressions are unmistakeably Dravidian, and probably from the Kannara- or Tulu-speaking areas of the Deccan. The *Manthānabhairava*, a work of the Deccan, knows the Krama, placing it, as we have seen, between the Trika and itself in its ascending hierarchy of revelation, even redacting in its *Siddhakhaṇḍa* a Krama scriptural text of 115 verses of which most are found in the *Devīdvyardhaśatikā*. Finally, the *Ūrmikaulārṇava*, also called *Bhogahasta*, teaches a version of the Krama that it associates with the sacred site of the goddess Mahālakṣmī at Kolhapur in the Deccan, saying that it had been brought by *siddha*s to this place from the site of its original revelation by Śrīnātha in Assam (Kāmarūpa).

The last of the four, the Dakṣiṇāmnāya, is presented by the *Ciñciṇīmata* as the cult of Kāmeśvari surrounded by Kāmadeva and the 11 goddesses known as the Nityās, a tradition of whose literature we now possess only a single incomplete manuscript of one work, the *Nityākaula*. This cult was eclipsed in time by its own outgrowth, the cult of the goddess Tripurā/Tripurasundarī (see → Śrīvidyā), which eventually became much the most widespread and popular form of Śākta worship, surviving with some vigour down to the present. This later form, whose primary scriptures are the *Nityāṣoḍaśikārṇava* and the *Yoginīhṛdaya*, did not assign itself to the Dakṣiṇāmnāya. Rather it claimed from the beginning that it transcends the Āmnāyas as the essence and embodiment of all four; and this stance was elaborated in the learned exegesis in the claim that the constituent parts of Tripurā's *maṇḍala* of nine intersecting triangles, known as the *śrīcakra*, are the embodiment of these four, equated with the four phases of emission (*sṛṣṭi*), stasis (*sthiti, avatāra*), retraction (*saṃhāra*), and the nameless (*anākhya*), a tetrad borrowed from the Krama, thus transforming the *maṇḍala* into a proof, as it were, of the cult's claim to encompass and surpass all the other Kaula traditions.

This claim that the four Āmnāyas are embodied in the constituent parts of the *śrīcakra* is purely theoretical or rhetorical, since no deities or *mantra*s from those traditions are incorporated. However, in the *Jñānārṇava*, a scriptural work of this tradition that shows additional elements not found in the system set out in the *Nityāṣoḍaśikārṇava* and *Yoginīhṛdaya* and which is no doubt later than both of them for this reason and because it is not cited by the early exegetes, an attempt has been made to provide a more graphic expression of this belief by working the goddesses of the four Āmnāyas into the liturgy as subordinates of Tripurā. What is striking in this, however, is not the mere fact that this has been done but the fact that in doing so the redactors of the tradition reveal that by their time while the concept of the four Āmnāyas was alive only the Paścimāmnāya and Uttarāmnāya out of the four identified by the *Ciñciṇīmata* were familiar to them as active traditions. This we can infer from the fact that Kubjikā and Kālī are given there as the goddesses of those two Āmnāyas with their root *mantras* correctly recorded, while the other two Āmnāyas are filled in with goddesses and *mantras* created or adopted for this purpose without precedent in those traditions as evidenced in early sources, namely with Unmanī in the Pūrvāmnāya and Bhoginī in the Dakṣiṇāmnāya. We may surmise that the Dakṣiṇāmnāya had disappeared from view through its transformation into this ascendant cult of Tripurasundarī. As for the Pūrvāmnāya, the earliest and least elaborate of these systems, it had perhaps died out as an independent tradition, outmoded in the face of these later Śākta developments.

Both this claim to transcend the four Āmnāyas and the obsolescence of the old Dakṣiṇāmnāya and Pūrvāmnāya are confirmed by another and independent account of the Āmnāya system found in the *Parātantra*, also referred to as the *Karavīrayāga*, a work probably composed within the Newar community of the Kathmandu valley at some time during the Malla period (1200–1768), probably in its latter half. It presents the four Āmnāyas as the traditions of the goddesses that preside over them and these goddesses as seated on lion thrones (*siṃhāsana*) located in the corresponding cardinal directions. Tripurā is introduced after chapters devoted to those four as the goddess of the upper lion throne (*ūrdhvasiṃhāsana*), as venerated in all the Āmnāyas and as embodied in (the teachings of) all four of the cardinal thrones, that is to say, as the goddess of the Ūrdhvāmnāya ("Upper Tradition"), transcending them just as the Siddhānta claimed its superiority within the Mantramārga by making its scriptures come forth from the mouth of Īśāna, the upward-gazing, upper face of Sadāśiva, and the Vāmatantra, Dakṣiṇatantras, Gāruḍatantras, and Bhūtatantras, from the mouths of the faces below that look out to the four directions. And here too, as in the *Jñānārṇava*, it is very clear that the redactor knew only the Paścimāmnāya and Uttarāmnāya as living traditions in the lineage of those outlined in the *Ciñciṇīmata*. It gives an accurate account of the cult of Kubjikā and Navātmabhairava for the first and of those of Siddhalakṣmī and Guhyakālī for the second. But for the Pūrvāmnāya and Dakṣiṇāmnāya it gives us two goddesses Pūrṇeśvarī and Niśeśvarī that have been concocted, it seems, in order to complete the set of four. For these two goddesses appear in the Śaiva tradition only in this text and its Nepalese derivatives such as the *Karmasāramahātantra*. I know no evidence of scriptural production that would attest that these traditions existed at any time in their own right and I consider it improbable that any will surface, though I do not exclude the possibility that we may encounter in the ill-explored mass of the Newars' Śākta Paddhatis evidence of the creation of liturgies for their independent worship after their invention in this artificial context. The *Parātantra* itself suggests their fictive character by reporting that the devotees of these two goddesses dwell on Plakṣadvīpa, Kuśadvīpa, Śākadvīpa, and Puṣkaradvīpa, that is to say, on four of the six concentric island continents that the cosmographers of the Purāṇas claim to lie beyond the salt water ocean that surrounds Jambudvīpa, the central continent centered on Mount Meru, within whose southern segment they located their known world.

The Tantras mentioned here as the two principal scriptural authorities of this neo-Śākta tradition, the *Nityāṣoḍaśikārṇava* and the *Yoginīhṛdaya*, came to be considered to be the prior and posterior halves of a single work, the *Vāmakeśvara*, the first devoted to external worship and the second to internal worship or rather to the inner meaning of the ritual, awareness of which was claimed to render the outer ritual effective. But the two works are of very different character. While the first is free of doctrinal or soteriological subtlety, the *Yoginīhṛdaya* was composed by an author who sought to encode the ritual system of Tripurā worship set out in the earlier work with the metaphysics of the Kashmirian Śaiva non-dualists. Therefore it cannot have been written before the 11th century. Indeed the earliest attestations of its existence known to me are a citation of it by Maheśvarānanda (c. 1275–1325) and the commentary on the text by Amṛtānanda (c. 1325–1375), who claims, I propose, that he is the first to have written a commentary on the work and was active in Andhra circa 1350. His predecessor Śivānanda, who flourished around 1225–1275, does not cite the text in his commentary on the *Nityāṣoḍaśikārṇava*, and this would be very surprising if the text had already existed in his time. As for the *Nityāṣoḍaśikārṇava*, we can say at present only that it had been existence for an undetermined period before it received a commentary from the Kashmirian Jayaratha, who flourished under Rājadeva, who ruled from 1213 to 1236, but probably not much earlier than the 11th century.

Exegetical Literature of the Kulamārga

For exegesis of the Kulamārga of the Pūrvāmnāya as represented in the literature of the Trika we have the Kashmirian Abhinavagupta's *Tantrāloka*, in particular its 28th and 29th chapters, and Jayaratha's commentary thereon. For the Anuttara subsystem of the Trika, based on the *Parātriṃśikā*, also known as the *Parātrīśikā* or *Anuttaratriṃśikā*, we have Abhinavagupta's *Parātriṃśikāvivaraṇa*, and the 22nd chapter of his *Tantrasāra* corresponding to the 29th of the *Tantrāloka*, in which he deviates from the latter by taking the *Parātriṃśikā* rather than the *Mālinīvijayottara* as the basis of his Kaula Paddhati.

We also have a number of texts from South India written within the conceptual framework of the Kashmirian Trika that show that this subsystem became established in that region in later times. This is the probable provenance of the commentary *Parātriṃśikālaghuvṛtti* or *Anuttaravimarśinī*. That too has been attributed to Abhinavagupta; but the two commentaries, this and Abhinavagupta's much longer and more complex *-vivaraṇa*, are of markedly different intellectual quality and diverge not only in their interpretations but also in their readings. That the *-laghuvṛtti* is a South Indian work is suggested by its manuscript transmission and by the existence of a body of South Indian material based on it, namely a commentary (*-laghuvṛttivimarśinī*) by Kṛṣṇadāsa, the successor of Madhurāja/Mādhurācārya ("The *Ācārya* of Madurai"), and a verse commentary, the *Parātrīśikātātparyadīpikā*, written in Chidambaram and of unknown authorship, and Paddhatis and other ancillary texts that attest to the enduring popularity of a tradition based on this commentary among South Indian Śākta-Śaivas: the *Anuttarasaṃvidarcanācarcā*, the **Parārcanakrama*, the **Parākramavāsanā* in the *Paramaśivādvaitakalpalatikā* of Śāmbhavānanda, the *Pūrvaparāpūjā*, the *Parāpūjā*, and the *Paraparāpūjā* that are chapters 8, 9, and 11 of the *Ānandakalpavallī* of Maheśvaratejānanda, the *Parāpūjāprayoga*, the *Mahārthamūlasaṃketasūtra* of Paraśambhudeva, the *Anuttaraprakāśapañcāśikā*, also called *Parāpañcāśikā*, attributed to Ādyanātha, the *Parāpraveśikā* of Nāgānanda, also known as *Svarūpaprakāśikā*, with a commentary (*Svarūpavimarśinī*) by one Cidānanda, and another (*Nāgānandasūtravivaraṇa*) by Heddase Hariharaśarman written for Basavappa Nāyaka of Keladi (Kēlaḍi) in Karnataka (r. 1697–1714), the *Anuttarapaddhati* of the *Paraśurāmakalpasūtra* with the commentary (*Saubhāgyasudhodaya*) of Rāmeśvara (1831), the parallel *Parāpaddhati* of Umānanda's *Nityotsava* (1745), the *Parāmantramāhātmya*, and the *Parāstuti* of Sahajānanda. There is also another probably South Indian commentary (*-vivaraṇa*) on the *Parātriṃśikā*, written by one by Sadānanda.

This tradition also reached Orissa, since it is the content of the *Parājapavidhi* and *Parāmantravidhi* in the *Āṅgirasakalpa* collection of the Oriya Paippalādin Atharvavedins. As to whether it reached Orissa through the spread of the tradition from the south up through Andhra or by some other route cannot be settled beyond doubt from the evidence now known to me. But the numerous correspondences in details of procedure between these texts and the South Indian Parākrama, not least the use of the visualization verse for the goddess Parā seen in those texts, make the former scenario the most probable. The least probable is transmission from Kashmir, since the part of the *Parātriṃśikā* incorporated in the Orissan *Parājapavidhi* agrees with the South Indian version of the text rather than the Kashmirian transmitted in Abhinavagupta's *-vivaraṇa*.

For the Uttarāmnāya, including the Krama, we have no running commentaries on its scriptures, but we do have a rich literature of professed human authorship setting out its ritual and meditational disciplines. That composed by Kashmirians, principally the three texts that share the title *Mahānayaprakāśa* (one anonymous, and the other two by Kulācārya Arṇasiṃha and Rājānaka Śitikaṇṭha) and the *Chummāsaṃketaprakāśa* of Niṣkriyānanda, has been covered by me in some detail in another publication (Sanderson, 2007b). From Chola Nadu (Cōḻanāṭu) in South India we have the *Mahārthamañjarī* in Maharashtri Prakrit with an elaborate Sanskrit autocommentary (*-parimala*) by Maheśvarānanda (c. 1300), and, of unknown provenance, the *Cidgaganacandrikā* of Śrīvatsa. From Nepal we have Vimalaprabodha's *Kālīkulakramārcana*, an exhaustive Paddhati of the early 13th century for the Krama worship of Guhyakālī, and the *Mahārthakramapañcakamantrapaddhati*, which gives the *mantra* text of this same liturgy.

For the cult of the goddess Kubjikā in the Paścimāmnāya we have in Nepalese manuscripts practical commentaries on both the *Kubjikāmata* (*-laghuṭippaṇī*) and the *Ṣaṭsāhasrakulālikāmnāya* (*-ṭippaṇī*) and at least three detailed Paddhatis by learned scholars: the *Nityāhnikatilaka* of Jaya, son of Śrīkaṇṭha, which reaches us in Nepalese and East Indian manuscripts, the earliest dated in 1268/1269, the *Nityaprakāśa* of Vīracandra, composed in 1072/1073, with the commentary *Nityaprakāśavivaraṇapañjikā*, also called *Nityakaumudī*, written by his chief disciple Gaṅgādhara at the request of the latter's pupil Śambhudatta, the personal physician of the Pala monarch Rāmapāla (r. c. 1072–1126); and the *Śrimatapaddhati*, also called *Siddhasaṃtānasopānapaṅkti*, of Jasorāja (Yaśorājacandra), of which we have an incomplete copy in a composite Nepalese codex of the 12th century and a copy in an east Indian manuscript dated in year 144 of the era of Lakṣmana(sena), that is to say, in 1263 or 1252.

From the Dakṣiṇāmnāya as defined by the *Ciñciṇīmata*, that is to say, from the cult of Kāmeśvarī attended by Kāmadeva and the 11 Nityās, no exegetical work has come to light. But from the Kaula cult of Tripurasundarī that developed from it have such an abundance of postscriptural sources that only the most influential will be mentioned. We have commentaries on the *Nityāṣoḍaśikārṇava* by the South Indians Śivānanda (c. 1225–1275; *-ṛjuvimarśinī*), Vidyānanda (*-artharatnāvalī*), probably his near contemporary, and by the Kashmirian Rājānaka Jayaratha (c. 1250; *Vāmakeśvarīmatavivaraṇa*), a commentary on the *Yoginīhṛdaya* by the South Indian Amṛtānanda (c. 1325–1375), and a commentary (*-setubandha*) on both Tantras, presented as the prior and posterior divisions of a single work, the *Vāmakeśvara*, by the Maharashtrian Deśastha Brahman Bhāskararāya (1690–1785). From Nāgabhaṭṭa we have the Paddhati *Tripurāsārasamuccaya*, from Śivānanda, who cites Nāgabhaṭṭa, two Paddhatis, *Subhagodaya* and *Subhagodayavāsanā*, one covering the ritual procedures and the other giving their inner meanings (*vāsanā*), the contemplation of which is held to animate the external actions. We also have a liturgical hymn of his: the *Saubhāgyahṛdayastotra*. From a Vidyānandanātha, who is probably identical with the Vidyānanda who wrote the (*-artharatnāvalī*), we have the Paddhati *Jñānadīpavimarśinī* of which we have a Nepalese manuscript dated in 1382/1383, and from Amṛtānanda the Paddhati *Saubhāgyasudhodaya* and a liturgical hymn, the *Cidvilāsa*. From his Guru Puṇyānanda we have the *Kāmakalāvilāsa*, with a commentary (*-cidvallī*) by Naṭanānanda.

We also have texts from the Ṣaḍanvayaśāmbhava system of worship, a secondary variant of the Paścimāmnāya, not mentioned by the *Ciñciṇīmata*, that flourished in conjunction with the cult of Tripurasundarī. We have its scripture *Śambhunirṇaya* and by way of exegesis a commentary (*-dīpikā*) on that text by Śivānanda, the author of the *-ṛjuvimarśinī* commentary on the *Nityāṣoḍaśikārṇava*. We also have for this system chapter 10 of the *Ānandakalpavallī* of Maheśvaratejānanda, the *Ṣaḍanvayaśāmbhavakrama* of Umākānta, a disciple of Amṛtānanda, and the anonymous Paddhati *Śāmbhavapūjāvidhāna*.

Salvific Alchemy and Procedures for Victory in Battle

Two further categories of Śaiva tantric literature may be mentioned. One, the *rasaśāstra* (→ *rasāyana*), teaches an initiatory tantric alchemical cult for the attainment of immortality and liberation through the use of mercurial elixirs, and is found in such Tantras as the *Rasārṇava*, the *Ānandakanda*, and the *Rasasvacchanda*, and such scripture-based works as the *Rasaratnasamuccaya* of Vāgbhaṭa. The other teaches rituals and prognosticatory procedures to secure victory in battle. Its fundamental scripture is the *Yuddhajayārṇava*, which reaches us in a manuscript of 1061. Based on this source we have Narapati's *Narapatijayacaryāsvarodaya*, completed in Aṇahillapattana (Patan), the capital of the Caulukyas in northern Gujarat, during the reign of Ajayapāla (1173/1174–1176/1177), and the anonymous *Saṃgrāmavijayodaya*, which claims to have been extracted from the *Yuddhajayārṇava* as its essence. Material from this tradition also found its way into the *Agnipurāṇa* as its chapters 123 to 150.

This martial tradition might have been mentioned above in the company of the Bhūtatantras and Gāruḍatantras, since like those traditions it is ancillary to the main Śaiva systems, and indeed is covered with them in the Keralan works *Īśānaśivagurudevapaddhati* and

Tantrasārasaṃgraha. It has been placed here, as has the tradition of tantric alchemy, because the cultic background on which both draw is that of the Kulamārga. Thus in the *Rasārṇava* and *Rasaratnasamuccaya* Kaula practice is rejected but Kaula terminology is frequently used and the pantheon draws on the Kaula cults. The iconography of Rasabhairava and Rasāṅkuśā, the central syzygy, reveal them to be ectypes of Svacchandabhairava and Tripurasundarī, and their innermost circuit of attendant deities comprises Mālinī, Parā, Parāparā, and Aparā, the core triad of the Trika with Mālinī as the transcendent fourth. Also present is the *mantra* of the Paścimāmnāya's goddess Kubjikā. The *Yuddhajayārṇava* too requires the worship of Kaula deities.

Pratyabhijñā and Spandapratyabhijna

The South Indian authors Śivānanda, Vidyānanda (either one or two), Puṇyānanda, Naṭanānanda, Amṛtānanda, Nāgānanda, Maheśvaratejānanda, Maheśvarānanda, Paraśambhudeva, Śāmbhavānanda, and Sahajānanda, all wrote within the philosophical and soteriological position formulated by Kashmirian Śākta-Śaiva scholars during the course of the 10th and into the early years of the 11th century. That development began with the *Śivadṛṣṭi*, of Somānanda (*fl.* c. 900–950 CE) and was refined by his pupil Utpaladeva in his commentary on that work, and in four independent treatises, namely the *Siddhitrayī* (*Īśvarasiddhi*, *Saṃbandhasiddhi*, and *Ajaḍapramātṛsiddhi*), and the *Īśvarapratyabhijñākārikā*. On the last of these he composed two commentaries: the *Vṛtti*, which survives, and the *Vivṛti*, of which we have only a few fragments. Abhinavagupta, pupil of Utpaladeva's pupil Lakṣmaṇagupta, composed his commentary *Īśvarapratyabhijñāvimarśinī* on the *Īśvarapratyabhijñākārikā* and his *Īśvarapratyabhijñāvivṛtivimarśinī* on the second of Utpaladeva's autocommentaries. From Abhinavagupta's pupil Kṣemarāja we have the *Pratyabhijñāhṛdaya*, in which he relates the doctrine of this philosophical corpus to the nondualistic practice of his Kaula tradition, drawing primarily on the Krama, which for him is the summit of the Śaiva revelation. On the *Īśvarapratyabhijñākārikā* we also have a commentary (*Pratyabhijñākaumudī*) by a Bhaṭṭāraka Sundara, a Kashmirian devotee of Tripurasundarī, and another by a certain Sadānanda (*Īśvarapratyabhijñātātparyānvayadīpikā*), probably a South Indian. On the *Īśvarapratyabhijñāvimarśinī* we have two commentaries, one, the *Bhāskarī*, written by the Kashmirian Bhāskarakaṇṭha towards the end of the 17th century, and the other, an anonymous *-vyākhyā*. The manuscript of the latter does not reveal the author's identity. But he is evidently a South Indian, since the sources that he quotes closely match those of other works of this tradition in the Tamilian region, such as the *Paramaśivādvaitakalpalatikā* of Śāmbhavānanda and the *Mahārthamañjarīparimala* of Maheśvarānanda; and he quotes South Indian works not known outside that region until recent times, such as the *Paryantapañcāśikā*, the *Parātriṃśikālaghuvṛtti*, and an unnamed work by Vādipralayabhairava, who is no doubt the Vādibhairava mentioned as a propagator of the Pratyabhijñā doctrine and as one of the teachers of Mādhurāja/Mādhurācārya in the opening verses of two other works of the Tamil country: the *Ānandakalpavallī* of Maheśvaratejānanda and the *Gurupaṅktistotra*. Since the author of the *-vyākhyā* quotes the *Mahārthamañjarī*, he cannot have been active before the 14th century.

Also influential on those assimilating the Kashmirian Śaiva nondualism and its terminology were the *Śivasūtra*, the *Spandakārikā*, and their commentaries by Kṣemarāja and others, these texts like the Pratyabhijñā corpus representing an attempt to establish a doctrine that transcends the liturgical and devotional specifics of such systems as the Trika and the Krama. Among the texts of this corpus is a work by a South Indian: the *Śivasūtravārttika* of Varadarāja, also called Kṛṣṇadāsa, which is a paraphrase in verse of Kṣemarāja's prose commentary (*-vimarśinī*) on the *Śivasūtra*.

These doctrines of the Pratyabhijñā and Spanda texts could then be applied, and were applied, to the exegesis of other tantric traditions in Kashmir and beyond, notably the cults of Svacchanda and Amṛteśvara, the Trika, the Krama, the cult of Tripurasundarī, the Ṣaḍanvayaśāmbhava variant of the Paścimāmnāya, the Vīraśaivism of the *Siddhāntaśikhāmaṇi* of Śivayogin, also called Reṇukācārya, and its commentary *Tattvapradīpikā* by Maritōṇṭadārya, and even beyond Śaivism, in the South Indian Pāñcarātrika Vaiṣṇava system seen in the *Lakṣmītantra* and *Ahirbudhnyasaṃhitā*.

Non-Saiddhāntika Śaiva Hymnography

Also instrumental in propagating the new Śākta-Śaiva nondualism of the Kashmirians among non-Saiddhāntika Śaivas of all liturgical persuasions was a literature of devotional hymns (*stotra, stuti, stava*) supported by learned commentaries. Notable are the *Bahurūpagarbhastotra* with the commentary of Anantaśakti, the hymn collections *Stavacintāmaṇi* of Bhaṭṭa Nārāyaṇa and *Śivastotrāvalī* of Utpaladeva, on both of which we have commentaries by Kṣemarāja, the *Sāmbapañcāśikā* with a commentary by the same, and the *Virūpākṣapañcāśikā* with commentaries by Vidyācakravartin and Heddase Hariharaśarman.

Later Developments

The map of Śaiva literature outlined here holds for the period up to about the 12th century, though many of its elements continued, as we have seen, to produce texts long after that. But it should not be thought that the 12th century marked the end of the Śaivas' capacity for innovation.

In the *Padyavāhinī* of Śaṅkara, a South Indian work probably of the first half of the 14th century, we encounter a novel form of syncretistic Śākta devotion in which the cult of Tripurasundarī, the Anuttara's cult of Parā, the Ṣaḍanvayaśāmbhava variant of the cult of Kubjikā, and the pantheon of the Krama system, that is to say, the elements that as distinct systems constitute the Śākta domain known to Śivānanda and Maheśvarānanda, are woven together into a single course of regular and occasional worship.

We have evidence of another such syncretistic development in South India in the literature of a cult of the goddess Lalitā/Kāmākṣī of Kanchipuram. Here she is worshipped as Tripurasundarī with ancillary cults of Gaṇapati and the goddesses Mātaṅgī (Śyāmalā), Vārāhī (Daṇḍinī), and Parā, the last adopted from of the Anuttara form of the Trika. This was prescribed in the *Paraśurāmakalpasūtra*, which pious tradition holds to be the last and shortest of a series of abridgements of an original *Dattasaṃhitā* of 18,000 verses. We have a Paddhati, the *Nityotsava*, composed in 1745 by the Maharashtrian Deśastha Brahman Jagannātha (initiated as Umānandanātha), a disciple of Bhāskararāya, who enjoyed the patronage of the Marathas of the Bhonsle dynasty then ruling from Thanjavur, an extensive commentary (*Saubhāgyasudhodaya*) composed in 1831 by the Maharashtrian Deśastha Brahman Rāmeśvara (initiated as Aparājitānandanātha), disciple of a disciple of a disciple of Bhāskararāya, and another by the Maharashtrian Koṅkaṇastha Brahman Lakṣmaṇa Rāṇade (*Sūtratattvavimarśinī*), completed in 1889. There was also a commentary (*Ratnāloka*) by the Deśastha Brahman Bhāskararāya (initiated as Bhāsurānandanātha), the *guru* of Jagannātha. But I do not know of any surviving manuscript of this work.

The system was provided with less ambiguously scriptural status in the *Paramānandatantra* and the *Tripurārahasya* with the minor difference that these works have replaced the Anuttara's goddess Parā with the cognate Bālā form of Tripurasundarī. The former work has reached us with a commentary (*Saubhāgyānandasaṃdoha*) by Maheśvarānandanātha, a resident of Banaras, written in 1828/1829, and the latter with a commentary written in 1832 by Śrīnivāsabhaṭṭa of Madurai in the far south. Also in this tradition, with Bālā in place of Parā, are the 18th-century Paddhati *Saubhāgyakalpadruma* of the Dravidian Brahman Lakṣmaṇa (initiated as Mādhavānandanātha) and, following it, the *Mahāyāgapaddhati* of the Dravidian Brahman Lakṣmīnātha (initiated as Ambikānandanātha) written at the request of Maharaja Sawai Raja Singh II of Jaipur (b. 1833; r. 1835–1880). All the literature of this cult is steeped in the tradition of the Kashmirian Śākta-Śaiva nondualists, and the commentaries frequently cite their works. How long before its 18th- and 19th-century exegesis this syncretistic variant of the cult of Tripurasundarī came into existence is uncertain. But it is probably this or a cult very close to it that is referred to in the 16th century in a verse that another Śrīnivāsabhaṭṭa, known also as Ratnakheṭa, has a Śākta named Śaktisiddhānta recite in his allegorical drama *Bhāvanāpuruṣottama*, invoking Bālā, Mātaṅgī (Mātaṅgakanyā), and Vārāhi.

Another influential development that is probably to be assigned to a date after the 12th century is seen in the *Kulārṇava*. This expounds a new form of Kaulism that it refers to as the Ūrdhvāmnāya ("Upper Tradition"), thereby claiming, like the cult of Tripurasundarī, superiority over the forms of Śākta-Śaivism that preceded it. This has little in common with the elaborate pantheons and *mantra* systems of the forms of the Kulamārga reviewed up to this point. For it teaches a radically simplified cult of Ardhanārīśvara with an icon that is a variant of the Trika's Parā (*KuT.* 4.112c–113b) but, as its name declares, is half Śiva and half the Goddess. This fusion is also expressed in the system's *mantras*. For these are the *prāsādaparā* (*hsauṃḥ*) and the *parāprāsāda* (*shauṃḥ*), which are the result of fusing the *mantra* of Parā (*sauḥ*), the high goddess of the Trika, with the *prāsāda* (*hauṃ*), the *mantra* of Śiva in the Saiddhāntika system on which most of the Saiddhāntika Paddhatis are based. However, apart from the *mantra* there is no discernible connection with the Trika and certainly no trace of awareness of the distinctive doctrines of the Kashmirian nondualistic exegesis of that tradition that permeated the South Indian exegesis of the cult of Tripurasundarī and related systems down to recent times. The latest stratum of the South Indian Śākta literature takes it into account by including it in a classification of the *mantra* pantheon into six Āmnāyas. In this the *Kulārṇava* tradition is accommodated in the Ūrdhvāmnāya division with a yet higher division, the Anuttarāmnāya ("Ultimate Tradition"), ranked above it and populated with *mantras* that include those proper to the worship of Tripurasundarī.

It was also during this period that there emerged out of the Kulamārga the tradition later known as the → Nāth Sampradāya, comprising lineages of Śākta-Śaiva "Kāpālikas" claiming spiritual descent from Gorakṣanātha (Gorakhnāth), whom they venerate as a disciple of Matsyendranātha, the Macchandanātha of the Pūrvāmnāya, the propagator of the Kulamārga during the present *kaliyuga*. The literature of this vigorous tradition, which appears to have had its origin in the Deccan, contains works such as the *Matsyendrasaṃhitā*, probably a South Indian work of the 13th century – this is also the date of the earliest references to Gorakṣanātha – which combines Kaula materials pertaining to the cults of Tripurasundarī and Kubjikā (particularly in its Ṣaḍanvayaśāmbhāva variant), and many works teaching a system of *yoga* that use Kaula terminology and concepts but tend to reject Kaula externals, such as the *Vivekamārtaṇḍa*, the *Gorakṣaśataka*, the *Amaraughaprabodha*, *Amaraughaśāsana*, and the *Khecarīvidyā*.

Related to this meta-Kaula Yoga literature are the *Amṛtasiddhi*, the *Amanaska*, the *Dattātreyayogaśāstra*, the *Śivasaṃhitā*, and works found variously grouped together in Kashmirian manuscripts alongside the *Gorakṣaśataka* and *Amaraughaśāsana*, namely the *Candrajñāna*, *Jñānasāra*, *Niruttaravāda*, *Nirvāṇayogottara*, *Paramārthasāra*, *Prāṇāgnihotra*, *Brahmasaṃdhāna*, *Matsyodarayogaśāstra*, *Sarvajñānottarayogaśāstra*, and *Haṃsasāra*.

In eastern India after the decline of Buddhism in that region, various goddesses not encountered in earlier Kaula/Śākta sources, namely Śyāmā (Dakṣiṇā, Dakṣiṇā Kālī, Dakṣiṇakālī), Tārā, Chinnamastā, Dhūmāvatī, Bagalā or Bagalāmukhī, and Bhuvaneśvarī, made their appearance in a new wave of Kaula scriptural literature, eventually forming with Tripurasundarī (Ṣoḍaśī, Śrīvidyā), Mātaṅgī, Kamalā, and Tripurabhairavī the ten *mahāvidyās*, with three of these the primary focus of devotion: Tripurasundarī, Tārā, and Dakṣiṇā Kālī. Notable Tantras of this East Indian Śākta tradition are the *Kaṅkālamālinī*, *Kāmadhenu*, *Kālīvilāsa*, *Kubjikā*, *Kumārī*, *Kulacūḍāmaṇi*, *Kaulāvalīnirṇaya*, *Guptasādhana*, *Jñānasaṃkalinī*, *Toḍala*, *Nigamakalpadruma*, *Nigamatattvasāra*, *Niruttara*, *Nirvāṇa*, *Picchilā*, *Phetkāriṇī*, *Bṛhadyoni*, *Bṛhannīla*, *Bhāvacūḍāmaṇi*, *Muṇḍamālā*, *Yoginī*, *Yoni*, *Rādhā*, *Varadā*, *Vīra*, *Samayācāra*, and *Saṃmohana*; a major early compendium drawing on many of these texts and thereby providing those with a *terminus ante quem* is the *Sarvollāsatantra* of Sarvānandanātha, probably compiled circa 1400; and important later scriptural sources are the *Śaktisaṃgamatantra*, probably of the 17th century, and the *Merutantra*, a work composed or at least completed in its present form after the arrival of the British in India. Notable among numerous later compendia and Paddhatis in this tradition are the 16th-century Bengali Brahmānandagiri's *Śāktānandataraṅgiṇī* and *Tārārahasya*, the former a general Śākta treatise and the latter on the worship of Tārā, his disciple Pūrṇānanda's *Śyāmārahasya* on the worship of Dakṣiṇā Kālī and *Śrītattvacintāmaṇī* on that of Tripurasundarī, the latter completed in 1577, the *Mantramahodadhi* of Mahīdhara, a Brahman of Ahicchatra residing in Banaras, completed in 1588, the *Tantrasāra* of the Bengali Kṛṣṇānanda Āgamavāgīśa, written in the 16th or 17th century, the *Śyāmārcanacandrikā* and *Kramacandrikā* of the Bengali Ratnagarbha Sārvabhauma, *guru* of Kedār Rāy, the *zamīndār* of Bikrampur near Dhaka killed in 1603, the *Tārābhaktisudhārṇava* of the Maithila Narasiṃha Ṭhakkura completed in 1668, the *Āgamatattvavilāsa* of the

Bengali Raghunātha Tarkavāgīśa (1687), the *Puraścaryārṇava* of Mahārāja Pratāp Singh Shāh of Nepal (r. 1774–1777), the 18th-century *Kālikārcanacandrikā* of the Bengali Keśava Nyāyabhūṣaṇa, the *Tārābhaktitaraṅgiṇī* of the Bengali Kāśīnātha (1815), the *Prāṇatoṣiṇī* of the Bengali Prāṇatoṣaṇa Vidyālaṅkāra (1821), the *Dīkṣāprakāśa* of the Maithila Jīvanātha (1869/1870), and the *Śāktapramoda* (1889) of Rāja Devanandan Singh, a *zamīndār* of Muzaffarpur in Bihar.

From late medieval Kashmir we have the syncretistic, Tripurā-centered Śākta tradition of the *Devīrahasya*, also called *Parārahasya*, which adapts this east Indian tradition in various ways, also working in Śārikā, Śāradā, Rājñī, and Jvālāmukhī, the lineage goddesses (*kuladevī*) of the Kashmirian Brahmans. From Sāhib Kaul, the 17th-century Śākta scholar of the Kashmirian Kaul lineage that originated in northern Bihar, we have detailed Paddhatis for the regular worship of three deities of this tradition: a *Śyāmāpaddhati* for Dakṣiṇā Kālī, a *Hṛllekhāpaddhati* for Bhuvaneśvarī, and a *Śrīvidyānityapūjāpaddhati* for Tripurasundarī.

Probably from Mithilā, we have the tradition of the *Mahākālasaṃhitā*, which, in the context of the east Indian Śākta tradition of the *mahāvidyā*s, teaches at great length the cults of two Kālīs, Kāmakalākālī and Guhyakālī in an expurgated form in which only Śūdras are allowed to offer and consume alcoholic liquor and meat in the worship of the Goddess, the twice-born being required to employ various tame substitutes. All the works of this east Indian neo-Śākta tradition lack the doctrinal underpinning provided by the earlier Śaiva and Śākta-Śaiva traditions reviewed here, reverting to a Smārta ontology based on the 25 *tattva*s of the → Sāṃkhya system, in which the Goddess (Śakti) is equated with → *prakṛti* and Śiva with → *puruṣa*.

Also to be mentioned as major developments of this period are the expurgated and internalized cult that called itself the Samayamata, expounded by Lakṣmīdhara, a courtier of Pratāparudra, the Gajapati ruler of Orissa, in the first decades of the 16th century, in his commentary on the Śākta hymn *Saundaryalaharī*, for those who wished to remain within the bounds of Brahmanical orthopraxy and orthodoxy, the eclectic, Smārta tantric tradition, probably originating in Orissa in the 12th century, of the *Prapañcasāra* and *Śāradātilaka*, and, following the latter, such texts as the *Śaivacintāmaṇi* of Lakṣmīdharamiśra, a late-17th-century Vaidiki Brahman of Bhubaneshwar under Gajapati Mukundadeva I. The *Śāradātilaka* reaches us in many manuscripts from all over the subcontinent, along with an exhaustive citation-rich commentary composed in Banaras in 1494 by Rāghavabhaṭṭa, a Deśastha brahmin whose father had migrated from Nasik to Banaras. Both the Samayamata and this tradition of the *Prapañcasāra* and *Śāradātilaka* have alligned themselves with Brahmanical orthodoxy by jettisoning the 36 *tattva* hierarchy of the classical Śaiva systems for that of the Sāṃkhya.

Nor was creativity after the 12th century limited to the Śākta side of Śaivism. The period from the close of the 12th century saw the emergence in the Deccan of the movement of the non-Brahman Vīraśaivas, also called → Liṅgāyats, who are now the largest community in Karnataka, forming about 15 percent of the population overall and up to a third in some areas. This produced its own literature in Kannara, Sanskrit, and, to a lesser extent, in Telugu and Marathi, from the 12th century down to modern times. The Kannara sources comprise collections of devotional poetic prose (*vacana*s) written in simple language by the saints (*śaraṇa*s) of this tradition, namely Allamaprabhu (Prabhuliṅga), → Basava, Cennabasava, Siddharāmayya, and numerous others, including women, such as → Akkāmahādevī, and hagiographical works such as the 12th-century *Śivagaṇadararagaḷe* of Harihara, the *Somanāthacaritre* and *Siddharāmapurāṇa* of Harihara's disciple Rāghavaṅka, the *Basavapurāṇa* of Bhīmakavi (1369), which is a Kannara translation of the 13th-century Telugu *Basavapurāṇamu* of Pālkuriki Somanātha, the *Prabhuliṅgalīle* of Cāmarasa (1430), the *Vīraśaivāmṛtapurāṇa* of Mallaṇārya (c. 1513), and the *Cennabasavapurāṇa* of Virūpākṣa (1584), the *Śivatattvacintāmaṇi* of Lakkaṇa Daṇḍēśa (1441), general and minister of Devarāya II of Vijayanagara, and the four versions of the *Śūnyasaṃpādane*, by Śivagaṇaprasādi Mahādēvayya (c. 1420), Keñcavīraṇṇodeyaru or his *guru* Halageya Dēvaru (c. 1495), Gummaḷāpurada Siddhaliṅgadēvaru (c. 1500), and Gūḷūra Siddhavīraṇāryaru (c. 1510), in which the *vacana*s of the saints are embedded in a narrative framework arranged to portray the stages of spiritual progress.

In Telugu notable Vīraśaiva works other than the 13th-century *Basavapurāṇamu* of Pālkuriki Somanātha mentioned above, are the same author's *Paṇḍitārādhyacaritramu, Anubhavasāramu, Caturvedasāramu*, and *Vṛṣādhipaśatakamu*, the *Śivatattvasāramu* of Paṇḍitārādhya, the *Haravilāsamu, Bhīmeśvarapurāṇamu*, also called *Bhīmakhaṇḍamu, Śivarātrimāhātmyamu, Kāśīkhaṇḍamu*, and *Paṇḍitārādhyacaritramu* of Śrīnātha (1365–1440), and the *Kāḷahastīśvaramāhātmyamu* and *Kāḷahastīśvaraśatakamu* of Dhūrjaṭi in the early 16th century.

Notable among Vīraśaiva works in Marathi are the 16th-century Śāntaliṅga's *Karṇahastaki, Vivekacintāmaṇi*, and *Śāntabodha*, and the *Paramarahasya, Jñānabodha, Anubhavānanda*, and other works of Manmatha (1560–1613).

The Sanskrit sources, which dominate in the areas of ritual and theological doctrine, comprise scriptural works such as the *Kāraṇa, Candrajñāna, Makuṭa, Pārameśvara, Vātulaśuddha*, and *Vīra* (*Vīrottara*) – these have the names of early Saiddhāntika scriptures in spite of their Vīraśaiva content, which is for the most part the detailed prescription of the rituals of daily worship and initiation – the doctrinal *Anubhavasūtra* of Māyideva, which claims to transmit the teaching of the scripture *Vātulottara*, and exegetical works such as the *Kriyāsāra* composed by Nīlakaṇṭhaśivācārya at some time between circa 1350 and 1530, when, he says, Śiva himself had appeared to him in a dream and commanded him to produce a summary of all the Śaiva scriptures, the *Siddhāntaśikhāmaṇi* of Śivayogin, probably of the 13th or early 14th century, together with its 17th-century commentary by Maritōṇṭadārya, both following in their metaphysics the nondualistic doctrine of the Kashmirian Śākta-Śaivas, Śrīpati's *Śrīkarabhāṣya*, a Vīraśaiva commentary (c. 1400) on the Brahmanical *Brahmasūtra*, the *Śivayogapradīpikā* of Cennasadāśivayogin (15th cent.), the 17th-century *Liṅgadhāraṇacandrikā* of Nandikeśvara, the *Pañcaratna* of Vīraṇārādhya and its commentary by Sosale Revaṇārādhya (c. 1650), the latter's *Pramathagaṇapaddhati*, the *Anādivīraśaivācārasaṃgraha* of Sampādanasiddha Vīraṇaśivayogin (c. 1600), the Paddhati-like *Vīraśaivācārasāroddhārabhāṣya* of Somanātha, the *Vīramāheśvarācārasaṃgraha* of Nīlakaṇṭhagaṇanātha, the *Vīraśaivasiddhāntottarakaumudī* of Vīrabhadrārādhya, and the *Vivekacintāmaṇi* of Liṅgarāja. This later literature is heavily dependent on the doctrinal sources of the Saiddhāntikas, both their scriptures and such exegetical or secondary works as the *Tattvaprakāśa*, the *Siddhāntaśekhara*, and the *Siddhāntasārāvalī*, but it also looks for support to the *Śivadharma*, the Śaiva Purāṇas, the Upaniṣads, and works on *yoga* such as the *Yogabīja* and the *Yogatārāvalī*.

The period after the 12th century also saw significant innovations among the Śaivas of the Tamil-speaking region. Here too we find a body of devotional poetry in the vernacular, but one whose earliest and most venerated collections predate that of the Vīraśaivas by several centuries. By the 11th century a closed canon of devotional literature in Tamil had been established. Arranged in 12 books, known as the *Tirumuṟai* (Sacred Treatises), it comprises primarily collections of Tamil hymns attributed to a number of poet-saints, expressing devotion (*bhakti*) to Śiva as manifest to these devotees in numerous sacred sites throughout the region. Books 1–3 contain the poems of Campantar (Tiruñāṉacampantamūrtti), books 4–6 those of Appar (Tirunāvukaracar), book 7 those of Cuntarar (Cuntaramūrtti) – the hymns of these three poets are known collectively as the *Tēvāram* – book 8 those of Māṇikkavācakar, and books 9 and 11 those of 21 other devotees, among them Nampi Āṇṭār Nampi and the poetess Kāraikkālammaiyār. To these collections were added the soteriological treatise *Tirumantiram* of Tirumūlar as book 10 and the *Periyapurāṇam* of Cēkkiḻār as book 12. The last, composed during the reign of the Chola Kulottuṅga II (r. 1133–1150), is a hagiographical narrative of the lives of these and other Tamil Śaiva saints, the 63 → Nāyaṉārs ("Lords"), of whom, according to this account, less than a fifth were Brahmans and three were women.

It is widely held that Appar and Campantar lived in the 7th century, Cuntarar and Māṇikkavācakar in the 9th, and, even earlier than these, Kāraikkālammaiyār in the 6th. It is at least clear that Cuntarar, who refers with reverence to both Campantar and Appar, was living before 913 CE, the last year of Pallava rule, since he refers to Śiva as punishing rulers who refuse to pay tribute to these kings. The *Tirumantiram* has been assigned various early dates, but its contents render a date long before the closure of this canon in the 12th century very unlikely.

After this corpus of sacred texts had been constituted there developed a body of neo-Saiddhāntika theological writing in Tamil, eventually forming a canon of 14 texts known as the Śāstras of Meykaṇṭār (*meykaṇṭacāttiraṅkaḷ*). The first two works, the *Tiruvuntiyār* of Tiruviyalūr

Uyyavantatēvanāyaṉār, and its expansion, the *Tirukkaḷiṟṟuppaṭiyār* of Tirukkatavūr Uyyavantatēvanāyaṉār, are transitional between the devotional poetry of the *Tirumuṟai* and the 12 theological treatises that followed. These are the *Civañāṉapōtam* of Meykaṇṭār, the *Civañāṉacittiyār* of Aruṇanti, a treatise elaborating the new doctrine, which attracted a number of Tamil commentaries, his *Irupāvirupaḥtu*, the *Uṇmaiviḷakkam* of Maṉavācakaṅkaṭantār, and eight works by Umāpaticiva: the *Civappirakācam, Tiruvaruṭpayaṉ*, the *Viṉāveṇpā*, the *Pōṟippaḥṟoṭai*, the *Koṭikkavi*, the *Neñcuviṭutūtu*, the *Uṇmaineṟiviḷakkamtukaḷaṟupōtam*, and the *Caṅkaṟpanirākaraṇam*. Dates have been assigned to all 14 texts, beginning with 1147 for the *Tiruvuntiyār* and 1177 for the *Tirukkaḷiṟṟuppaṭiyār*. But the authority for the dates assigned to the first 13 works is obscure. Only the last, the *Caṅkaṟpanirākaraṇam*, is securely dated, in 1313.

This Tamil corpus and its exegesis were complemented in the 16th century by Sanskrit works along the same lines, notably the *Pauṣkarabhāṣya* of another Umāpatiśiva on the *Pauṣkarajñānapāda*, the latter claiming to be the doctrinal section of the *Pauṣkarapārameśvara*, one of the early Saiddhāntika scriptures, the *Śaivaparibhāṣā* of Śivāgrayogīndra Jñānaśivācārya, the same author's *Saṃgrahabhāṣya* and *Vistarabhāṣya* on the *Śivajñānabodha*, and, of uncertain date, the *Devīkālottara*, a short text claiming scriptural status as a redaction of the *Kālottara*, though of very different content and spirit from the early *Kālottara* versions, which are genuine redactions of a single work, probably the *Sārdhatriśatika*.

This new tradition in Tamil and Sanskrit propagated a rapprochement with the language of vedantic nondualism. It was not nondualistic in the sense of the Advaita Vedānta or the Pratyabhijñā. For it continued to adhere to the doctrine of the plurality of souls and the reality of the material universe. However it rephrased the Saiddhāntika definition of Śiva's causality in a manner that enabled it to appear to escape the criticism of Śaivism enshrined in the *Brahmasūtra* (2.2.35; *patyur asāmañjasyāt*), namely that it claims that Śiva is only the efficient cause of the universe (*nimittakāraṇa*) and not also its material cause (*upādānakāraṇa*). We are now told that Śiva is both causes, being the former per se and the latter through association with the two → *māyā*s that provide the matter of the pure and impure universes. It also shifted the emphasis from rites to devotion and liberating knowledge, claiming that the latter alone can complete the soul's liberation, and this gnostic reorientation is already apparent in what is said to be the earliest of the *meykaṇṭacāttiraṅkaḷ*, the *Tiruvuntiyār*. There are is another respect in which the neo-Siddhānta comes closer to Smārta doctrine. For it has redefined liberation not as the manifestation (*abhivyakti*) of the soul's equality with Śiva (*śivasāmya*), the doctrine of the Kashmirian Saiddhāntikas and their South Indian followers, but as the direct experience of the bliss of Śiva through oneness with him. Further it stressed the neo-Siddhānta's congruence with Brahmanical orthopraxy, and accordingly condemned as delusive the Atimārga and the non-Saiddhāntika forms of the Mantramārga. In all these ways it sought to draw itself closer to the dominant Smārta Śaiva tradition of the region. It also reached out to the uninitiated majority by shifting the emphasis from the Siddhānta's tantric *mantra*s, accessible only to initiates, to the universal Śaiva *mantra* advocated for lay devotees in the Śivadharma corpus and the Śaiva Purāṇas, namely the *pañcākṣara* (five-syllable) *namaḥ śivāya*, a feature that the neo-Siddhānta shares with the Vīraśaiva movement.

It was no doubt in the same spirit that in the 16th century Vedajñāna I translated the *Śivadharmottara* and Śivayogīndra Jñānaśivācārya the *Devīkālottara* and *Sarvajñānottara* into Tamil, and that Tamil was used for many of the Sthalapurāṇas, texts in praise of particular sacred sites, that were composed during this period, such as the *Kōyiṟpurāṇam* of Umāpaticiva glorifying Chidambaram, the *Kamalālayacciṟappu* and *Aruṇakiripurāṇam* of Vedajñāna I in praise of Thiruvarur and Thiruvannamalai, the *Tiruvaiyyāṟṟuppurāṇam* of Ñāṉakūttār, and the numerous such works produced by Ellappa Nāvalar in the 17th century. We may note also that Vedajñāna I produced the *Caivasamayaneṟi* and other works in Tamil on aspects of Śaiva observance, thus ending the monopoly of Sanskrit in this domain too.

During the same centuries the Sanskrit Saiddhāntika literature of the Tamil zone expanded greatly through the creation, redaction, or compilation of numerous scriptures such as the *Aṃśumat, Ajita, Kāmika, Kāraṇa, Candrajñāna, Cintyaviśvasādākhya, Dīpta, Makuṭa, Yogaja, Raurava, Vijaya/Vijayottara, Vīra, Śarvottara, Saṃtāna, Sāhasra, Siddha, Suprabheda*, and *Sūkṣma*. These too, like the Sanskrit scriptures of the Vīraśaivas, have titles contained in the old lists of the Tantras of the Siddhānta found in our early sources; but they too are unlikely to be, or are certainly not, works of that period. There is no trace of them in the North Indian and Nepalese manuscript collections and where an early work under one of these titles has been cited or excerpted in the early exegetical literature, as is the case with the *Kāmika, Makuṭa*, and *Sāhasra*, the text passages so preserved do not establish identity with the works assigned the same titles in late southern sources. Moreover, the manifest purpose of much of this material is to provide scriptural authority for the specifics of the tradition of Śaiva temple worship that had developed in that region under the Tamil Ādiśaiva priesthood, whose hereditary and exclusive right to officiate in the temples of Śiva is much stressed in this literature.

Nonetheless, one should not conclude that the traditions reflected in these materials are entirely South Indian. For instance, the *Kāmika*, probably among the earliest of these neo-Saiddhāntika Tantras, is aware also of an east Indian context, ruling in its coverage of temple worship that devotional songs should be sung either in the Gauḍa language or the Drāviḍa, that is to say, in the vernacular of Bengal or Tamil. This prescription may be understood in the context of textual and epigraphic evidence that east Indian (*gauḍadeśīya*) Saiddhāntikas were involved in the propagation of the Saiddhāntika tradition in Tamil Nadu, a phenomenon of which we have seen an example above in the ascetic Brahmaśiva who carried the Saiddhāntika tradition of the Golagī Maṭha in central India south to Thiruvarur.

The corpus of Śaiva literature from the Tamil-speaking region also includes works that accommodate a more Śākta perspective. This trend, which may be correlated with the widespread construction throughout the region from the 12th century onwards of separate temples known as *kāmakkoṭṭam* for Śiva's consort in Śaiva temple complexes, a phenomenon that has been thought to be a consequence of the growing influence of the non-Brahman, Vēḷāḷa agriculturalist castes as patrons of religion during this period, appears in one of the Tamil *Tirumuṟai*, namely the *Tirumantiram* of Tirumūlar, and also in such Sanskrit works as the *Jñānasiddhyāgama* and the *Siddhāntapaddhati* of a certain Jñānaśivācārya, all showing a similar admixture of the Tamil Śaiva Siddhānta, Śāktism, and Vedānta. A Śaiva-Śākta-Vaidika fusion is also enacted in the system of worship followed in the Chidambaram temple by its Dīkṣita (non-Ādiśaiva) priesthood seen in their Paddhatis for regular and festival worship, namely the *Cidambareśvaranityapūjāsūtra* and *Citsabheśotsavasūtra* of the *Cidambarakṣetrasarvasva*.

The desire of certain South Indian Śaivas to increase their acceptability in the eyes of the Smārtas may also account for the *Śrīkaṇṭhabhāṣya*, a Śaiva commentary on the *Brahmasūtra* composed by Nīlakaṇṭha, also called Śrīkaṇṭha. For this work goes beyond the stance of the Tamil neo-Saiddhāntikas to expound a vedantic Śaiva nondualism in which Śiva qualified by his power of consciousness (*cicchaktiviśiṣṭaśivādvaita*) is said, in keeping with vedantic orthodoxy, to be both the efficient and the material cause of the world, drawing for this purpose not only on the usual Brahmanical sources but also on the works of the Kashmirian Śākta-Śaivas, quoting the *Īśvarapratyabhijñākārikā* of Utpaladeva and the *Bodhapañcadaśikā* and *Tantrāloka* of Abhinavagupta, though without identifying the authors or works by name. In the 16th century Appayya Dīkṣita wrote the *Śivārkamaṇidīpikā*, an elaborate commentary on this work, and an independent treatise, the *Śivādvaitanirṇaya*, in which he contended that Nīlakaṇṭha's doctrine is ultimately indistinguishable from the pure nondualism (*śuddhādvaita*) of the Smārtas. This interpretation is implausible and it was not universally accepted: it was resisted by Brahmavidyādhvarīndra in his *Vedāntasarvasvaśivadarpaṇa*. But whatever the truth of this, we learn that it was possible at this time to be a Saiddhāntika in one's ritual life while adhering to Smārta orthodoxy in one's metaphysics. For Appayya Dīkṣita, as we have seen above, was also the author of an exhaustive Saiddhāntika Paddhati, the *Śivārcanacandrikā*.

Nonprescriptive Evidence

In this survey of the Śaiva literature I hope to have shown something of the richness and diversity of our surviving textual record and its great range both in time and geographical distribution. But I cannot end without pointing to this record's limitations as evidence of the traditions that produced it. The foremost of these is that the sources are almost entirely prescriptive. This means that they tell Śaivas what to do and what to think (and sometimes why they should do so) but disclose very little about the prevalence of the practices and beliefs that they advocate, of where or when they originated, of where and when they spread, or of the institutional infrastructure and patronage that enabled and sustained these developments. Anyone undertaking the study of this literature with an historian's perspective should be aware of this problem and work towards its alleviation by confronting the texts with various forms of non-prescriptive evidence.

Some of this evidence is to be found within the texts themselves, especially in those of professed human authorship, in the form of accounts of lineages and institutional affiliations and in reports of what other groups were actually doing and thinking. There is also a certain amount of information that can be gleaned outside the Śaiva literature, from portrayals of Śaivas in dramas, historical Kāvyas, local chronicles, satirical works, narrative fiction, and reports of their practices and beliefs in non-Śaiva religious literature.

But we also have nonliterary evidence. We have the material evidence provided by what survives of temples, monasteries, and images of deities in the various regions; we have ethnographic records of Śaiva groups from the 19th century onwards; and above all we have the evidence of the very numerous inscriptions on stone and copper plates found in the subcontinent and Southeast Asia that record donations made by rulers and others to religious beneficiaries, establishing temples and installing deities, and providing endowments to finance their worship and the support of ascetics and priests. These data, material, ethnographic, and epigraphic, enable us to learn much more than the prescriptive texts reveal about the date, spread, and patronage of the Śaiva movements in India and beyond, to gain insight into their relative strength in various regions and periods, and to see important elements of these traditions and their institutions that are not mentioned in the prescriptive literature or if mentioned are not emphasized, and in some cases to find in our texts evidence whose significance is not evident until the texts are reread in the light of the nonprescriptive record.

The most effective work on the Śaiva record will be that which not only transcends the limitation long prevalent of focus on one artificially constructed territory such as "→ Kashmir Śaivism" or "South Indian Śaivism" to the exclusion of others, not to mention neglect of the position of these coexisting and often cofunctioning traditions in the broader picture of Brahmanical, Buddhist, and Jaina religion, but also transcends the limitation that has tended to separate those able to read and understand the prescriptive and theoretical literature of religious traditions from those who concentrate their attention on epigraphic and material or ethnographic data. It is only by attempting to encompass all these forms of evidence that we can hope to escape to some extent at least from the limitations of each.

(This essay is essentially Sanderson, 2014, stripped of its extensive annotation and slightly expanded through the incorporation of some material from that annotation. I thank Professors Fujii and Yokochi, the editors of Kyoto University's *Journal of Indological Studies*, in which that study was published, for their kind permission to adapt that publication for this encyclopedia. Readers may consult the original publication for the evidence supporting the main text and for the bibliographical details of the works, primary and secondary, on which it rests.)

Bibliography

Blake Michael, R., *The Origins of Vīraśaiva Sects: A Typological Analysis of Ritual and Associated Patterns in the Śūnyasaṃpādane*, Delhi, 1992.

Dhavamony, M., *Love of God According to the Śaiva Siddhānta: A Study in the Mysticism of Theology of Śaivism*, Oxford, 1971.

Goodall, D., *The Parākhyatantra: A Scripture of the Śaiva Siddhānta: A Critical Edition and Annotated Translation*, CI 98, Pondicherry, 2004.

Goodall, D., "Problems of Name and Lineage: Relationships Between South Indian Authors of the 'Śaiva Siddhānta'" (a review of *Somaśambhupaddhati: Rituels dans la tradition śivaïte selon Somaśambhu: Quatrième partie: rituels optionnels: pratiṣṭhā* by H. Brunner-Lachaux), *JRAS* 3/10, 2000, 205–216.

Goodall, D., *Bhaṭṭa Rāmakaṇṭha II's Commentary on the Kiraṇatantra: Volume I: chapters 1–6: Critical Edition and Annotated Translation*, PDI 86/1, Pondicherry, 1998.

Goodall, D., & H. Isaacson, "Workshop on the Niśvāsatattvasaṃhitā: The Earliest Surviving Śaiva Tantra?", *NNGMCP* 3, 2007, 4–6.

Goudriaan, T., & S. Gupta, *Hindu Tantric and Śākta Literature*, HIL II/2, Wiesbaden, 1981.

Hara, M., "Materials for the Study of Pāśupata Śaivism," diss., Harvard University, 1966.

Mallinson, J., "Nāth Sampradāya," in: K.A. Jacobsen *et al.*, eds., *Brill's Encyclopedia of Hinduism*, vol. III, Leiden, 2011, 409–428.

Sanderson A., "The Śaiva Literature," *JIS* 24–25, 2014, 1–113.

Sanderson, A., "The Impact of Inscriptions on the Interpretation of Early Śaiva Literature," *IIJ* 56, 2013, 211–244.

Sanderson, A., "The Śaiva Age: An Explanation of the Rise and Dominance of Śaivism During the Early Medieval Period," in: S. Einoo, ed., *Genesis and Development of Tantrism*, Tokyo, 2009, 41–349.

Sanderson, A., "The Śaiva Exegesis of Kashmir," in D. Goodall & A. Padoux, eds., *Mélanges tantriques à la mémoire d'Hélène Brunner / Tantric Studies in Memory of Hélène Brunner*, CI 106, Pondicherry, 2007a, 231–442; 551–582.

Sanderson, A., "Atharvavedins in Tantric Territory: The Āṅgirasakalpa Texts of the Oriya Paippalādins and their Connection with the Trika and the Kālīkula, With Critical Editions of the Parājapavidhi, the Parāmantravidhi, and the *Bhadrakālīmantravidhiprakaraṇa," in: A. Griffiths & A. Smiedchen, eds., *The Atharvaveda and its Paippalāda Śākhā: Historical and Philological Papers on a Vedic Tradition*, Aachen, 2007b, 195–311.

Sanderson, A., "The Lākulas: New Evidence of a System Intermediate Between Pāñcārthika Pāśupatism and Āgamic Śaivism," *IPA* 26, 2006, 143–217.

Sanderson, A., "The Śaiva Religion Among the Khmers, Part I," *BÉFEO* 90, 2003, 352–464.

Sanderson, A., "History Through Textual Criticism in the Study of Śaivism, the Pañcarātra and the Buddhist Yoginītantras," in: F. Grimal, ed., *Les sources et le temps/ Sources and Time*, PDI 91, Pondicherry, 2001, 1–47.

Sanderson, A., "Meaning in Tantric Ritual," in: A.M. Blondeau & K. Schipper, eds., *Essais sur le Rituel II: Colloque du Centenaire de la Section des Sciences religieuses de l'École Pratique des Hautes Études*, Louvain-Paris, 1995, 15–95.

Shulman, D.D., *Songs of the Harsh Devotee: The Tēvāram of Cuntaramūrttināyaṉār*, Philadelphia, 1990.

Shulman, D.D., *Tamil Temple Myths: Sacrifice and Divine Marriage in the South Indian Śaiva Tradition*, Princeton, 1980.

Slouber, M., "Gāruḍa Medicine: A History of Snakebite and Religious Healing in South Asia," diss., University of California, Berkeley, 2012.

Stainton, H., "Poetry and Prayer: Stotras in the Religious and Literary History of Kashmir," diss., Columbia University, 2013.

Törzsök, J., "The Doctrine of Magic Female Spirits: A Critical Edition of Selected Chapters of the Siddhayogeśvarīmata(tantra) with Annotated Translation and Analysis," diss., University of Oxford, 1999.

Vasudeva, S., *The Yoga of the Mālinīvijayottaratantra, Chapters 1–4, 7, 11–17: Critical Edition, Translation and Notes*, CI 97, Pondicherry, 2004.

Viswanathan Peterson, I., *Poems to Śiva: The Hymns of the Tamil Saints*, Delhi, 1991.

Watson, A., *The Self's Awareness of Itself: Bhaṭṭa Rāmakaṇṭha's Arguments Against the Buddhist Doctrine of No-Self*, DNRL 32, Vienna, 2006.

Yokochi, Y., *The Skandapurāṇa*, vol. III: *Adhyayas 34.1–61, 53–69: The Vindhyavāsinī Cycle*, Groningen, 2013.

Alexis Sanderson

Hinduism and Judaism

The term "Judaism" refers to the religion and culture whose teachings and practices are derived from the Hebrew Bible and the rabbinic tradition. Contrary to popular views that see Hinduism and Judaism at opposite ends of the religious landscape, there are compelling symmetries and affinities between → Veda and Torah, and between rabbinic and Brahmanical traditions. Interactions between Hindus and Jews can be traced back in Jewish sources to the Hebrew Bible. Jews and Judaism represent one of the earliest extrinsic religions and cultures to arrive in India. Constituting and remaining a religious minority in India since the 1st millennium CE, Jews have lived in different locales in India with no instances of persecution from the majority Hindus. In contrast to other parts of the world, India is remarkable for the absence of anti-Semitism and its legacy of loyalty and benevolence toward its Jewish community.

Indo-Judaic Studies and the Jews of India

The historiography of the Jewish community in India is an integral area in the academic field of Indo-Judaic Studies drawing upon local oral traditions as well as documents and artifacts. The literature and material objects suggest a flourishing Jewish community that enjoyed amicable relationships with their Indian neighbors. The encounters between Jews and the people of ancient India began with commerce and trade, which over time fostered cultural and religious exchanges. Tablets found in Babylonia serve as evidence of trade and other cultural interactions between Indians and Israelites. In the biblical Book of Esther, India is mentioned in reference to King Ahasuerus, who reigned from Hodu (India) to Cush (Ethiopia). In later periods, we find references to trade with India in the Talmud and other Jewish texts. In Jewish Hellenistic writings such as those of Josephus Flavius and Philo of Alexandria, there are positive references to Indian philosophy; other thinkers such as Aristotle believed that Jews descended from Brahmans and that, like the philosophers of Greece, they represent an elite intellectual community. Documents found in the Cairo Genizah include travelogues from the medieval period, by such explorers as Benjamin of Tudela and other Jewish merchants and philosophers who visited India and reported on its Jewish community. Objects such as copper plates from Malabar, the earliest of which dates from 843 CE, and a later one given to the leader of the Jewish community of Kochi (Cochin) by the king in the year 1001 provide further evidence for Jewish life in India from the 9th century onward.

The oldest group is the Jews in and around Kochi in the state of Kerala, whose origins in India according to local historical traditions can be traced to the year 70 CE, when the Romans destroyed Jerusalem and the Second Temple. They first settled in Shingly (present-day Kodungallur), where they were welcomed and given land by the local kings, who bestowed royalty on their leader, Joseph Rabban. Consequently the community enjoyed prosperity and religious freedom. They became prosperous as merchants, built synagogues, and developed their unique style of liturgy. Upon the arrival of the Portuguese in the 14th century, the Jews of Shingly migrated to Kochi, where they established themselves economically and culturally. Under Dutch rule in the 17th century, Kochi Jewry enjoyed a renewal of literary and liturgical creativity that drew on their places of origins that include Syria, Afghanistan, and Persia, as well as local Indian culture (Katz & Goldberg, 1993; Johnson, 2007).

This intercultural symbiosis includes poetic and liturgical compositions, and customs emulating local royal and priestly symbols. Unique Kochi *minhagim* (Heb. customs) include celebrating the Jewish fall holiday of Simchat Torah (lit. Joy of Torah) by placing the Torah scroll in a temporary ark and parading on the streets with it. The Jewish spring holiday of Passover, known for its joyful feast of the Seder (the ritual meal), is a paradigmatic family holiday commemorating the Israelites' Exodus from Egypt. Unlike Jews in other places around the world, for whom this is an occasion in which children are active participants, the Kochi Jews have cultivated a more somber view toward this holiday according to which children are not given a role in the recitation of the story, and fasting and other austerities are integral to their celebration of this eight-day holiday. These examples represent adaptations of rules and practices that Kochi Jews share with their Hindu neighbors who hold priestly and royal symbols, especially those of → purity, in highest esteem and incorporate these into their holiday observances. Another testimony to the integration of Jews into the Hindu culture is Jewish women's songs from Kochi. Sung in Malayalam, they are striking in their praise of the friendship between the Jews and their Hindu neighbors. Since the 1950s, most of the Kochi Jews have immigrated to Israel, with only a few elderly members remaining today who maintain their beautiful synagogue in Kochi (Katz & Goldberg, 1993; Katz, 2000; Johnson, 2007).

The largest group of Indian Jews is the Bene Israel, who has lived mostly in Mumbai and also in Pune, Ahmedabad, and New Delhi. They trace their history in India to a group of survivors of a shipwreck on the Konkan coast. According to their legends, they are descendants of one of the lost tribes of Israel, having left Palestine fleeing persecution by Antiochus Epiphanes around 175 BCE. Others offer the theory that the Bene Israel came to India in the 5th or 6th century CE from either southern Arabia or Persia. The only written reference to the Bene Israel is a letter from the 18th century written by a Christian missionary who claims that the only Hebrew prayer that they knew was the *Shema*. Having been isolated from the rest of the Jewish world and without access to the Torah and the Talmud, the Bene Israel remarkably maintained essential Jewish practices such as dietary laws, circumcision, the Sabbath, and the major holidays. They worked as oil pressers and in farming and refrained from working on the Sabbath. Their unique rituals include the celebration of Eliyahoo Hannabi (Elijah the Prophet), who according to them ascended to heaven from the village of Khandalla in the Konkan. Without compromising their distinctive Jewish identity, the Bene Israel integrated into the local community by speaking Marathi and absorbing local practices such as the naming ceremony on the occasion of the birth of a girl. Since their discovery by a Kochi Jew two hundred years ago, the Bene Israel built synagogues and deepened their knowledge of Hebrew and Jewish teachings. In the 19th and 20th centuries, many served as officers in the British army and government, while others entered the professions as journalists, architects, writers, physicians, lawyers, social workers, engineers, and teachers. British presence in the army and government, as well as American Congregationalist missionaries that established educational institutions, enabled Bene Israel accessibility to the English language, which facilitated its acceptance and embrace by the Jewish community worldwide (Roland, 1998). Two well-known members of the Bene Israel are Nissim Ezekiel, one of India's leading poets writing in English, and Esther David, a novelist of international renown. Since the establishment of the State of Israel in 1948, the majority of Bene Israel has immigrated to Israel. Today approximately 50,000 Bene Israel are in Israel, while in India they number around 5,000.

The most recent group to settle in India is the Iraqi Jews known as the Baghdadis, merchant traders who arrived in the 18th century and established their community primarily in Mumbai and Kolkata. In the early 1830s, David Sassoon, scion of a wealthy family from Baghdad whose political influence and fortunes in Iraq were threatened, arrived in Bombay. The Sassoons initially established themselves in the textile trade and later in real estate and in building, together with the British, India's ports. Their name became synonymous with the history of the Baghdadi community in India and in other parts of South and Southeast Asia, not only because of their wealth and social rank among the British but also due to their generosity and philanthropy both in the Jewish community and beyond. The Sassoons built synagogues and educational and cultural institutions, and were revered for their charitable donations. With their support, most Baghdadi Jews led comfortable lives, enjoying prosperity while maintaining their religious identity. In their effort to gain acceptance by the British both economically and socially, the Baghdadis adopted English as their first language, joined British clubs that excluded Indians, and separated themselves even from their fellow Bene Israel Jews. At their peak, they numbered around 5,000, whereas today their community has dwindled to approximately 100 persons (Roland, 2009).

Interestingly, the largest Jewish community in India at any given time is Israeli backpackers and tourists, whose number is estimated to be between 50,000 and 60,000 (see also → tourism). Their presence has resulted in the establishment of Chabad Houses, an international Jewish outreach organization throughout India and other parts of Asia, which dedicate themselves to serving the spiritual needs of the indigenous Jewish community as well as tourists, businesspeople, and other short-term residents. While representing a variety of age groups, the majority of these Israelis are people in their early twenties who, following their military service, flock to India for spiritual and recreational reasons alike. For those among them who are observant, India is an attractive destination for a number of reasons, including dietary ones, given the strictly vegetarian Hindu diet prevailing in India, which accommodates *kashrut* (Jewish dietary) laws.

The Comparative Study of Hinduism and Judaism

Ethnography of Indian Jewish communities by scholars such as N. Katz, who is also the founder and editor of the *Journal of Indo-Judaic Studies*, provide case studies that bring to light the relationship between religious behavior and ethnic identity, and between religion and culture. Analytic categories such as these enable and further the academic area of the comparative study of Hinduism and Judaism. This area was established nearly two decades ago at the American Academy of Religion, offering analytical categories through which South Asian and Judaic scholars delineate and explicate elements of Hindu and Jewish traditions. At its inception, scholars such as B.A. Holdrege (1996) and P. Morris, who founded this academic group, articulated their rationale in defining this academic study as providing an alternative to the protestant Christian paradigm of comparative religion, which privileges certain categories of analysis, such as belief, faith, and theology, while undermining others such as ritual (Holdrege, 2007). Focusing on purity laws and rituals, for example, serves to delineate the religio-legal parameters that operate in both traditions.

The comparative study of Hinduism and Judaism encompasses a wide range of topics of research and scholarship including Veda and Torah, rabbinic and Brahmanical traditions, → *bhakti* and Hasidic movements, and Hindu and Jewish diasporas. The volume *Between Jerusalem and Benares: Comparative Studies in Judaism and Hinduism*, published in 1994, is the first attempt by a group of scholars of Hinduism and Judaism to take seriously the cross-cultural affinities between these traditions. These essays explore the historical connections and influences between the two cultures; highlight resonances of concepts and practices; and feature comparative themes such as → *dharma* and Halacha (or Halakhah), → *guru* and zaddiq, and tantric and kabbalistic notions of union with the divine.

The premise of this area of comparative study is that unlike other traditions that are missionizing and therefore aim toward absorbing all cultures, the teachings and practices of Hinduism and Judaism are grounded in and aim to preserve the history, land, and language of the two ethno-religious groups and traditions. Jews and Hindus have traditionally ascribed identity in their respective groups on the basis of birth, thus setting boundaries that distinguish them from outsiders. Veda and Torah are revealed scriptures whose teachings and interpretations by their religious leadership and intellectual elite shaped the beliefs and practices of their respective ethno-religious groups. These traditions accept the sacredness of Sanskrit and Hebrew, the holiness of the lands of India and Israel, the transmission of religious identity through birth, and the revealed truths of Veda and Torah.

The term "Torah" in Hebrew is derived from the root *yrh-*, "to teach." The term in its narrow sense refers to the Pentateuch or the Five Books of Moses (Genesis, Exodus, Leviticus, Numbers, and Deuteronomy). A broader meaning of Torah is the entire Hebrew Bible, which includes Nevi'im (Prophets) and Ketuvim (Writings). The all-encompassing meaning of Torah includes not only the written Torah but also the oral Torah, which according to tradition was integral to the revelation at Sinai. The oral Torah is the tradition of interpretation of all the teachings and laws in the written Torah initially transmitted orally and then written down in the Talmud and Midrash, thus forming a vast body of thought and literature that spans over two millennia. Similarly, the term "Veda," in its narrow sense, refers to the four primary Saṃhitas, the *Ṛgveda, Sāmaveda, Yajurveda*, and *Atharvaveda*. Subsequent writings have been assimilated into the tradition, and the Veda expanded to a body of literature much larger than the core texts.

Representations of the Veda and Torah also include cosmological principles that transcend their common meaning as sacred texts. The word of god/God in both traditions is perceived not only as the written text with its cognitive content but also as the sound or vocalization of its words. Torah and Veda signify not only knowledge of the divine but also the embodiment of the divine. Moreover, the word of God/god as manifested in Torah and Veda is both its source and its expression. The Veda is described as the collection of *mantras* for the Brahmanical performance of the sacrifices (*yajñas*), as the essence of *brahman* and thus ultimate reality embodied in the word, and as the blueprint used by the creator in the process of creation.

The creative power of the divine speech is explicit in chapter 1 in the Book of Genesis, in which God speaks the world into creation. While certain rabbinic texts connect the Torah as the word of God with the notion of the blueprint of the creation of the cosmos, a fuller expression of this idea is found in kabbalistic texts in the medieval period. In the Kabbala, the Torah is conceived as the word or name of God (*HaShem*, lit. the name), which is revealed in the created world. The Torah is also personified as primordial wisdom that enabled creation. The Torah is perceived as divine language as well and is linked with the vision of creation according to which God "looked into" the Torah as an architect examines a blueprint:

> It is written in the Torah: "In the beginning God created the heavens and the earth"; He looked at this expression and created heaven and earth. In the Torah it is written: "Let there be light"; He looked at these words and created light; and in this manner was the whole world created. (Zohar II.161a)

Concepts and textual representations of god/God are similar in vedic and Jewish thought. In vedic philosophy, god, the supreme being, is infinite and beyond form. As the principle of absolute truth, god is called *brahman*, signifying the source of everything, permeating every aspect of existence, yet remaining unknowable. In the Jewish prayer book, metaphors describe God as without beginning and without end; as unknown, indescribable, and inexhaustible; and as hidden, yet the cause of all there is and permeating all there is.

Hinduism and Judaism also approach and represent the divine in poetry that celebrates the love of the human and the divine in intimate and erotic imagery. The Song of Songs (Shir ha-Shirim) and the *Gītagovinda* occupy a paramount position in their respective cultures and traditions as representing spiritual love. Despite the attribution of the Song of Songs' authorship to King Solomon, modern scholars agree that the Song of Songs most likely dates to the 1st century CE, when it was accepted into the Jewish scriptures, though it may contain material that is much older.

The *Gītagovinda*, a great devotional (*bhakti*) text composed in Sanskrit, is a lyrical poem written in the 12th century by the poet → Jayadeva. According to tradition, Jayadeva was associated with the temple to the god Jagannāth in the east Indian city of Puri, → Orissa. The *Gītagovinda* has been translated into many European languages. One 19th-century translation by E. Arnold is titled *The Indian Song of Songs*. Whereas the *Gītagovinda* conveys the love between Lord → Kṛṣṇa and his beloved → Rādhā, both believed to be divine beings, the Song of Songs identifies the lover with Solomon and the beloved with the mysterious Shulamit. The commentaries to the Song of Songs often interpret it allegorically as the love between God and the community of Israel, and between God and the soul.

The leitmotif in both poems is the physical separation of the lovers from each other and the passionate desire for their union. Eros in both songs comprises absence and longing for the presence of the beloved, including emotional and physical wounds inflicted on each other. The setting and nuanced features of erotic love in the songs represent unmistakable geographic locations and historical/mythological narratives. In the Song of Songs, the lovers are assimilated into their environment and are associated with specific locations in the land of Israel, foremost among them Jerusalem. In the *Gītagovinda*, Kṛṣṇa and Rādhā's encounters occur in the forest in Vrindavan, on the banks of the river Yamunā, and at the Man Sarovar Lake in Braj. These locations are sacred and are integral, according to their respective traditions, to the holiness of the lands of India (Bhārat) and Israel (Eretz ha-Kodesh). Despite the numerous parallels between the two poems, the lover in the Hebrew text is, more often than not, absent; in the *Gītagovinda*, however, after the painful separation, Kṛṣṇa and Rādhā achieve blissful union. Whereas spiritual bliss (*ānanda*) is an achievable goal in Hindu teachings, the longing for the divine is a dominant motif in Jewish texts.

Hindu-Jewish Dialogues

The establishment and growth of Indo-Judaic studies and the comparative studies of Hinduisms and Judaisms in the last decades attest to the significance of exposing and explicating the relationship between these ethno-religious thought systems. A recent volume, *Indo-Judaic Studies in the Twenty-First Century: A View from the Margin*, provides a context for a discourse on the role of theology and the relationship between doctrine and practice in Hindu-Jewish dialogue (Katz, 2007). This volume features the common strands of the two traditions as orthopraxic religions with hereditary priesthood, sacrifices, and strict dietary and purity laws. Additionally, it underscores significant social symmetries that exist in Hindu-Jewish relations, especially outside of India, where both have been subject to religious oppression. Communities that are just now becoming diasporized and/or modernized such as Hindus and Tibetan Buddhists look to Jews for guidance in the process of diasporization and modernization. As minorities in countries such as the United States, both communities can cooperate in shared challenges such as warding off missionaries.

More recently, interreligious encounters of religious leaders representing the two traditions took place in 2007 and 2008, and declarations of mutual acceptance were signed proclaiming common spiritual values and goals. Peaceful coexistence of Jews and Hindus throughout for the past two millennia has played an important role in Jewish-Hindu dialogue as attested by the 2007 meeting in Delhi at which the delegation of the Chief Rabbinate of Israel convened with major religious leaders of Hindu Dharma Acharya Sabha. At the first Hindu-Jewish Leadership Summit, delegates of both groups met for a historic interfaith dialogue to acknowledge their mutual values and objectives. At this meeting, a declaration of common vision was articulated and signed by the delegates. The document proclaims that "the religious identities of both Jewish and Hindu communities are related to components of Faith, Scripture, Peoplehood, Culture, Religious Practices, Land and Language" (*Proceedings of the First Hindu-Jewish Leadership Summit*, 2007). This comprehensive statement is further nuanced in other assertions in this document and in the second declaration produced at the groups' subsequent meeting in Israel in 2008.

A central feature of the summits' discussions is the recognition of common attitudes toward proselytizing. As highlighted in the declaration, neither religion

> seeks to proselytize, nor undermine or replace in any way the religious identities of other faith communities... Both the Hindu and Jewish traditions affirm the sanctity of life and aspire for a society in which all live in peace and harmony with one another. Accordingly, they condemn all acts of violence in the name of any religion or against any religion. (*Proceedings of the First Hindu-Jewish Leadership Summit*, 2007)

Other key statements made at the meeting recognize that both traditions have given birth to other world religions as Hinduism gave birth to Buddhism and Jainism, and Judaism is the mother of Christianity and Islam. Delegates spoke of both traditions as revealed: the Vedas are not merely books; they are revealed truths by → *ṛṣi*s who are the seers of the *mantra*s, not their authors, similarly to the prophet Moses who received the Torah from God. As traditions deeply embedded in orthopraxy, Hinduism and Judaism share an adherence to purity laws and to strict dietary laws. Other correspondences that were highlighted include the lunar calendar and the fast holidays of Yom Kippur and *navarātri* as well as the spring holidays of Purim and *holī*. The delegates expressed support for self-preservation, partnership, and mutual education in the areas of Hebrew, Torah, Sanskrit, and Veda.

As the summits and subsequent dialogues between the two groups indicate, dialogues regarding multiple interpretations of foundational beliefs, symbols, and practices were prominent. A central issue in this interfaith encounter is the representations and worship of the divine in Hinduism and Judaism. This topic raised extensive and provocative questions, including from the Jewish perspective the issue of idolatry (Heb. *avodah zarah*). While Judaism affirms not only the transcendent God but also the immanence of the divine, it has held since the biblical period a deeply engrained stance of defining itself over and against the practices of idolatry. This repudiation of idolatry is reflected in the second commandment of the Decalogue as well as in the Talmud, which has an entire tractate called *Avodah Zarah*, devoted to delineating rules of conduct pertaining to all aspects of contact with idol worshippers. According to Jewish law, Jews are forbidden to enjoy any benefits of contact with idol-worshipping religious institutions and individuals, whose practices are considered blasphemous. Even the Noahide Laws in the Hebrew Bible, a set of seven laws directed toward the nations of the world, include, along with prohibition of murder and theft, the ban against idolatry.

In the course of the dialogue, members of the Hindu Dharma Acharya Sabha clarified what to them has been a fundamentally inaccurate and flawed view of their tradition. They explained on the basis of the Vedas that their traditions teach of one supreme being who created the world; along with highlighting this essential truth, they elaborated that the multiplicity of gods and goddesses are manifestations of the godhead. Hindu traditions may agree that there is one supreme being yet they can differ widely on the nature of that being and its relationship to the world and the individual. The concept of one supreme being – in contrast to one God – is open to different interpretations within Hinduism while also representing the Jewish concepts of the divine. Contrary to the view that the topic of idolatry may represent an obstacle in Hindu-Jewish dialogue, it appears that not only was it addressed in Delhi, but also, in fact, members of the Jewish delegation displayed genuine openness and trust toward their Hindu dialogical partners with regards to this topic and accepted the self-definition of their Hindu partners without imposing their own definitions.

The second declaration was a product of the groups' summit in Israel and does not present any new theological ideas. However, a more nuanced and elaborate formulation of the monotheistic nature of Hindu belief is expressed in the first affirmation of the second declaration. Accordingly, the Rabbinate recognized the following:

> One Supreme Being, both in its formless and manifest aspects, has been worshipped by Hindus over the millennia. This does not mean that Hindus worship "gods" and "idols." The Hindu relates to only the One Supreme Being when he/she prays to a particular manifestation. (*Proceedings of the Second Hindu-Jewish Leadership Summit*, 2008)

Still, in explicating this statement, Jewish delegates underscored the differences between established Hindu theology and popular Hindu religion, thereby aligning their stance only with those beliefs espoused by Hindu scholars derived from → Advaita Vedānta and Vaiṣṇava canonical texts.

The conversations in the second meeting also highlighted specific concerns of the Hindu delegation. For example, the first declaration affirmed the need to understand each other's religious symbols, culture, and philosophy and to be understood by other faith communities. The seventh affirmation of the second declaration addresses this concern in a specific way by focusing on the misunderstanding of the ancient Hindu symbol of the → *svastika*:

> Swastika is an ancient and greatly auspicious symbol of the Hindu tradition. It is inscribed on Hindu temples, ritual altars, entrances, and even account books. A distorted version of the sacred symbol was misappropriated by the Third Reich in Germany, and abused as an emblem under which heinous crimes were perpetrated against humanity, particularly against the Jewish people. The participants recognize that this symbol is, and has been sacred to Hindus for millennia, long before its misappropriation. (*Proceedings of the Second Hindu-Jewish Leadership Summit*, 2008)

As stated above, it is clear that the *svastika* is a sensitive symbol for both communities and could generate a possible point of contention in Hindu-Jewish dialogue. In the case of the Hindus, a distortion and misunderstanding of this religious symbol is embarrassing; for Jews, the *svastika* (albeit in its distorted form) is a painful reminder of the cruelest crimes committed against them in history. The seventh affirmation not only informs of and elaborates on the original and true meaning of the *svastika* for Hindus but also recognizes its painful association for Jews. In this way, it assuages both communities' sensitivities to this symbol.

The significance of both summits can be further appreciated in light of Indo-Judaic and comparative religious studies. Despite their distinct enterprises, ethos, and rules of engagement, interfaith dialogue as seen in the Hindu-Jewish summits and the comparative study of Indo-Judaic civilizations begin with similar questions: what do these traditions share and what is gained from this comparison and dialogue? A common perception of Judaism and Hinduism is the apparent contradiction between Hindu iconocentric polytheism and Jewish iconoclastic monotheism. However, as indicated in the Hindu-Jewish summits and the burgeoning field of Indo-Judaic studies, examples of cultural and religious resonances and affinities between the two traditions are compelling and worthy of further scholarship. The expertise and commitment of eminent scholars from disciplines such as history, linguistics, philosophy, sociology, anthropology, and comparative religion promise growth of this innovative interdisciplinary field and deepening of Hindu-Jewish encounters and relations.

Bibliography

Arnold, E., *Light of Asia and the Indian Song of Songs*, Bombay, 1949.

Bloch, A., & C. Bloch, *The Song of Songs: A New Translation*, Berkeley, 1995.

Chakravarti, R., "Reaching out to Distant Shores: Indo-Judaic Trade Contacts (up to CE 1300)," in: N. Katz *et al.*, eds., *Indo-Judaic Studies in the Twenty-first Century: A View from the Margin*, New York, 2007, 19–43.

Egorova, Y., *Jews and India: Perceptions and Image*, London, 2006.

Goodman, H., ed., *Between Jerusalem and Benares: Comparative Studies in Judaism and Hinduism*, Albany, 1994.

Greenberg, Y.K., "The Languages of Love and Desire in the Gitagovinda and the Song of Songs," *JVS* 22/1, 2013, 69–78.

Greenberg, Y.K., "Hindu-Jewish Summits (2007–2008): A Postmodern Religious Encounter," *II* 7/1, 2009, 26–39.

Holdrege, B.A., "Hindu-Jewish Encounters," in: C. Cornille, ed., *The Wiley-Blackwell Companion to Inter-Religious Dialogue*, London, 2013, 410–437.

Holdrege, B.A., "Beyond Hegemony: Hinduisms, Judaisms, and the Politics of Comparison," in: N. Katz *et al.*, eds., *Indo-Judaic Studies in the Twenty-first Century: A View from the Margin*, New York, 2007, 77–92.

Holdrege, B.A., *Veda and Torah: Transcending the Textuality of Scripture*, Albany, 1996.

Johnson, B., "New Research, Discoveries and Paradigms: A Report on the Current Study of Kerala Jews," in: N. Katz *et al.*, eds., *Indo-Judaic Studies in the Twenty-first Century: A View from the Margin*, New York, 2007, 129–146.

Katz, N., *Who are the Jews of India?*, Berkeley, 2000.

Katz, N. *et al.*, eds., *Indo-Judaic Studies in the Twenty-first Century: A View from the Margin*, New York, 2007.

Katz, N., & E. Goldberg, *The Last Jews of Cochin: Jewish Identity in Hindu India*, Columbia, 1993.

Marks, R.G., "Hindus and Hinduism in Medieval Jewish Literature," in: N. Katz *et al.*, eds., *Indo-Judaic Studies in the Twenty-first Century: A View from the Margin*, New York, 2007, 57–73.

Nir, E., *Me-Hodu ve-cad kan: Hogim Yisre'elim kotvim cal Hodu ve-ha-yahadut shelahem* (From India till Here: Israeli Thinkers Write about Their Conception of Judaism and India), Jerusalem, 2006 (Heb.).

Proceedings of the Second Hindu-Jewish Leadership Summit, unpubl. ms., Jerusalem, 2008.

Proceedings of the First Hindu-Jewish Leadership Summit, unpubl. ms., Delhi, 2007.

Roland, J., "The Baghdadi Jews of India: Perspectives on the Study and Portrayal of a Community," in: N. Katz *et al.*, eds., *Indo-Judaic Studies in the Twenty-first Century: A View from the Margin*, New York, 2007, 158–180.

Roland, J., *The Jewish Communities of India: Identity in a Colonial Era*, New Brunswick, ^{2}1998.

Shingly, L.A., "Cochin Jewish Memory and in Eyewitness Accounts," *JIJS* 3, 2000, 7–21.

Stoler Miller, B., ed., *Love Song of the Dark Lord: Jayadeva's Gitagovinda*, New York, 1977.

Weil, S., *India's Jewish Heritage: Ritual, Art and Life-Cycle*, Mumbai, ^{1}2002, ^{3}2009.

Weinstein, B., "Jewish Traders in the Indian Ocean – Tenth to Thirteenth Centuries: A Review of Published Documents from the Cairo Genizah," *JIJS* 4, 2001, 79–94.

Yudit Kornberg Greenberg

Secularism

Secularism and Religion-State Relations in Modern India

In the Anglo-American tradition, the word "secularism" commonly indicates the principled detachment of religion from the institutions of public life (Levy, 2001). Degrees of detachment vary, from the absence of a state-sponsored or "established" religion, to the building of a "wall of separation" that prohibits religion from influencing governance and vice versa, to the exclusion of religious symbolism from contexts or actions associated with public life (Eisgruber & Sager, 2007). In India, however, secularism is understood to entail the state's equal treatment of all religions. Indian secularism thus encompasses non-establishment, but disavows separation and exclusion.

The development of this unique understanding of secularism and its manifestation in the government of India are significantly tied to the British colonial period. British efforts to avoid disrupting the colonial economy spurred the identification, preservation, and later the attempted reformation of local religious customs and institutions. Colonial courts interpreted religious texts and practices, and made pronouncements regarding the "true nature" of local religions, particularly Hinduism and Islam (Lariviere, 1989). Additionally, and especially in South India, British officials came to exercise considerable control over the administration of Hindu temples.

Although much of this administrative and judicial infrastructure carried over into the post-Independence era, the Indian Constitution indicated that the country would have no official state religion. In 1976, the Constitution was amended to include the word "secular." However, almost seventy years after Independence, the relationship between religion, law, and the state continues to be extremely complex. In particular, tensions have arisen as a result of the perceived conflict between the Constitution's guarantee of freedom of religion to individuals and denominations, its grant of equality between denominations, and the continued and varied regulation of religion through courts and bureaucracies. For instance, the rise of Hindu → nationalism in the second half of the 20th century was fueled in large part by a belief that Hinduism had been unfairly singled out for government interference. Similarly, the task of ensuring the equality of persons with respect to → gender and → caste has been complicated by the fact that Indian secularism may require the state to enforce, rather than prohibit, certain discriminatory religious norms.

Meanings of Secularism

As a term, "secularism" has relatively recent origins: the British reformer G.J. Holyoake coined it in the 1840s (Holyoake, 1896). In his usage, secularism described an emphasis on the present world rather than a distancing from other, divine, worlds. While the stronger understanding of secularism as the detachment of religion from public life has no single origin, reference is commonly made to European Enlightenment thinkers. Indeed, the popular definition of secularism as a "wall of separation" between religion and state originates in an 1802 letter by Thomas Jefferson to the Danbury Baptist Association (Jefferson, 1802). Importantly, many Enlightenment thinkers were Deists who argued against the relevance of religion in social governance rather than for the nonexistence of divine powers altogether.

Given this tension between ontological truths and social governance, the presence of multiple secularisms is unsurprising. The United States, Britain, France, and India exemplify just a few forms of secular statehood. All four confer freedom of religion upon their citizens in some manner. However, Britain has an official state religion, France prohibits the wearing of certain religious symbols in schools and other public places, the United States only recognizes some religious communities for tax purposes (calling them all "churches") and criminalizes some religious practices, while state officials in India govern many large Hindu temples. Characterizing Indian secularism as a variant of a basic form is thus highly problematic, particularly given the humanist and Deist tendencies of paradigmatic western secularists.

At the same time, the government of India has undoubtedly been remarkable in its desire to not exclude religion from public life. Variously described as a "principled distance," collective authorization (specifically when referring to state involvement in Hinduism), and "religious freedom, celebratory neutrality, and reformatory justice," modern India's approach to secularism owes much in practice, if not in spirit, to colonial institutions (Bhargava, 2005; Mehta, 2005; Dhavan, 2001). And, although the rest of this article will refer exclusively to Hinduism, much of what is said is also applicable to other religions.

Religion and State in the Colonial Era

When Warren Hastings became the first governor-general of Bengal in 1774, he had already issued a judicial plan that called for natives to be governed by their own systems of law as far as "personal" matters were concerned (Rocher, 1972; Rocher, 2010). To correctly interpret and apply those laws, colonial officials would first have to identify and translate them. Texts were viewed as facilitating the uniform application of law in the face of diverse customary practices, and also as repositories of earlier norms that had degenerated over time into a myriad of beliefs. Additionally, mastery over native texts could free colonial officials from dependence on the native scholar-translators whom they relied upon in courts but whose skills and motivations they mistrusted. Enforcing the contents of native religious texts was thus ideologically and strategically advantageous to the early colonial regime. Importantly, Warren Hastings' motivations themselves were not easily categorized. On the one hand, he viewed noninterference as economically sound since it would minimize unrest and market disruptions. On the other hand, he argued that natives possessed their own laws, and that these laws formed a more suitable basis for local governance.

The texts selected by Warren Hastings and his officials were considerably more varied in the case of Hinduism than Islam, for which British officials could rely on the *Qur'ān* and the Hadīth with relative confidence. In the decades following Warren Hastings's 1772 pronouncement, several scholar-administrators worked to identify, compile, and translate the texts most crucial to a British judge seeking to implement Hindu law. In 1776, Nathaniel Halhed compiled the first catalogue of translated Hindu laws, while philologists like William Jones and H.T. Colebrooke produced Sanskrit grammars in 1786 and 1806, as well as a monumental digest of Hindu laws. H.T. Colebrooke's view that Hindu law could be divided into different schools of thought came to dominate the colonial government, and his translations of the two texts he viewed as seminal to Hinduism's two main schools – Vijñāneśvara's *Mitākṣarā* and Jīmūtavāhana's *Dāyabhāga* – were influential for generations.

In the process of collecting and enforcing textual norms, the colonial government naturally left its own imprint upon the very religious laws it sought to leave untouched. The British favored Smṛti ("remembered" texts like the *Manusmṛti*) over Śruti (revealed or "heard" texts like the → Vedas), and Nibandhas (digests containing thematically arranged excerpts from Smṛti texts with commentary) over Smṛti. However, the broad → *dharmaśāstra* canon held the reverse. Similarly, the authority of individual Smṛti texts was hardly uniform since they were both collections of traditions and of expert reflections on traditions, and frequently local in nature. Perhaps most significantly, the British emphasis on implementing the more "authentic" principles found in Sanskrit texts ran contrary to previous Hindu legal tradition, which consisted of interpreting and applying customary law (*ācāra*) with an eye to *dharmaśāstra* jurisprudence. In addition to the rediscovery of ostensibly purer Hindu laws, this devaluation of customary law suited the Common Law's prioritization of generally applicable principles, as well as the more mundane goal of streamlining justice.

With time the unquestionable influence of the state on religion became more overt and self-conscious, and acquired more explicitly normative overtones. This shift, usually referenced as the move from Orientalism to Anglicism, was never linear or continuous. Elements of the move towards greater British involvement in native religion are evident from as early as 1817, when Regulation VII of the Madras Code sanctioned greater East India Company participation in the management of Hindu religious institutions, particularly in the Madras Presidency. There, decades of alliance building founded upon temple patronage had led the East India Company to occasionally arbitrate temple related disputes. Likewise, in neighboring Chittoor in Andhra Pradesh, the so-called Bruce's Code – a set of 42 regulations created in 1820 and named after the commissioner of Chittoor District – represented British involvement in the very wealthy → Veṅkaṭeśvara Temple at Tirupati.

By the mid-1800s, the colonial state's gradual move away from noninterference was indisputable. Perhaps nowhere was this more evident than in the government's approach to the "women's question": the issues of → *satī* (widow immolation), polygamy, widow remarriage, and the age of consent (Chatterjee, 1993). *Satī* was abolished in 1829, albeit on the grounds that it was "nowhere enjoined by the Hindoo faith" (Regulation XVII, 1829). Widows, especially those of high caste who had been required to remain celibate after their husbands' deaths, were granted the statutory right to remarry in 1856. And in the 1929, after much debate, an age of consent was established. Polygamy was never legally abolished, although successive campaigns against it led by native reformers rendered it virtually nonexistent by the late 19th century.

Much of the impetus for this more assertive approach to Hinduism came from William Bentinck, who was inaugurated as the first governor-general of India in 1833, and from Thomas Macaulay, who sat on the governor's council between 1834 and 1838. Both men sought to overhaul the infrastructure and underlying principles of the failing East India Company. Among their primary targets was the previously dominant idea that native subjects were to be ruled according to their own laws and values; under William Bentinck and Thomas Macaulay, Hindu principles were increasingly tested and modified using English principles.

This attitudinal shift was reflected in codifications that sought to go beyond the old Orientalist goal of capturing Hindu tradition. The Sepoy rebellion of 1857 prompted a shift from Company to Crown, which was announced by the Government of India Act, 1858. An extensive new bureaucratic infrastructure sprang up to cope with the governance of the new imperial possession. For instance, both the Indian Penal Code, which served as a model for Britain's other colonies and even exists to this day, and the Indian Civil Service (the "steel frame" of the empire) were established in 1860 and 1861, respectively. In 1862, high courts were established in the presidency cities of Madras, Bombay, and Calcutta, marking a sea change in the resolution of native disputes.

The late 19th-century establishment of British-style courts affected both the kinds of texts judges would use as well as the principles by which those texts would be judged. Instead of the *dharmaśāstra*, judges now looked to case law created by their own courts or to codified statutes like The Religious Endowments Act and The Religious Societies Act. As a result, they no longer needed the help of Sanskrit experts and translators, who were dispensed in 1864. This is not to say that British judges were no longer concerned with the protection of Hindu customs, but rather that these customs were now protected by and subject to integration within a broader Anglo-Indian legal system.

Predictably, this integration was neither fluid nor unproblematic. The close relationship between colonial administrators and the native – especially Hindu – religious institutions, in which they were often patrons and arbitrators, was not always well received in Britain. British observers often complained that the colonial state's involvement in native religion mirrored the relationship between the government at home and the Anglican Church. This in itself was undesirable, but given the growth of British missionary efforts in India, colonial support for native religion was considered especially inappropriate.

However, neither the colonial government nor many of the native religious elites were eager to disrupt a relationship that was decades old and had proven beneficial in many ways. Temples and other religious institutions had become important sites of colonial power brokering, since the state's authority over land and tax revenue drew it into struggles between priests, patrons, and worshippers. Likewise, native participants in temple life viewed the colonial state as providing the administrative oversight hitherto provided by local rulers. Attempts at disentangling the colonial power from native religion, like The Religious Endowments Act, thus met with hostility from both sides.

In addition to codified laws, the relationship between religion, law, and governance was significantly affected by the strengthening of the Common Law. Although they had never been entirely absent from Anglo-Indian courts, Common Law concepts like *stare decisis* (whereby the outcomes of earlier cases are binding upon substantially similar later cases) and *locus standi* (whereby plaintiffs must have suffered a sufficiently direct harm to bring suit) began to apply with full force after the creation of the high courts. Moreover, the Common Law employed a winner-takes-all approach to conflicts that were discrete and separable from broader interpersonal and social tensions. It also created outcomes that were sometimes the opposite of what was intended, as it did in the case of litigation pertaining to Act XX. This was a radical departure from the *dharmaśāstra*-inspired adjudication, which created no binding authority from one case to the next, and which emphasized the ongoing mediation of disputes whose contours shifted with time.

The creation of a national legal system entailed unprecedented consequences for the way in which judicial authority moved both horizontally and vertically. Not only were the decisions of higher courts binding upon lower courts: the decisions were binding across all of British India. Thus, for instance, opinions issued by the Bombay High Court with regards to religious institutions and practices were applicable within the jurisdiction of the Madras High Court. Although religious life in the subcontinent continued to be characterized by immense diversity across sectarian, caste, and geographic lines, the cross application of judicial decisions ignored or papered over many of these differences. The contrast between this new system and pre-Anglophone adjudication was striking, since dispute resolution under systems like the *Dāyabhāga* and *Mitākṣarā* did not create any binding precedent, much less precedent that was potentially applicable throughout the subcontinent. Increasingly, the formalized authority of Anglo-Indian jurisprudence created something that could be called "Hindu law."

The development of legal codes, bureaucratic structures, and a binding, national body of case law cemented the already strong relationship between the colonial state and native religion. Additionally, colonial officials helped administer native religious institutions, adjudicated disputes over religion using a mixture of principles derived from native texts and the Common Law, and frequently tried to reform Hindu practices. However, reform was by no means the sole prerogative of colonial officials. Native reformers like → Rammohun Roy, Ishwar Chandra Vidyasagar, and Keshub Chandra Sen pressed for reforms both within the native community and via the colonial legal system. Others pressed Hindus to revisit and purify their faith themselves, including → Dayananda Saraswati (founder of the → Arya Samaj) and various members of the → Tagore family who, like Keshub Chandra Sen, acted prominently through the → Brahmo Samaj. And of course, attempts at reforming Hinduism from within became the hallmark of Gandhian agitation at the turn of the century. As the probability of independence increased, it became clear that Indians would have to find ways to integrate the system they would receive from the British into a new approach towards religion-state relations.

Independence and the Constitution

In the early 20th century, facing the growing likelihood of independence, nationalists began to consider how religion and governance would intersect in the new nation. The Indian National Congress, which had been at the forefront of the independence struggle, encompassed such a range of political and religious viewpoints that no answer clearly presented itself. By the time of Independence, Congress and the bulk of the nationalist movement had firmly adopted the position that India would be a nation of many communities rather than a Hindu country. Nevertheless, this too did not answer how Indians, both Hindu and non-Hindu, would relate to their state as far as laws, rights, and political representation were concerned. These issues produced some of the most dramatic debates in the Constituent Assembly, which discussed the content of a new Indian constitution and doubled as India's first parliament after Independence in 1947.

That religion-state relations in independent India present problems for which there are no easy solutions is evident from the fact that the word "secular" was only added to the Constitution in 1976, and that there continues to be no uniform civil code applicable to all Indian citizens. As far as civil matters like marriage and inheritance are concerned, independent India has continued the practice initiated by Warren Hastings in 1774, and governs individuals according to the laws of the religious communities into which they were born. However, Article 44 of the Directive Principles of the Constitution keeps alive the idea of a uniform civil code by stipulating that the country will strive towards its development; although the Directive Principles are not actionable as laws, Nehru and other prominent members of Congress insisted upon its inclusion for symbolic purposes.

The tension between the individual and the group as the unit of politics underlay much of the Constituent Assembly debates. The colonial government was clear in its community-based approach to governance, but members of the Constituent Assembly were also significantly committed to the idea of the individual as the base unit of political life. The Constitution they produced, which was adopted on January 26, 1950, included extensive protection for individual liberties like freedom of speech and conscience, a right to life, and equality before the law. Via traditionally liberal provisions like these, the framers of the Constitution sought to ensure that individuals, regardless of their religious affiliation, would enjoy the same relationship with the state.

At the same time, religious communities continued to play an important role in the Constitution. Just after individuals are guaranteed freedom of religion (Article 25), Article 26 grants communities the right to manage their own religious affairs and to establish their own educational and religious institutions. More significantly, Article 17 and clause (2)(b) of Article 25 demonstrate two of the most enduring and challenging assumptions of the Constitution: that social change is best effected via communities, and that it may require treating communities differently. Article 17 abolishes → untouchability in its entirety; although many non-Hindu communities in India practice some form of caste discrimination, there is no question that Article 17 is directed at eradicating a Hindu practice preventing millions of individuals from participating as equal members of the Indian nation. Meanwhile, Article 25(2)(b) provides "for the social welfare and reform or the throwing open of Hindu religious institutions of a public character" (Constitution of India). Moreover, it defines "Hindu" as also encompassing Sikhs, Jains, and Buddhists. The recognition that community life is worthy of political, even constitutional, recognition *and* that Hindus occupy an inescapably unique position within India has affected legislative, executive, and judicial approaches to governance in modern India (see also → modern legal framework).

Legislatively, the early years after Independence were marked by, among other things, the development and eventual passage of the Hindu Code bills, which attempted to synthesize and codify Hindu law. To begin with, the state required an accurate and uniform understanding of Hindu laws if it was to use these laws to govern Hindus (like other communities) by community standards in personal matters. Moreover, in the wake of Partition and the deepening of divisions along religious, linguistic, class, and caste lines, the Congress Party viewed the synthesis of Hindu law as a first step in national unification. If Hindus could be made to overcome their internal divisions, so it was thought, then eventually the various communities within Indian society could be united as well. Finally, others (see Mehta, 2005) have suggested that given the absence of a Hindu ecclesiasty as well as the over-representation of Hindus in parliament, the Indian Parliament is effectively a Hindu parliament capable of legitimately passing laws for Hindus.

Four bills were passed between 1955 and 1956: the Hindu Marriage Act, the Hindu Succession Act, the Hindu Minority and Guardianship Act, and the Hindu Adoptions and Maintenance Act. The content of the bills actually dated back to the early 1940s, when the colonial government appointed a committee led by B.N. Rau to study earlier reform efforts. However, it was not until 1955, after multiple revisions and concessions, that Nehru was able to have the bills passed. The bills devised a set of laws that would be applicable to all Hindus across India, and still form the basis of Hindu personal law today.

Executive control over Hinduism underwent a similar period of rapid transformation and consolidation in the years after Independence, especially via the management of Hindu institutions. Public temples or temples not owned and operated by a single family, as well as monasteries and their associated endowments, required supervision since the informal networks of colonial patronage and arbitrage no longer existed. The need for governmental oversight was especially strong in South India, where temples were larger, richer, and more embedded in systems of local governance. South Indian states were the first to develop large scale forms of executive control over Hindu institutions (see also → religious endowments).

In many cases, this supervision had been formalized to some degree prior to 1947. For instance, the precursor to the contemporary Tamil Nadu Hindu Religious and Charitable Endowments Department was originally founded in 1925 as the Hindu Religious and Charitable Endowments Board of Madras. Since the Madras Presidency, and later Madras state, encompassed parts of four of the five contemporary South Indian states, the pattern set there carried influence across the region. Nevertheless, whereas Madras (later Tamil Nadu) created a central department represented within the state government by a cabinet minister, Andhra Pradesh has created a handful of temple boards to govern major temples like the one in Tirupati, Karnataka has appointed a central commissioner, and Kerala has a cabinet minister, department in the state government, and five regional temple boards.

The duties of these administrative bodies vary considerably by state, temple, and context, but generally they exercise significant control over the finances of individual temples, and temples must receive permission for expenditures above a certain threshold. Indeed, one of the central functions of state-wide temple governance is to apportion the income derived from devotees among all temples under state control. Many temples do not earn enough to support themselves and, given the absence of a central religious organization able to disperse funds, would not survive without the state's facilitation. Roadside shrines, one-room neighborhood temples, and even moderate size temples in poorer or rural areas frequently receive much of their annual budgets from a state fund that, in turn, is primarily filled by the great pilgrimage centers of South India. In Kerala, for instance, temples are still classified according to either a three-tier system devised in the 19th century or a four-tier system proposed in 1990, based on the number of daily and seasonal rituals they perform as well as their real property assets.

The courts have also been influential in interpreting and constructing the unique relationship between Hinduism and the Indian state. India's powerful higher judiciary has sought to uphold both the Constitution's support for religious freedom and its vision of a society less encumbered by faith-based divisions and religiously inspired discrimination. In doing so, the judiciary has wrestled with defining what Hinduism exactly is, which practices are essential to Hinduism (such that they deserve constitutional protection), and which practices are essentially Hindu (such that observing them indicates someone is Hindu regardless of their assertions to the contrary). The latter two questions gave rise to especially influential cases for several decades after Independence, as communities seeking to exclude untouchables and low caste persons from their temples sought to argue that doing so was essential to their faith or, alternatively, that they were not Hindu and thus exempt from Article 25(2)(b).

The courts are thus involved in a process of gradually changing Hinduism from outside. Because so many judges have been learned in Sanskrit and possess a deep knowledge of relevant texts, their opinions frequently intermingle constitutional and Hindu textual exegesis. In *Venkataramana Devaru v. State of Mysore*, for instance, the Supreme Court held that the practice of excluding untouchables from a Brahman temple was actually a misinterpretation of relevant Sanskrit texts that, when correctly interpreted, only required that untouchables have an insignificant role in the worship ritual.

However, even as judges sometimes have implemented a more inclusive vision of Hinduism, the judiciary draws significantly on the colonial era precedent it has inherited, to occasionally interesting effect. In 2011, the discovery of immense wealth in the underground vaults of a temple in Kerala prompted an investigation and a court case involving the local, state, and central government. The Kerala High Court, acting in reliance on a theory of divine personhood and property ownership developed by colonial courts and frequently employed since then, eventually decreed that the wealth belonged to the presiding deity of the temple. But the colonial jurists who had developed this idea saw the deity's ownership as a way to prevent donors from accessing assets once they were granted to temple endowments, while simultaneously avoiding the taint of hoarding that was at that time strongly associated with the Hindu joint family inheritance structure. In this sense, many of the contemporary problems pertaining to Hinduism and law, as well as many of the solutions devised by all branches of Indian government, have deep ties to their colonial predecessors. However, the concluding section of this article will briefly indicate some recent developments that are, perhaps, produced by the structure of the nation-state.

Contemporary Practices and Problems

Although group identities have never been unimportant in Indian politics, they have been especially strong in the decades after the Emergency of 1975–1977. The Mandal Report, published in 1980, advocated for a system of caste-based reservations in government controlled educational institutions and for government jobs. The report sparked a wave of protests from opponents who argued that it discriminated against upper-castes, favored birth over merit, and was paternalistic; several upper-caste Hindu college students immolated themselves after 1989 when Prime Minister V.P. Singh attempted to implement some of its recommendations.

Political debate has also been changed by the rise of Hindu nationalism as represented by the Bharatiya Janata Party (BJP), the Rashtriya Swayamsevak Sangh (a non-political umbrella organization), and their affiliates. The Hindu nationalist claim that India is really not secular because it treats Hinduism differently from other religions – that successive Congress governments have promoted a pseudo-secularism catering to minorities and dividing Hindus according to caste – gained significant traction as reservations and other benefits were increasingly viewed as benefiting everyone except ordinary Hindus. In 1992–1993, the Bābrī Masjid in Ayodhya (believed to be both the site of a Mughal era mosque and the birthplace of the Hindu god Rām) was destroyed by Hindu extremists and there were retaliatory bombings by Muslims in Bombay. In 2002, a train was burned in Godhra, Gujarat, killing Hindu pilgrims who were returning from Ayodhya and prompting widespread retaliation against Muslims. Narendra Modi's election as Prime Minister in 2014 has generated uncertainty about how the central government will approach Hindu-Muslim relations in the near future. Modi, a member of the BJP, was the chief minister of Gujarat at the time of the Godhra massacre and is widely believed to have ignored if not encouraged the retaliatory violence against Muslims.

It is undeniable that secular governance has meant different things to Indians who are Hindu, as opposed to Muslim, Sikh, or Christian. Non-Hindu institutions experience far less government regulation, and courts do not regularly interpret non-Hindu sacred texts. But the critique that Indian secularism is pseudo-secularism wrongly presumes that secularism is a static concept with specific requirements. The number of approaches to simultaneously separating and integrating Hinduism and public life since the colonial era itself suggests that secular governance changes with society. Indian secularism, developed and adapted for its special context via translators, judges, temple boards, and legislators, has sought to preserve religious institutions and practices without permitting them to become obsolete.

Bibliography

Appadurai, A., *Worship and Conflict under Colonial Rule: A South Indian Case*, Cambridge UK, 2008.

Austin, G., *The Indian Constitution: Cornerstone of a Nation*, New Delhi, 2008.

Bajpai, R., *Minority Rights in the Indian Constituent Assembly Debates, 1946–1949*, QEHWPS 30, 2002.

Bhargava, R., "India's Secular Constitution," in: Z. Hasan, E. Sridharan & R. Sudarshan, eds., *India's Living Constitution: Ideas, Practices, Controversies*, London, 2005, 105–133.

Birla, R., *Stages of Capital: Law, Culture, and Market Governance in Late Colonial India*, Durham, 2009.

Chatterjee, P., *The Nation and Its Fragments: Colonial and Postcolonial Histories*, Princeton, 1993.

Cohn, B., "Law and the Colonial State in India," in: J. Starr & J.F. Collier, eds., *History and Power in the Study of Law: New Directions in Legal Anthropology*, Ithaca, 1989, 131–152.

Davis Jr., D.R., "A Historical Overview of Hindu Law," in: T. Lubin, D.R. Davis Jr. & J.K. Krishnan, eds., *Hinduism and Law: An Introduction*, Cambridge UK, 2010, 17–27.

Derrett, J.D.M., *Religion, Law and the State in India*, London, 1968.

Dhavan, R., "The Road to Xanadu: India's Quest for Secularism," in: G. Larson, ed., *Religion and Personal Law in Secular India*, Bloomington, 2001, 301–329.

Eisgruber, C.L., & L.G. Sager, *Religious Freedom and the Constitution*, Cambridge MA, 2007.

Frykenberg, R.E., "The Construction of Hinduism as a 'Public' Religion: Looking Again at the Religious Roots of Company Raj in South India," in: K.E. Yandell & J.J. Paul, eds., *Religion and Public Culture: Encounters and Identities in Modern South India*, Richmond, 2000, 3–26.

Fuller, C.J., "Hinduism and Scriptural Authority in Modern Indian Law," *CSSH* 30, 1988, 225–248.

Galanter, M., "Hinduism, Secularism, and the Indian Judiciary," *PEW* 21/4, 1971, 467–487.

Galanter, M., "Secularism East and West," *CSSH* 7, 1965, 133–159.

Good, A., *Worship and the Ceremonial Economy of a Royal South Indian Temple*, Lewiston, 2004.

Holyoake, G.J., *Origin and Nature of Secularism*, London, 1896.

Jacobsohn, G.J., "Chapter Seven: The Sounds of Silence: Militant and Acquiescent Constitutionalism," in: S. Kautz *et al.*, eds., *The Supreme Court and the Idea of Constitutionalism*, Philadelphia, 2009, 131–161.

Jefferson, T., "Letter to the Danbury Baptists," http://www.loc.gov/loc/lcib/9806/danpre.html.

Lariviere, R.W., "Justices and Panditas: Some Ironies in Contemporary Readings of the Hindu Legal Past," *JAS* 48/4, 1989, 757–769.

Levy, Leonard W., *Origins of the Bill of Rights*, New Haven, 2001.
Mahajan, G., "Religion and the Indian Constitution: Questions of Separation and Equality," in: R. Bhargava, ed., *Politics and Ethics of the Indian Constitution*, New Delhi, 2008, 297–310.
Mani, L., *Contentious Traditions: The Debate on Sati in Colonial India*, Berkeley, 1998.
Mehta, P.B., "Reason, Tradition, Authority: Religion and the Indian State," in: I. Jaising, ed., *Men's Laws, Women's Lives: A Constitutional Perspective on Religion, Common Law and Culture in South Asia*, New Delhi, 2005, 56–86.
Presler, F.A., *Religion under Bureaucracy: Policy and Administration for Hindu Temples in South India*, Cambridge UK, 1987.
Price, P.G., *Kingship and Political Practice in Colonial India*, Cambridge UK, 2008.
Rocher, L., "Indian Response to Anglo-Hindu Law," *JAOS* 92/3, 1972, 419–424.
Rocher, R., "The Creation of Anglo-Hindu Law," in Lubin, T. et al., eds. *Hinduism and Law: An Introduction*, Cambridge, 2010, 78–88.
Sen, R., *Legalizing Religion: The Indian Supreme Court and Secularism*, Washington, 2007.
Smith, D.E., *India as a Secular State*, Princeton, 1963.

Deepa Das Acevedo

Secularism: A Search for Conceptual Spaces

It is frequently argued that secularism is born out of the dialectic between Protestantism and the European Enlightenment, and that therefore it does not sit easily with Hinduism. How correct is this view? Can we argue that at least some features or some forms of Hinduism are compatible with secularism? The success of secularism depends on the availability of certain background conditions within the cultural and intellectual landscape of the religion in question. Are certain aspects or elements of Hinduism a constitutive part of these background conditions? Which conceptual spaces in these background conditions facilitate secularism? Which features of the Hindu traditions inhibit the growth of secularism? This essay focuses on these questions, giving far less space to the equally important question of which features of the Hindu traditions inhibit the growth of secularism. Some preliminary remarks are in order on the two key terms that form the title of this essay: Hinduism and secularism.

The term "secularism" has different senses. It is used for (a) various forms of exclusive humanisms and atheisms, and (b) a political, frequently state-driven normative project that is best called political secularism. In this essay my principal concern is with the latter.

What is political secularism? Broadly speaking, political secularism anywhere in the world presupposes or means the separation of organized religion from organized political power (state) inspired by a specific set of values, principally a common identity as citizens including equality of citizenship and religious freedom. In this general sense, it is or can be a universal ideal. However, its constitutive elements can be differently interpreted giving rise to multiple secularisms. For example, in the French model, separation is understood as one-sided exclusion of religion from the state for the sake of a common identity as citizens of republic. The state can interfere in religion, but no religion can interfere in the affairs of the state or demand that it be formally recognized in the public domain. In the United States, separation is interpreted as mutual exclusion of state and religion for the sake primarily of liberty. Because of a wall of separation between the two, neither state nor religion may help or hinder one another. They must restrict themselves to their own domain of jurisdiction. Even within India, there exists not one but at least two conceptions of secularism. This fact is not always noticed. Many scholars and ideologues, both those who defend and those who oppose secularism frequently, share common assumptions about the doctrine, perhaps even the same mistaken conception. Most people believe that

- there is just one secularism;
- that it developed in the West;
- that it meant a strict separation between church and state, possibly between religion and state, and in some cases, between religion and

public life altogether where separation means exclusion.

Secularism entails, it is assumed, that religion ought to be a private matter. Defenders believe that it is a worthy ideal, and opponents believe that it is undesirable, unworkable in the cultural context of India, or both.

Is this conception really embedded in the best practices of the Indian state, or in the Indian constitution? It is my claim that the actual contours of Indian secularism are different. To outline its difference and distinctiveness from Western conceptions and to specify its distinctiveness is what I propose to do in the first section of this essay. Indeed I claim that there emerged two such conceptions, each of which was distinctive. Perhaps it is best to contrast it with the mainstream European conception. To do so, I focus on the background conditions presupposed by European secularism, and which in turn shape it.

Background Conditions

First, European secularism developed after a great deal of religious homogeneity had already occurred or brought about. Religious diversity was virtually extinguished. After religious wars, the boundaries of the state were drawn along sectarian and confessional lines, following the principle "one king, one law, one faith." Wars were followed by the birth of a confessional state.

Another way to tell the story involves the use of categories of self and the other. In this narrative, religious homogenization came in the wake of a persistent, deep, and pervasive anxiety about the other, about both the other outside one's religion and, potentially, the other within. The other was viewed and felt as an existential threat. So doctrinal differences were not mere intellectual disagreements but were cast in order to undermine basic trust in one another. Even in the largely middle belt, which eventually come to have by-confessional states, others were tolerated, but toleration frequently meant what N. Gole in a different context has called "invisibilization," (personal communication). These vulnerable/dominated religious groups were expelled not from the territory (hence toleration) but from the main public square. So churches of other vulnerable minority confessions could not be on the same high street where the church of the dominant confession stood. Rather, it was tucked away in by-lanes, frequently lodged in buildings that could not look like a church but were residential halls, for instance.

Thus Europe was divided into predominantly single-religion societies or at least a society whose public life was captured by one confession. So, England became Anglican, France became Catholic, Holland became Calvinist, Denmark became Lutheran, and so on.

Another important constituent of this background condition was this: the institutional separation of church and state had already occurred in such societies to a very large degree, which of course is one reason why it is profoundly mistaken to identify secularism with mere church-state separation. The state has already wrested a lot of power from the church. Yet it did not even occur to any one that in order to become secular the state needs to more thoroughly severe its link with the church.

It was inconceivable at that time that the state would not be religious. So most states retained a formal and legal tie with religion. There were strongly institutionalized religious (confessional) states (when secularism was born) – this did not really occur until the 19th–20th centuries – it meant deconfessionalization in single-religion societies and involved a further weakening of ties of the state with the church. The church came increasingly to be seen as a very repressive component of the wider social domain, which, along with the state, threatened the freedom of and equality between individuals. Henceforth, secularism became part of an emancipatory agenda, one which emerged in response to what one might call intrareligious domination. Thus Western secularism was an individualist secularism, born in a religiously homogeneous society.

The background conditions in India were different, at least till the advent of colonial modernity. For a start, different faiths, modes of worship, philosophical outlooks, and ways of practicing existed. Deep diversity was accepted as part of the natural landscape – Syrian Christians, Zoroastrians, Jews, Muslims (Arab traders on the Malabar coast), Turks, and Afghans, who came initially as conquerors – not to speak of a variety of South Asian faiths.

In short, the presence of the other was not questioned. There was no deep anxiety, instead a basic level of comfort existed. The other did not present an existential threat. This is not to say that there were no deep intellectual disagreements and conflicts, some of which led even to violent skirmishes, but these did not issue in major wars or religious persecution. There was no collective physical assault on the other on a major scale.

The need for secularism was not felt till colonial modernity unsettled this background condition – it was only when religious coexistence could not be taken for granted and became a problem that the problematic issue was spoken about and articulated. An explicit invocation and defense of the idea became necessary that all religions must be at peace with one another, that there should be trust, a basic level of comfort, and that confidence must be restored. This was put sometimes normatively and sometimes merely affirmed. The term used by → Gandhi for this was "communal harmony." Soon after Independence (see → independent India), this idea found political articulation as secularism, strictly speaking, political secularism. The state must show *sarva dharma sambhāv*, should be equally well disposed to all paths, god, or gods, the ultimate good, or toward all religions. But this should not be confused with what is called multiple establishment, where the state has formal ties with all religions, endorses all of them, and helps all of them, and where it allows each to flourish in the direction in which it found them, to let them grow with all their excrescences, for example, the Millet system, the imperial → British rule, and so on.

Rather its task as an entity separate from all religions was to ensure trust between religious communities, to restore basic confidence if and when it was undermined. This happens under conditions when there is a threat of interreligious domination, when a majority religion threatens to marginalize minority religions. So here secularism is pitted against communalism.

To generalize even more, secularism came to be used for a certain stance comportment of the state, whereby its primary function is to promote a certain quality of sociability, to foster a certain quality of relations among religious communities, under conditions of deep religious diversity.

A second conception also developed, even more ambitious, that tried to combine the emancipatory agenda of secularism with its other major aim of fostering better quality of social relations – or to put it differently, to confront and fight both interreligious and intrareligious domination, simultaneously. This is constitutional secularism of India.

Its main features are: active respect for all religions and religious freedom for all individuals and groups, but also disrespect for some features of each of the religions. This is a complex dialectical attitude to religion that I have called critical respect. So, on the one hand, the state protects all religions, makes them feel equally at home, especially vulnerable religious communities, by granting them community-specific rights. For instance, the right to establish and maintain their own educational institutions and the provision of subsidies to schools run by religious communities. But the state also hits hard at religion-based oppression, exclusion, and discrimination. Thus the state is committed to actively abolishing the hierarchical → caste order. It has banned → untouchability and forcibly opened all Hindu temples to ex-untouchables (→ Dalits), should they wish to enter them.

So, in this model, the state does not identify with any religion. There is neither a wall of separation nor one-sided exclusion. Nor finally is their exclusive support to one religion. There is support for all, but equally a potential to restrict aspects of every religion if they violate certain constitutional goals. Separation is replaced here by or reinterpreted as what I have called principled distance – a flexible strategy that engages with religion or engages from it, engages positively or negatively, and engages with one more than the other depending upon which of these reduces interreligious and intrareligious domination, improves relation between religious communities, or quality of well-being of individuals (Bhargava, 2006; Dryzek, Honnig & Philips, 2006).

Thus, we have two different conceptions, each very different from all the mainstream Western variants. As can be seen, the second encompasses the first and is conceptually richer. The first protects religious freedom and encourages respect for all religions. The second makes religious freedom a right of individuals and communities and embodies the value of equal critical respect for all religions.

Hinduism

For understanding the modern concept of Hinduism, it is helpful to make a distinction between (1) the religious practices and beliefs of ancient Indian peoples; (2) a fairly coherent set of beliefs and practices of people who to different degrees view themselves as Hindus and distinguish themselves from others, principally Muslims; and finally (3) a body of beliefs marked by an aspiration for unity among the people who hold these beliefs, central to which is the idea that such unity can be achieved in a political form, largely by the political acts of all those who wish to achieve this unity.

The term "Hinduism" can be applied

1. anachronistically and therefore with considerable distortion;
2. to something akin to "Hinduism," starting around the 15th century;
3. to the "Hinduism" of Hindu nationalists from the 19th century on.

The term may be is distorting because it imposes a unity that was nonexistent both in thought and practice in premodern phases of Indian history. It is not until the 15th century that we find the term "Hindu" in textual sources of Hindus themselves. In 15th-century Kashmir, the term "Hindu" is employed by the Śaiva historian Śrīvara to distinguish Muslims from non-Muslims. The term was also used in Sanskrit and Bengali Vaiṣṇava sources in the 16th century to denote those who were not Yāvanas (see → foreigner) or Muslims (Flood, 2005, 1–4). While textual evidence suggests the birth of the term "Hindu" in the 15th–16th century, it is possible to presume that a vague concept was born earlier. Around the time of the permanent settlement of Muslim rulers and the affirmation by the *ʿulamā* of the distinction of Islam from the beliefs and practices of the native population, which was clearly non-Muslim. At any rate, it is only during this period between the 13th and 15th centuries that something akin to Hinduism in sense (2) began to emerge. However, the occurrence of the term "Hindu" in this sense does not imply either that the word was in common usage or that it clearly signified anything other than that it differentiates a group of people from Muslims or Yāvanas. What people within the group share with one another is not clearly articulated. A lucid statement or detailed portrayal of what specific features distinguish Hindus from Muslims is not provided.

This vague deployment of the term "Hindu" continues till the 18th century when it was adopted by the British. In the 19th century, when the public presence of a more robustly self-conscious Christian community begins to interact with this group does Hinduism (2) properly emerge, followed quickly by the emergence of Hinduism (3). The processes that form Hinduism and Hindu nationalism crisscross and overlap, and their origins could not have been too far apart.

Hinduism in sense (2) may also be called "prenational," but Hinduism in sense (3) includes within it elements of (2), but only after reproducing them from within a particular political vision, that is, → nationalism. This is political or nationalist Hinduism for which the term *hindutva* is not inappropriate.

The Idea of Conceptual Spaces

This brings me to my principal concern: to explore the link between Indian conceptions of secularism and the beliefs and practices of the peoples of India, including those who saw themselves as Hindus or profess Hinduism. To undertake this task, an additional issue needs exploration. Sometimes it is assumed that a close connection exists between concepts and their background conditions. I reject this view, because it undermines the idea of the open-endedness of concepts, forecloses the possibility of their novel and plural interpretations, and does not take cognizance of the idea of conceptual spaces. In my view, at certain crucial junctures in Indian history, certain conceptual spaces were opened up which could contribute, under certain conditions, to the growth of modern Indian secularism.

I have used the word conceptual space in the plural. I mean here that some spaces must be opened up simultaneously or over regular intervals of time, which enables multiple historical agents to imagine new concepts, provided they have the motivation to do so. A conceptual space may be opened up and remain wholly unutilized for long periods of time, sometimes so long that it may even recede out of our background, totally forgotten. Or else, it may get filled up by concepts, though these concepts may be in different stages of articulacy, some clearly formed, others only half done, still others barely born. Some concepts in the space may have a very short life – they get made, are used, and destroyed. Others have a much longer period of gestation. Most are revived, modified, recast, recycled, or reappropriated. Some are even mutated. The important thing is they are available in the conceptual stock as a resource, for use, dissemination, and, under certain conditions, for mobilization.

A reasonably articulated and complex concept draws elements from multiple conceptual spaces, provided there are agents with the motivation to do so. This usually happens over long periods of time. This conceptual work is never fully finished and frequently never fully related to one another. So, one may find different concepts generated over different periods of time that retrospectively belong to one family or strongly resemble one another. Seen teleologically, some older conceptual elements may even be seen as evolving into something that is seen now to be well formed. At key moments in the history of a society, all these elements drawn from different periods of history and therefore from different conceptual spaces may be forged together to form a broad conception. Such a conception may even crystallize around a single word. Often the same word is used as the foci of the crystallization of many related conceptions. One can trace their different trajectories and offer a narrative of the different sources of a concept and a term associated with it (or many concepts and a term associated with it or one concept with many terms associated with it). So, my only ambition is to sow the seeds of a non-teleological conceptual history of what we today call secularism. I begin to take the first faltering steps toward an initial survey of the field – by exploring the relationship of political power and religion in early modern India and in greater detail to a much earlier period, a couple of centuries after the birth of Buddhism. I hope to have shown that conceptual spaces in multiple Indian traditions existed where elements were formed, opposed, and reinvented, and out of which modern Indian secularism was constructed.

This shows neither that India has always been secular, in some or the other sense of the term, nor that there is some evolutionary growth of Indian secularism. The story of the concept I wish to construct contains scattered presences of diverse, disconnected elements and long absences. I wish to argue that spaces were opened up in the 1st millennium bce, clearly articulated in the 3rd century bce by Aśokan edicts, and filled by the conception of *dhamma* (Skt. *dharma*). They may have been dormant for several centuries thereafter. But these were filled again by concepts developed in the → *bhakti*, Sufi, and *guru-pīr* tradition, articulated once again first by Akbar and later by social reformers of the 19th and 20th century. During and after Independence, it was transformed by figures such as Gandhi to mean communal harmony and by Ambedkar and Nehru into modern constitutional secularism, according to which the state must keep a principled distance from all public or private, individual-oriented or community-oriented, religious institutions (not to exclude religion from itself or exclude itself from religion) for the sake of the equally significant (and sometimes conflicting) values of peace, this-worldly goods, dignity, liberty, and equality (in all its complicated individualistic or non-individualistic versions).

Background Conditions of Religious Freedom in the Ancient Hindu World

What in India were the broader contexts within which religions/secularities were chosen, entered into, or exited from? How could people cohabit amid such diversity? What did it mean to have an option or choice between rival world views? What did it mean to choose a religion? And to exit one?

I begin this discussion by R. Gombrich's characterization of religion in India (Gombrich, 1988). According to him, "religion" might refer to *mārga*, a path, providing an answer to the question, "What must I do to be saved?" In short, religion might be a soteriology, a meaning endowing perspective specifying ultimate goals, which gives individual life its point and direction, especially when confronted with the certainty of death. Equally, it refers to those embedded beliefs and practices that structure the social life and normative expectations of individuals, particularly in relations to one another. Rituals, rites of passage, rules of hygiene, and traditional norms can also be subsumed under this conception of religion. R. Gombrich calls it communal religion.

This distinction is important because it enables us to see how it is possible in India and more generally in Asia for many individuals to belong to two or more religions, for they can be attached at once to one of the many soteriologies (religion 1) and to a quite different set of communal practices (religion 2). They could continue to follow the set of practices they participated in before the new attachment. Hinduism has over time spawned many soteriologies but with minor regional variations has tended to keep a stable set of communal practices. These communal religious elements have sometimes been so entrenched that even conversion to other religions, those which claim to perform both soteriological and communal functions, has not unsettled them. Thus, many Muslims and Christians for long continued with "communal" aspects of Hinduism, despite a change in their soteriology. Many Buddhists believe in gods but claim that this has nothing to do with, and therefore is not inconsistent with, their religion (soteriology). Gods, for them, have much to do with their this worldly concerns but have no bearing on their pursuit of *nibbāna* (Skt. *nirvāṇa*). This also allows a ruler to respect all "faiths." Since one might without contradiction follow the soteriological beliefs of one religion and the communal practices of another, one must respect both, and so must the ruler who himself may follow one or many "religions." It is clear that one should not view Hinduism and Buddhism as two mutually exclusive religions. To do so would be to utterly distort both.

What are the conditions of the possibility of moving easily from one religion (soteriology) to another? Three immediately come to mind. First, the religion in question must not impose heavy costs or forbid movement across religions. It should contain conceptual resources of ideological freedom rather than unfreedom. This is primarily a cognitive but also an emotional matter. Second, closely related to the first, it must not possess an internal institutional structure with enormous social power. This is matter of social organization, of loose or tight internal social relations, of openness and flexibility within. Third, it must not provide direct legitimation to political power, not become too closely aligned to it. Neither political rule nor political violence must be sanctioned by religion. This is an issue of the relationship between religion and political power, a matter of toleration or political secularity. The absence of political restrictions on religious and philosophical dissent, formation of opposing alternatives to mainstream faiths and philosophies, or on movement from one philosophical/religious outlook to another. This condition seems to be frequently present in ancient India. A glorious illustration is to be found in the edicts of Aśoka, the builder of a large empire in the 3rd century BCE. Under Aśoka no single philosophia legitimated a political rule, and therefore the distance between state power and religion/philosophy was always maintained (for a detailed discussion, see Bhargava, 2014). I believe this point is of a piece with S. Pollock's view that nothing compels us to believe that "legitimation, or its higher form, ideology...have anything like the salience in non capitalist non modernity that scholars have attributed to them" (see Pollock, 2006, 517; Pollock's account is far more complex than suggested here).

In conjunction with other conditions, a continuing tradition of refusal to use any religious outlook for political legitimation helped both religious diversity and accommodation as well as freedom of movement from one religion to another – conceptual elements that were important ingredients for modern Indian secularism.

Secular Elements in the Pre-nationalist World of Hindus

A major contribution in the development of new conceptual spaces was the *bhakti* movement(s), which arose in 6th–7th century in southern India led by the → Nāyaṉārs and the → Āḻvārs in Tamil Nadu, spread to western India in the 13th century, and reached northern and eastern parts of the country between the 14th and 17th centuries.

During much of this period, the focus of attention shifted from elite vedic religion to popular worship of → Kṛṣṇa and → Rāma. Passionate *bhakti* replaced sacrificial rites; ecstatic religion replaced vedic philosophy. Group singing (→ *kīrtan*) of devotional songs emerged as a popular religio-cultural form and pushed Sanskrit aside from the public space. This movement shaped many modern Indian vernacular literatures, which were essentially for the masses. Brahmanical socio-ritualistic order lost much of its spiritual authority, which passed to the *sants*-*gurus*-*pīrs*. This new devotional religion, within the existing social framework, introduced alternative space for the ideas of brotherhood, equality, and individual *bhakti* saints (Jordens, 1975, 266). Secondly, vedic Brahmanism got "transformed into a new sort of syntheses" (Singh, 2008, 509) as politico-cultural traditions were contested within spaces that were opened up as Muslim power and pre-Muslim practices confronted one another. Normative and textual Islam arrived in India and found itself in a dialogue with changing socio-political institutions, individuals, and ideas leading to a new narrative (see Alam, 2004). "*Bhakti*," (a generic term) meaning a sentiment of loving devotion or attachment, had distinct and sometimes contradictory features highlighting both the intrareligious and interreligious eclecticism of the period (Sharma, 2004, 291–327).

Bhakti had two broad strands: First, → *nirguṇa bhaktas* like → Kabīr and Nānak rejected caste distinctions, religious differentiation, and contributed toward political rapprochement as Muslims began their political dominance in India. Second, *saguṇa bhaktas* like → Tulsīdās and → Rāmānuja upheld caste sanctity, had a predominant Hindu appeal and served to galvanize religious fervor. In fact, Tulsīdās was particularly successful in marginalizing the revolutionary impulses of the *nirguṇa* movement through appropriation (Grewal, 2006, 9). Later, in the 17th century, Kabīr was Vaiṣṇavized as well. Notably, *bhakti* did not necessarily bring together different religious groups; sometimes they led to their proliferation such as the rise of Sikhism from the non-sectarian teachings of Nānak (Sharma, 2004, 291–327).

It is doubtless true that the critical edge of dissenting forms of *bhakti* was blunted with their assimilation into mainstream upper-caste worship. But "even if it did not substantially break the boundaries of high traditions, it redefined these in content, modality and address... the language remained evocative precisely because its experiential base had altered but not disappeared" (Grewal, 2006, 16). Thus, one can safely say that much of *bhakti* ultimately aimed at the liberation from rebirth and the miseries of this worldly existence, and some of its strands opened up a conceptual space for a novel and radical normative imagery that would influence the later development of secular ideals.

One particular *bhakti* movement, the → Liṅgāyats/Vīraśaivas led by the Karnataka saint → Basava and popularized by the *vacana* writers in the 12th century, was the most radical. Although a Brahman, Basava revolted against Brahmanical orthodoxy, ritualism, and discrimination on the basis of caste, creed, and gender. His movement gave special place to women and became the predominant factor in overturning Brahamanical superiority and, to some extent, patriarchal values. The female with her powers of creation and nurturing became more important than the male, and the lower castes devoid of the trappings of wealth and power were considered nearer to the god than Brahmans (Ramaswamy, 1996, 147). Worshipping → Śiva, the movement rejected vedic authority, even the rite of cremation, favoring burial instead. It propagated widow remarriage, condemned child marriage and arranged marriage, and did not class women as polluted during menstruation (Jones, 1994, 11). While the initial radicalism and the anti-sanskritization of the Vīraśaivas did not last beyond the 12th century, and inherent socio-economic inequality retrenched caste hierarchies, patriarchy, and gender inequality (Ramaswamy, 1996, 192), three things stand out in the early phases of this movement: first, a defence of social equality and a rejection of both caste hierarchies and gender inequality leading toward a new religious community; second, an emphasis on individual choice and responsibility in religious matters including liberation unmediated by social authority or institution thus developing the conceptual repertoire for socio-religious freedom for individuals; and, finally, this freedom was not only a challenge to established authority but also a platform for radical dissent.

Likewise, another exponent of *bhakti*, → Mīrābāī (1498–1550), gave voice to the subordinated classes (in particular the weaving communities in the 16th century) of Saurashtra and Rajasthan against feudal privilege and caste norms, stood for a cultural resistance to socially imposed marital relationship, and gave refuge to the repressed (see Mukta, 1994; Sangari, 1990, 1464–1475, 1537–1552). Both Basava and Mīrābāī to some degree undermined the idea of closely bounded communities and rendered religious boundaries flexible.

Guru-Pīr Tradition

Although the radicalism of *bhakti* perhaps can be traced back to late Buddhist *siddhas* and Nāth *yogīs* (see → Nāth Sampradāya; McLeod, 1968, 159), the coming of Islam also had a profound impact on the development of what R. Thapar calls the *guru-pīr* tradition. Indeed the popular monotheistic movements of neither Kabīr nor Gurū Nānak can be understood without the disavowal of esoteric ritualism and an egalitarianism reinforced by popular Islam (Vaudeville, vol. I, 1974, 94; as "Sufi preachings had already spread... in Kabir's and Nanak's time" they must have influenced them). Furthermore, these movements differed from both Hinduism and Islam and "cannot be... explained away as the off-spring of a marriage between Hinduism and Islam" (Habib, 1965). There were innovations (the Sufi tradition of the hagiographic *ta̱dkira* genre) as well as continuities, which must be recognized (Lawrence, 1987, 372). *Nirguṇa bhakti*, in particular, "distanced itself from distinctive Hindu and Muslim symbols and encouraged a selfless love for God" (Metcalf & Metcalf, 2002, 12).

Like *bhakti*, Sufism asserted the freedom of the individual to experiment with Islamic religious truth, even if it entailed a questioning of the *šarīʿah*. The rejection of the caste by radical *bhakti* paralleled the Islamic propagation of social and religious equality. Both popular Islam and Hinduism showed remarkable proclivity toward individual religious idiosyncrasy, rejection of social institutions, and their power. The teachings of → Rāmānanda exemplify this. He not only taught egalitarianism but also accepted disciples regardless of their castes. Kabīr, one of his pupils, even more radically argued that each devotee should seek god directly. His views envisioning an egalitarian order were endorsed by broad sections of society including peasants, artisans, and untouchables. His poetry saw no difference between Rām and Raḥīm, Hari and Ḥażrat, and Mahādeva and Muḥammad.

Similar to the *bhakti* emphasis on individual choice, devotion, and *guru-sant* (e.g. the *ācārya* tradition of Nāthmuni; see → Śrīvaiṣṇavism), the Sufis too gave prominence to *pīr*s and *faqīr*s. Over time the fluid teachings of the *bhakti* saints and the Sufi *pīr*s loosened the formal boundaries of socio-religious distinctions. As different regions came under the spell of Sufis, Sufism too got indigenized through the use of regional languages and traditions (Grewal, 2006, 27).

The religious needs of the lower levels of society were fulfilled by the so-called *guru-pīr* tradition, which emphasized individual choice and dissent, social equality, and welfare; sustained the fluidity of elite religious boundaries; taught "toleration" and a form of limited but sincere universal social ethic; and emerged as a popular "religious attempt at social reconciliation and integration" (Sharma, 1974, 189; see also Jha, 1987, 388). Modern Indian secularism is believed to draw its conceptual resources from this tradition. Key Sufi thinkers were: ʿAṭṭār, Rūmī, Jāmī, Ibn ʿArabī (1165–1240), and ʿAbd al-Qādir al-Jīlānī (1365–1428); influential Sufi orders were: Čištī (13th–18th cents.), Suhrawardī (13th–14th cents.), Firdawsī (13th–14th cents.), Kubrawī (13th–14th cents.), Qādirī (15th–16th cents.), Šaṭṭārī (15th–16th cents.) and Naqšbandī (15th–17th cents.). Sufis are often portrayed as a vital link between Hindus and Muslims mitigating, to some extent, the harshness of the Turko-Muslim and Afghan-Muslim military conquest of the subcontinent (Sherwani, 1963; Chand, 1965, 96–100; 1963; Khan, 1956, 252; Yasin, 1958, 51). They are also identified as important agents in the conversion to Islam (Arnold, 1913, 270–271; Ahmed, 1964, 83–84); Habibullah, 1967, 305–306; Mujeeb, 1967, 22; Nizami, 1966, 92; Rashid, 1969, 192–193; Srivastava, 1964, 78; Titus, 1959, 48–49).

In the ultimate analysis then, the quintessence of Sufi mystic teachings, namely, "unity of godhead," "brotherhood of men," "moral equilibrium against slavery, black-marketing, profiteering, venery brought in the wake of the urban revolution of 13–14th centuries," "social service," "rejection of worldly goods and glory," and "pacifism and non-violence" facilitated the evolution of a common exchange of ideas (see Nizami, 1966). "While political strife and social conflict brought forth . . . uncompromising reactions, the periods of political stability . . . and social harmony tended to strengthen the moderate opinion" (Grewal, 2006, 21).

Akbar

I have spoken of Sufis in a discussion of Hinduism and secularism. This in the Indian context is inevitable. India has been marked for much too long with a mind-boggling religious diversity. The coexistence of multiple religions means that virtually nothing in society or politics has a direct impact on any one religion and is almost always mediated by other religions. Moreover, all religions in India are in constant dialogue with one another, mutually influencing, borrowing from, imitating, or opposing one another. In many cases, therefore, it is hard to say that they belong exclusively to Hindus or Muslims. Since they belong to both, they can be included in the discussion of either (see → Hinduism and Islam). This is true in some important respects for some beliefs and practices developed by the → Mughal emperor, Akbar.

For a start, the sheer presence of Hindus influenced the direction in which Islamic thought developed. In a context where the religious views of rulers failed to coincide with the religion of the subjects, dissenters within Sunni Islam continued to invoke the *šarīʿah* but altered its meaning, using it to legitimize an ideal city as one that is composed of diverse religious and social practices and an ideal ruler to be one who ensured the well-being of not only Muslims but also the entire people consisting of diverse religious groups. For these dissenters, *šarīʿah* was not to be interpreted in narrow juridical terms but in broader philosophical terms (Alam, 2004). It became a more flexible concept of practical political philosophy rather than a rigid concept of law. In the narrow juridical interpretation found for instance in the works of Żiyāʾ al-Dīn Baranī and Aḥmad Sirhindī, the rule of the *šarīʿah* meant not only the total dominance by Muslims but also, if not their elimination, at the very least the humiliation of infidels. To those who interpreted *šarīʿah* more philosophically, for example, some of the Mughals, the *šarīʿah* came to be synonymous with the *nāmūs* (from Gk. *nomos*, divine law) the most important task of which was to ensure a balance of conflicting interests, of harmony between groups and communities, and of noninterference in their personal belief.

Akbar creatively deployed resources from this tradition to invent his own policies that enhanced the value of what he had inherited. Since the sultanate was equated with the caliphate in India, every Muslim ruler was dependent on the religious guidance of the *ʿulamā*. The *ṣadr us-ṣadūr* was the chief theologian of the state – responsible for the interpretation and application of the *šarīʿah* and invariably an exponent of the narrow juridical view. When it came into conflict with the broader, philosophical interpretation, Akbar claimed that as a just ruler, he was not bound by any particular interpretation of *šarīʿah*, and if there was any disagreement on a point of law, he had full authority to give a legally binding interpretation – in conformity with the injunctions of the *Qurʾān* and the prophet. In fact, in 1579, Akbar drastically reduced the powers of the *ṣadr us-ṣadūr*.

An eclectic man, Akbar's *ṣulḥ-i kul* (absolute/universal peace) was to be his basis for the fraternity of faiths (Rizvi, 1992, 3–21). When it failed to appease the Muslim orthodoxy, the subsequent years from 1581 to 1605 saw the emergence of Dīn-i Ilāhī ("Divine Faith") – independent of either orthodox Islam or Hinduism and questioning both with a neutral terminology for both intra-controversies and inter-controversies – heavily influenced by pantheism: "God creates visible differences whereas the Reality is the same." Pursuit of empire and spirit of syncretism saw the steady evolution of mutually consistent religious ideas from a multiplicity of sources.

Akbar's liberal religious outlook is also considered to be the motive force of his Rajput policy. His close relationship with the Rajputs was, initially, essentially political, based on an elite commonality of interests. Subsequently, it symbolized a broad liberal social tolerance. This alliance strengthened cultural rapprochement and opened space for the Sufi concept of *waḥdat al-wajūd* (monism as a reality/unity of being) as well as the *nirguṇa bhakti* emphasis on religious unity and social equality.

Akbar's contact with Šayẖ Tāj al-Dīn Ajodhanī in 1578 moved him to a realm of his own (Ahmad, 1964, 167–81). He forbade forcible conversions to Islam, removed restrictions on the building of temples, and appointed Hindus in high places. He organized religious discourses, initially only for the *ʿulamā*, open to the Hindus, Jains, Parsis, and Christians after 1578. In 1575, he gave orders for the erection of an *ibādatẖāna* (house of worship) for religious discussions. Between 1579 and 1605, Akbar hosted three Jesuit missions, but his profound faith in *waḥdat al-wajūd/ṣulḥ-i kul* as the state policy remained deeply rooted.

Between 1579 and 1582, Akbar passed through the most critical years of his spiritual experiences leading to profound changes. Matrimonial alliances across religions were pursued, and the *Mahābhārata* and the → Upaniṣads were translated into Persian. *Jizya* (pilgrimage tax) was abolished again in 1580. Various Hindu festivals were celebrated in Akbar's court. Following Hindu *yogī*s, Akbar abstained from eating meat and had the center of his head shaved. He named his own household servants *celā*s (disciples of *yogī*s were known as *celā*s). He appointed a Brahman, Puruṣotta, as translator and showed interest in the worship of fire and the sun. He had always permitted his Hindu wives to worship their idols within the palace and now showed some interest in the idea of reincarnation. He also venerated the Virgin Mary and gave permission to construct churches.

Akbar developed and implemented the Sufi doctrine of *ṣulḥ-i kul* for which all religions were equal, and therefore festivals of all religious communities were to be publicly observed. This tradition of equal respect and impartiality developed in Akbar's times toward all religions was continued in large measure even by the British. In medieval India, a broad theme of "religious eclecticism" (Shrimali, 2007, 29) can be detected, which embraced Akbar's imperial and aristocratic innovations as well as numerous popular monotheism(s) and mysticism(s), and it is not far-fetched to conclude that while the Europeans learnt the idea of toleration of other sects from their own experience, the conceptual space for the idea of impartiality toward all faiths was created in the subcontinent and learnt by Europe, if at all, from colonial encounters and the legacy they inherited from the polities of their colonial subjects.

Unorthodox Social Movements in the 19th and Early 20th Century

Finally in order to further identify those spaces where conceptual elements forging modern Indian secularism were invented or strengthened, I would like to examine socio-religious movements of the 19th and early 20th century. Here, I would focus on internal democratization within Hinduism. By internal democratization, I mean the following: (1) an attack on religious orthodoxy, (2) an attempt to expand the base of the religion by its deliberate popularization, and (3) a marked concern for the poor, the lower castes, and less frequently for women by offering them forceful visions of individual self-respect and collective self-confidence. Internal democratization in a religion occurs when some members challenge the view that religion is the prerogative of upper-class or/and caste males. It aims at radical interpretation of scripture or occasionally its outright rejection. It results in relocation of authority.

Egalitarian movements that challenged the rigidity of the caste order are many. In their weaker versions (→ Rāmānandīs and Arya Samajis), they encourage a loosening of caste ties. The stronger versions reject the caste structure. Some of these, such as → Ad Dharm, declare themselves to be separate from Hinduism. Others radically reinterpret what is perceived as central tenets of the Hindus found in their preferred scripture and mode of worship (Ramnamis; see → *rām*). A third incorporate elements from Christianity and Islam. Such hybrid faiths are of two kinds. Some, like the → Arya Samaj, emulate other religions but simultaneously stigmatized them obsessively emphasizing their minute differences. Others, like the → Radhasoamis, are more comfortable with what it has borrowed and mark their difference but do not stress opposition.

The Rāmānandīs and Ramnamis

The Rāmānandīs took the name from the founder Rāmānanda who championed Tulsīdās's epic *Rāmcaritmānas* as a primary scripture, as the fifth Veda, representing the language of the common people and the distilled spiritual wisdom preserved in the Sanskrit scriptures of the past. Rāmānandīs are considered among the most liberal of Vaiṣṇava ascetics, who took as their slogan a couplet of Rāmānanda, "Do not inquire of anyone concerning his caste or community: whoever worships the lord belongs to him" (van der Veer, 1996, 267–268). Rāmānandīs embrace relaxed policies on inter-caste commensality and on the initiation of women, low castes, and even Muslims. Such policies contribute to their success. P. van der Veer argues that such theological malleability and liberality was the result precisely of their adherence to the *Rāmcaritmānas*, because it is a syncretic text, which lends itself to radically different interpretations. Hitherto, the *Rāmcaritmānas* was believed to uphold the Brahmanical hierarchical order. The Rāmānandīs interpreted it in a way that attracted lower classes and groups, turning the *Rāmcaritmānas* into an inspirational scripture of caste uplift and upward mobility.

This did not make Rāmānandīs into radical egalitarians; their message was couched in what they themselves saw as an orthodox idiom, and their influence on their patrons showed many features characteristic of what is today known as Sanskritization.

However, the Rāmānandī proselytization is not restricted to caste Hindus or even to Śūdras. This is illustrated by the Ramnamis, founded in the 1890s by Parsuram. Although their practices center on the rhythmic chanting of the name *rām* and thus differ little from those of other *nirguṇa* oriented groups, the *Rāmcaritmānas* figured prominently. Initially the Ramnamis overlooked those verses in the *Rāmcaritmānas* that insulted the Śūdras and flattered the Brahmans, possibly because they were illiterate and knew the epic only through selected verses learned from upper-caste *sādhus*. However, in the last century, the Chamars have not only acquired the ability to read the epic, but also have reinterpreted its contents and even altered verses they found unacceptable. In short, they have successfully created their own *Rāmcaritmānas*, demonstrating that the spirit of the → *Rāmāyaṇa* can appeal to the most marginalized groups (van der Veer, 1996, 272).

Some of these new movements of the outcastes are so vehement in their rejection of the caste order that they separate themselves from all other Hindu traditions, even from the Arya Samaj. For example, the Ad Dharm founded in Punjab by Mangoo Ram.

Ad Dharm

The central motif of the Ad Dharm is the idea that untouchables constitute a *qaum*, a distinct religious community similar to those of Muslims, Hindus, and Sikhs, and that the *qaum* had existed from time immemorial. In convincing the untouchables that they are a part of a great *qaum* with a mythical past and not simply the village Chamars, the Ad Dharm leaders want ordinary people to believe in their equal status (Juergensmeyer, 1982, 45–50).

Whenever there is mention of god in any of the Ad Dharm literature, there is a certain impersonal intent to it, which reflects the influence of the → Sants and their poetry on the Ad Dharm leadership and particularly → Ravidās (c. 1450–1520 CE; see also → Ravidāsīs). He was probably born in Varanasi, as a Chamar, and stated that his trade was low and labor degrading, and that his caste was not honored (Zelliot & Mokashi-Punekar, 2005, 35–39). More than organization and strategy, it is the continuity between the Ad Dharm and the old and familiar realities as expressed in the devotional songs of Ravidās that touched the untouchables. The Ad Dharm appropriated the figure of Ravidās, used his picture as its emblem, poetry and aphorism as its sacred text, and stories about his life as illustrations of lower-caste pride and power. It touches the heart of the cultural tradition of lower-caste Punjab (Juergensmeyer, 1982, 83). His message is very similar to that of Kabīr or Rāmānanda. All of them preached *bhakti* and all of them held that spiritual fulfillment depends entirely on an individual and interior search. None believed that this search was related in any way to ascetic ritual practices or to the obligations of caste. The Ravidās culture being promoted by the Ad Dharm is an emblem of the changing values that the Chamar leadership is eager to establish. These values that the Ad Dharm stands for the objectives of modern society: equal opportunity, reward based on merit, reverence, temperance, and reason.

A critique of intrareligious domination is the hallmark of many of these popular religious movements. Some of these movements also make extensive use of resources with the Hindu traditions that allows free borrowing from other faiths and even free movements from one sect to another. Thus they encourage the principles of both religious freedom and interreligious and intrareligious equality. In doing so, they help provide ingredients to what constitutes a distinctively modern Indian secularism.

Ancient Ideas in New Forms: Gandhian Secularism

With the advent of colonial modernity and the formation of Hindus and Muslims as national communities, religious coexistence in India was severely unsettled. Religious coexistence could now no longer be taken for granted, doubts about coexistence forced themselves upon the public arena, and religious coexistence became a problematic issue to be spoken about and publically articulated. An explicit invocation and defence of the idea became necessary that all religions must be at peace with one another, that there should be trust, a basic level of comfort among them, and if undermined mutual confidence must be restored. And trust and confidence requires that everyone, particularly the state, has equal regard for all religions. This might be called the communal harmony (*sarvadharma sambhāva*) model of secularism.

The source of this conception can be found in Gandhi (1963). Gandhi begins by accepting religious pluralism as the inevitable and healthy destiny of human kind. He affirms, "there is endless variety in all religions" and "interminal religious differences," and states "some go on a pilgrimage and bathe in the sacred river, others go to Mecca; some worship him in temples, others in mosques, some just bow their heads in reverence; some read the Vedas, others the Quran.... some call themselves Hindus, others Muslims..." There is, for Gandhi, not only diversity *of* religions but also diversity within them: "While I believe myself to be a Hindu, I know that I do not worship God in the same manner as any one or all of them" (Gandhi, 1963, 42). Given this deep religious diversity, "the need of the moment is not one religion, but mutual respect and tolerance of the devotees of different religions," indeed to entertain "equal regard for other religions and their followers" (Gandhi, 1963, 43). Eventually, this theological mode of coping with diversity can be enlarged to include soteriologies that do not depend on gods. One can deploy the more general term "ethic of self-realization" that includes both god-dependent and god-free ethics pertaining to humans and even non-human selves. Each of these ethics can be treated as a way of being or relating to the ultimate, in whichever way the latter is defined or understood.

This moral-practical attitude of equal regard for all religions is a (practical) entailment of a deeper epistemic grasp of the fundamental unity of all religions. For Gandhi,

> The soul of religion is one, but it is encased in a multitude of forms. The latter will persist to the end of time. Wise men will ignore the outward crust and see the same soul living under a variety of crusts. (Gandhi, 1963, 41)

The basic reference of all religions is the same: god or truth.

> All religions are true and also that all have some error in them and that whilst I hold by my own, I should hold others as dear as Hinduism, from which it logically follows that we should hold all as dear as our nearest kith and kin and that we should make no distinction between them. (Gandhi, 1963, 57)

This move towards inclusive monotheism flows directly from the most ancient aspects of Indian polytheistic traditions, as mentioned above, a trait they share with other religious traditions of the ancient world. Thus, "all worship the same God although under different names" (Gandhi, 1963, 41). Although Gandhi drew the opposite conclusion that the move to another religion is redundant, this inclusive monotheism also permits easy movement across religions. If different names refer to the same god or the same god has different cultural backgrounds, then why create too much fuss about leaving one and embracing another? Indeed, why not embrace both, even all? Multiple allegiances have been fairly common in India (see Chatterjee, 1994). Three more things follow. First, "to revile one another's religion, to make reckless statements, to utter untruth, to break the heads of innocent men, to desecrate temples or mosques *is* a denial of God." Second, "it is wrong for anyone to say that his God is superior to that of another's. God is one and the same for all" (Gandhi, 1963, 43). At one level, there is a fundamental unity among all religions and precisely because of it they must be regarded as equal. Third, contrary to some of Gandhi's own pronouncements, but implicit in Gandhi's views is a deeper pluralism – what K. Rose (2010), drawing on the work of A. Sharma (2005), calls nonexclusive pluralism. The principle underlying nonexclusive pluralism, drawn from the Upaniṣads, is that of a non-exclusive both/and approach rather than an exclusive either/or approach, an approach that includes within pluralism the possibility that either inclusivism or exclusivism may be true and that pluralism may be false. The political implication of all this is that "it is the duty of the government to offer protection to all who look up to it, wherever they are and to whatever religion they belong" (Gandhi, 1963, 43).

Soon after Independence, this idea found articulation in public discourse as secularism, strictly speaking, political secularism. The state must show *sarvadharma sambhāva* (i.e. be equally disposed to all paths, god, or gods, all religions, even all philosophical conceptions of the ultimate good). The central task of the state as an entity separate from all religions is to ensure trust between religious communities, to restore basic confidence if and when it was undermined. This happens under conditions when there is a threat of interreligious domination, when a majority religion threatens to marginalize minority religions. So here secularism is pitted against what in India is pejoratively called communalism – a sensibility or ideology where a community's identity, its core beliefs, practices, and interests are constitutively opposed to the identity and interests of another community or of all.

Political Hinduism and Political Secularism

Several decades ago, D.E. Smith (1963) wrote that two features of Hinduism undermine political secularism. First, Hinduism still demonstrates a powerful capacity for the detailed ordering of the social life through caste and Hindu law. Though there exist views that Hindu social institutions have resulted from certain historical factors and are in no way concerned with religion, the fact remains that many Hindus still continue to believe and act as if the hierarchical caste order exists. Such a view is bound to inhibit political secularism that is against intrareligious domination. Second, an important aspect of Hinduism that is not so favorable to a secular state is that

Hinduism in the main has not been and is not an international missionary religion. Hinduism in India has a strong tendency to become closely identified with national culture. The promotion of national ideals by the state thus tends to become the promotion of majority religion, which poses a more subtle challenge to the secular state. In recent years, this Hindu nationalism has become more political and more militant.

Now political Hinduism is a view that begins with acknowledging a lack of unity among Hindus. Their political project, therefore, is firstly to constitute a unity among all Hindus. They try to do so by constructing a unifying narrative that stigmatizes and excludes Muslims and Christians. Since under modern conditions this unity can be imagined only within the frame of the nation, the creation of a unified Hindu nation is the second objective of political Hinduism. Finally, since nationalism is guided by the principle that every nation must have its own state, a third objective of political Hinduism is to propel suitably politicized Hindus to capture state power.

In most of its variants, proponents of political Hinduism define the nation in exclusivist terms. The unifying narrative is built by excluding some important groups. Thus V.D. Savarkar famously envisaged the Hindu nation as consisting of all those people who were born in Hindustan and crucially whose religions too were born there. Thus, those counted among Hindus included Jains, Buddhists, and Sikhs but not Muslims and Christians. This political Hinduism, which is indistinguishable from one prominent brand of Hindu nationalism, insists that only Hindus can have a common identity as citizens in the Indian nation state, indeed even in the Indian republic. Muslims and Christians cannot be citizens, unless they see themselves as Hindus. At best they can have a derivate, secondary citizenship. In this strong version, political Hinduism is incompatible with any version of secularism. At best, however, political Hinduism can accommodate Muslims and Christians as long as they cease to bring their collective religious identity in the public domain and come there as bare individuals with only individual rights. These forms of political Hinduism would be quite happy with the American or the French version of political secularism but would remain deeply uncomfortable with Indian constitutional secularism. Why so? Because, political Hinduism is uncomfortable with: (1) interreligious equality, (2) wants the privatization of other religions and the dominant presence of Hinduism in the public domain, and (3) opposes the presence of Christians and Muslims as collectivities in the public domain.

None of this is compatible with Indian constitutional secularism. There is a great deal of empirical evidence showing why political secularism and political Hinduism have an uneasy relationship.

Hindu culture, previously tolerant with respect to doctrines, and syncretic but also always lacking a clear center, a clear- cut identity, unity, and sense of cohesion, has probably now come into itself, as a nation, through the Rāmjanmabhūmi/ Bābrī Masjid issue, or so at least the Vishwa Hindu Parishad (VHP) rhetoric went (Hansen, 1999, 172–185). Through the collective worship of Rām posed as a latent nationalist practice, the Hindus have come together on a common platform and have made the Hindu nation manifest not as a series of "lacks" as in the orientalist renditions, but as a positivity.

With this discursive operation, the VHP tried to transgress both the classical problem of identifying a positive "core" in Hinduism and to transgress the strategies of the Hindu reform movements. The greatness of Hindu culture, according to the VHP, was exactly its antiquity, its continuity, and its doctrinal breath. Hinduism is a culture, a "way of life," and not a religion organized as an institution or a set of doctrines with all the intolerance and fanaticism that is implied. The religious modality of the VHP's discourse was aimed at popularizing the idea of Hindus as a "people nation" engaged in perennial conflict with alien and intolerant semitic faiths.

A vigorous campaign of religious exclusion of Christians and Muslims has been a feature, particularly since the late 1980s. Much of this is justified by the claim that this is legitimate anger against conversion of Hindus to Christianity and Islam. Since 1984, the VHP engineered the revival of a movement to liberate sacred Hindu sites believed to have been usurped by Muslims – an issue that has persistently excited and invigorated Hindu nationalists. In 1992, a well-armed mob led by VHP activists reduced the Bābrī Masjid to rubble as senior Bharatiya Janata Party (BJP) leaders looked on. The Rāmjanmabhūmi campaign was less about god Rām and more about Hindu consolidation, it was about showing Muslims their place in a Hindu country. This exclusionary intent has sometimes turned violent. Though, Hindu-Muslim riots have an old pedigree. their incidents appear to have increased over the last four decades (Akbar, 1988; Varadarajan, 2002; Dharkar, 2002 ; Varshney, 2002; Nandy, 1997). In a majority of cases, as in Moradabad, Delhi, Mumbai, and in central Gujarat, the worst sufferers have been the minorities.

It must be kept in mind that though political Hinduism is opposed to secularism, it has also tried to find a place for it within its discourse. In doing so, it has altered the meaning of the term "secular." Secularism now connotes a political strategy underpinning the practices of a non-theocratic state by which it maintains peace between communities and under certain conditions, within specified limits, protects the religious liberty of individuals. The BJP frequently cites the absence of communal rioting during its tenure as evidence of the secular character of states governed by it. However, by persistently attacking the social and cultural rights of religious minorities, Hindu nationalists have snapped the link between secularism and community specific minority rights, namely, resources to combat interreligious domination. If secularism is to maintain peace and prevent religious liberty, it is fully compatible with the privatization and depoliticization of non-Hindu religions and the deprivatization and repoliticization of Hinduism. Full citizenship rights now depend on ethno-religious allegiance and need not be distributed equally. Principled distance too can now be reinterpreted to mean the distance of the state from religious institutions for the sake of communal peace and religious liberty of individuals and is compatible with the public-political presence of the majority religious community. In short, secularism is now indistinguishable from the ideology of states with established religions. Much of the spade work for this complete distortion of secularism was affected by the gradual fudging of the difference between secularism and multiple-establishment (a confusion also generated by publicizing secularism as equal respect of all religions) and then due to a further distortion of the meaning of multiple establishment. The complicity and practice of most political parties ensured that multiple establishment became a system that pampers the self-appointed, wholly non-accountable leadership of the fanatical fringe of almost every religious group. Secularism was now identified with the alternating appeasement of extremist religious groups. Once the connection of secularism with norms of equality and justice was obliterated and secularism identified with this peculiar form of multiple establishment, not much conceptual work was required to force the term to mean simply a non-theocratic state with an overwhelming allegiance to the dominant religious group that, under conditions of inequality, still manages to maintain a modicum of peace.

Once secularism and democracy were conceptually complementary, now they are presented as mutually exclusive of which we must choose only one. If democracy means the rule of an ethno-religious majority, a view that is part of middle-class/upper-caste common sense, and further, if the conceptual link cannot after all be snapped between secularism and equality (and therefore equality of citizenship/minority rights), an association also part of their common sense, then, given the current conjuncture of meanings, a choice between democracy and secularism is inescapable. This truncates the conceptual spaces of secularism. And herein lies the crisis of secularism induced by political Hinduism.

Bibliography

Ahmed, A., *Studies in the Islamic Culture in the Indian Environment*, Oxford, 1964.

Akbar, M.J., *Riot After Riot*, New Delhi, 1988.

Alam, M., *The Languages of Political Islam in India c. 1200–1800*, Delhi, 2004.

Arnold, T.W., *The Preaching of Islam: A History of the Propagation of the Muslim Faith*, London, 1913.

Bhargava, R., "Beyond Toleration: Civility and Principled Coexistence in Asokan Edicts," in: A. Stepan & C. Taylor, eds., *Boundaries of Toleration*, New York, 2014.

Bhargava, R., "The distinctiveness of Indian Secularism," in: T.N. Srinivasan, ed., *The Future of Secularism*, 2006a.

Bhargava, R., "Political Secularism," in: J. Dryzek, B. Honnig & A. Philips, eds., *A Handbook of Political Theory*, Oxford, 2006b.

Chand, T., *Society and State in the Mughal Period*, Delhi, 1965.

Chand, T., *Influence of Islam on Indian Culture*, Allahabad, 1963.

Chatterjee, M., "Reflections on Religious Pluralism in the Indian Context," *JHCS* 7/1, 1994; repr. http://digitalcommons.butler.edu/jhcs/vol7/iss1.

Damning Verdict, publ. the Justice B.N. Srikrishna Commission, Mumbai, 1998.

Dharkar, A., *Crime against Humanity*, New Delhi, 2002.

Gandhi, M.K., *The Way to Communal Harmony*, Ahmedabad, 1963.

Gombrich, R., *Theravada Buddhism: A Social History from Ancient Benares to Modern Colombo*, London, 1988.

Grewal, J.S., *Religious Movements and Institutions in Medieval India*, New Delhi, 2006.

Flood, G., *The Blackwell Companion to Hinduism*, Oxford, 2005.
Habib, I., "The Historical Background of the Popular Monotheistic Movement of the 15th–17th Centuries," *Seminar on Ideas: Medieval India*, Delhi, 1965.
Habibullah, A.B.M., *The Foundation of Muslim Rule in India*, Allahabad, 1967.
Hanse, T.B., *The Saffron Wave: Democracy and Hindu Nationalism in Modern India*, New York, 1999.
Hatch, N., *The Democratization of American Christianity*, New Haven, 1989.
Jha, D.N., *Feudal Social Formation in Early India*, Delhi, 1987.
Jones, K., *Socio-religious Reform Movements in British India*, Cambridge UK, 1994.
Jordens, J.T.F., "Medieval Hindu Devotionalism," in: A.L. Basham, ed., *A Cultural History of India*, Oxford, 1975.
Juergensmeyer, M., *Religion as Social Vision*, Berkeley, 1982.
Kesavan, M., *Secular Common Sense*, New Delhi, 2001.
Khan, Y.H., "Sufism in India," *IsC* 30, 1956, 252.
Lawrence, B., "The Sant Movement and North Indian Sufis," in: K. Schomer, ed., *Sants of Devotional India*, Delhi, 1987.
McLeod, W.H., *Guru Nanak and the Sikh Religion*, Oxford, 1968.
Metcalf, B., & T. Metcalf, *A Concise History of India*, Cambridge UK, 2002.
Mujeeb, M., *The Indian Muslims*, London, 1967.
Mukta, P., *Upholding a Common Life: The Community of Mira Bai*, Delhi, 1994.
Nandy, A., *Shikha Trivedy, Shail Mayaram, Achyut Yagnik, Creating a Nationality*, Delhi, 1997.
Nizami, K.A., *Studies in Medieval Indian History and Culture*, Allahabad, 1966.
Ramaswamy, V., *Divinity and Deviance: Women in Virasaivism*, New Delhi, 1996.
Rashid, A., *Society and Culture in Medieval India*, Calcutta, 1969.
Rose, K., "Religious Pluralism and the Upanishads," *JVS* 19/1, 2010, 23–48.
Sangari, K., "Mira Bai and the Spiritual Economy of Bhakti," *EPW* 7, 1990, 1464–1475, 1537–1552.
Sharma, A., "Can There Be More Than One Kind of Pluralism?," in F. Knitter, ed., *The Myth of Religious Superiority*, New York, 2005.
Sharma, K., "Towards a New Perspective," in: D. Lorenzen, ed., *Religious Movement in South Asia 600–1800*, Oxford, 2004, 291–327.
Sharma, R.S., *Indian Society: Historical Probings*, Delhi, 1974.
Sherwani, H.K., "Cultural Synthesis in Medieval India," *JIH* 41/1, 1963.
Singh, U., *A History of Ancient and Early Medieval India*, Delhi, 2008.
Smith, D.E., *India as a Secular State*, Princeton, 1963.
Srivastava, A.L., *Medieval Indian Culture*, Agra, 1964.
Taylor, C., *A Secular Age*, Cambridge MA, 2007.
Titus, M.T., *Islam in India and Pakistan*, Calcutta, 1959.
Varadarajan, S., *Gujarat: The Making of a Tragedy*, Gujarat, 2002.
Varshney, A., *Ethnic Conflict and Civic Life*, New Delhi, 2002.
Vaudeville, C., *Kabir*, vol. I, Oxford, 1974.
Veer, P. van der, "The Politics of Devotion to Rama," in: D. Lorenzen, ed., *Bhakti Religion in North India*, New Delhi, 1996, 267–268.
Yasin, M., *A Social History of Islamic India (1605–1748)*, Lucknow, 1958.
Zelliot E., & R. Mokashi-Punekar, *Untouchable Saints*, New Delhi, 2005.

Rajeev Bhargava

Nāgas

Rituals devoted to the propitiation and supplication of snakes, *nāgas*, have been practiced on the South Asian subcontinent for more than two millennia and have spread far beyond India to such places as Tibet, Cambodia, and Indonesia. Moreover, these ritual practices remain relevant for people up to the present day. During *nāgapañcamī*, the annual festival devoted to the deified snakes in Banaras, for example, thousands of people crowd into the area around Naga Kuan ("Snake Pool"), which is situated in the northwestern sector. At this festival, which takes place during the rainy season in the month of *śrāvana* (Jul–Aug), bathers are drawn to the deep, dark pool believed to provide access to the Nāgaloka, the magnificently luxurious underwater world of the *nāgas*. Worshippers honor these supernatural snakes in order that these deities might ensure a variety of boons, mostly related to human and earthly fertility, such as the birth of healthy children and the provision of bountiful harvests.

While *nāgas* are specially equipped with supernatural powers, any snake can potentially be a *nāga*, although in narratives and representations from the Common Era, *nāgas* are depicted specifically as cobras – cobras, moreover, who have the capacity to take on human form but always with some feature of the snake remaining, such as the cobra's hood or tail. J. Williams notes that, in some cases, representations of *nāgas* reflect the dress customs of the time, for the *nāga* statues in Nagauri and Gulgaon appear wearing stone turbans. In relation to these *nāgas*, "Williams has argued that the Nagarui and Gulgaon *nāgas* belong to a 'localized' style, which gives the impression of a folk tradition not fully accustomed to working in stone" (Shaw, 2004, 22).

In present times, women, particularly those desiring to become pregnant, worship *nāgas*. As part of these devotional rituals, women cover *nāga* statues with fresh flowers or sprinkle them with water. In Banaras, one site that is very popular for such activities is at the top of Chauki Ghat in the southeastern sector of the city, where several *nāga* statues are situated beneath a huge tree. Women also dominate the ritual spaces associated with these practices. For example, on Saturday evenings in Banaras, the *nāga* temple called Nāg Kuān – site of the *nāgapañcamī* annual festival – is filled with women who, according to first-hand reports, have been coming to the temple every Saturday night for decades, as had their mothers before them.

A. Allocco notes that women in South India are also the primary worshippers at temples and sites devoted to snake worship: "During the Tamil month of *āṭī* (July–August), a vibrant festival season… I witnessed crowds of women arranging abundant offerings in front of these *nāga* images" (Allocco, 2013, 233). Snakes as ubiquitous, powerful denizens of the earth's surface provide constant and easy access to anyone who might wish to approach them as objects of religious devotion – a crucial feature for those disenfranchised by orthodox traditions. It comes as no surprise, moreover, that these rituals in both North and South India occur during the rainy months, for it is during this time that snakes tend to emerge from their usual abodes and join humans on porches, gardens, and the interior of houses. Thus, an important feature of *nāga* worship recognizes the power of these beings and attempts to ritually propitiate them when they are most active.

The earliest representation of a snake comes from the → Indus Valley civilization in the form of a pottery tablet found at Harappa circa 2300–1750 BCE. On this tablet, two snakes are painted poised behind two kneeling men, each flanking a seated figure. T.V. Mahalingam (1965, 4) refers to the seated figure as a "seated deity," but from the evidence, it could just as easily be a royal personage. Other archaeological artifacts from the Indus Valley civilization include pottery pieces painted with snakes, the carved figure of a snake, a clay amulet with a snake situated in front of a stool on which there appears to be an offering of some sort, and an amulet picturing two snakes and a bird (Heras, 1953, 364). From this evidence, what can be said about the representation of snakes during the pre-vedic period is that they seem to be associated at times with divine and/or sovereign power, and they seem to be objectified in a positive fashion.

The earliest ethnographic evidence that we have of snake worship is documented in conjunction with the 4th-century-BCE visit of Alexander the Great to India:

Fig. 1: *Nāga* worship in the Bhramarāmbā temple complex at Srisailam (photo by Ivo Belandi, used by courtesy).

> When Alexander was assaulting some of the cities in India and capturing others, he found in many of them, besides other animals, a snake which the Indians, regarding as sacred, kept in a cave and worshipped with much devotion. (McCrindle, 1971, 45)

And as noted by R. Gombrich,

> [There is] epigraphic and archaeological evidence for the worship of *nāga*s, supernatural snakes, in shrines and temples. Härtel has excavated a *nāga* temple at Sonkh, near Mathurā, which he dates to the Kuṣāṇa period. He considers that the area around Rājagṛha known as Maṇiyār Maṭha has been securely identified by excavators as a *nāga* shrine; its oldest strata are dated to the second or first century BC... [I]t is about as old as the evidence for any Indian shrine or temple, so it seems reasonable to extrapolate by projecting the cult back a couple of centuries. (Gombrich, 1996, 72)

The excavation and dating of such places are essential because the sites traditionally associated with the worship of the supernatural snake are either → *tīrtha*s or *caitya*s, neither of which leave much in the way of archaeological traces. *Tīrtha*s are places where one might literally cross (verb *tṝ-*) a body of water and thereby gain access to the deities living under the water in their palatial homes in the Nāgaloka – a luxurious underwater world built and decorated with all the → gemstones of the earth. *Caitya*s, however, are sacred spots marked by a pool or body of water, a stone, or a tree. Supernatural snakes are also associated with anthills. In a recent ethnography, looking at contemporary *nāga* worship in South India, A. Allocco notes the following:

> The snake goddess takes the form of an anthill (*puṟṟu*, sometimes referred to as a termite hill or white-ant hill), which is conceived by some to be a *svayambhū* (self-manifest) eruption of the goddess from the earth. These conical earthen mounds may be relatively small or grow to be as many as six or more feet in height and are often decorated with vermilion and turmeric powders, *nīm* fronds, and flower garlands. (Allocco, 2013, 232)

It is fortunate that we have some of these *nāgī* statues ensconced in temples, for, not surprisingly, these statues do not survive intact out in the natural world. Either they are beaten down by the weather over the centuries, or they are sometimes stolen. According to J. Shaw,

> The earliest known serpent sculptures in the area come from Gulgaon, a settlement (and modern village) around two kilometers to the west of Sanchi. Here a *nāga/nāginī* couple originally stood on the embankment of an ancient irrigation reservoir. During the 1980's the *nāga* was shifted to the Sanchi Archaeological Museum following the theft of the *nāginī* partner. (Shaw, 2004, 22)

Given the natural contours of *caitya*s, *tīrtha*s, and anthills, and the problems associated with statues left to nature and the avaricious inclinations of human nature, very little exists to mark the historical worship of these figures. However, we can draw forth some of the historical traces of snake worship by looking at the orthodox texts of the Hindu tradition. Whether contextualized in a negative, neutral, or positive fashion, the Brahman redactors of these texts end up encompassing an enormous amount of material concerning the development of snake worship over the centuries: information such as what ritual elements comprised these practices, what social groups may have been involved in these practices, and what brought them to choose the snake as an object of religious devotion.

Even a cursory examination of the Hindu and Buddhist textual traditions goes a long way today answering this last question. From its earliest appearance in the *Ṛgveda*, the snake consistently displays the following three features: it is portrayed as an earthly sovereign, it is endowed with supernatural powers over earthly elements, and it responds (both positively and negatively) to human desires. Moreover, these texts also give us a great deal of information as to how snake-centered rituals were conducted and possibly by whom, thus contributing to and preserving the ritual tradition associated with snake worship.

The *Ṛgveda* (c. 1200 BCE) is made up of 1,028 hymns or chants. The divine order in the *Ṛgveda* is led by Vajradhara ("He Who Wields the Thunderbolt"; i.e. Indra), who is declared to be king of the vedic gods (*ṚV*. 1.32.15). In order to be legitimated as exclusive controller of the natural world, Indra is pitted against an opponent characterized as having dominion over earthly and atmospheric elements: Vṛtra, a supernatural snake.

Vṛtra is so named because he encloses/covers up (verb *vṛ-*) things, particularly water. In several hymns, he is called *apovṛt* (the encloser of the waters) and *nadīvṛt* (the encloser of the rivers) (*ṚV*. 1.32). Vṛtra is also depicted as having "the lightning and thunder, rain, and hail" at his command (*ṚV*. 1.32.13). In addition to controlling both earthly and atmospheric waters, Vṛtra maintains the highest point of the earth as he "lay on the mountain" (*ṚV*. 1.32.2). And while this association with mountains has led some scholars to describe Vṛtra as a high-flying dragon rather than a snake, one need only turn to rgvedic hymns 4.18 and 1.32 – in which Vṛtra is described respectively as *vyaṃsa* and as *anaṃsa*, both meaning "shoulderless" – to find that only a snake would fit that description. Interestingly, this descriptor recurs across space and time, for in present-day Mississippi, another region abounding in snakes, these creatures are often referred to as "Mr. No-Shoulders."

It is also in the *Ṛgveda* that we see the first of what will be a historical succession of signifiers given to this sovereign snake. In hymns 1.32 and 1.2, we see the name Vṛtra used interchangeably with the term *ahi* (snake). *Ahi* is not merely descriptive but rather carries a negative connotation: it comes from the verb *aṃh-* (to press together, to strangle), which forms other words such as *aṃhati* and *aṃhas* (anxiety or distress).

In the late-vedic texts, we find a great deal of information about *nāga*s and *nāga* worship such as the following: the supernatural snake's hybrid nature, the rituals conducted by and for supernatural snakes, the first reference to a supernatural snake as a *nāga*, their ability to tame their non-supernatural brethren, their divine nature, their ability to help humans against enemies, and their expanded powers over the natural world. We are able to glean so much information about supernatural snakes in the late-vedic texts because the redactors of these texts appear most interested in compiling all of the various ritual means available for controlling nature and valorize the supernatural snake as one of those means.

While the rgvedic redactors constructed powerful snakes as demonic beings, the late-vedic redactors constructed powerful snakes as divine beings. They began this process by shifting the negative *ahi* to the neutral *sarpa*, and finally to the *nāga*. *Sarpa* comes from the verb *sṛp-*, "to glide," and thus highlights the unique, reptilian nature of the snake. This shift in signifier, however, does not signal the snake's impotence; in these texts, a constant association is made between snakes and their inherent powers, especially the power to render a poisonous bite. In the *Śatapathabrāhmaṇa*, for instance, poison is declared to be the primary factor in elevating the snake to the status of a divine being (*ŚBr.* 10.5.2.20). Beyond their poisonous prowess, the late-vedic snakes are depicted as capable of amazing feats such as stopping the world from spinning on its axis and protecting the four corners of the earth. And the *sarpanāma* (snake-naming) *mantra*s proclaim the fact that "these worlds are ruled by snakes" (*ŚBr.* 7.4.1.25–30).

In hymn 12.3 of the *Atharvaveda*, the redactors again enhanced the snake's supernatural powers over the entire earth as they portrayed snakes as guardians of the four quarters: the eastern quarter has Asita as protector; the southern quarter has Tiraściräji as protector; the western quarter has Pṛdāku; and the northern quarter has Svaja. Each of these names describes their reptilian characteristics: *asita* (black), *tiraścirāji* (striped across), *pṛdāku* (adder), and *svaja* (viper). This hymn thus highlights the fact that the snake's power, its capacity to act as a world ruler and protector, is grounded in its reptilian being. While functioning as a celestial guardian, each of these creatures is characterized first and foremost as a snake.

Having made a strong association between snakes and their inherent powers, and having enhanced the snakes' supernatural powers, the redactors made a further assertion: because they are powerful, snakes are worthy of deification. In another hymn from the *Atharvaveda*, it is stated that snakes should be regarded as gods because of their mordacious powers.

> May the snake not kill us along with our children and our people. If its jaws are closed, let them not open, if they are opened, let them not close. Honor to the god people. Honor to Asita, honor to Tiraścirāji, honor to Svaja, [and] honor to Babhru [i.e. the son of Arjuna and the *nāgī* princess Citrāṅgadā], honor to the god people. I seal up your teeth, your jaws, your tongue, and your mouth. (*AV.* 6.56; trans. by author)

It is no wonder that the worship of supernatural snakes is replete with ambivalence. While they are regarded as divine and capable of providing riches and fertility to their worshippers, they are also efficient killing machines. This duality forms the foundation on which these snakes are characterized as hybrid beings, for "these creatures... are represented as having the capacity to bless as well as curse" (Allocco, 2013, 232). Moreover, while

Fig. 2: *Nāgakal*s (snake stones) in the Bhramarāmbā temple complex at Srisailam (photo by Ivo Belandi, used by courtesy).

they are perceived by worshippers as controlling water and providing "sufficient rain for healthy crops, they also had the power to cause destructive storms" (Shaw, 2004, 17–18).

Regardless of the constant threat posed by the snake, killing a snake is considered to be a horrific action and one that will have terrible karmic consequences in not only this life but also future lives. "A number of authors note that killing a snake is regarded as a sin and detail the lengths that individuals may go to in order to avoid injuring a snake as *nāga*s are believed to deliver formidable curses with far-reaching implications" (Allocco, 2013, 231).

The *Śatapathabrāhmaṇa* first uses the word that comes to signify the supernatural snake: *nāga*. "The wise Śvetaketu Āruṇeya said, 'To the one who will know the splendor of the preliminary offerings, people in future days will come in droves as if desiring to see a great Nāga'" (*ŚBr*. 11.2.7.12). While the term *nāga* is also sometimes used in these texts to signify an elephant, the *Śatapathabrāhmaṇa*'s commentary explicitly states that the *nāga* in question is a *mahāsarpa* (great snake; *ŚBr*. 11.2.7.12). What is striking about the term *nāga* as it is first employed in the above passage is that, unlike *ahi* or *sarpa*, it signifies a snake that is differentiated explicitly from the average reptile: a snake that is exceptional due to its great size, its great powers, or perhaps both. This term thus captures the dual nature of an exceptional being.

It is also in the *Śatapathabrāhmaṇa* that we first hear of the *sarpavidyā* (the science of snakes). This science is taught to the *vid*s (knowers) of *sarpa*s (snakes) in order for them to understand and control snakes. C. Minkowski makes an interesting point when he speculates that orthodox "commentators [link] the *sarpavidyā* with the vast network of Indian snake lore, the science of how to avoid harm from snakes, which escapes the limits of even Sanskrit literature" (Minkowski, 1991, 394). Given the on-the-ground reality of poisonous snakes in India, it is to be expected that others, in addition to the redactors (possibly farmers tending their fields or women tending their homes), would have been interested in the issue of controlling snakes. Another snake-centered ritual deserves mention at this juncture: the *sarpasattra* – the term *sarpasattra* literally means "snake sacrifice," and in the late-vedic version of this ritual, this term denotes a sacrifice performed by snakes functioning in the role of Brahmans. The late-vedic version of the *sarpasattra* also incorporates a cosmogonic myth explaining how snakes became both powerful biters and wonderfully heroic. In performing this ritual, the *Baudhāyanagṛhyasūtra* promises benefits such as sons, cattle, and snakebite protection. It also states that you need not be a Brahman to perform this ritual, nor must one perform the entire ritual to gain protection against poisonous snakes. One need only recite the names of Arbuda, and the other Brahman-snake officiates, saying, "Let there be homage paid to the snakes," to be protected from dangerous snakes (*BauGS*. 3.10). The short version of this ritual thus allows the average householder to benefit from performing this ritual act.

Many of the supernatural snakes listed in the late → Vedas have names that link them to specific regional areas. For example, Dhṛtarāṣṭra Airāvata's name ties him to the Irāvatī River region located in the Punjab. And in relation to Takṣaka Vaiśāleya, his name ties him to the town of Vaiśalī. The name Vaiśāleya also turns up in the *Karṇaparvan* of the → *Mahābhārata* to signify a tribe of Nāga people – those who took the divine snake as a totem or who believed themselves to be descendants of divine snakes (*MBh*. 8.63.37). While various royal principalities took the *nāga* as a symbol of their power, it is important to note that the people of Nagaland have no association with the supernatural snake. As noted by K.R. Dikshit quoting Lieutenant Colonel R.G. Woodthorpe, "The word 'Naga' is quite foreign to and unrecognized by the Naga [people] themselves" (Dikshit & Dikshit, 2013, 310). K.R. Dikshit goes on to say, "The situation has changed, and though the term 'Naga' may have been used by the plains' people, its use is firmly established today in the society, government and even internationally" (Dikshit & Dikshit, 2013, 310). Regardless of its use as a socially unifying name, it remains distinct from any association with the supernatural *nāga* discussed here.

As one views the rituals with which these snakes are associated, one apprehends why the snake regents were and continue to be valued by local inhabitants: for in addition to guarding the populace from dangerous snakes, they also purify the earth. In fact, the late Vedas explicitly associate the snake Arbuda Kādraveya with the earth – Kādraveya being a matronymic for Kadrū, that is, "the earth personified" according to the Brāhmaṇas. This chthonic connection continues as snakes are propitiated to ensure the protection of those things built on the earth. As such, there is a specific ritual listed in the *Sāmavidhānabrāhmaṇa* in which the snake Vāsuki is addressed through the ceremony of the *vāstupraśamana* – a ceremony specifically designed to purify the earth and make it fit for human habitation (*SāViBr.* 3.3.7). In the *Gobhilagṛhyasūtra*, Vāsuki is asked to ensure the propitious setting of a foundation stone for a new house (*GobhGS.* 4.71.41). In the *Kauśikasūtra*, both Takṣaka Vaiśaleya and Vāsuki are invoked as protectors of the house, as the supernatural snake stands on the limen between the civilized world and the natural world (*KauS.* 74.8).

The *Mahābhārata*, one of two great epics, was redacted over several centuries and is usually dated somewhere around 300 BCE–300 CE. While the late-vedic redactors positioned the supernatural snake as a powerful deity worthy of both fear and reverence, the first book of the *Mahābhārata*, the *Ādiparvan*, positions supernatural snakes as troublesome deceivers bent on destruction. Thus, the redactors of the *Ādiparvan* strip the snakes of the very powers for which they are revered in the late Vedas: they lose their regional place names; they lose their status as independent demigods as they are made dependent on established gods such as Indra; their powers over the natural elements are diminished; they are provided with an overpowering natural enemy in the form of the great Garuḍa bird; and they are presented as a threatening multitudinous force that deserves to die. In fact, the *Ādiparvan* both begins and ends with the attempted destruction of all snakes in a blazing fire. One cannot help but wonder why supernatural snakes are depicted in such a negative fashion in this text. Perhaps, snake worship had become popularized to the extent that it was perceived as a threat by the orthodox redactors of the *Ādiparvan*. Whatever the reason, the redactors emphasize the need to destroy these creatures not only by giving them a powerful, voracious enemy in the form of Garuḍa but also by attempting to annihilate the snakes first in a snake sacrifice, a *sarpasattra*, and second through the destruction of their home in the Khāṇḍava Forest.

The *Ādiparvan* introduces the mighty Garuḍa in a myth depicting the origin of the *nāgas*. In this myth, Kadrū, the earth, is depicted as the mother of all *nāgas*, while her sister, Vinatā, is presented as the mother of Garuḍa. According to this myth, Kadrū gives birth to a "Thousand *nāgas*... all equal

Fig. 3: *Nāgakals* in the Bhramarāmbā temple complex at Srisailam (photo by Ivo Belandi, used by courtesy).

in brilliant energy," while "just at the appropriate time, Garuḍa is born – he who destroys snakes" (*MBh.* 1.14.5–23; trans. by author). As featured in the epic, Garuḍa attends to his task with zeal, for in addition to his vigorous appetite for snakes, in one episode, he attempts to burn the *nāgas* by flying them into the sun's rays. Garuḍa's role is not without precedents, for the enmity between snakes and birds is mentioned as far back as the *Ṛgveda* (2.38). Moreover, both the *Atharvaveda* (4.6.3) and the *Śaṃkhāyanagṛhyasūtra* (1.22.15) mention a particular Garutmat ("One Who Has Wings") who is the happy imbiber of poison, the snakes' singular weapon.

The destruction of the snakes by fire, however, is a particularly powerful motif in this text as noted by W. Doniger:

> It begins with King Janamejaya's attempt to murder all the snakes in the world in revenge for his father's death by snake bite...To the ancient Indians, a snake sacrifice must have been an abomination, for though Hindus have worshiped snakes from time immemorial, they do so by making small offerings of milk to them, not by killing them. (Doniger, 2009, 266)

And it is particularly ironic that in the late-vedic version of the *sarpasattra*, the sacrifice is depicted as one performed by snakes, whereas in the *Ādiparvan*, it is depicted as a sacrifice of snakes. The *Ādiparvan* describes this event in lurid detail as Brahman officiants, "having put on black robes and with eyes red from the smoke," offer the snakes to the mouth of Agni:

> Then they offered all of the snakes into the mouth of the fire, causing terror to roil in the minds of all those snakes. The snakes fell into the blazing fire, coiling around themselves, weeping, and crying out to each other. Falling heavily into the lustrous fire they died, trembling and hissing, writhing about with their heads and their tails. White, black, blue, old, and young screeching horrible screams, they fell into the radiant flames. Hundreds of thousands and millions and tens of millions of snakes were destroyed completely against their will. (*MBh.* 1.47.20–24; trans. by author)

At the end of the *Ādiparvan*, snakes again are targeted for destruction as Agni moves to burn down their home in the Khāṇḍava Forest. However, Agni is incapable of achieving this task on his own because "Indra's friend lives there with his people, the Snake Takṣaka, and for his sake, the Thunderbolt-Wielder (Indra) protects it from burning" (van Buitenen, 1973, 415). Having secured the help of Arjuna and Kṛṣṇa, Agni almost succeeds in killing all of the snakes except for Takṣaka, who has removed himself to the field of the Kurus.

While much of the *Ādiparvan* focuses on the destruction of snakes, it also gives us a great deal of information about snakes:

1. the term *nāga* has evolved over the centuries to become the dominant modifier associated with the supernatural snake;
2. we have our first appearance of the Nāgaloka, a beautiful, bejeweled, underwater kingdom that is described as the home of the *nāgas*;
3. the *nāgas* of the *Mahābhārata* are able to shift their shape into any form they desire such as a tiny worm or an anatomically correct human being;
4. the *Mahābhārata* introduces its audience to *nāgīs*, the feminine term for *nāga*, and these *nāgīs* appear as beautiful, sensual, mermaid-like beings who are always adorned with a brilliant jewel in the middle of their foreheads;
5. snakes such as Takṣaka Vaiśāleya and Dhṛtarāṣtra Airāvata are stripped of their matronymics/patronymics, and as such, they are stripped of their familial connection to a regional locale; and lastly
6. we are introduced to a new snake that comes to be extremely important in both popular practice and Hindu textual sources: Śeṣa, whose alternative name is Ananta ("Endless") – the *nāga* whose coils are "without end."

On introduction, Śeṣa is positioned at a *tīrtha*, a place where *nāgas* are ritually invoked to assist the worshipper in gaining the powers of fertility or the riches of the earth. The practice of worshipping *nāgas* and other deities at *tīrthas* is not a foreign element in the *Mahābhārata*, for the *Tīrthayātrāparvan* goes into great detail on this subject. In this *parvan*, which extends for more than 70 sections, we learn of not only all the different *tīrthas* of the east, south, west, and north but also the benefits that accrue from bathing at these sites, such as the capacity to hear far distant sounds, the knowledge of all the worlds, freedom from snakebites, and the capacity to cross over to the *nāgaloka* at the *tīrthas* called Nāgobheda and Sarpadarvī. In this *parvan*, moreover, the redactors compare *tīrtha* worship to sacrificial rituals and laud the former as a type of religiosity that might be more generally accessible to a broader range of people. "One might wish to sacrifice with the 'Praise of Agni' [i.e. *agniṣṭoma*] ritual or with other rites that require extensive fees, yet not obtain the reward [that accrues] from visiting the *tīrthas*" (*MBh.* 3.80.40; trans. by author).

As the *Mahābhārata* features Śeṣa as a powerful figure susceptible to granting human wishes, it is not surprising that a recent ethnography reports that Śesa has taken on Vāsuki's late-vedic role as the *nāga* charged with helping human beings situate the foundation stone for a house.

> If one digs over Śeṣnāg's head, there will be harm to one's parents; and if one digs over the back there will be fear, disease, and pain; and if one digs over the tail there will be harm to the three *gotras*. But whoever digs over an empty space will obtain the benefits of wife, sons, and wealth (Goodwin-Raheja, 1988, 55)

As indicated in the above quote, G. Goodwin-Raheja notes the care that must be taken in digging out a foundation; this is due to the fact that, in India, situating a house is linked both to → astrology and to astronomy – fields that are not nearly as disconnected in India as they are in the West. The linkage occurs as Śeṣnāg's body moves in conjunction with the earth's rotation around the sun. "During each three-month period, Śeṣnāg moves ninety degrees clockwise, and the 'empty space,' where the digging should always be done, changes accordingly" (Goodwin-Raheja, 1988, 80). A. Allocco also notes that there is a linkage between harming a snake and astrology in her ethnographic research in South India.

> [T]he popular belief that disturbing, harming, or killing a snake, whether knowingly or inadvertently, in this life or in a previous birth, produces a condition called *nāga dōṣam* (snake blemish). This astrological flaw, which manifests in inauspicious planetary configurations in an individual's horoscope (*jatakam*), is primarily faulted for delayed marriage and infertility but may also be blamed for an array of additional negative effects. (Allocco, 2013, 239)

The *Ādiparvan* also brings the beautiful, sensual *nāgī* princesses into focus and describes the practice of intermarriage between *nāga*s and humans. While this interspecies marriage in the *Ādiparvan* features none other than Vāsuki's sister and a rather worn-out old Brahman, another example from the *Mahābhārata* is the marriage of Arjuna and the *nāgī* princess Ulūpī. Kālidāsa's *Raghuvaṃśa* also includes a *nāgī*-human intermarriage: the union of Kuśa and the *nāgī* princess Kumudvatī. And the poet Guṇāḍhya, purported author of the *Bṛhatkathā*, is said himself to be the progeny of a mortal mother and a *nāga*. All descriptions of *nāgī*s portray them as having the following characteristics: they are of royal heritage; they are fabulously beautiful and sexually irresistible; they have healthy sexual appetites and are often driven to find a mortal man in order to satisfy these cravings; and they are forever fertile, often giving birth to a host of sons.

The matrimonial union between a mortal and a *nāgī* crosses the line from the mythological to the historical, as a large number of royal dynasties claim that there is a *nāgī* ancestress somewhere in their lineage. Having a *nāgī* in one's genealogical history is seen as exceptionally desirable; it conveys not only a sense of sovereignty but also a promise of perpetual progeny. Thus, as chronicled by J.P. Vogel, the kings of the Swat Valley (Udyāna), Kashmir, Bhardarva, Chhotanagpur, and Manipur; of Gonds and Bastar; Cholas; Pallavas; and also kings from as far afield as Cambodia and China all claim that there is a *nāgī* princess somewhere in their family tree (Vogel, 1926, 35–37). In fact, as noted by J. Shaw, evidence of various clan affiliations with *nāga*s can be found on coins:

> [L]arge hoards of tiny copper *nāga* coins have been retrieved from the ancient [2nd-cent. CE Vidisha] city mounds. Analyses of these coins and other numismatic, epigraphical, and textual evidence, have led to the suggestion that the [Nāga] dynasty originated during the second half of the second century CE in Vidisha, from where it moved north to Mathura, Pawaya, and Kantipurya, the three major *nāga* centers mentioned in the *Viṣṇu Purāṇa*... I also suggest that the *nāga* sculptures in the area doubled as symbols of the *nāga* clan and, in particular, their patronage of major irrigation projects in the area. (Shaw, 2004, 10–11)

To bring us back to the present day, one can still visit *nāga* temples or sites encompassing *nāga* statues in India and beyond. In her ethnography of South India, A. Allocco notes the following:

> The snake goddess takes multiple manifestations and is accessible to devotees in a range of physical forms. She is perhaps most represented anthropomorphically, typically as a black stone

> head with a crown of snake hoods arranged around her face. When she is installed in the inner sancta of temples in this form she may be accompanied by a full-body image as well, either carved from the same black stone or cast in a variety of metals. (Allocco, 2013, 235)

Or if one visits the tremendous compound of Angkor Wat in → Cambodia, one will experience the following:

> Cambodian builders placed serpent balustrades along the bridges that crossed the surrounding moats, for as water symbols, serpents linked heaven and earth...Heaven's blessings then flowed outward from the temple, the centre of the universe or world of the gods, through the arched gate and across the serpent-railed bridge, to the benefit of humankind. (Fisher, 1993, 170)

Whether one might visualize "the rainbow as a large, sometimes two-headed snake" (Wessing, 2006, 213) or take *darśan* at a Vaiṣṇava temple wherein one experiences Śeṣnāg holding fast to the sleeping Viṣṇu, *nāgas* excite our attention in a myriad of ways. Thus, whatever statue, ritual, image, or reptile stirs one's senses, it is clear that humans have a long, creative relationship with *nāgas*: a reciprocal relationship within which humans recognize and propitiate the *nāga*'s tremendous power "for the benefit of humankind" (Fisher, 1993, 170).

Bibliography

Allocco, A., "Fear, Reverence, and Ambivalence: Divine Snakes in Contemporary South India," *RSA* 7, 2013, 230–248.

Bloss, L., "The Buddha and the Nāga: A Study of Folk Religiosity," *HR* 13, 1973, 36–53.

Cozad, L., *Sacred Snakes: Orthodox Image of Indian Snake Worship*, Aurora, 2004.

Dikshit, K.R., & J. Dikshit, *North-East India: Land, People, and Economy*, New York, 2013.

Doniger, W., *The Hindus: An Alternative History*, London, 2009.

Fisher, R., *Buddhist Art and Architecture*, London, 1993.

Gombrich, R., *How Buddhism Began*, London, 1996.

Goodwin-Raheja, G., *The Poison in the Gift*, Chicago, 1988.

Heras, H., *Studies in Proto-Indo-Mediterranean Culture*, Bombay, 1953.

Mackay, E., *The Indus Civilization*, London, 1935.

Mahalingam, T.V., "The Nagas in Indian History and Culture," *JIH* 43, 1965, 1–69.

McCrindle, J.S., *Ancient India as Described in Classical Literature*, Amsterdam, 1971.

Minkowski, C., "Snakes, Sattras, and the Mahābhārata," in: A. Sharma, ed., *Essays on the Mahābhārata*, New York, 1991.

Shaw, J., "Nāga Sculptures in Sanchi's Archaeological Landscape: Buddhism, Vaiṣṇavism, and Local Agricultural Cults in Central India, First Century BCE to Fifth Century CE," *ArtA* 64, 2004, 5–59.

Singh, U., "Cults and Shrines in Early Historical Mathura (c. 200 BC–AD 200)," *WA* 36/3, 2004, 378–398.

Vargas-O'Bryan, I., "Falling Rain, Reigning Power in the Reptilian Affairs: The Balancing of Religion and the Environment," *RSA* 7, 2013, 110–125.

Vogel, J.P., *Indian Serpent Lore or the Nāgas in Hindu Legend and Art*, London, 1926.

Wessing, "Symbolic Animals in the Land between the Waters: Markers of Place and Transition," *AFS* 65/2, 2006, 205–239.

Westerkamp, W., "From Singa to Naga Padoha, the Making of a Magical Creature," *IMW* 37/108, 2009, 163–181.

Williams, J.G., "New Naga Images from the Sanchi Area," *OA* 22, 1976, 174–179.

LAURIE ANN COZAD

Trimūrti

Trimūrti (lit. having three forms) is a conception that posits a supreme deity manifesting itself in three particular shapes in order to perform the basic cosmological functions: as Brahmā he emits the world, as Viṣṇu he preserves it, and as Śiva he annihilates it. The grouping together of Brahmā, Viṣṇu, and Śiva – albeit not always in this order – and the emphasis on their specific yet complementary roles emerged in the first centuries of the Common Era. This was the result of a theological and cosmological synthesis that was already implied in the *Mahābhārata* and *Harivaṃśa* but reached its fullest expression in the literature of the Purāṇas.

It has been hypothesized that the *trimūrti* concept might have developed under the influence of Mahāyāna Buddhism and its triads: one is reminded of the Buddha's three bodies, that is, the *dharmakāya* ("*dharma* body," the unconceivable aspect of the Buddha corresponding to the perfectly pure reality of *nirvāṇa*), *sambhogakāya* ("enjoyment body," the glorified body that the Buddha attained as a reward for his *bodhisattva* practices), and *nirmāṇakāya* ("apparition body" the Buddha's bodily form), as well as of the emanation of *dhyānibuddhas* (celestial *buddhas* engaged in contemplation), *dhyānibodhisattvas* (celestial *bodhisattvas* engaged in contemplation), and *mānuṣibuddhas* (human *buddhas*) from the supreme Ādibuddha (the original Buddha). Be that as it may, the *trimūrti* of Brahmā, Viṣṇu, and Śiva is linked to the rise of devotional, *bhakti* movements and to the integration of their supreme deities – mainly Viṣṇu and Śiva – within a cosmological framework combining the outward (*pravṛtti*) and inward (*nivṛtti*) poles, that is, involvement in the world through its manifestation and maintenance and withdrawal from it through its annihilation. This integrative effort was the product of theological speculation, a somewhat artificial attempt that never became popular among the masses, nor did it trigger a specific worship. Even in the Purāṇas, the focus is placed on its individual members rather than on their cooperative ensemble as a triad. Due to sectarian reasons, the one supreme deity that manifests itself in the three forms is identified with a particular god or even a particular goddess (*devī*), that is, with one's chosen deity (*iṣṭadevatā*). This supreme godhead is often one of the three members of the *trimūrti* itself, typically Viṣṇu or Śiva, who in his transcendent reality is conceived as none other than the absolute *brahman*, utterly detached from the lower cosmological functions of manifestation, preservation, and annihilation.

G. Bailey (1979) has argued that the *trimūrti* concept fits well with the trifunctional Indo-European pattern – he cites *Kathāsaritsāgara* 8.4.46–48 as a revealing passage – even though he underlines that trifunctionalism is not the only or even the most important influence in the characterization of the group of the three gods: Brahmā is understood as the representative of vedic religion and of the Brāhmaṇa *varṇa*; Viṣṇu is said to characterize kingship and the Kṣatriya *varṇa*; and Śiva is linked to the power of fertility and to the Vaiśya *varṇa*.

Historical Development

The first occurrence of the three forms of the *trimūrti* – though not explicitly identified as creator, preserver, and destroyer of the cosmos – is found in three places of the late and composite *Maitrāyaṇīyopaniṣad* (4.5–6; 5.1–2; 6.5). In *Maitrāyaṇīyopaniṣad* 4.5–6, Brahmā, Rudra (= Śiva), and Viṣṇu – in this order – are mentioned together with two other triads (Agni, Vāyu, and Āditya [i.e. fire, air, and sun]; and time, *prāṇa*, and food) as being objects of meditation, the chief bodies of the immortal, disembodied *brahman*. Moreover, *Maitrāyaṇīyopaniṣad* 6.5 states that Agni, Vāyu, and Āditya are *brahman*'s luminous body and that through Brahmā, Rudra, and Viṣṇu, its body has sovereign deities. In particular, 5.1–2 correlates the triad of gods with the three *guṇas* of Sāṃkhya, each god being identified with one particular quality: Rudra with the dark, inert *tamas*, Brahmā with the active, passionate *rajas*, and Viṣṇu with the luminous, pure *sattva*.

The *trimūrti* is not the only nor indeed the earliest triad in Indian literature. From vedic times, there has been a tendency to recognize several triads of divine powers. The above-mentioned triad of Agni, Vāyu (or Indra), and Āditya (or Sūrya) is found in the earliest vedic sources, being related to the assumption that Agni ("Fire") manifests himself in three forms: as sun in the sky, as lightning in the atmosphere, and as fire on earth. Even the 33 deities of the vedic pantheon are distinguished into 3 classes of 11 gods supposed to dwell in the 3 regions of space: the celestial *ādityas* in the heavens, the aerial *rudras* in the intermediate atmosphere, and the terrestrial *vasus* on earth (see vedic gods). It seems reasonable to suppose that these vedic triads were influential in the elaboration of the *trimūrti* concept. J. Gonda remarked the following:

> The Trimūrti idea of Hinduism seems to have developed from ancient cosmological and ritualistic speculations about the triple character of an individual god, in the first place of Agni, whose births are three or threefold and who is threefold light, has three bodies and three stations, etc. (Gonda, 1968, 218)

In the Brāhmaṇas, even the creator god Prajāpati exhibits a threefold character, being identified with various gods such as Vāyu, Puruṣa, and Agni. The *trimūrti* concept appears to be adumbrated already in the solemn definition of *Taittirīyopaniṣad* 3.1.1, where the transcendent *brahman*, described as triune, is characterized by the three functions of manifestation, maintenance, and dissolution of the world and its creatures: "That from which these beings are born; on which, once born, they live; and into which they pass upon death – seek to perceive that! That is *Brahman*!" (trans. Olivelle, 1998, 190). The *trimūrti* is also linked to the syllable *oṃ*, the three gods being interpreted as its constituent phonemes, that is, *a*, *u*, and *m*. The late *Māṇḍūkyopaniṣad*, which identifies the *oṃ* with *brahman*, the *ātman*, and the world, and the three phonemes with the waking, dreaming, and deep-sleep states, respectively, states: "He is the Lord of all; he is the knower of all; he is the inner controller; he is the womb of all – for he is the origin and the dissolution of beings" (*MāṇḍU.* 6; trans. Olivelle, 1998, 289).

Traditionally, the triad of Brahmā, Viṣṇu, and Śiva is microcosmically equated to the ages of man, that is, childhood, youth, and old age as well as to the stages of life (→ *āśramas*): the student's celibate life (*brahmacarya*), the householder's life (*gārhasthya*), and the renouncer's life (*saṃnyāsa*).

Turning to the epic materials, it must be observed that each of the three cosmological functions is not consistently assigned to the same deity: for instance, Brahmā is said to act as destroyer as well as preserver, and Viṣṇu is extolled as creator as well as destroyer. If in the *Rāmāyaṇa* there is no mention whatsoever of the *trimūrti*, in the entire *Mahābhārata*, there is only one passage in which the three functions of the triad of gods are openly stated. This is found in the third book of the *Vanaparvan*, regarded as an interpolation by the editors of the BORI critical edition, where Śiva extols Viṣṇu as the supreme god of gods, the primordial principle assuming all forms: "As Brahmā he emits (*sṛjate*) the world, as Puruṣa (i.e. Viṣṇu) he protects (*rakṣate*) it, and as Rudra (= Śiva) he destroys (*śamayet*) it: these are the three states (*tisro'vasthāḥ*) of Prajāpati" (*MBh.* 3, app. I, 27, 35–36; trans. by author).

Despite this sole and possibly late reference to the *trimūrti*, the epic poets concern themselves at various points with the theological and cosmological configurations of Brahmā, Viṣṇu, and Śiva as well as of another triad, namely, that of Viṣṇu, Śiva, and Devī (Mahādevī). Although the intricate mythological network of the *Mahābhārata* tends to establish multiple associations rather than one-to-one correspondences, A. Hiltebeitel has persuasively argued that the epic triad of Kṛṣṇa, Arjuna, and Draupadī (the so-called three Kṛṣṇas) stands for the *bhakti* triad of Viṣṇu, Śiva, and the Goddess, and that the triad of Kṛṣṇa, Arjuna, and Vyāsa is evocative of the three gods of the *trimūrti*, given that Vyāsa exhibits affinities with Brahmā (Hiltebeitel, 1984, 5–6).

To be sure, in the *Mahābhārata* there are various episodes in which Brahmā, Viṣṇu, and Śiva cooperate in view of a common goal. In the story of the Arjuna-Karṇa duel narrated in the *Karṇaparvan*, the help that Brahmā and Śiva offer to Kṛṣṇa (i.e. Viṣṇu) and Arjuna evidences the mutually supportive interests of the three gods: their solidarity is indicative of an already significant interplay. When Arjuna finally decides to kill the evil Karṇa, he first asks permission from Kṛṣṇa, Bhava (= Śiva), and Brahmā (*MBh.* 8.65.3). The gods of the *trimūrti* are also evoked in *Mahābhārata* 9.52, where Brahmā, Viṣṇu, and Śiva send the warriors who die on the battlefield of Kurukṣetra straight to heaven. Even in the *Nārāyaṇīya* section of the *Śāntiparvan* (*MBh.* 12.335.11–18; 12.337.16–36), there appears to be an implicit recognition of the *trimūrti* scheme.

If Kṛṣṇa is a manifestation of Viṣṇu, then by the same token Arjuna in his destructive impetus is an alter ego of Śiva operating world dissolution (*pralaya*). As the *Mahābhārata* insists on the ultimate identity of Kṛṣṇa and Arjuna, it also highlights the interdependence and ontological unity of Viṣṇu and Śiva, of Hari and Hara. As A. Hiltebeitel has noted,

> it is not surprising that Kṛṣṇa should subordinate himself to Arjuna as his charioteer. For he is, in fact, subordinating himself to Arjuna in his destructive dimension as a form of Śiva. But again, one must not forget the double soteriological language. For not only do they mutually subordinate themselves to each other as alternate representations of *puruṣa* and Mahāpuruṣa. They also ride together as the two Kṛṣṇas on the one chariot of the "impartial" Brahmā, the Brahmā with whom Kṛṣṇa is compared, and the Brahmā who can be "superior to the gods," even Śiva or Viṣṇu, only because he is the personification of the *Brahman* in which all hierarchies and distinctions merge and cease. (Hiltebeitel, 1984, 26)

In the *Harivaṃśa*, possibly dating to the 2nd or 3rd century CE, one comes across complementary triads of divinities: on a cosmic plane, the triad of Viṣṇu, Śeṣa, and the goddess Nidrā, to which on the earthly plane corresponds the triad of Kṛṣṇa, Saṃkarṣaṇa, and Ekānaṃśā. The three gods are represented on an equal footing and as an interdependent whole. Viṣṇu-Kṛṣṇa is the creator god; Nidrā-Ekānaṃśā plays either a protective or a destructive role; and Śeṣa-Saṃkarṣaṇa personifies either the world's support or the world's quiescence.

Harivaṃśa 2.125.31–35 – which again the authors of the BORI edition interpret as a late interpolation – offers a remarkable passage on the *trimūrti*. The text is part of the *Hariharamāhātmya* (*HV*. 2.125.29–57), extolling the identity of Viṣṇu and Śiva:

> I (i.e. Mārkaṇḍeya) shall declare to thee (i.e. Brahmā) that form composed of Hari and Hara combined that is without beginning, middle, or end and that is imperishable, undecaying. He who is Viṣṇu is Rudra; he who is Rudra is Pitāmaha ("The Grandfather"; i.e. Brahmā). Rudra, Viṣṇu, and Pitāmaha: three gods in one form (*ekā mūrtis trayo devā rudraviṣṇupitāmahāḥ*). They are the benefactors, the makers of the worlds, the protectors of the worlds, and the self-existent ones. They are Ardhanārīśvara and intent on severe observances. As water thrown in water is nothing but water, so when Viṣṇu enters Rudra, he is wholly Rudra. As when fire enters fire, there is nothing but fire, so when Rudra enters Viṣṇu, he is wholly Viṣṇu. (*HV*. 2.125.31–35; trans. by author)

As noted already, the proclamation of the oneness of Viṣṇu and Śiva is not at all exceptional, being found in various places of the *Mahābhārata* (3.39.76–77; 12.342). Following the seminal works of M. Biardeau (1981–1994) and A. Hiltebeitel (1984), the analysis of *Harivaṃśa* 2.125.31–35 and of other epic passages leads to the following conclusions:

1. A characteristic of both the *Mahābhārata* and the *Harivaṃśa* is their aim to present the two major *bhakti* gods Viṣṇu and Śiva on an equal footing, as per Smārta theology.
2. Their rivalry in the epic accounts betrays their complementary character: if they differ in function, they are nonetheless regarded as ontologically identical.
3. The *trimūrti* is related to the synthetic, dual icons of Harihara and Ardhanārīśvara, the lord who is half female, that is, Śiva-Śakti. The Harihara icon appears as the logical antecedent of the *trimūrti* concept, which will then be extended to include Brahmā, though the latter's significance in the *bhakti* context of both the epics and the Purāṇas is much more limited.

In the Purāṇas, the joint actions of the three gods – both upholding one another and competing among themselves for supremacy – are numerous. Indeed, it is here that the *trimūrti* scheme is explicitly and repeatedly affirmed, often in combination with the theory of the three *guṇas*. The puranic narratives of the triad of gods reflect a variety of sectarian concerns. Though even here one meets with the idea that Śiva and Viṣṇu are identical (*SauP*. 29.48ff.; 31.57ff.), depending on the Śaiva or Vaiṣṇava orientation of any given Purāṇa, either Śiva or Viṣṇu is presented as superior, being identified as the transcendent godhead: thus for Śaivas, Śiva is verily the sole god, and Brahmā and Viṣṇu are but attributes or particular manifestations of him. By the same token, Vaiṣṇavas uphold the superiority of Viṣṇu, who is said to encompass all names and forms. For instance, the *Viṣṇupurāṇa* states, "The only God, Janārdana ['Tormentor of Men'; i.e. Viṣṇu], takes the designation of Brahmā, Viṣṇu and Śiva, accordingly as he creates, preserves, or brings to an end" (*ViP.* 1.2.62; trans. Gonda, 1968, 221).

Exceptionally, a few Purāṇas magnify Brahmā as the highest godhead, though he is admittedly a secondary figure whose cult had already declined by the 4th–5th centuries CE. A noteworthy illustration in which Brahmā is extolled as supreme is found in the *Mārkaṇḍeyapurāṇa*:

> As I (i.e. Mārkaṇḍeya) have told you (i.e. Krauṣṭuki), when the unmanifest nature (*pradhāna*) is agitated, the god called Brahmā is born, situated in the cavity of the egg. At first he is the agitator, and then he, who is the husband of nature (*prakṛti*), is that which should be agitated. He is the *pradhāna*, with its contraction and manifestation. Though born he is the source of the universe. Though he is without *guṇas*, he takes on the *guṇa rajas* in order to engage in creation and thus becomes Brahmā. As Brahmā he emits creatures; then, having an excess of the *guṇa sattva*, he becomes Viṣṇu and righteously protects all creatures; thereafter, having an excess of the *guṇa tamas*, he becomes Rudra, dissolves the three worlds, and sleeps. Though he possesses the three *guṇas*, he is devoid of them... As Brahmā he manifests the worlds, as Rudra he dissolves them, and as Viṣṇu he holds a neutral position. These are the three states of the self-existent. The lord of the worlds as Brahmā is *rajas*, as Rudra *tamas*, and as Viṣṇu *sattva*: these are the three gods, these are the three *guṇas*. (*MārP.* 46.11–18; trans. by author)

The *trimūrti*'s role is specifically linked to the cyclical emission, preservation, and annihilation of the world and is thus assimilated to the sphere of transmigration (*saṃsāra*). The three gods are not involved with the original manifestation (*sarga*, *prākṛtasarga*) taking place at the beginning of each life of Brahmā (*mahākalpa*; see cosmic cycles). Instead, they are thought to operate at the inferior level of the secondary re-manifestation (*pratisarga*) of the universe, which occurs at the beginning of each day of Brahmā. This seems to be the reason why the *trimūrti* as such has never been the object of worship. If in the Purāṇas Viṣṇu and Śiva rise to the level of *puruṣa*, of *brahman*, and are therefore worshipped in their own terms as both the transcendent and the immanent godhead, Brahmā – with rare exceptions such as the one reported above – is confined to the *pratisarga* level. Being linked to the law of *karman* and to the unending cycles of births and deaths at both a cosmological and a human level, the creator god is the emblem of inexorable fate (*daiva*): he is the personification of *vidhi*, that is, ritual injunction, the upholder of the Vedas and of Brahmanical orthodoxy, not of *bhakti* and liberation (*mokṣa*).

In epic and puranic sources, the male triad is not infrequently flanked by a triad of goddesses understood to be their spouses. Vāc or Sarasvatī accompanies Brahmā, Śrī-Lakṣmī accompanies Viṣṇu, and Umā-Pārvatī or Durgā/Kālī accompanies Śiva. From the perspective of Devī worshippers, the goddess as Parāśakti is identified with the transcendent *brahman* as well as with *prakṛti*, that is, she is thought to be the very source of Brahmā, Viṣṇu, and Śiva. She is then revered as the mother of the male gods and of all creatures. Triads of goddesses are known from vedic times. For instance, in the *Āprī* hymns of the *Ṛgveda*, we find mention of Bhāratī, Iḍā, and Sarasvatī (e.g. see *ṚV.* 2.1.11, where they are associated with Agni).

Through an accurate survey of the main cosmological divergences in puranic materials, H. Brinkhaus (1999) has put forward the thesis that what he calls the *trimūrti* doctrine was preceded by an older, quite different doctrine of the three states (*tryavasthā*). He suggests that in both the epic and the puranic accounts, we are faced with the juxtaposition of two competing cosmological and theological schemes. The *tryavasthā* doctrine, also traceable in the *Manusmṛti* (1.5ff.), postulates the supreme reality of Brahmā as Svayaṃbhū, the self-existent lord of the universe, who is characterized by three states:

1. as the demiurge Brahmā, he is in charge of creation (the *guṇa rajas* then predominates);
2. as *kāla*, that is, inexorable time, he is in charge of annihilation (the *guṇa tamas* then predominates); and
3. as *puruṣa*, he remains inactive, that is, he rests as Nārāyaṇa on the waters of the primeval ocean (the *guṇa sattva* then predominates).

This scheme embraces the cyclical alternation of the unfolding and reabsorption of the world and is more comprehensive than the *trimūrti* scheme that concerns itself with only one period of manifestation/maintenance/destruction.

Whereas in the *tryavasthā* design, the emphasis is on the cosmic pause of inactivity, that is, the state of absorption between a destruction and a remanifestation of the world, in the *trimūrti* pattern, the emphasis is on the intermediate, active phase of upholding the cosmos between manifestation and destruction. As M. Biardeau (1981, 55–57) has noticed, in the various cosmogonic accounts it is the role of the *guṇa sattva* (i.e. Puruṣa/Viṣṇu) that appears puzzling, since it serves different purposes: as Puruṣa/Nārāyaṇa, following the *tryavasthā* scheme, it is linked to stagnation; as Viṣṇu, following the *trimūrti* scheme, it is linked to maintenance.

H. Brinkhaus posits that the distant, inexorable god Brahmā came to be admitted as a member of the *trimūrti* for the simple reason that he was the main figure in the older and perhaps original *tryavasthā* framework. According to him, the overlapping of the *tryavasthā* and *trimūrti* schemes is detectable in the seminal passage of the *Vanaparvan* quoted above, in which the "three states" (*tisro 'vasthāḥ*) of the supreme god Prajāpati are openly described for the first time. He observes that immediately preceding this explicit mention of the *trimūrti* (*MBh.* 3, app. I, 27.35–36) is an account of the three cosmic phases as per the *tryavasthā* scheme (vv. 5–34): first *kāla* destroys the world (v. 5); then Puruṣa retires to rest (vv. 16–17); and finally Brahmā springs out of Puruṣa's navel in order to newly manifest the world (vv. 28–30).

The *Mahābhārata* passage would thus mirror the superimposition of the *trimūrti* scheme – set within the framework of *bhakti* and witnessing the affirmation of the great gods Viṣṇu and Śiva – on an older conception of a fatalistic, supreme god (i.e. Brahmā), destined to become a more and more remote deity and a *deus otiosus*. In fact, H. Brinkhaus suggests that Viṣṇu and Śiva were not really appropriate for the triadic scheme, which was originally tailored for prototypes of fate such as Brahmā and *kāla*. He further argues that a similar blending of the two doctrines can be found in the older Purāṇas, such as the *Mārkaṇḍeyapurāṇa*.

Apparently, the *tryavasthā* and *trimūrti* schemes were both prominent side by side for a certain time. H. Brinkhaus sees proof of this in two works of Kālidāsa (5th cent. CE), the *Kumārasaṃbhava* and the *Raghuvaṃśa*. In chapter 2 of the *Kumārasaṃbhava*, in which Indra and other deities praise Brahmā, he interprets the poet's eulogy of the triple-formed (*trimūrtaye*) creator god who differentiated himself in accordance with the three *guṇas* (*guṇatrayavibhāgāya*; *KumS.* 2.4ff.) as evidence of a Brahmā-based theology following the *tryavasthā* scheme. In this regard, the most significant verse is the following:

> Bringing forth [your] greatness in three states (*tisṛbhis tvam avasthābhir*), you are the sole cause of the dissolution, stagnation and creation (*pralayasthitisargāṇām*) [of the world]. (*KumS.* 2.6; trans. Brinkhaus, 1999, 44n55)

In order to strengthen his hypothesis, H. Brinkhaus translates *sthiti* as "stagnation" rather than "maintenance" or "preservation" as per the classic *trimūrti* scheme. However, in two other verses of the *Kumārasaṃbhava*, the *trimūrti* is clearly evoked. In the first verse, Śiva is extolled as the godhead who manifests himself in the three forms of Brahmā, Visnu, and Śiva:

> What form of you is this? The one by which you create (*sṛjasi*) the manifest universe? Or the one by which you support (*bibharṣi*) it? Or, indeed, the one that destroys (*saṃhartā*) it? (*KumS.* 6.23; trans. Smith, 2005, 217)

In the second verse, the equality of the triad of gods is emphasized:

> There is just one form, which divided three ways (*tridhā*). Each of them might appear first or last, sometimes Śiva the Destroyer before Viṣṇu, sometimes Yellow Viṣṇu before him, the Creator having his praises sung by them both, or both of them by the Creator. (*KumS.* 7.44; trans. Smith, 2005, 271)

Kālidāsa also mentions the *trimūrti* in two verses of the *Raghuvaṃśa*, in which Śiva and Viṣṇu, respectively, are extolled as the godhead performing the three functions of the triad: (1) "[you (i.e. Śiva) are] the cause of the creation, preservation and destruction" (*sargasthitipratyavahārahetuḥ*; *RaghV.* 2.44; trans. Brinkhaus, 1999, 45n57); (2) "Hail to you [i.e. Viṣṇu], the creator of the universe (*namo viśvasṛje*)... preserving the universe (*viśvam... anubibhrate*)... the destroyer of the universe" (*viśvasya saṃhartre tubhyam; RaghV.* 10.16; trans. Brinkhaus, 1999, 45n56).

Iconographic Testimonies

Representations of the triad of Brahmā, Viṣṇu, and Śiva – each with his own distinctive marks (*lakṣaṇas*) – emerge from around the 6th to 7th centuries CE. The Harihara and Ardhanārīśvara images of the Kushana and Gupta periods were probably a pioneering inspiration for them. The different ways in which the *trimūrti* is portrayed in sculpture have been classified by T.A. Gopinatha Rao (1916) as follows:

1. Śiva, clear as crystal, with three eyes and four arms, standing erect with only one leg, usually on a lotus pedestal (*padmapīṭha*): from the right and left of Śiva's body emanate Brahmā (with four heads and four arms) and Viṣṇu (with four arms). This form is known as *ekapādatrimūrti*. The gods' vehicles may also be represented in it – Śiva's bull, Brahmā's *haṃsa*, and Viṣṇu's Garuḍa;
2. Brahmā and Viṣṇu issuing forth from either side of a *liṅga* (i.e. Śiva);
3. Brahmā, Viṣṇu, and Śiva standing erect side by side, often on three separate *padmapīṭhas*. A fine example dating to circa the 6th century CE is found in Ellora, cave 29 (Śiva, however, may also take the central position, as in Ellora, cave 16);
4. Each of the gods has a shrine reserved to him, and these shrines are contiguous: typically Brahmā is placed to the right, the *liṅga* (i.e. Śiva) stands at the center, and Viṣṇu is placed to the left.

With the exception of number 3, the main deity of these portrayals is Śiva, from whom Brahmā and Viṣṇu issue forth in both number 1 and number 2. Even stone reliefs of the Hindu triad from Kashmir typically present the sequence Brahmā-Śiva-Viṣṇu, with Śiva or the *liṅga* occupying the central, most important position.

Having never gained popularity among the masses, specimens of the *trimūrti* are altogether scarce in Indian art, even though images of the three gods combined together have been found as far as Java and Cambodia. In fact, the iconographical representations of the *trimūrti* never became a well-defined genre. The uncertainty with respect to the identity of various composite figures – that is, whether they should be regarded as the *trimūrti* – is revealing in this respect. A striking case of misinterpretation is the colossal three-faced bust (6th-7th cents. CE) located in the cave shrine of the Elephanta Island near Mumbai. For a long time, this famous sculpture was erroneously thought to represent Brahmā, Viṣṇu, and Śiva – even nowadays it is publicized as the Indian *trimūrti* – though it is actually a composite form of Śiva Mahādeva: at the center, looking east, is his gentle, auspicious (*saumya*) face; on the proper right, looking south, is his terrific (*ghora*) face; on the proper left, looking north, is the face of his consort Umā, that is, his *śakti*.

Moreover, the individual figures making up the triad may change and the group of gods may even be extended to incorporate a fourth or a fifth deity. In particular, the sun-god Sūrya sometimes takes the place of Brahmā, more seldom of Viṣṇu and Śiva, and we know of triads in which Sūrya figures as the main deity. Enlarged, composite images include Śiva, Viṣṇu, Brahmā, and Sūrya or else Śiva, Viṣṇu, Devī, and Sūrya. We even come across representations of various kinds of pentads, among which is the Smārta pentad of Viṣṇu, Śiva, Devī, Sūrya, and Gaṇeśa.

Although the *trimūrti* as such did not start a cult, there are individual gods who have come to be worshipped as the triad of Brahmā, Viṣṇu, and Śiva. A notable example is that of Datta or Dattātreya, a minor *avatāra* of Viṣṇu and a puranic integrative deity whose worship is centered in the Marathi cultural area but whose icons and temples are found all across the subcontinent, in Kashmir as well as Nepal. Dattātreya has come to be identified with the three gods of the *trimūrti* standing side by side, an icon usually referred to as Hari-Hara-Pitāmaha. From around the 11th-12th centuries, he is sculptured as Viṣṇu seated in *yoga* posture, his triple nature being indicated by the emblems and vehicles of Brahmā, Viṣṇu, and Śiva. In the mid-16th century, the modern and nowadays most popular three-headed (*trimukhī*) portrayal of Dattātreya emerged: he is represented as either standing or seated in *padmāsana*, with three heads – the central one being that of Viṣṇu – and six arms bearing the emblems of the *trimūrti*. He is often depicted as an ascetic attended by three or four dogs, said to symbolize the Vedas, and by a cow, said to symbolize mother earth.

Western Encounters

The first European author to mention the Hindu triad was the Portuguese Duarte Barbosa (1480–1521). Significantly, he superimposed the Christian doctrine of the Trinity on the *trimūrti* concept, which he saw akin to it. In his travel book he wrote:

> These Brahmans greatly honour the number trine: they hold that there is a God in three persons, and who is not more than one. All their

> prayers and ceremonies are in honour of the trinity, and they, so to say, figure it in their rites, and the name by which they call it is this, Berma [i.e. Brahmā] Besnu [i.e. Viṣṇu] Maycereni [i.e. Maheśvara, that is, Śiva], who are three persons and one sole god. (Barbosa, 1995, 122–123)

Along the centuries, European missionaries conceded that the Indians possessed a pristine, natural knowledge of the one God, and even postulated that within Hinduism there were remnants of a lost Christianity, which had been later supplanted by Islam. In their search for analogies, they were naturally fascinated by the *trimūrti*. The Italian Jesuit missionary Roberto de Nobili (1577–1656), though condemning the Hindu triad as a confusion disseminated by Satan, found an adumbration of the "recondite mystery of the most Holy Trinity" (*mysterium reconditum Sanctissimae Trinitatis*) in the *Taittirīyopaniṣad* (1.6.1; Amaladass & Clooney, 2005, 98–99). And the French physician and traveler François Bernier (1620–1688) observed the following:

> With respect to these three Beings [of the *trimūrti*], I have met with some European missionaries, who pretend that the Heathens have some idea of the Mystery of the Trinity; and say that it is expressly declared in their Books, that they are three Persons in one God. I myself have frequently discoursed with the Brahmins on this Subject, but they expressed themselves so confusedly, that I never could understand their Meaning perfectly. (Lockman, vol. II, 1743, 246)

In his influential *Hindu Manners, Customs and Ceremonies*, the abbé J.A. Dubois (1765–1848) interpreted the *trimūrti* as the personification of the elements earth, water, and fire and concluded that "even granted... that the primitive Hindus intended to transmit... the idea of the Trinity under the form and attributes of the *Trimurti*... the result has been a sadly distorted presentation of this great mystery" (Dubois, 1990, 554).

Throughout the 18th and 19th centuries, the Trinity was debated between missionaries and Hindu authorities. The missionaries took pains to translate their complex notion of the tri-natured God (*trirūpakeśvara*), while Hindus understood the Trinity in their own terms, namely viewing the Christian doctrine of the triune God as analogous to the ultimate oneness in *brahman* of a plural number of deities.

To be sure, the parallel that Western travelers and missionaries had originally instituted between the Trinity and the *trimūrti* influenced the way in which Hindus looked at the triad of Brahmā, Viṣṇu, and Śiva. Nonetheless, while in the West debates arose whether the *trimūrti* should be understood as a derivation from the Christian Trinity or whether, as Louis Jacolliot (1837–1890) argued, it were actually the Christians who acquired the Trinity from India, Hindus themselves did not upgrade the *trimūrti* concept into a full-fledged doctrine (*vāda*). And when in the 19th century Hindu apologists responded to John Muir's (1810–1882) Sanskrit treatise *Mataparīkṣā* (1839), a critique of the religious and philosophical teachings of Hinduism from a Christian point of view, their positive assessment of the Trinity was not argued by pointing at the analogy with the *trimūrti* but rather by having recourse to the two-tiered epistemology of Advaita Vedānta – in other words, via the recognition that *brahman* is apprehended as a variously manifested Īśvara at the lower level of relative truth (*vyāvahārikasatya*) and as one, ineffable reality at the upper level of supreme truth (*pāramārthikasatya*; Young, 1981, 119–120n125).

In time, the Trinity came to be linked to the vedantic triad of *sat, cit*, and *ānanda*. The Brāhma Samāj reformer Keshub Chandra Sen (1838–1884), in his lecture "That Marvelous Mystery – the Trinity" (Jan. 1882), was apparently the first to correlate the Father, Son, and Spirit of the Christian Trinity to the notions of *sat, cit*, and *ānanda*, respectively, which he explained as truth, intelligence, and joy (Scott, 1979, 39–40, 228, 245; Clooney, 2011, 316–317). Inspired by such correspondence, in 1950 the Benedictine monks Jules Monchanin alias Svāmin Paramārubyānanda (1895–1957) and Henry Le Saux alias Svāmin Abhiṣiktānanda (1910–1973) founded an *āśram* in Shantivanam, Tamil Nadu, which they dedicated to the Trinity – namely, the Saccidānanda *āśram*. In his approach to the experience of non-duality (*advaita*), Father Monchanin magnified India as the land of the Trinity itself (Monchanin, 1957, 37). He remarked the following:

> Only the mystery of the Trinity is capable of resolving the antinomies which cause Hindu thought to swing endlessly between monism and pluralism, between a personal and an impersonal God. (Boyd, 1969, 219)

Even Christians, however, fail to penetrate the glorious mystery of the Trinity. Father Le Saux has observed that this is precisely the reason why it is usually downgraded to an inferior *trimūrti*:

> The liturgy struggles helplessly today in its efforts to celebrate the Trinity. Mass and office are very poor. There is no understanding of or feeling for the Trinity in the composition of this office. The Trinity, a crude, second-rate *Trimūrti* for the common run of Christians and theologians. (Abhishiktananda, 1998, 102)

In a philosophical perspective, comparisons of the *trimūrti* concept with the Christian doctrine of the Trinity are found in the thought of G.W.F. Hegel (1770–1831). In his *Lectures on the Philosophy of Religion*, G.W.F. Hegel, for whom Hinduism appears as the prototype of the principle of substantiality (*Substantialität*), observes that, although the idea of the *trimūrti* is laudable and worthy of attention, "having the abstract form to become the concrete characterization of the spirit," it is a "superficial personification" of *brahman* not "elevated unto the concept" (Viyagappa, 1980, 121) – in other words, it is nothing but abstract unity. If the gods of the *trimūrti* appear as independent beings (*selbständige Wesenheiten*), distinguished from the simple substance, which is *brahman*, they still disappear in the one, which means that they are ultimately untrue and they do not form a community of the one. In the *trimūrti*, he argues, Śiva is only the moment of destruction and not the return and reconciliation of the separated. For G.W.F. Hegel, Indian thought fails to unfold the idea of the person, the autonomous individual subject. Although he recognizes that between the *trimūrti* and the Christian Trinity there is a "common element of conceptualization," he observes that there is an essential difference between the two since "in true Trinity," besides a unity, there is a community – "a conclusion unto the unity full of content and actuality, which in its total concreteness is spirit" (Viyagappa, 1980, 184–186).

In his *Philosophy of Mythology*, F.W.J. Schelling (1775–1854) claims that, although the Indian tradition exhibits a deep yearning toward unity, there is not an originally pure notion of divine oneness in Hinduism. According to him, the abstract principle of *brahman* is not to be equated with the God of monotheism but is rather a philosophical afterthought, a secondary phenomenon. He notes that the Hindu tradition appears dominated by the separation of the *trimūrti*'s three principles. F.W.J. Schelling underlines the primacy of Śiva, whereas Brahmā, the "real God," is but a lost and forgotten god, and Viṣṇu, though he may seem to restore the lost and destroyed unity, cannot recover the true sense of monotheism: indeed, Viṣṇu and Śiva appear as sectarian, mutually exclusive principles (Halbfass, 1988, 103).

On his part, A. Schopenhauer (1788–1860) interprets the *trimūrti* in terms of his own philosophy of the will to live, in which Śiva's *liṅga* is a symbol of generation as well as annihilation. In *The World as Will and Idea*, he writes the following:

> Thus the will to live appears just as much in suicide (Śiva) as in the satisfaction of self-preservation (Viṣṇu) and in the sensual pleasure of procreation (Brahmā). This is the inner meaning of the unity of the *trimūrti*, which is embodied in its entirety in every human being, though in time it raises now one, now another, of its three heads. (Schopenhauer, vol. I, [7]1909, 510)

Conclusion

Over the centuries, the Western fascination with the *trimūrti*, the insisted comparison and correlation of this integrative concept with the Christian doctrine of the Trinity, determined a significant modification of its original meaning and function (see Slaje, 2012). The European assessment of the *trimūrti* brought about a process of re-enculturation, through which the Hindu self-understanding of the concept was subject to inevitable transformations. Particularly in the 20th century, the *trimūrti* scheme has become increasingly popular, part and parcel of the vedantic inclusivistic framework of neo-Hinduism. Nowadays this development is plainly illustrated in the many introductory books to Hinduism, both in India and in the West, which present the triad of Brahmā, Viṣṇu, and Śiva as one of the religion's cornerstone features. In contemporary iconography, one even witnesses the emergence of new *trimūrti*s such as that of Lakṣmī, Gaṇeśa, and Sarasvatī: with the traditional male triumvirate as its inspiring model, this recent triad appears to stand for lucre, luck, and learning, respectively – three concrete goals toward which most humans aspire (Smith, 1999).

Bibliography

Abhishiktananda, S., *Ascent to the Depth of the Heart: The Spiritual Diary (1948–1973) of Swami Abhishiktānanda (Dom H. Le Saux)*, Delhi, 1998.

Abhishiktananda, S., *Saccidānanda: A Christian Approach to Advaitic Experience*, Delhi, 1974.

Amaladass, A., & F.X. Clooney, *Preaching Wisdom to the Wise: Three Treatises by Roberto de Nobili, S.J. Missionary, Scholar and Saint in 17th Century India*, Chennai, 2005.

Bailey, G., "Trimūrti," in: D. Cush, C. Robinson & M. York, eds., *Encyclopedia of Hinduism*, London, 2008, 453.

Bailey, G., *The Mythology of Brahmā*, Delhi, 1983.

Bailey, G., "Trifunctional Elements in the Mythology of the Hindu *Trimūrti*," *Numen* 26/2, 1979, 152–163.

Banerjea, J.N., "A 'Viṣṇudharmottara' Passage and the 'So-called Trimūrti' of Elephantā," *AA* 3/2, 1956, 130–133.

Banerjea, J.N., "The So-called Trimūrti of Elephantā," *AA* 2/2, 1955, 121–126.

Barbosa, D., *A Description of the Coasts of East Africa and Malabar in the Beginning of the Sixteenth Century*, New Delhi, [1]1866, repr. 1995.

Basham, A.L., *The Wonder That Was India*, Calcutta, [1]1954, repr. 1989.

Bhan, J.L., *Kashmir Sculptures: An Iconographical Study of Brāhmanical Sculptures*, vols. I–II, New Delhi, 2010.

Bhattacharji, S., *The Hindu Theogony*, London, 1970.

Bhattacharyya, H.D., "Minor Religious Sects," in: R.C. Majumdar, ed., *The History and Culture of the Indian People: The Age of Imperial Kanauj*, Bombay, 1955, 326–336.

Biardeau, M., *Études de mythologie hindoue*, 2 vols., Paris, 1981–1994.

Boyd, R.H.S., *An Introduction to Indian Christian Theology*, Madras, 1969.

Brinkhaus, H., "Cyclical Determinism and the Development of the *trimūrti*-Doctrine," in: M. Brockington & P. Schreiner, eds., *Composing a Tradition: Concepts, Techniques and Relationships*, Zagreb, 1999, 35–47.

Calza, S., *La contemplazione: via privilegiata al dialogo cristiano-induista. Sulle orme di J. Monchanin, H. Le Saux, R. Panikkar e B. Griffiths*, Milan, 2001.

Carpenter, J.E., *Theism in Medieval India: Lectures Delivered in Essex Hall, October-December 1919*, London, 1921.

Clooney, F.X., "Trinity and Hinduism," in: P.C. Phan, ed., *The Cambridge Companion to the Trinity*, Cambridge UK, 2011, 309–324.

Collins, C.D., *The Iconography and Ritual of Śiva at Elephanta*, Albany, 1988.

Couture, A., & C. Schmid, "The *Harivaṃśa*, the Goddess Ekānaṃśā, and the Iconography of the Vṛṣṇi Triads," *JAOS* 121/2, 2001, 173–192.

Dhavamony, M., *Classical Hinduism*, Rome, 1982.

Diserens, H., "A Stone Relief of the Hindu Triad," *SAA* 11, 1991, 389–400.

Dubois, J.A., *Hindu Manners, Customs, and Ceremonies*, New Delhi, [1]1906, repr. 1990.

Gonda, J., *Triads in the Veda*, Amsterdam, 1976a.

Gonda, J., *Viṣṇuism and Śivaism: A Comparison*, New Delhi, [1]1970, repr. 1976b.

Gonda, J., "The Hindu Trinity," *Anthropos* 63, 1968, 212–226.

Gupta, S.M., *Vishnu and His Incarnations*, Bombay, 1974.

Hacker, P., "The Idea of the Person in the Thinking of Vedānta Philosophers," in: W. Halbfass, ed., *Philology and Confrontation: Paul Hacker on Traditional and Modern Vedānta*, Albany, 1995, 153–175.

Halbfass, W., *India and Europe: An Essay in Understanding*, Albany, 1988.

Hegel, G.W.F., *Vorlesungen über die Philosophie der Religion*, 3 vols., Leipzig, 1925–1929; ET: *Lectures on the Philosophy of Religion*, 3 vols., Berkeley, 1984–1987.

Hiltebeitel, A., "The Two Kṛṣṇas on One Chariot: Upaniṣadic Imagery and Epic Mythology," *HR* 24/1, 1984, 1–26.

Hopkins, E.W., *Epic Mythology*, Delhi, [1]1915, repr. 1986.

Hopkins, E.W., *The Religions of India*, New Delhi, [1]1885, repr. 1970.

Jacolliot, L., *The Bible in India: Hindoo Origin of Hebrew and Christian Revelation*, New York, 1868.

Kalidos, R., "*Vāmacāra* Viṣṇu in Hindu Iconography: A Problem in Sociological Values," *EW* 44/2–4, 1994, 275–291.

Kane, P.V., *History of Dharmaśāstra (Ancient and Medieval Religious and Civil Law)*, vol. II, Poona, 1941.

Keith, A.B., "Trimūrti," in: J. Hastings, ed., *Encyclopædia of Religion and Ethics*, vol. XII, New York, [1]1921, [3]1954, 457–458.

Lockman, J., *Travels of the Jesuits into Various Parts of the World*, vol. II, London, 1743.

Long, J.B., "Trimurti," in: K. Crim, ed., *The Perennial Dictionary of World Religions*, San Francisco, 1989, 766–767.

Mackenzie Brown, C., *The Triumph of the Goddess: The Canonical Models and Theological Visions of the Devī-Bhāgavata Purāṇa*, Albany, 1990.

Mathothu, K., *The Development of the Concept of Trimūrti in Hinduism*, Palai, 1974.

Mattam, J., *Land of the Trinity: A Study of Modern Christian Approaches to Hinduism*, Bangalore, 1975.

Moeller, V., "Trinität," in: H.W. Haussig, ed., *Götter und Mythen des indischen Subkontinents*, Stuttgart, 1984, 176–178.

Monchanin, J., *Mystique de l'Inde, mystère chrétien*, Paris, 1974.

Monchanin, J., *Ecrits spirituels*, Paris, 1957.

Nakamura, G., "Die Auslegung der indischen Dreieinigkeit 'Trimurti' bei Hegel und Schelling," *GJJ* 47, 2005, 57–71.

Olivelle, P., trans., *Upaniṣads*, Oxford, [1]1996, repr. 1998.

Paine, L.L., *The Ethnic Trinities and Their Relations to the Christian Trinity*, Boston, 1901.

Pal, P., "A Brahmanical Triad from Kashmir and Some Related Icons," *AAA* 27, 1973–1974, 33–45.

Panikkar, R., *The Trinity and the Religious Experience of Man: Icon-Person-Mystery*, New York, 1973.

Pathak, V.S., *Smārta Religious Tradition (Being a Study of the Epigraphic Data on the Smārta Religious Tradition of Northern India c. 600 A.D. to c. 1200 A.D.)*, Meerut, 1987.

Pathak, V.S., *History of Śaiva Cults in Northern India from Inscriptions (700 A.D. to 1200 A.D.)*, Varanasi, 1960.

Patton, L.L., "The Transparent Text: Purāṇic Trends in the *Bṛhaddevatā*," in: W. Doniger, ed., *Purāṇa Perennis: Reciprocity and Transformation in Hindu and Jaina Texts*, Albany, 1993, 3–29.

Prabhu, J., "Trinity: Unity and Pluralism in the Thought of Raimon Panikkar and Bede Griffiths," in: K. Acharya, M. Carrara Pavan & W. Parker, eds., *Fullness of Life*, Mumbai, 2008, 191–214.

Rao, T.A.G., *Elements of Hindu Iconography*, vol. II/2, Madras, 1916.

Renou, L., & J. Filliozat, *L'Inde classique: Manuel des études indiennes*, vol. I, Paris, [1]1947, repr. 1985.

Rigopoulos, A., *Dattātreya: The Immortal Guru, Yogin, and Avatāra: A Study of the Transformative and Inclusive Character of a Multi-faceted Hindu Deity*, Albany, 1998.

Schelling, F.W.J., *Sämmtliche Werke*, vol. II/1–2: *Philosophie der Mythologie*, Stuttgart, 1856–1857; ET: *Philosophy of Mythology*, Albany, 2007.

Schmithausen, L., "Trimurti," in: J. Ritter & K. Gründer, eds., *Historisches Wörterbuch der Philosophie*, vol. X, Basel, 1998, 1492.

Schopenhauer, A., *Die Welt als Wille und Vorstellung*, Leipzig, 1818–1819; ET: *The World as Will and Idea*, vol. I, London, [7]1909.

Scott, D.C., ed., *Keshub Chunder Sen*, Bangalore, 1979.

Sharma, A., *Classical Hindu Thought: An Introduction*, New Delhi, 2000.

Singh, S.B., *Brahmanical Icons in Northern India (A Study of Images of Five Principal Deities from Earliest Times to circa 1200 A.D.)*, New Delhi, 1977.

Slaje, W., *Trimūrti. Zur Verwandlung eines inklusivistischen Dominanzbegriffs in eine monotheistische Trinitätslehre*, Stuttgart, 2012.

Smith, D., *The Birth of Kumāra by Kālidāsa*, New York, 2005.

Smith, H.D., "A Contemporary Iconic Tradition: Lakṣmī, Gaṇeśa, Sarasvatī: An Emerging, 'New' Hindu Trimūrti," in: P.K. Mishra, ed., *Studies in Hindu and Buddhist Art*, Delhi, 1999, 11–48.

Viyagappa, I., *G.W.F. Hegel's Concept of Indian Philosophy*, Rome, 1980.

Young, R.F., *Resistant Hinduism: Sanskrit Sources on Anti-Christian Apologetics in Early Nineteenth-Century India*, Vienna, 1981.

Antonio Rigopoulos

Austria

There have been contacts between Austria and the Indian subcontinent since the early 20th century, when some Indian students came mainly to Vienna. But these contacts were rather limited and remained restricted to individuals. When in 1963 an Austrian-Indian cultural society was established, some exchange in the fields of arts and music started, followed up by the creation of associations such as the World Malayalee Council, Kerala Cultural Society, and the Association of Nepalese in Austria. Because of the United Nations Office in Vienna Indian diplomats reside there, but they come from different areas of India and do not share a common regional background. Additionally, people from Nepal and Bangladesh live in Austria, and it is important to note that practically no Tamil refugees from Sri Lanka have sought asylum in Austria. Of course, not all of the people from South Asia are Hindus. The documented history of Hinduism in Austria only started in 1980. According to the census of 2001, there were 3,629 Hindus in Austria, but this number might have been too low already then. Mukundrabhai Joshi, a member of the Hindu Mandir Gesellschaft (Hindu Mandir Association) in Vienna, puts the unofficial number of Hindus in Austria today at 11,000–12,000 (see "The Hindu Diaspora within Continental Europe," 2014, 9). Presently, there are at least five Hindu communities offering regular services to their members in various places.

"Hindus" and the "Hindu Religious Organization Austria"

According to Austrian law, religions are handled in three different ways: besides (1) low-scale organized associations, (2) a group of religions (e.g. the major Christian confessions, Judaism, Islam, and Buddhism) has obtained full official acknowledgment (starting in 1874) by the state, and (3) a further legislation (effective since 1998) gives secondary, limited, state recognition to another group of religions, which are labeled *Religiöse Bekenntnisgemeinschaften*, a very vague wording coined as an umbrella term covering rather diverse religious communities. This last category also includes Hinduism, with its umbrella organization acknowledged as the Hinduistische Religionsgesellschaft in Österreich (HRÖ, Hindu Religious Organisation Austria) in December 1998 (see Büeler, 2001, 87; see also Wallner, 2007, 300–304). As Hinduism is a broad term, the HRÖ gives the following definition of who can be considered "Hindu" in Austria, as is written in the constitution of the HRÖ:

> A person can be considered a Hindu, who is either Hindu by family or who is initiated through *dīkṣā* into a *sampradāya*, or who has chosen Hinduism by personal belief. (*Verfassung der HRÖ*, 2002, 85, § 3.1; trans. by author)

This threefold definition of persons as Hindus is interesting, as it opens the way for "Western Hindus" to join Hinduism in Austria besides people of South Asian origin who have been born or have been raised as "Hindus." The Śrī Śrī Rādhā-Govinda Mandir in Vienna, catering for many Western Vaiṣṇavas, can be considered to represent Hindus of this third category of HRÖ's definition who feel affiliated to the HRÖ; other groups, communities, or individuals with a (neo-)Hindu background (e.g. → Brahma Kumaris and → Sathya Sai Baba followers) in Austria, though belonging to the same third category, feel hardly attracted to the HRÖ (see Hutter, 2001, 53–56; Strobl, 2010, 335–341). Moreover, it should be noted that individual "Hindus by family tradition and/or *dīkṣā*" apply for membership to the HRÖ in limited numbers only, which explains the difference between numbers from the census and the estimate given by the community.

Because of its official acknowledgment, the HRÖ is an incorporate entity that can manage Hindu affairs in the public arena – for example fostering a project to build a temple in Austria. The legal situation allows for individuals to have their religion mentioned as Hinduism in official documents. School certificates, for example, may mention that a child has taken part in Hindu religious education (comparable to those of other children who, for example, want to have their Christian, Buddhist, or Islamic religious education mentioned). But – in contrast to Christian, Buddhist, or Islamic religious instruction, which is offered as a standard school subject – Hindu religious instruction is not offered (or financed) in public schools. This is due to the legal status of Hindus as *Bekenntnisgemeinschaft* versus the full acknowledgment of other religions. It is also difficult for the Hindu community to obtain visas and working permits for Hindu priests from Asia for a long-term stay in Austria, whereas fully acknowledged religions like Islam have more rights to import religious specialists and teachers to serve the community. So, Hindus are still struggling to raise their legal position to the same rank as Christianity, Buddhism, and Islam.

Besides working for the benefits of individual Hindus in Austria, the HRÖ mentions a number of goals to be achieved for the Hindu community and for Hinduism in general (*Verfassung der HRÖ*, 2002, 95f.; see Hutter, 2010, 8f.; Strobl, 2010, 302). The main goal is the establishment and improvement of places at which to provide knowledge of Hinduism to Hindus and non-Hindus alike and to make the religion known to the general public through social, cultural, and interreligious activities. Building a temple in Indian style either in the suburbs of Vienna or in the adjacent areas of the Federal State of Lower Austria and establishing a Hindu University in Europe are important goals for the long run. To achieve such goals, the HRÖ fosters various institutions that help to promote diverse facets and aspects of Hinduism under the umbrella of the HRÖ. The following institutions are mentioned in § 2.3 of the constitution: "*mandir*s, *ashram*s, *math*s, *peetham*s, missions, *sanatana dharma* groups, *yoga* centres" (*Verfassung der HRÖ*, 2002, 84, 98–100; see also Hutter, 2010, 9f.; Strobl, 2010, 301). This paragraph suggests possibilities for growth and organization of Hinduism in Austria; if new institutions come into being, then they could be easily integrated into the umbrella organization of the HRÖ. To highlight the cooperation among the different communities, in November 2010, the HRÖ organized a special *pūjā* celebrating the 30th anniversary of the founding of Hinduism in Austria.

Hindu Mandir Gemeinschaft (Hindu Mandir Community), Vienna

On the evening before *dīvālī*, on Nov 8, 1980, Dr. Bimal Kundu, an Indian chemist by profession living in Austria, arranged a → *pūjā* for the goddess Kālī and inaugurated a room at the premises of the Afro Asiatisches Institut (African Asian Institute) in Vienna (which is run by the Roman Catholic Church and houses dormitories and apartments for students from Africa and Asia) as the first Hindu temple. This celebration can be taken as the starting point of the Hindu Mandir Gemeinschaft in Vienna and of Hinduism in an organized form in Austria. Bimal Kundu, the founder of the community, wanted to offer an opportunity for Hindus to practice their religion as a community in addition to performing rituals at home for their family deity, but also to make the Austria public aware of Hinduism as one of the religions in Austria. This temple of the community has since then become the center of their activities, with a regular *pūjā* every Saturday evening. On average, 20–30 people meet there on a Saturday evening; on special days and during festivals, the number rises to about one hundred. Besides religious services, festivals are organized by the community in larger halls. A report on the *holī* festival at the end of the 1990s gives an impression of how Hindus try to organize themselves in diasporic surroundings:

> Though normally the festival is done outdoors, we arranged a large hall for it. At the full moon day of Holi, we celebrate the rituals in the temple and dedicate the colours used in the festival to the gods. The main festival – attracting Austrians and Indians alike – will be celebrated on the weekend with music and dance, and at the end, multiple colours are spread on everybody as a token of joy. To keep the hall clean, all the walls had been protected by fixing plastic sheets beforehand which can be removed after the event. Thanks to many helpers, at the end of the festival, all the room is left in clean condition. (Kundu, 1998, 23)

One additional aspect should be mentioned: the location of the temple in premises belonging to the Roman Catholic Church has since long helped establish intensive contacts between the community and representatives of the church on the level of interreligious dialogue.

Hindu Mandir Gesellschaft (Hindu Mandir Association), Vienna

In 1990 Hindu families managed to found another temple in Vienna. By law, this community is organized as an association, and, to differentiate itself from the before-mentioned community, this group labels itself as the Hindu Mandir Gesellschaft. In contrast to the Hindu Mandir Gemeinschaft, the association is organized in a formal way, about five hundred Hindu families having acquired formal membership in the association. As the first temple room soon proved to be too small, on Feb 14, 1999, on the eve of the *śivarātri* festival, a new temple was inaugurated. Besides the main temple room, also a kitchen, offices, and a small library are available. Such facilities help the association to promote Hinduism on a cultural, political, and social level. Not only is the HRÖ using the facilities of the association, but both organizations are also working closely together in conveying Hinduism to the Austrian public in a more visible way, as is the case with the Hindu Mandir Gemeinschaft. Every year cultural events, in particular combined wih the *dīvālī* festival, are held by the association in large rented halls, and these attract many Austrians. Even though these are successful events, the association is aware of the restrictions of such halls for the use during these types of cultural and religious festivals. Therefore the association (together with the HRÖ) has for one decade been looking for a possibility to build an "original" Hindu temple, including large facilities to house crowds at festivals and cultural events in or near Vienna. The regular temple service takes place every Sunday afternoon and runs for about two hours. Every meeting starts with *bhajan*s and → *kīrtan*s, followed by religious instruction or sermons. The evening ends with *āratī* to all the gods. The temple is dedicated to the *sarvā devatā* (all deities) and is therefore sometimes referred to as the Sarvā Devatā Temple by its members. This means that the association wants to attract all Hindus, irrespective of their tradition or school, to its services. As a consequence the Hindu Mandir Gesellschaft is presently attracting more Hindus at regular services, catering for 60–70 persons on the average Sunday afternoon.

Bochasanwasi Akshar Purushottam Sanstha

The Hindu organization → Bochasanwasi Akshar Purushottam Sanstha (BAPS) was founded in 1906, representing one branch of the → Swaminarayan Sampradāya, which has its European center in London. Since 1995, a (relatively small) group of Swaminarayans have been practicing their religion as a community, meeting privately in the devotees' homes. Starting from 2011, they use the rooms of the Hindu Mandir Gesellschaft for their service every Saturday afternoon. Regularly ten to fifteen person (from four or five Gujarati families) attend this service. On the linguistic and social level, it is noteworthy that – besides English – only Gujarati is used in the service especially when reading from the (authoritative) scriptures of the Swaminarayan tradition. Thus BAPS' temple service (weekly as well as special women's meetings once a month) – in contrast to the services of the other groups practicing Hinduism – is mostly restricted to members of this Sampradāya, which is until now only attracting Hindus of Gujarati background while other Hindus in Austria are scarcely aware of the existence of BAPS here.

Śrī Śrī Rādhā-Govinda Mandir (Gaudiya Math Vienna)

The driving force behind this temple is a native Austrian, who three and a half decades ago converted to Vaiṣṇavism, following the tradition of the Bengal mystic → Caitanya (d. 1533) and especially the Gaudiya Math tradition established in 1920 by → Bhaktisiddhanta Saraswati to spread (*kṛṣṇa-*)*bhakti* in India and in the Western world. This means that this temple in Vienna is clearly Vaiṣṇava and thus less all embracing than the Hindu Mandir Gesellschaft. Furthermore, this temple attracts a greater number of Western Hindus than the other temples in Vienna, including people who had joined or followed → ISKCON earlier but who, due to the disappearance of ISKCON in organized form in Austria in the early 3rd millennium, now practice in the Rādhā-Govinda Mandir. However, Vaiṣṇavas of Indian origin also frequent this temple, which is a formal member of the HRÖ. The main service is held every Sunday afternoon, with *bhajan*s, lectures from Vaiṣṇava scriptures, and *ārati*, with about 50 people attending on average. As a few members of the community are living in the temple, there is also a daily morning service (starting at 4:30 am), which is mostly attended only by the residents of the temple; a few guests also take part in the daily evening *pūjā*. The most recent development of the temple community is the successful building of a new temple structure south of Vienna in the Federal State of Lower Austria. In January 2014, they managed to attain permission to start building a temple at an estate measuring about 8,000 m^2. According to the architectural layout, a two-story building is planned, with not only the main temple room but also rooms for teaching Hinduism, meditation, and living quarters for some residents. The temple area will be surrounded by a garden with smaller shrines. After laying the foundation stone in April, on May 2, 2014, Ananta-Śeṣa, the serpent deity on whom Viṣṇu is resting, was installed at the temple. The ongoing building process shall come to its end in autumn 2015, when the official inauguration is scheduled. Once this temple is finished, it will be the first Hindu structure in Austria, built for religious purposes, that is not just adapting a previously used building as a temple. Thus this temple will mark an important step in the development of Hinduism in Austria, as was recently mentioned by some representatives of the HRÖ (personal communication).

Śrī Hari Oṃ Sanātan Dharm Mandir

At present, there exists only one Hindu community outside of Vienna, namely the Śrī Hari Oṃ Sanātan Dharm Mandir in Salzburg. In the early 1990s, an Indian woman running an Indian restaurant in Salzburg turned a room into a temporary temple, thus making religious activities for Hindus living in Salzburg possible. By the end of the decade, the community rented some rooms to convert them into a small temple. The temple community is organized as an association, and the temple is also a formal member of the HRÖ. Despite this, one has to concede that the temple's public visibility is small; mostly every Sunday morning, one Hindu family arranges the service in the temple, with fire waving, singing, reading from Hindu scriptures, and the final *prasāda*, which also serves as a common meal and meeting opportunity for the small number of Hindus in Salzburg. In this way, the *mandir* also functions as a social institution, as the Hindus can arrange birthday or marriage celebrations in the temple rooms. Even though people who are engaged in managing this temple are also active in local interreligious dialogues and guiding schoolchildren in the temple, it is hardly known to the public.

Conclusion

Hinduism in Austria becomes visible – at least partly – thanks to the above five temple communities providing regular religious services. As could be seen, there is no balance countrywide, and, mostly, the (few) Hindus living outside Vienna have to restrict their religious service to their home shrines or house altars. However, they try to take part in festivals based on Hindu culture, sometimes also arranged along ethnic or national lines, and in recent years also with the help of the HRÖ. In this way, the HRÖ as a legal institution tries to contribute to the development of Hinduism in Austria without eliminating the diversity within Hinduism, because Hinduism – according to the constitution of the HRÖ – is a broad term under whose umbrella many practices find shelter.

Bibliography

Büeler, G., "Hinduistische Religionsgesellschaft in Österreich (HRÖ) – eine universelle geistig-kulturelle Gemeinschaft," in: J. Hirnsperger, C. Wessely & A. Bernhard, eds., *Wege zum Heil? Religiöse Bekenntnisgemeinschaften in Österreich. Selbstdarstellung und theologische Reflexion*, Graz, 2001, 87–99.

Hutter, M., "Hindus asiatischer Herkunft in Österreich," in: M. Klöcker & U. Tworuschka, eds., *Handbuch der Religionen*, suppl. vol. XXIII, entry VIII-25, Munich, 2010, 1–13.

Hutter, M., "Hinduismus in Österreich. Rechtliche Stellung und Aktivitäten," in: M. Hutter, ed., *Buddhisten und Hindus im deutschsprachigen Raum*, Frankfurt, 2001, 47–59.

Kundu, B., "Das indische Holi-Fest," *RU* 4/1, 1998, 22–23.

Strobl, A., *Was Graz glaubt. Religion in der Stadt*, Innsbruck, 2010.

"The Hindu Diaspora within Continental Europe," *HT*, 2014, 1–11.

"Verfassung der Hinduistischen Religionsgesellschaft in Österreich," in: J. Hirnsperger & C. Wessely, eds., *Wege zum Heil? Religiöse Bekenntnisgemeinschaften in Österreich. Verfassung und Statuten*, Graz, 2002, 83–100.

Wallner, L., *Die staatliche Anerkennung von Religionsgemeinschaften. Die historische und aktuelle Umsetzung der religiösen Vereinigungsfreiheit in Österreich unter Berücksichtigung des deutschen Religionsrechts*, Frankfurt, 2007.

Manfred Hutter

Germany

At the end of the first decade of the 21st century, approximately 67,000 people of Indian origin lived in Germany with a German passport, and about 43,000 Indian citizens. Such data can only be a general estimate, because people who originally came as Tamil refugees from → Sri Lanka or as "Indians" from → Afghanistan are sometimes also included in such numbers. Another inaccuracy appears as persons of the second and partly already the third generation of migrants from the Indian subcontinent are included as well. Therefore an exact number of how many "Hindus" are presently living in Germany is difficult to arrive at, but, taking "Hindu" in a broad sense, it may be 100,000 to 120,000 people, also including "Western converts" to new religious movements with Indian background or to global movements of Indian origin (see Bergunder, 2006) – but the number of these Westerners is only small.

"Indian" Migration to Germany

The first Indians to come to Germany were mainly students, arriving after World War I. Some of them were active in the Indian independence movements. As Germany had no colonial history with India, the country was appealing to some independence fighters, for example, Subhas Chandra Bose in the 1930s. After World War II, students – generally single males – came and often married German women, finding employment as academics; already in the 1960s, these Indians were running a temple in Frankfurt am Main. A significant rise in the number of Hindus started in 1978, as a result of the civil war in Sri Lanka, which brought refugees and people seeking political asylum to Germany (see Baumann *et al.*, 2003, 44–48). Their migration route led from South Asia to the German Democratic Republic, where they could obtain a transit for their onward journey to the Federal Republic of Germany. Another group of refugees were Hindus from Afghanistan, who since the 1980s, due to the instable political situation, sought asylum in Germany; they found help from Afghan Hindus, who since the 1970s had come as students to Germany. A last wave of Indian immigrants reached Germany between the last years of the 20th century and 2003, when highly specialized experts in computer technology received working permits. These diverse origins of migrants also contributed to the pluralism of Hinduism in Germany (for Indian migrants in Germany in general, see Brosius & Goel, 2006). In this diversity, the Hindu migrants in Germany can be well compared to those in Switzerland (Neubert, 2013, 318); the situation in neighboring Austria is a bit different, as there are no significant numbers there of Hindus of Tamil background from Sri Lanka (Hutter, 2010, 3).

Low-scale Organizations as Associations

The Hindu community as a whole is not organized in a common body, as it is the case, for example, in Austria with the Hinduistische Religionsgesellschaft Österreich, which in 1998 obtained recognition by the government according to Austrian law (Hutter, 2010, 8–10). Maybe the reason for the lack of an umbrella organization covering all Hindu communities lies in the diverse ethnic, linguistic, social, and historical background of the local communities. Efforts to create a common body – mainly headed by Tamils – have not yet led to results. Therefore we find – if ever – only local associations of temple communities with two noteworthy exceptions: the Vishwa Hindu Parishad (VHP) and the Rhein-Main Bengali Cultural Association.

VHP has been active since 1984, when they first founded a German branch of the Indian association in Frankfurt, mainly to cater to the cultural, social, and religious needs of Indians – many of them of Bengali background; in 1989 they founded a religious center in Frankfurt for a maximum of about 150 persons. But generally one has to admit that the activities of the VHP focused more on North Indian culture than on regular (daily) temple practices. Despite the efforts of the VHP to be an overall association for Indians, many of them do not support the VHP but stick to local associations instead.

The Rhein-Main Bengali Cultural Association is active in the greater Frankfurt area (Dech, 2000); its main activity since the 1980s is the organization of the yearly *durgāpūjā* in September or

October – a huge cultural (and religious) event attracting not only Bengalis but also Hindus in general as well as Germans who take part in it as an Indian cultural festival.

Related to the Bengali Association in its focus on the *durgāpūjā* is the Indian cultural association Bharat Samiti in Cologne, mainly active in organizing a yearly cultural festival in September. Another important association, starting in 1991 in Cologne, has been the Hindu-Sikh-Verein (Hindu Sikh Association), which founded the first temple for Hindu refugees who came from Afghanistan to Germany. In 2002 both Hindus and Sikhs of Afghan background managed to establish the Afghan Hindu and Sikh Society of Germany as a registered association by law. It covered the needs of Afghan refugees and was highly engaged in helping them to get political asylum in Germany and thus preventing their deportation to Afghanistan by making the German public aware of the dangerous situation for religious minorities there. As far as the Tamil side in Germany is concerned, one can see that until today the large number of Tamil Hindus (and also Christians) in Germany has not managed to form a common society, but there are more than 20 local registered communities (see Back, 2007, 30–33) who are responsible for Tamil Hindu temples. As temple communities, they not only run small temples but also intend to care for the members of the community in general. In conclusion it can be said that – unlike the legal situation in → Austria – there is no registered association representing all Hindus in Germany that could serve as a dialogue partner for political or religious institutions, and Hindus are mainly organized on a local, sometimes only low-scale, level.

Temples and Communities of Tamil Hindus

The first religious "temple services" of Tamil Hindus in Germany were performed in private houses or rented rooms for special religious occasions, but in the mid-1980s, the first communities managed to arrange rooms as "temples" by adapting abandoned halls, formerly used, for example, as factories. Initially such temples were situated, for example, e.g. in Schwerte, Hattingen, Hamm, or Essen – all located in the federal state of North-Rhine Westphalia, as this federal state was more receptive of foreign refugees than other federal states at the time. These early communities also attracted additional Hindus, and new temples were set up in the 1990s in other locations. But some of them were admittedly rather short lived, and addresses frequently changed. Despite such uncertainties, temples became centers of community building and the focal point of religious practices and rituals. The daily routine largely followed Tamil practices of the homeland, as far as possible, with *pūcai* (Skt. *pūjā*; offerings), *apiṣēkam* (Skt. *abhiṣeka*; ritual purification with water), *hōmam* (Skt. *homa*; offering fire), and *arccaṉai* (Skt. *arcanā*; private devotion or reverence to the deities). Performing such temple ceremonies three times a day was the exception, though, because many communities could only afford – due to a lack of priestly manpower – one ritual per day or even per week, usually on a Friday.

The best-known place of Tamil Hinduism in Germany is the Sri Kamadchi Ampal (Śrī Kāmāṭci Ampāḷ) Temple (Baumann *et al.*, 2003, 125f., 246–250; Wilke, 2013) in Hamm, which – thanks to the efforts of its priest, who was trained in priesthood already during his childhood in Jaffna (Sri Lanka) – was established in 1989. The first temple festival, with a chariot ride through some adjacent streets (see Luchesi, 2008; Wilke, 2013), was performed in 1993, attracting up to three hundred devotees. This event two decades ago brought, for the first time, greater public attention to Hinduism in Germany, and the following years brought not only growth to both the community and the temple in Hamm but also some resistence from the public, when the growing number of attendants rose to several thousands. This growth created traffic problems, and people complained about the disturbance brought by this visibility of lived Hinduism. But the problems were solved by moving the temple and the festival to the suburbs of Hamm, where suitable space was available for building the first Hindu temple in Germany, following Sri Lankan Hindu and South Indian temple architecture rather than just adapting and converting buildings like houses, shop rooms, or storehouses. Through the cooperation between a German and an Indian architect under the supervision of the priest, the temple was inaugurated on Jul 7, 2002. Since then this temple has been the main focal point for many Tamil Hindus, and especially for the main festival in May or June. In recent years, up to 15,000 people have come to Hamm, from Germany and neighboring countries. Hindus of diverse ethnic origins and even a small community of German "converts" are active in the festival, aside from the tourists who also attend the main ceremony.

Even if the temple in Hamm with its activities is the best known in Germany, Hinduism cannot be confined to this center, as there are about 25 other Tamil Hindu temples all over the country. Geographically they concentrate in the area of the federal states of Lower Saxony and North-Rhine Westphalia, but nearly all larger cities now house such a temple; the most recently inaugurated ones are located in Bielefeld (January 2013) and Berlin (September 2013), both dedicated to → Murukaṉ. All of these Tamil temples have their own followers, who still remember their roots in Sri Lanka and who keep to their local traditions, which differ in everyday practice – even if the temple in Hamm with its public attraction and efforts to create networks and cooperation between the communities intends to shape a harmonized form of Hinduism of Tamil origin and thus a common "Hindu identity." But still the idea of keeping one's own tradition is not forgotten, and sometimes signs of competition are visible (see e.g. Meisig, 2001, 230–233; Baumann *et al.*, 2003, 159f.). So we clearly have to deal with a plurality among Tamil Hindus (see also the documentation of several larger temples all over Germany by Back, 2007, 64–109).

Afghan Hindus

A minority among the Hindu population in Germany are those Hindus (and Sikhs) who came from Afghanistan. They clearly stick to religious and cultural traditions that originated in northwestern India and → Pakistan, so they are closely related to Punjabis and Sindhis. Currently about seven to ten thousand Afghan Hindus and Sikhs are living in Germany, and they run six temples (and three *gurdvārā*s). They founded the first temple in 1991 in Cologne but – due to distinct local traditions that can be traced back to either Kandahar (or even to their homeland in Multan, Pakistan) or Kabul – the community split two years later. This led in 1993 to the creation of the Afghan Hindu community Hari Om Mandir from the Kandahari side and the Afghan Hindu cultural association Sanatan Hari Om Mandir from the Kabuli side. Both have a temple of their own until today in Cologne. More houses converted to temples for the need of different communities in the following years in Essen, Hamburg, and Frankfurt.

These temples are not absolutely distinct from one another, and, as a whole, they cater for a special "Afghan Hinduism" in Germany, dissociating themselves from the Tamil side. Notable is the array of statues (*mūrti*s) in these temples, most of which have been dedicated by the priest Pujya Shree Rambaba, who has lived in the United Kingdom since 1970. Having taken part in the inauguration of these temples, Pujya Shree Rambaba is indirectly the source of some uniformity among the Afghans in Germany. The temples house the Vaiṣṇava *mūrti*s of → Hanumān, → Rāma, his brother Lakṣmaṇa, and his wife Sītā; statues of → Rādhā and → Kṛṣṇa; the Śaiva *mūrti*s of → Śiva, → Pārvatī, Gaṇeśa; and → *liṅga*s. Thus, we find the prominent North Indian gods and goddesses of both Śaivaism and Vaiṣṇavism.

In addition, however, a clear local setting is established, referring to the origin of the forefathers of the community from the northwest Indian provinces Punjab and Sindh, by displaying the *mūrti*s of Jhūlelāl (the *iṣṭadevatā* of the Sindhi community), → Shirdi Sai Baba, and Gurū Nānak as well (see Hutter, 2012, 358–360). The last one – mostly taken as the founding *gurū* of Sikhism – is a special case. Although Hindus from Pakistan, northwestern India, and Afghanistan are aware of the Indian saint, he gives rise to some estrangement among community members: especially the Hari Om Mandir is running a practice that is blending more elements of northwest Indian Hinduism and Sikhism by not only revering Gurū Nānak in the temple but also reciting texts from the *Gurū Granth Sāhib* of the Sikh tradition besides texts of North Indian Hindu tradition in the religious service on Sunday, including Sikh → *kīrtans* as well. Among the main festivals celebrated in the Hari Om Mandir, besides *durgāpūjā* in September or October and *dīpāvalī* in October or November, *baisākhī* in April or May is also celebrated as a festival clearly inspired by Sikh tradition. Thus generally speaking, the Hari Om Mandir is open to both traditions, which breeds discontent. On the one hand, Sikhs visiting the temple feel uncomfortable with the Hindu statues, and, on the other hand, some Hindus express their concern that reading from the *Gurū Granth Sāhib* and seeing the picture of Gurū Nānak is not suitable for Hindu rituals. From this point of view, Hari Om Mandir is a unique place of worship for Afghans in Germany (Hutter, 2012, 354–357). The other Afghan temple in Cologne, the Sanatan Hari Om Mandir, several other Afghan Hindu temples, and the three Afghan *gurdvārās* in Germany keep a purer Hindu or Sikh tradition, without incorporating elements of the other tradition.

All the Afghan temples – like the Tamil temples above – function not only as religious centers but also as places of social commitment, integrating Afghan Hindus into German society and preserving Hindu identity and culture for the younger generation. Thus during religious services, Hindi is widely used in order to keep language skills among the younger people alive; Hindi classes are arranged by the temple management. However, German-language courses are also offered to provide (elder) members of the community with knowledge of the local language as a tool of integration into German society. As a consequence, after just two and a half decades of living in Germany, Afghan Hindus are well integrated into the local society.

Further Tokens of Plurality

North Indians run fewer temples than Tamils, and – compared to the Afghan Hindus, who are fewer in number than the North Indians – the visibility of North Indian temple communities is limited. The assemblies mentioned above, who organize Indian cultural events and the *durgāpūjā*, are not engaged in regular temple services. There is one notable exception. Since 2005 the Sri Ganesha Hindu Temple Association in Berlin has been struggling to build a huge Hindu temple in North Indian architectural style; there are plans – approved by the local building authorities – for a temple, which would then be the third-largest Hindu architecture in Europe, after the → Swaminarayan Temple in London and the Sri Kamadchi Ampal Temple in Hamm. But since the foundation-stone ceremony, done in 2008 and repeated in 2010, there has been no significant construction work, because the association is short of money. As a consequence, it uses a former storehouse on the building ground as a temporary temple. The fact that – as mentioned above – a Tamil temple dedicated to Murukaṉ was erected and inaugurated in 2013 only a few kilometers away from the place intended to house the Gaṇeśa temple in the future is seen neither as competition nor as an opportunity for cooperation, because the North Indians in Berlin clearly want to have their own temple, promoting North Indian traditions (Wobbe, 2014).

Another side of "Hinduism" is represented by two Balinese Hindu temples; one was inaugurated in May 2012 in Berlin, the other one in May 2010 in Hamburg. Each of the two temples serves approximately eight hundred Balinese in Germany. Both temples were constructed in Bali and shipped to Germany, where they were erected on public ground. The Hamburg temple is adjacent to the Museum für Völkerkunde (The Ethnological Museum) and works in close cooperation with the museum to promote Balinese culture in Germany. The Berlin temple is situated inside the Gärten der Welt (Gardens of the World), a huge park and green area in Berlin. The location of both temples shows that the – relatively small – Balinese community in Germany has been cooperating with public institutions to highlight its own cultural and religious tradition and to make these two temples the homelands of Balinese migrants to Germany.

Conclusion: Hindus in Public Society

The different Hindu communities in Germany are rather small in number and, on the organizational level, still widely fragmented, missing an umbrella organization. Public perception of most of the temples is rather inconspicuous, but there are no significant frictions between the Hindu communities and the German host society. The migrant Hindus, who have been coming to Germany in considerable numbers for more than three decades, are still on the way to fully establishing, structuring, and organizing themselves as religious communities, but Hinduism as part of the cultural heritage connects the second (and with children already a third) generation with their South Asian origin.

Bibliography

Back, C., *Hindu-Tempel in Deutschland. Eine Untersuchung tamilisch-hinduistischer Strukturen in der Diaspora*, Marburg, 2007.

Baumann, M. *et al.*, eds., *Tempel und Tamilen in zweiter Heimat. Hindus aus Sri Lanka im deutschsprachigen und skandinavischen Raum*, Würzburg, 2003.

Bergunder, M., ed., *Westliche Formen des Hinduismus in Deutschland. Eine Übersicht*, Halle, 2006.

Brosius, C., & U. Goel, *Masala.de - Menschen aus Südasien in Deutschland*, Heidelberg, 2006.

Dech, M., "Rhein-Main Bengali Cultural Association e.V.," in: M. Klöcker & U. Tworuschka, eds., *Handbuch der Religionen*, suppl.vol. IV, entry VIII-18, Munich, 2000, 1–4.

Hutter, M., "'Half Mandir and Half Gurdwara': Three Local Hindu Communities in Manila, Jakarta, and Cologne," *Numen* 59, 2012, 344–365.

Hutter, M., "Hindus asiatischer Herkunft in Österreich," in: M. Klöcker & U. Tworuschka, eds., *Handbuch der Religionen*, suppl. vol. XXIII, entry VIII-25, Munich, 2010, 1–13.

Luchesi, B., "Parading Hindu Gods in Public: New Festival Traditions of Tamil Hindus in Germany," in: K.A. Jacobsen, ed., *South Asian Religions on Display: Religious Processions in South Asia and the Diaspora*, London, 2008, 178–190.

Meisig, K., "Tamilischer Hinduismus in Deutschland. Ein Rundgang durch den Vighneśvara-Tempel in Hamm (Westfalen)," *MARG* 14, 2001, 229–249.

Neubert, F., "Switzerland," in: K.A. Jacobsen *et al.*, eds., *Brill's Encyclopedia of Hinduism*, vol. V, Leiden, 2013, 317–323.

Wilke, A., "Tamil Temple Festival Culture in Germany: A New Hindu Pilgrimage Place," in: U. Hüsken & A. Michaels, eds., *South Asian Festivals on the Move*, Wiesbaden, 2013, 369–395.

Wobbe, L., "Der Wettlauf von Ganesha und Murugan. Zwei Hindugötter erobern Berlin," *MEZW* 77, 2014, 210–218.

Manfred Hutter

Brahma Kumaris and Dada Lekhraj

The origins of the Brahma Kumaris – officially the Brahma Kumaris World Spiritual University (BKWSU), a nongovernmental organization affiliated with the United Nations – go back to the mid-1930s when the organization formed in India. From there it spread to many other countries from the 1970s onward. Founded by Dada Lekhraj, a diamond merchant in Hyderabad, Sindh (now Pakistan), with a Hindu background, who came to be known as Brahma Baba, the Brahma Kumaris ("Daughters of Brahma") started as a small group, called Om Mandali, which eventually (in the early 1950s) transferred to Mount Abu, in Rajasthan, where the headquarters of this international organization are now located. One of its distinctive features is the emphasis on women's leadership, with the sisters (referred to as *dādīs*) who had formed the core group around Brahma Baba taking the most senior positions. Another distinctive aspect of the Brahma Kumaris is the continuing communication with Dada Lekhraj: since his death in 1969, his teachings continue to be relayed via the medium of one of the *dādīs*.

The teachings and beliefs of the Brahma Kumaris are broadly Hindu, Hindu-related or Hindu-orientated (Bowker, 1997, 163); for example, they adhere to the belief in reincarnation and → *karma* and celebrate some of the Hindu → festivals. The Hindu-related character is also reflected in the Brahma Kumaris' concept of membership insofar as there are no formal or distinct rituals to undergo in order to attain membership. Although the discourses of the founder form the core sources on which the Brahma Kumaris draw, the teachings of the traditional Hindu scriptures, such as the *Bhagavadgītā*, blend with Brahma Kumari belief and practice. Other aspects of the Brahma Kumaris, such as their attitude toward education, other faiths, and the natural environment (educational initiatives and a strong interfaith element form part of their outreach activities), can also be seen within a broadly Hindu worldview.

Founder Dada Lekhraj and His Vision

The Brahma Kumaris were founded in 1937 in India by Dada Lekhraj (1877–1969), who at the age of 60 gave up his diamond business to devote himself entirely to spiritual matters after he had experienced a series of visions. Up to that point, he had been a well-known businessman with a family, known as Lekhraj Khubchand Kirpalani, who studied Hindu scriptures, such as the → Vedas, at the feet of a number of *gurus*. Then the visions started, the first being of the soul consciousness (see below) flowing out of his body. The second was a vision of Viṣṇu: an image of god, but as a perfect human being, the incarnation of god in man, who told him "That one, I am you." After these visions, Dada Lekhraj went to Calcutta (where his business was based), where he gained a different perception of the world, seeing it as a cycle of time; he also experienced visions of destruction, followed by a vision of heaven. All this made him wonder, and it upset his life. One day, Dada Lekhraj retired to his room, which he saw as filled with golden light, burning his eyes. He heard a voice saying, "I am the blissful one, I am Śiva, I am the incarnation of light. I am Śiva." The way in which Dada Lekhraj explained what happened is the following: "[t]here was an immense power and presence. I was not aware of what was being said." He interpreted that "immense power and presence" to be "Śiva Bābā" (god), who then came regularly to speak through Dada Lekhraj, as a result of which he began to attract a following. In Brahma Kumari thought, Dada Lekhraj put into practice what he was taught by Śiva. He was Ādi Dev ("First Man") of a new era, thus the founder of the BKWSU (see Chander, 1983).

After having set out on this path, Dada Lekhraj surrendered his wealth to his followers, handing everything over to eight trustees. In traditional Hindu thought, Dada Lehhraj's renunciation of worldly status and goods can be seen to mark his transition from the stage of householder to the stage of hermit or ascetic. His wealth was such that it sustained the community for 14 years. The members of this community lived in a closed environment, comparable to a monastic setting, until 1969, when Dada Lekhraj is said to have "left the body." According to the Brahma Kumaris' teachings, he did so because he realized that the speed with which he could teach was too slow. Having gone into the light, he could now work at the speed of light, as an angel who can awaken people individually. After Dada Lekhraj had "left the body," Śiva Bābā – through Dada Lekhraj – returned in the body of one of the members, first every three days, then less and less. Initially, Dada Lekhraj/ Śiva Bābā used various people as the channel for his message, but he then settled on just one person.

Now referred to as Prajapita Brahma or Brahma Baba, the Brahma Kumaris describe Dada Lekhraj as a visionary ahead of his time, who

> founded a spiritual movement which has grown from a few hundred people to a highly respected worldwide organisation ... [his] vision was of a new world founded on the values of peace, harmony and love. His dedication towards achieving it has inspired and continues to inspire people from diverse cultures and backgrounds to make that vision a reality through the transformation of their own lives. (BKWSU promotional materials)

Dada Lekhraj's vision also included the idea that women can and should have leadership roles, in both an administrative and a spiritual sense.

The time when Dada Lekhraj was alive formed what might be called the dormant period in the development of the Brahma Kumaris as a group or organization, a time during which the community of his followers slowly took shape and found its physical and spiritual footing (see Arweck, 2002). Until his death in 1969, Brahma Baba acted as a channel for god (Śiva Bābā), who communicated his messages known as *murlīs* (i.e. flutes [of knowledge]). As a body of written documents, these include all the Brahma Kumaris' teachings and instructions and thus form the canon of Brahma Kumari writings. The practice of communicating spiritual messages still continues through the mediumship of one of the *dādīs*.

There are two types of *murlī*:

1. the *sakar murlī*, communicated through Brahma Baba when he was still alive (practical in nature, giving advice about how to live); and
2. the *avyakt murlī*, communicated through the Brahma Kumari sister who now acts as Brahma Baba's mouthpiece (poetic in nature, giving "angelic" messages).

Both types have a formal beginning (a blessing) and end (an expression of love, a remembrance, and a *namaste*). During the last five years of Brahma Baba's life, the *murlīs* were written down to be preserved, and, given the continued additions, the corpus of *murlīs* is growing. *Avyakt murlīs* are delivered on fixed dates, occasions that attract large numbers of members (12,000–15,000 people).

A considerable number of those in charge of Brahma Kumari centers are women, as are the most senior members of the organization, most of whom have been with the movement for a long time, having joined at an early age as children or teenagers; most of them are now in their 80s. They are referred to and addressed as *dādīs* (elder sisters, although in Hindi, the word *dādī* literally means "paternal grandmother"), with *dādī* being used as an honorific (e.g. Dadi Prakashmani). Other female members are addressed as "sister" (e.g. Sister Maureen). Although each *dādī* has a specific role in the organization, the collective of the *dādīs* directs the organization; they are deeply respected by members and hold charismatic authority. The collective nature of the leadership and the fact that the organization has a male founder preclude the identification of the *dādīs* with female *gurus*, although they share some characteristics (see e.g. Charpentier, 2010; see also Pechilis, 2004). The status of the *dādīs* accounts for a certain hierarchy in the organization, with the female members who were directly taught by Dada Lekhraj forming the apex of the leadership and bestowing high authority and charisma to those immediately surrounding them. These in turn pass on some of these powers to those in their immediate sphere of activities, who in their turn do likewise, with charismatic authority cascading down the ranks of leadership.

After Dada Lekhraj had passed away, Dadi Prakashmani, one of the original trustees, assumed leadership as the administrative head of the organization worldwide; she was subsequently joined by Dadi Janki, who had joined the movement at the very beginning, as additional administrative head. In recent years, the number of the *dādīs* has dwindled, given their advanced ages (for example, Dadi Prakashmani died in 2007). However, younger members have risen to senior positions, such as Sister Jayanti, who combines a number of roles, including director of the organization in London and representative of the Brahma Kumaris at the United Nations in Geneva. The unusual prominence of women in an organization of this kind has been a focus of attention for both the Brahma Kumaris themselves (see Sister Sudesh, 1993) and scholars studying them (see Babb, 1984; Skultans, 1993; Howell, 1998; Lourenço, 2013; see also Puttick, 1997).

The Early Years: Om Mandali and the Move to Mount Abu

The following that Dada Lekhraj began to attract in 1936 as a result of his visions consisted mostly of women and children. Known as Om Mandli or Om Mandali, the group first gathered in Hyderabad, where Dada Lekhraj had started to hold *satsaṅg*s in his own house. In line with his vision of female leadership, he formed a committee of eight young women, who were entrusted with managing the trust to which Dada Lekhraj transferred all his material wealth. One of them, Radha, a cousin of Dada Lekhraj's wife, who became known as Om Radhe and later Mama, became the public face and spokeswoman of the new institution. It is also at this time that the members' outward appearance began to reflect the ideas and principles that Dada Lekhraj was teaching: they exchanged their usual bright garments for white cotton clothes, the former being associated with wealth and status, especially of their families, the latter considered a low-grade fabric worn by the poor and by widows. Members also changed their names to mark the transition from their former lives to members of Om Mandali – a practice associated with monastic life. Also, given the number of children who joined the community, a boarding school, called Om Nivas, was put in place. Its timetable included meditation as well as school work and play and thus reflected the spiritual and temporal discipline of the group.

Although Om Mandali represents the so-called dormant period of the organization (the Brahma Kumaris refer to it as the *yagya* [lit. sacrificial fire]), living self-sufficiently engaged in study, meditation, and self-transformation, this was also the period in which dissonance arose between the group and its surrounding social environment. The teachings of a pure and spiritual life led some young unmarried women to refuse marriage and women who were already married to refuse their husbands' conjugal rights, which resulted in disturbances, arson attacks, and court cases. An Anti Om Mandli committee formed with the aim of closing the institution and discrediting Dada Lekhraj. The print media of the time reported some of these events, taking both favorable and negative stances toward Om Mandali and using the term "cult" to refer to the group (e.g. *The Illustrated Weekly of India*, July 1938). Eventually, in late 1938, the case ended up in the high court in Karachi, where proceedings to restrict Om Mandali were squashed (see Hodgkinson, 1999, 31). However, despite being free to continue as before, the group decided to move to Karachi for a fresh start, only to find itself embroiled in further lawsuits, instigated by both the Anti Om Mandli committee and the Sindh government, who still sought to outlaw the organization; when these measures failed, an attack was made on Dada Lekhraj's life (see Hodgkinson, 1999, 33–36). None of these actions succeeded, and Om Mandali was thereafter left alone, allowing the 250–300 members (of which 50–60 were men) to pursue their spiritual lives undisturbed (see Hodgkinson, 1999, 36). It was at this point that they changed their name to Brahma Kumaris (see also Chander, 1983; Babb, 1986).

After Partition in 1947, Sindh became part of Pakistan. Although the Brahma Kumaris experienced no hostility or ill-treatment in the mainly Muslim country, to which many of the Hindu community had fled in anticipation of persecution, they felt that they belonged to India. Thus, in 1950, the group moved to Mount Abu, a hill station situated in the northwest of India in the state of Rajasthan. Given its long-standing association with seers and sages, Mount Abu was deemed a suitable location. During the 1950s, the Brahma Kumaris' expansion slowly began in India, with Dada Lekhraj sending sisters to Delhi and Bombay where they started Raja Yoga centers.

The Teachings of the Brahma Kumaris

The Brahma Kumaris adhere to the idea of reincarnation and *karma*, the belief that a person is a soul rather than a body (hence the Brahma Kumaris' speaking of "soul consciousness") and that leading a pure life (which includes eating vegetarian or *sāttvika* food, celibacy, and daily meditation) will rid one of all the obstacles or vices that prevent one from achieving union with god. There are five vices (lust, ego, anger, greed, and attachment), which are the enemy – called "Rāvaṇ," the main adversary in the → *Rāmāyaṇa*.

The notion of leading a pure life links with the idea of *karma*, of which according to the Brahma Kumaris there are three kinds: neutral, wasteful (nonproductive, although not necessarily harmful), and negative (causing pain for oneself and others). The Brahma Kumaris believe that the body leaves impressions on the soul according to the actions and thoughts that it has performed. The vices obviously lead to bad *karma*, with lust, associated with sex, being considered the most destructive, as it affects the soul for many rebirths. Dada Lekhraj declared sex to be "the greatest vice which needs to be totally renounced" (Puttick, 1997, 109) and "the dreaded enemy of the man of knowledge" (Chryssides, 1999, 196), as it entails – in terms of the individual – identification with the body and thus hinders the forging of the spiritual relationship with god. It also entails socially undesirable consequences, such as overpopulation (in the Brahma Kumaris' view, India's biggest problem), rape, promiscuity, and pornography. Sex is also considered the root cause of inequality in the relationships between men and women, as wives are traditionally expected to be subservient to their husbands (see Chryssides, 1999, 196–197). Hence the practice of celibacy for core members or chastity for married members, the segregation of the genders, and the use of "brother" and "sister" as titles for Brahma Kumari members, which denotes the relationship among them as that of members of a family.

Leading a pure life also links with the idea of giving service or → *sevā*, which not only means doing good or charitable work, and thereby creating good *karma*, but also ties in with the notion that everything one does is in the service of god or worship. The Brahma Kumaris follow the idea of the detached observer, involving detachment from the world while taking part in it, and celebrate some of the festivals in the Hindu calendar, such as *dīvāli*, *śivarātri*, and *rākhi* (*rakṣābandhan*).

The Brahma Kumaris' teachings are called Raja Yoga (see also → Rāja Yoga); through them, one is to realize one's essential nature as a soul or to develop soul consciousness. Apart from borrowing concepts and practices from the Hindu tradition, which undoubtedly stems from Dada Lekhraj's study of the Hindu scriptures, the Brahma Kumaris hold beliefs that are quite distinct to them, including the law of entropy (according to which deterioration is inevitable), the millenarian perspective of the cycle of time, and the intervention of god at the very end of the cycle (the so-called age of confluence), when god chooses a medium or channel (i.e. Dada Lekhraj) through which to send his messages, and a strong emphasis on the relationship with god/Śiva Bābā, which is established and maintained through meditation. Other religions and their founders are acknowledged as well as incorporated in the Brahma Kumaris' narrative of the cycle of time (in Brahma Kumaris' words, the "world drama"), which implies that, according to the Brahma Kumaris, their worldview transcends all other religions. In their own understanding, the Brahma Kumaris' teachings do not amount to a religion but take the form of a university that promotes spirituality – however defined (see e.g. Rose, 2001; King & Beattie, 2001).

The Brahma Kumaris' belief and practice are taught in an introductory course in meditation (see also O'Donnell, 1987) – a set of seven sessions usually offered by Brahma Kumari centers, to be taken in person or as a correspondence course. Although the introduction to Raja Yoga consists of a standard set of materials, it depends on the particular Brahma Kumari who teaches it how the material is conveyed. When presented to a group, the course is taught in interaction with the participants. All the sessions include meditation, usually guided visualization with music. It starts with exercises, which are to relax the body, and then focuses on the space in one's head that is the seat of one's thoughts, the so-called third eye, as a source of light. It ends with the course leader intoning *oṃ śanti* (*oṃ* peace), a key notion and phrase in Brahma Kumari thought – female members wear badges imprinted with *oṃ śanti*. At the end of some meditation sessions, especially when senior members or one of the *dādī*s lead it, the attention of the meditation leader focuses on each of those present in turn, a practice known as *dṛṣṭi*, the transmission of a spiritual quality or blessing through a gaze, generally from teacher to student (see Howell, 1997, 152), which J. Chander (1983) calls "a donation of power through the third eye." The Brahma Kumaris meditate with their eyes open. The reason that they give for this is that it prevents one from falling asleep, that we do not see other things when we are in deep thought, and that it is a natural state for human beings to be in. Meditation is, in their understanding, the gateway to seeing reality as it is and to experiencing the qualities within, such as happiness and peace. It is the process by which we remember – a journey back in time when we knew that we are a soul rather than a body. The soul consists of knowledge (which is based on observation and trust), energy (of which there is an eternal flow), and bliss (our natural state of being). From these three, we derive peace, love, and wisdom. The soul is seen as a light, the point of consciousness that is situated in the forehead – the third eye. Soul consciousness increases our respect for other people, because we can see the divinity of others, while body consciousness brings stress and tiredness, which are reflections of the material world we live in.

The soul needs the human body, but it loses its perfect state over time, because we identify with the body, and the soul loses awareness of itself by the attractions outside. Therefore, the Brahma Kumaris believe that we should live in the world but also need to be detached. Meditation helps to develop the detached observer: the more aware we are that we are detached, the more we can develop love and compassion. The Brahma Kumaris believe that we see the world of matter as solid around us but believe that the actual world in which we live is one of pure energy. According to Brahma Kumaris we are exposed to everything because of vibrations. We need to become positive so that our positive vibrations can have an effect on the world. In that sense, we are totally responsible for the state of the world. An important aspect of Brahma Kumaris' spirituality is the realization that we can be masters of our own world and have creative power over it. Hence the Brahma Kumaris' motto "when we change, the world changes" and their claim that "any transformation of the world begins with the transformation of the self."

We live in the three dimensions, but the soul dwells in the golden red light, an unlimited field of light and pure energy, which refers to Dada Lekhraj's experience of the room filled with golden light; hence the Brahma Kumaris' distinction between the three dimensions of the physical world, the subtle world (of thoughts and feelings), and the soul world, which is golden red light. Therefore, in Brahma Kumari centers in which there is a separate meditation room, this room is often suffused in red golden light during meditation, because in meditation, the golden glow is felt – it is regarded as their own home and the home of god, the supreme soul. There is no image of god; he is only a point of light, multifaceted. He has no weight, is as fast as the wind, and has the depth of stillness and quiet. God has no desires and no focus. He is gentle and loving, knowledgeable and sharp, teacher and friend, and mother and father.

The world drama cycle begins with the golden age in which the world is perfect. This is followed by the silver age, a time of civilization. Then deterioration sets in during the copper age: the soul forgets and loses consciousness; there is misuse of science and nature – this is the time of idol worship. Then comes the emergence of organized religions, in the iron age. Thereafter the night approaches until it is total (the period that we experience now) – the confluence age (which overlaps with the *kaliyuga*), when all the religions are waiting for the messiah. However, all the while, god observes. At some point, which is unpredictable, at the extreme of irreligiousness, god knows that the time has come to act (see the *Bhagavadgītā*). He comes assuming the body of a person. Being outside the drama of the cycle, supreme Śiva is the only entity that can intervene at this point. He gives the signal of a new dawn, which mankind catches, albeit in its own time. The transformation of the world is then the transformation of our consciousness, and the cycle starts again. Thus, this cyclical revolution of history involves "amnesia and remembrance" (Babb, 1982).

The world drama is represented as both cycle (spanning five thousand years and 84 rebirths, in which world history and geography repeat themselves) and tree, the tree of humanity, narrating the story of the ages (golden, silver, copper, iron, and confluence), moving from civilization to diversification (with the creation of other religions) and expansion, ending in deterioration and destruction (see also Babb, 1986).

Despite their millenarian and apocalyptic outlook of the world, which they see as consisting in the world drama cycle of gradual degradation followed by salvation, the Brahma Kumaris embrace the amenities and advantages of modernity. The buildings and extensive grounds at its headquarters, for example, are designed and constructed to high specification, with attention to ecological concerns. At the Brahma Kumari centers, offices and meetings rooms are furnished with computers with Internet, sound and lighting equipment, recording devices, and so on. Both the main organization and its branches maintain Web sites that disseminate information as well as extend the reach of lectures and presentations. Members can stay in touch in various ways, for example, by following lectures and seminars on the Web sites, subscribing to alerts about courses and events, subscribing to the "thought for the day," distributed daily by e-mail (e.g. "The biggest disease of the mind is over-thinking, especially too much thinking about others. Thinking too much is like eating too much. The heaviness makes it impossible to remain light and flexible."), or joining Internet discussion groups. Important meetings on Mount Abu can be attended by members across the globe through conference links. Thus technology allows for centers and members to be interconnected at almost any given time and widens the range of the audiences, as the *dādīs* can address multiple audiences at any given time, either directly or through recorded material on the Web sites. Thus, while rejecting some of the worldly goods and the materialistic attitude that goes with them, the Brahma Kumaris enthusiastically accept and make use of those aspects of modernity that serve their purposes; hence J. Walliss's (1999) assessment of the Brahma Kumaris' attitude toward the world as ambivalent.

Membership and Practice

Those who embrace the teachings of the Brahma Kumaris dedicate themselves to leading a pure life by including in their lives the practice of celibacy or chastity, vegetarian food, abstention from any kind of stimulants, and regular meditation. The inner state of purity is often reflected outwardly by wearing white clothes and, especially in the case of women, a white saree. The Brahma Kumaris' concept of membership does not involve formal or outward rituals that would-be followers undergo in order to attain membership. Membership is a question of identifying oneself as a Brahma Kumari and then following the practices (both individually and communally), taking part in activities, embracing the beliefs, and leading a simple lifestyle. The Brahma Kumaris themselves refer to members as "regular students." The notion of enrolling students in the courses that the Brahma Kumaris offer opens the path to membership to anyone, including those who may have a commitment to other religious communities. Despite the prevalence of women in the leadership and the emphasis on feminine qualities, the Brahma Kumaris offer self-growth and personal development programs to both men and women and attract followers of both genders. At center level, both men and women lead meditations and seminars and teach Raja Yoga courses. However, consonant with Dada Lekhraj's vision, the Brahma Kumaris promote "traditionally feminine virtues" for which, they state, there is an increasing need:

> The soundness of his decision to choose women and young girls as administrators and spiritual teachers has been born [*sic*] out by the Brahma Kumaris World Spiritual University (BKWSU) becoming a respected global institution under their leadership. Brahma Baba also correctly foresaw that core values based on traditionally feminine qualities – patience, tolerance, sacrifice, kindness and love – would increasingly become the foundation of progress in personal growth, human relations, and the development of caring communities. (BKWSU, 2014)

These qualities point to maternal characteristics, such as nurture, care, protection, understanding, and compassion rather than traditionally masculine traits such as strength and aggressiveness (see also Puttick, 1997, 194).

Similar to other organizations, membership in the Brahma Kumaris is tiered in concentric circles. The core of the membership consists of those who dedicate most or all their time to the organization; they tend to live communally, either in or close to a Brahma Kumari center. The core members are single (because they either never married or are no longer in a relationship) and celibate; they live together, like a family, as brothers and sisters, but segregated, and follow a daily rhythm of practices, which have features of monastic life, with mundane tasks alternating with periods of contemplation, reading, and reflection. The majority of members, however, live in the wider community and visit a Brahma Kumari center regularly – ideally every day.

Members rise at 4:00 am to meditate, usually on their own. At 6:00 am, there is more meditation (communal for those attending a center) and then the reading of a *murlī*, followed by a discussion of the reading. *Murlīs* are read as a cycle of texts, of which there is a sufficient number to make a cycle of five years. There is further meditation in the evening between 6:30 and 7:30 pm. Those who have gone through the introductory course are invited to join these meditation sessions as well as the separate *murlī* readings in the evening. However, there is no obvious coercion or pressure to do so. On the third Sunday of the month, the hour of meditation is declared the world-meditation hour and is open to the public. It is a continuation of an initiative, the "million minutes of peace," which the Brahma Kumaris dedicated to the United Nation's International Year of Peace in 1986. The appeal asked people to pledge time in meditation, positive thinking, and prayers for peace.

The Movement Today

The international headquarters of the movement on Mount Abu have developed and grown over the years in terms of their size and the range of activities and outreach programs. This site now forms an extensive campus, with a range of facilities that serve the various purposes of the organization's activities. Apart from the original building of the complex, which is known as Madhuban or Pandav Bhavan, where the senior sisters are located when in residence, there are later additions, such as the Global Hospital and Research Centre (founded in 1991), Gyan Sarovar or the Academy for a Better World (inaugurated in the mid-1990s to celebrate the 60th anniversary of the organization), the Peace Park (a formally laid-out garden), and Taleti (which includes Shantivan). An extension of the Global Hospital is the Village Outreach Program, which is aimed at treating people in the surrounding villages and includes primary healthcare education. Respectively described as "a modern village-style complex in a rural setting" and "a sprawling collection of buildings," Gyan Sarvar and Shantivan serve the Brahma Kumaris' educational outreach in offering residential programs in spiritual education and training, having capacity to accommodate very large numbers of people. Another focal point on Mount Abu is the memorial to the founder – the Tower of Peace, a tribute to Prajapita Brahma and to the service he did for humanity.

As the physical and spiritual center of the organization – the hub from which all the spokes radiate into the wider world – Mount Abu attracts thousands of people every year, both members and nonmembers. For members, it is a place of pilgrimage, the epicenter of their belief and practice. For nonmembers, it is a meeting place and conference center for various project and an opportunity to experience Indian culture and traditions.

Apart from the headquarters on Mount Abu, the Brahma Kumaris have a network of centers in India and across the world, having branched out across the globe since 1969. The first country outside India to have a Brahma Kumari branch is the United Kingdom, where the movement has been present since 1971. The UK headquarters, located in the Global Co-operation House in London (opened in 1991) also represents the group's European center. Another flagship center in the United Kingdom is the Global Retreat Centre, an 18th-century country house on the Thames River, with grounds designed by Capability Brown, which opened in 1993. Like other religious organizations and new religious movements, the Brahma Kumaris exemplify aspects of globalization in the way in which they take account of both global and local conditions in embedding themselves in various countries and cultures, adapting and adjusting to different cultural and social conventions (see e.g. Arweck, 2007; see also Howell & Nelson, 1997). Despite its deep roots in Indian culture, the organization thus has a distinct international dimension, which is reflected in its various activities and the global circulation of its members, including the *dādīs*, who travel extensively. The Brahma Kumaris claim to have 5,000 branches in 87 countries and half a million regular students (Arweck, 2002; Harris, *et al.*, 1993, 311), with the number of branches and the size of their membership seemingly growing year on year, as, in the early 1990s, the organization had reported 3,000 branches in 62 countries (BKWSU, 1993a) and, in 1995, 3,500 centers in 65 countries (see BKWSU, 1995, 107). In the Brahma Kumaris' own terms, the BKWSU has been "working towards world peace through personal change."

Another aspect of the Brahma Kumaris' international presence and range of activities is the BKWSU's status as a nongovernmental organization affiliated with the United Nations and their connection with UNESCO. This connection consists of general consultative status with the United Nations Economic and Social Council, consultative status with UNICEF, and affiliation to the United Nations Department of Public Information, a link that started to develop as early as 1980, with a number of initiatives following. For example, in 1986, the United Nations International Year of Peace, an appeal was made to donate a "million minutes of peace" through meditation or prayer. This was followed, in 1988, by "Global Co-operation for a Better World," a "Peace Messenger Initiative," which sought to elicit responses to the question "What is your vision of a better world?" resulting in "The Global Vision Statement" (see e.g. BKWSU, 1995, 69) and *Visions of a Better World* (BKWSU, 1993b). The Brahma Kumaris are also the recipients of seven United Nations Messenger of Peace awards.

The range of the Brahma Kumaris' outreach programs and activities includes disaster relief in India and other countries (see e.g. Ramsay, 2009; Ramsay, Manderson & Smith, 2010), health care (e.g. through the Janki Foundation for Global Health Care, a United Kingdom-based charity), interreligious dialogue, youth programs, prison outreach, social work, and men's groups. The strong interfaith element in the Brahma Kumaris' activities is based on the conviction that all religions share common traits and that their teachings incorporate those of all other religions. There is thus a claim to universality, which the Brahma Kumaris share with other (world) religions and religious groups.

Bibliography

Arweck, E., "Globalization and New Religious Movements," in: P. Berger & L. Beaman, eds., *Religion, Globalization, and Culture*, Leiden, 2007, 253–280.

Arweck, E., "New Religious Movements," in: L. Woodhead, *et al.*, eds., *Religions in the Modern World: Traditions and Transformations*, London, 2002.

Babb, L.A., "Dada Lekhraj and the Daughters of Brahma," in: L.A. Babb, ed., *Redemptive Encounters: Three Modern Styles in the Hindu Tradition*, Berkeley, 1986, 93–155.

Babb, L.A., "Indigenous Feminism in a Modern Hindu Sect," *SJWCS* 9/3, 1984, 399–416.

Babb, L.A., "Amnesia and Remembrance in a Hindu Theory of History," *AFS* 41/1, 1982, 49–66.

Bowker, J., *The Oxford Dictionary of World Religions*, Oxford, 1997.

Brahma Kumaris World Spiritual University, 2014, http://www.brahmakumaris.org/uk/whoweare/headquarters.

Brahma Kumaris World Spiritual University, *Living Values: A Guidebook*, London, 1995.

Brahma Kumaris World Spiritual University, *Practical Meditation*, London, 3 1993a.

Brahma Kumaris World Spiritual University, *Visions of a Better World*, London, 1993b.

Chander, J., & Brahma Kumaris World Spiritual University, *Adi Dev: The First Man*, Mount Abu, 1983.

Charpentier, M.-T., *Indian Female Gurus in Contemporary Hinduism: A Study of Central Aspects and Expressions of Their Religious Leadership*, Turku, 2010.

Chryssides, G.D., *Exploring New Religions*, London, 1999.

Harris, I., *et al., Contemporary Religions: A World Guide*, Harlow, 1993.

Hodgkinson, L., *Peace and Purity: The Story of the Brahma Kumaris: A Spiritual Revolution*, London, 1999.

Howell, J.D., "Gender Role Experimentation in New Religious Movements: The Case of the Brahma Kumaris," *JSSR* 37/3, 1998, 453–461.

Howell, J.D., "ASC Induction Techniques, Spiritual Experiences, and Commitment to New Religious Movements," *SOR* 58/2, 1997, 141–164.

Howell, J.D., & P.L. Nelson, "Structural Adaptation and 'Success' in the Transplantation of an Asian New Religious Movement: The Brahma Kumaris in the Western World, Part I," *RSSSR* 8, 1997, 1–33.

King, U., & T. Beattie, *Spirituality and Society in the New Millennium*, Brighton, 2001.

Lourenço, I., "Gender and Power: Brahma Kumaris Spirituality and Hinduism in Portugal," in: A. Fedele & K.E. Knibbe, *Gender and Power in Contemporary Spirituality: Ethnographic Approaches*, New York, 2013, 160–178.

O'Donnell, K., *New Beginnings: Raja Yoga Meditation Course*, London, 1987.

Pechilis, K., *The Graceful Guru: Hindu Female Gurus in India and the United States*, New York, 2004.

Puttick, E., *Women in New Religions: In Search of Community, Sexuality and Spiritual Power*, Basingstoke, 1997.

Ramsay, T., "Custodians of Purity: An Ethnography of the Brahma Kumaris," diss., Monash University, 2009.

Ramsay, T., L. Manderson & W. Smith, "Changing a Mountain into a Mustard Seed: Spiritual Practices and Responses to Disaster among New York Brahma Kumaris," *JCR* 25/1, 2010, 89–105.

Rose, S., "Is the Term 'Spirituality' a Word that Everyone Uses but Nobody Knows What Anyone Means by It?" *JCR* 16/2, 2001, 193–207.

Sister Sudesh, "Women as Spiritual Leaders in the Brahma Kumaris," in: E. Puttick & P.B. Clarke, eds., *Women as Teachers and Disciples in Traditional and New Religions*, Lampeter, 1993, 39–45.

Skultans, V., "The Brahma Kumaris and the Role of Women," in: E. Puttick & P.B. Clarke, eds., *Women as Teachers and Disciples in Traditional and New Religions*, Lampeter, 1993, 47–62.

Walliss, J., "From World Rejection to Ambivalence: The Development of Millenarianism in the Brahma Kumaris," *JCR* 14/3, 1999, 375–386.

ELISABETH ARWECK

General Index

Index terms that coincide with article titles are displayed in bold. Proper names, texts, and films begin with a capital letter. Foreign and transliterated terms and titles of texts and films are italicized. The numbers refer to volume and page where the index term appears (e.g. V: 237 = volume V, page 237); bold numbers refer to the volume and pages of articles whose title coincides with the respective index terms. When a page number is followed by f., the index term can be found on the indicated page as well as on the following page. When a page number is followed by ff., the index term is relevant throughout the remainder of the article. Circled numbers refer to the following index categories:

① astronomical
② botanical
③ calendrical
④ community (Hindu, Muslim, etc.)
⑤ cinematographic
⑥ gods, goddesses, and powers
⑦ dynasty
⑧ festival
⑨ groups of gods, goddesses, and powers
⑩ language/script
⑪ literary genre/feature
⑫ medical
⑬ musical genre/feature
⑭ musical instrument
⑮ performance tradition
⑯ poet, teacher, saint (pre-1900)
⑰ poet, teacher, saint (post-1900)
⑱ *rāga*
⑲ religious and/or philosophical tradition (pre-1900)
⑳ religious specialist/role
㉑ religious tradition (post-1900)
㉒ ritualistic
㉓ ritual, life-cycle
㉔ river
㉕ royalty (historical)
㉖ *ṛṣi*
㉗ scholarly tradition
㉘ tribe

N.B. boundaries between the index categories can be fluid (e.g. a performance tradition might be a festival as well without necessary being indicated as such).

A

① astronomical ② botanical ③ calendrical ④ community (Hindu, Muslim, etc.) ⑤ cinematographic ⑥ gods, goddesses, and powers ⑦ dynasty ⑧ festival ⑨ groups of gods, goddesses, and powers ⑩ language/script ⑪ literary genre/feature ⑫ medical ⑬ musical genre/feature ⑭ musical instrument

⑮ performance tradition ⑯ poet, teacher, saint (pre-1900) ⑰ poet, teacher, saint (post-1900) ⑱ *rāga* ⑲ religious and/or philosophical tradition (pre-1900) ⑳ religious specialist/role ㉑ religious tradition (post-1900) ㉒ ritualistic ㉓ ritual, life-cycle ㉔ river ㉕ royalty (historical) ㉖ *ṛṣi* ㉗ scholarly tradition ㉘ tribe

① astronomical ② botanical ③ calendrical ④ community (Hindu, Muslim, etc.) ⑤ cinematographic ⑥ gods, goddesses, and powers ⑦ dynasty ⑧ festival ⑨ groups of gods, goddesses, and powers ⑩ language/script ⑪ literary genre/feature ⑫ medical ⑬ musical genre/feature ⑭ musical instrument

⑮ performance tradition ⑯ poet, teacher, saint (pre-1900) ⑰ poet, teacher, saint (post-1900) ⑱ *rāga* ⑲ religious and/or philosophical tradition (pre-1900) ⑳ religious specialist/role ㉑ religious tradition (post-1900) ㉒ ritualistic ㉓ ritual, life-cycle ㉔ river ㉕ royalty (historical) ㉖ *ṛṣi* ㉗ scholarly tradition ㉘ tribe

① astronomical ② botanical ③ calendrical ④ community (Hindu, Muslim, etc.) ⑤ cinematographic ⑥ gods, goddesses, and powers ⑦ dynasty ⑧ festival ⑨ groups of gods, goddesses, and powers ⑩ language/script ⑪ literary genre/feature ⑫ medical ⑬ musical genre/feature ⑭ musical instrument

⑮ performance tradition ⑯ poet, teacher, saint (pre-1900) ⑰ poet, teacher, saint (post-1900) ⑱ *rāga* ⑲ religious and/or philosophical tradition (pre-1900) ⑳ religious specialist/role ㉑ religious tradition (post-1900) ㉒ ritualistic ㉓ ritual, life-cycle ㉔ river ㉕ royalty (historical) ㉖ *ṛṣi* ㉗ scholarly tradition ㉘ tribe

① astronomical ② botanical ③ calendrical ④ community (Hindu, Muslim, etc.) ⑤ cinematographic ⑥ gods, goddesses, and powers ⑦ dynasty ⑧ festival ⑨ groups of gods, goddesses, and powers ⑩ language/script ⑪ literary genre/feature ⑫ medical ⑬ musical genre/feature ⑭ musical instrument

⑮ performance tradition ⑯ poet, teacher, saint (pre-1900) ⑰ poet, teacher, saint (post-1900) ⑱ *rāga* ⑲ religious and/or philosophical tradition (pre-1900) ⑳ religious specialist/role ㉑ religious tradition (post-1900) ㉒ ritualistic ㉓ ritual, life-cycle ㉔ river ㉕ royalty (historical) ㉖ *ṛṣi* ㉗ scholarly tradition ㉘ tribe

① astronomical ② botanical ③ calendrical ④ community (Hindu, Muslim, etc.) ⑤ cinematographic ⑥ gods, goddesses, and powers ⑦ dynasty ⑧ festival ⑨ groups of gods, goddesses, and powers ⑩ language/script ⑪ literary genre/feature ⑫ medical ⑬ musical genre/feature ⑭ musical instrument

⑮ performance tradition ⑯ poet, teacher, saint (pre-1900) ⑰ poet, teacher, saint (post-1900) ⑱ *rāga* ⑲ religious and/or philosophical tradition (pre-1900) ⑳ religious specialist/role ㉑ religious tradition (post-1900) ㉒ ritualistic ㉓ ritual, life-cycle ㉔ river ㉕ royalty (historical) ㉖ *ṛṣi* ㉗ scholarly tradition ㉘ tribe

① astronomical ② botanical ③ calendrical ④ community (Hindu, Muslim, etc.) ⑤ cinematographic ⑥ gods, goddesses, and powers ⑦ dynasty ⑧ festival ⑨ groups of gods, goddesses, and powers ⑩ language/script ⑪ literary genre/feature ⑫ medical ⑬ musical genre/feature ⑭ musical instrument

① astronomical ② botanical ③ calendrical ④ community (Hindu, Muslim, etc.) ⑤ cinematographic ⑥ gods, goddesses, and powers ⑦ dynasty ⑧ festival ⑨ groups of gods, goddesses, and powers ⑩ language/script ⑪ literary genre/feature ⑫ medical ⑬ musical genre/feature ⑭ musical instrument

⑮ performance tradition ⑯ poet, teacher, saint (pre-1900) ⑰ poet, teacher, saint (post-1900) ⑱ *rāga* ⑲ religious and/or philosophical tradition (pre-1900) ⑳ religious specialist/role ㉑ religious tradition (post-1900) ㉒ ritualistic ㉓ ritual, life-cycle ㉔ river ㉕ royalty (historical) ㉖ *ṛṣi* ㉗ scholarly tradition ㉘ tribe

① astronomical ② botanical ③ calendrical ④ community (Hindu, Muslim, etc.) ⑤ cinematographic ⑥ gods, goddesses, and powers ⑦ dynasty ⑧ festival ⑨ groups of gods, goddesses, and powers ⑩ language/script ⑪ literary genre/feature ⑫ medical ⑬ musical genre/feature ⑭ musical instrument

⑮ performance tradition ⑯ poet, teacher, saint (pre-1900) ⑰ poet, teacher, saint (post-1900) ⑱ *rāga* ⑲ religious and/or philosophical tradition (pre-1900) ⑳ religious specialist/role ㉑ religious tradition (post-1900) ㉒ ritualistic ㉓ ritual, life-cycle ㉔ river ㉕ royalty (historical) ㉖ *ṛṣi* ㉗ scholarly tradition ㉘ tribe

① astronomical ② botanical ③ calendrical ④ community (Hindu, Muslim, etc.) ⑤ cinematographic ⑥ gods, goddesses, and powers ⑦ dynasty ⑧ festival ⑨ groups of gods, goddesses, and powers ⑩ language/script ⑪ literary genre/feature ⑫ medical ⑬ musical genre/feature ⑭ musical instrument

⑮ performance tradition ⑯ poet, teacher, saint (pre-1900) ⑰ poet, teacher, saint (post-1900) ⑱ *rāga* ⑲ religious and/or philosophical tradition (pre-1900) ⑳ religious specialist/role ㉑ religious tradition (post-1900) ㉒ ritualistic ㉓ ritual, life-cycle ㉔ river ㉕ royalty (historical) ㉖ *ṛṣi* ㉗ scholarly tradition ㉘ tribe

① astronomical ② botanical ③ calendrical ④ community (Hindu, Muslim, etc.) ⑤ cinematographic ⑥ gods, goddesses, and powers ⑦ dynasty ⑧ festival ⑨ groups of gods, goddesses, and powers ⑩ language/script ⑪ literary genre/feature ⑫ medical ⑬ musical genre/feature ⑭ musical instrument

⑮ performance tradition ⑯ poet, teacher, saint (pre-1900) ⑰ poet, teacher, saint (post-1900) ⑱ *rāga* ⑲ religious and/or philosophical tradition (pre-1900) ⑳ religious specialist/role ㉑ religious tradition (post-1900) ㉒ ritualistic ㉓ ritual, life-cycle ㉔ river ㉕ royalty (historical) ㉖ *ṛṣi* ㉗ scholarly tradition ㉘ tribe

B

① astronomical ② botanical ③ calendrical ④ community (Hindu, Muslim, etc.) ⑤ cinematographic ⑥ gods, goddesses, and powers ⑦ dynasty ⑧ festival ⑨ groups of gods, goddesses, and powers ⑩ language/script ⑪ literary genre/feature ⑫ medical ⑬ musical genre/feature ⑭ musical instrument

⑮ performance tradition ⑯ poet, teacher, saint (pre-1900) ⑰ poet, teacher, saint (post-1900) ⑱ *rāga* ⑲ religious and/or philosophical tradition (pre-1900) ⑳ religious specialist/role ㉑ religious tradition (post-1900) ㉒ ritualistic ㉓ ritual, life-cycle ㉔ river ㉕ royalty (historical) ㉖ *ṛṣi* ㉗ scholarly tradition ㉘ tribe

① astronomical ② botanical ③ calendrical ④ community (Hindu, Muslim, etc.) ⑤ cinematographic ⑥ gods, goddesses, and powers ⑦ dynasty ⑧ festival ⑨ groups of gods, goddesses, and powers ⑩ language/script ⑪ literary genre/feature ⑫ medical ⑬ musical genre/feature ⑭ musical instrument

① astronomical ② botanical ③ calendrical ④ community (Hindu, Muslim, etc.) ⑤ cinematographic ⑥ gods, goddesses, and powers ⑦ dynasty ⑧ festival ⑨ groups of gods, goddesses, and powers ⑩ language/script ⑪ literary genre/feature ⑫ medical ⑬ musical genre/feature ⑭ musical instrument

⑮ performance tradition ⑯ poet, teacher, saint (pre-1900) ⑰ poet, teacher, saint (post-1900) ⑱ *rāga* ⑲ religious and/or philosophical tradition (pre-1900) ⑳ religious specialist/role ㉑ religious tradition (post-1900) ㉒ ritualistic ㉓ ritual, life-cycle ㉔ river ㉕ royalty (historical) ㉖ *ṛṣi* ㉗ scholarly tradition ㉘ tribe

① astronomical ② botanical ③ calendrical ④ community (Hindu, Muslim, etc.) ⑤ cinematographic ⑥ gods, goddesses, and powers ⑦ dynasty ⑧ festival ⑨ groups of gods, goddesses, and powers ⑩ language/script ⑪ literary genre/feature ⑫ medical ⑬ musical genre/feature ⑭ musical instrument

⑮ performance tradition ⑯ poet, teacher, saint (pre-1900) ⑰ poet, teacher, saint (post-1900) ⑱ *rāga* ⑲ religious and/or philosophical tradition (pre-1900) ⑳ religious specialist/role ㉑ religious tradition (post-1900) ㉒ ritualistic ㉓ ritual, life-cycle ㉔ river ㉕ royalty (historical) ㉖ *ṛṣi* ㉗ scholarly tradition ㉘ tribe

⑮ performance tradition ⑯ poet, teacher, saint (pre-1900) ⑰ poet, teacher, saint (post-1900) ⑱ *rāga* ⑲ religious and/or philosophical tradition (pre-1900) ⑳ religious specialist/role ㉑ religious tradition (post-1900) ㉒ ritualistic ㉓ ritual, life-cycle ㉔ river ㉕ royalty (historical) ㉖ *ṛṣi* ㉗ scholarly tradition ㉘ tribe

① astronomical ② botanical ③ calendrical ④ community (Hindu, Muslim, etc.) ⑤ cinematographic ⑥ gods, goddesses, and powers ⑦ dynasty ⑧ festival ⑨ groups of gods, goddesses, and powers ⑩ language/script ⑪ literary genre/feature ⑫ medical ⑬ musical genre/feature ⑭ musical instrument

⑮ performance tradition ⑯ poet, teacher, saint (pre-1900) ⑰ poet, teacher, saint (post-1900) ⑱ *rāga* ⑲ religious and/or philosophical tradition (pre-1900) ⑳ religious specialist/role ㉑ religious tradition (post-1900) ㉒ ritualistic ㉓ ritual, life-cycle ㉔ river ㉕ royalty (historical) ㉖ *ṛṣi* ㉗ scholarly tradition ㉘ tribe

① astronomical ② botanical ③ calendrical ④ community (Hindu, Muslim, etc.) ⑤ cinematographic ⑥ gods, goddesses, and powers ⑦ dynasty ⑧ festival ⑨ groups of gods, goddesses, and powers ⑩ language/script ⑪ literary genre/feature ⑫ medical ⑬ musical genre/feature ⑭ musical instrument

① astronomical ② botanical ③ calendrical ④ community (Hindu, Muslim, etc.) ⑤ cinematographic ⑥ gods, goddesses, and powers ⑦ dynasty ⑧ festival ⑨ groups of gods, goddesses, and powers ⑩ language/script ⑪ literary genre/feature ⑫ medical ⑬ musical genre/feature ⑭ musical instrument

⑮ performance tradition ⑯ poet, teacher, saint (pre-1900) ⑰ poet, teacher, saint (post-1900) ⑱ *rāga* ⑲ religious and/or philosophical tradition (pre-1900) ⑳ religious specialist/role ㉑ religious tradition (post-1900) ㉒ ritualistic ㉓ ritual, life-cycle ㉔ river ㉕ royalty (historical) ㉖ *ṛṣi* ㉗ scholarly tradition ㉘ tribe

① astronomical ② botanical ③ calendrical ④ community (Hindu, Muslim, etc.) ⑤ cinematographic ⑥ gods, goddesses, and powers ⑦ dynasty ⑧ festival ⑨ groups of gods, goddesses, and powers ⑩ language/script ⑪ literary genre/feature ⑫ medical ⑬ musical genre/feature ⑭ musical instrument

① astronomical ② botanical ③ calendrical ④ community (Hindu, Muslim, etc.) ⑤ cinematographic ⑥ gods, goddesses, and powers ⑦ dynasty ⑧ festival ⑨ groups of gods, goddesses, and powers ⑩ language/script ⑪ literary genre/feature ⑫ medical ⑬ musical genre/feature ⑭ musical instrument

⑮ performance tradition ⑯ poet, teacher, saint (pre-1900) ⑰ poet, teacher, saint (post-1900) ⑱ *rāga* ⑲ religious and/or philosophical tradition (pre-1900) ⑳ religious specialist/role ㉑ religious tradition (post-1900) ㉒ ritualistic ㉓ ritual, life-cycle ㉔ river ㉕ royalty (historical) ㉖ *ṛṣi* ㉗ scholarly tradition ㉘ tribe

C

⑮ performance tradition ⑯ poet, teacher, saint (pre-1900) ⑰ poet, teacher, saint (post-1900) ⑱ *rāga* ⑲ religious and/or philosophical tradition (pre-1900) ⑳ religious specialist/role ㉑ religious tradition (post-1900) ㉒ ritualistic ㉓ ritual, life-cycle ㉔ river ㉕ royalty (historical) ㉖ *ṛṣi* ㉗ scholarly tradition ㉘ tribe

① astronomical ② botanical ③ calendrical ④ community (Hindu, Muslim, etc.) ⑤ cinematographic ⑥ gods, goddesses, and powers ⑦ dynasty ⑧ festival ⑨ groups of gods, goddesses, and powers ⑩ language/script ⑪ literary genre/feature ⑫ medical ⑬ musical genre/feature ⑭ musical instrument

① astronomical ② botanical ③ calendrical ④ community (Hindu, Muslim, etc.) ⑤ cinematographic ⑥ gods, goddesses, and powers ⑦ dynasty ⑧ festival ⑨ groups of gods, goddesses, and powers ⑩ language/script ⑪ literary genre/feature ⑫ medical ⑬ musical genre/feature ⑭ musical instrument

⑮ performance tradition ⑯ poet, teacher, saint (pre-1900) ⑰ poet, teacher, saint (post-1900) ⑱ *rāga* ⑲ religious and/or philosophical tradition (pre-1900) ⑳ religious specialist/role ㉑ religious tradition (post-1900) ㉒ ritualistic ㉓ ritual, life-cycle ㉔ river ㉕ royalty (historical) ㉖ *ṛṣi* ㉗ scholarly tradition ㉘ tribe

① astronomical ② botanical ③ calendrical ④ community (Hindu, Muslim, etc.) ⑤ cinematographic ⑥ gods, goddesses, and powers ⑦ dynasty ⑧ festival ⑨ groups of gods, goddesses, and powers ⑩ language/script ⑪ literary genre/feature ⑫ medical ⑬ musical genre/feature ⑭ musical instrument

⑮ performance tradition ⑯ poet, teacher, saint (pre-1900) ⑰ poet, teacher, saint (post-1900) ⑱ *rāga* ⑲ religious and/or philosophical tradition (pre-1900) ⑳ religious specialist/role ㉑ religious tradition (post-1900) ㉒ ritualistic ㉓ ritual, life-cycle ㉔ river ㉕ royalty (historical) ㉖ *ṛṣi* ㉗ scholarly tradition ㉘ tribe

⑮ performance tradition ⑯ poet, teacher, saint (pre-1900) ⑰ poet, teacher, saint (post-1900) ⑱ *rāga* ⑲ religious and/or philosophical tradition (pre-1900) ⑳ religious specialist/role ㉑ religious tradition (post-1900) ㉒ ritualistic ㉓ ritual, life-cycle ㉔ river ㉕ royalty (historical) ㉖ *ṛṣi* ㉗ scholarly tradition ㉘ tribe

① astronomical ② botanical ③ calendrical ④ community (Hindu, Muslim, etc.) ⑤ cinematographic ⑥ gods, goddesses, and powers ⑦ dynasty ⑧ festival ⑨ groups of gods, goddesses, and powers ⑩ language/script ⑪ literary genre/feature ⑫ medical ⑬ musical genre/feature ⑭ musical instrument

D

⑮ performance tradition ⑯ poet, teacher, saint (pre-1900) ⑰ poet, teacher, saint (post-1900) ⑱ *rāga* ⑲ religious and/or philosophical tradition (pre-1900) ⑳ religious specialist/role ㉑ religious tradition (post-1900) ㉒ ritualistic ㉓ ritual, life-cycle ㉔ river ㉕ royalty (historical) ㉖ *ṛṣi* ㉗ scholarly tradition ㉘ tribe

① astronomical ② botanical ③ calendrical ④ community (Hindu, Muslim, etc.) ⑤ cinematographic ⑥ gods, goddesses, and powers ⑦ dynasty ⑧ festival ⑨ groups of gods, goddesses, and powers ⑩ language/script ⑪ literary genre/feature ⑫ medical ⑬ musical genre/feature ⑭ musical instrument

① astronomical ② botanical ③ calendrical ④ community (Hindu, Muslim, etc.) ⑤ cinematographic ⑥ gods, goddesses, and powers ⑦ dynasty ⑧ festival ⑨ groups of gods, goddesses, and powers ⑩ language/script ⑪ literary genre/feature ⑫ medical ⑬ musical genre/feature ⑭ musical instrument

⑮ performance tradition ⑯ poet, teacher, saint (pre-1900) ⑰ poet, teacher, saint (post-1900) ⑱ *rāga* ⑲ religious and/or philosophical tradition (pre-1900) ⑳ religious specialist/role ㉑ religious tradition (post-1900) ㉒ ritualistic ㉓ ritual, life-cycle ㉔ river ㉕ royalty (historical) ㉖ *ṛṣi* ㉗ scholarly tradition ㉘ tribe

① astronomical ② botanical ③ calendrical ④ community (Hindu, Muslim, etc.) ⑤ cinematographic ⑥ gods, goddesses, and powers ⑦ dynasty ⑧ festival ⑨ groups of gods, goddesses, and powers ⑩ language/script ⑪ literary genre/feature ⑫ medical ⑬ musical genre/feature ⑭ musical instrument

⑮ performance tradition ⑯ poet, teacher, saint (pre-1900) ⑰ poet, teacher, saint (post-1900) ⑱ *rāga* ⑲ religious and/or philosophical tradition (pre-1900) ⑳ religious specialist/role ㉑ religious tradition (post-1900) ㉒ ritualistic ㉓ ritual, life-cycle ㉔ river ㉕ royalty (historical) ㉖ *ṛṣi* ㉗ scholarly tradition ㉘ tribe

⑮ performance tradition ⑯ poet, teacher, saint (pre-1900) ⑰ poet, teacher, saint (post-1900) ⑱ *rāga* ⑲ religious and/or philosophical tradition (pre-1900) ⑳ religious specialist/role ㉑ religious tradition (post-1900) ㉒ ritualistic ㉓ ritual, life-cycle ㉔ river ㉕ royalty (historical) ㉖ *ṛṣi* ㉗ scholarly tradition ㉘ tribe

① astronomical ② botanical ③ calendrical ④ community (Hindu, Muslim, etc.) ⑤ cinematographic ⑥ gods, goddesses, and powers ⑦ dynasty ⑧ festival ⑨ groups of gods, goddesses, and powers ⑩ language/script ⑪ literary genre/feature ⑫ medical ⑬ musical genre/feature ⑭ musical instrument

⑮ performance tradition ⑯ poet, teacher, saint (pre-1900) ⑰ poet, teacher, saint (post-1900) ⑱ *rāga* ⑲ religious and/or philosophical tradition (pre-1900) ⑳ religious specialist/role ㉑ religious tradition (post-1900) ㉒ ritualistic ㉓ ritual, life-cycle ㉔ river ㉕ royalty (historical) ㉖ *ṛṣi* ㉗ scholarly tradition ㉘ tribe

① astronomical ② botanical ③ calendrical ④ community (Hindu, Muslim, etc.) ⑤ cinematographic ⑥ gods, goddesses, and powers ⑦ dynasty ⑧ festival ⑨ groups of gods, goddesses, and powers ⑩ language/script ⑪ literary genre/feature ⑫ medical ⑬ musical genre/feature ⑭ musical instrument

E

⑮ performance tradition ⑯ poet, teacher, saint (pre-1900) ⑰ poet, teacher, saint (post-1900) ⑱ *rāga* ⑲ religious and/or philosophical tradition (pre-1900) ⑳ religious specialist/role ㉑ religious tradition (post-1900) ㉒ ritualistic ㉓ ritual, life-cycle ㉔ river ㉕ royalty (historical) ㉖ *ṛṣi* ㉗ scholarly tradition ㉘ tribe

① astronomical ② botanical ③ calendrical ④ community (Hindu, Muslim, etc.) ⑤ cinematographic ⑥ gods, goddesses, and powers ⑦ dynasty ⑧ festival ⑨ groups of gods, goddesses, and powers ⑩ language/script ⑪ literary genre/feature ⑫ medical ⑬ musical genre/feature ⑭ musical instrument

F

G

⑮ performance tradition ⑯ poet, teacher, saint (pre-1900) ⑰ poet, teacher, saint (post-1900) ⑱ *rāga* ⑲ religious and/or philosophical tradition (pre-1900) ⑳ religious specialist/role ㉑ religious tradition (post-1900) ㉒ ritualistic ㉓ ritual, life-cycle ㉔ river ㉕ royalty (historical) ㉖ *ṛṣi* ㉗ scholarly tradition ㉘ tribe

① astronomical ② botanical ③ calendrical ④ community (Hindu, Muslim, etc.) ⑤ cinematographic ⑥ gods, goddesses, and powers ⑦ dynasty ⑧ festival ⑨ groups of gods, goddesses, and powers ⑩ language/script ⑪ literary genre/feature ⑫ medical ⑬ musical genre/feature ⑭ musical instrument

⑮ performance tradition ⑯ poet, teacher, saint (pre-1900) ⑰ poet, teacher, saint (post-1900) ⑱ *rāga* ⑲ religious and/or philosophical tradition (pre-1900) ⑳ religious specialist/role ㉑ religious tradition (post-1900) ㉒ ritualistic ㉓ ritual, life-cycle ㉔ river ㉕ royalty (historical) ㉖ *ṛṣi* ㉗ scholarly tradition ㉘ tribe

① astronomical ② botanical ③ calendrical ④ community (Hindu, Muslim, etc.) ⑤ cinematographic ⑥ gods, goddesses, and powers ⑦ dynasty ⑧ festival ⑨ groups of gods, goddesses, and powers ⑩ language/script ⑪ literary genre/feature ⑫ medical ⑬ musical genre/feature ⑭ musical instrument

⑮ performance tradition ⑯ poet, teacher, saint (pre-1900) ⑰ poet, teacher, saint (post-1900) ⑱ *rāga* ⑲ religious and/or philosophical tradition (pre-1900) ⑳ religious specialist/role ㉑ religious tradition (post-1900) ㉒ ritualistic ㉓ ritual, life-cycle ㉔ river ㉕ royalty (historical) ㉖ *ṛṣi* ㉗ scholarly tradition ㉘ tribe

① astronomical ② botanical ③ calendrical ④ community (Hindu, Muslim, etc.) ⑤ cinematographic ⑥ gods, goddesses, and powers ⑦ dynasty ⑧ festival ⑨ groups of gods, goddesses, and powers ⑩ language/script ⑪ literary genre/feature ⑫ medical ⑬ musical genre/feature ⑭ musical instrument

① astronomical ② botanical ③ calendrical ④ community (Hindu, Muslim, etc.) ⑤ cinematographic ⑥ gods, goddesses, and powers ⑦ dynasty ⑧ festival ⑨ groups of gods, goddesses, and powers ⑩ language/script ⑪ literary genre/feature ⑫ medical ⑬ musical genre/feature ⑭ musical instrument

⑮ performance tradition ⑯ poet, teacher, saint (pre-1900) ⑰ poet, teacher, saint (post-1900) ⑱ *rāga* ⑲ religious and/or philosophical tradition (pre-1900) ⑳ religious specialist/role ㉑ religious tradition (post-1900) ㉒ ritualistic ㉓ ritual, life-cycle ㉔ river ㉕ royalty (historical) ㉖ *ṛṣi* ㉗ scholarly tradition ㉘ tribe

① astronomical ② botanical ③ calendrical ④ community (Hindu, Muslim, etc.) ⑤ cinematographic ⑥ gods, goddesses, and powers ⑦ dynasty ⑧ festival ⑨ groups of gods, goddesses, and powers ⑩ language/script ⑪ literary genre/feature ⑫ medical ⑬ musical genre/feature ⑭ musical instrument

⑮ performance tradition ⑯ poet, teacher, saint (pre-1900) ⑰ poet, teacher, saint (post-1900) ⑱ *rāga* ⑲ religious and/or philosophical tradition (pre-1900) ⑳ religious specialist/role ㉑ religious tradition (post-1900) ㉒ ritualistic ㉓ ritual, life-cycle ㉔ river ㉕ royalty (historical) ㉖ *ṛṣi* ㉗ scholarly tradition ㉘ tribe

① astronomical ② botanical ③ calendrical ④ community (Hindu, Muslim, etc.) ⑤ cinematographic ⑥ gods, goddesses, and powers ⑦ dynasty ⑧ festival ⑨ groups of gods, goddesses, and powers ⑩ language/script ⑪ literary genre/feature ⑫ medical ⑬ musical genre/feature ⑭ musical instrument

⑮ performance tradition ⑯ poet, teacher, saint (pre-1900) ⑰ poet, teacher, saint (post-1900) ⑱ *rāga* ⑲ religious and/or philosophical tradition (pre-1900) ⑳ religious specialist/role ㉑ religious tradition (post-1900) ㉒ ritualistic ㉓ ritual, life-cycle ㉔ river ㉕ royalty (historical) ㉖ *ṛṣi* ㉗ scholarly tradition ㉘ tribe

① astronomical ② botanical ③ calendrical ④ community (Hindu, Muslim, etc.) ⑤ cinematographic ⑥ gods, goddesses, and powers ⑦ dynasty ⑧ festival ⑨ groups of gods, goddesses, and powers ⑩ language/script ⑪ literary genre/feature ⑫ medical ⑬ musical genre/feature ⑭ musical instrument

⑮ performance tradition ⑯ poet, teacher, saint (pre-1900) ⑰ poet, teacher, saint (post-1900) ⑱ *rāga* ⑲ religious and/or philosophical tradition (pre-1900) ⑳ religious specialist/role ㉑ religious tradition (post-1900) ㉒ ritualistic ㉓ ritual, life-cycle ㉔ river ㉕ royalty (historical) ㉖ *ṛṣi* ㉗ scholarly tradition ㉘ tribe

① astronomical ② botanical ③ calendrical ④ community (Hindu, Muslim, etc.) ⑤ cinematographic ⑥ gods, goddesses, and powers ⑦ dynasty ⑧ festival ⑨ groups of gods, goddesses, and powers ⑩ language/script ⑪ literary genre/feature ⑫ medical ⑬ musical genre/feature ⑭ musical instrument

⑮ performance tradition ⑯ poet, teacher, saint (pre-1900) ⑰ poet, teacher, saint (post-1900) ⑱ *rāga* ⑲ religious and/or philosophical tradition (pre-1900) ⑳ religious specialist/role ㉑ religious tradition (post-1900) ㉒ ritualistic ㉓ ritual, life-cycle ㉔ river ㉕ royalty (historical) ㉖ *ṛṣi* ㉗ scholarly tradition ㉘ tribe

① astronomical ② botanical ③ calendrical ④ community (Hindu, Muslim, etc.) ⑤ cinematographic ⑥ gods, goddesses, and powers ⑦ dynasty ⑧ festival ⑨ groups of gods, goddesses, and powers ⑩ language/script ⑪ literary genre/feature ⑫ medical ⑬ musical genre/feature ⑭ musical instrument

⑮ performance tradition ⑯ poet, teacher, saint (pre-1900) ⑰ poet, teacher, saint (post-1900) ⑱ *rāga* ⑲ religious and/or philosophical tradition (pre-1900) ⑳ religious specialist/role ㉑ religious tradition (post-1900) ㉒ ritualistic ㉓ ritual, life-cycle ㉔ river ㉕ royalty (historical) ㉖ *ṛṣi* ㉗ scholarly tradition ㉘ tribe

① astronomical ② botanical ③ calendrical ④ community (Hindu, Muslim, etc.) ⑤ cinematographic ⑥ gods, goddesses, and powers ⑦ dynasty ⑧ festival ⑨ groups of gods, goddesses, and powers ⑩ language/script ⑪ literary genre/feature ⑫ medical ⑬ musical genre/feature ⑭ musical instrument

⑮ performance tradition ⑯ poet, teacher, saint (pre-1900) ⑰ poet, teacher, saint (post-1900) ⑱ *rāga* ⑲ religious and/or philosophical tradition (pre-1900) ⑳ religious specialist/role ㉑ religious tradition (post-1900) ㉒ ritualistic ㉓ ritual, life-cycle ㉔ river ㉕ royalty (historical) ㉖ *ṛṣi* ㉗ scholarly tradition ㉘ tribe

J

① astronomical ② botanical ③ calendrical ④ community (Hindu, Muslim, etc.) ⑤ cinematographic ⑥ gods, goddesses, and powers ⑦ dynasty ⑧ festival ⑨ groups of gods, goddesses, and powers ⑩ language/script ⑪ literary genre/feature ⑫ medical ⑬ musical genre/feature ⑭ musical instrument

⑮ performance tradition ⑯ poet, teacher, saint (pre-1900) ⑰ poet, teacher, saint (post-1900) ⑱ *rāga* ⑲ religious and/or philosophical tradition (pre-1900) ⑳ religious specialist/role ㉑ religious tradition (post-1900) ㉒ ritualistic ㉓ ritual, life-cycle ㉔ river ㉕ royalty (historical) ㉖ *ṛṣi* ㉗ scholarly tradition ㉘ tribe

① astronomical ② botanical ③ calendrical ④ community (Hindu, Muslim, etc.) ⑤ cinematographic ⑥ gods, goddesses, and powers ⑦ dynasty ⑧ festival ⑨ groups of gods, goddesses, and powers ⑩ language/script ⑪ literary genre/feature ⑫ medical ⑬ musical genre/feature ⑭ musical instrument

① astronomical ② botanical ③ calendrical ④ community (Hindu, Muslim, etc.) ⑤ cinematographic ⑥ gods, goddesses, and powers ⑦ dynasty ⑧ festival ⑨ groups of gods, goddesses, and powers ⑩ language/script ⑪ literary genre/feature ⑫ medical ⑬ musical genre/feature ⑭ musical instrument

K

① astronomical ② botanical ③ calendrical ④ community (Hindu, Muslim, etc.) ⑤ cinematographic ⑥ gods, goddesses, and powers ⑦ dynasty ⑧ festival ⑨ groups of gods, goddesses, and powers ⑩ language/script ⑪ literary genre/feature ⑫ medical ⑬ musical genre/feature ⑭ musical instrument

⑮ performance tradition ⑯ poet, teacher, saint (pre-1900) ⑰ poet, teacher, saint (post-1900) ⑱ *rāga* ⑲ religious and/or philosophical tradition (pre-1900) ⑳ religious specialist/role ㉑ religious tradition (post-1900) ㉒ ritualistic ㉓ ritual, life-cycle ㉔ river ㉕ royalty (historical) ㉖ *ṛṣi* ㉗ scholarly tradition ㉘ tribe

① astronomical ② botanical ③ calendrical ④ community (Hindu, Muslim, etc.) ⑤ cinematographic ⑥ gods, goddesses, and powers ⑦ dynasty ⑧ festival ⑨ groups of gods, goddesses, and powers ⑩ language/script ⑪ literary genre/feature ⑫ medical ⑬ musical genre/feature ⑭ musical instrument

⑮ performance tradition ⑯ poet, teacher, saint (pre-1900) ⑰ poet, teacher, saint (post-1900) ⑱ *rāga* ⑲ religious and/or philosophical tradition (pre-1900) ⑳ religious specialist/role ㉑ religious tradition (post-1900) ㉒ ritualistic ㉓ ritual, life-cycle ㉔ river ㉕ royalty (historical) ㉖ *ṛṣi* ㉗ scholarly tradition ㉘ tribe

① astronomical ② botanical ③ calendrical ④ community (Hindu, Muslim, etc.) ⑤ cinematographic ⑥ gods, goddesses, and powers ⑦ dynasty ⑧ festival ⑨ groups of gods, goddesses, and powers ⑩ language/script ⑪ literary genre/feature ⑫ medical ⑬ musical genre/feature ⑭ musical instrument

⑮ performance tradition ⑯ poet, teacher, saint (pre-1900) ⑰ poet, teacher, saint (post-1900) ⑱ *rāga* ⑲ religious and/or philosophical tradition (pre-1900) ⑳ religious specialist/role ㉑ religious tradition (post-1900) ㉒ ritualistic ㉓ ritual, life-cycle ㉔ river ㉕ royalty (historical) ㉖ *ṛṣi* ㉗ scholarly tradition ㉘ tribe

① astronomical ② botanical ③ calendrical ④ community (Hindu, Muslim, etc.) ⑤ cinematographic ⑥ gods, goddesses, and powers ⑦ dynasty ⑧ festival ⑨ groups of gods, goddesses, and powers ⑩ language/script ⑪ literary genre/feature ⑫ medical ⑬ musical genre/feature ⑭ musical instrument

⑮ performance tradition ⑯ poet, teacher, saint (pre-1900) ⑰ poet, teacher, saint (post-1900) ⑱ *rāga* ⑲ religious and/or philosophical tradition (pre-1900) ⑳ religious specialist/role ㉑ religious tradition (post-1900) ㉒ ritualistic ㉓ ritual, life-cycle ㉔ river ㉕ royalty (historical) ㉖ *ṛṣi* ㉗ scholarly tradition ㉘ tribe

① astronomical ② botanical ③ calendrical ④ community (Hindu, Muslim, etc.) ⑤ cinematographic ⑥ gods, goddesses, and powers ⑦ dynasty ⑧ festival ⑨ groups of gods, goddesses, and powers ⑩ language/script ⑪ literary genre/feature ⑫ medical ⑬ musical genre/feature ⑭ musical instrument

⑮ performance tradition ⑯ poet, teacher, saint (pre-1900) ⑰ poet, teacher, saint (post-1900) ⑱ *rāga* ⑲ religious and/or philosophical tradition (pre-1900) ⑳ religious specialist/role ㉑ religious tradition (post-1900) ㉒ ritualistic ㉓ ritual, life-cycle ㉔ river ㉕ royalty (historical) ㉖ *ṛṣi* ㉗ scholarly tradition ㉘ tribe

① astronomical ② botanical ③ calendrical ④ community (Hindu, Muslim, etc.) ⑤ cinematographic ⑥ gods, goddesses, and powers ⑦ dynasty ⑧ festival ⑨ groups of gods, goddesses, and powers ⑩ language/script ⑪ literary genre/feature ⑫ medical ⑬ musical genre/feature ⑭ musical instrument

⑮ performance tradition ⑯ poet, teacher, saint (pre-1900) ⑰ poet, teacher, saint (post-1900) ⑱ *rāga* ⑲ religious and/or philosophical tradition (pre-1900) ⑳ religious specialist/role ㉑ religious tradition (post-1900) ㉒ ritualistic ㉓ ritual, life-cycle ㉔ river ㉕ royalty (historical) ㉖ *ṛṣi* ㉗ scholarly tradition ㉘ tribe

① astronomical ② botanical ③ calendrical ④ community (Hindu, Muslim, etc.) ⑤ cinematographic ⑥ gods, goddesses, and powers ⑦ dynasty ⑧ festival ⑨ groups of gods, goddesses, and powers ⑩ language/script ⑪ literary genre/feature ⑫ medical ⑬ musical genre/feature ⑭ musical instrument

⑮ performance tradition ⑯ poet, teacher, saint (pre-1900) ⑰ poet, teacher, saint (post-1900) ⑱ *rāga* ⑲ religious and/or philosophical tradition (pre-1900) ⑳ religious specialist/role ㉑ religious tradition (post-1900) ㉒ ritualistic ㉓ ritual, life-cycle ㉔ river ㉕ royalty (historical) ㉖ *ṛṣi* ㉗ scholarly tradition ㉘ tribe

① astronomical ② botanical ③ calendrical ④ community (Hindu, Muslim, etc.) ⑤ cinematographic ⑥ gods, goddesses, and powers ⑦ dynasty ⑧ festival ⑨ groups of gods, goddesses, and powers ⑩ language/script ⑪ literary genre/feature ⑫ medical ⑬ musical genre/feature ⑭ musical instrument

⑮ performance tradition ⑯ poet, teacher, saint (pre-1900) ⑰ poet, teacher, saint (post-1900) ⑱ *rāga* ⑲ religious and/or philosophical tradition (pre-1900) ⑳ religious specialist/role ㉑ religious tradition (post-1900) ㉒ ritualistic ㉓ ritual, life-cycle ㉔ river ㉕ royalty (historical) ㉖ *ṛṣi* ㉗ scholarly tradition ㉘ tribe

① astronomical ② botanical ③ calendrical ④ community (Hindu, Muslim, etc.) ⑤ cinematographic ⑥ gods, goddesses, and powers ⑦ dynasty ⑧ festival ⑨ groups of gods, goddesses, and powers ⑩ language/script ⑪ literary genre/feature ⑫ medical ⑬ musical genre/feature ⑭ musical instrument

⑮ performance tradition ⑯ poet, teacher, saint (pre-1900) ⑰ poet, teacher, saint (post-1900) ⑱ *rāga* ⑲ religious and/or philosophical tradition (pre-1900) ⑳ religious specialist/role ㉑ religious tradition (post-1900) ㉒ ritualistic ㉓ ritual, life-cycle ㉔ river ㉕ royalty (historical) ㉖ *ṛṣi* ㉗ scholarly tradition ㉘ tribe

① astronomical ② botanical ③ calendrical ④ community (Hindu, Muslim, etc.) ⑤ cinematographic ⑥ gods, goddesses, and powers ⑦ dynasty ⑧ festival ⑨ groups of gods, goddesses, and powers ⑩ language/script ⑪ literary genre/feature ⑫ medical ⑬ musical genre/feature ⑭ musical instrument

L

① astronomical ② botanical ③ calendrical ④ community (Hindu, Muslim, etc.) ⑤ cinematographic ⑥ gods, goddesses, and powers ⑦ dynasty ⑧ festival ⑨ groups of gods, goddesses, and powers ⑩ language/script ⑪ literary genre/feature ⑫ medical ⑬ musical genre/feature ⑭ musical instrument

⑮ performance tradition ⑯ poet, teacher, saint (pre-1900) ⑰ poet, teacher, saint (post-1900) ⑱ *rāga* ⑲ religious and/or philosophical tradition (pre-1900) ⑳ religious specialist/role ㉑ religious tradition (post-1900) ㉒ ritualistic ㉓ ritual, life-cycle ㉔ river ㉕ royalty (historical) ㉖ *ṛṣi* ㉗ scholarly tradition ㉘ tribe

① astronomical ② botanical ③ calendrical ④ community (Hindu, Muslim, etc.) ⑤ cinematographic ⑥ gods, goddesses, and powers ⑦ dynasty ⑧ festival ⑨ groups of gods, goddesses, and powers ⑩ language/script ⑪ literary genre/feature ⑫ medical ⑬ musical genre/feature ⑭ musical instrument

⑮ performance tradition ⑯ poet, teacher, saint (pre-1900) ⑰ poet, teacher, saint (post-1900) ⑱ *rāga* ⑲ religious and/or philosophical tradition (pre-1900) ⑳ religious specialist/role ㉑ religious tradition (post-1900) ㉒ ritualistic ㉓ ritual, life-cycle ㉔ river ㉕ royalty (historical) ㉖ *ṛṣi* ㉗ scholarly tradition ㉘ tribe

M

① astronomical ② botanical ③ calendrical ④ community (Hindu, Muslim, etc.) ⑤ cinematographic ⑥ gods, goddesses, and powers ⑦ dynasty ⑧ festival ⑨ groups of gods, goddesses, and powers ⑩ language/script ⑪ literary genre/feature ⑫ medical ⑬ musical genre/feature ⑭ musical instrument

⑮ performance tradition ⑯ poet, teacher, saint (pre-1900) ⑰ poet, teacher, saint (post-1900) ⑱ *rāga* ⑲ religious and/or philosophical tradition (pre-1900) ⑳ religious specialist/role ㉑ religious tradition (post-1900) ㉒ ritualistic ㉓ ritual, life-cycle ㉔ river ㉕ royalty (historical) ㉖ *ṛṣi* ㉗ scholarly tradition ㉘ tribe

① astronomical ② botanical ③ calendrical ④ community (Hindu, Muslim, etc.) ⑤ cinematographic ⑥ gods, goddesses, and powers ⑦ dynasty ⑧ festival ⑨ groups of gods, goddesses, and powers ⑩ language/script ⑪ literary genre/feature ⑫ medical ⑬ musical genre/feature ⑭ musical instrument

⑮ performance tradition ⑯ poet, teacher, saint (pre-1900) ⑰ poet, teacher, saint (post-1900) ⑱ *rāga* ⑲ religious and/or philosophical tradition (pre-1900) ⑳ religious specialist/role ㉑ religious tradition (post-1900) ㉒ ritualistic ㉓ ritual, life-cycle ㉔ river ㉕ royalty (historical) ㉖ *ṛṣi* ㉗ scholarly tradition ㉘ tribe

① astronomical ② botanical ③ calendrical ④ community (Hindu, Muslim, etc.) ⑤ cinematographic ⑥ gods, goddesses, and powers ⑦ dynasty ⑧ festival ⑨ groups of gods, goddesses, and powers ⑩ language/script ⑪ literary genre/feature ⑫ medical ⑬ musical genre/feature ⑭ musical instrument

⑮ performance tradition ⑯ poet, teacher, saint (pre-1900) ⑰ poet, teacher, saint (post-1900) ⑱ *rāga* ⑲ religious and/or philosophical tradition (pre-1900) ⑳ religious specialist/role ㉑ religious tradition (post-1900) ㉒ ritualistic ㉓ ritual, life-cycle ㉔ river ㉕ royalty (historical) ㉖ *ṛṣi* ㉗ scholarly tradition ㉘ tribe

① astronomical ② botanical ③ calendrical ④ community (Hindu, Muslim, etc.) ⑤ cinematographic ⑥ gods, goddesses, and powers ⑦ dynasty ⑧ festival ⑨ groups of gods, goddesses, and powers ⑩ language/script ⑪ literary genre/feature ⑫ medical ⑬ musical genre/feature ⑭ musical instrument

⑮ performance tradition ⑯ poet, teacher, saint (pre-1900) ⑰ poet, teacher, saint (post-1900) ⑱ *rāga* ⑲ religious and/or philosophical tradition (pre-1900) ⑳ religious specialist/role ㉑ religious tradition (post-1900) ㉒ ritualistic ㉓ ritual, life-cycle ㉔ river ㉕ royalty (historical) ㉖ *ṛṣi* ㉗ scholarly tradition ㉘ tribe

① astronomical ② botanical ③ calendrical ④ community (Hindu, Muslim, etc.) ⑤ cinematographic ⑥ gods, goddesses, and powers ⑦ dynasty ⑧ festival ⑨ groups of gods, goddesses, and powers ⑩ language/script ⑪ literary genre/feature ⑫ medical ⑬ musical genre/feature ⑭ musical instrument

① astronomical ② botanical ③ calendrical ④ community (Hindu, Muslim, etc.) ⑤ cinematographic ⑥ gods, goddesses, and powers ⑦ dynasty ⑧ festival ⑨ groups of gods, goddesses, and powers ⑩ language/script ⑪ literary genre/feature ⑫ medical ⑬ musical genre/feature ⑭ musical instrument

⑮ performance tradition ⑯ poet, teacher, saint (pre-1900) ⑰ poet, teacher, saint (post-1900) ⑱ *rāga* ⑲ religious and/or philosophical tradition (pre-1900) ⑳ religious specialist/role ㉑ religious tradition (post-1900) ㉒ ritualistic ㉓ ritual, life-cycle ㉔ river ㉕ royalty (historical) ㉖ *ṛṣi* ㉗ scholarly tradition ㉘ tribe

⑮ performance tradition ⑯ poet, teacher, saint (pre-1900) ⑰ poet, teacher, saint (post-1900) ⑱ *rāga* ⑲ religious and/or philosophical tradition (pre-1900) ⑳ religious specialist/role ㉑ religious tradition (post-1900) ㉒ ritualistic ㉓ ritual, life-cycle ㉔ river ㉕ royalty (historical) ㉖ *ṛṣi* ㉗ scholarly tradition ㉘ tribe

⑮ performance tradition ⑯ poet, teacher, saint (pre-1900) ⑰ poet, teacher, saint (post-1900) ⑱ *rāga* ⑲ religious and/or philosophical tradition (pre-1900) ⑳ religious specialist/role ㉑ religious tradition (post-1900) ㉒ ritualistic ㉓ ritual, life-cycle ㉔ river ㉕ royalty (historical) ㉖ *ṛṣi* ㉗ scholarly tradition ㉘ tribe

① astronomical ② botanical ③ calendrical ④ community (Hindu, Muslim, etc.) ⑤ cinematographic ⑥ gods, goddesses, and powers ⑦ dynasty ⑧ festival ⑨ groups of gods, goddesses, and powers ⑩ language/script ⑪ literary genre/feature ⑫ medical ⑬ musical genre/feature ⑭ musical instrument

⑮ performance tradition ⑯ poet, teacher, saint (pre-1900) ⑰ poet, teacher, saint (post-1900) ⑱ *rāga* ⑲ religious and/or philosophical tradition (pre-1900) ⑳ religious specialist/role ㉑ religious tradition (post-1900) ㉒ ritualistic ㉓ ritual, life-cycle ㉔ river ㉕ royalty (historical) ㉖ *ṛṣi* ㉗ scholarly tradition ㉘ tribe

① astronomical ② botanical ③ calendrical ④ community (Hindu, Muslim, etc.) ⑤ cinematographic ⑥ gods, goddesses, and powers ⑦ dynasty ⑧ festival ⑨ groups of gods, goddesses, and powers ⑩ language/script ⑪ literary genre/feature ⑫ medical ⑬ musical genre/feature ⑭ musical instrument

⑮ performance tradition ⑯ poet, teacher, saint (pre-1900) ⑰ poet, teacher, saint (post-1900) ⑱ *rāga* ⑲ religious and/or philosophical tradition (pre-1900) ⑳ religious specialist/role ㉑ religious tradition (post-1900) ㉒ ritualistic ㉓ ritual, life-cycle ㉔ river ㉕ royalty (historical) ㉖ *ṛṣi* ㉗ scholarly tradition ㉘ tribe

⑮ performance tradition ⑯ poet, teacher, saint (pre-1900) ⑰ poet, teacher, saint (post-1900) ⑱ *rāga* ⑲ religious and/or philosophical tradition (pre-1900) ⑳ religious specialist/role ㉑ religious tradition (post-1900) ㉒ ritualistic ㉓ ritual, life-cycle ㉔ river ㉕ royalty (historical) ㉖ *ṛṣi* ㉗ scholarly tradition ㉘ tribe

① astronomical ② botanical ③ calendrical ④ community (Hindu, Muslim, etc.) ⑤ cinematographic ⑥ gods, goddesses, and powers ⑦ dynasty ⑧ festival ⑨ groups of gods, goddesses, and powers ⑩ language/script ⑪ literary genre/feature ⑫ medical ⑬ musical genre/feature ⑭ musical instrument

N

⑮ performance tradition ⑯ poet, teacher, saint (pre-1900) ⑰ poet, teacher, saint (post-1900) ⑱ *rāga* ⑲ religious and/or philosophical tradition (pre-1900) ⑳ religious specialist/role ㉑ religious tradition (post-1900) ㉒ ritualistic ㉓ ritual, life-cycle ㉔ river ㉕ royalty (historical) ㉖ *ṛṣi* ㉗ scholarly tradition ㉘ tribe

① astronomical ② botanical ③ calendrical ④ community (Hindu, Muslim, etc.) ⑤ cinematographic ⑥ gods, goddesses, and powers ⑦ dynasty ⑧ festival ⑨ groups of gods, goddesses, and powers ⑩ language/script ⑪ literary genre/feature ⑫ medical ⑬ musical genre/feature ⑭ musical instrument

⑮ performance tradition ⑯ poet, teacher, saint (pre-1900) ⑰ poet, teacher, saint (post-1900) ⑱ *rāga* ⑲ religious and/or philosophical tradition (pre-1900) ⑳ religious specialist/role ㉑ religious tradition (post-1900) ㉒ ritualistic ㉓ ritual, life-cycle ㉔ river ㉕ royalty (historical) ㉖ *ṛṣi* ㉗ scholarly tradition ㉘ tribe

① astronomical ② botanical ③ calendrical ④ community (Hindu, Muslim, etc.) ⑤ cinematographic ⑥ gods, goddesses, and powers ⑦ dynasty ⑧ festival ⑨ groups of gods, goddesses, and powers ⑩ language/script ⑪ literary genre/feature ⑫ medical ⑬ musical genre/feature ⑭ musical instrument

① astronomical ② botanical ③ calendrical ④ community (Hindu, Muslim, etc.) ⑤ cinematographic ⑥ gods, goddesses, and powers ⑦ dynasty ⑧ festival ⑨ groups of gods, goddesses, and powers ⑩ language/script ⑪ literary genre/feature ⑫ medical ⑬ musical genre/feature ⑭ musical instrument

⑮ performance tradition ⑯ poet, teacher, saint (pre-1900) ⑰ poet, teacher, saint (post-1900) ⑱ *rāga* ⑲ religious and/or philosophical tradition (pre-1900) ⑳ religious specialist/role ㉑ religious tradition (post-1900) ㉒ ritualistic ㉓ ritual, life-cycle ㉔ river ㉕ royalty (historical) ㉖ *ṛṣi* ㉗ scholarly tradition ㉘ tribe

① astronomical ② botanical ③ calendrical ④ community (Hindu, Muslim, etc.) ⑤ cinematographic ⑥ gods, goddesses, and powers ⑦ dynasty ⑧ festival ⑨ groups of gods, goddesses, and powers ⑩ language/script ⑪ literary genre/feature ⑫ medical ⑬ musical genre/feature ⑭ musical instrument

⑮ performance tradition ⑯ poet, teacher, saint (pre-1900) ⑰ poet, teacher, saint (post-1900) ⑱ *rāga* ⑲ religious and/or philosophical tradition (pre-1900) ⑳ religious specialist/role ㉑ religious tradition (post-1900) ㉒ ritualistic ㉓ ritual, life-cycle ㉔ river ㉕ royalty (historical) ㉖ *ṛṣi* ㉗ scholarly tradition ㉘ tribe

① astronomical ② botanical ③ calendrical ④ community (Hindu, Muslim, etc.) ⑤ cinematographic ⑥ gods, goddesses, and powers ⑦ dynasty ⑧ festival ⑨ groups of gods, goddesses, and powers ⑩ language/script ⑪ literary genre/feature ⑫ medical ⑬ musical genre/feature ⑭ musical instrument

⑮ performance tradition ⑯ poet, teacher, saint (pre-1900) ⑰ poet, teacher, saint (post-1900) ⑱ *rāga* ⑲ religious and/or philosophical tradition (pre-1900) ⑳ religious specialist/role ㉑ religious tradition (post-1900) ㉒ ritualistic ㉓ ritual, life-cycle ㉔ river ㉕ royalty (historical) ㉖ *ṛṣi* ㉗ scholarly tradition ㉘ tribe

① astronomical ② botanical ③ calendrical ④ community (Hindu, Muslim, etc.) ⑤ cinematographic ⑥ gods, goddesses, and powers ⑦ dynasty ⑧ festival ⑨ groups of gods, goddesses, and powers ⑩ language/script ⑪ literary genre/feature ⑫ medical ⑬ musical genre/feature ⑭ musical instrument

O

⑮ performance tradition ⑯ poet, teacher, saint (pre-1900) ⑰ poet, teacher, saint (post-1900) ⑱ *rāga* ⑲ religious and/or philosophical tradition (pre-1900) ⑳ religious specialist/role ㉑ religious tradition (post-1900) ㉒ ritualistic ㉓ ritual, life-cycle ㉔ river ㉕ royalty (historical) ㉖ *ṛṣi* ㉗ scholarly tradition ㉘ tribe

P

① astronomical ② botanical ③ calendrical ④ community (Hindu, Muslim, etc.) ⑤ cinematographic ⑥ gods, goddesses, and powers ⑦ dynasty ⑧ festival ⑨ groups of gods, goddesses, and powers ⑩ language/script ⑪ literary genre/feature ⑫ medical ⑬ musical genre/feature ⑭ musical instrument

① astronomical ② botanical ③ calendrical ④ community (Hindu, Muslim, etc.) ⑤ cinematographic ⑥ gods, goddesses, and powers ⑦ dynasty ⑧ festival ⑨ groups of gods, goddesses, and powers ⑩ language/script ⑪ literary genre/feature ⑫ medical ⑬ musical genre/feature ⑭ musical instrument

⑮ performance tradition ⑯ poet, teacher, saint (pre-1900) ⑰ poet, teacher, saint (post-1900) ⑱ *rāga* ⑲ religious and/or philosophical tradition (pre-1900) ⑳ religious specialist/role ㉑ religious tradition (post-1900) ㉒ ritualistic ㉓ ritual, life-cycle ㉔ river ㉕ royalty (historical) ㉖ *ṛṣi* ㉗ scholarly tradition ㉘ tribe

① astronomical ② botanical ③ calendrical ④ community (Hindu, Muslim, etc.) ⑤ cinematographic ⑥ gods, goddesses, and powers ⑦ dynasty ⑧ festival ⑨ groups of gods, goddesses, and powers ⑩ language/script ⑪ literary genre/feature ⑫ medical ⑬ musical genre/feature ⑭ musical instrument

⑮ performance tradition ⑯ poet, teacher, saint (pre-1900) ⑰ poet, teacher, saint (post-1900) ⑱ *rāga* ⑲ religious and/or philosophical tradition (pre-1900) ⑳ religious specialist/role ㉑ religious tradition (post-1900) ㉒ ritualistic ㉓ ritual, life-cycle ㉔ river ㉕ royalty (historical) ㉖ *ṛṣi* ㉗ scholarly tradition ㉘ tribe

① astronomical ② botanical ③ calendrical ④ community (Hindu, Muslim, etc.) ⑤ cinematographic ⑥ gods, goddesses, and powers ⑦ dynasty ⑧ festival ⑨ groups of gods, goddesses, and powers ⑩ language/script ⑪ literary genre/feature ⑫ medical ⑬ musical genre/feature ⑭ musical instrument

⑮ performance tradition ⑯ poet, teacher, saint (pre-1900) ⑰ poet, teacher, saint (post-1900) ⑱ *rāga* ⑲ religious and/or philosophical tradition (pre-1900) ⑳ religious specialist/role ㉑ religious tradition (post-1900) ㉒ ritualistic ㉓ ritual, life-cycle ㉔ river ㉕ royalty (historical) ㉖ *ṛṣi* ㉗ scholarly tradition ㉘ tribe

① astronomical ② botanical ③ calendrical ④ community (Hindu, Muslim, etc.) ⑤ cinematographic ⑥ gods, goddesses, and powers ⑦ dynasty ⑧ festival ⑨ groups of gods, goddesses, and powers ⑩ language/script ⑪ literary genre/feature ⑫ medical ⑬ musical genre/feature ⑭ musical instrument

⑮ performance tradition ⑯ poet, teacher, saint (pre-1900) ⑰ poet, teacher, saint (post-1900) ⑱ *rāga* ⑲ religious and/or philosophical tradition (pre-1900) ⑳ religious specialist/role ㉑ religious tradition (post-1900) ㉒ ritualistic ㉓ ritual, life-cycle ㉔ river ㉕ royalty (historical) ㉖ *ṛṣi* ㉗ scholarly tradition ㉘ tribe

① astronomical ② botanical ③ calendrical ④ community (Hindu, Muslim, etc.) ⑤ cinematographic ⑥ gods, goddesses, and powers ⑦ dynasty ⑧ festival ⑨ groups of gods, goddesses, and powers ⑩ language/script ⑪ literary genre/feature ⑫ medical ⑬ musical genre/feature ⑭ musical instrument

⑮ performance tradition ⑯ poet, teacher, saint (pre-1900) ⑰ poet, teacher, saint (post-1900) ⑱ *rāga* ⑲ religious and/or philosophical tradition (pre-1900) ⑳ religious specialist/role ㉑ religious tradition (post-1900) ㉒ ritualistic ㉓ ritual, life-cycle ㉔ river ㉕ royalty (historical) ㉖ *ṛṣi* ㉗ scholarly tradition ㉘ tribe

① astronomical ② botanical ③ calendrical ④ community (Hindu, Muslim, etc.) ⑤ cinematographic ⑥ gods, goddesses, and powers ⑦ dynasty ⑧ festival ⑨ groups of gods, goddesses, and powers ⑩ language/script ⑪ literary genre/feature ⑫ medical ⑬ musical genre/feature ⑭ musical instrument

① astronomical ② botanical ③ calendrical ④ community (Hindu, Muslim, etc.) ⑤ cinematographic ⑥ gods, goddesses, and powers ⑦ dynasty ⑧ festival ⑨ groups of gods, goddesses, and powers ⑩ language/script ⑪ literary genre/feature ⑫ medical ⑬ musical genre/feature ⑭ musical instrument

⑮ performance tradition ⑯ poet, teacher, saint (pre-1900) ⑰ poet, teacher, saint (post-1900) ⑱ *rāga* ⑲ religious and/or philosophical tradition (pre-1900) ⑳ religious specialist/role ㉑ religious tradition (post-1900) ㉒ ritualistic ㉓ ritual, life-cycle ㉔ river ㉕ royalty (historical) ㉖ *ṛṣi* ㉗ scholarly tradition ㉘ tribe

① astronomical ② botanical ③ calendrical ④ community (Hindu, Muslim, etc.) ⑤ cinematographic ⑥ gods, goddesses, and powers ⑦ dynasty ⑧ festival ⑨ groups of gods, goddesses, and powers ⑩ language/script ⑪ literary genre/feature ⑫ medical ⑬ musical genre/feature ⑭ musical instrument

⑮ performance tradition ⑯ poet, teacher, saint (pre-1900) ⑰ poet, teacher, saint (post-1900) ⑱ *rāga* ⑲ religious and/or philosophical tradition (pre-1900) ⑳ religious specialist/role ㉑ religious tradition (post-1900) ㉒ ritualistic ㉓ ritual, life-cycle ㉔ river ㉕ royalty (historical) ㉖ *ṛṣi* ㉗ scholarly tradition ㉘ tribe

① astronomical ② botanical ③ calendrical ④ community (Hindu, Muslim, etc.) ⑤ cinematographic ⑥ gods, goddesses, and powers ⑦ dynasty ⑧ festival ⑨ groups of gods, goddesses, and powers ⑩ language/script ⑪ literary genre/feature ⑫ medical ⑬ musical genre/feature ⑭ musical instrument

⑮ performance tradition ⑯ poet, teacher, saint (pre-1900) ⑰ poet, teacher, saint (post-1900) ⑱ *rāga* ⑲ religious and/or philosophical tradition (pre-1900) ⑳ religious specialist/role ㉑ religious tradition (post-1900) ㉒ ritualistic ㉓ ritual, life-cycle ㉔ river ㉕ royalty (historical) ㉖ *ṛṣi* ㉗ scholarly tradition ㉘ tribe

Q

R

① astronomical ② botanical ③ calendrical ④ community (Hindu, Muslim, etc.) ⑤ cinematographic ⑥ gods, goddesses, and powers ⑦ dynasty ⑧ festival ⑨ groups of gods, goddesses, and powers ⑩ language/script ⑪ literary genre/feature ⑫ medical ⑬ musical genre/feature ⑭ musical instrument

① astronomical ② botanical ③ calendrical ④ community (Hindu, Muslim, etc.) ⑤ cinematographic ⑥ gods, goddesses, and powers ⑦ dynasty ⑧ festival ⑨ groups of gods, goddesses, and powers ⑩ language/script ⑪ literary genre/feature ⑫ medical ⑬ musical genre/feature ⑭ musical instrument

⑮ performance tradition ⑯ poet, teacher, saint (pre-1900) ⑰ poet, teacher, saint (post-1900) ⑱ *rāga* ⑲ religious and/or philosophical tradition (pre-1900) ⑳ religious specialist/role ㉑ religious tradition (post-1900) ㉒ ritualistic ㉓ ritual, life-cycle ㉔ river ㉕ royalty (historical) ㉖ *ṛṣi* ㉗ scholarly tradition ㉘ tribe

① astronomical ② botanical ③ calendrical ④ community (Hindu, Muslim, etc.) ⑤ cinematographic ⑥ gods, goddesses, and powers ⑦ dynasty ⑧ festival ⑨ groups of gods, goddesses, and powers ⑩ language/script ⑪ literary genre/feature ⑫ medical ⑬ musical genre/feature ⑭ musical instrument

⑮ performance tradition ⑯ poet, teacher, saint (pre-1900) ⑰ poet, teacher, saint (post-1900) ⑱ *rāga* ⑲ religious and/or philosophical tradition (pre-1900) ⑳ religious specialist/role ㉑ religious tradition (post-1900) ㉒ ritualistic ㉓ ritual, life-cycle ㉔ river ㉕ royalty (historical) ㉖ *ṛṣi* ㉗ scholarly tradition ㉘ tribe

⑮ performance tradition ⑯ poet, teacher, saint (pre-1900) ⑰ poet, teacher, saint (post-1900) ⑱ *rāga* ⑲ religious and/or philosophical tradition (pre-1900) ⑳ religious specialist/role ㉑ religious tradition (post-1900) ㉒ ritualistic ㉓ ritual, life-cycle ㉔ river ㉕ royalty (historical) ㉖ *ṛṣi* ㉗ scholarly tradition ㉘ tribe

① astronomical ② botanical ③ calendrical ④ community (Hindu, Muslim, etc.) ⑤ cinematographic ⑥ gods, goddesses, and powers ⑦ dynasty ⑧ festival ⑨ groups of gods, goddesses, and powers ⑩ language/script ⑪ literary genre/feature ⑫ medical ⑬ musical genre/feature ⑭ musical instrument

① astronomical ② botanical ③ calendrical ④ community (Hindu, Muslim, etc.) ⑤ cinematographic ⑥ gods, goddesses, and powers ⑦ dynasty ⑧ festival ⑨ groups of gods, goddesses, and powers ⑩ language/script ⑪ literary genre/feature ⑫ medical ⑬ musical genre/feature ⑭ musical instrument

① astronomical ② botanical ③ calendrical ④ community (Hindu, Muslim, etc.) ⑤ cinematographic ⑥ gods, goddesses, and powers ⑦ dynasty ⑧ festival ⑨ groups of gods, goddesses, and powers ⑩ language/script ⑪ literary genre/feature ⑫ medical ⑬ musical genre/feature ⑭ musical instrument

S

① astronomical ② botanical ③ calendrical ④ community (Hindu, Muslim, etc.) ⑤ cinematographic ⑥ gods, goddesses, and powers ⑦ dynasty ⑧ festival ⑨ groups of gods, goddesses, and powers ⑩ language/script ⑪ literary genre/feature ⑫ medical ⑬ musical genre/feature ⑭ musical instrument

⑮ performance tradition ⑯ poet, teacher, saint (pre-1900) ⑰ poet, teacher, saint (post-1900) ⑱ *rāga* ⑲ religious and/or philosophical tradition (pre-1900) ⑳ religious specialist/role ㉑ religious tradition (post-1900) ㉒ ritualistic ㉓ ritual, life-cycle ㉔ river ㉕ royalty (historical) ㉖ *ṛṣi* ㉗ scholarly tradition ㉘ tribe

① astronomical ② botanical ③ calendrical ④ community (Hindu, Muslim, etc.) ⑤ cinematographic ⑥ gods, goddesses, and powers ⑦ dynasty ⑧ festival ⑨ groups of gods, goddesses, and powers ⑩ language/script ⑪ literary genre/feature ⑫ medical ⑬ musical genre/feature ⑭ musical instrument

⑮ performance tradition ⑯ poet, teacher, saint (pre-1900) ⑰ poet, teacher, saint (post-1900) ⑱ *rāga* ⑲ religious and/or philosophical tradition (pre-1900) ⑳ religious specialist/role ㉑ religious tradition (post-1900) ㉒ ritualistic ㉓ ritual, life-cycle ㉔ river ㉕ royalty (historical) ㉖ *ṛṣi* ㉗ scholarly tradition ㉘ tribe

① astronomical ② botanical ③ calendrical ④ community (Hindu, Muslim, etc.) ⑤ cinematographic ⑥ gods, goddesses, and powers ⑦ dynasty ⑧ festival ⑨ groups of gods, goddesses, and powers ⑩ language/script ⑪ literary genre/feature ⑫ medical ⑬ musical genre/feature ⑭ musical instrument

⑮ performance tradition ⑯ poet, teacher, saint (pre-1900) ⑰ poet, teacher, saint (post-1900) ⑱ *rāga* ⑲ religious and/or philosophical tradition (pre-1900) ⑳ religious specialist/role ㉑ religious tradition (post-1900) ㉒ ritualistic ㉓ ritual, life-cycle ㉔ river ㉕ royalty (historical) ㉖ *ṛṣi* ㉗ scholarly tradition ㉘ tribe

① astronomical ② botanical ③ calendrical ④ community (Hindu, Muslim, etc.) ⑤ cinematographic ⑥ gods, goddesses, and powers ⑦ dynasty ⑧ festival ⑨ groups of gods, goddesses, and powers ⑩ language/script ⑪ literary genre/feature ⑫ medical ⑬ musical genre/feature ⑭ musical instrument

⑮ performance tradition ⑯ poet, teacher, saint (pre-1900) ⑰ poet, teacher, saint (post-1900) ⑱ *rāga* ⑲ religious and/or philosophical tradition (pre-1900) ⑳ religious specialist/role ㉑ religious tradition (post-1900) ㉒ ritualistic ㉓ ritual, life-cycle ㉔ river ㉕ royalty (historical) ㉖ *ṛṣi* ㉗ scholarly tradition ㉘ tribe

① astronomical ② botanical ③ calendrical ④ community (Hindu, Muslim, etc.) ⑤ cinematographic ⑥ gods, goddesses, and powers ⑦ dynasty ⑧ festival ⑨ groups of gods, goddesses, and powers ⑩ language/script ⑪ literary genre/feature ⑫ medical ⑬ musical genre/feature ⑭ musical instrument

⑮ performance tradition ⑯ poet, teacher, saint (pre-1900) ⑰ poet, teacher, saint (post-1900) ⑱ *rāga* ⑲ religious and/or philosophical tradition (pre-1900) ⑳ religious specialist/role ㉑ religious tradition (post-1900) ㉒ ritualistic ㉓ ritual, life-cycle ㉔ river ㉕ royalty (historical) ㉖ *ṛṣi* ㉗ scholarly tradition ㉘ tribe

① astronomical ② botanical ③ calendrical ④ community (Hindu, Muslim, etc.) ⑤ cinematographic ⑥ gods, goddesses, and powers ⑦ dynasty ⑧ festival ⑨ groups of gods, goddesses, and powers ⑩ language/script ⑪ literary genre/feature ⑫ medical ⑬ musical genre/feature ⑭ musical instrument

(15) performance tradition (16) poet, teacher, saint (pre-1900) (17) poet, teacher, saint (post-1900) (18) *rāga* (19) religious and/or philosophical tradition (pre-1900) (20) religious specialist/role (21) religious tradition (post-1900) (22) ritualistic (23) ritual, life-cycle (24) river (25) royalty (historical) (26) *ṛṣi* (27) scholarly tradition (28) tribe

① astronomical ② botanical ③ calendrical ④ community (Hindu, Muslim, etc.) ⑤ cinematographic ⑥ gods, goddesses, and powers ⑦ dynasty ⑧ festival ⑨ groups of gods, goddesses, and powers ⑩ language/script ⑪ literary genre/feature ⑫ medical ⑬ musical genre/feature ⑭ musical instrument

⑮ performance tradition ⑯ poet, teacher, saint (pre-1900) ⑰ poet, teacher, saint (post-1900) ⑱ *rāga* ⑲ religious and/or philosophical tradition (pre-1900) ⑳ religious specialist/role ㉑ religious tradition (post-1900) ㉒ ritualistic ㉓ ritual, life-cycle ㉔ river ㉕ royalty (historical) ㉖ *ṛṣi* ㉗ scholarly tradition ㉘ tribe

① astronomical ② botanical ③ calendrical ④ community (Hindu, Muslim, etc.) ⑤ cinematographic ⑥ gods, goddesses, and powers ⑦ dynasty ⑧ festival ⑨ groups of gods, goddesses, and powers ⑩ language/script ⑪ literary genre/feature ⑫ medical ⑬ musical genre/feature ⑭ musical instrument

⑮ performance tradition ⑯ poet, teacher, saint (pre-1900) ⑰ poet, teacher, saint (post-1900) ⑱ *rāga* ⑲ religious and/or philosophical tradition (pre-1900) ⑳ religious specialist/role ㉑ religious tradition (post-1900) ㉒ ritualistic ㉓ ritual, life-cycle ㉔ river ㉕ royalty (historical) ㉖ *ṛṣi* ㉗ scholarly tradition ㉘ tribe

① astronomical ② botanical ③ calendrical ④ community (Hindu, Muslim, etc.) ⑤ cinematographic ⑥ gods, goddesses, and powers ⑦ dynasty ⑧ festival ⑨ groups of gods, goddesses, and powers ⑩ language/script ⑪ literary genre/feature ⑫ medical ⑬ musical genre/feature ⑭ musical instrument

⑮ performance tradition ⑯ poet, teacher, saint (pre-1900) ⑰ poet, teacher, saint (post-1900) ⑱ *rāga* ⑲ religious and/or philosophical tradition (pre-1900) ⑳ religious specialist/role ㉑ religious tradition (post-1900) ㉒ ritualistic ㉓ ritual, life-cycle ㉔ river ㉕ royalty (historical) ㉖ *ṛṣi* ㉗ scholarly tradition ㉘ tribe

① astronomical ② botanical ③ calendrical ④ community (Hindu, Muslim, etc.) ⑤ cinematographic ⑥ gods, goddesses, and powers ⑦ dynasty ⑧ festival ⑨ groups of gods, goddesses, and powers ⑩ language/script ⑪ literary genre/feature ⑫ medical ⑬ musical genre/feature ⑭ musical instrument

⑮ performance tradition ⑯ poet, teacher, saint (pre-1900) ⑰ poet, teacher, saint (post-1900) ⑱ *rāga* ⑲ religious and/or philosophical tradition (pre-1900) ⑳ religious specialist/role ㉑ religious tradition (post-1900) ㉒ ritualistic ㉓ ritual, life-cycle ㉔ river ㉕ royalty (historical) ㉖ *ṛṣi* ㉗ scholarly tradition ㉘ tribe

⑮ performance tradition ⑯ poet, teacher, saint (pre-1900) ⑰ poet, teacher, saint (post-1900) ⑱ *rāga* ⑲ religious and/or philosophical tradition (pre-1900) ⑳ religious specialist/role ㉑ religious tradition (post-1900) ㉒ ritualistic ㉓ ritual, life-cycle ㉔ river ㉕ royalty (historical) ㉖ *ṛṣi* ㉗ scholarly tradition ㉘ tribe

① astronomical ② botanical ③ calendrical ④ community (Hindu, Muslim, etc.) ⑤ cinematographic ⑥ gods, goddesses, and powers ⑦ dynasty ⑧ festival ⑨ groups of gods, goddesses, and powers ⑩ language/script ⑪ literary genre/feature ⑫ medical ⑬ musical genre/feature ⑭ musical instrument

⑮ performance tradition ⑯ poet, teacher, saint (pre-1900) ⑰ poet, teacher, saint (post-1900) ⑱ *rāga* ⑲ religious and/or philosophical tradition (pre-1900) ⑳ religious specialist/role ㉑ religious tradition (post-1900) ㉒ ritualistic ㉓ ritual, life-cycle ㉔ river ㉕ royalty (historical) ㉖ *ṛṣi* ㉗ scholarly tradition ㉘ tribe

⑮ performance tradition ⑯ poet, teacher, saint (pre-1900) ⑰ poet, teacher, saint (post-1900) ⑱ *rāga* ⑲ religious and/ or philosophical tradition (pre-1900) ⑳ religious specialist/role ㉑ religious tradition (post-1900) ㉒ ritualistic ㉓ ritual, life-cycle ㉔ river ㉕ royalty (historical) ㉖ *ṛṣi* ㉗ scholarly tradition ㉘ tribe

⑮ performance tradition ⑯ poet, teacher, saint (pre-1900) ⑰ poet, teacher, saint (post-1900) ⑱ *rāga* ⑲ religious and/or philosophical tradition (pre-1900) ⑳ religious specialist/role ㉑ religious tradition (post-1900) ㉒ ritualistic ㉓ ritual, life-cycle ㉔ river ㉕ royalty (historical) ㉖ *ṛṣi* ㉗ scholarly tradition ㉘ tribe

⑮ performance tradition ⑯ poet, teacher, saint (pre-1900) ⑰ poet, teacher, saint (post-1900) ⑱ *rāga* ⑲ religious and/or philosophical tradition (pre-1900) ⑳ religious specialist/role ㉑ religious tradition (post-1900) ㉒ ritualistic ㉓ ritual, life-cycle ㉔ river ㉕ royalty (historical) ㉖ *ṛṣi* ㉗ scholarly tradition ㉘ tribe

① astronomical ② botanical ③ calendrical ④ community (Hindu, Muslim, etc.) ⑤ cinematographic ⑥ gods, goddesses, and powers ⑦ dynasty ⑧ festival ⑨ groups of gods, goddesses, and powers ⑩ language/script ⑪ literary genre/feature ⑫ medical ⑬ musical genre/feature ⑭ musical instrument

① astronomical ② botanical ③ calendrical ④ community (Hindu, Muslim, etc.) ⑤ cinematographic ⑥ gods, goddesses, and powers ⑦ dynasty ⑧ festival ⑨ groups of gods, goddesses, and powers ⑩ language/script ⑪ literary genre/feature ⑫ medical ⑬ musical genre/feature ⑭ musical instrument

⑮ performance tradition ⑯ poet, teacher, saint (pre-1900) ⑰ poet, teacher, saint (post-1900) ⑱ *rāga* ⑲ religious and/or philosophical tradition (pre-1900) ⑳ religious specialist/role ㉑ religious tradition (post-1900) ㉒ ritualistic ㉓ ritual, life-cycle ㉔ river ㉕ royalty (historical) ㉖ *ṛṣi* ㉗ scholarly tradition ㉘ tribe

⑮ performance tradition ⑯ poet, teacher, saint (pre-1900) ⑰ poet, teacher, saint (post-1900) ⑱ *rāga* ⑲ religious and/or philosophical tradition (pre-1900) ⑳ religious specialist/role ㉑ religious tradition (post-1900) ㉒ ritualistic ㉓ ritual, life-cycle ㉔ river ㉕ royalty (historical) ㉖ *ṛṣi* ㉗ scholarly tradition ㉘ tribe

① astronomical ② botanical ③ calendrical ④ community (Hindu, Muslim, etc.) ⑤ cinematographic ⑥ gods, goddesses, and powers ⑦ dynasty ⑧ festival ⑨ groups of gods, goddesses, and powers ⑩ language/script ⑪ literary genre/feature ⑫ medical ⑬ musical genre/feature ⑭ musical instrument

T

① astronomical ② botanical ③ calendrical ④ community (Hindu, Muslim, etc.) ⑤ cinematographic ⑥ gods, goddesses, and powers ⑦ dynasty ⑧ festival ⑨ groups of gods, goddesses, and powers ⑩ language/script ⑪ literary genre/feature ⑫ medical ⑬ musical genre/feature ⑭ musical instrument

⑮ performance tradition ⑯ poet, teacher, saint (pre-1900) ⑰ poet, teacher, saint (post-1900) ⑱ *rāga* ⑲ religious and/or philosophical tradition (pre-1900) ⑳ religious specialist/role ㉑ religious tradition (post-1900) ㉒ ritualistic ㉓ ritual, life-cycle ㉔ river ㉕ royalty (historical) ㉖ *ṛṣi* ㉗ scholarly tradition ㉘ tribe

① astronomical ② botanical ③ calendrical ④ community (Hindu, Muslim, etc.) ⑤ cinematographic ⑥ gods, goddesses, and powers ⑦ dynasty ⑧ festival ⑨ groups of gods, goddesses, and powers ⑩ language/script ⑪ literary genre/feature ⑫ medical ⑬ musical genre/feature ⑭ musical instrument

⑮ performance tradition ⑯ poet, teacher, saint (pre-1900) ⑰ poet, teacher, saint (post-1900) ⑱ *rāga* ⑲ religious and/or philosophical tradition (pre-1900) ⑳ religious specialist/role ㉑ religious tradition (post-1900) ㉒ ritualistic ㉓ ritual, life-cycle ㉔ river ㉕ royalty (historical) ㉖ *ṛṣi* ㉗ scholarly tradition ㉘ tribe

① astronomical ② botanical ③ calendrical ④ community (Hindu, Muslim, etc.) ⑤ cinematographic ⑥ gods, goddesses, and powers ⑦ dynasty ⑧ festival ⑨ groups of gods, goddesses, and powers ⑩ language/script ⑪ literary genre/feature ⑫ medical ⑬ musical genre/feature ⑭ musical instrument

① astronomical ② botanical ③ calendrical ④ community (Hindu, Muslim, etc.) ⑤ cinematographic ⑥ gods, goddesses, and powers ⑦ dynasty ⑧ festival ⑨ groups of gods, goddesses, and powers ⑩ language/script ⑪ literary genre/feature ⑫ medical ⑬ musical genre/feature ⑭ musical instrument

⑮ performance tradition ⑯ poet, teacher, saint (pre-1900) ⑰ poet, teacher, saint (post-1900) ⑱ *rāga* ⑲ religious and/or philosophical tradition (pre-1900) ⑳ religious specialist/role ㉑ religious tradition (post-1900) ㉒ ritualistic ㉓ ritual, life-cycle ㉔ river ㉕ royalty (historical) ㉖ *ṛṣi* ㉗ scholarly tradition ㉘ tribe

① astronomical ② botanical ③ calendrical ④ community (Hindu, Muslim, etc.) ⑤ cinematographic ⑥ gods, goddesses, and powers ⑦ dynasty ⑧ festival ⑨ groups of gods, goddesses, and powers ⑩ language/script ⑪ literary genre/feature ⑫ medical ⑬ musical genre/feature ⑭ musical instrument

⑮ performance tradition ⑯ poet, teacher, saint (pre-1900) ⑰ poet, teacher, saint (post-1900) ⑱ *rāga* ⑲ religious and/or philosophical tradition (pre-1900) ⑳ religious specialist/role ㉑ religious tradition (post-1900) ㉒ ritualistic ㉓ ritual, life-cycle ㉔ river ㉕ royalty (historical) ㉖ *ṛṣi* ㉗ scholarly tradition ㉘ tribe

⑮ performance tradition ⑯ poet, teacher, saint (pre-1900) ⑰ poet, teacher, saint (post-1900) ⑱ *rāga* ⑲ religious and/or philosophical tradition (pre-1900) ⑳ religious specialist/role ㉑ religious tradition (post-1900) ㉒ ritualistic ㉓ ritual, life-cycle ㉔ river ㉕ royalty (historical) ㉖ *ṛṣi* ㉗ scholarly tradition ㉘ tribe

① astronomical ② botanical ③ calendrical ④ community (Hindu, Muslim, etc.) ⑤ cinematographic ⑥ gods, goddesses, and powers ⑦ dynasty ⑧ festival ⑨ groups of gods, goddesses, and powers ⑩ language/script ⑪ literary genre/feature ⑫ medical ⑬ musical genre/feature ⑭ musical instrument

⑮ performance tradition ⑯ poet, teacher, saint (pre-1900) ⑰ poet, teacher, saint (post-1900) ⑱ *rāga* ⑲ religious and/or philosophical tradition (pre-1900) ⑳ religious specialist/role ㉑ religious tradition (post-1900) ㉒ ritualistic ㉓ ritual, life-cycle ㉔ river ㉕ royalty (historical) ㉖ *ṛṣi* ㉗ scholarly tradition ㉘ tribe

V

⑮ performance tradition ⑯ poet, teacher, saint (pre-1900) ⑰ poet, teacher, saint (post-1900) ⑱ *rāga* ⑲ religious and/or philosophical tradition (pre-1900) ⑳ religious specialist/role ㉑ religious tradition (post-1900) ㉒ ritualistic ㉓ ritual, life-cycle ㉔ river ㉕ royalty (historical) ㉖ *ṛṣi* ㉗ scholarly tradition ㉘ tribe

① astronomical ② botanical ③ calendrical ④ community (Hindu, Muslim, etc.) ⑤ cinematographic ⑥ gods, goddesses, and powers ⑦ dynasty ⑧ festival ⑨ groups of gods, goddesses, and powers ⑩ language/script ⑪ literary genre/feature ⑫ medical ⑬ musical genre/feature ⑭ musical instrument

⑮ performance tradition ⑯ poet, teacher, saint (pre-1900) ⑰ poet, teacher, saint (post-1900) ⑱ *rāga* ⑲ religious and/or philosophical tradition (pre-1900) ⑳ religious specialist/role ㉑ religious tradition (post-1900) ㉒ ritualistic ㉓ ritual, life-cycle ㉔ river ㉕ royalty (historical) ㉖ *ṛṣi* ㉗ scholarly tradition ㉘ tribe

① astronomical ② botanical ③ calendrical ④ community (Hindu, Muslim, etc.) ⑤ cinematographic ⑥ gods, goddesses, and powers ⑦ dynasty ⑧ festival ⑨ groups of gods, goddesses, and powers ⑩ language/script ⑪ literary genre/feature ⑫ medical ⑬ musical genre/feature ⑭ musical instrument

⑮ performance tradition ⑯ poet, teacher, saint (pre-1900) ⑰ poet, teacher, saint (post-1900) ⑱ *rāga* ⑲ religious and/or philosophical tradition (pre-1900) ⑳ religious specialist/role ㉑ religious tradition (post-1900) ㉒ ritualistic ㉓ ritual, life-cycle ㉔ river ㉕ royalty (historical) ㉖ *ṛṣi* ㉗ scholarly tradition ㉘ tribe

① astronomical ② botanical ③ calendrical ④ community (Hindu, Muslim, etc.) ⑤ cinematographic ⑥ gods, goddesses, and powers ⑦ dynasty ⑧ festival ⑨ groups of gods, goddesses, and powers ⑩ language/script ⑪ literary genre/feature ⑫ medical ⑬ musical genre/feature ⑭ musical instrument

⑮ performance tradition ⑯ poet, teacher, saint (pre-1900) ⑰ poet, teacher, saint (post-1900) ⑱ *rāga* ⑲ religious and/or philosophical tradition (pre-1900) ⑳ religious specialist/role ㉑ religious tradition (post-1900) ㉒ ritualistic ㉓ ritual, life-cycle ㉔ river ㉕ royalty (historical) ㉖ *ṛṣi* ㉗ scholarly tradition ㉘ tribe

⑮ performance tradition ⑯ poet, teacher, saint (pre-1900) ⑰ poet, teacher, saint (post-1900) ⑱ *rāga* ⑲ religious and/or philosophical tradition (pre-1900) ⑳ religious specialist/role ㉑ religious tradition (post-1900) ㉒ ritualistic ㉓ ritual, life-cycle ㉔ river ㉕ royalty (historical) ㉖ *ṛṣi* ㉗ scholarly tradition ㉘ tribe

⑮ performance tradition ⑯ poet, teacher, saint (pre-1900) ⑰ poet, teacher, saint (post-1900) ⑱ *rāga* ⑲ religious and/or philosophical tradition (pre-1900) ⑳ religious specialist/role ㉑ religious tradition (post-1900) ㉒ ritualistic ㉓ ritual, life-cycle ㉔ river ㉕ royalty (historical) ㉖ *ṛṣi* ㉗ scholarly tradition ㉘ tribe

① astronomical ② botanical ③ calendrical ④ community (Hindu, Muslim, etc.) ⑤ cinematographic ⑥ gods, goddesses, and powers ⑦ dynasty ⑧ festival ⑨ groups of gods, goddesses, and powers ⑩ language/script ⑪ literary genre/feature ⑫ medical ⑬ musical genre/feature ⑭ musical instrument

① astronomical ② botanical ③ calendrical ④ community (Hindu, Muslim, etc.) ⑤ cinematographic ⑥ gods, goddesses, and powers ⑦ dynasty ⑧ festival ⑨ groups of gods, goddesses, and powers ⑩ language/script ⑪ literary genre/feature ⑫ medical ⑬ musical genre/feature ⑭ musical instrument

⑮ performance tradition ⑯ poet, teacher, saint (pre-1900) ⑰ poet, teacher, saint (post-1900) ⑱ *rāga* ⑲ religious and/or philosophical tradition (pre-1900) ⑳ religious specialist/role ㉑ religious tradition (post-1900) ㉒ ritualistic ㉓ ritual, life-cycle ㉔ river ㉕ royalty (historical) ㉖ *ṛṣi* ㉗ scholarly tradition ㉘ tribe

① astronomical ② botanical ③ calendrical ④ community (Hindu, Muslim, etc.) ⑤ cinematographic ⑥ gods, goddesses, and powers ⑦ dynasty ⑧ festival ⑨ groups of gods, goddesses, and powers ⑩ language/script ⑪ literary genre/feature ⑫ medical ⑬ musical genre/feature ⑭ musical instrument

⑮ performance tradition ⑯ poet, teacher, saint (pre-1900) ⑰ poet, teacher, saint (post-1900) ⑱ *rāga* ⑲ religious and/or philosophical tradition (pre-1900) ⑳ religious specialist/role ㉑ religious tradition (post-1900) ㉒ ritualistic ㉓ ritual, life-cycle ㉔ river ㉕ royalty (historical) ㉖ *ṛṣi* ㉗ scholarly tradition ㉘ tribe

① astronomical ② botanical ③ calendrical ④ community (Hindu, Muslim, etc.) ⑤ cinematographic ⑥ gods, goddesses, and powers ⑦ dynasty ⑧ festival ⑨ groups of gods, goddesses, and powers ⑩ language/script ⑪ literary genre/feature ⑫ medical ⑬ musical genre/feature ⑭ musical instrument

W

⑮ performance tradition ⑯ poet, teacher, saint (pre-1900) ⑰ poet, teacher, saint (post-1900) ⑱ *rāga* ⑲ religious and/or philosophical tradition (pre-1900) ⑳ religious specialist/role ㉑ religious tradition (post-1900) ㉒ ritualistic ㉓ ritual, life-cycle ㉔ river ㉕ royalty (historical) ㉖ *ṛṣi* ㉗ scholarly tradition ㉘ tribe

X

Y

① astronomical ② botanical ③ calendrical ④ community (Hindu, Muslim, etc.) ⑤ cinematographic ⑥ gods, goddesses, and powers ⑦ dynasty ⑧ festival ⑨ groups of gods, goddesses, and powers ⑩ language/script ⑪ literary genre/feature ⑫ medical ⑬ musical genre/feature ⑭ musical instrument

⑮ performance tradition ⑯ poet, teacher, saint (pre-1900) ⑰ poet, teacher, saint (post-1900) ⑱ *rāga* ⑲ religious and/or philosophical tradition (pre-1900) ⑳ religious specialist/role ㉑ religious tradition (post-1900) ㉒ ritualistic ㉓ ritual, life-cycle ㉔ river ㉕ royalty (historical) ㉖ *ṛṣi* ㉗ scholarly tradition ㉘ tribe

① astronomical ② botanical ③ calendrical ④ community (Hindu, Muslim, etc.) ⑤ cinematographic ⑥ gods, goddesses, and powers ⑦ dynasty ⑧ festival ⑨ groups of gods, goddesses, and powers ⑩ language/script ⑪ literary genre/feature ⑫ medical ⑬ musical genre/feature ⑭ musical instrument

Z

Additional Indices

Gods, Goddesses, and Powers

Abge Bonga
Abhijit
Abhiṣekalakṣmī
Acalā
Acyuta
Adharma
Adhiparaśakti
Ādhivarāha
Adhvagh
Ādi
Ādi Purkh
Ādibuddha
Ādigaṇeś
Ādināth
Ādinātha
Ādiparāśakti
Ādiśakti
Ādiśeṣa
Aditi
Āditya
Ādiviṣṇu
Ādya Bhuvaneśvarī
Ādya Sundarī
Ādya Tāriṇī
Ādyādevī
Ādyakālī
Ādyakālīkā
Ādyaśakti
Ādyaśakti Kālī
Ādyaśakti Mahāmāyā
Ādyavidyā Kālī
Aešma
Aghora
Aghoreśvarī
Agnāyī
Agni
Agni Jātavedas
Agni Saucika
Agni Sviṣṭakṛt
Agni Vaiśvānara
Ahi
Ahiṃsā
Ahirāvaṇa
Ahīśa
Ahoī Mātā
Ahura Mazdā
Aindrī
Airāvata
Airiiaman
Aiśvaryalaksṃī
Aiyan
Aiyaṉār
Ajātaśatru
Ajitā
Akāl
Akal Purakh
Akhilāṇḍeśvarī
Akilāṇṭēcuvari
Akṣamālā
Akṣayā
Akṣobhyā
Akśobya
Alaimakaḷ
Alakh
Aḻakiyamaṇavāḷaṉ
Alakṣmī
Ālambaradundubhi
Alekha Puruṣa
Allāh
Allāh Mālik
Alopi Devī
Amarakaṇṭakeśvara
Ambā
Ambākālī
Ambalikā
Ambikā
Ambujā
Amitābha
Ammaṉ
Amoghasiddhi
Ampāḷ
Amṛtadhāraka
Amṛtāharaṇa
Amṛtalakṣmī
Amṛteśabhairava
Amṛteśvarabhairava
Aṃśa
Anādyadeva
Anāhitā
Ānakadundubhi
Anām
Ānandabhairava
Anaṅga
Ananta
Anantapadmanābha
Anantaśakti
Anantaśayana
Anantaśāyin

Batantī
Batara Guru
Bāthau
Bāthau Śivrāi
Baṭukabhairava
Bemmeru
Bhadrā
Bhadrakālī
Bhaga
Bhagautī
Bhagavān
Bhagavān Svayam
Bhagavant
Bhagavatī
Bhagavatī Bālasundrī
Bhagwati
Bhāgyādhirohiṇī
Bhairav
Bhairava
Bhairavācārya
Bhairavasadbhāva
Bhairavī
Bhairavnāth
Bhairon
Bhākīrājabhairava
Bhakti
Bhallāṭa
Bhaṇḍāsura
Bhānu
Bhānumatī
Bhāradī
Bharaṇī
Bhārat Devī
Bhārat Mātā
Bhārata Mātā
Bhāratī
Bharma
Bhāskareśvara
Bhasman
Bhasmāsura
Bhattāra Da Tonta
Bhattāra Guru
Bhattāra Hyang Putrajaya
Bhattāri Dewi Danu
Bhattāri Mandul
Bhaukadevī
Bhauma
Bhaumāsura
Bhava
Bhavānī
Bhavatāriṇī
Bhayānanā
Bheḍā
Bherujī
Bherūnāth
Bhikṣāṭana
Bhīmasena
Bhīmavaktrā
Bhivāī
Bhoga Śrīnivāsa
Bhoginī
Bhramarāmbā
Bhṛgu
Bhṛṅgarāja
Bhṛṅgin
Bhṛśa
Bhū
Bhūdevī
Bhujaga
Bhūmā
Bhūmi
Bhūṅkhāl
Bhūṅkhāl Devī
Bhūtabhavyabhavatprabhu
Bhūtakṛt
Bhūtamaheśvara
Bhūteśvara
Bhūthathan
Bhūtnāth
Bhuvanamālinī
Bhuvaneśī
Bhuvaneśvara
Bhuvaneśvarī
Bibhīṣaṇa
Biḍālī
Bitthula
Bomma
Brahmā
Brahma Nāyuḍu
Brahmā Sahampati
Brahmā Sanatkumāra
Brahmadeva
Brahmaṇaḥsvāmin
Brahmaṇaspati
Brahmaṇī
Brahmāśāstṛ
Bṛhaspati
Bṛhatkṣata
Bṛhatkukṣī
Buddhi
Budha
Buḍi Mā

Bukit Dharma
Buṃgadya
Buṛhi Ṭhākurāṇī
Buruma Deva
Burzāwand Yazd

Cakrahasta
Cakrapāṇī
Cakti
Calon Arang
Camuṇḍā
Camuṇḍākālī
Cāmuṇḍeśvarī
Caṇḍa
Caṇḍakāpālin
Caṇḍākāpālinī
Caṇḍākṣī
Caṇḍāsidhāra
Caṇḍeśvara
Caṇḍī
Caṇḍikā
Candra
Candra Bhagvān
Candraghaṇṭā
Candrahāsinī
Candramas
Candranāth
Candraśekhara
Candrāvalī
Caṅkani Kaṟuppu
Caṅkilikaṟuppaṉ
Cannamallikārjuna
Cāpara Ṣaṣṭhī
Cārumaṉ
Caturātmakeśava
Cauḍeśvari
Ceṅgamuṛi
Ceṅkamalavalli
Cennamallikārjuna
Cetanya Jhāṃkī
Cēttirapālaṉ
Cevvēḷ
Ceyōṉ
Chāmuṇḍā
Chando
Chatracaṇḍeśvara
Chāyā
Cheiron
Chinnamastā
Cītai
Citi
Citrā
Citragupta
Citraketu
Citrāṅgadā
Citrarathasvāmin
Civaṉ
Codalamadan
Cōmi
Cūr
Cūraṉ
Cūrapatumaṉ

Dadhibāmana
Dadhivāhana
Ḍākinī
Dakṣa
Dakṣayani
Dakṣiṇā
Dakṣiṇa Rāya
Dakṣiṇakālī
Dakṣiṇāmūrti
Dāmodar
Dāmodara
Dānava
Danāyu
Daṇḍadhāra
Daṇḍahastā
Daṇḍinī
Danteśvarī
Danturā
Danu
Dariapīr
Dārika
Dathan
Dātṛ
Datta
Dattātreya
Dauvārika
Dayāmayī
Dee Baba
Dev Nārāyaṇ
Devahūti
Devakī
Devanāyaka
Devasenā
Devatrāsa
Devavrata
Devī
Devī Asthān
Devī Vasundharā
Devīdurgā

Devkī Kṛṣṇa
Devnārāyaṇ
Dewi Pretiwi
Dhanvantari
Dharma
Dharmādharmamaya
Dharmarāja
Dharmasaṃvardhanī
Dharmaṭhākura
Dharmesh
Dharmo
Dhārtimātā
Dhātṛ
Ḍhebo
Ḍholyā
Dhorom
Dhṛtarāṣṭra Airāvata
Dhruva
Dhruveśa
Dhuḷobā
Dhūmāvatī
Dhūmorṇā
Dhūmralocana
Dīkṣādevī
Diti
Docā Mujā
Draupadī
Draupadiyamma
Dundubhi
Durga
Durgā
Durga Ranini
Durgā Ṣaṣṭhī
Durgādevī
Durgama
Durgāparameśvarī
Durgī
Durjayā
Durlabhasvāmin
Dyaus
Dyauṣpitṛ

Ekajaṭā
Ekānaṃśā
Ekanetra
Ekāntavāsinī
Ekapādabhairava
Ekārṇavaśaya
Ekarudra
Ekaśṛṅgatanu
Ekavrātya
Ekliṅgjī
Ekvirā Devī
Ellaiyammaṉ
Ellamma
Ē<u>l</u>umalai
Ē<u>l</u>umalaiyaṉ
Enki
Erukamma
Erulan
Ezhakathipītam

Gabriel
Gadādhara
Gahaneśa
Gajakarṇa
Gajalakṣmī
Gajendra
Gaṇādhipa
Gaṇapati
Gandah
Gandharva
Gandharvī
Gandhavatī
Gaṇeśa
Gaṅgāmma
Gaṇpatī
Garbhodakaśāyin
Gariaya
Garuḍa
Garutmat
Gaurī
Gawan Deoti
Gayāsura
Gāyatrī
Ghaga
Ghanśyām
Ghanśyāma
Ghaṭotkaca
Gheraṇḍa
Ghoraghoratarā
Ghṛtācī
Girdevī
Giridhar
Giridhar Gopāl
Girisutā
Gītā
Gobardhan
Gogo
Gogo Cauhān
Goludev
Gomātā

Jayantī
Jhūlelāl
Jīvandevatā
Jñāna
Jñānodayinī
Jugal Kiśor
Jumādi Daiva
Jvālāmukhī
Jvalatparaśudhṛk Rāma
Jvālpā Devī
Jvara
Jvarāsura
Jvareśvara
Jvarī
Jyeṣṭhā
Jyeṣṭheśvara

Ka
Ka blei Synshar
Kabandha
Kabin Mahāphrom
Kaca
Kachiyabhairav
Kadrū
Kaikasī
Kainthīvālī Mātā
Kaiṭabha
Kaivalyadāyinī
Kākacaṇḍeśvarī
Kāl
Kāl Bhairav
Kāla
Kālā
Kālā Rām
Kālabhairava
Kālabhairavī
Kālāgni
Kālahastīśvara
Kālakarṇī
Kalal De
Kālanemi
Kālanemighna
Kālarātrī
Kālarūpin
Kālasaṃkarṣiṇī
Kālasaṃkarṣiṇīkālī
Kālbhaironāth
Kālī
Kālī Jogeśvarī
Kālī Mā
Kali Mai
Kālī Mātā
Kālikā
Kaliṅgā
Kāḷiya
Kāliya
Kalkattevalī
Kalki
Kalki Viṣṇuyaśas
Kalleśvara
Kalyāṇasundara
Kāma
Kāmadeva
Kāmadhenu
Kāmakalākālī
Kāmākhya
Kāmākṣi
Kamalā
Kāmamardana
Kāmeśvara
Kāmeśvari
Kanakadurgā
Kandasvāmī
Kaṇṇaṉ
Kantacāmi
Kantaṉ
Kāntātman
Kanyākumārī
Kapāleśa
Kāpālin
Kapālīśabhairava
Kapil Muni
Kapilā
Kapila Mahābrahmā
Kapilādhenu
Karālā
Karālī
Karaṅkiṇī
Kardama
Kardama Prajāpati
Karkoṭaka
Karmaśreṣṭha
Karṇamoṭī
Kartṛ
Kārttikai
Kārttikeya
Karumāriyammaṉ
Karuṇāmaya
Karuppa
Karuppacāmi
Karuppan
Karuṭan

Kāśī Viśvanāth
Kāśī Viśvanātha
Kaśyapa
Kāṭamarāju
Kaṭavuḷ
Kātyāyanī
Kaumārī
Kauśikī
Kāvērī Amman̲
Kavi
Kecāi Khāti
Kelbāī
Kerār Bīr
Keśava
Ketakā
Ketu
Kētu
Khaḍgarāvaṇa
Khaṇḍobā
Khaśā
Khecarī
Khoḍiyār
Khongkhā
Kiśorī
Kolārammā
Koṅkaṇā
Kor̲r̲avai
Kōšīdār
Kōtaṇṭa Rāma
Koterie
Kottiyāvattai
Kroḍātman
Krodhā
Krodhanā
Krodheśvara
Kṛṣṇa
Kṛṣṇā Draupadī
Kṛṣṇa Govardhana
Kṛṣṇa Veṇugopāla
Kṛṣṇābāī
Kṛṣṇavartman
Kṛttikā
Kṣapaṇā
Kṣayā
Kṣema
Kṣemaṅkarī
Kṣemarājabhairava
Kṣetrapāl
Kṣetrapāḷ
Kṣetrapāla
Kṣīrodaputrī
Kubera
Kubjikā
Kūḍala Saṅgama
Kuhū
Kulamārtaṇḍabhairava
Kuleśvara
Kuleśvarī
Kumāra
Kumārī
Kumbha
Kumbhakarṇa
Kumbhaśyāma
Kumpan̲
Kumudvatī
Kunalā
Kuṇḍalinī
Kuñjabihārinī
Kuṅkuṇāmbā
Kūrma
Kurubhairava
Kurukullā
Kuśa
Kuśadhavaja
Kuṣmāṇḍā
Kusṃāṇḍī
Kusumadanta
Kūttāṇṭavar
Kuvalayāpīṭam

Lābha
Lāhirai
Lajjā Gaurī
Lakṣmana
Lakṣmī
Lālasā
Lalitā
Lalitāmbikā
Lambodara
Laṅgūrvīr
Laṅkeśvarī
Lārilī
Lāṭbhairava
Lava
Lavaṇa
Layā
Liṅgapuruṣa
Liṅgarāja
Lohaka
Lohitākṣa
Lokaguru
Lokamātṛ

Lokanātha
Lolā
Lolupā
Lotan Ṣaṣṭhī
Luktum Budhi
Luktum Haram
Luv

Macakruka
Mada
Madanamohana
Madanmohanjī
Madanpīṭam
Mādhava
Madhusūdana
Madhyamā
Madirā
Mādrī
Maduraivīran
Maghā
Mahābala
Mahābalā
Mahābhairava
Mahadeo
Mahādev
Mahādeva
Mahādevī
Mahadewa
Mahāgaṇapati
Mahākāl
Mahākāl Kālkā
Mahākāla
Mahākālī
Mahākrūrā
Mahālakṣmī
Mahāliṅgeśvara
Mahāmāyā
Mahapeinnay Nat
Mahaprabhu
Mahāpuruṣa
Mahāśani
Mahāsarasvatī
Mahāsena
Mahāsurī
Mahāsvacchandabhairava
Māhātmyaśarīra
Mahātripurasundarī
Mahāviṣṇu
Mahāyogin
Maheśa
Maheśvara
Maheśvarī
Mahiṣa
Mahiṣamardinī
Mahiṣāsura
Mahiṣāsuramardinī
Mahiṣavāhana
Mahocchuṣmā
Mailāra
Mailāradeva
Mailāraliṅga
Maithilī
Māl
Malaimakaḷ
Malaiyappaṉ
Mālaṇ
Malarmakaḷ
Male Mādeśvara
Mālik Devatā
Mālinī
Malla
Mallamkam Kāḷipītam
Mallaṇṇa
Mallāri
Mallayya
Mallikārjuna
Manasā
Manasādevī
Manda
Mandinmātā
Maṅgalā
Maṅgala
Maṅgalacaṇḍī
Mangeśa
Maṇi
Māṇicara
Mañjunātha
Maṅkharāja
Manmatha
Manoja
Manthānabhairava
Mantraḍāmarikā
Mantramātṛkā
Manu
Manusiṃha Nat
Manyu
Māra
Maran Buru
Marduk
Marī
Mārīca
Marīci I

Marīci II
Māriyamma
Māriyamman̲
Mārtāṇḍa
Mārtāṇḍa Vivasvant
Mārtaṇḍabhairava
Marut
Māruti
Mārutī
Maruttaš
Maryādāpuruṣottama
Matacakreśvarī
Mātājī
Mātali
Mātaṅga
Mātaṅgakanyā
Mātaṅgi
Mātaṅgī
Mātariśvan
Mātṛsadbhāva
Matsya
Mātumai Ampāl
Maturai Vīran̲
Maulī
Maya
Māyā
Māyāmoha
Mayilirāvaṇa
Māyōn̲
Mazdā
Meghanāda
Meghnād
Meghayantī
Mehājī
Melādimātā
Menā
Menakā
Merā
Mhāḷsā
Mhāḷsā Devī
Mhasobā
Mihireśvara
Mīnākṣī
Mīnāṭci
Mitra
Mitra-šil
Miθra
Mohan
Mohinī
Momāī
Momāī Mātājī
Morzāī
Mṛga
Mṛgaśīrsạ̄
Mṛtyu
Mucilinda
Mūkāmbikā
Mukhya
Muktākeśava
Muktasvāmin
Mukunda
Mūlā
Mūla Ṣaṣṭhī
Muṇḍa
Mun̲iyāṇṭi
Mun̲n̲ēcuvaram
Muṇṭakaṇṇiyamman̲
Mura
Murāri
Murkatwa
Murukan̲
Mūtēvi
Muvva Gopāla

Nācciyār
Nāciketa
Nāciketas
Nādaśakti
Nāgabhūṣaṇa
Nāgarī
Nageśa
Nairiiō.saŋha
Nairṛteśvarī
Nākapūcaṇi
Nakura
Nalinī
Namuci
Nanā
Nān̲ampāḷ
Nanaya
Nandā
Nandādevī
Nandi
Nandikeśvara
Nandikeśvarabhairava
Nandin
Nandirudra
Nandīśvara
Nā̊ŋhaiθiia
Nappin̲n̲ai

Nara
Naraka
Narakāsura
Nāraṇaṉ
Narāśaṃsa
Narasiṃha
Nārasimhī
Nārāyaṇa
Nārāyaṇī
Našatiya
Našatiya-nna
Nāsatya
Naṭakeśavabhairava
Naṭarāja
Naṭeśa
Nāthjī
Navātmabhairava
Navātman
Navnitpriyājī
Nāyiṉācāriyaṉ
Neṭiyōṉ
Netrabhaṭṭāraka
Nidrā
Nikalaṅk
Nikumbha
Nīlā
Nīla Ṣaṣṭhī
Nīḷā
Nīlagrīva
Nīlakaṇṭha
Nīlalohita
Nīlasarasvatī
Nīlātā
Nīḷātevī
Nimi
Nin-ti
Nirañjana
Nirṛti
Nirṛtidevī
Niśeśvarī
Niṣkalasvacchanda
Niśumbha
Nityākālī
Nṛsiṃha
Nṛvarāha
Nyagrodhaśāyin
Nyāy kā Devtā

Oēšo
Olābībī

Pābūjī
Padmā
Padma
Padmājā
Padmanābha
Padmasvāmin
Padmāvatī
Padmāvatī Tāyār
Padminī
Pampā
Pan
Pañcajana
Pāñcālī
Pañcaśikha
Pāṇḍurang
Paṅkajā
Pāpanāśinī
Pāpāntakāriṇī
Pāpayakṣman
Parā
Parabrahmā
Paramaśiva
Paramātmā
Parameśvar
Parameśvara
Parameśvarī
Parāparā
Paraśurāma
Parihāsakeśava
Pārijātahara
Parjanya
Pārmakaḻ
Parṇaśavarī
Parvata
Pārvatī
Paśu Yama
Paśupati
Paśupatināth
Paśupatinātha
Pātāi Ṣaṣṭhī
Pātāladhāraka
Pātālaśayana
Paṭitāṇṭātapatnī
Patitapābana
Pattiṉi
Pattirakālīyāmmaṉ
Pavanputra
Periya Pirāṭṭi
Perumāḷ
Pēycciyammaṉ
Phra Īsuan

Phra Khaphung
Phra Nārāi
Phra Phikkhanēt
Phra Phrām
Phra Phūm
Picuvaktrā
Pīlā
Pilch Budhi
Pilcu Haram
Piḷḷaiyār
Pinākin
Piṅgākṣī
Piṅgala
Piṅgalaka
Piśāci
Piśitāśā
Pitāmaha
Po Nagar
Pōlāli
Pōrmaṉṉaṉ
Poseidon
Pōtu Rāju
Pracaṇḍogrā
Pradhā
Pradhānapuruṣeśa
Pradyumna
Prahlāda
Prajāpati
Prajāpati Viśvarūpa
Prāṇa
Praṇavasvarūpiṇī
Prapañcikā
Pratibhā
Pratyakṣadaiva
Pravāhaṇa Jaivali
Pravareśvara
Pṛdāku
Premasvarūpiṇī
Pretāsana
Pretrāj
Pṛthivī
Pṛthivīmātṛ
Pṛthvī
Pṛthvīdhara
Pṛthvīmātṛ
Punarvasu
Puṇḍarīka
Pūrṇarājānaka
Pūrṇeśvarī
Puruṣa
Puruṣāmirukam
Puruṣamṛga
Puruṣottama
Puruṭāmirukam
Pūrvabhadrapadā
Pūrvaphalgunī
Pūrvāṣāḍhā
Pūṣan
Puṣkara
Puṣpadanta
Puṣpadantarājabhairava
Puṣya
Pūtanā

Rādhā
Rādhākānta
Rādhāramaṇa
Rādhāvallabha
Rādhikā Rāṇī
Rāghava
Raghunāth
Raghupati
Raḥīm
Raḥmān
Rāhu
Rāhujit
Raireśvar
Rājaputra
Rājarājeśvara
Rājarājeśvarī
Rājayakṣman
Rājña
Rājñī
Rājyalakṣmī
Rākā
Rakhumāī
Rākṣasī
Raksel
Rakselin
Raktā
Raktabatī
Raktabīja
Raktākṣī
Rām
Rāma
Ramā
Rāma Dhanurdhara
Rāma Jāmadagnya
Rāmacandra
Rāmanātha
Rambhā
Rāmlāla

Raṇachoḍa
Raṇasvāmin
Raṇeśvara
Raṅganātha
Raṅganāyaki
Rantideva
Rasāṅkuśā
Rasāṅkuśī
Rasasaṃgrāhī
Rašnu
Rāṣṭrādhipati
Rati
Ratiśekhara
Rātri
Raudrī
Rāvaleśa
Rāvalnāth
Rāvaṇa
Rāvaṇānugraha
Ravi
Ṛbhu
Ṛddhi
Reṇukā
Revanta
Revatī
Ṛkṣakarṇī
Rodasī
Roga
Rohiṇī
Rohireśvar
Rohita
Rōkiṇi
Rongo Ruji
Rudra
Rudrapatnī
Rukmiṇī
Ruru
Rurujit

Śabda
Saccidānandarūpin
Saccikā
Śacī
Śacīpati
Sadāśiva
Sadāviṣṇu
Sadguru
Sadgurū
Sadyojāta
Sāgara
Śailaputrī
Śailūṣā
Sakalasvacchanda
Śākambharī
Sakka
Śakra
Śakti
Śaktyātman
Śakuntalā
Śalihotra
Saman
Samarasvāmin
Sāmba
Śambara
Śambhu
Saṃdhīśvara
Saṃdhyā
Saṃkarṣaṇa I
Saṃkarṣaṇa II
Saṃvid
Śanaiścara
Sanamahee
Sanatsujāta
Śāṇḍilī
Śāṇḍilya
Saṅgamēśvara
Śani
Śanideva
Śaṅkara
Śaṅkareśvara
Śaṅkarī
Saṅkaṭā
Ṣaṇmukha
Śāntādurgā
Santāna Gopāla
Śāntātman
Santoṣi Mā
Saptakotīśvara
Saptakotīśvarī
Sārā
Śarabha
Sarabkāl
Śāradā
Saramā
Saramā Devaśunī
Saraṇyū
Sārasvata
Sarasvatī
Śārikā
Sarojā
Sarojinī
Sārparājñī

Subrahmaṇya
Sugrīva
Sūkarā
Śukra
Sūkṣma
Sumanā
Śumbha
Sunda
Sundarī
Suparṇī
Surabhī
Sūrapadma
Śūrpanakhā
Sūrya
Sūryavarcas
Suśīlā
Śuṣṇa
Suvarṇā
Suvarṇākarṣaṇabhairava
Svacchandabhairava
Svāhā
Svaja
Svāminī
Svarbhānu
Svasthānī
Svāti
Svayaṃ Bhagavān
Śveta
Śyāma
Śyāmā
Śyāmākālī
Śyāmalā
Śyāmasundara

Takṣaka
Takṣaka Vaiśāleya
Taleju
Taleju Bhavānī
Tālujihvikā
Tāmasī
Tamilttāy
Taṇṭapāṇi
Taṇṭāyutapāṇi
Tanūnapāt
Tāpanī
Tārā
Tāraka
Tārakanātha
Taralā
Taṭciṇāmūrtti
Tatpuruṣa
Tāyār
Tejājī
Tejīśa
Tejīśa Rudra
Tejojī
Tevayāṉai
Thakur
Thakur Deo
Ṭhākur
Ṭhākura
Thakuranī
Tilottamā
Tiraścirāji
Tiru
Tirumakaḷ
Tirumāl
Tiruveṅgalanātha
Tiruveṅkaṭamuṭaiyāṉ
Tiruveṅkaṭattāṉ
Tookay
Toṣalā
Trailokyaḍāmarā
Tribhuvanasvāmin
Tribhuvaneśvarī
Trijaṭā
Trilocana
Trinetra
Tripurā
Tripurabhairavī
Tripurāntaka
Tripurasundarī
Tripureśvara
Trita
Trivikrama
Tuhan Yang Maha Ésa
Tulasī
Tuḷjāpur Bhavānī
Tulsī
Tulsībīr
Tumburu
Tuṅgeśvara
Tuṟkai
Turuṣkarājānaka
Tvaṣṭṛ

Uccaiḥśravas
Ugra
Ugratārā
Ugreśvara
Ulūpī
Umā

Umā Haimavatī
Umāpati
Ūmasahitaśiva
Unmanī
Upasunda
Upendra
Upulvan
Uruna-šil
Ušah
Uṣas
Utpalasvāmin
Uttarabhadrapadā
Uttaraphalgunī
Uttarāṣāḍhā

Vāc
Vaḍabāmukhī
Vadakkunnāthan
Vaḍavāvaktra
Vāgbhaveśvarī
Vāgdevī
Vāgīśī Kālī
Vāgīśvara
Vāgīśvarī
Vāhigurū
Vahni
Vaidyanātha
Vaiiu
Vaikharī
Vaikuṇṭha
Vaikuṇṭhanātha
Vairāgya
Vairavar
Vairocana
Vairochana
Vaiṣṇavī
Vaiṣṇo Devī
Vaiśravaṇa
Vaiśvānara
Vaitaraṇī
Vajrabhairava
Vajradhara
Vajrahastā
Vajrayoginī
Vākdevī
Vākpati
Vakra
Vālā
Vāliyōn
Vaḷḷī
Vāmā
Vāmadeva
Vāmana
Vāmanī
Vāmeśvarī
Vanadevī
Vanadurgā
Vanaspati
Vāṇī
Vañjuḷavaḷḷi
Varada
Varadarāja
Varāha
Vārāhī
Varalakṣmī
Varapradā
Vareśvara
Varṇinī
Varuṇa
Varuṇaṉ
Vasanta
Vaṣaṭ
Vaṣaṭkāra
Vasu Uparicara
Vāsudeva
Vasudhārā
Vāsukī
Vasundharā
Vāta
Vaṭivēlaṉ
Vatsa
Vaṭuka
Vāyu
Vayuš
Vāyusūnu
Vāyuvegā
Vedavid
Vēl
Veṅkaṭacalapati
Veṅkaṭarāma
Veṅkaṭeśvara
Veṇugopāla
Vərəthragna
Vərəthrajan
Vetāḷ
Vibhīṣaṇa
Vibhu
Vidhātṛ
Vidyā
Vidyādhideva
Vidyālakṣmī
Vidyāvidyeśvarī

Vidyujjihvā
Vihaṅgama
Vijayā
Vijayantikā
Vikala
Vikrameśvara
Vikṛtā
Vikṛtānanā
Vilohita
Vimalā
Vīṇādhārī
Vīṇāpāṇī
Vinatā
Vināyaka
Vināyakaṉ
Vindhyavāsinī
Vipulā
Vipulakeśava
Vīrabhadra
Vīrabhairava
Virādha
Virāj
Virajā
Vīralakṣmī
Vīrāmmakālī
Virocana
Virūpākṣa
Viśākha
Viśālaka
Viśālākṣī
Viṣṇu
Viṣṇu Anantaśāyin
Viṣṇu Narendrasvāmin
Viṣṇu Raṇārambhasvāmin
Viṣṇu Vaikuṇṭha
Viśva
Viśvā
Viśvakarma
Viśvakarman
Viśvaksena
Viṣvaksena
Viśvanāth
Viśvanātha
Viśvarādhya
Viśvarūpa
Viśvarūpā
Viśvarūpikā
Viśvāvasu
Viśveśvara
Viṭaiyūrti
Vitastā
Vitatha
Viṭhāī
Viṭhobā
Viṭṭhal
Viṭṭhala
Viṭṭhalanāth
Viṭṭhalanātha
Vivasvant
Vivasvant Mārtāṇḍa
Vivasvat
Vṛka
Vṛndā
Vṛndāvaneśvarī
Vṛṣabhānu
Vṛṣabhānunandinī
Vṛṣabhārūḍha
Vṛṣākapi
Vṛtra
Vṛtraghnī
Vṛtrahan
Vyādhibhakṣa
Vyāpin

Wēšparkar

Yaidyanātha
Yajña Prājāpatya
Yājñasenī
Yākaceṉi
Yakṣi
Yama
Yama Vaivasvata
Yamajihvā
Yamarāja
Yamarājan
Yamī
Yamī Vaivasvatī
Yaśodā
Yavakrī
Yima
Yimak
Yogamāyā
Yoganidrā
Yogeśvara
Yogeśvarī

Zeus

Groups of Gods, Goddesses, and Powers

ādityas
ahuras
aməša spəṇtas
apsarās
apsarases
arhants
arhats
asārās
aṣṭabhairavas
aṣṭadikpālas
aṣṭalakṣmīs
aṣṭamātṛkās
aṣṭavināyaks
asuras
atrins
āvaraṇadevatās
avatārs
avatāras
āyudhapuruṣas

baladevas
bālagrahas
bangas
bhaginīs
bhaṭṭijīs
bhavanis
bhomiyās
bhūcarīs
bhūts
bhūtas
bhūtanāthas
bhūtapretas
bhuteśvaras
bhūtprets
bhuvanadevatās
bodhisattvas
bogas
bongas
brahms
brahmarākṣasas
brahmarṣis
buddhas
buḍis
burus
buru bongas
būtas

caturvyūhas
churails
curins

dains
daiteyas
daityas
daivas
daivats
daivyavrātyas
ḍākans
ḍākinīs
dakṣakanyās
dānavas
dārudevatās
dāsas
dasyus
dessaulis
devas
devagaṇas
devakulas
devakulikas
devalogs
devapatnīs
devatās
devīs
dewa dewas
dhyānibodhisattvas
dhyānībuddhas
dihs
dikcarīs
dikpālas
dvārapālas
dvārpālas

firištas

gaṇas
gaṇapas
gandharvas
gaṇeśvaras
ghāṇṭikayakṣas
gocarīs
gossaiyans
grahas
grahaṇīs

grahīs
grāmadevatās
grāmadevīs
grāmdevtās
grāmpuruṣas
guhyakas
guṇāvatāras

hārdāvatāras

iṣṭadaivats
iṣṭadevatās
iṣṭadevīs
iṣṭatēvams

jakhaiyās
jakkhas
jakkhiṇīs
jakkus
jakkulus
jhūnjhārjīs
jinas
jinns
jogīṇīs
jūñjhunos

kabandas
kālakeyas
kāmois
kaṉṉimārs
karam rānīs
kāval taivams
khecarīs
khuntkattidars
kiṃnaras
kiṃnarīs
kiṃpuruṣas
kṛttikās
kṣetrapālas
kula taivams
kuladevas
kuladevatās
kuladevīs
kulajs
kulanāgas
kuldevs
kuldevatās
kuldevīs
kulpuruṣas
kumāras
kuttichātans

leyaks
līlāvatāras
lokapālas

mahārṣis
mahāvidyās
māmās
mandehas
mānuṣibuddhas
maris
maruts
maśāns
mātṛs
mātṛkās
māvalayās
māyās
monreko turuikos

nāgas
nāgīs
nāginīs
nats
navadurgās
navagrahas
navapatrikās
nityās
nityasūris

pañcakṛṣṇas
pañcāyatanas
paramarṣis
parīs
parivāradevatās
phīs
piśācas
pisācus
pīṭheśvarīs
pitṛs
pracetases
prādurbhāvas
prajāpatis
pramathas
prativāsudevas
pratyaṅgirās
prets
pretas
pū yā tā yāis
pūrṇāvatāras

rājandaivas
rājaputras

rakṣases
rākṣasas
rākṣasīs
raṅgāvataraṇas
rāṣṭradevatās
rāṣṭradevīs
ṛṣis
rudras
rudrabhedas
rudrakannikes

sādhyas
sagasjīs
sagasjī baojīs
saguṇa avatārs
saptabhāunīs
saptamātṛs
saptamātṛkās
saptarṣis
śāsanadevatās
sātī āsarās
siddhavidyās
śiṣṇadevas
śivabhedas
skandagrahas
sthānayoginīs
śucis
sūris
śuṣṇas

tathāgatas
teyvams
thēwadās
tīrthaṅkaras

vājas
vālakhilyas
vaṃśadevīs
vāṇamantaras
vasus
vāsudevas
vetālas
vidyādevīs
vidyādharas
vidyeśvaras
vigraheśvaras
vināyakas
viśvadevas
viśvasṛjs
viśvedevas
vodils
vouns
vrātyas
vyantaras
vyūhas
vyūhāntaras
yakkhas
yakkhinīs
yakṣas
yakṣīs
yakṣiṇīs
yātus
yazatas
yogeśvarīs
yoginīs
yugadevīs
yuganāthas
yugāvatāras

zolmis

Religious and/or Philosophical Traditions (pre-1900)

Ādinātha Sampradāya
Acintyabhedābheda
Ādivaiṣṇava
Advait Brahm
Advaita Vedānta
Āgamasiddhānta
Aghorī
Āī Panth
Ājīvika
Akali Dal
Alakh Panth
Āḻvār
Anādivaiṣṇava
Ānanda
Anuttarāmnāya
Araṇya
Āśrama
Aṭal
Atibāḍi Sampradāya
Atimārga
Aulūkya
Āvāhan
Avāntaravaiṣṇava

Baṛā Pañcāyatī Udāsī
Bārah Bhāī Dāriyā
Bārah Panth
Bārhaspatya
Basantīya
Bauddha
Bāul
Bāvrī
Bene Israel
Bhāgavata
Bhāmatī
Bhāratī
Bhartṛhari Bairāg Panth
Bhaṭmārg
Bhedābheda
Bhīm log
Bhogavāra
Bhurivāra
Bhūtavāda
Bihārījī kā Bagicā
Bījā Mārg
Bisṇoī
Brahmamīmāṃsā

Caitanya Sampradāya
Caityaka
Cao Dai Buddhism
Caraṇdāsī
Cārvāka
Chaudah Bhāī Mahātyāgī
Choṭā Pañcāyatī Udāsī
Cīnācāra
Čištī
Cittāntacaivam

Dādūpanth
Dakṣiṇācāra
Dakṣiṇagharāmnāya
Dakṣiṇāmnāya
Darśanī
Dāsakūṭa Sampradāya
Daśanāmī
Datta Sampradāya
Dawudī Būrah
Devīnaya
Dharmanāth Panth
Dhir Maliā
Digambara
Dīn-i-Ilahī
Dvaita Vedānta
Dvaitādvaita Vedānta

Ek Nām Śaran Dharm
Ekānta

Fakir
Firdawsī

Gaṇapatitantra
Gāṇapatya
Gaṅganāth Panth
Gauḍīya Vaiṣṇavism
Giri
Gorakhnāthpanth
Gūdaḍ Panth

Haridāsa Sampradāya
Haridāsī Sampradāya
Haṭha Yoga
Hīnayāna
Hoa Hao

Icchāntika
Ismāʿīlī

Jalālī
Jasnāthī Panth
Jūnā
Junaydī

Kabīrpanthī
Kālāmukha
Kālīkula
Kāmarāja Sampradāya
Kāmarḍiyā Panth
Kāñchlī Panth
Kānphaṭā
Kāpālika
Kāpḍia
Karma Mīmāṃsā
Karmamīmāṃsā
Kartābhajā
Kashmir Śaivism
Kāśmīravaibhāṣika
Kāṭhiya
Kaula
Kāulacārī
Kaumāra
Khūja Ismā'īlī
Kirātadharma
Krama
Kubrawī
Kūkā
Kulamārga
Kuṇḍā Panth

Lākula
Lāl Panth
Lāldāsī Sampradāy
Liṅgāyat
Lokāyata

Madāri
Madhva Gaureśvara Sampradāya
Mādhva Sampradāya
Madhyamaka
Mahānaya
Mahānubhāv
Mahāpanth
Mahārtha
Mahāsāṅghika
Mahāvrata
Mahāyāna
Mahdawī
Mahīśāsaka
Mailā Panth
Maithila Kaul
Mantramārga
Mantrasiddhānta
Mantrayāna
Maṭhāmnāya
Maṭṭamayūra
Mazhabi
Mīmāṃsā
Mīnā
Mūlasarvāstivāda
Mundiyā
Musalī

Nāmasiddhānta
Nāmdhārī
Nānakpanth
Nānaksar
Nandinātha Sampradāya
Naqšbandī
Nāth Sampradāya
Nāthpanth
Navyanyāya
Nayā Pañcāyatī Udāsī Akhāṛā
Nāyaṉār
Nazarani
Nihaṅg
Nijārpanthī
Nimbārka Sampradāya
Nirañjanī
Nirmal Pañcāyatī
Nirmalā
Nirmohī
Nirvāṇī
Niẓāmī
Nizār Panth
Nizārī Ismā'īlī
Nyāya

Pāñcakālika
Pāñcarātra
Pañcārtha
Parākrama
Parama Advaita
Parsi
Pārvata
Paścimāmnāya
Pāśupata
Pātañjala Yoga

Pāvpanth
Phakīr
Phūl Sāhib
Prabhākara
Prakāśa
Pramāṇa
Prāṇnāthī
Pratyabhijñā
Purī
Pūrvakaula
Pūrvamīmāṃsā
Pūrvāmnāya
Puṣṭimārg

Qādirī

Rādhāvallabh Nirmohī
Rādhāvallabha Sampradāya
Rāja Yoga
Rājagirika
Rām Digambar
Rām Rāiyā
Rāmānandī
Rāmāvat
Rāmdāsī
Rāmnāthī
Rāmrasik Sampradāya
Rāmsnehī Sampradāya
Raseśvara
Rāval Panth
Ravidāsī
Rawšānī
Rifāʿī
Rišī

Ṣābirī
Ṣaḍanvayaśāmbhava
Sādh
Sadhāru
Sāgarīya
Sahajiyā
Śāhpurā Rāmsnehī Sampradāy
Śaiva Siddhānta
Śākta Vedānta
Samayamata
Śāmbhava
Saṃhitāpāñcarātra
Sāṃkarṣaṇapāñcarātra
Sāṃkhya
Sāṃkhyayoga

Sanakādi Sampradāya
Sant
Sant Mat
Santoṣī
Sārasvatī
Śārīrakamīmāṃsā
Sarvāstivāda
Satnāmī
Šaṭṭarī
Sāttvata
Sātvata
Satyanāth Panth
Saura
Sautrāntika
Seśvarasāṃkhya
Sevāpanth
Šīʿa
Siddha
Siddhānta
Sipāsī
Śivaśāsana
Smārta
Somasiddhānta
Spanda
Śramaṇa
Śrī Sampradāya
Śrīkula
Śrīvaiṣṇavism
Śrīvidyā
Śuddhādvaita Brahmavāda-Nirguṇa-Puṣṭibhakti Mārg
Śuddhādvaita Vedānta
Suhrawardī
Śuk Sampradāy
Sunni
Sūri
Sūta
Svābhāvika
Svarūpa
Śvetāmbara
Śyām Digambar

Tantrāntarasiddhānta
Tantrasiddhānta
Tapasī Śākhā
Teṉkalai
Terah Bhāī Tyāgī
Theravāda
Tīrtha
Trika

Trika Viśiṣṭādvaita
Trikajātīya

Ubhaya Vedānta
Udāsī
Udāsīna Karsiṇī
Ujjainīya
Ūrdhvāmnāya
Uttara Kaula
Uttaramīmāṃsā
Uttarāmnāya

Vaibhāṣika
Vaibhāṣika
Vaikhānasa
Vaimala
Vaiśeṣika
Vaitikacaivam
Vajrayāna
Vallabha Sampradāya
Vāmācāra
Vāna
Vārkarī Sampradāy
Vaśapāśupata
Vaṭakalai
Vedānta
Vīraśaiva
Vīravrata
Viśiṣṭādvaita Vedānta
Vivaraṇa Vedānta
Vyākaraṇa

Yamila
Yāpanīya
Yogācāra
Yoginī Kaula

Zen

Religious Specialists/Roles

abuddhi
ācārya
adhvaryu
ādi udāsī
adūraga
afsūngar
ali
ʿamil
anirodhaka
ārādhya
araiyar
araṇyaka
aravāṉi
arcaka
asambhakta
āsthānapaṇḍita
atīt
augharṛ
avadhūta(ka)
awliyā

bābā
bācabaṭh
baiga
baigā
bairāgī
bairāginī
bālāvadhuta
balian
bālsaṃnyāsin
bhagat
bhagavadīya
bhāgavata
bhāgavatar
bhaiśa bhaṭṭa
bhaktarālu
bhaṇḍārī
bhāṭ
bhaṭṭāra
bhaṭṭāraka
bhikkunī
bhikṣu
bhītariyā
bhopā
bhopī
bhopo
bhrūmadhyaga
bhujangga waisnawa
bhuva
bhuvī
bīr bābā
brahmacārin
brahmacariṇī
brahman
brāhmaṇa
brahmavādinī
braj videhī mahant
buā
buī
būva
buyya

cāmi
cāmiyāṭi
celā
cinnamēḷam
cīrā guru
cittar
copdār

dādī
daita
ḍāk
ḍaṅgariya
darvīš
deodhā
deśika
devala
devalaka
devṛṣī
dhāmī
dhāriṇī
dihuri
dīkṣāguru
dissari
dūraga
dūtī
dyaḥ waimha

ekārṣya

faqīr

gaṇaka
ganinnans
gāyen
ġāzī
gharbārī sādhu

ghāṭiyā
gondhalī
gor
gorava
goravamma
goravappa
gosāīṃ
gotipua
granthi
granthika
guṇī
guniar
guṇin
gur
guru
gurū
gurubhāī
gurumātā
gurusvāmi

ḫādim
ḥakīm
hijṛā
hotar
hotṛ
huṛdaṅg

ida mpu

jādūgar
jādūgarnī
jagadācārya
jagadguru
jāgariya
jan guru
jaṅgama
jaṭila
jhāḍ
jhāḍṇevālā
jhākrī
jhelā
jhuṇḍī mahant
jīvanmukti
jīvanvratī
jōgamma
jōgappa
jogī
jyotirvid
jyotiṣī

kañchavīra
kaṇṇi
kaṇṇisvāmi
kāryakartā
kathākār
kathāvācak
kāṭiyā
kāya cittar
khālsā mahant
kimīdin
kīrtankār
kulapurohita
kumāra

lohiyā

magi
mahāmaṇḍaleśvara
mahānāyaka mahanta
mahant
mahāpatra
mahārāja
mahārājaguru
mahārtvij
mahat
mahātma
mahātyāgī
maiba
maṇḍaleśvar
mantiravāti
mantravid
mārgaga
maṭādhipati
maṭhādhipati
maṭhdhārī
mati
mati deonra
mativah
māyin
mpu
mujavar
mukhiyā
mullā
muṇḍa
muni
muñjiyā
murīd
murmu
muršid

nabī
nācnevālā
naeke
nāgā

ñāṉa cittar
neṣṭṛ
nirodhaka

ojha
ojhā
ōtuvār

padanda
pahan
pamangku
pāṇaṉār
paṇḍā
paṇḍit
paṇḍitā
paṇḍitkavi
pangiwa
pañjikar
paṇṭāram
paramahaṃsa
paricāra
parihar
parikramāvāsī
parivrājaka
parivrājikā
parivrāṭ
parśād
pārṣad
pārṣadā
pāṭiṉi
pāṭṭiyār
pedanda
pedanda bauddha
pedanda siwa
periyasvāmi
phalāhārī
phām
phra mahārātchakhrū
pīr
puchvari
pūjaka
pūjāpaṇḍā
pujārī
pujāriṇī
purohita

quṭb

rāja
rājaguru
rājapurohita
rājguru
resi
rojā
ṛtvij

sabhāpati
saciv
sādak
sadguru
sādhu
sādhu mātā
sādhvī
sadyovadhū
šahīd
sāhir
sāmīpya
saṃkhyayoginī
saṃnyāsaguru
saṃnyāsī mahātma
saṃnyāsī
saṃnyāsin
saṃnyāsinī
sāṃvatsara
sāṃvatsarapāṭhin
sāṃvatsarika
saṅgha guru
śaṅkarācārya
sanmārga cittar
santkavi
śaraṇa
sāraṅga
sarūpa
sayana
šayḫ
sevaka
sevāvratī
siddha
siddha yogī
śikṣāguru
sisa
sisya
śiṣya
sokhā
śrī mahant
svāmī
svāmin

tantri
tapasī
tapasvī
tapasvin

tapasvinī
tēcikar
tēvaraṭiyār
ṭonhā
ṭonhī
turīyātīta
tyāgī
tyāginī

udgātṛ
upādhyāyānī
ūrdhvaretās tapasvī
ustād
uttarādhā

vaidya
vaikhānasa
vairāgī
vairāginī
vaṇ toṇṭaṉ
vānaprasthī
vēlaṉ
veḷicappāṭu
vimārgaga
vipra
vīra
virakta
viṟali
viṟalipāṭiṇi
vīravidyavantulu
vīrulu
vyās

yati
yātrī
yātumat
yoga
yogī
yogin
yogirāja

Poets, Teachers, Saints (pre-1900)

ʿAbd al-Ḥaqq
ʿAbd al-Karīm Kašmīrī
ʿAbd Allāh Ḫān Fīrūz-Jang
ʿAbd al-Qādir al-Jīlānī
ʿAbd al-Qādir Badāʾūnī
ʿAbd al-Quddus Gangohi
ʿAbd al-Quddus Ḥajjī Imdād Allāh
ʿAbd al-Raḥmān Čištī
Abhay Rām Dās
Abhayadattaśrī
Abhinada
Abhinava Pampa
Abhinavagupta
Abū al-Fażl ʿAllāmī
Acintanātha
Acyutānanda Dāsa
Acyutaprekṣa
Adhokṣaja
Adhyāpaka
Ādi Śaṅkara
Ādityadarśana
Advaitācārya
Ādyanātha
Agastyasiṃha
Aggavaṃsa
Aghoraśiva
Aghornāth
Agniveśa
Agradās
Aḥmad Šāh Bahmanī
Aḥmad Sirhindī
Aḥmad Zayn al-Dīn
Āī Mātā
Āījī
Ajita Keśakambalin
Āju Gosāīn
Ākā Adhyāru
Ākiñcanadāsa
Akkamahādēvi
Akṣapāda
Alaśiṅgabhaṭṭa
Āḷavantār
Al-Bīrūnī
Allama Prabhu
Amar Dās
Amarasiṃha
Amaru
Ambikānandanātha
Amitagati
Amṛta Devī
Amṛtānanda
Ānand Rām Muḫlis
Ānanda
Ānandabodhendra Sarasvatī
Ānandagiri
Ānandarāyamakhin
Ānandatīrtha
Ānandavana
Ānandavardhana
Anantānanda
Anantaśambhu
Anantdās
Ānāya Nāyaṉār
Aṅgad
Annamācārya
Annamayya
Aṇṇaṉ Svāmi
Āṇṭāl
Anūpgiri
Aparāditya
Aparājitānandanātha
Āpastamba
Appar
Appayya Dīkṣita
Arjan
Arṇasiṃha
Aromal Cēvakār
Ārtabhāga
Aruḷnanticivācārya
Aruṇakiri
Aruṇanti
Āryabhaṭa
Āryadeva
Asahāya
Aśudhir
Aśvaghoṣa
ʿAṭā ʾAllāh Rašīdī
Ativallabh
Ativaṇ Caṭakōpaṉ
Atrigupta
ʿAṭṭār
Āulcāṅd
Aupadhenava
Aupajaṅghani
Aurabhra
Auvaiyār
Avadhūta
Avalokita

Aviddhakarṇa
Avvaiyār
Āyyāval

Baḍa Khān Gājī
Bādarāyaṇa
Baḍu Caṇḍīdās
Bahā' al-Dīn Šaṭṭār
Bahiṇābāī
Bahman Qay Qobād Sanjāna
Bāhubala
Bāhubali
Bāidevbās
Baijnāth
Baijū Bāvrā
Bakhśū
Baladeva Vidyābhūṣana
Bālaka
Bālānanda
Bālarūpa
Bālgundāī
Bālkṛṣṇa Alī
Ballāla
Ballālasena
Bālnāth
Balrām Dās
Bammera Pōtana
Bāṇa
Bāṇabhaṭṭa
Bānārsīdās
Baṅkā
Banvārīdās
Basava
Baudhāyana
Bāvrī Sāhibā
Bāyāṇ Sā
Bāyāzīd Anṣārī
Bechu Bīr
Bedil
Beṇimādhavdās
Bhadrabāhu
Bhadrācalam Rāmadās
Bhagat Gir
Bhagavānprasād Rūpkalā
Bhagavat Mudita
Bhāgavatācārya Devadhara
Bhāgavatotpala
Bhagīratha Ṭhakkura
Bhagūdās Dhanautī
Bhagvāndās
Bhaiṣajyaguru
Bhāllavins
Bhāmaha
Bhāṇ
Bharata
Bharatamuni
Bhāravi
Bharthari
Bhartṛhari
Bhartṛprapañca
Bhartṛyajña
Bhāruci
Bhāsa
Bhāsarvajña
Bhāskara I
Bhāskara II
Bhāskara III
Bhāskarakaṇṭha
Bhāskararāya
Bhāsurānandanātha
Bhaṭobās
Bhaṭṭa Bhāskara
Bhaṭṭa Jayanta
Bhaṭṭa Lollaṭā
Bhaṭṭa Nārāyaṇa
Bhaṭṭa Nārāyaṇakaṇṭha
Bhaṭṭa Rāmakaṇṭha
Bhaṭṭa Śivottama
Bhaṭṭa Vādīndra
Bhaṭṭamalla
Bhaṭṭanāyaka
Bhaṭṭar
Bhaṭṭāraka Ānanda
Bhaṭṭāraka Sundara
Bhaṭṭi
Bhaṭṭoj Dikṣita
Bhāvabhūti
Bhavadāsa
Bhavadeva
Bhāvamiśra
Bhāvānanda
Bhavanātha
Bhavāṇi Prasāda Kara
Bhavasvāmin
Bhāviveka
Bhāvivikta
Bhavya
Bheḍa
Bhela
Bheḷa
Bhikhārīdās
Bhīmakavi

Bhīmasoma
Bhīmasvāmī Śirgāvkar
Bhoja
Bhojadeva
Bhojarāja
Bihārīlāl
Bihārinīdās
Bilās Khān
Bilhaṇa
Bīrbhan
Bodhāyana
Bodhendra
Brahmagupta
Brāhmaṇabala
Brahmānanda
Brahmānandagiri
Brahmaśambhu
Brahmaśiva
Brahmavidyādhvarīndra
Braj Jīvana
Bṛhaspati
Bu ston Rin chen grub
Buddha
Buddhabhadra
Buddhaghoṣa
Buddhamitra
Buḍḍhan
Buddhapāla
Bulī Šāh
Bulle Śāh

Cācā Vṛndābandās
Caitanya
Caitanyanātha
Cākkiyar
Cakradhar
Cakrapāṇī
Cakrapāṇidatta
Cāmarasa
Campantar
Cāṇakya
Caṇḍeśvara
Caṇḍīdāsa
Candradatta
Candrakīrti
Candramati
Candrānanda
Cāṅgdev Rāuḷ
Cangranghācah
Cannabasava
Cannabasavānka
Caṇṭēcuraṉ
Caṇṭīcaṉ
Caraka
Caraṇdās
Carpaṭ
Carpaṭi
Caṭakōpaṉ
Cattiyār
Caturbhuj al-Hind
Caturbhuj Miśra
Caturbhujdās
Caturcintāmaṇi
Caturdās
Cauraṅgīnāth
Cāvuṇḍarāya
Cēkkiḻār
Cennabasava
Cennasadāśivayogin
Cetandās
Chavillākara
Cidānanda
Cidvilāsa
Citsukha
Citsvāmi
Civavākkiyar
Cokhāmeḷā
Cuntarar

Dādū Dayāl
Daityāri Ṭhākura
Ḍalhaṇa
Dāmodar Svāmī
Dāmodara
Dāmodara Dās
Dāmodaradāsa Harsānī
Daṇḍin
Daṇḍin Kāñci
Danghyang Nirartha
Dariyāvjī
Dāsānidās
Dāsimaiah
Dāsopant
Dattila
Dayā Bāī
Dayā Nāth
Devācāraja
Devācārya
Devakīnandana Dāsa
Devanandin

Devaṇṇabhaṭṭa
Devapāla
Dēvara Dāsimayya
Devarāja
Devaśarman
Devasvāmin
Dhairyarāśi
Dhāmeśvara
Dhanā
Dharamnāth
Dhareśvara
Dharmadās Darveś
Dharmakīrti
Dharmapāla
Dharmarāja
Dharmaśiva
Dharmasvāmin
Dharmdās
Dharmottara
Dhir Mal
Dholan Satī
Dhoyī
Dhruvadās
Dhruvdās
Dhūrjaṭi
Dhyānacandra Gosvāmī
Dignāga
Dñyāndev
Dñyāneśvar
Ḍohara Kakkayya
Dṛḍhabala
Duddu
Dūdh Pīr
Dulālcānda
Durvekamiśra

Ekānta Rāmayya
Ekāyana Ojaka
Ekāyanācārya Nārāyaṇagarbha
Eknāth
Ekorāmārādhya
Ellappa Nāvalar
E<u>l</u>uttacchan

Fakīrdās
Fānī
Farīd
Fāṭimah
Faxian
Fażl ʿAbbās Mūsā ʿĀšiqān
Fażl Allāh

Gadādhar Bhaṭṭ
Gāgābhaṭṭa
Gahinīnāth
Gaṇanātar
Gaṇapati Dēva
Gaṅgādhara
Gaṅgeśa
Gārgī
Garībdās
Garuḍavāhana
Gauḍapāda
Gaura
Gaurāṅga
Gau<u>r</u>anna
Gaurasundara
Gaurībāī
Gauridāsa
Gaurīkāntanta
Gautama I
Gautama II
Gautama III
Gāvbā
Ġawṯ ʿAlī Šāh Qalandar
Ġawwāṣī
Ġāzī Miyān
Gesūdarāz
Ghamaṇḍa
Ghanānanda
Ghāzī Bābā
Giridhara
Gīsūdirāz
Gobind Dās Kabirāj
Gobind Siṅgh
Gogā
Goindā
Gokulnāth
Gōmaṭa
Gondā
Gōpāl
Gopāl Nāik
Gopāla Bhaṭṭa
Gopāla Bhañja
Gopālaka Rājāna
Gopāldās
Gopīcand
Gopīnāth Kavirāj
Gopīnāth
Gopurarakṣita
Gorā
Gorakhnāth
Gorākṣa

Gosāi Gopāl
Gotama
Govardhana
Govindadās
Govinda Bhaṭṭa
Govindabhagavatpāda
Govindacandra
Govindācārya
Govindapāda
Govindaprabhu
Govindarāja
Govindasvāmī I
Govindasvāmī II
Govindgiri
Gūga Pīr
Guggā Pīr
Gulābrām
Gulāl
Gūḷūra Siddhavīraṇāryaru
Gummaḷāpurada Siddhaliṅgadēvaru
Guṇāḍhya
Guṇamati
Guṇarāja Khān
Guṇaratna
Guṇḍam Rāuḷ
Gurdās
Gurditā
Guru Besnao
Gurudas Phakir
Gurukkal Govindankutty Nayar
Gyān Nāth Saʿādatmand

Ḥājj Sulṭān Thāneswarī
Ḥājji Ratan
Ḥakīm Ġulām ʿAlī
Halageya Dēvaru
Hamdānī
Ḥamīd al-Dīn Nagawrī
Haṃsamiṭṭhu
Hanumaddās
Hāpojī
Haradatta
Harakiṅkara
Hardās
Hargobind
Haribhadra
Haridās I
Haridās II
Harideva
Harihara
Harirām Vyās
Harirāmdās
Harirāya
Hariṣeṇa
Harīśvara
Hārīta I
Hārīta II
Harivarman
Harivyās
Hariyānanda
Harṣadatta
Harṣakīrti
Hasan
Hastāmalaka
Hastiruci
Hāure
Ḥaydar Šayḫ
Ḥażrat ʿAbbās
Heddase Hariharaśarman
Helārāja
Heliodorus
Hemacandra
Hemāḍpant
Hemādri
Himmat Bahādur
Hīr
Hiraṇyadāma
Hiraṇyakeśin
Hit Harivaṃś
Hit Rūplāl
Hṛdayaśiva
Hṛdayrām
Hṛṣikeśa
Hṛṣikeśatīrtha

Ibn ʿArabī
Ibn Baṭṭūṭa
Icaiñāniyār
Iḷaṅkō Aṭikaḷ
Iḷattu Pūtandēvaṉār
Imām Ḥusayn
Iṟaiyaṉār
Irāmatēvar
ʿIsā Ḫān
Īśānaśiva
Īśvara Puri
Īśvarakṛṣṇa
Īśvarasena

Jadrūp
Jagaddhara
Jagadguru

Jagadindu
Jagadīśa Bhaṭṭācārya
Jagannāth
Jagannātha Dās
Jagannātha Paṇḍita
Jagjivandās
Jāhnavā
Jāhnavī
Jaimini
Jaitrām
Jalāl al-Dīn
Jalāl al-Dīn Muḥammed Rūmī
Jālandhari
Jālandharnāth
Jambheśvara
Jāmbhojī
Jāmī
Janābāī
Janārdan
Jangopāl
Jasnāth
Jasorāja
Jaṭādhara
Jatūkarṇa
Jaya
Jayadeva
Jayadratha
Jayānanda
Jayantabhaṭṭa
Jayarāma Śeṣa
Jayarāśi
Jayaratha
Jāyasī
Jayatīrtha
Jaymal
Jejjaṭa
Jījī Devī
Jīmūtavāhana
Jina
Jinadāsa
Jinasena
Jitendriya
Jīva Gosvāmī
Jīvaka
Jīvanātha
Jizang
Jñān Dās
Jñānaprakāśa
Jñānarāja
Jñānaśiva
Jñānaśrī
Jñāndev
Jñāneśvar
Jonarāja
Jujhar Siṅgh
Jvālendra
Jyotirīśvara

Kabīr
Kacchapeśvaraśiva
Kacciyappa Civācāriar
Kaivalyāśrama
Kakuda Kātyāyana
Kalhaṇa
Kālī Mirjā
Kālīdāsa
Kallaṭa
Kallinātha
Kalyāṇamalla
Kalyāṇavarman
Kāmadeva
Kamalākānta Bhaṭṭācārya
Kamalākara Bhaṭṭa
Kāmandaki
Kāmarūpeśa
Kambalāśvatara
Kampaṉ
Kaṇabhakṣa
Kaṇabhuj
Kaṇacara
Kaṇāda
Kanakadāsa
Kānhopātrā
Kaṇṇappan
Kapilar
Karaikkālammaiyār
Karasthaḷa Basavideva
Karavīrya
Karmabāī
Karmameḷā
Karṇakagomin
Kartā Mā
Kartṛ
Kāśīnātha
Kāśīrām Dās
Kaśyapa
Kāśyapa Basavarasa
Kātya
Kātyāyana
Kauṇḍinya
Kauṭilya
Kautsa

Kavi Keśav
Kavi Vallabha
Kavi Vijaya Gupta
Kavikaṅkaṇa
Kavikarṇapūra
Kavīndra
Kavirāja
Kavīśvar
Keñcavīraṇṇodeyaru
Keśakambala
Keśava Bhaṭṭa
Keśava Bhāratī
Keśava Nyāyabhūṣaṇa
Keśava Vyās
Keśavdās
Keśavsvāmī
Kesobās
Ketakādāsa
Kevalarāma
Kevalrām
Kheṭabāla
Khiḍiyā Cānaṇ
Kinnara Brahmayya
Kiśorīdās
Kōcceṅkaṭ Cōḻār
Kokkoka
Kokokka
Kōtai
Koṭali Pa
Koṭṭārakkara Tampurān
Kṛṣṇa Caitanya
Kṛṣṇacandra
Kṛṣṇadās Bābā
Kṛṣṇadās Payahāri
Kṛṣṇadās Payāhārī
Kṛṣṇadās
Kṛṣṇadāsa Adhikārī
Kṛṣṇadāsa Kavirāja
Kṛṣṇadvaipāyana Vyāsa
Kṛṣṇamiśra
Kṛṣṇānanda Āgamavāgīśa
Kṛṣṇaram Dās
Kṛṣṇasvāmī
Kṛttibās
Kṛttivāsa
Kṣārapāṇi
Kṣemarāja
Kṣemendra
Kṣetrajña
Kṣetrayya
Kṣīrasvāmin
Kuiji
Kulācārya Arṇasiṃha
Kulacēkarāḻvār
Kullūka
Kūḻukkuppāti
Kumarakuruparacuvāmikal
Kumāralāta
Kumārila
Kumbha
Kumbhandās
Kuṇika
Kuñjan Nambyār
Kūrattāḻvāṉ
Kureśa
Kuśika
Kutsa

Lagadha
Lāguḍi
Lakkamma
Lakkaṇa Daṇḍēśa
Lakṣmana
Lakṣmaṇa Rāṇade
Lakṣmaṇadeśika
Lakṣmaṇagupta
Lakṣmīdhara
Lakṣmīdharamiśra
Lakṣmīnātha
Lakulīśa
Lāl Beg
Lālan Šāh
Lāldās
Lālgiri
Lalitkiśorīdās
Lalitmohanīdās
Lalla
Lallā
Lalleśvarī
Lallūlāl
Lāparagopāla
Līla Śukha
Locanadāsa
Lokānanda
Lokanātha Gosvāmī
Loknāth Brahmacārī

Macchaghna
Macchandanātha
Madanagopāla
Mādhava I
Mādhava II

Mādhava III
Mādhava Kandali
Mādhava Mukunda
Mādhava Vidyāraṇya
Mādhavadeva
Mādhavakāra
Mādhavānandanātha
Mādhavayogin
Mādhavdās
Mādhavdās Jagannāthī
Mādhavendra
Mādhurācārya
Madhurāja
Madhusūdana Sarasvatī
Madhusūdana Vācaspati
Madhusūdanasarasvatī
Madhva
Mādhyandina
Maḍivāḷa Mācayya
Magha
Mahādeva Bhaṭṭa Vādīndra
Mahādēviyakka
Mahādēviyamma
Mahājajñu
Mahāvīra
Mahendranath Gupta
Maheśvarānanda
Maheśvarānandanātha
Maheśvaratīrtha
Mahīdhara
Mahīpati
Makkhali Gosāla
Mālādhara Basu
Mallaṇārya
Mallavādin
Mallikārjuna Paṇḍitārādhya
Mallināth Rathore
Mallinātha
Mālūkdās
Māmājī
Mānāṅka
Mānatuṅga
Maṉavācakaṅkaṭantār
Maṇavāḷamāmuṉi
Manaveda
Maṇḍanamiśra
Maṇibhadra
Maṇika Datta
Maṇikkavācakar
Māṇikrām Gāṅgulī
Maṇirāma
Mañjulāli Mañjarī
Maṅkaiyarkkaraciyar
Maṅkha
Manoda
Manohara
Manush Kali
Maṟaiñāṉacampantar
Māṟaṉ
Mardānā
Mardānfarrox
Maritōṇṭadārya
Maruḷnīkkiyār
Maskarin
Maskīndās
Mastnāth
Mataṅga
Mathurādās
Maticandra
Mātṛceṭa
Matsyendra
Maturaiccivappirakācar
Maturakavi
Maudgalya
Maulānā Dāūd
Mawlā ʿAlī
Māyāprasād Śāstri
Māyideva
Mayūra
Medhātithi
Melattur Veṅkaṭarāma Śāstri
Meykaṇṭār
Mīhān Sāhib
Mīān Sāhib
Mīnanāth
Mīr ʿAbd al-Wāhid Bilgrāmī
Mīr Muḥammad Hāšim Buḫārī
Mīr Sayyid Manjhan
Mīr Taqī Mīr
Mīra Dātār
Mīrabāī
Mirzā Asad Allāh Ḫān Ġālib
Mīrzā Ḫān ibn Faḫr
Mīrzā Maẓhar Jān-I Jānān
Miyān Mīr
Moggallāna
Mohandās Daftarī
Mokkhali Gosāla
Mōḷigeya Mārayya
Molla
Mpu Kanwa
Mpu Panuluh

Mpu Prapanca
Mpu Tantular
Mritunjaya
Muḥammad
Muḥammad Ġawṯ
Muḥammad Ghaus
Muḥammad Kabīr
Muḥammad Kāẓimī
Muḥammad Malik Jāyasī
Muḥammad Qāsim Firišta
Mu'īn al-Dīn Čištī
Muktā
Muktābāī
Mukteśvar
Mukundadeva
Mukundarāja
Mukundarāma Cakravartī
Mu'min 'Ārif
Muntajib al-Dīn
Murāribhaṭṭa
Murārigupta
Mūsan
Muttusvāmi Dīkṣitar

Nābhādās
Nāgabhaṭṭa
Nāgacandra
Nāgājī
Nāgānanda
Nāgaridās
Nāgārjuna I
Nāgārjuna II
Nāgdev
Nageśa
Nageśa Bhaṭṭa
Nāgoji Bhaṭṭa
Nāgrīdās
Nakkīrar
Nakulīśa
Nāma Yaśvant
Nāmdev
Namisādhu
Nammāḻvār
Nampi Āṇṭār Nampi
Nampi Ārūr
Ñāṉacampantar
Nānak
Ñāṉakūttār
Nandadās
Nandana
Nandapaṇḍita
Nandarāma
Nanddās
Nandi
Nandi Timmana
Nandikeśvara I
Nandikeśvara II
Nandīśvara
Nannaya
Nannechōda
Nantaṉār
Naracandrasūri
Narahari
Narahari Cakravartī
Narahari Sārkara
Naraharitīrtha
Narapati
Narasiṃha Mehtā
Narasiṃha Ṭhakkura
Nārāyaṇa Bhaṭṭa
Nārāyaṇa Paṇḍitācārya
Nārāyaṇa Tīrtha
Nārāyaṇakaṇṭha
Nārāyaṇī Satī
Narharī
Narottamadās
Narsi Mehtā
Nātamuṉi
Naṭanānanda
Nātaputta
Nāthamuni
Nehī Nāgaridās
Nemināth
Neryōsang Dhaval
Nigamajñāna I
Nigamajñāna II
Nigaṇṭha Nāthaputta
Nīlakaṇṭha
Nīlakaṇṭha Somayājin
Nīlakaṇṭhagaṇanātha
Nīlakaṇṭhaśivācārya
Nimbārka
Nimbarkasharana
Niṉṟacīr Neṭumāran
Nirmalā
Nirmalamaṇi
Niṣkriyānanda
Nityānanda Cakravartī
Nityānanda Ghoṣa
Nityānanda
Nityanāth
Nivṛtti

Niẓām al-Dīn Awliyā᾽
Niẓām al-Dīn Awrangābādī
Nṛsiṃha Sarasvatī
Nṛsiṃha Vājapeyin
Nūnd Riši
Nūr al-Dīn
Nūr Jahān

Ohrmazddād
Oṃkārnāth Ṭhākur
Oṭṭakkūttaṉ

Padmamihira
Padmanābha Miśra
Padmanābhatīrtha
Padmapāda
Padmaśrī
Padmatīrtha
Padmāvati
Pakṣadhara
Pakṣilasvāmin
Pakudha Kaccāyana
Pālkuriki Sōmanātha
Palṭū
Pampa
Pañcādhikaraṇa
Paṇḍitārādhya
Pāṇḍudāsa
Pāṇini
Pāñja
Pāṇṭipperumāl
Paramānand(a)dās
Paramaśrotriya Sadāśiva
Parameśvar
Parameśvara Dāsa
Paraśambhudeva
Parāśara I
Parāśara II
Parāśara Bhaṭṭar
Paraśarām
Paraśarāmbās
Parisā Bhāgavata
Paritoṣamiśra
Parśurāmdevācārya
Pārśva
Pārthasārathimiśra
Patañjali I
Patañjali II
Pauṣkalāvata
Periyāḻvār
Periyavāccaṉ Piḷḷai
Pēy
Phūl Pīr
Piḷḷai Lokācārya
Piṉpaḻakiya Perumāḷ Jīyar
Pīpā
Piṭāmbardās
Pōkar
Poṉmutiyār
Ponna
Poṉṉaṭikkaḷ Jīyar
Ponnayya
Poykai
Prabhākara
Prabhānandasūri
Prabhuliṅga
Prabodhānanda Sarasvati
Prabodhaśiva
Prahlāddās
Prakāśānanda Sarasvatī
Prakāśātman
Prakāśdās
Prāṇatoṣaṇa Vidyālaṅkāra
Praśastapāda
Pratāp Siṅgh Śāh
Prativādi Bhayaṅkaram Aṇṇan
Premadāsa
Priyādās
Pṛtham Dās
Pṛthi Cand
Pṛthuyaśas
Pūcalār
Pūjyapāda
Puṇḍarika Pūrī
Puṇḍarīkākṣa
Puṉitavati
Pūntānam Nambūtiri
Puṇyānanda
Pūraṇ Bhagat
Pūraṇa Kāśyapa
Purandara
Purandaradāsa
Pūrṇānanda
Puruṣottomācārya
Puṣkarasādi
Pūtam
Pyāre Satī

Qāżī Qādan

Rādhākṛṣṇa Gosvāmī
Rādhākṛṣṇadāsa
Rādhāvallabh Dās
Rāghavabhaṭṭa
Raghavadās
Rāghavānanda
Rāghavaṅka
Raghunandana
Raghunātha Śiromaṇi
Raghunātha Tarkavāgīśa
Raghunāthabhaṭṭa
Raghunāthadāsa
Raghupatibhaṭṭācārya
Ragunātha Śiromaṇi
Raidās
Rajab
Rājānaka Bhāskara
Rājānaka Bhullaka
Rājānaka Jayaratha
Rājānaka Śitikaṇṭha
Rājānaka Takṣakavarta
Rājaśekhara
Rājaśekharasūri
Rajjabdās
Rām Dās
Rām Dāss
Rām Pīr
Rāma Brāhmam
Rāma Pīr
Rāmacandra
Rāmacandrabudhendra
Rāmacandrācārya
Rāmadāsu
Rāmadeva
Rāmāi Paṇḍita
Rāmakṛṣṇa
Ramakṛṣṇa Dās
Rāmakṛṣṇānanda
Rāmāmātya
Rāmamiśra
Rāmānanda
Rāmānanda Rāya
Rāmānandī Jayatarāma
Rāmanātha
Rāmānātha Śrauti
Rāmānuja
Rāmarāya Prabhu
Rāmatīrthayati
Rāmbhadra
Rāmcaraṇjī
Rāmdās I
Rāmdās II
Rāmdās Cauhān
Rāmdev Pīr
Rāmeśvara
Rāmprasād Sen
Rāmrāy
Rāmšāh Pīr
Rāṇī Bhatiyānī
Rāṇī Piṅgalā
Rāṇī Satī
Rāñjha
Ranna
Raṇsi Tanvar Siṅgh
Rasikdās
Raskhān
Ratan
Ratannāth
Ratnagarbha Sārvabhauma
Ratnākara
Ratnaketu
Ratnakheṭa
Ratnākīrti
Ratnasambhava
Rāvaṇa I
Rāvaṇa II
Ravi
Ravidās
Raviṣeṇa
Rawšan ʿAlī Šāh
Reṇukācārya
Revaṇārādhya
Rucidattamiśra
Rudrāśiva
Rudrasoma
Rudraṭa
Rūmī
Rūpa Gosvāmī
Rūparāma
Rūpkalā
Rūpnāth

Śabara
Saccidānanda
Sadānanda
Sadāśivācārya
Sadgurusvāmī
Sadhāru
Sadnā Pīr
Sadyojyotis
Šāh ʿAbd al-Laṭīf
Šāh Ahl Allāh

Šāh ʿĀlam
Šāh Dātār
Šāh Muḥammad Farmūlī
Šāh Walī Allāh
Sahacari Sukh
Sahajānanda
Sāhib Kaul
Sāhib Rām
Sahjo Bāī
Sai Baba
Śākalya
Sākhī Sarvār
Sākina
Śaktisiddhānta
Śālikanāthamiśra
Salīm Čištī
Sāmarāja Dīkṣita
Samārth Rāmdās
Śāmbhavānanda
Śambhudatta
Śambhunātha
Sampādanasiddha Vīraṇaśivayogin
Šāṃs Pīr
Sanātana Gosvāmī
Sanātana Miśra
Saṅgat Sāhib
Saṅghabhadra
Saṅgharakṣa
Śaṅkara Bhagavatpāda
Śaṅkara Miśra
Śaṅkara
Śaṅkarabhaṭṭa
Śaṅkaradeva
Śaṅkaran Nampūtiri
Śaṅkarasvāmin
Śaṅkuka
Śāntarakṣita
Santdāsjī
Santokh Dās
Šaraf al-Dīn Manerī
Saraldās
Śaraṇa
Sāraṅgadeva
Sāraṅgadhara
Sāraṅgapāṇi
Sarasdās
Sarasvatī Gaṅgādhār
Sariputta
Śārṅgadeva
Śārṅgadhāra
Sārvabhauma Bhaṭṭācārya
Sarvajñanārāyaṇa
Sarvajñātman
Sarvānandanātha
Sarvātmaśambhu
Śarvavarmin
Śāstṛ
Satyapīr
Saudā
Sāvant Siṅgh
Sāvatā Māḷi
Sāyaṇa
Sayyid Salmān Čištī
Sayyid Sulṭān
Sen
Sen Nāī
Senā
Sevakjī
Shin Agga Thamadi
Shin Arahan
Siddharāma
Siddhārtha Gautama
Siddhasena Divākara
Siddhendra Yogi
Śiḍila Brahmadeva
Sikandar Šāh
Siṃhabhūpāla
Siṃhagupta
Siṃharāja
Siṃhasūri
Śiṃpī Nāma
Sītādevī
Śivāditya
Śivagaṇaprasādi Mahādēvayya
Śivāgrayogī Jñānaśivācārya
Śivānanda
Śivarāmasvamin
Śivasvāmin
Śivayogin
Śivayogīndra Jñānaśivācārya
Śivodāsa
Śivopadhyāya
Skandasvāmin
Somadeva
Somadevasūri
Somānanda
Somaśambhu
Somaśarman
Someśa
Somibhaṭṭāraka
Sonti Veṅkaṭaramanayya
Sopān

Sosale Revaṇārādhya
Soyrābāī
Srī Cand
Śrībhaṭṭa
Śrīdhar Vyās
Śrīdhara
Śrīdharasvāmin
Śrīkaṇṭha
Śrīkaṇṭhaśambhu
Śrīkumāra
Śrīnāth
Śrīnātha Cakravartī
Śrīnivāsa
Śrīnivāsa Dīkṣita
Śrīnivāsabhaṭṭa
Śrīpād Śrivallabh
Śrīpādarāya
Śrīpati
Śrīpati Paṇḍita
Śrīvāsa
Śrīvatsa
Śrīvijaya
Śṛṅgadeva
Śrotriya
Sthiramati
Subandhu
Sucaritamiśra
Sudarśanārya
Śūdraka
Śukadeva
Sukhā
Sukhānand
Śūlapāṇi
Sulaymān Mandawī
Sundarabhaṭṭa
Sundararāja
Sundardās Bhaṭnāgar
Sundardās the Elder
Sundardās the Younger
Surasurānanda
Sūratgopal
Sūrdās
Sureśvara
Sūrkiśor
Sursuranand
Sursurī
Suśruta
Suvarṇa
Svabhūrāma
Svacchandabhairava
Svarūpa Dāmodara
Svātmārāma
Śyāmānanda
Śyāmaśāstri

Tāj al-Dīn Ajodhanī
Takṣakavarta
Tānsen
Taqī
Tārābāī
Taraṇ Svāmī
Tarigoṇḍa Vēṅgamāmbā
Tāyumāṉavar
Tejasoma
Ṭhākura Haridās
Theghnāth
Tikkana
Tirukkatavūr Uyyavantatēvanāyaṉār
Tirukkōnēri Dāsyai
Tirukkurukaippirāṉ Piḷḷāṉ
Tirukōṭṭiyūrnampi
Tirumalācārya
Tirumaḻicai
Tirumaṅkai
Tirumūlar
Tirunāḷaippōvār
Tiruñānacampantar
Tirunāvukkaracar
Tirunīlakaṇṭayāḻpāṇar
Tiruppāṉ
Tiruttakkatevār
Tiruvaḷḷuvar
Tiruvaraṅkattu Amutanār
Tiruviyalūr Uyyavantatēvanāyaṉār
Tolkāppiyaṉ
Toṇṭaraṭippoṭi
Toṭaka
Trilocan
Trimallabhaṭṭa
Trivikrama
Tryambakaśambhu
Tryambakayajvan
Tukārām
Tulasīdāsa Lāljī
Tulsīdās
Tyāgarāja

U Aung Phyo
Udaidās
Udayana
Udbhaṭa
Uddhav

Uddyotakara
Uditācārya
Udyotanasūri
Ugrabhairava
Ulūka
Umākānta
Umānanda
Umānandanātha
Umāpaticiva
Umāpatidhara
Umāpatiśiva
Umaṟuppulavar
Umāsvāti
Umbeka
Upaniṣad Brahmam
Upaniṣadbrahmayogin
Upavarṣa
Utpaladeva
Uttama Dās
Uttuṅgaśiva
Uyyakkoṇṭār

Vācaspatimiśra
Vādibhairava
Vādirāja
Vāgbhaṭa
Vāgīśa
Vaidyanātha
Vaitaraṇa
Vākīcamuṉivar
Vākpatirāja
Vakreśvara Paṇḍita
Vaktraśambhu
Vāladhārin
Vallabha
Vaḷḷuvar
Vāman Paṇḍit
Vāmanadatta
Vanacandra
Vānamāmalai Periya Rāmānuja Jīyar
Vaṉṟoṇṭar
Varadarāja
Varāhamihira
Vardhamāna
Vardhamāna Mahāvīra
Vāris Śāh
Varma Rāja
Vārṣagaṇya
Varuṇaśiva
Vasubandhu
Vāsudeva Sarvabhauma
Vāsudevamiśra
Vasugupta
Vaṭakkuttiruvītippiḷḷai
Vaṭivaḻakiya Nampi Tācar
Vātsyāyana I
Vātsyāyana II
Vāyilār
Vedajñāna I
Vedajñāna II
Vedāntadeśika
Veḷḷiyampalavāṇattampirāṉ
Vēmana
Veṅkaṭamakhi
Veṅkaṭarāmana
Vibhūticandra
Vidyācakravartin
Vidyākaṇṭha
Vidyānanda
Vidyāpati
Vidyāraṇya
Vidyātīrtha
Vihārabhadra
Vijayabāhu
Vijayendra Saraswathi
Vijñānabhikṣu
Vijñāneśvara
Villiputtūr Aḻvār
Vilvamaṅgala
Vimalacandra
Vimalācārya
Vimalaprabodha
Vimalaśiva
Vimalasūrī
Vimuktātman
Vindhyavāsin
Vipradāsa
Vīrabhadradeva
Vīrabhadrārādhya
Vīracandra
Vīraṇārādhya
Virūpākṣa
Viśākhadatta
Viṣṇu
Viṣṇubhaṭṭa
Viṣṇucittaṉ
Viṣṇudās Nām
Viṣṇudāsa
Viṣṇugupta
Viṣṇupuri
Viṣṇusvāmī
Viṣṇutīrthā

Visobhā Khecara
Viśuddhamuni
Viśvambhara
Viśvanātha Cakravartī
Vīśvanātha Kavirāja
Viśvanātha Nyāyapañcānana
Viśvarūpa
Viśvāvarta
Viśveśvara
Viśveśvara Sarasvatī
Viṭhā Reṇukānandan
Viṭṭhal Vipul
Viṭṭhalanāth
Viṭṭhaldās
Vivaraṇakāra Śaṅkara
Vohita
Vopadeva
Vraja Mohana
Vṛddhajīvaka
Vṛndāvanadās
Vṛndāvanadeva
Vyāḍi
Vyākhyānikācārya
Vyāsa I
Vyāsa II
Vyāsadāsa
Vyāsarāya
Vyāsatīrtha
Vyomācārya
Vyomaśiva

Xuanzang

Yādavaprakāśa
Yadunandana
Yadunātha
Yaḥyā al-Kābulī
Yakoppu
Yāmuna
Yārī Sāhab
Yāska
Yaśodhara
Yaśomitra
Yaśorājacandra
Yaśovanta Dāsa
Yaśovijaya
Yeṛṛāprgaḍa
Yijing
Yogīśvara
Yugaleradāsa

Ẓahīr al-Dīn Rūmī
Ẓahīr Pīr
Zar Zarī Zar Baḫš
Zarathustra
Zaynab
Żiyāʾ al-Dīn Baranī
Żiyāʾ al-Dīn Naḫšabī

Festivals

adhyayanotsava
agnijāgaraṇ
akṣayatṛtīya
akti
ambubachi melā
anantacaturdaśī
aṇitirumañcaṉam
annakūṭa
ārdrādarśana
ārttirātaricaṉam
āti
āṭipūram
āṭṭukālpoṅgāla
ayūdhapūja

baha
baheriamelā
baisākhī
bakr ʿīd
basanta
basantpañcamī
bhāgavatamēḷa
bhajan melā
bhavyadūj
bhūṅkhāl
bikhpantsaṃkrānt
bisketjātrā
bohāgbihū
bōnālu
brahmotsava
buddha jayantī

caitra
caitranavarātri
cetī cand
chathadeo
chathpūjā
chaumos
chenda meḷam
chhaparmelā
cittirai
cūrṇotsava

daśaharā
daśahrā
dasai
dasarā
dasehrā
dashain
devālī
devdīpāvalī
dhanateras
dīpāvalī
dīvālī
ḍol
ḍola
ḍolasammelana
durgāpūjā
duśehrā

eknāth ṣaṣṭhī

galungan
gaṇeśacaturthī
gaṅgādaśaharā
gaṅgāmahāratī
gaṅgāsaptamī
gaṅgaur
gaurapūrṇimā
gaurītṛtiyā
ghoḍejātrā
gopāṣṭamīgrīṣmaṛtujal vihār
guḍī pāḍvā
guggānavamī
gurpurab
gurupūrṇimā

hanumān jayantī
hariharkṣetramelā
hariśayana ekadaśī
hita badhāī
holā
holī
hostila huṇṇime jātre

ʿīd al-fitr
indrajātrā
indramaha
indrotsava

jakhaiyā
janmāṣṭamī
jaragmelā
jhāñpāna
jhūlan
jhūlanā

jhūlnā

kālarātri
kālīpūjā
kalyāṇotsava
kantacaṭṭi
karaga
karam
kārttikapūjā
kate
khecimāvas
khicarī utsav
khicṛī
kṛṣṇajanmāṣṭamī
kumbhamelā
kuningan

lailat ul-qadr
lakṣmīpūjā
lohśī
lòikrathong

madanotsava
māghamelā
mahākumbhamelā
mahallā
mahānavamī
mahāsaptamī
mahāśivarātri
mahāṣṭamī
mahotsava
makarajyoti
makarasaṃkrānti
makaraviḷakku
makōṟcavam
manasāpūjā
mārkaḻitiruvāturai
maturaiccittirai
mohanī
muḥarram
mysore dasarā

nāgapañcamī
nāgpāncamī
nandotsav
navānna
navarātra
navarātri
navarāttiri
navavarṣotsava
navrātri
nēma
norta

onam

paṅkuṉi uttiram
paṭotsava
perahara
phāg
phulpati
poṅgāla
poṅkal
prabodhinī
puṣkar kā melā
puttāṇṭu

rādhāṣṭamī
rāj jāt yātrā
rājasaṃkrānti
rākhī
rakṣābandhan
rāmalīlā
rāmanavamī
rāmānujajayantī
rāmnaomipūjā
rāmnaumi
rāmnavamī
randoli
rathayātrā
rathotsava
rathyātrā
rāto matsyendranātha jātrā

šaʿbān
śabarotsava
šab-i barāt
sahrul
salheśmelā
śamipūjā
saṅgrānd
sarasvatīpūjā
sarhul
sāvaṇ tīj
sevak badhāī
śibcaturdaśīmelā
śivarātri
śivrātri
skandaṣaṣṭhi
snānayātrā
sohrae
sonepurmelā

songkrān
śraddhotsava
śrāvaṇ
śrīpañcamī
srivenkatewara kalyanam
sūryaṣaṣṭī
svasthānī
śyāmāpūjā

taipūcam
tērōṭṭattiruviḻā
tet
thin-gyan
tīj
tilsaṃkrānt
tirukkārttikai
tiruviḻā
tīyāṅ
trissurpūram

ugādi

vaikāci vicākam
vaikuṇṭhaikādāśī
vasantapañcamī
vasantotsava
vasumelā
vijayadaśamī
vijayādaśamī
vijaydaśamī
vijayotsava
vināyakacaturtti
viruppaṉtirunāḷ
viṣu
vivāhapañcamī
vṛkṣotsava

yakṣarātri
yakṣeśvarapūjā
yāmadvitīya
yamunājayantī
yugādi

Performance Traditions

abhinaya
aṅkatari
aṅkiyanāṭ
araiyar cēvai
araṅgukēḷi
arappukai
aṣṭapadiyāṭṭam
āṭa
avatāram

bahurūpi
bāṇayuddham
bayalāṭa
bhāgavatam
bhāgavatara āṭa
bhagavatī teyyam
bhāonā
bharatanāṭyam
bhāratlīlā
bihū
bommalāṭam
buḍir jāt
burrakathā

cākyārkūttu
cāmuṇḍi teyyam
catir kaccēri
catirāṭṭam
chhau
cindu bhāgavatam
cindu madiga yakṣagānam
cindu yakṣagānam

daṇḍīyara
dāsarāṭa
daśāvatāra āṭa
dāsiyāṭṭam
dāskāṭhiā
dhalo
dhanāśi
dhanuyātra
dīpagarbha
doḍḍāṭa

fugddi

gambhira
garbha
gauralīlā
gondhal
goṣṭhalīlā

harake āṭa
hastābhinayam
hun lakhon lek

jāgaraṇa
jāgarāta
jāgraṇ
jāgrat

kaikoṭṭikaḷi
kaḷamezhuttu
kaḷarippayaṭṭu
kāḷi teyyam
kāmatamāśā
katā kālakṣepam
kathābhinayam
kathaka
kathakaḷi
kēḷi
kēḷi abbara
kēḷikkayyu
kēḷikoṭṭu
kolatāriyaṅkam
kṛṣṇalīlā
kṛṣṇanāṭṭam
kūcipuḍi
kuravai
kūtiyāṭṭam

lalit

mach
mañch
manipuri
meippayaṭṭu
melappādam
mohiniyāṭṭam
muṭiyēṭṭu

naṅgyārkūttu
nāṭakī
naṭṭuvamēḷa
nāṭya
nāṭyamēḷa
nauṭaṅkī
nityarās

nṛtta
nṛtya

oḍḍōlaga
odissi
ojā pali
oṭṭan thullal

padayani
padyanāṭakam
pāṇḍavalīlā
pānīhārinlīlā
paratanāṭṭiyam
paṟayan tuḷḷal
pārijāta
paṭayaṇi
paṭuyā saṅgīt
payaṭṭu
pillatanni
prahlādanāṭaka

rādhānāṭa
rāmanāṭṭam
rāmlīlā
rāsa
rāsakrīḍa
rāsalīlā
rāslīlā

saṇṇāṭa
sansenba
sattrīya
sēve āṭa
śītaṅkan tuḷḷal
śrīkṛṣṇapārijāta

ṭakkar
tamāśa
tatkar
terukkūttu
teyvam aṭumākkal
teyyam
teyyāṭṭam
thaṅgta
totayam
tuḷḷal

vāg
vaitari
varaviḷī
varmakalai
vatten tirippu
verumkai
vīragase
vīthināṭakam
voggukathā

wayang kulit

yakṣagāna
yakṣagāna prasaṅga
yātra
yātrā
yokethay thabin

Primary Sources

Abhidhānacintāmaṇi
Abhidharmakośa
Abhidharmakośabhāṣya
Abhidharmakośakārikā
Abhidharmakośavyākhyā
Abhidharmamahāvibhāṣā
Abhidharmavibhāṣā
Abhidharmavibhāṣāśāstra
Abhijñānaśakuntala
Abhinavabhāratī
Abhinayadarpaṇa
Ācārāṅgasūtra
Ācāryacarita
Acintyaviśvasādākhyāgama
Ādarśa
Adbhutarāmāyaṇa
Ādeśapadavyākhyā
Adhyātmapalavivaraṇa
Adhyātmarāmāyaṇa
Ādi Upadeś
Ādigranth
Ādiguru Vāṇī Granth
Ādikāvya
Ādiparvan
Ādipurāṇa
Ādisaṃhitā
Ādityahṛdaya
Advaitasiddhi
Afsāna-yi-šāhan
Āgamaḍambara
Āgamaprāmāṇya
Āgamasāra
Āgamaśāstra
Āgamatattvavilāsa
Agaññasutta
Agastimata
Agastyasaṃhitā
Aghoreśvarīsvacchanda
Agnikāryapaddhati
Agnipurāṇa
Agniveśatantra
Ahirbudhnyasaṃhitā
Aikkiyaviyal
A'in-Akbarī
Aiṅkuṟunūṟu
Aitareya
Aitareyabrāhmaṇa
Aitareyāraṇyaka
Aitareyopaniṣad
Ajaḍapramātṛsiddhi
Ajitā
Ajita/Ajitāgama
Ajitapurāṇa
Ājyaśāstra
Akāl Ustat
Akanāṉūru
Akapporuḷ
Akattiyam
Akbar-nāma
Ākhyātacandrikā
Ākhyāyikādhyāya
Akulavīratantra
Alakhbānī
Alaṃkārakaustubha
Āḻvārkaḷ Vaipavam
Alli Aracāṇi Mālai
Amalaṉātippirāṉ
Amanaskayoga
Amarakośa
Amaraughaprabodha
Amaraughaśāsana
Āmardakamāhātmya
Āmbhāv Bhārat
Amṛtabhairavārcanavidhi
Amṛtakaṇikodyotanibandha
Amṛtakataka
Amṛtakuṇḍa
Amṛtalaharī
Amṛtānubhava
Amṛtarasāvalī
Amṛtasiddhi
Amṛtasūryapūjāvidhi
Amṛtasūryārcanavidhi
Amṛteśavidhāna
Amṛteśvarapūjāgnikāryavidhāna
Amṛteśvarapūjana
Amṛtīśabhairavabhaṭṭārakāhnikavidhi
Aṃśumadbhedāgama
Aṃśumat
Aṃtagaśadasāo
Āmuktamālyada
Anādivīraśaivācārasaṃgraha
Anāmikajātaka
Ānanda Sāgara
Ānandabhairava
Ānandabhāṣya
Ānandakalpavallī
Ānandakanda

Ānandalaharī
Ānandamaṭh
Ānandānubhav
Ānandarāmāyaṇa
Ānandasaṃhitā
Anaṅgaraṅga
Anāsaktiyoga
Anbhaivāṇī
Āndhra Mahābhāgavatamu
Āṅgirasakalpa
Aṅguttaranikāya
Aniruddhasaṃhitā
Annapūrṇastotra
Anteṣṭividhi
Antyeṣṭipaddhati
Antyeṣṭiprakaraṇa
Aṇubhāṣya
Anubhavāmṛt
Anubhavānanda
Anubhavasāramu
Anubhavasūtra
Anubhūtiprakāśa
Anugītā
Anukramaṇī
Aṇumadhvacarita
Aṇumadhvavijaya
Anurāgsāgar
Anuśāsanaparvan
Anuttarapaddhati
Anuttaraprakāśapañcāśikā
Anuttarasaṃvidarcanācarcā
Anuttaratriṃśikā
Anuttaravimarśinī
Anuvyākhyāna
Āpaddharmaparvan
Aparārka
Aparokṣānubhūti
Āpastambadharmasūtra
Āpastambagṛhyasūtra
Āpastambaśrautasūtra
Āpastambaśulbasūtra
Aponaptrīya
Apratihatamahādīkṣāsuṭippaṇaka
Āprī
Āraṇyakakāṇḍa
Āraṇyagāṇa
Āraṇyakaparvan
Āratī
Āṟāyirappaṭi
Arcanānavanīta
Arddhakathānak
Argalā
Arjyamanjuśrīmūlakalpa
Aṟputattiruvantāti
Arthaśāstra
Aruṇācalamāhātmya
Aruṇācalapurāṇam
Aruṇakiripurāṇam
Āryabhaṭīya
Aryabhaṭīyabhāṣya
Āryalaṅkāvatāravṛtti
Āryāstava
Āsanayogagrantha
Āśaucacandrikā
Āśaucadīpikā
Aṣṭadaś Siddhānta
Aṣṭadhyāyī
Aṣṭakālīyalīlāsmaraṇamaṅgalastotra
Aṣṭalakṣmīstrotra
Aṣṭāṅgahṛdayasaṃhitā
Aṣṭāṅgasaṃgraha
Aṣṭapadī
Aṣṭasāhasrikāprajñāpāramitā
Aṣṭaślokī
Aṣṭāvakragītā
Ātharvāṅgirasa
Atharvapariśiṣṭa
Atharvaśikhopaniṣad
Atharvaśiropaniṣad
Atharvaveda
Atharvavedapariśiṣṭha
Ātmabodha
Ātmārthapūjāpaddhati
Ātmasiddhi
Ātmasūkta
Ātmasvarūpamanana
Ātmatattva
Ātreyatantra
Atrisaṃhitā
Atrismṛti
Ātticūṭi
Avadhūtagītā
Avantikhaṇḍa
Avantisundarīkathā
Avantisundarīkathāsāra
Āvaśyakacūrṇi
Avesta
Avimāraka
Avvaikkuṟal
Ayātgār ī Žāmāspik

Bhīmarūpīstotra
Bhīmāyan
Bhīmeśvarapurāṇamu
Bhīṣmaparvan
Bhogahasta
Bhogakārikā
Bhramaragīta
Bhṛgubharadvājasaṃvāda
Bhṛgusaṃhitā
Bhṛṅgīśasaṃhitā
Bhūstuti
Bhuśuṇḍirāmāyaṇa
Bhūtanāthopākhyā
Bhūtiprakaraṇa
Bicitra Nātak
Bījabheda
Bījagaṇita
Bījak
Bijjaḷarāyacarite
Bijjaḷarāyapurāṇa
Bilātyatrāpratiṣedha
Birudāvalīlakṣaṇa
Bodhapañcadaśikā
Brahmacārisūkta
Brāhmadharma
Brahmajalasutta
Brahmāṇḍapurāṇa
Brahmapurāṇa
Brahmarātra
Brahmaśambhupaddhati
Brahmasaṃdhāna
Brahmasaṃhitā
Brahmasiddhi
Brāhmasphuṭasiddhānta
Brahmasūtra
Brahmasūtrabhāṣya
Brahmavaivartapurāṇa
Brahmayāmala
Brahmotsavānukramaṇikā
Bṛhadāraṇyakopaniṣad
Bṛhadbhāgavatāmṛta
Bṛhadbhāṣya
Bṛhadbrahmasaṃhitā
Bṛhaddeśī
Bṛhaddevatā
Bṛhaddharmapurāṇa
Bṛhadyogavāsiṣṭha
Bṛhadyoni
Bṛhajjābālopaniṣad
Bṛhajjātaka
Bṛhallaghupañjikā
Bṛhannāradīyapurāṇa
Bṛhannīla
Bṛhaspatirātra
Bṛhaspatismṛti
Bṛhaspatisūtra
Bṛhatī
Bṛhatkālottara
Bṛhatkathā
Bṛhatkathāmañjarī
Bṛhatkathāślokasaṃgraha
Bṛhatkhecarīprakāśa
Bṛhatsaṃhitā
Bṛhatśṛṅgadharapaddhati
Bṛhatstotraratnākara
Bṛhaṭṭīkā
Buddhacarita

Caitanyabhāgavata
Caitanyacandrāmṛta
Caitanyacandrodayanāṭaka
Caitanyacaritāmṛta
Caitanyacaritāmṛtamahākāvya
Caitanyamaṅgala
Caitanyamatamañjuṣā
Caivasamayaneṟi
Caivatūṣaṇaparikāram
Cāṇakyarājanīti
Caṇḍabhairava
Caṇḍāsidhārakalpa
Candāyan
Caṇḍīmāhātmya
Caṇḍīśataka
Candrajñāna
Candranāthmāhātmya
Candraśekhar kāhinī bā candranāth māhātmya
Candrāvalokana
Cāṅgdevpāsaṣṭī
Cangranghācah-Nāmah
Caṅkaṟpanirākaraṇam
Cannabasavapurāṇa
Carakapratisaṃskṛta
Carakasaṃhitā
Cārvākasūtra
Caṭakōparantāti
Catuḥśataka
Catuḥśatī
Catuḥśatika
Catuḥślokī
Catuḥślokī Bhāgavat
Caturaśitisiddhapravṛtti
Cāturī

Caturvargacintāmaṇi
Caturvedasāramu
Caturviṃśatistava
Caurāsī Baiṭhak Caritra
Caurāsī Vaiṣṇavan kī Vārtā
Caurāsīpad
Ceitiya Jātaka
Cēkkiḻārnāyaṉārpurāṇam
Ceñcu Nāṭakamu
Cennabasavapurāṇa
Chāndogyopaniṣad
Chauṣaṭhi Ratibandha
Chummāsaṃketaprakāśa
Cidambarakṣetrasarvasva
Cidambaramāhātmya
Cidambareśvaranityapūjāsūtra
Cidgaganacandrikā
Cidvilāsa
Cikitsāsārasaṃgraha
Cikitsāsthāna
Cilappatikāram
Ciñcinīmatasārasamuccaya
Cintāmaṇiṭīkā
Cintyāgama
Cintyaviśvasādākhya
Cīṟāppurāṇam
Ciṟiyatirumaṭal
Citrakūṭamahātmya
Citrasūtra
Citsabheśotsavasūtra
Cīvakacintāmaṇi
Civālayataricaṉaviti
Civañāṉacittiyār
Civañāṉapōtam
Civappirakācam
Civatarumōttaram
Cūḷadukkhakkhandhasutta

Dabistān-i maḏāhib
Dādūjanmalīlā
Dādūvāṇī
Daivikabhāga
Ḍākinīkalpa
Dakṣiṇa Rāya Pāñcālī
Dakṣiṇāmūrtistotra
Dānacandrikā
Dānadharmaparvan
Dānakāṇḍa
Dānakelikaumudī
Dānakhaṇḍa
Dānasāgara
Daṇḍaviveka
Dāṇḍirāmāyaṇ
Daodejing
Darraṅg Rajvaṃśāvali
Daśabhūmikavibhāṣāśāstra
Dāsabodha
Daśakumāracarita
Dasam Granth
Daśapadārthaśāstra
Daśapadārthī
Dasarathajātaka
Daśaślokī
Daśāvatāracarita
Dasaveyāliyasutta
Dāsbodh
Dastūr al-aṭibbāʾ
Dattamāhātmya
Dattapurāṇa
Dattasaṃhitā
Dattātreyakalpa
Dattātreyapūjāpaddhati
Dattātreyatantra
Dattātreyayogaśāstra
Dattātreyopaniṣad
Dattila
Dāyabhāga
Debī Caudhurāṇī
Dehasthadevatācakrastotra
Dēnkard
Deśīnāmamālā
Deśopadeśa
Devalakakathāmṛt
Devalasmṛti
Devāmṛtapāñcarātra
Devanāyakapañcāśat
Devapūjāpaddhati
Devatrāsakalpa
Devatrāsatantra
Devībhāgavatapurāṇa
Devīdvyārdhaśatikā
Devīgītā
Devīkālottara/Devīkālottarāgama
Devīkavaca
Devīmāhātmya
Devīnāmavilāsa
Devīpañcaka
Devīpañcaśataka
Devīpurāṇa
Devīrahasya
Devīstotra
Devīsūkta

Devītantrasadbhāva
Devyāmata
Devyaparādhakṣamāpana
Devyāyāmala
Dhammapada
Dhammasaṅgaṇi
Dharmamaṅgala
Dharmaparīkṣā
Dharmaputrikā
Dharmaratna
Dharmgraṃ thoṃ kā Punarpāṭh
Dharmottapradīpa
Dhātupāṭha
Dhātusaṃgraha
Ḍhol Sāgar
Dhuṃdh se Uṭhtī Dhun
Dhūrtākhyāna
Dhvanyāloka
Dhvanyālokalocana
Dhyānabindūpaniṣad
Dhyānaratnāvalī
Digdarśinī
Dīghanikāya
Dīkṣādarśa
Dīkṣāprakāśa
Dīkṣātattvaprakāśa
Dīkṣottara
Dīpālikā
Dīpta
Divyasūricarita
Dohāvalī
Drāhyāyaṇaśrautasūtra
Drāviḍa Veda
Droṇaparvan
Dṛṣṭāntapāṭha
Dummedha Jātaka
Durgamasaṃgamanī
Durgāśaptasatī
Durgāstava
Durgāstotra
Durgotsavaviveka
Dvādaśāranayacakra
Dvādaśasāhasra
Dvādaśastotra
Dvārakākṣetramāhātmya
Dvātriṃśikā
Dvayasaṃpattivārttika
Dvipadabhāgavatamu
Dvīpamata
Dvīpottara
Dvīsahasri
Dviśatika

Eka Ślokī
Ekākṣarasūkta
Ekākṣaropaniṣad
Ekaliṅgamāhātmya
Eknāthcaritra
Eknāthībhāgavat
Eṭṭutokai

Fatāwā-yi ʿĀlamgīrī

Gadāyuddha
Gadyatraya
Gaṇakārikā
Gaṇeśagītā
Gaṇeśamahimnaḥstotra
Gaṇeśapurāṇa
Gaṇeśasahasranāma
Gaṅgālaharī
Gaṅgāstava
Gaṅgāstuti
Gaṅgāvatāraṇa
Garbhalakṣana
Garbhopaniṣad
Gargasaṃhitā
Gārgīyajyotiṣa
Garuḍapurāṇa
Garudeya
Gāthā
Gāthāsaptaśatī
Gauḍapādakārikā
Gauḍavaho
Gauragaṇoddeśadīpikā
Gauragovindārcanasmaraṇapaddhati
Gautam Candrikā
Gautamadharmasūtra
Gautamatantra
Gautamīmāhātmya
Gautamīyatantra
Gayatrīmantravivṛtti
Gāyatrītantra
Gāyatrīvyākhyā
Gāθā
Ghaṇṭakarṇa Mantra Stotra
Ghatajātaka
Gheraṇḍasaṃhitā
Gītābhāṣya
Gītagovinda
Gītāñjalī
Gītārthasaṃgraha

Gītātātparya
Gītāvalī
Gītavitān
Gobhilagṛhyasūtra
Godāstuti
Godāvarīmāhātmya
Goindval Pothī
Gokaruṇānidhi
Gopālacampū
Gopālarājavaṃśāvalī
Gopālatāpanyupaniṣad
Gopālavirudāvalī
Gopathabrāhmaṇa
Gorakhbāṇī
Gorakṣ Upaniṣad
Gorakṣagītā
Gorakṣasahasranāmastotra
Gorakṣasaṃhitā
Gorakṣaśataka
Gorakṣasiddhāntasaṃgraha
Gorakṣavijaya
Gosāīṃ Carit
Govardhanadharaṇa
Govindabirudāvalī
Govindalīlāmṛta
Grāmageyagāna
Gṛhyapaddhati
Guḍhārthadīpikā
Guṇamāla
Ġunyat al-munya
Guptasādhana
Gurū Granth Sāhib
Gurucaritra
Gurugītā
Gurunāthaparāmarśa
Gurupaṅktistotra
Guruparamparāprabhāvam
Gurupustikā
Gurusaṃhitā
Gurustuti
Gurvaṣṭaka
Gyānalīlā
Gyānatilaka
Gyānsamudra

Haft aḥbāb
Haṃsadūta
Haṃsasaṃdeśa
Haṃsasāra
Hanumadrahasya
Hanumān Cālīsā
Hanumānbāhuk
Hanumānupāsnā
Hanumatkavaca
Haqāyaq-i Hindī
Haracaritacintāmaṇi
Haraprasādakiraṇāvalīdarpaṇa
Haravijaya
Haravilāsamu
Haribhaktiśuddhodaya
Haribhaktivilāsa
Harigītā
Hariharamāhātmya
Harimīḍestotra
Harināmāmṛtavyākaraṇa
Haripāṭh
Harivaṃśa
Harivaṃśapurāṇa
Harṣacarita
Hastābhinaya
Hastalakṣaṇadīpikā
Hastāmalak
Hastamudrādīpikā
Haṭhapradīpikā
Haṭhapradīpikājyotsnā
Haṭharatnāvalī
Haṭhasaṃketacandrikā
Haṭhatattvakaumudī
Haṭhayogapradīpikā
Hayaśīrṣapañcarātra
Ḫazīna al-āṣafiyya
Hemakūṭakhaṇḍa
Hevajratantra
Hikāyat Siri Rām
Himavatkhaṇḍa
Hindū-Turk Saṃvād
Hīr Rāñjhā
Hiraṇyagarbhasūkta
Hitacaritra
Hitopadeśa
Horāsāra
Hṛllekhāpaddhati
Ḥujjat al-hind
Humāyūn-nāma

Indrarātra
Indriyasthāna
Irāmāvatāram
Iraṇṭām Tiruvantāti
Irupāvirupaḥtu
Īśānaśivagurudevapaddhati
Īśopaniṣad

Iṣṭasiddhi
Īśvaragītā
Īśvarapratyabhijñākārikā
Īśvarapratyabhijñākārikāvṛtti
Īśvarapratyabhijñātātparyānvayadīpikā
Īśvarapratyabhijñāvimarśinī
Īśvarapratyabhijñāvivṛtivimarśinī
Īśvarasaṃhitā
Īśvarasiddhi

Jagamohana Rāmāyaṇa
Jaiminīyabrāhmaṇa
Jaiminīyaśrautasūtra
Jaiminīyopaniṣadbrāhmaṇa
Jaimīyanyāyamālā
Jainendravyākaraṇa
Jalabheda
Jāmbavati Kalyāṇa
Jāmbhavāṇī
Jambūdvīpasaṃgrahaṇī
Janmacarita
Janmakhaṇḍa
Janmalīlā
Jātakakarmapaddhati
Jātakapārijāta
Jatūkarṇatantra
Javasakuṇa Jātaka
Jawāmiʿ al-kalim
Jaya
Jayadrathayāmala
Jayadrathayāmalaprastāramantrasaṃgraha
Jayākhya
Jayamaṅgalā
Jayarāśi
Jayottaratantra
Jitaṃtestotra
Jīvancaritra
Jīvanmuktagītā
Jñāna Vāsiṣṭha Rāmāyaṇamu
Jñānabodha
Jñānadīpavimarśinī
Jñānakhaṇḍa
Jñānāmṛtasārasaṃhitā
Jñānapañcāśikā
Jñānaprasthāna
Jñānārṇavatantra
Jñānasaṃhitā
Jñānasaṃkalinī
Jñānasāra
Jñānasiddhyāgama
Jñānāvaraṇabhāṣya
Jñāndevī
Jñāneśvarī
Jogpradīpakā
Jyotiṣavedāṅga

Kabikāhinī
Kabīr Granthāvalī
Kabīr Manśūr
Kabīr Parcāī
Kaḍacā
Kadalīmañjunāthamāhātmya
Kādambarī
Kādimatatantra
Kahāṃ jāise
Kaivalyadīpikā
Kaivalyapāda
Kaivalyopaniṣad
Kākacaṇḍeśvarīmata
Kakawin Arjunawijaya
Kakawin Arjunawiwaha
Kakawin Bharatayudha
Kakawin Ghatotkacāśraya
Kakawin Hariwangsa
Kakawin Kunjarakarna
Kakawin Parthayajna
Kakawin Ramayana
Kakawin Sutasoma
Kakṣapuṭa
Kalādīkṣāpaddhati
Kāḷahastīśvaramāhātmyamu
Kāḷahastīśvaraśatakamu
Kālamṛgayā
Kalānidhi
Kālanirṇaya
Kālaviveka
Kaḷaviyal Eṉṟa Iṟaiyaṉār Akapporuḷ
Kālikākrama
Kālikākulapañcaśataka
Kālikāpurāṇa
Kālikārcanacandrikā
Kālīkīrtan
Kālīkulakramārcana
Kālīkulakramasadbhāva
Kālīkulapañcaśatika
Kalittokai
Kālīvilāsa
Kāliyadamana
Kāḷiyamarddanam
Kālottara
Kalpacintāmaṇi
Kalpanāmaṇḍitikā Dṛṣṭāntapaṅkti

Kalpasthāna
Kalyāṇ Tīrthaṅk
Kalyāṇamandirastotra
Kalyāṇasaugandhikam
Kāmadhenu
Kāmakalāvilāsa
Kāmākhyātantra
Kamalālayaccirappu
Kāmasūtra
Kāmika/Kāmikāgama
Kaṃsavadham
Kaṇādarahasya
Kaṇādasūtravārttika
Kaṇādasūtravivṛti
Kanakadharastotra
Kāñcīmāhātmya
Kāñcipurāṇam
Kandarpacūḍāmaṇi
Kanhāvat
Kaṅkālamālinī
Kaṇṇinuṇciruttāmpu
Kantapurāṇam
Kantaralaṅkāram
Kantaranapūti
Kantarkaliveṉpā
Kaṇvatantra
Kapilagītā
Kapilāśramīyapātañjalayogadarśana
Kapilāsurisaṃvāda
Kapilatantra
Kapilopadeśa
Kapiṣṭhala
Kapiṣṭhalabrāhmaṇa
Kāraṇa/Kāraṇāgama
Karavīrayāga
Karmasāramahātantra
Karṇabhāra
Karṇahastaki
Karṇāndana
Karṇaparvan
Karpūrādistotra
Kārttikāśramamāhātmya
Kārttikkamāhātmya
Karuṇālaharī
Karuṇāṣṭaka
Kāśīkhaṇḍa
Kāśīkhaṇḍamu
Kāśīmāhātmya
Kāśmīrāgamaprāmāṇya
Kāśmīratīrthasaṃgraha
Kāśyapajñānakāṇḍa
Kāśyapasaṃhitā
Kāśyapaśilpaśāstra
Kaṭandī
Kātantra
Kāṭhabrāhmaṇa
Kāṭhakabrāhmaṇa
Kāṭhakagṛhyasūtra
Kāṭhakasaṃhitā
Kāṭhakayajñasūtra
Kaṭhapaniṣad
Kāṭhāraṇyaka
Kaṭhasaṃhitā
Kathāsaritsāgara
Kaṭhaśikṣopaniṣad
Kaṭhopaniṣad
Kaṭhopaniṣadbhāṣya
Kātyāyanaśrautasūtra
Kātyāyanasmṛti
Kaulajñānanirṇaya
Kaulakamala
Kaulāvalīnirṇaya
Kauśikasūtra
Kauṣītakibrāhmaṇa
Kauṣītakyāraṇyaka
Kauṣītakyupaniṣad
Kāverīkhaṇḍa
Kavirājamārga
Kavitāvalī
Kāvyādarśa
Kāvyālaṃkāra
Kāvyamīmāṃsā
Kāvyanirṇaya
Kāyābelī
Kedārakhaṇḍa
Kekawin Arjunawiwaha
Keligopāla
Kelimālā
Kenopaniṣad
Keralopathi
Khaḍgamālāstotra
Khaḍgarāvaṇakalpa
Khādiragṛhyasūtra
Khaṇḍanakhaṇḍakhādya
Khaṇḍanatraya
Khañjinīmata
Kharanādasaṃhitā
Kharapuccha
Khecarīvidyā
Kheyā
Khilādhikāra
Kidung Sudamala

Kīlaka
Kiraṇa/Kiraṇāgama
Kiraṇāvalī
Kiraṇāvalībhāskara
Kiraṇāvalīprakāśa
Kiraṇāvalīprakāśavivṛti
Kirātārjunīya
Kirimirivadham
Kīrtanaghoṣa
Kiṣkindhākāṇḍa
Kitāb fī tārīx mā li-l-Hind
Kitāb taḥqīq mā li ʾl-Hind
Kokasāra
Kokaśāstra
Kokkokaśāstra
Koṉṟaivēntaṉ
Korawāśrama
Koṭikkavi
Kōyaṃbēḍu
Kōyiloḻuku
Kōyiṟpurāṇam
Kramacandrikā
Kramadīpikā
Kramanayapradīpikā
Kramasadbhāvatantra
Kramasandarbha
Kramastava
Kramastotra
Krishnayana
Kristāpurāṇa
Kristubhāgavatam
Kristusahasranāma
Kriyādhikāra
Kriyākālaguṇottaratantra
Kriyākāṇḍa
Kriyākāṇḍakramāvalī
Kriyākramadyotikā
Kriyāsaṃgrahapaddhati
Kriyāsaṃgrahapañjikā
Kriyāsāra
Krodhabhairava
Kṛṣṇacaitanyacaritāmṛta
Kṛṣṇacaitanyacaritāmṛtamahākāvya
Kṛṣṇacaitanyasahasranāma
Kṛṣṇacaritra
Kṛṣṇagītāvalī
Kṛṣṇagītī
Kṛṣṇajanmatithividhi
Kṛṣṇakarṇāmṛta
Kṛṣṇakīrtan
Kṛṣṇāmṛtamahārṇava
Kṛṣṇapādapadmacihna
Kṛṣṇasaṃhitā
Kṛṣṇasandarbha
Kṛṣṇayajurveda
Kṛṣṇāyan
Kṛtyakalpataru
Kṛtyaratnākara
Kṣetrapālapaddhati
Kṣīrasāgaramanthana
Kṣīrodamathana
Kubjikāmatatantra
Kulacūḍāmaṇi
Kulakrīḍāvatāra
Kulālikāmata
Kulālikāmnāya
Kulānanda
Kulapañcāśikā
Kularatnoddyota
Kulārṇavatantra
Kulasāra
Kumārakhaṇḍa
Kumārasambhava
Kumāratantra
Kumārī
Kuñcitāṅghristava
Kūrmapurāṇa
Kusāñjali Jātaka
Kūṭadantasutta
Kuvalaymālā

Laghubhagavatāmṛta
Laghuṭīkā
Laghuvaiṣṇavatoṣaṇī
Laghuyogavāsiṣṭha
Laghvī
Laghvikāmnāya
Lahajāt-i Sikandar-šāhī
Lakṣaṇasaṃgraha
Lakṣaṇāvalī
Lakṣmīlaharī
Lakṣmīsahasranāma
Lakṣmītantra
Lakṣmīviśiṣṭādvaitabhāṣya
Lakṣmyaṣṭottara
Lalitamādhava
Lalitāsahasranāma
Lalitasvacchanda
Lalitavistara
Lalitopākhyāna

Laṅkākāṇḍa
Laṅkavatārasūtra
Lāṭyāyanaśrautasūtra
Laugākṣigṛhyasūtra
Laẓat al-nisāʾ
Līlācaritra
Līlātilakam
Līlāvatī
Liṅgadhāraṇacandrikā
Liṅgapurāṇa
Locanarocanī
Lokatattvanirṇaya

Maʿdan al-šifāʾ-i Sikandar-šāhī
Madanaratna
Mādhavakula
Mādhavamahotsava
Mādhavanidāna
Madhumālatī
Mādhuryakadambinī
Madhvavijayabhāvaprakāśika
Madhyalīlā
Madhyamakahṛdaya
Madhyamakahṛdayakārikā
Madhyāntavibhāgakārikābhāṣya
Madhyāntavibhāgaśāstra
Madhyāntavibhāgasūtrabhāṣya
Mahābhāgavatamu
Mahābhāgavatapurāṇa
Mahābhairavamaṅgalā
Mahābhārata
Mahābhāratamu
Mahābhāratatātparyanirṇaya
Mahābhāṣya
Mahābhāṣyadīpikā
Mahābhāṣyaṭīkā
Mahācīnatantra
Mahādēviyakkanapurāna
Mahākālasaṃhitā
Mahālakṣmīstotra
Mahāmanthana
Mahāmāyūrī
Mahānārāyaṇopaniṣad
Mahānayaprakāśa
Mahānirvāṇatantra
Mahānuśāsana
Mahāpīṭhanirūpaṇa
Mahāprajñāpāramitāśāstra
Mahāprasthānaparvan
Mahāpūrvapakṣa
Mahāraudra
Mahārthakramabheda
Mahārthakramapañcakamantrapaddhati
Mahārthamañjarī
Mahārthamañjarīparimala
Mahārthamūlasaṃketasūtra
Mahāsammoha
Mahāsiddhānta
Mahāvaṃśa
Mahāvāṇī
Mahāvastu
Mahāvibhāṣā
Mahāvīracarita
Mahāyāgapaddhati
Mahimnaḥstava
Mahiṣāsuramardinīstotra
Mahotsavavidhi
Maḫzan al-ʿulūm
Maitrāyaṇī
Maitrāyaṇīsaṃhitā
Maitrayaṇīyopaniṣad
Maitreyyupaniṣad
Maitryupaniṣad
Majjhimanikāya
Majmaʿ al-baḥrayn
Makuṭa
Mālatīmādhava
Malāvikāgnimitra
Mālinīślokavārttika
Mālinīvijayavārttika
Mālinīvijayottaratantra
Mallapurāṇa
Mallārimāhātmya
Manāceślok
Manaḥśikṣā
Mānamanohara
Mānasāra
Manasāvijaya
Mānasīsevā
Mānasollāsa
Mānaspīyūṣ
Mānavadharmaśāstra
Mānavagṛhyasūtra
Mānavaśrautasūtra
Maṇḍalabrāhmaṇopaniṣad
Maṇḍūkasūkta
Māṇḍūkyopaniṣad
Māṇḍūkyopaniṣatkārikā
Maner Mānuṣ
Mangeśamāhātmya
Maṇimañjari
Maṇimēkalai

Maṇiprabhā
Mānmañjarī
Manorathapūraṇī
Manthānabhairavatantra
Mantraḍāmarikāpaṭala
Mantramahodadhi
Mantrapīṭhasvacchanda
Mantrapraśna
Mantravimarśinī
Manubhāṣya
Manubṛhaspatisaṃvāda
Manuśāstravivaraṇa
Manusmṛti
Māpāṭiyam
Marāṭhyāñcyā Itihāsācīṃ Sādhaneṃ
Mārgaśīrṣamāsamāhātmya
Marīcisamhitā
Mārkāṇḍeyapurāṇa
Mārkaṇḍeyasaṃhitā
Mātājī rā Chand
Mataṅgapārameśvarāgama
Mataparīkṣā
Matasāra
Māṭharavṛtti
Mathurāmahātmya
Mathurāmaṅgala
Mātrā
Mātṛkabhedatantra
Mātṛsadbhāva
Matsyapurāna
Matsyendrasaṃhitā
Matsyodarayogaśāstra
Mattavilāsa
Maturaikkāñci
Mausalaparvan
Maya Machhindra
Mayamata
Mayasaṃgraha
Māyāvādakhaṇḍana
Meghadūta
Meghnādbādhakāvya
Merutantra
Meymmolicaritai
Milindapañha
Mīmāṃsābhāṣya
Mīmāṃsānayaviveka
Mīmāṃsānukramaṇikā
Mīmāṃsāsūtra
Mīmāṃsāsūtrabhāṣyanibandhana
Mīmāṃsāsūtrabhāṣyavivaraṇa
Mīrā Janma Patrī
Mir'āt al-ḥaqā'iq
Mitākṣarā
Mohammad Bodh
Mohamudgara
Mohaśūrottara
Mokṣadharma
Mokṣadharmaparvan
Mokṣakārikā
Mokṣopāya
Mokṣopāyapradīpikā
Mokṣopāyaṭīkā
Mollarāmāyaṇam
Mṛcchakaṭika
Mṛgendra/Mṛgendrāgama
Mṛgendrapaddhati
Mṛgendravṛttidīpikā
Mrigāvatī
Mṛtitattvānusmaraṇa
Mṛtyujit
Mudgalapurāṇa
Mudrārākṣasa
Muhūrtadīpikā
Mukha
Muktāphala
Muktikopaniṣad
Mukundamālā
Mūl Gosāīṃ Carit
Mūlamadhyamakārikā
Mūlarāmāyāṇa
Mūlasarvāstivādavinaya
Muluki Ain
Mummaṇikkōvai
Mumukṣācatuṣka
Mumukṣupadi Sārārtha Dīpikā
Muṇḍakopaniṣad
Muṇḍamālā
Mūṉṟām Tiruvantāti
Mūrtirahasya
Mutal Tiruvantāti
Muttiniccayam
Mūturai

Nabīvaṃśa
Nācciyār Tirumoḻi
Nādabindūpaniṣad
Nādupai Palikēru
Nāgānandasūtravivaraṇa
Nagarakertagama
Nāgarakhaṇḍa
Nagarapurāṇa
Nāgarasarvasva

Naimittikakriyānusaṃdhāna
Naiṇsī rī Khyāt
Naiṣkarmyasiddhi
Nālāyira Divya Prabandham
Nālāyira Tivya Pirapantam
Nalvaḻi
Nāmaghoṣa
Nāmaliṅgānuśāsana
Nāmāyan
Nāṉ Yār
Ñānāmirutam
Nandanar Charitram
Nandikṣetramāhātmya
Nandīśvarāvatāra
Nāṉmukaṉ Tiruvantāti
Nannu Brovakanu
Nāradabhaktisūtra
Nāradabhāṣya
Nāradapāñcarātra
Nāradaparivrājakopaniṣad
Nāradapurāṇa
Nāradaśikṣā
Nāradasmṛti
Nāradīyaharibhaktisudhodaya
Nāradīyapurāṇa
Nāradīyasaṃhitā
Nāradīyāśikṣā
Narapatijayacaryāsvarodaya
Narasiṃhapurāṇa
Nārāyaṇasūkta
Nārāyaṇavarman
Nārāyanīstuti
Nārāyanīyam
Nārāyaṇīyaparvan
Nareśvaraparīkṣā
Nareśvaraparīkṣāprakāśa
Narmadāmāhātmya
Narottamavilāsa
Narsī jī ro Māhero
Nāsadīyasūkta
Nāṭakacandrikā
Naṭarājapaddhati
Nāṭyaśāstra
Nāṭyaveda
Naukācaritram
Naukākhaṇḍa
Navadvīpāṣṭaka
Navanāthabhaktisāra
Navanāthacaritra
Navanāthacaritramu
Navanīt
Navarattiṉamālai
Nāyādhammakahāo
Nayatattvasaṃgraha
Nayottara
Nemicarita
Neñcuviṭutūtu
Nepālamāhatmya
Netratantra
Netroddyota
Nibandhasaṃgraha
Nidānasthāna
Nidānasūtra
Nigamacūḍādarpaṇa
Nigamajñānadeśika
Nigamakalpadruma
Nigamakalpatara
Nigamatattvasāra
Nighaṇṭu
Nighaṇṭuśeṣa
Nigūḍhārthaprakāśāvalī
Niḥśvāsatattvasaṃhitā
Nijmat Siddhānta
Nikuñjarahasyastava
Nīlakēci
Nīlamatapurāṇa
Nirantarapadavyākhyā
Nirodhalakṣaṇa
Nirukta
Niruttaratantra
Niruttaravāda
Nirvāṇa
Nirvāṇayogottara
Nirvāṇopaniṣad
Niśīthacūrṇi
Niśvāsaguhya
Niśvāsakārikā
Niśvāsamukha
Niśvāsamūla
Niśvāsanaya
Niśvāsatattvasaṃhitā
Niśvāsottara
Nītipañcatantrākhyāyika
Nītiprakāśika
Nītisāra
Nītiśataka
Nītitattvāvirbhāva
Nītivākyāmṛta
Nityādisaṃgraha
Nityagrantha
Nityāhnikatilaka
Nityakarmavidhi

Nityākaula
Nityakaumudī
Nityakriyānusaṃdhāna
Nityaprakāśa
Nityaprakāśavivaraṇapañjikā
Nityāṣoḍaśikārṇava
Nityotsava
Niẓām al-qulūb
Nizāmī Dakanī
Nṛsiṃhapurāṇa
Nṛsimhaśatakamu
Nūr-nāmā
Nūṟṟantāti
Nyāyabhāṣya
Nyāyabhūṣaṇa
Nyāyakandalī
Nyāyakandalīpañjikā
Nyāyakandalīsāra
Nyāyakumudacandra
Nyāyakusumāñjali
Nyāyalīlāvatī
Nyāyalīlāvatīkaṇṭhābharaṇa
Nyāyamañjarī
Nyāyamañjarigranthibhaṅga
Nyāyāmṛta
Nyāyānusāra
Nyāyapraveśa
Nyāyasiddhāñjana
Nyāyasudhā
Nyāyasūtra
Nyāyasūtrabhāṣya
Nyāyatattva
Nyāyavārttika
Nyāyavivaraṇa

Pacurappatirāmāyaṇam
Padaprasaṅgmālā
Padārthadharmasaṃgraha
Padārthadharmasaṃgrahaṭīkā
Padāvalī
Padmacarita
Padmapurāṇa
Pādmasaṃhitā
Pādmatantra
Padmāvat
Padmodbhavatantra
Padyavāhinī
Padyāvalī
Paitāmahasiddhānta
Paḻaṉittalapurāṇam
Palnāṭi Vīrula Kathā
Pamancangah
Pampa Bhārata
Pampa Rāmāyaṇa
Pampāmāhātmya
Pañc Mātrā
Pañcacāmaraśekhara
Pañcāmṛta
Pañcapādikā
Pañcapādikāvivaraṇa
Pañcaprakriyā
Pañcapurāṇam
Pañcarakṣā
Pañcaratna
Pāñcarātrarakṣā
Pañcārtha
Pañcārthabhāṣya
Pañcārthabhāṣyadīpikā
Pañcārthapramāṇa
Pañcasāyaka
Pañcasiddhāntikā
Pañcastavī
Pañcatantra
Pañcavāṇī
Pañcāvaraṇārcanavidhipaṭala
Pañcāvaraṇastava
Pañcaviṁśabrāhmaṇa
Pañcnāmā
Pañcvāṇī
Pāṇḍavacarita
Pāṇḍavapurāṇa
Pāṇḍavavijaya
Paṇḍitārādhyacaritamu
Pandun ka Kara
Pāṇinīyaśikṣā
Paṉṉirunāmam
Pantalsēvam
Parājapavidhi
Parākhya/Parākhyāgama/Parākhyatantra
Parākramavāsanā
Paramānandatantra
Parāmantramāhātmya
Parāmantravidhi
Paramarahasya
Paramasaṃhitā
Paramaśivādvaitakalpalatikā
Paramatantra
Paramātmasandarbha
Pāramātmika
Pāramātmikopaniṣad
Paramātmuḍu
Pārameśvarasaṃhitā

Paramokṣanirāsakārikā
Paramōpatēcam
Parāpaddhati
Parāpañcāśikā
Paraparāpūjā
Parāprāveśikā
Parāpūjā
Parāpūjāprayoga
Parārahasya
Parārcanakrama
Pārāśaramādhavīya
Parāśarasaṃhitā
Parāśarasmṛti
Parāstuti
Paraśurāmakalpasūtra
Paraśurāmasagara
Parātantra
Parātriṃśikā
Parātriṃśikālaghuvṛtti
Parātriṃśikāvivaraṇa
Parātrīśikā
Parātrīśikātātparyadīpikā
Parātrīśikāvivaraṇa
Parcaī/Paricāī
Paribhāṣenduśekhara
Pārijāta
Parimala
Paripāṭal
Pariśiṣṭa
Pārthivāvalī
Pārvatīkhaṇḍa
Pārvatīmaṅgal
Paryantapañcāśikā
Pasāyadān
Pāśupatāgama
Pāśupatasūtra
Pātañjalayogaśāstravivaraṇa
Patipacupācappaṉuval
Patittupāṭṭu
Pātravidhi
Pattuppāṭṭu
Paumacariya
Pauṇḍrakhaṇḍa
Paurandarasūtra
Pauṣkarabhāṣya
Pauṣkarāgama
Pauṣkarajñānapāda
Pauṣkarapārameśvara
Pauṣkarasaṃhitā
Pāvamānī
PeriyāḻvārTirumoḻi
Periyapurāṇam
Periyatirumaṭal
Periyatirumoḻi
Periyatirumuṭi Aṭaivu
Periyatiruvantāti
Perumāḷ Tirumoḻi
Petavatthu
Pettalēm Kuṟavañci
Phatteśāhaprakāśa
Phetkāriṇī
Phra Lak Phra Lam
Phra Rātchaphithī Sip Sòng Düan
Phuṭkar
Picchilātantra
Picumata
Piṅgalāmata
Pīṭhanirṇaya
Pitṛkalpa
Pitṛmedhasūtra
Pōṟṟippaḥṟoṭai
Pō̃t Pratū Kailāt
Prabhākaravijaya
Prabhāsakhaṇḍa
Prabhātiyāṃ
Prabhuliṅgalīle
Prabodhacandrodaya
Prādhānikarahasya
Pradyumnacarit
Prahlād Līlā
Prahlāda Bhakti Vijayam
Prajñāpanā
Prajñāpāramitāhṛdaya
Prakaraṇapañcikā
Prakīrṇādhikāra
Pramāṇa
Pramāṇalakṣaṇa
Pramāṇapaddhati
Pramāṇavārttikālaṃkāra
Pramāṇavārttikavṛtiṭīkā
Pramāṇaviniścaya
Pramathagaṇapaddhati
Prāṇāgnihotra
Praṇavopaniṣad
Prapañcamithyātvānumānakhaṇḍana
Prapañcasāra
Prasād Prasaṅga
Prasaṅga Pārijāt
Prasannapadā
Praśastapādabhāṣya
Praśnamārga
Praśnatantra

Praśnavyākaraṇa
Praśnopaniṣad
Pratimānāṭaka
Prātimokṣasūtra
Pratisargaparvan
Pratiṣṭhālakṣaṇasārasamuccaya
Pratiṣṭhāncaritra
Pratiṣṭhāsārapaddhati
Pratiṣṭhāvidhidarpaṇa
Pratyabhijñāhṛdaya
Pratyabhijñākaumudī
Pratyaṅgirāstotra
Prāyaścittasaṃgraha
Prāyaścittasamuccaya
Prāyaścittavidhi
Prayogamañjarī
Prayuktākhyātamañjarī
Prem Ambodh Pothī
Premagītā
Premavilāsa
Premsāgar
Pretakalpa
Prītisandarbha
Priypravās
Pṛthvīsūkta
Pūjākāṇḍa
Pūjāprakāśa
Pulipalasēvam
Puṇyāham
Puṟanāṉūṟu
Purāṇasaṃhitā
Puraścaryārṇava
Puruṣamāhātmya
Puruṣanirṇaya
Puruṣasūkta
Puruṣottamamāhātmya
Puruṣottamasaṃhitā
Pūrvamīmāṃsāsūtra
Pūrvaparāpūjā
Pūrvārcika
Puṣkaramāhātmya

Qeṣṣe-yi Sanjān
Qiyāfa-šināsī

Rādhākṛṣṇagaṇoddeśadīpikā
Rādhākṛṣṇārcanadīpikā
Rādhikā Śantvanamu
Rādhikāpādapadmacihna
Rāgavartmacandrikā
Rāghavapāṇḍavīya
Raghuvaṃśa
Rahasyatrayasāra
Rahit Maryādā
Raidās Kabīr Goṣṭī
Raidāsvāṇī
Rājadharmaparvan
Rājamārtaṇḍavṛtti
Rajamārttaṇḍa
Rājataraṅgiṇī
Rājayogāmṛtasāramu
Rajitōtsavasaṃcika
Rām Cālīsā
Rāmacandracaritrapurāṇa
Rāmacaritam
Rāmagītā
Rāmājñāpraśna
Rāmakerti
Rāmakian/Rāmakien
Rāmānanda kī hindī racnāeṃ
Rāmānandajanmotsava
Rāmānuja Nūṟṟantāti
Rāmapūrvatāpanīyopaniṣad
Rāmarahasyopaniṣad
Rāmarakṣāstotra
Rāmārcana Candrikā
Rāmārcanapaddhati
Rāmaśakunāvali
Rāmaśalākā
Rāmāṣṭaka
Rāmavijaya
Rāmāyaṇa
Rāmāyaṇabhūṣaṇa
Rāmcaritmānas
Rāmlalā Nahachū
Rāmopākhyāna
Rāmottaratāpinīyopaniṣad
Rāmprasādī Saṅgīt
Rāṇāyaṇīya
Raṅganātharāmāyaṇam
Rasagaṅgādhara
Rasahṛdayatantra
Rasamañjarī
Rasapañcādhyāya
Rasaprakāśasudhākara
Rasaratnākara
Rasaratnasamuccaya
Rasārṇavatantra
Rasārṇavasudhākāra
Rasasāra
Rasasvacchanda
Rasendracūḍāmaṇi

Sāmaveda
Sāmavedārcika
Sāmavidhānabrāhmaṇa
Samayācāra
Sambād Prabhākar
Sambandhasiddhi
Sāmbapañcāśikā
Sāmbapurāṇa
Śāmbhavapūjāvidhāna
Śambhunirṇaya
Saṃdhyārati
Saṃdhyāsaṅgīt
Saṃgrahabhāṣya
Saṃgrahacūḍāmaṇi
Saṃgrāmavijayodaya
Saṃhitāsāra
Saṃkalpakalpadruma
Saṃkalpasūryodaya
Saṃkarṣakāṇḍa
Saṃkarṣaṇasūtra
Sāṃkhyakārikā
Sāṃkhyakārikābhāṣya
Sāṃkhyapravacana
Saṃkhyasaptativṛtti
Sāṃkhyasāra
Sāṃkhyasūtra
Sāṃkhyasūtrapravacanabhāṣya
Sāṃkhyatattvāloka
Sāṃkhyavṛtti
Saṃkṣepabhāgavatāmṛta
Saṃkṣepaśārīrakam
Sammohanatantra
Saṃnyāsanirṇaya
Sampūrṇa Mahābhārata
Saṃskārakāṇḍa
Saṃskāravidhi
Saṃtāna
Samudramanthana
Samudrayānagamanadoṣamīmāṃsā
Samūrtārcanādhikaraṇa
Saṃvitprakāśa
Saṃvitsiddhi
Saṃyuktaratnapiṭakasūtra
Saṃyuttanikāya
Sanatkumārasaṃhitā
Sanatkumāratantra
Śāṇḍīlyabhaktisūtra
Śāṇḍilyasaṃhitā
Śāṇḍilyopaniṣad
Sanghyang Kemahāyānikan
Saṅgītaratnākara
Saṅgītopaniṣatsāroddhāra
Śaṅkarabhāṣya
Śaṅkaradevamādhavadevar Jīvanacaritra
Śaṅkaradigvijaya
Śaṅkaravijaya
Śaṅkaravijayavilāsa
Śaṅkhalikhitadharmasūtra
Śaṅkhāyanagṛhyasūtra
Śāṅkhāyanāraṇyaka
Śāṅkhāyanaśrautasūtra
Sant guṇ sāgar
Sant Nāmdev kī Hindī Padāvalī
Śāntabodha
Santānagopalan
Santavijaya
Śāntikalpa
Śāntimayūkha
Śāntiparvan
Śāntipurāṇa
Śāntistava
Saptapadārthī
Saptaśatika
Saptatiratnamālikā
Śāradātilakatantra
Sarala Sāṃkhyayoga
Śaraṇacaritamānasa
Śaranniśā
Sārasamuccaya
Sarasī Ruhanayana
Sarasvatīpurāṇa
Sarasvatīrahasyopaniṣad
Sarasvatīstotra
Sārāvalī
Sārdhaśatika
Sārdhatriśatika
Śārikāstava
Śārīrashtāna
Śārṅgadharapaddhati
Śārṅgadharasaṃhitā
Sāroddhāra
Saromāhātmya
Sartavadupaṭṭu
Sarvadarśanasaṃgraha
Sarvajñānottara/Sarvajñānottarāgama
Sarvajñānottarayogaśāstra
Sarvamūlagrantha
Sarvāṅgī
Sarvānukramaṇī
Sarvapratiṣṭhāvidhidarpaṇa
Sarvārthasiddhi
Sarvasaṃvādinī

Śivajñānabodhopanyāsa
Śivamahimnaḥstava
Śivamahimnaḥstotra
Śivamānasapūjā
Śivānandalaharī
Śivanirvāṇapaddhati
Śivapañcākṣarastotra
Śivapūjāstava
Śivapurāṇa
Śivarahasya
Śivarātra
Śivarātrimāhātmyamu
Śivarātripūjāpaddhati
Śivarātrirahasya
Śivārcanacandrikā
Śivārkamaṇidīpikā
Śivasahasranāmastotra
Śivaśaktistotra
Śivasaṃhitā
Śivastotra
Śivastotrāvalī
Śivasūtra
Śivasūtravārttika
Śivasūtravimarśiṇī
Śivatanu
Śivatattvacintāmaṇi
Śivatattvasāra
Śivatattvasāramu
Śivayogapradīpikā
Śivayogasāramu
Śivopaniṣad
Śivsiṃh Saroj
Škand Gumānīg Wizār
Skandapurāṇa
Skandayāmala
Ślokavārttika
Smaradīpikā
Smṛticandrikā
Smṛtiratnākara
Smṛtisaṃdarbha
Smṛtisaṃgraha
Smṛtisthaḷa
Smṛtitattva
Ṣoḍaśagrantha
Somanāthacaritre
Somaśambhupaddhati
Spandakārikā
Spandapradīpikā
Sphuṭavāṇī
Śrāmaṇyaphalasūtra
Śrautakośa
Śrī Bayālīs Līlā
Śrī Canvar Purāṇ
Śrī Hita Rādhāvallabhīya Sahityā Ratnāvali
Śrī Kṛṣṭāsaṅgitā
Śrī Mastnāth Adbhut Līlā Prakāś
Śrī Mastnāth Carit
Śrī Mukh Pātrī
Śrī Nāmdev Gāthā
Śrī Nāthajī Prākaṭya kī Vārtā
Śrī Rādhāvallabhjī ka Varṣotsava
Śrī Santoṣi Mātā Pūjā kā Vratkathā
Śrībhāṣya
Śrīharilīlāmṛta
Śrihitaharivaṃśacandrāṣṭaka
Śrīkaṇṭhabhāṣya
Śrīkarabhāṣya
Śrīkhaṇḍyākhyān
Śrīkṛṣṇakīrtana
Śrīkṛṣṇāśraya
Śrīkṛṣṇavijaya
Śrīmadbhagavadarcāprakaraṇa
Śrīmadvādirājaguruvaracaritāmṛta
Śrīmahādevagadya
Śrimatapaddhati
Śrīmatottara
Śrīmatvikanasacaritram
Śrīmukh Patrī
Śrīnāradapañcarātra
Śrīnivāsadīkṣitacarita
Śrīpaprīya Saṅgītopāsana
Śrīpraśnasaṃhitā
Śrīrādhā(rasa)sudhānidhi
Śrīraṅgarājastava
Śrīrudra
Śrīsakaḷasantgāthā
Śrīstuti
Śrīsūkta
Śrītattvacintāmaṇī
Śrītattvanidhi
Śrīvacanabhūṣanam
Śrīvaikānasam
Śrīvaikhānasadharmacaṃdrika
Śrīvaikhānasapatrika
Śrīvaikhānasaśatābdasaṃcika
Śrīvallabhadigvijaya
Śrīvāsiṣṭhamahārāmāyaṇatātparyaprakāśa
Śrīvidyāmantravivṛti
Śrīvidyāpaddhati
Śrīvidyārṇavatantra
Śrīvikanasapriyā
Śrīvikhanasācāryavarṣavardhanōtsavasaṃcika

Tantrāloka
Tantrālokaviveka
Tantramahārṇava
Tantramantrotpatti
Tantrarāja
Tantrarājabhaṭṭāraka
Tantrarājatantra
Tantrarājatantrāvatārastotra
Tantrasadbhāvatantra
Tantrasamuccaya
Tantrasāra
Tantrasārasaṃgraha
Tantravārttika
Tāntrikābhidhānakośa
Tārābhaktisudhārṇava
Tārābhaktitaraṅgiṇī
Tārārahasya
Tārātantra
Tarigoṇḍa Nṛsimhaśatakamu
Tarkajvālā
Tarkarahasyadīpikā
Tarkasāgara
Tarkatāṇḍava
Tātparyacandrikā
Tātparyadīpikā
Tattuvaviḷakkam
Tattvabindu
Tattvacintāmaṇi
Tattvakaumudī
Tattvamasistotra
Tattvamuktākalāpa
Tattvapradīpa
Tattvapradīpikā
Tattvaprakāśa
Tattvaratnāvalī
Tattvārthādhigamabhāṣya
Tattvārthadhigamasūtra
Tattvārthadīpanibandha
Tattvārthadīpanibandhaprakāśa
Tattvārthasūtra
Tattvasamāsasūtra
Tattvasaṃgraha
Tattvasaṃgrahapañjikā
Tattvasandarbha
Tattvasiddhi
Tattvaṭīkā
Tattvatrayanirṇaya
Tattvavaiśāradī
Tattvavṛtti
Tattvopaplavasiṃha
Tautātitamatatilaka
Tēmpāvaṇi
Tēvāram
Theragāthā
Ṭibb-i šifā-yi Maḥmūd-šāhī
Tilakaṭīkā
Timirodghāṭana
Timṯāl-i ašyā᾽ wa azhār al-adwiya
Tirāviḍavētam
Tīrthacintāmaṇi
Tīrthakamalākara
Tīrthaprakāśa
Tīrthavaḷī
Tīrthavīvecanakāṇḍa
Tīrthayātrāparvan
Tīrthenduśekhara
Tiru Ammāṉai
Tirucāḻāl
Tiruccantaviruttam
Tirukkaḷiṟṟuppaṭiyār
Tirukkōvaiyār
Tirukkuṟaḷ
Tirukkuṟuntāṇṭakam
Tirumālai
Tirumantiram
Tirumuṟai
Tirumuṟaikaṇṭapurāṇam
Tirumurukāṟṟuppaṭai
Tiruneṟiviḷakkam
Tiruneṭuntāṇṭakam
Tiruporcuṇṇam
Tiruppallāṇṭu
Tiruppaḷḷiyeḻucci
Tiruppāvai
Tirupoṉṉūcal
Tiruppukaḻ
Tiruppūvalli
Tiruteḷḷēṇam
Tiruttōṇōkkam
Tiruttoṇṭarpurāṇam
Tiruttoṇṭartiruvantāti
Tiruttoṇṭartokai
Tiruvācakam
Tiruvāciriyam
Tiruvaiyyāṟṟuppurāṇam
Tiruvālaṅkāṭṭumūttatirupatikam
Tiruvaḷḷuvamālai
Tiruvaruṭpayaṉ
Tiruvāymoḻi
Tiruveḻukūṟṟirukkai
Tiruvempāvai
Tiruvicaippā

Vaikṛtikarahasya
Vairāgya Sandīpinī
Vairāgyaśataka
Vaiśeṣikakaṭandī
Vaiśeṣikasetu
Vaiśeṣikasūtra
Vaiśeṣikasūtravākya
Vaiśeṣikasūtravārttika
Vaiśeṣikasūtravṛtti
Vaiśeṣikasūtravyākhyā
Vaiśeṣikasūtropaskāra
Vaishnav Jān To Tene Kahiye Je Pīr Parai Jāne Re
Vaiṣṇavajana
Vaiṣṇavamatābjabhāskara
Vaiṣṇavatoṣaṇī
Vaiṣṇavavandanā
Vaitānaśrautasūtra
Vaitānika
Vājasaneyiprātiśākhya
Vājasaneyisaṃhitā
Vajracchedikāprajñāpāramitāsūtra
Vākyapadīya
Vākyapadīyavṛtti
Vākyārthamātṛkā
Vālakhilya
Vālakhilyastava
Vaḷḷal Cāttiram
Vāmadevya
Vāmakeśvara
Vāmakeśvarīmata
Vāmakeśvarīmatavivaraṇa
Vāmanapurāṇa
Vaṃśānucarita
Vanaparvan
Vanphūl
Varadā
Varadarājastāva
Varāhapurāṇa
Vārāhaśrautasūtra
Varāhopaniṣad
Vāraṅ Bhāī Gurdās
Vāridhi Nīku
Varivasyārahasya
Varmacuṭṭiram
Varṇaratnākara
Varṇārhavarṇastotra
Varṇāśramacandrikā
Vārttika
Varuṇapaddhati
Vāsādhikāra
Vasantarājaśakuna
Vasiṣṭhadharmaśāstra
Vasiṣṭhadharmasūtra
Vasiṣṭhasaṃhitā
Vassantara Jātaka
Vāstusūtropaniṣad
Vasudevahiṇḍi
Vāsudevakalpa
Vaṭakkan Paṭṭukal
Vātāpi Gaṇapati
Vaṭeśvarasiddhānta
Vātulānāthasūtra
Vātulaśuddha
Vātulottara
Vāvar Mahātmayam
Vāyavīyasaṃhitā
Vāyupurāṇa
Vedabhāṣya
Vedāṅkuśa
Vedāntadīpa
Vedāntakaustubha
Vedāntakaustubhaprabhā
Vedāntaparibhāṣa
Vedāntapārijātasaurabha
Vedāntaratnamañjuṣā
Vedāntasāra
Vedāntasarvasvaśivadarpaṇa
Vedāntasūtra
Vedārthasaṃgraha
Vedavākyamaṇi
Veṅkaṭācalamāhātmyamu
Vibhāṣāśāstra
Vibhūtipāda
Vicāracaṅkirakam
Vidagdhamādhava
Vīdēvdād
Vidhavavivāha
Vidhirasāyana
Vidhiviveka
Viduranīti
Vidvanmanorañjanī
Vidyābheda
Vidyāmādhavīya
Vidyāpāda
Vidyāpariṇaya
Vidyāsundar
Vigrahavyāvartanī
Vijaya/Vijayottara
Vijñānabhairava

Vijñānakaumudī
Vijñāpana
Vikramacarita
Vikramāṅkadevacarita
Vikramārjunavijaya
Vikramorvaśīya
Vīlacōḻiyam
Villipāratam
Vimalāvatī
Vimānārcanakalpa
Vinanti Patra
Vīṇāśikhatantra
Vīṇāśikhottara
Viṉāveṇpā
Vināyakamāhātmya
Vināyakarakavaḷ
Vinayapiṭaka
Vinaypatrikā
Viprapatnīnāṭa
Vīra
Virahakhaṇḍa
Vīramāheśvarācārasaṃgraha
Vīramitrodaya
Vīraśaivācārasāroddhārabhāṣya
Vīraśaivāmṛtapurāṇa
Vīraśaivasiddhāntottarakaumudī
Virāṭaparvan
Vīrāvalī
Vīrāvalīkula
Vīravarīya
Vīrottara
Virūpākṣapañcāśikā
Viṣṇu Cittiyam
Viṣṇu Pārijātamu
Viṣṇudharma
Viṣṇudharmasūtra
Viṣṇudharmottarapurāṇa
Viṣṇumahimnaḥstava
Viṣṇumahimnaḥstotra
Viṣṇupañcaka
Viṣṇupurāṇa
Viṣṇusahasranāma
Viṣṇusaṃhitā
Viṣṇusmṛti
Viṣṇustotra
Viṣṇustuti
Viṣṇutattvavinirṇaya
Viṣṇuyāmala
Visperad
Viśrām Sāgar
Vistarabhāṣya
Vistṛtabhāṣya
Visuddhimagga
Viśvādya
Viśvakarmavāstuśāstra
Viśvaksenasaṃhitā
Viśvāmitrasaṃhitā
Viśvasārottara
Vitastāmāhātmya
Vivādacintāmaṇi
Vivartavilāsa
Vivekacintāmaṇi
Vivekacūḍāmaṇi
Vivekamārtaṇḍa
Vivekasindhū
Vividavadham
Viyāhapannatti
Vrātya
Vṛddhahārīta
Vṛddhajīvakatantra
Vṛddhasvacchanda
Vṛndāvanamahimāmṛta
Vṛṣādhipaśatakamu
Vṛṣasārasaṃgraha
Vṛttikāragrantha
Vyāsabhāṣya
Vyāsavāṇī
Vyavahāramayūkha
Vyavahāranirṇaya
Vyomamatī
Vyomavatī
Vyomavyāpistava

Yādavābhyudaya
Yajñādhikāra
Yajñadulu
Yajñasūtra
Yājñavalkyasmṛti
Yājñikyopaniṣad
Yajurveda(saṃhitā)
Yakoppu Cuṇṇam
Yāmā
Yamadaṇḍa
Yamagītā
Yamunāṣṭaka
Yantracintāmaṇi
Yāpparuṅkalakkārikai
Yaśastilaka
Yasna
Yasna Haptaŋhāiti

Yaśodharā
Yatidharmaprakāśa
Yatidharmasaṃgraha
Yatidharmasamuccaya
Yatiliṅgasamarthana
Yavanajātaka
Yogabhāṣya
Yogabīja
Yogācārabhūmi
Yogacintāmaṇi
Yogacūḍāmaṇyupaniṣad
Yogaja
Yogakāṇḍa
Yogakārikā
Yogakuṇḍalyupaniṣad
Yogakuruṇṭa
Yōgāngatrividhi
Yogāñjalisāram
Yogarahasya
Yogarājopaniṣad
Yogaratnākara
Yogaratnamālā
Yogaratnāvalī
Yogasaṃcāra
Yogasārasaṃgraha
Yogasārastava
Yogaśāstra
Yogasiddhāntacandrikā
Yogasiddhāntapaddhati
Yogaśikhopaniṣad
Yogasūtra
Yogasūtrabhāṣyavivaraṇa
Yogasūtrapāṭha
Yogataraṅgiṇī
Yogatārāvalī
Yogatattvopaniṣad
Yogavallī
Yogavārttika
Yogavāsiṣṭha
Yogavāsiṣṭharāmāyaṇa
Yogaviṣaya
Yogayājñavalkya
Yogayātrā
Yoginītantra
Yoginīhṛdaya
Yoginīhṛdayadīpikā
Yoginījālaśaṃvara
Yoginīsaṃcāra
Yogisaṃpradāyāviṣkṛti
Yonitantra
Yonigahvara
Yuddhajayārṇava
Yuddhakāṇḍa
Yugalaśataka
Yugapurāṇa
Yugayatra
Yuktidīpikā
Yuktikalpataru
Yuktisnehaprapūraṇī